Pro Drupal Development

Second Edition

John K. VanDyk

Apress®

Pro Drupal Development, Second Edition

Copyright © 2008 by John K. VanDyk

ISBN-13 (paperback): 978-1-4302-0989-8

ISBN-13 (electronic): 978-1-4302-0990-4

Printed and bound in the United States of America 9 8 7 6 5 4 3 2

Lead Editor: Matt Wade
Technical Reviewer: Robert Douglass
Editorial Board: Clay Andres, Steve Anglin, Ewan Buckingham, Tony Campbell, Gary Cornell,
    Jonathan Gennick, Matthew Moodie, Joseph Ottinger, Jeffrey Pepper, Frank Pohlmann,
    Ben Renow-Clarke, Dominic Shakeshaft, Matt Wade, Tom Welsh
Project Manager: Beth Christmas
Copy Editors: Heather Lang and Damon Larson
Associate Production Director: Kari Brooks-Copony
Production Editor: Laura Esterman
Compositor: Linda Weidemann, Wolf Creek Press
Proofreaders: April Eddy and Linda Siefert
Indexer: John Collin
Cover Designer: Kurt Krames
Manufacturing Director: Tom Debolski

Distributed to the book trade worldwide by Springer-Verlag New York, Inc., 233 Spring Street, 6th Floor, New York, NY 10013. Phone 1-800-SPRINGER, fax 201-348-4505, e-mail orders-ny@springer-sbm.com, or visit http://www.springeronline.com.

For information on translations, please contact Apress directly at 2855 Telegraph Avenue, Suite 600, Berkeley, CA 94705. Phone 510-549-5930, fax 510-549-5939, e-mail info@apress.com, or visit http://www.apress.com.

Apress and friends of ED books may be purchased in bulk for academic, corporate, or promotional use. eBook versions and licenses are also available for most titles. For more information, reference our Special Bulk Sales–eBook Licensing web page at http://www.apress.com/info/bulksales.

The source code for this book is available to readers at http://www.apress.com.

For the Great Architect
and to my incredibly patient wife and children

Contents at a Glance

Contents

Foreword

Less than two years ago, I wrote the foreword for the first edition of this book. What was missing at that time was a developer book for Drupal. By writing the first version of this book, John VanDyk and Matt Westgate made an incredible contribution to Drupal's steady growth. I don't think I know a single Drupal developer who doesn't own a copy of the first *Pro Drupal Development* book.

Drupal, through its open source nature, has become much greater than I ever imagined it would. The Drupal developer community has a healthy desire to innovate, to respond to the ever-changing landscape of web development, and to provide web developers an almost infinite amount of flexibility. Change is a constant in the Drupal community and key to our success.

Since the first edition of this book was published, we released Drupal 6, a big step forward, with new and improved APIs. In fact, Drupal 6 had over 700 individual contributors who have patches included in the core code. Together, we've made important theme system improvements, better support for multilingual web sites, an improved menu system, form API improvements, JavaScript goodies, and much more. The net result is that Drupal 6 is an even better web application development platform than Drupal 5.

Probably to John and Matt's despair (sorry!), all of the chapters of the original edition of *Pro Drupal Development* went partially out of date.

Fortunately, the second edition of this book fixes all that. This book covers all of the capabilities and developer facilities in Drupal 6 and provides deep insight into the inner workings and design choices behind Drupal 6. Every time we release a new major version of Drupal, Drupal attracts more users and developers. So, if anything was missing for Drupal 6, it was this book, and I'm indebted to John for revising and expanding it.

Armed with this book and a copy of Drupal's source code, you can participate in the Drupal community and contribute to Drupal's development. If you have figured out how to do something better, with fewer lines of code or more elegantly and faster than before, let us know because we are completely and utterly focused on making Drupal rock even more. I'd love to review and commit your Drupal core patches, and I'm sure many of the other maintainers would too.

Dries Buytaert
Drupal founder and project lead

About the Author

**JOHN VANDYK** began his work with computers on a black Bell and Howell Apple II by printing out and poring over the BASIC code for Little Brick Out in order to increase the paddle width. Later, he manipulated timing loops in assembly to give Pac-Man a larger time slice than the ghosts. Before discovering Drupal, John was involved with the UserLand Frontier community and used Plone before writing his own content management system (with Matt Westgate) using Ruby.

John is a senior web architect at Lullabot, a Drupal education and consulting firm. Before that, John was a systems analyst and adjunct assistant professor in the entomology department at Iowa State University of Science and Technology. His master's thesis focused on cold tolerance of deer ticks, and his doctoral dissertation was on the effectiveness of photographically created three-dimensional virtual insects on undergraduate learning.

John lives with his wife Tina in Ames, Iowa. They homeschool their passel of children, who have become used to bedtime stories like "The Adventures of a Node Revision in the Land of Multiple Joins."

About the Technical Reviewer

 **ROBERT DOUGLASS**'s Drupal adventure started in 2003 with the creation of his personal web site, RobsHouse.net. In 2005, Robert coauthored the book *Building Online Communities with Drupal, phpBB, and WordPress* (Apress). As the first book to be published that covered Drupal in depth, *Building Online Communities* has proven to be a valuable guide to Drupal newcomers and experienced Drupallers alike.

Robert has been responsible for Drupal's involvement in the Google Summer of Code program, has spoken about Drupal at numerous conferences, has published dozens of Drupal-related articles online, and is the founder of the Köln/ Bonn Drupal users group in Germany.

As senior Drupal advisor at Acquia, Robert is working to make Drupal more accessible, fun, and productive for a wider range of people and organizations. Robert loves classical music and open source software dearly and looks to each as a source for motivation and optimism.

Acknowledgments

First of all, thanks to my family members for their understanding and support during the writing of this book, especially as a "simple revision" turned into a project as large as the first edition.

Drupal is essentially a community-based project. This book could not have happened without the selfless gifts of the many people who write documentation, submit bug reports, create and review improvements, and generally help Drupal to become what it is today.

But among the many, I'd like to thank those few who went above and beyond what could have been expected.

Those include the members of the #drupal Internet Relay Chat channel, who put up with the constant questioning of how things worked, why things were written a certain way, and whether a bit of code was brilliant or made no sense at all. Significant contributions came from Brandon Bergren, Øivind Binde, Larry "Crell" Garfield, Dmitri Gaskin, Charlie Gordon, Gerhard Killesreiter, Greg Knaddison, Druplicon, Rob Loach, Chad Phillips, and Oleg Terenchuck. Sincere apologies to the many who contributed but whose names I have missed here.

A special thanks to Robert Douglass, Károly Négyesi, Addison Berry, Angela Byron, Heine Deelstra, Jeff Eaton, Nathan Haug, Kevin Hemenway, Gábor Hojtsy, Barry Jaspan, Earl Miles, and James Walker for their critical review of parts of the manuscript.

Thanks to Joel Coats at Iowa State University for believing that this book was a worthwhile investment of time, and thanks to the amazing team at Lullabot.

Thanks to the Apress team for showing grace when code examples needed to be changed yet again and for magically turning my drafts into a book.

And of course, thanks to Dries Buytaert for sharing Drupal with the world.

Introduction

The journey of a software developer is an interesting one. It starts with taking things apart and inspecting the isolated components to try to understand the whole system. Next, you start poking at and hacking the system in an attempt to manipulate its behavior. This is how you learn—by hacking.

You follow that general pattern for some time until you reach a point of confidence where you can build your own systems from scratch. You might roll your own content management system, for example, deploy it on multiple sites, and think you're changing the world.

But there comes a critical point, and it usually happens when you realize that the maintenance of your system starts to take up more time than building the features, when you wish that you knew back when you started writing the system what you know now. You begin to see other systems emerge that can do what your system can do and more. There's a community filled with people who are working together to improve the software, and you realize that they are, for the most part, smarter than you. And even more, the software is free.

This is what happened to me, and maybe even you, upon discovering Drupal. It's a common journey with a happy ending—hundreds of developers working together on one simultaneous project. You make friends; you make code; and you are still recognized for your contributions just as you were when you were flying solo.

This book was written for three levels of understanding. First and most importantly, there are pretty pictures in the form of diagrams and flowcharts; those looking for the big picture of how Drupal works will find them quite useful. At the middle level are code snippets and example modules. This is the hands-on layer, where you get your hands dirty and dig in. I encourage you to install Drupal, work along with the examples (preferably with a good debugger) as you go through the book, and get comfortable with Drupal. The last layer is the book as a whole: the observations, tips, and explanations between the code and pictures. This provides the glue between the other layers.

If you're new to Drupal, I suggest reading this book in order, as chapters are prerequisites for those that follow.

Lastly, you can download this book's code examples as well as the flowcharts and diagrams from http://drupalbook.com or http://www.apress.com.

Good luck and welcome to the Drupal community!

■ ■ ■

## CHAPTER 1

How Drupal Works

In this chapter, I'll give you an overview of Drupal. Details on how each part of the system works will be provided in later chapters. Here, we'll cover the technology stack on which Drupal runs, the layout of the files that make up Drupal, and the various conceptual terms that Drupal uses, such as nodes, hooks, blocks, and themes.

What Is Drupal?

Drupal is used to build web sites. It's a highly modular, open source web content management framework with an emphasis on collaboration. It is extensible, standards-compliant, and strives for clean code and a small footprint. Drupal ships with basic core functionality, and additional functionality is gained by enabling built-in or third-party modules. Drupal is designed to be customized, but customization is done by overriding the core or by adding modules, not by modifying the code in the core. Drupal's design also successfully separates content management from content presentation.

Drupal can be used to build an Internet portal; a personal, departmental, or corporate web site; an e-commerce site; a resource directory; an online newspaper; an image gallery; an intranet, to mention only a few possibilities. It can even be used to teach a distance-learning course.

A dedicated security team strives to keep Drupal secure by responding to threats and issuing security updates. A nonprofit organization called the Drupal Association supports Drupal by improving the drupal.org web site infrastructure and organizing Drupal conferences and events. And a thriving online community of users, site administrators, designers, and web developers work hard to continually improve the software; see http://drupal.org and http://groups.drupal.org.

Technology Stack

Drupal's design goals include both being able to run well on inexpensive web hosting accounts and being able to scale up to massive distributed sites. The former goal means using the most popular technology, and the latter means careful, tight coding. Drupal's technology stack is illustrated in Figure 1-1.

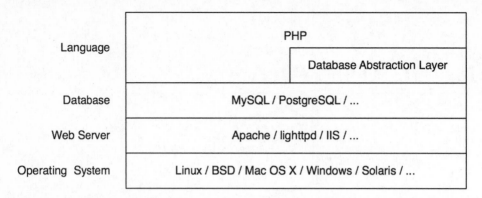

Figure 1-1. *Drupal's technology stack*

The operating system is at such a low level in the stack that Drupal does not care much about it. Drupal runs successfully on any operating system that supports PHP.

The web server most widely used with Drupal is Apache, though other web servers (including Microsoft IIS) may be used. Because of Drupal's long history with Apache, Drupal ships with .htaccess files that secure the Drupal installation. *Clean URLs*—that is, those devoid of question marks, ampersands, or other strange characters—are achieved using Apache's mod_rewrite component. This is particularly important because when migrating from another content management system or from static files, the URLs of the content need not change, and unchanging URIs are cool, according to Tim Berners-Lee (http://www.w3. org/Provider/Style/URI). Clean URLs are available on other web servers by using the web server's URL rewriting capabilities.

Drupal interfaces with the next layer of the stack (the database) through a lightweight database abstraction layer. This layer handles sanitation of SQL queries and makes it possible to use different vendors' databases without refactoring your code. The most widely tested databases are MySQL and PostgreSQL, though support for Microsoft SQL Server and Oracle is increasing.

Drupal is written in PHP. Since PHP is an easy language to learn, there are many PHP programs written by beginners. The quality of beginner's code has given PHP a bad reputation. However, PHP can also be used to write solid code. All core Drupal code adheres to strict coding standards (http://drupal.org/nodes/318) and undergoes thorough review through the open source process. For Drupal, the easy learning curve of PHP means that there is a low barrier to entry for contributors who are just starting out, and the review process ensures this ease of access comes without sacrificing quality in the end product. And the feedback beginners receive from the community helps to improve their skills.

Core

A lightweight framework makes up the Drupal *core*. This is what you get when you download Drupal from drupal.org. The core is responsible for providing the basic functionality that will be used to support other parts of the system.

The core includes code that allows the Drupal system to bootstrap when it receives a request, a library of common functions frequently used with Drupal, and modules that provide basic functionality like user management, taxonomy, and templating as shown in Figure 1-2.

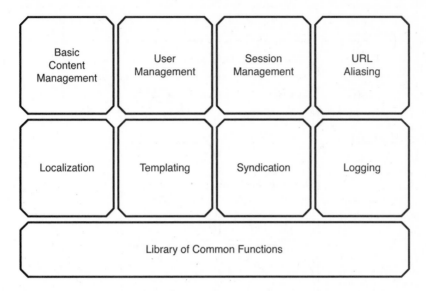

Basic Content Management	User Management	Session Management	URL Aliasing
Localization	Templating	Syndication	Logging
Library of Common Functions			

Figure 1-2. *An overview of the Drupal core (not all core functionality is shown)*

Administrative Interface

The administrative interface in Drupal is tightly integrated with the rest of the site and, by default, uses the same visual theme. The first user, user 1, is the superuser with complete access to the site. After logging in as user 1, you'll see an Administer link within your user block (see the "Blocks" section). Click that, and you're inside the Drupal administrative interface. Each user's block will contain different links depending on his or her access levels for the site.

Modules

Drupal is a truly modular framework. Functionality is included in *modules*, which can be enabled or disabled (some required modules cannot be disabled). Features are added to a Drupal web site by enabling existing modules, installing modules written by members of the Drupal community, or writing new modules. In this way, web sites that do not need certain features can run lean and mean, while those that need more can add as much functionality as desired. This is shown in Figure 1-3.

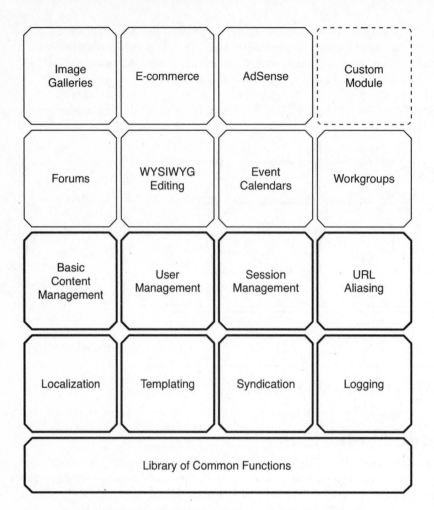

Figure 1-3. *Enabling additional modules gives more functionality.*

Both the addition of new content types such as recipes, blog posts, or files, and the addition of new behaviors such as e-mail notification, peer-to-peer publishing, and aggregation are handled through modules. Drupal makes use of the *inversion of control* design pattern, in which modular functionality is called by the framework at the appropriate time. These opportunities for modules to do their thing are called *hooks*.

Hooks

Hooks can be thought of as internal Drupal events. They are also called *callbacks*, though because they are constructed by function-naming conventions and not by registering with a listener, they are not truly being called back. Hooks allow modules to "hook into" what is happening in the rest of Drupal.

Suppose a user logs into your Drupal web site. At the time the user logs in, Drupal fires the user hook. That means that any function named according to the convention *module name* plus *hook name* will be called. For example, `comment_user()` in the comment module, `locale_user()` in the locale module, `node_user()` in the node module, and any other similarly named functions will be called. If you were to write a custom module called `spammy.module` and include a function called `spammy_user()` that sent an e-mail to the user, your function would be called too, and the hapless user would receive an unsolicited e-mail at every login.

The most common way to tap into Drupal's core functionality is through the implementation of hooks in modules.

■**Tip** For more details about the hooks Drupal supports, see the online documentation at `http://api.drupal.org/api/6`, and look under Components of Drupal, then "Module system (Drupal hooks)."

Themes

When creating a web page to send to a browser, there are really two main concerns: assembling the appropriate data and marking up the data for the Web. In Drupal, the theme layer is responsible for creating the HTML (or JSON, XML, etc.) that the browser will receive. Drupal can use several popular templating approaches, such as Smarty, Template Attribute Language for PHP (PHPTAL), and PHPTemplate.

The important thing to remember is that Drupal encourages separation of content and markup.

Drupal allows several ways to customize and override the look and feel of your web site. The simplest way is by using a cascading style sheet (CSS) to override Drupal's built-in classes and IDs. However, if you want to go beyond this and customize the actual HTML output, you'll find it easy to do. Drupal's template files consist of standard HTML and PHP. Additionally, each dynamic part of a Drupal page (such as a box, list, or breadcrumb trail) can be overridden simply by declaring a function with an appropriate name. Then Drupal will use your function instead to create that part of the page.

Nodes

Content types in Drupal are derived from a single base type referred to as a *node*. Whether it's a blog entry, a recipe, or even a project task, the underlying data structure is the same. The genius behind this approach is in its extensibility. Module developers can add features like ratings, comments, file attachments, geolocation information, and so forth for nodes in general without worrying about whether the node type is blog, recipe, or so on. The site administrator can then mix and match functionality by content type. For example, the administrator may choose to enable comments on blogs but not recipes or enable file uploads for project tasks only.

Nodes also contain a base set of behavioral properties that all other content types inherit. Any node can be promoted to the front page of the web site, published or unpublished, or even searched. And because of this uniform structure, the administrative interface is able to offer a batch editing screen for working with nodes.

Blocks

A *block* is information that can be enabled or disabled in a specific location on your web site's template. For example, a block might display the number of current active users on your site. You might have a block containing links to the most popular content on the site, or a list of upcoming events. Blocks are typically placed in a template's sidebar, header, or footer. Blocks can be set to display on nodes of a certain type, only on the front page, or according to other criteria.

Often blocks are used to present information that is customized to the current user. For example, the user block only contains links to the administrative areas of the site to which the current user has access, such as the "My account" page. Regions where blocks may appear (such as the header, footer, or right or left sidebar) are defined in a site's theme; placement and visibility of blocks within those regions is managed through the web-based administrative interface.

File Layout

Understanding the directory structure of a default Drupal installation will teach you several important best practices such as where downloaded modules and themes should reside and how to have different Drupal installation profiles. A default Drupal installation has the structure shown in Figure 1-4.

Figure 1-4. *The default folder structure of a Drupal installation*

Details about each element in the folder structure follow:

The `includes` folder contains libraries of common functions that Drupal uses.

The `misc` folder stores JavaScript and miscellaneous icons and images available to a stock Drupal installation.

The `modules` folder contains the core modules, with each module in its own folder. It is best not to touch anything in this folder (or any other folder except `profiles` and `sites`). You add extra modules in the `sites` directory.

The `profiles` folder contains different installation profiles for a site. If there are other profiles besides the default profile in this subdirectory, Drupal will ask you which profile you want to install when first installing your Drupal site. The main purpose of an installation profile is to enable certain core and contributed modules automatically. An example would be an e-commerce profile that automatically sets up Drupal as an e-commerce platform.

The `scripts` folder contains scripts for checking syntax, cleaning up code, running Drupal from the command line, and handling special cases with `cron`. This folder is not used within the Drupal request life cycle; these are shell and Perl utility scripts.

The `sites` directory (see Figure 1-5) contains your modifications to Drupal in the form of settings, modules, and themes. When you add modules to Drupal from the contributed modules repository or by writing your own, they go into `sites/all/modules`. This keeps all your Drupal modifications within a single folder. Inside the `sites` directory will be a subdirectory named `default` that holds the default configuration file for your Drupal site—`default.settings.php`. The Drupal installer will modify these original settings based on the information you provide and write a `settings.php` file for your site. The default directory is typically copied and renamed to the URL of your site by the person deploying the site, so your final settings file would be at `sites/www.example.com/settings.php`.

The `sites/default/files` folder doesn't ship with Drupal by default, but it is needed to store any files that are uploaded to your site and subsequently served out. Some examples are the use of a custom logo, enabling user avatars, or uploading other media associated with your new site. This subdirectory requires read and write permissions by the web server that Drupal is running behind. Drupal's installer will create this subdirectory if it can and will check that the correct permissions have been set.

The `themes` folder contains the template engines and default themes for Drupal. Additional themes you download or create should not go here; they go into `sites/all/themes`.

`cron.php` is used for executing periodic tasks, such as pruning database tables and calculating statistics.

`index.php` is the main entry point for serving requests.

`install.php` is the main entry point for the Drupal installer.

update.php updates the database schema after a Drupal version upgrade.

xmlrpc.php receives XML-RPC requests and may be safely deleted from deployments that do not intend to receive XML-RPC requests.

robots.txt is a default implementation of the robot exclusion standard.

Other files not listed here are documentation files.

Figure 1-5. *The sites folder can store all your Drupal modifications.*

Serving a Request

Having a conceptual framework of what happens when a request is received by Drupal is helpful, so this section provides a quick walk-through. If you want to trace it yourself, use a good debugger, and start at index.php, which is where Drupal receives most of its requests. The sequence outlined in this section may seem complex for displaying a simple web page, but it is rife with flexibility.

The Web Server's Role

Drupal runs behind a web server, typically Apache. If the web server respects Drupal's .htaccess file, some PHP settings are initialized, and the URL is examined. Almost all calls to Drupal go through index.php. For example, a call to http://example.com/foo/bar undergoes the following process:

1. The mod_rewrite rule in Drupal's .htaccess file looks at the incoming URL and separates the base URL from the path. In our example, the path is foo/bar.

2. This path is assigned to the URL query parameter q.

3. The resulting URL is http://example.com/index.php?q=foo/bar.

4. Drupal treats foo/bar as the internal Drupal path, and processing begins in index.php.

As a result of this process, Drupal treats http://example.com/index.php?q=foo/bar and http://example.com/foo/bar exactly the same way, because internally the path is the same in both cases. This enables Drupal to use URLs without funny-looking characters in them. These URLs are referred to as clean URLs.

In alternate web servers, such as Microsoft IIS, clean URLs can be achieved using a Windows Internet Server Application Programming Interface (ISAPI) module such as ISAPI Rewrite. IIS version 7 and later may support rewriting directly.

The Bootstrap Process

Drupal bootstraps itself on every request by going through a series of bootstrap phases. These phases are defined in bootstrap.inc and proceed as described in the following sections.

Initialize Configuration

This phase populates Drupal's internal configuration array and establishes the base URL ($base_url) of the site. The settings.php file is parsed via include_once(), and any variable or string overrides established there are applied. See the "Variable Overrides" and "String Overrides" sections of the file sites/all/default/default.settings.php for details.

Early Page Cache

In situations requiring a high level of scalability, a caching system may need to be invoked before a database connection is even attempted. The early page cache phase lets you include (with include()) a PHP file containing a function called page_cache_fastpath(), which takes over and returns content to the browser. The early page cache is enabled by setting the page_cache_fastpath variable to TRUE, and the file to be included is defined by setting the cache_inc variable to the file's path. See the chapter on caching for an example.

Initialize Database

During the database phase, the type of database is determined, and an initial connection is made that will be used for database queries.

Hostname/IP-Based Access Control

Drupal allows the banning of hosts on a per-hostname/IP address basis. In the access control phase, a quick check is made to see if the request is coming from a banned host; if so, access is denied.

Initialize Session Handling

Drupal takes advantage of PHP's built-in session handling but overrides some of the handlers with its own to implement database-backed session handling. Sessions are initialized or reestablished in the session phase. The global $user object representing the current user is also initialized here, though for efficiency not all properties are available (they are added by an explicit call to the user_load() function when needed).

Late Page Cache

In the late page cache phase, Drupal loads enough supporting code to determine whether or not to serve a page from the page cache. This includes merging settings from the database into the array that was created during the initialize configuration phase and loading or parsing module code. If the session indicates that the request was issued by an anonymous user and page caching is enabled, the page is returned from the cache and execution stops.

Language Determination

At the language determination phase, Drupal's multilingual support is initialized and a decision is made as to which language will be used to serve the current page based on site and user settings. Drupal supports several alternatives for determining language support, such as path prefix and domain-level language negotiation.

Path

At the path phase, code that handles paths and path aliasing is loaded. This phase enables human-readable URLs to be resolved and handles internal Drupal path caching and lookups.

Full

This phase completes the bootstrap process by loading a library of common functions, theme support, and support for callback mapping, file handling, Unicode, PHP image toolkits, form creation and processing, mail handling, automatically sortable tables, and result set paging. Drupal's custom error handler is set, and all enabled modules are loaded. Finally, Drupal fires the init hook, so that modules have an opportunity to be notified before official processing of the request begins.

Once Drupal has completed bootstrapping, all components of the framework are available. It is time to take the browser's request and hand it off to the PHP function that will handle it. The mapping between URLs and functions that handle them is accomplished using a callback registry that takes care of both URL mapping and access control. Modules register their callbacks using the menu hook (for more details, see Chapter 4).

When Drupal has determined that there exists a callback to which the URL of the browser request successfully maps and that the user has permission to access that callback, control is handed to the callback function.

Processing a Request

The callback function does whatever work is required to process and accumulate data needed to fulfill the request. For example, if a request for content such as `http://example.com/q=node/3` is received, the URL is mapped to the function `node_page_view()` in `node.module`. Further processing will retrieve the data for that node from the database and put it into a data structure. Then, it's time for theming.

Theming the Data

Theming involves transforming the data that has been retrieved, manipulated, or created into HTML (or XML or other output format). Drupal will use the theme the administrator has selected to give the web page the correct look and feel. The resulting output is then sent to the web browser (or other HTTP client).

Summary

After reading this chapter, you should understand in general how Drupal works and have an overview of what happens when Drupal serves a request. The components that make up the web page serving process will be covered in detail in later chapters.

■■■

## CHAPTER 2

Writing a Module

In many open source applications, you can customize the application by modifying the source code. While this is one method for getting the behavior you desire, it is generally frowned upon and considered a last resort in the Drupal community. Customizing code means that with each update of Drupal, you must perform more work—you must test to see that your customization still works as expected. Instead, Drupal is designed from the ground up to be modular and extensible.

Drupal is a very lean framework for building applications and the default installation is referred to as the Drupal core. Functionality is added to the core by enabling modules, which are files that contain PHP code. Core modules reside in the modules subdirectory of your Drupal installation. Take a look at that directory now, and compare it to the list of modules you see when you navigate to Administer ➤ Site building ➤ Modules on your Drupal site.

In this chapter, we are going to build a module from scratch. As you build the module, you'll learn about the standards to which modules must adhere. We need a realistic goal, so let's focus on the real-world problem of annotation. When looking through the pages of a Drupal web site, users may comment on content if the administrator has enabled the comment module. But what about making an annotation (a type of note that only the user can see) to a web page? This might be useful for confidentially reviewing content (I know it seems contrived, but bear with me).

Creating the Files

The first thing we are going to do is to choose a name for the module. The name "annotate" seems appropriate—it's short and descriptive. Next, we need a place to put the module. We could put it in the modules directory along with the core modules, but that would make maintenance more difficult, because we'd have to remember which modules are core modules and which are ours. Let's put it in sites/all/modules to keep it separate from the core modules.

Create the sites/all/modules directory if necessary. Create a subdirectory called custom in sites/all/modules and a subdirectory called annotate in sites/all/modules/custom. This will keep the custom modules you develop separate from third-party modules you download. This organization is up to you but can be helpful to orient another developer should you need to hand off your site. We create a subdirectory and not just a file named annotate.module because we're going to include other files besides the module file in our module distribution. For example, we'll need a README.txt file to explain to other users what our module does and how to use it, and an annotate.info file to provide some information about our module to Drupal. Ready to begin?

Our annotate.info file follows:

```
; $Id$
name = Annotate
description = Allows users to annotate nodes.
core = 6.x
package = Pro Drupal Development
```

The file is in a simple format that defines keys and values. We start with a concurrent versions system (CVS) identification tag. If we want to share our module with others by checking it into Drupal's contributed modules repository, this value will automatically be replaced by CVS. Then we provide a name and description for Drupal to display in the module administration section of the web site. We explicitly define which major version of Drupal our module is compatible with; in this case, version 6.x. Drupal 6 and later will not allow incompatible modules to be enabled. Modules are displayed in groups, and the grouping is determined by the package; thus, if we have three different modules that have package = Pro Drupal Development, they will display in one group. We could assign optional values in addition to those listed previously. Here's an example of a module that requires PHP 5.2 and the forum and taxonomy modules:

```
; $Id$
name = Forum confusion
description = Randomly reassigns replies to different discussion threads.
core = 6.x
dependencies[] = forum
dependencies[] = taxonomy
package = "Evil Bob's Forum BonusPak"
php = 5.2
```

Note You might be wondering why we need a separate .info file. Why not just have a function in our main module that returns this metadata? Because when the module administration page loads, it would have to load and parse every single module whether enabled or not, leading to memory use far higher than normal and possibly over the memory limit assigned to PHP. With .info files, the information can be loaded quickly and with minimal memory use.

Now we're ready to create the actual module. Create a file named annotate.module inside your sites/all/modules/custom/annotate subdirectory. Begin the file with an opening PHP tag and a CVS identification tag, followed by a comment:

```
<?php
// $Id$
```

```
/**
 * @file
 * Lets users add private annotations to nodes.
 *
 * Adds a text field when a node is displayed
 * so that authenticated users may make notes.
 */
```

First, note the comment style. We begin with /**, and on each succeeding line, we use a single asterisk indented with one space (*) and */ on a line by itself to end a comment. The @file token denotes that what follows on the next line is a description of what this file does. This one-line description is used so that api.module, Drupal's automated documentation extractor and formatter, can find out what this file does. After a blank line, we add a longer description aimed at programmers who will be examining (and no doubt improving) our code. Note that we intentionally do not use a closing tag (?>); these are optional in PHP and, if included, can cause problems with trailing whitespace in files (see http://drupal.org/node/545).

■**Note** Why are we being so picky about how everything is structured? It's because when hundreds of people from around the world work together on a project, it saves time when everyone does things one standard way. Details of the coding style required for Drupal can be found in the "Coding standards" section of the *Developing for Drupal Handbook* (http://drupal.org/node/318).

Our next order of business is to define some settings so that we can use a web-based form to choose which node types to annotate. There are two steps to complete. First, we'll define a path where we can access our settings. Then, we'll create the settings form.

Implementing a Hook

Recall that Drupal is built on a system of hooks, sometimes called callbacks. During the course of execution, Drupal asks modules if they would like to do something. For example, when determining which module is responsible for the current request, it asks all modules to provide the paths that the modules will handle. It does this by making a list of all the modules and calling the function that has the name of the module plus _menu in each module. When it encounters the annotate module (which it will early on, since the listing is alphabetical by default), it calls our annotate_menu() function, which returns an array of menu items. Each item (we only have one at this point) is keyed by the path, in this case, admin/settings/annotate. The value of our menu item is an array consisting of keys and values describing what Drupal should do when this path is requested. We'll cover this in detail in Chapter 4, which covers Drupal's menu/callback system. Here's what we'll add to our module:

```
/**
 * Implementation of hook_menu().
 */
function annotate_menu() {
  $items['admin/settings/annotate'] = array(
    'title' => 'Annotation settings',
    'description' => 'Change how annotations behave.',
    'page callback' => 'drupal_get_form',
    'page arguments' => array('annotate_admin_settings'),
    'access arguments' => array('administer site configuration'),
    'type' => MENU_NORMAL_ITEM,
    'file' => 'annotate.admin.inc',
  );

  return $items;
}
```

Don't worry too much about the details at this point. This code says, "When the user goes to http://example.com/?q=admin/settings/annotate, call the function drupal_get_form(), and pass it the form ID annotate_admin_settings. Look for a function describing this form in the file annotate.admin.inc. Only users with the permission administer site configuration may view this menu item." When the time comes to display the form, Drupal will ask us to provide a form definition (more on that in a minute). When Drupal is finished asking all the modules for their menu items, it has a menu from which to select the proper function to call for the path being requested.

Note If you're interested in seeing the function that drives the hook mechanism, see the module_invoke_all() function in includes/module.inc.

You should see now why we call it hook_menu() or the menu hook. Drupal hooks are always created by appending the name of the hook to the name of your module.

Tip Drupal's hooks allow modification of almost any aspect of the software. A complete list of supported hooks and their uses can be found at the Drupal API documentation site (http://api.drupal.org).

Adding Module-Specific Settings

Drupal has various node types (called *content types* in the user interface), such as stories and pages. We will want to restrict the use of annotations to only some node types. To do that, we need to create a page where we can tell our module which node types we want to annotate. On that page, we will show a set of check boxes, one for each content type that exists. This will let the end user decide which content types get annotations by checking or unchecking the check boxes (see Figure 2-1). Such a page is an administrative page, and the code that composes it need only be loaded and parsed when needed. Therefore, we will put the code into a separate file, not in our `annotate.module` file, which will be loaded and run with each web request. Since we told Drupal to look for our settings form in the `annotate.admin.inc` file, create that file at `sites/all/modules/custom/annotate/annotate.admin.inc`, and add the following code to it:

```php
<?php
// $Id$

/**
 * @file
 * Administration page callbacks for the annotate module.
 */

/**
 * Form builder. Configure annotations.
 *
 * @ingroup forms
 * @see system_settings_form().
 */
function annotate_admin_settings() {
  // Get an array of node types with internal names as keys and
  // "friendly names" as values. E.g.,
  // array('page' => 'Page', 'story' => 'Story')
  $options = node_get_types('names');

  $form['annotate_node_types'] = array(
    '#type' => 'checkboxes',
    '#title' => t('Users may annotate these content types'),
    '#options' => $options,
    '#default_value' => variable_get('annotate_node_types', array('page')),
    '#description' => t('A text field will be available on these content types to
      make user-specific notes.'),
  );

  return system_settings_form($form);

}
```

Forms in Drupal are represented as a nested tree structure; that is, an array of arrays. This structure describes to Drupal's form rendering engine how the form is to be represented. For readability, we place each element of the array on its own line. Each form property is denoted with a pound sign (#) and acts as an array key. We start by declaring the type of form element to be `checkboxes`, which means that multiple check boxes will be built using a keyed array. We've already got that keyed array in the `$options` variable.

We set the options to the output of the function node_get_types('names'), which conveniently returns a keyed array of the node types that are currently available in this Drupal installation. The output would look something like this:

```
'page' => 'Page', 'story' => 'Story'
```

The keys of the array are Drupal's internal names for the node types, with the friendly names (those that will be shown to the user) on the right. If your Drupal installation had a node type called Savory Recipe, the array might look like this:

```
'page' => 'Page', 'savory_recipe' => 'Savory Recipe', 'story' => 'Story'
```

Therefore, in our web form, Drupal will generate check boxes for the page and story node types.

We give the form element a title by defining the value of the #title property.

Note Any returned text that will be displayed to the user (such as the #title and #description properties of our form field) is inside a t() function, a function provided by Drupal to facilitate string translation. By running all text through a string translation function, localization of your module for a different language will be much easier. We did not do this for our menu item because menu items are translated automatically.

The next directive, #default_value, will be the default value for this form element. Because checkboxes is a multiple form element (i.e., there is more than one check box) the value for #default_value will be an array.

The value of #default_value is worth discussing:

```
variable_get('annotate_node_types', array('page'))
```

Drupal allows programmers to store and retrieve any value using a special pair of functions: variable_get() and variable_set(). The values are stored to the variables database table and are available anytime while processing a request. Because these variables are retrieved from the database during every request, it's not a good idea to store huge amounts of data this way. But it's a very convenient system for storing values like module configuration settings. Note that what we pass to variable_get() is a key describing our value (so we can get it back) and a default value. In this case, the default value is an array of which node types should allow annotation. We're going to allow annotation of story node types by default.

Tip When using system_settings_form(), the name of the form element (in this case, annotate_node_types) must match the name of the key used in variable_get().

Lastly, we provide a description to tell the site administrator a bit about the information that should go into the field.

Save the files you have created, and go to Administer ➤ Site building ➤ Modules. Your module should be listed at the end of the list in a group titled Pro Drupal Development (if not, double-check the syntax in your annotate.info and annotate.module files; make sure they are in the sites/all/modules/custom directory). Go ahead and enable your new module.

Now that the annotate module is enabled, navigating to Administer ➤ Site Configuration ➤ Annotate should show us the configuration form for annotate.module (see Figure 2-1).

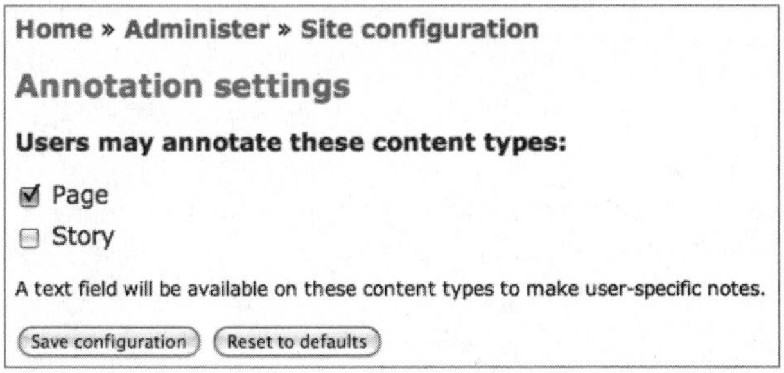

Figure 2-1. *The configuration form for annotate.module is generated for us.*

In only a few lines of code, we now have a functional configuration form for our module that will automatically save and remember our settings! OK, one of the lines was pretty long, but still, this gives you a feeling of the power you can leverage with Drupal.

Adding the Data Entry Form

In order for the user to enter notes about a web page, we're going to need to provide a place for the notes to be entered. Let's add a form for notes to annotate.module.

```
/**
 * Implementation of hook_nodeapi().
 */
function annotate_nodeapi(&$node, $op, $teaser, $page) {
  global $user;
  switch ($op) {
    // The 'view' operation means the node is about to be displayed.
    case 'view':
      // Abort if the user is an anonymous user (not logged in) or
      // if the node is not being displayed on a page by itself
      // (for example, it could be in a node listing or search result).
      if ($user->uid == 0 || !$page) {
        break;
      }
      // Find out which node types we should annotate.
      $types_to_annotate = variable_get('annotate_node_types', array('page'));
```

```
      // Abort if this node is not one of the types we should annotate.
      if (!in_array($node->type, $types_to_annotate)) {
        break;
      }

      // Add our form as a content item.
      $node->content['annotation_form'] = array(
        '#value' => drupal_get_form('annotate_entry_form', $node),
        '#weight' => 10
      );
      break;
  }
}
```

This looks complicated, so let's walk through it. First, note that we are implementing yet another Drupal hook. This time it's the nodeapi hook, and it's called when Drupal is doing various activities with a node, so that other modules (like ours) can modify the node before processing continues. We are given a node through the $node variable. The ampersand in the first parameter shows that this is actually a *reference* to the $node object, which is exciting because it means any modification we make to the $node object here in our module will be preserved. Since our objective is to append a form, we are glad that we have the ability to modify the node.

We're also given some information about what is going on in Drupal at the moment our code is called. The information resides in the $op (operation) parameter and could be insert (the node is being created), delete (the node is being deleted), or one of many other values. Currently, we are only interested in modifying the node when it is being prepared to be viewed; the $op variable will be view in this case. We structure our code using a switch statement, so that we can easily add cases and see what our module will do in each case.

Next, we quickly check for situations in which we don't want to display the annotation field. One case is when the user viewing the node is not logged in (notice that we used the global keyword to bring the $user object into scope so we could test if the current user is logged in). Another time we want to avoid displaying the form is when the $page parameter is not TRUE. If the $page parameter is FALSE, this node is not being displayed by itself but is being displayed in a list, such as in search engine results or a list of recently updated nodes. We are not interested in adding anything in such cases. We use the break statement to exit from the switch statement and avoid modifying the page.

Before we add the annotation form to the web page, we need to check whether the node being processed for viewing is one of the types for which we enabled annotation on our settings page, so we retrieve the array of node types we saved previously when we implemented the settings hook. We save it in a variable with the nicely descriptive name $types_to_annotate. As the second parameter of the variable_get() call, we still specify a default array to use in case the site administrator has not yet visited the settings page for our module to enter settings. The next step is to check if the node we are working with is, indeed, of a type contained in $types_to_annotate; again, we bail out using the break statement if it's a type of node we don't want to annotate.

Our final task is to create the form and add it to the $node object. First, we'll need to define the form so that we have something to add. We'll do that in annotate.module in a separate function whose sole responsibility is to define the form:

```
/**
 * Define the form for entering an annotation.
 */
function annotate_entry_form($form_state, $node) {
  // Define a fieldset.
  $form['annotate'] = array(
    '#type' => 'fieldset',
    '#title' => t('Annotations'),
  );

  // Define a textarea inside the fieldset.
  $form['annotate']['note'] = array(
    '#type' => 'textarea',
    '#title' => t('Notes'),
    '#default_value' => isset($node->annotation) ? $node->annotation : '',
    '#description' => t('Make your personal annotations about this content here.
      Only you (and the site administrator) will be able to see them.')
  );

  // For convenience, save the node ID.
  $form['annotate']['nid'] = array(
    '#type' => 'value',
    '#value' => $node->nid,
  );

  // Define a submit function.
  $form['annotate']['submit'] = array(
    '#type' => 'submit',
    '#value' => t('Update'),
  );
  return $form;
}
```

The function takes two parameters. The first, $form_state, is passed automatically by Drupal to all form functions. We'll ignore it for now; for details, see Chapter 10 where the form API is discussed in detail. The second parameter is the $node object that we passed into drupal_get_form() inside our nodeapi hook implementation previously.

We create the form the same way we did in our annotate_admin_settings() function, by creating a keyed array—only this time we want to put our text box and Submit button inside a fieldset so that they are grouped together on the web page. First, we create an array, set #type to be 'fieldset', and give it a title. Then we create the array that describes the textarea. Note that the array key of the textarea array is a member of the fieldset array. In other words, we use $form['annotate']['note'] instead of $form['note']. This way, Drupal can infer that the textarea element is a member of the fieldset element. We use the ternary operator to prepopulate the textarea with an existing annotation or, if no current annotation exists, with an empty string. Last, we create the submit button and return the array that defines our form.

Back in the annotate_nodeapi() function, we appended the form to the page's content by adding a value and weight to the node's content. The value contains what to display, and the weight tells Drupal where to display it in relation to other content the node may have. We want our annotation form to be low on the page, so we assign it a relatively heavy weight of 10. What we want to display is our form, so we call drupal_get_form() to change our form from an array describing how it should be built to the finished HTML form. Note how we pass the $node object along to our form function; we'll need that to get any previous annotation and prefill the form with it.

Create and view a Page node in your web browser, and you should see that the form has been appended with the annotations form (see Figure 2-2).

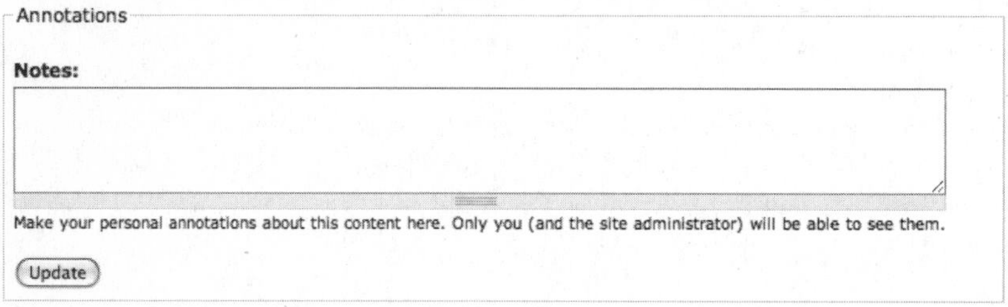

Figure 2-2. *The annotation form as it appears on a Drupal web page*

What will happen when we click the Update button? Nothing, because we haven't written any code to do anything with the form contents yet. Let's add that now. But before we do, we have to think about where we're going to store the data that the user enters.

Storing Data in a Database Table

The most common approach for storing data used by a module is to create a separate database table for the module's data. That keeps the data separate from the Drupal core tables. When deciding what fields to create for your module, you should ask yourself: What data needs to be stored? If I make a query against this table, what fields and indices would I need? And finally, what future plans do I have for my module?

The data we need to store are simply the text of the annotation, the numeric ID of the node it applies to, and the user ID of the user who wrote the annotation. It might also be useful to save a timestamp, so we could show a list of recently updated annotations ordered by timestamp. Finally, the main question we'll ask of this table is, "What is the annotation for this user for this node?" We'll create a compound index on the uid and nid fields to make our most frequent query as fast as possible. The SQL for our table will look something like the following statement:

```
CREATE TABLE annotations (
  uid int(11) NOT NULL,
  nid int(11) NOT NULL,
  note longtext NOT NULL,
  created int(11) NOT NULL default 0,
  PRIMARY KEY (uid, nid)
);
```

We could just provide this SQL in a README.txt file with our module, and others who want to install the module would have to manually add the database tables to their databases. Instead, we're going to take advantage of Drupal's facilities for having the database tables created at the same time that your module is enabled. We'll create a special file; the filename should begin with your module name and end with the suffix .install, so for the annotate.module, the filename would be annotate.install. Create sites/all/modules/custom/annotate/annotate.install, and enter the following code:

```php
<?php
// $Id$

/**
 * Implementation of hook_install().
 */
function annotate_install() {
  // Use schema API to create database table.
  drupal_install_schema('annotate');
}

/**
 * Implementation of hook_uninstall().
 */
function annotate_uninstall() {
  // Use schema API to delete database table.
  drupal_uninstall_schema('annotate');
  // Delete our module's variable from the variables table.
  variable_del('annotate_node_types');
}

/**
 * Implementation of hook_schema().
 */
function annotate_schema() {
  $schema['annotations'] = array(
    'description' => t('Stores node annotations that users write.'),
    'fields' => array(
      'nid' => array(
```

```
      'type' => 'int',
      'unsigned' => TRUE,
      'not null' => TRUE,
      'default' => 0,
      'description' => t('The {node}.nid to which the annotation applies.'),
    ),
    'uid' => array(
      'type' => 'int',
      'unsigned' => TRUE,
      'not null' => TRUE,
      'default' => 0,
      'description' => t('The {user}.uid of the user who created the annotation.')
    ),
    'note' => array(
      'description' => t('The text of the annotation.'),
      'type' => 'text',
      'not null' => TRUE,
      'size' => 'big'
    ),
    'created' => array(
      'description' => t('A Unix timestamp indicating when the annotation
        was created.'),
      'type' => 'int',
      'not null' => TRUE,
      'default' => 0
    ),
  ),
  'primary key' => array(
    'nid', 'uid'
  ),
);

  return $schema;
}
```

When the annotate module is first enabled, Drupal looks for an annotate.install file and runs the annotate_install() function, which reads the schema that is described in our implementation of the schema hook. We describe the database tables and fields we want Drupal to create, and it translates them into standard SQL for the database we are using. For more information on how this works, see Chapter 5. If everything goes well, the database tables will be created. Let's try this now. Because we already enabled the module with no database tables, we need to reinstall our module with our new .install file. Do that now as follows:

1. Disable the module on the Administer ➤ Site building ➤ Modules page.

2. Uninstall the module using the Uninstall tab on the Administer ➤ Site building ➤ Modules page. This causes Drupal to forget about database tables, if any, that are associated with a module.

3. Enable the module. This time Drupal will create the tables while the module is being enabled.

Tip If you made a typo in your .install file or execution fails for another reason, you can make Drupal forget about your module and its tables by disabling the module at Administer ➤ Site building ➤ Modules and by uninstalling the module's tables using the Uninstall tab. As a last resort, deleting the module's row from the system table of the database will do the trick.

After Drupal has created the annotations table to store the data, we'll have to make some modifications to our code. For one thing, we'll have to add some code to handle the processing of the data once the user enters an annotation and clicks the Update button. Our function for form submittal follows:

```
/**
 * Handle submission of the annotation form and saving
 * of the data to the database.
 */
function annotate_entry_form_submit($form, $form_state) {
  global $user;

  $note = $form_state['values']['note'];
  $nid = $form_state['values']['nid'];

  db_query('DELETE FROM {annotations} WHERE nid = %d AND uid = %d',
    $nid, $user->uid);
  db_query("INSERT INTO {annotations} (nid, uid, note, created) VALUES
    (%d, %d, '%s', %d)", $nid, $user->uid, $note, time());
  drupal_set_message(t('Your annotation has been saved.'));
}
```

Since we're allowing only one annotation per user per node, we can safely delete the previous annotation (if any) and insert our own into the database. There are a few things to notice about our interactions with the database. First, we don't need to worry about connecting to the database, because Drupal has already done this for us during its bootstrap sequence. Second, whenever we refer to a database table, we put it inside curly brackets. This is so that table prefixing can be done seamlessly (for more on table prefixing, see the notes in sites/default/settings.php). And third, we use placeholders in our queries and then provide the variables to be placed, so that Drupal's built-in query sanitizing mechanism can do its part to prevent SQL injection attacks. We use the %d placeholder for integers and '%s' for strings. Then, we use drupal_set_message() to stash a message in the user's session, which Drupal will display as a notice on the next page the user views. This way, the user gets some feedback.

Finally, we need to change our nodeapi hook code so that if there's an existing annotation, it gets pulled from the database and is used to prefill our form. Just before we assign our form to $node->content, we add the following lines, shown in boldface type:

```
/**
 * Implementation of hook_nodeapi().
 */
function annotate_nodeapi(&$node, $op, $teaser, $page) {
  global $user;
  switch ($op) {
    // The 'view' operation means the node is about to be displayed.
    case 'view':
      // Abort if the user is an anonymous user (not logged in) or
      // if only the node summary (teaser) is being displayed.
      if ($user->uid == 0 || !$page) {
        break;
      }
      // Find out which node types we should annotate.
      $types_to_annotate = variable_get('annotate_node_types', array('page'));

      // Abort if this node is not one of the types we should annotate.
      if (!in_array($node->type, $types_to_annotate)) {
        break;
      }

      // Get the current annotation for this node from the database
      // and store it in the node object.
      $result = db_query('SELECT note FROM {annotations} WHERE nid = %d
        AND uid = %d', $node->nid, $user->uid);
      $node->annotation = db_result($result);

      // Add our form as a content item.
      $node->content['annotation_form'] = array(
        '#value' => drupal_get_form('annotate_entry_form', $node),
        '#weight' => 10
      );
      break;

    case 'delete':
      db_query('DELETE FROM {annotations} WHERE nid = %d', $node->nid);
      break;
  }
}
```

We first query our database table to select the annotation for this user and this node. Next, we use db_result(), a function that gets only the first field of the first row from the result set. Since we're only allowing one note per user per node, there should only ever be one row.

We've also added a case for the delete operation of the nodeapi hook, so when a node is deleted the annotations for that node will be deleted as well.

Test your module. It should be able to save and retrieve annotations. Pat yourself on the back—you've made a Drupal module from scratch. You're on your way to becoming a core Drupal developer!

Defining Your Own Administration Section

Drupal has several categories of administrative settings, such as content management and user management, that appear on the main administration page. If your module needs a category of its own, you can create that category easily. In this example, we create a new category called "Node annotation." To do so, we modify our module's menu hook to define the new category:

```
/**
 * Implementation of hook_menu().
 */
function annotate_menu() {
  $items['admin/annotate'] = array(
    'title' => 'Node annotation',
    'description' => 'Adjust node annotation options.',
    'position' => 'right',
    'weight' => -5,
    'page callback' => 'system_admin_menu_block_page',
    'access arguments' => array('administer site configuration'),
    'file' => 'system.admin.inc',
    'file path' => drupal_get_path('module', 'system'),
  );
  $items['admin/annotate/settings'] = array(
    'title' => 'Annotation settings',
    'description' => 'Change how annotations behave.',
    'page callback' => 'drupal_get_form',
    'page arguments' => array('annotate_admin_settings'),
    'access arguments' => array('administer site configuration'),
    'type' => MENU_NORMAL_ITEM,
    'file' => 'annotate.admin.inc',
  );

  return $items;
}
```

The results of our code changes, namely a new category with our module's setting link in it, are shown in Figure 2-3.

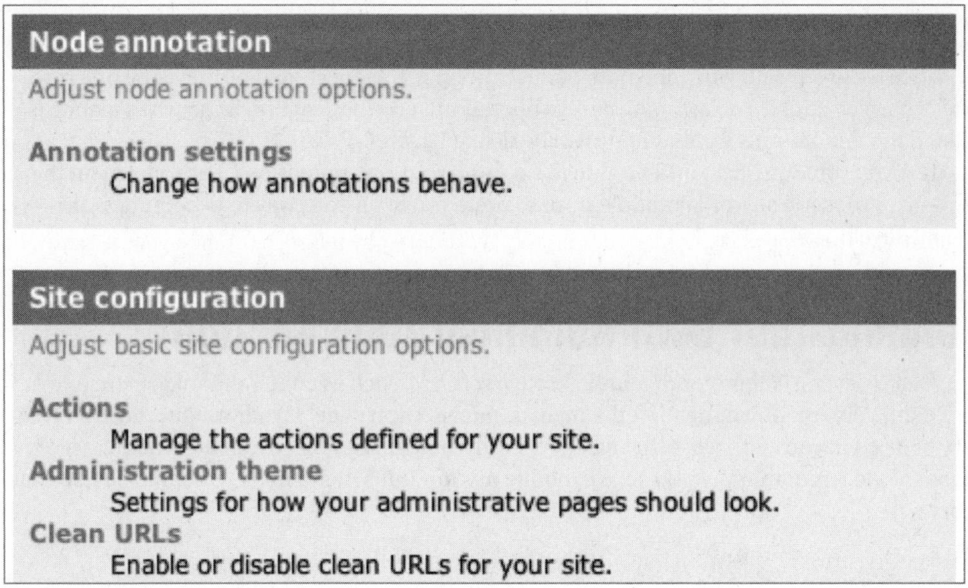

Node annotation

Adjust node annotation options.

Annotation settings
    Change how annotations behave.

Site configuration

Adjust basic site configuration options.

Actions
    Manage the actions defined for your site.
Administration theme
    Settings for how your administrative pages should look.
Clean URLs
    Enable or disable clean URLs for your site.

Figure 2-3. *The link to the annotation module settings now appears as a separate category.*

If you're following along at home, you'll need to clear the menu cache to see the link appear. You can do this by truncating the cache_menu table or by clicking the "Rebuild menus" link that the Drupal development module (devel.module) provides or by using the Clear cached data button at Administer ➤ Site configuration ➤ Performance.

■Tip The development module (http://drupal.org/project/devel) was written specifically to support Drupal development. It gives you quick access to many development functions, such as clearing the cache, viewing variables, tracking queries, and much more. It's a must-have for serious development. If you do not have it installed, download it, and place the folder at sites/all/modules/devel, then turn on the Development block at Administer ➤ Site building ➤ Blocks.

We were able to establish our new category in two steps. First, we added a menu item that describes the category header. This menu item has a unique path (admin/annotate). We declare that it should be placed in the right column with a weight of -5, because this places it just above the "Site configuration" category, which is handiest for the screenshot shown in Figure 2-3.

The second step was to tell Drupal to nest the actual link to annotation settings inside the "Node annotation" category. We did this by changing the path of our original menu item, so that instead of admin/settings/annotate, the path is now admin/annotate/settings. Previously, the menu item was a child of admin/settings, which is the path to the "Site configuration" category, as shown in Table 2-1. When Drupal rebuilds the menu tree, it looks at the paths to establish relationships among parent and child items and determines that, because admin/annotate/settings is a child of admin/annotate, it should be displayed as such. Nest module menu item paths underneath one of the paths shown in Table 2-1 to make those modules appear in that category on Drupal's administration page.

Drupal loads only the files that are necessary to complete a request. This saves on memory usage. Because our page callback points to a function that is outside the scope of our module (i.e., the function system_admin_menu_block_page() in system.module), we need to tell Drupal to load the file modules/system/system.admin.inc instead of trying to load sites/all/modules/custom/annotate/system.admin.inc. We did that by telling Drupal to get the path of the system module and put the result in the file path key of our menu item.

Of course, this is a contrived example, and in real life, you should have a good reason to create a new category to avoid confusing the administrator (often yourself!) with too many categories.

Table 2-1. *Paths to Administrative Categories*

Path	Category
admin/content	Content management
admin/build	Site building
admin/settings	Site configuration
admin/user	User management
admin/reports	Reports

Presenting a Settings Form to the User

In the annotate module, we gave the administrator the ability to choose which node types would support annotation (see Figure 2-1). Let's delve into how this works.

When a site administrator wants to change the settings for the annotate module, we want to display a form so the administrator can select from the options we present. In our menu item, we set the page callback to point to the drupal_get_form() function and set the page arguments to be an array containing annotate_admin_settings. That means that when you go to http://example.com/?q=admin/annotate/settings, the call drupal_get_form ('annotate_admin_settings') will be executed, which essentially tells Drupal to build the form defined by the function annotate_admin_settings().

Let's take a look at the function defining the form, which defines a check box for node types (see Figure 2-1), and add two more options. The function is in sites/all/modules/custom/annotate/annotate.admin.inc:

```
/**
 * Form builder. Configure annotations.
 *
 * @ingroup forms
 * @see system_settings_form().
 */
```

```
function annotate_admin_settings() {
  // Get an array of node types with internal names as keys and
  // "friendly names" as values. E.g.,
  // array('page' => 'Page', 'story' => 'Story')
  $options = node_get_types('names');

  $form['annotate_node_types'] = array(
    '#type' => 'checkboxes',
    '#title' => t('Users may annotate these content types'),
    '#options' => $options,
    '#default_value' => variable_get('annotate_node_types', array('page')),
    '#description' => t('A text field will be available on these content types
    to make user-specific notes.'),
  );

  $form['annotate_deletion'] = array(
    '#type' => 'radios',
    '#title' => t('Annotations will be deleted'),
    '#description' => t('Select a method for deleting annotations.'),
    '#options' => array(
      t('Never'),
      t('Randomly'),
      t('After 30 days')
    ),
    '#default_value' => variable_get('annotate_deletion', 0) // Default to Never
  );

  $form['annotate_limit_per_node'] = array(
    '#type' => 'textfield',
    '#title' => t('Annotations per node'),
    '#description' => t('Enter the maximum number of annotations allowed per
      node (0 for no limit).'),
    '#default_value' => variable_get('annotate_limit_per_node', 1),
    '#size' => 3
  );

  return system_settings_form($form);
}
```

We add a radio button to choose when annotations should be deleted and a text entry field to limit the number of annotations allowed on a node (implementation of these enhancements in the module is left as an exercise for you). Rather than managing the processing of our own form, we call system_settings_form() to let the system module add some buttons to the form and manage validation and submission of the form. Figure 2-4 shows what the options form looks like now.

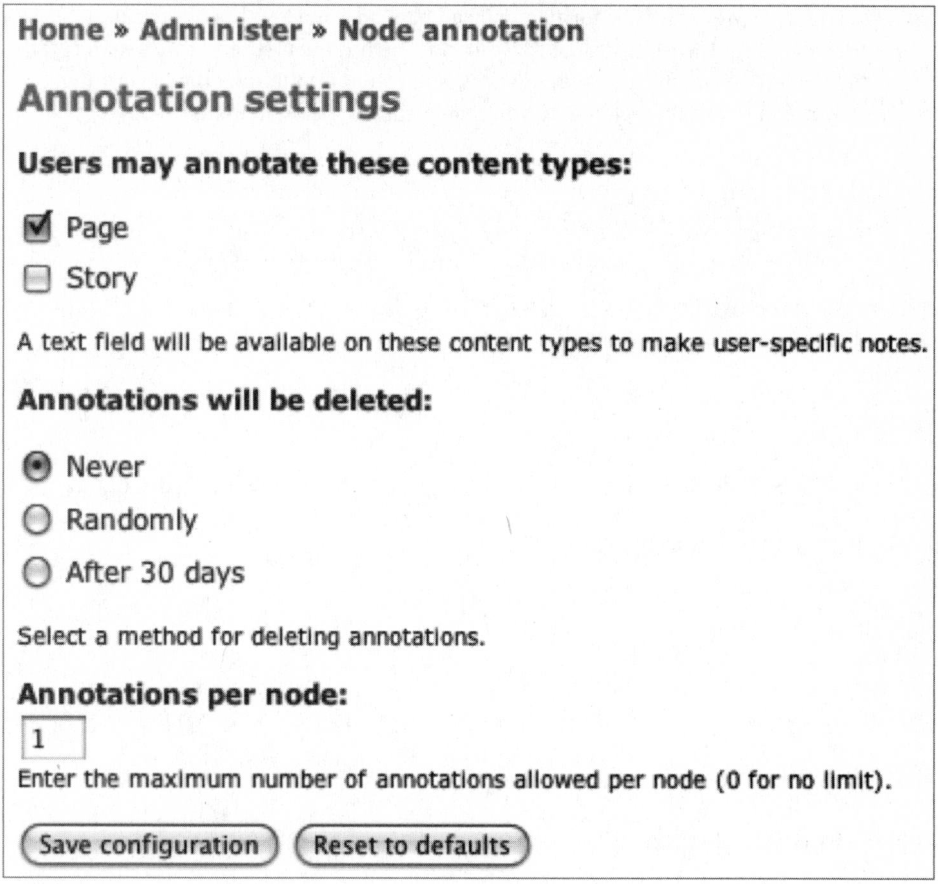

Home » Administer » Node annotation

Annotation settings

Users may annotate these content types:

☑ Page

☐ Story

A text field will be available on these content types to make user-specific notes.

Annotations will be deleted:

◉ Never

○ Randomly

○ After 30 days

Select a method for deleting annotations.

Annotations per node:

```
1
```

Enter the maximum number of annotations allowed per node (0 for no limit).

(Save configuration)   (Reset to defaults)

Figure 2-4. Enhanced options form using check box, radio button, and text field options

Validating User-Submitted Settings

If system_settings_form() is taking care of saving the form values for us, how can we check whether the value entered in the "Annotations per node" field is actually a number? Can we hook into the form submission process somehow? Of course we can. We just need to define a validation function in sites/all/modules/custom/annotate/annotate.admin.inc and use it to set an error if we find anything wrong.

```
/**
 * Validate the annotation configuration form.
 */
function annotate_admin_settings_validate($form, $form_state) {
  $limit = $form_state['values']['annotate_limit_per_node'];
  if (!is_numeric($limit)) {
    form_set_error('annotate_limit_per_node', t('Please enter a number.'));
  }
}
```

Now when Drupal processes the form, it will call back to `annotate_admin_settings_validate()` for validation. If we determine that a bad value has been entered, we set an error against the field where the error occurred, and this is reflected on the screen in a warning message and by highlighting the field containing the error, as shown in Figure 2-5.

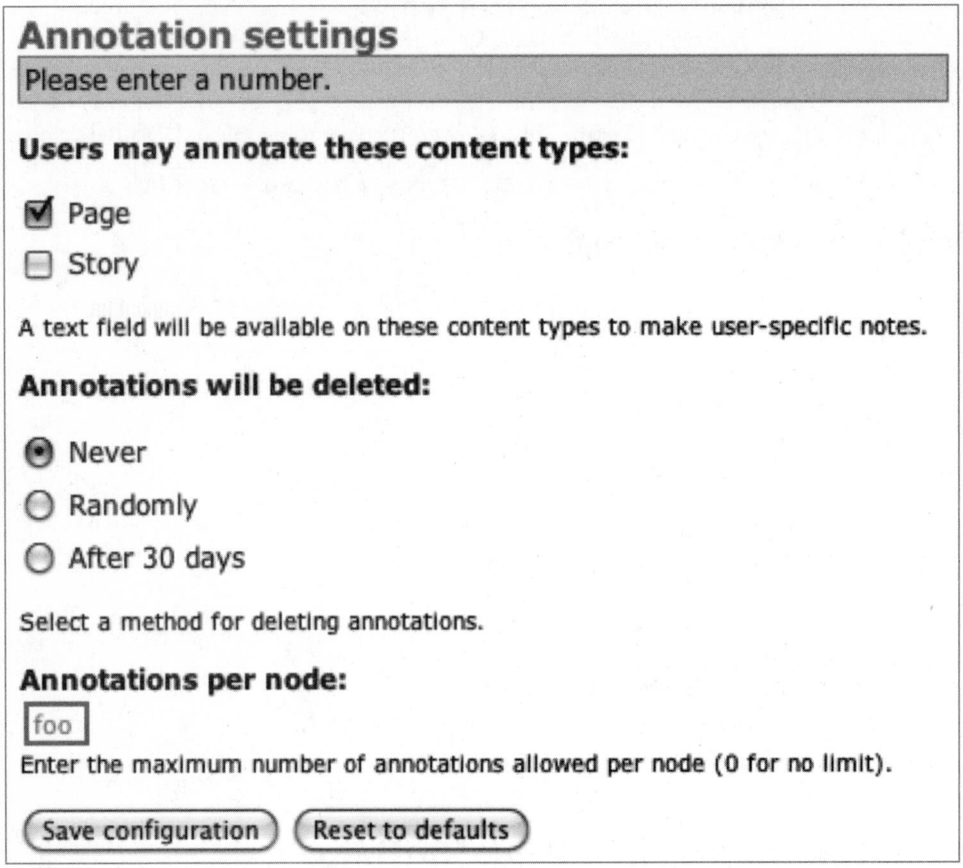

Annotation settings

Please enter a number.

Users may annotate these content types:

☑ Page
☐ Story

A text field will be available on these content types to make user-specific notes.

Annotations will be deleted:

◉ Never

○ Randomly

○ After 30 days

Select a method for deleting annotations.

Annotations per node:

`foo`

Enter the maximum number of annotations allowed per node (0 for no limit).

(Save configuration) (Reset to defaults)

Figure 2-5. *The validation script has set an error.*

How did Drupal know to call our function? We named it in a special way, using the name of the form definition function (`annotate_admin_settings`) plus `_validate`. For a full explanation of how Drupal determines which form validation function to call, see Chapter 10.

Storing Settings

In the preceding example, changing the settings and clicking the "Save configuration" button works. If the "Reset to defaults" button is clicked, the fields are reset to their default values. The sections that follow describe how this happens.

Using Drupal's variables Table

Let's look at the "Annotations per node" field first. Its `#default_value` key is set to

```
variable_get('annotate_limit_per_node', 1)
```

Drupal has a `variables` table in the database, and key-value pairs can be stored using `variable_set($key, $value)` and retrieved using `variable_get($key, $default)`. So we're really saying, "Set the default value of the 'Annotations per node' field to the value stored in the `variables` database table for the variable `annotate_limit_per_node`, but if no value can be found, use the value 1." So when the "Reset to defaults" button is clicked, Drupal deletes the current entry for the key `annotate_limit_per_node` from the variables table and uses the default value of 1.

■**Caution** In order for the settings to be stored and retrieved in the `variables` table without namespace collisions, always give your form element and your variable key the same name (e.g., `annotate_limit_per_node` in the preceding example). Create the form element/variable key name from your module name plus a descriptive name, and use that name for both your form element and variable key.

The "Annotations will be deleted" field is a little more complex, since it's a radio button field. The `#options` for this field are the following:

```
'#options' => array(
  t('Never'),
  t('Randomly'),
  t('After 30 days')
)
```

When PHP gets an array with no keys, it implicitly inserts numeric keys, so internally the array is really as follows:

```
'#options' => array(
  [0] => t('Never'),
  [1] => t('Randomly'),
  [2] => t('After 30 days')
)
```

When we set the default value for this field, we use

```
'#default_value' => variable_get('annotate_deletion', 0) // Default to Never
```

which means, in effect, default to item 0 of the array, which is `t('Never')`.

Retrieving Stored Values with variable_get()

When your module retrieves settings that have been stored, `variable_get()` should be used:

```
// Get stored setting of maximum number of annotations per node.
$max = variable_get('annotate_limit_per_node', 1);
```

Note the use of a default value for `variable_get()` here also, in case no stored values are available (maybe the administrator has not yet visited the settings page).

Further Steps

We'll be sharing this module with the open source community, naturally, so a `README.txt` file should be created and placed in the annotations directory alongside the `annotate.info`, `annotate.module`, and `annotate.install` files. The `README.txt` file generally contains information about who wrote the module and how to install it. Licensing information need not be included, as all modules uploaded to `drupal.org` are GPL licensed and the packaging script on `drupal.org` will automatically add a `LICENSE.txt` file. Next, you could upload it to the contributions repository on `drupal.org`, and create a project page to keep track of feedback from others in the community.

Summary

After reading this chapter, you should be able to perform the following tasks:

- Create a Drupal module from scratch.

- Understand how to hook into Drupal's code execution.

- Store and retrieve module-specific settings.

- Create and process simple forms using Drupal's forms API.

- Store and retrieve data using your module's database table.

- Create a new administrative category on Drupal's main administration page.

- Define a form for the site administrator to choose options using check boxes, text input fields, and radio buttons.

- Validate settings and present an error message if validation fails.

- Understand how Drupal stores and retrieves settings using the built-in persistent variable system.

CHAPTER 3

■ ■ ■

Hooks, Actions, and Triggers

A common goal when working with Drupal is for something to happen when a certain event takes place. For example, a site administrator may want to receive an e-mail message when a message is posted. Or a user should be blocked if certain words appear in a comment. This chapter describes how to hook into Drupal's events to have your own code run when those events take place.

Understanding Events and Triggers

Drupal proceeds through a series of events as it goes about its business. These internal events are times when modules are allowed to interact with Drupal's processing. Table 3-1 shows some of Drupal's events.

Table 3-1. *Examples of Drupal Events*

Event	Type
Creation of a node	Node
Deletion of a node	Node
Viewing of a node	Node
Creation of a user account	User
Updating of a user profile	User
Login	User
Logout	User

Drupal developers refer to these internal events as *hooks* because when one of the events occurs, Drupal allows modules to *hook into* the path of execution at that point. You've already met some hooks in previous chapters. Typical module development involves deciding which Drupal event you want to react to, that is, which hooks you want to implement in your module.

Suppose you have a web site that is just starting out, and you are serving the site from the computer in your basement. Once the site gets popular, you plan to sell it to a huge corporation and get filthy rich. In the meantime, you'd like to be notified each time a user logs in. You decide that when a user logs in you want the computer to beep. Because your cat is sleeping and would find the beeps annoying, you decide to simulate the beep for the time being with a simple log entry. You quickly write an `.info` file and place it at `sites/all/modules/custom/beep/beep.info`:

```
; $Id$
name = Beep
description = Simulates a system beep.
package = Pro Drupal Development
core = 6.x
```

Then it's time to write `sites/all/modules/custom/beep/beep.module`:

```php
<?php
// $Id$
/**
 * @file
 * Provide a simulated beep.
 */

function beep_beep() {
  watchdog('beep', 'Beep!');
}
```

This writes the message "Beep!" to Drupal's log. Good enough for now. Next, it's time to tell Drupal to beep when a user logs in. We can do that easily by implementing hook_user() in our module and catching the `login` operation:

```php
/**
 * Implementation of hook_user().
 */
function beep_user($op, &$edit, &$account, $category = NULL) {
  if ($op == 'login') {
    beep_beep();
  }
}
```

There; that was easy. How about beeping when new content is added, too? We can do that by implementing hook_nodeapi() in our module and catching the `insert` operation:

```php
/**
 * Implementation of hook_nodeapi().
 */
function beep_nodeapi(&$node, $op, $a3 = NULL, $a4 = NULL) {
  if ($op == 'insert') {
    beep_beep();
  }
}
```

What if we wanted a beep when a comment is added? Well, we could implement `hook_comment()` and catch the `insert` operation, but let's stop and think for a minute. We're essentially doing the same thing over and over. Wouldn't it be nice to have a graphical user interface where we could associate the action of beeping with whatever hook and whatever operation we'd like? That's what Drupal's built-in trigger module does. It allows you to associate some action with a certain event. In the code, an event is defined as a unique hook-operation combination, such as "user hook, login operation" or "nodeapi hook, insert operation." When each of these operations occurs, `trigger.module` lets you trigger an action.

To avoid confusion, let's clarify our terms:

- *Event*: Used in the generic programming sense, this term is generally understood as a message sent from one component of a system to other components.

- *Hook*: This programming technique, used in Drupal, allows modules to "hook into" the flow of execution.

- *Operation*: This refers to the specific process that is being performed within a hook. For example, the `login` operation is an operation of the user hook.

- *Trigger*: This refers to a specific combination of a hook and an operation with which one or more actions can be associated. For example, the action of beeping can be associated with the `login` operation of the user hook.

Understanding Actions

An *action* is something that Drupal does. Here are some examples:

- Promoting a node to the front page

- Changing a node from unpublished to published

- Deleting a user

- Sending an e-mail

Each of these cases has a clearly defined task. Programmers will notice the similarity to PHP functions in the preceding list. For example, you could send e-mail by calling the `drupal_mail()` function in `includes/mail.inc`. Actions sound similar to functions, because actions *are* functions. They are functions that Drupal can introspect and loosely couple with events (more on that in a moment). Now, let's examine the trigger module.

The Trigger User Interface

Navigate to Administer ➤ Site building ➤ Modules, and enable the trigger module. Then go to Administer ➤ Site building ➤ Triggers. You should see an interface similar to the one shown in Figure 3-1.

Home » Administer » Site building » Triggers

Triggers

| Comments | **Content** | Cron | Taxonomy | Users |

Triggers are system events, such as when new content is added or when a user logs in. Trigger module combines these triggers with actions (functional tasks), such as unpublishing content or e-mailing an administrator. The Actions settings page contains a list of existing actions and provides the ability to create and configure additional actions.

Below you can assign actions to run when certain content-related triggers happen. For example, you could remove a post from the front page when the post is updated.

[more help...]

Trigger: When either saving a new post or updating an existing post

| Choose an action ▼ | Assign |

Choose an action
node
    Publish post
    Unpublish post
    Make post sticky
    Make post unsticky
    Promote post to front page
    Remove post from front page

▼ | Assign |

▼ | Assign |

Trigger: After deleting a post

| Choose an action ▼ | Assign |

Trigger: When content is viewed by an authenticated user

| Choose an action ▼ | Assign |

Figure 3-1. *The trigger assignment interface*

Notice the tabs across the top. Those correspond to Drupal hooks! In Figure 3-1, we are looking at the operations for the nodeapi hook. They've all been given nice names; for example, the `delete` operation of the nodeapi hook is labeled "After deleting a post." So each of the hook's operations is shown with the ability to assign an action such as "Promote post to front page" when that operation happens. Each action that is available is listed in the "Choose an action" drop-down.

■Note Not all actions are available for all triggers, because some actions do not make sense in certain contexts. For example, you wouldn't run the "Promote post to front page" action with the trigger "After deleting a post." Depending on your installation, some triggers may display "No actions available for this trigger."

Some trigger names and their respective hooks and operations are shown in Table 3-2.

Table 3-2. *How Hooks, Operations, and Triggers Relate in Drupal 6*

Hook	Operation	Trigger Name
comment	insert	After saving a new comment
comment	update	After saving an updated comment
comment	delete	After deleting a comment
comment	view	When a comment is being viewed by an authenticated user
cron	run	When cron runs
nodeapi	presave	When either saving a new post or updating an existing post
nodeapi	insert	After saving a new post
nodeapi	update	After saving an updated post
nodeapi	delete	After deleting a post
nodeapi	view	When content is viewed by an authenticated user
taxonomy	insert	After saving a new term to the database
taxonomy	update	After saving an updated term to the database
taxonomy	delete	After deleting a term
user	insert	After a user account has been created
user	update	After a user's profile has been updated
user	delete	After a user has been deleted
user	login	After a user has logged in
user	logout	After a user has logged out
user	view	When a user's profile is being viewed

Your First Action

What do we need to do in order for our beep function to become a full-fledged action? There are two steps:

1. Inform Drupal which triggers the action should support.

2. Create your action function.

The first step is accomplished by implementing hook_action_info(). Here's how it should look for our beep module:

```
/**
 * Implementation of hook_action_info().
 */
```

```
function beep_action_info() {
  $info['beep_beep_action'] = array(
    'type' => 'system',
    'description' => t('Beep annoyingly'),
    'configurable' => FALSE,
    'hooks' => array(
      'nodeapi' => array('view', 'insert', 'update', 'delete'),
      'comment' => array('view', 'insert', 'update', 'delete'),
      'user' => array('view', 'insert', 'update', 'delete', 'login'),
      'taxonomy' => array('insert', 'update', 'delete'),
    ),
  );

  return $info;
}
```

The function name is beep_action_info(), because like other hook implementations, we use our module name (beep) plus the name of the hook (action_info). We'll be returning an array with an entry for each action in our module. We are only writing one action, so we have only one entry, keyed by the name of the function that will perform the action: beep_beep_action(). It's handy to know when a function is an action while reading through code, so we append _action to the name of our beep_beep() function to come up with beep_beep_action().

Let's take a closer look at the keys in our array.

- type: This is the kind of action you are writing. Drupal uses this information to categorize actions in the drop-down select box of the trigger assignment user interface. Possible types include system, node, user, comment, and taxonomy. A good question to ask when determining what type of action you are writing is, "What object does this action work with?" (If the answer is unclear or "lots of different objects!" use the system type.)

- description: This is the friendly name of the action that will be shown in the drop-down select box of the trigger assignment user interface.

- configurable: This determines whether or not the action takes any parameters.

- hooks: In this array of hooks, each entry must enumerate the operations the action supports. Drupal uses this information to determine where it is appropriate to list possible actions in the trigger assignment user interface.

We've described our action to Drupal, so let's go ahead and write it:

```
/**
 * Simulate a beep. A Drupal action.
 */
function beep_beep_action() {
  beep_beep();
}
```

That wasn't too difficult, was it? Before continuing, go ahead and delete beep_user() and beep_nodeapi(), since we'll be using triggers and actions instead of direct hook implementations.

Assigning the Action

Now, let's revisit Administer ➤ Site building ➤ Triggers. If you've done everything correctly and embedded the Beep Module, your action should be available in the user interface, as shown in Figure 3-2.

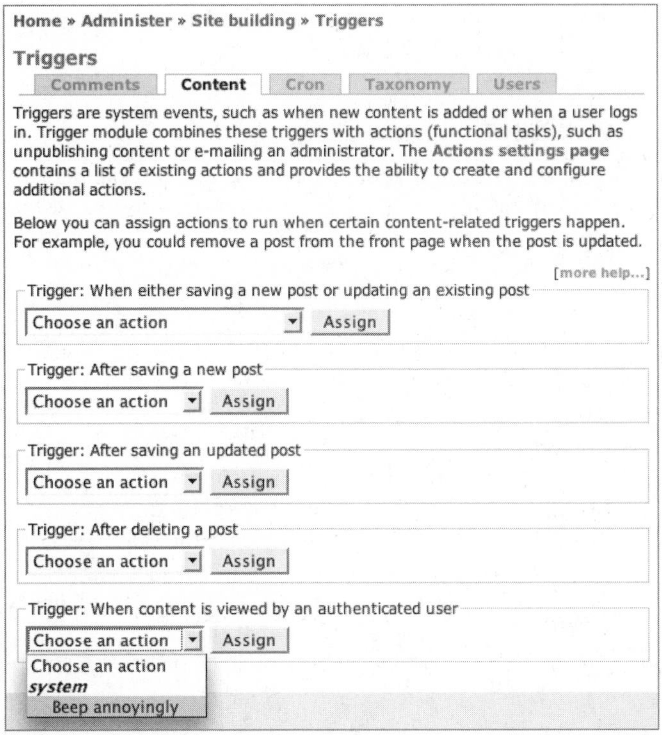

Home » Administer » Site building » Triggers

Triggers

| Comments | **Content** | Cron | Taxonomy | Users |

Triggers are system events, such as when new content is added or when a user logs in. Trigger module combines these triggers with actions (functional tasks), such as unpublishing content or e-mailing an administrator. The **Actions settings page** contains a list of existing actions and provides the ability to create and configure additional actions.

Below you can assign actions to run when certain content-related triggers happen. For example, you could remove a post from the front page when the post is updated.

[more help...]

Trigger: When either saving a new post or updating an existing post

[Choose an action ▾] [Assign]

Trigger: After saving a new post

[Choose an action ▾] [Assign]

Trigger: After saving an updated post

[Choose an action ▾] [Assign]

Trigger: After deleting a post

[Choose an action ▾] [Assign]

Trigger: When content is viewed by an authenticated user

[Choose an action ▾] [Assign]

Choose an action
system
  Beep annoyingly

Figure 3-2. *The action should be selectable in the triggers user interface.*

Changing Which Triggers an Action Supports

If you modify the values that define which operations this action supports, you should see the availability change in the user interface. For example, the "Beep" action will be available only to the "After deleting a post" trigger if you change beep_action_info() as follows:

```
/**
 * Implementation of hook_action_info().
 */
```

```
function beep_action_info() {
  $info['beep_beep_action'] = array(
    'type' => 'system',
    'description' => t('Beep annoyingly'),
    'configurable' => FALSE,
    'hooks' => array(
      'nodeapi' => array('delete'),
    ),
  );

  return $info;
}
```

Actions That Support Any Trigger

If you don't want to restrict your action to a particular trigger or set of triggers, you can declare that your action supports any trigger:

```
/**
 * Implementation of hook_action_info().
 */
function beep_action_info() {
  $info['beep_beep_action'] = array(
    'type' => 'system',
    'description' => t('Beep annoyingly'),
    'configurable' => FALSE,
    'hooks' => array(
      'any' => TRUE,
    ),
  );

  return $info;
}
```

Advanced Actions

There are essentially two kinds of actions: actions that take parameters and actions that do not. The "Beep" action we've been working with does not take any parameters. When the action is executed, it beeps once and that's the end of it. But there are many times when actions need a bit more context. For example, a "Send e-mail" action needs to know to whom to send the e-mail and what the subject and message are. An action like that requires some setup in a configuration form and is called an *advanced action*, also called a *configurable action*.

Simple actions take no parameters, do not require a configuration form, and are automatically made available by the system (after visiting Administer ➤ Site building ➤ Modules). You tell Drupal that the action you are writing is an advanced action by setting the configurable key to TRUE in your module's implementation of hook_action_info(), by providing a form to configure the action, and by providing an optional validation handler and a required submit handler to process the configuration form. The differences between simple and advanced actions are summarized in Table 3-3.

Table 3-3. *Summary of How Simple and Advanced Actions Differ*

	Simple Action	Advanced Action
Parameters	No*	Required
Configuration form	No	Required
Availability	Automatic	Must create instance of action using actions administration page
Value of `configure` key in `hook_action_info()`	FALSE	TRUE

* *The $object and $context parameters are available if needed.*

Let's create an advanced action that will beep multiple times. We will be able to specify the number of times that the action will beep using a configuration form.

First, we will need to tell Drupal that this action is configurable. Let's add an entry for our new action in the action_info hook implementation of `beep.module`:

```
/**
 * Implementation of hook_action_info().
 */
function beep_action_info() {
  $info['beep_beep_action'] = array(
    'type' => 'system',
    'description' => t('Beep annoyingly'),
    'configurable' => FALSE,
    'hooks' => array(
      'nodeapi' => array('delete'),
    ),
  );
  $info['beep_multiple_beep_action'] = array(
    'type' => 'system',
    'description' => t('Beep multiple times'),
    'configurable' => TRUE,
    'hooks' => array(
      'any' => TRUE,
    ),
  );

  return $info;
}
```

Let's quickly check if we've done the implementation correctly at Administer ➤ Site configuration ➤ Actions. Sure enough, the action should show up as a choice in the advanced actions drop-down select box, as shown in Figure 3-3.

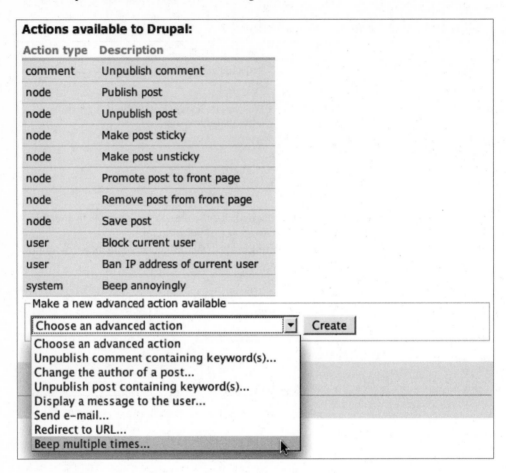

Figure 3-3. *The new action appears as a choice.*

Now, we need to provide a form so that the administrator can choose how many beeps are desired. We do this by defining one or more fields using Drupal's form API. We'll also write functions for form validation and submission. The names of the functions are based on the action's ID as defined in hook_action_info(). The action ID of the action we are currently discussing is beep_multiple_beep_action, so convention dictates that we add _form to the form definition function name to get beep_multiple_beep_action_form. Drupal expects a validation function named from the action ID plus _validate (beep_multiple_beep_action_validate) and a submit function named from the action ID plus _submit (beep_multiple_beep_action_submit).

```
/**
 * Form for configurable Drupal action to beep multiple times.
 */
function beep_multiple_beep_action_form($context) {
  $form['beeps'] = array(
    '#type' => 'textfield',
    '#title' => t('Number of beeps'),
    '#description' => t('Enter the number of times to beep when this action
      executes.'),
    '#default_value' => isset($context['beeps']) ? $context['beeps'] : '1',
    '#required' => TRUE,
  );
  return $form;
}

function beep_multiple_beep_action_validate($form, $form_state) {
  $beeps = $form_state['values']['beeps'];
  if (!is_numeric($beeps)) {
    form_set_error('beeps', t('Please enter a numeric value.'));
  }
  else if ((int) $beeps > 10) {
    form_set_error('beeps', t('That would be too annoying. Please choose fewer
      than 10 beeps.'));
  }
}

function beep_multiple_beep_action_submit($form, $form_state) {
  return array(
    'beeps' => (int) $form_state['values']['beeps']
  );
}
```

The first function describes the form to Drupal. The only field we define is a single text field so that the administrator can enter the number of beeps. When the administrator chooses to add the advanced action "Beep multiple times," as shown in Figure 3-3, Drupal will use our form field to present a full action configuration form, as shown in Figure 3-4.

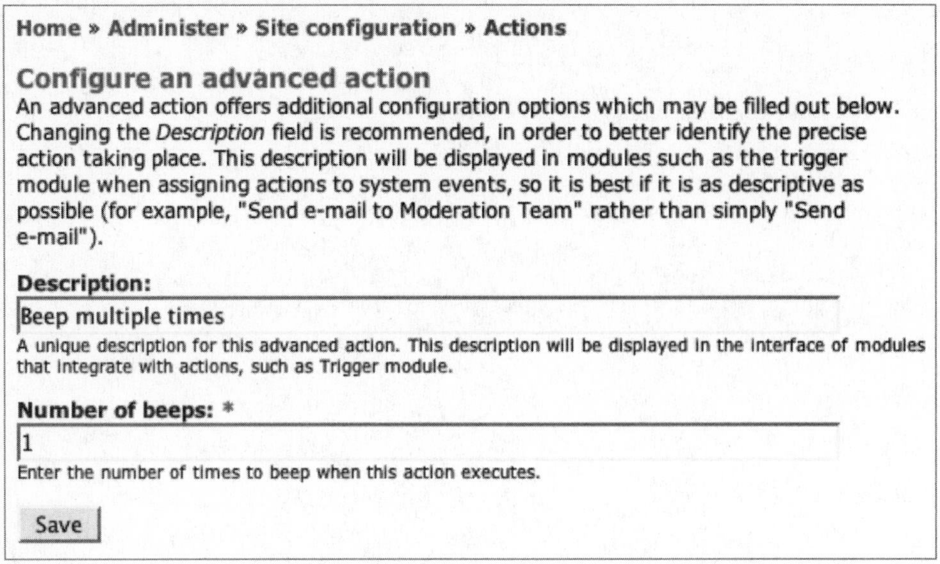

Home » Administer » Site configuration » Actions

Configure an advanced action

An advanced action offers additional configuration options which may be filled out below. Changing the *Description* field is recommended, in order to better identify the precise action taking place. This description will be displayed in modules such as the trigger module when assigning actions to system events, so it is best if it is as descriptive as possible (for example, "Send e-mail to Moderation Team" rather than simply "Send e-mail").

Description:

Beep multiple times

A unique description for this advanced action. This description will be displayed in the interface of modules that integrate with actions, such as Trigger module.

Number of beeps: *

1

Enter the number of times to beep when this action executes.

Save

Figure 3-4. *The action configuration form for the "Beep multiple times" action*

Drupal has added a Description field to the action configuration form. The value of this field is editable and will be used instead of the default description that was defined in the action_info hook. That makes sense, because we could create one advanced action to beep two times and give it the description "Beep two times" and another that beeps five times with the description "Beep five times." That way, we could tell the difference between the two advanced actions when assigning actions to a trigger. Advanced actions can thus be described in a way that makes sense to the administrator.

Tip These two actions, "Beep two times" and "Beep five times," can be referred to as instances of the "Beep multiple times" action.

The validation function is like any other form validation function in Drupal (see Chapter 10 for more on form validation). In this case, we check to make sure the user has actually entered a number and that the number is not excessively large.

The submit function's return value is special for action configuration forms. It should be an array keyed by the fields we are interested in. The values in this array will be made available to the action when it runs. The description is handled automatically, so we only need to return the field we provided, that is, the number of beeps.

Finally, it is time to write the advanced action itself:

```
/**
 * Configurable action. Beeps a specified number of times.
 */
function beep_multiple_beep_action($object, $context) {
  for ($i = 1; $i < $context['beeps']; $i++) {
    beep_beep();
  }
}
```

You'll notice that the action accepts two parameters, $object and $context. This is in contrast to the simple action we wrote earlier, which used no parameters.

■**Note** Simple actions can take the same parameters as configurable actions. Because PHP ignores parameters that are passed to a function but do not appear in the function's signature, we could simply change the function signature of our simple action from beep_beep_action() to beep_beep_action ($object, $context) if we had a need to know something about the current context. All actions are called with the $object and $context parameters.

Using the Context in Actions

We've established that the function signature for actions is example_action($object, $context). Let's examine each of those parameters in detail.

- $object: Many actions act on one of Drupal's built-in objects: nodes, users, taxonomy terms, and so on. When an action is executed by trigger.module, the object that is currently being acted upon is passed along to the action in the $object parameter. For example, if an action is set to execute when a new node is created, the $object parameter will contain the node object.

- $context: An action can be called in many different contexts. Actions declare which triggers they support by defining the hooks key in hook_action_info(). But actions that support multiple triggers need some way of determining the context in which they were called. That way, an action can act differently depending on the context.

How the Trigger Module Prepares the Context

Let's set up a scenario. Suppose you are running a web site that presents controversial issues. Here's the business model: users pay to register and may leave only a single comment on the web site. Once they have posted their comment, they are blocked and must pay again to get unblocked. Ignoring the economic prospects for such a site, let's focus on how we could implement this with triggers and actions. We will need an action that blocks the current user. Examining user.module, we see that Drupal already provides this action for us:

```
/**
 * Implementation of hook_action_info().
 */
function user_action_info() {
  return array(
    'user_block_user_action' => array(
      'description' => t('Block current user'),
      'type' => 'user',
      'configurable' => FALSE,
      'hooks' => array(),
    ),
    'user_block_ip_action' => array(
      'description' => t('Ban IP address of current user'),
      'type' => 'user',
      'configurable' => FALSE,
      'hooks' => array(),
    ),
  );
}
```

However, these actions do not show up on the triggers assignment page, because they do not declare any supported hooks; the hooks key is just an empty array. If only we could change that! But we can.

Changing Existing Actions with hook_action_info_alter()

When Drupal runs the action_info hook so that each module can declare the actions it provides, Drupal also gives modules a chance to modify that information—including information provided by other modules. Here is how we would make the "Block current user" action available to the comment insert trigger:

```
/**
 * Implementation of hook_drupal_alter(). Called by Drupal after
 * hook_action_info() so modules may modify the action_info array.
 *
 * @param array $info
 *    The result of calling hook_action_info() on all modules.
 */
function beep_action_info_alter(&$info) {
  // Make the "Block current user" action available to the
  // comment insert trigger. If other modules have modified the
  // array already, we don't stomp on their changes; we just make sure
  // the 'insert' operation is present. Otherwise, we assign the
  // 'insert' operation.
  if (isset($info['user_block_user_action']['hooks']['comment'])) {
    array_merge($info['user_block_user_action']['hooks']['comment'],
      array('insert'));
  }
```

```
  else {
    $info['user_block_user_action']['hooks']['comment'] = array('insert');
  }
}
```

The end result is that the "Block current user action" is now assignable, as shown in Figure 3-5.

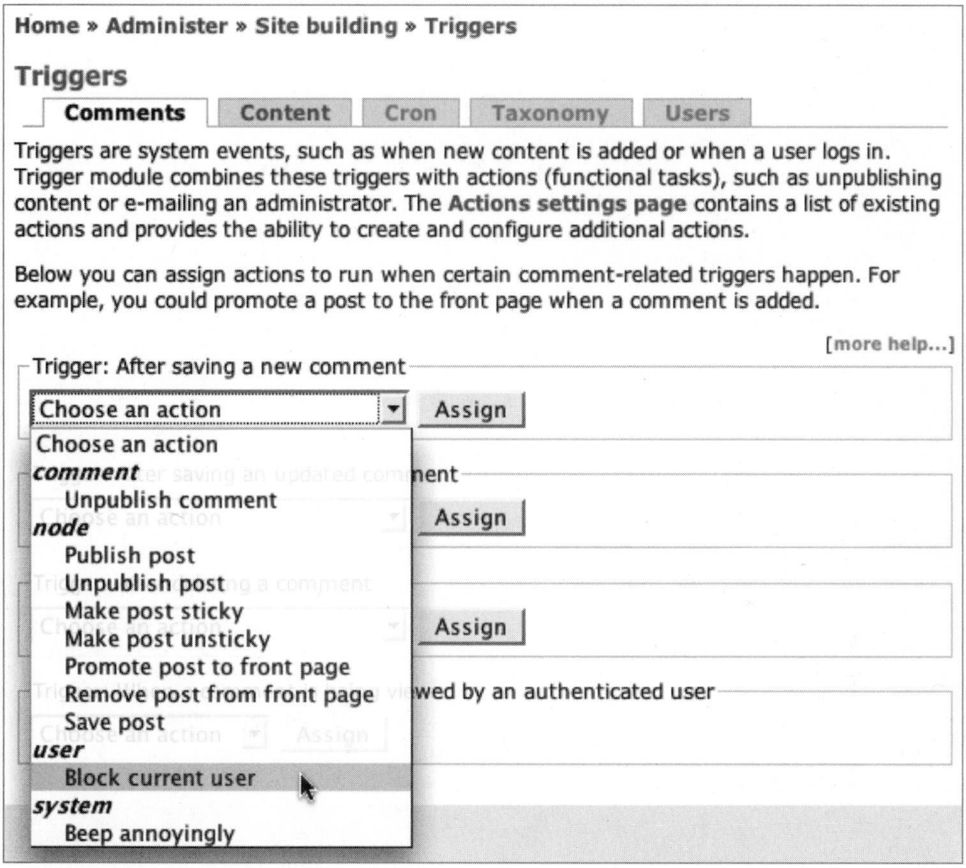

Figure 3-5. *Assigning the "Block current user" action to the comment insert trigger*

Establishing the Context

Because of the action we have assigned, when a new comment is posted, the current user will be blocked. Let's take a closer look at how that happens. We already know that Drupal's way of notifying modules that certain events are happening is to fire a hook. In this case, it is the comment hook. The particular operation that is happening is the insert operation, since a new comment is being added. The trigger module implements the comment hook. Inside this hook, it asks the database if there are any actions assigned to this particular trigger. The database gives it information about the "Block current user" action that we assigned. Now the trigger module gets ready to execute the action, which has the standard action function signature example_action($object, $context).

But we have a problem. The action that is about to be executed is an action of type user, not comment. It expects the object it receives to be a user object! But here, a user action is being called in the context of a comment hook. Information about the comment was passed to the hook, not information about the user. What should we do? What actually happens is that the trigger module determines that our action is a user action and loads the $user object that a user action expects. Here is code from modules/trigger/trigger.module that shows how this happens:

```
/**
 * When an action is called in a context that does not match its type,
 * the object that the action expects must be retrieved. For example, when
 * an action that works on nodes is called during the comment hook, the
 * node object is not available since the comment hook doesn't pass it.
 * So here we load the object the action expects.
 *
 * @param $type
 *    The type of action that is about to be called.
 * @param $comment
 *    The comment that was passed via the comment hook.
 * @return
 *    The object expected by the action that is about to be called.
 */
function _trigger_normalize_comment_context($type, $comment) {
  switch ($type) {
    // An action that works with nodes is being called in a comment context.
    case 'node':
      return node_load($comment['nid']);

    // An action that works on users is being called in a comment context.
    case 'user':
      return user_load(array('uid' => $comment['uid']));
  }
}
```

When the preceding code executes for our user action, the second case matches so the user object is loaded and then our user action is executed. The information that the comment hook knows about (for example, the comment's subject) is passed along to the action in the $context parameter. Note how the action looks for the user's ID first in the object and then the context, and finally falls back to the global $user:

```
/**
 * Implementation of a Drupal action.
 * Blocks the current user.
 */
```

```
function user_block_user_action(&$object, $context = array()) {
  if (isset($object->uid)) {
    $uid = $object->uid;
  }
  elseif (isset($context['uid'])) {
    $uid = $context['uid'];
  }
  else {
    global $user;
    $uid = $user->uid;
  }
  db_query("UPDATE {users} SET status = 0 WHERE uid = %d", $uid);
  sess_destroy_uid($uid);
  watchdog('action', 'Blocked user %name.', array('%name' =>
    check_plain($user->name)));
}
```

Actions must be somewhat intelligent, because they do not know much about what is happening when they are called. That is why the best candidates for actions are straightforward, even atomic. The trigger module always passes the current hook and operation along in the context. These values are stored in $context['hook'] and $context['op']. This approach offers a standardized way to provide information to an action.

Examining the Context

The fact that the hook and operation are available in the context is invaluable. An example of an action that makes heavy use of this is the "Send e-mail" action. It's an action of type system and can be assigned to many different triggers.

The "Send e-mail" action allows certain tokens to be replaced during the composition of the e-mail. For example, you might want to include the title of a node in the body of the e-mail or have the author of a node be the recipient of the e-mail. But depending on which trigger the action is assigned to, the recipient may not be available. For example, if e-mail is sent during the user hook, no node is available and thus no node author is available to be a recipient. The "Send e-mail" action in modules/system/system.module spends some time examining the context to determine what is available. Here, it is making sure that it has a node so node-related substitutions can happen:

```
/**
 * Implementation of a configurable Drupal action. Sends an e-mail.
 */
function system_send_email_action($object, $context) {
  global $user;
```

```
  switch ($context['hook']) {
    case 'nodeapi':
      // Because this is not an action of type 'node' (it's an action
      // of type 'system') the node will not be passed as $object,
      // but it will still be available in $context.
      $node = $context['node'];
      break;
    case 'comment':
      // The comment hook provides nid, in $context.
      $comment = $context['comment'];
      $node = node_load($comment->nid);
    case 'user':
      // Because this is not an action of type 'user' the user
      // object is not passed as $object, but it will still be
      // available in $context.
      $account = $context['account'];
      if (isset($context['node'])) {
        $node = $context['node'];
      }
      elseif ($context['recipient'] == '%author') {
        // If we don't have a node, we don't have a node author.
        watchdog('error', 'Cannot use %author token in this context.');
        return;
      }
      break;
    default:
      // We are being called directly.
      $node = $object;
  } ...
```

How Actions Are Stored

Actions are functions that run at a given time. Simple actions do not have configurable parameters. For example, the "Beep" action we created simply beeped. It did not need any other information (though of course $object and $context are available if needed). Contrast this action with the advanced action we created. The "Beep multiple times" action needed to know how many times to beep. Other advanced actions, such as the "Send e-mail" action, may need even more information: whom to send the e-mail to, what the subject of the e-mail should be, and so on. These parameters must be stored in the database.

The actions Table

When an instance of an advanced action is created by the administrator, the information that is entered in the configuration form is serialized and saved into the parameters field of the actions table. A record for the simple "Beep" action would look like this:

```
aid: 'beep_beep_action'
type: 'system'
callback: 'beep_beep_action'
parameters:
description: Beep
```

In contrast, the record for an instance of the "Beep multiple times" action would look like this:

```
aid: 2
type: 'system'
callback: 'beep_beep_action'
parameters: (serialized array containing the beeps parameter with its value, i.e.,
  the number of times to beep)
description: Beep three times
```

Just before an advanced action is executed, the contents of the `parameters` field are unserialized and included in the `$context` parameter that is passed to the action. So the number of beeps in our "Beep multiple times" action instance will be available to `beep_multiple_beep_action()` as `$context['beeps']`.

Action IDs

Notice the difference in the action IDs of the two table records in the previous section. The action ID of the simple action is the actual function name. But obviously we cannot use the function name as an identifier for advanced actions, since multiple instances of the same action are stored. So a numeric action ID (tracked in the `actions_aid` database table) is used instead.

The actions execution engine determines whether or not to go through the process of retrieving stored parameters for an action based on whether or not the action ID is numeric. If it is not numeric, the action is simply executed and the database is not consulted. This is a very quick determination; Drupal uses the same approach in `index.php` to distinguish content from menu constants.

Calling an Action Directly with actions_do()

The trigger module is only one way to call actions. You might want to write a separate module that calls actions and prepare the parameters yourself. If so, using `actions_do()` is the recommended way to call actions. The function signature follows:

```
actions_do($action_ids, &$object, $context = array(), $a1 = NULL, $a2 = NULL)
```

Let's examine each of these parameters.

- `$action_ids`: The action(s) to execute, either a single action ID or an array of action IDs

- `$object`: The object that the action will act upon, if any

- $context: Associative array containing information the action may wish to use, including configured parameters for advanced actions

- $a1 and $a2: Optional additional parameters that, if passed to actions_do(), will be passed along to the action

Here's how we would call our simple "Beep" action using actions_do():

```
$object = NULL; // $object is a required parameter but unused in this case
actions_do('beep_beep_action', $object);
```

And here is how we would call the "Beep multiple times" advanced action:

```
$object = NULL;
actions_do(2, $object);
```

Or, we could call it and bypass the retrieval of stored parameters like this:

```
$object = NULL;
$context['beeps'] = 5;
actions_do('beep_multiple_beep_action', $object, $context);
```

■**Note** Hardcore PHP developers may be wondering, "Why use actions at all? Why not just call the function directly or just implement a hook? Why bother with stashing parameters in the context, only to retrieve them again instead of using traditional PHP parameters?" The answer is that by writing actions with a very generic function signature, code reuse can be delegated to the site administrator. The site administrator, who may not know PHP, does not have to call on a PHP developer to set up the functionality to send an e-mail when a new node is added. The site administrator simply wires up the "Send e-mail" action to the trigger that fires when a new node is saved and never has to call anyone.

Defining Your Own Triggers with hook_hook_info()

How does Drupal know which triggers are available for display on the triggers user interface? In typical fashion, it lets modules define hooks declaring which hooks the modules implement. For example, here's the implementation of hook_hook_info() from comment.module. The implementation of hook_hook_info() is where the trigger descriptions are defined.

```
/**
 * Implementation of hook_hook_info().
 */
```

```
function comment_hook_info() {
  return array(
    'comment' => array(
      'comment' => array(
        'insert' => array(
          'runs when' => t('After saving a new comment'),
        ),
        'update' => array(
          'runs when' => t('After saving an updated comment'),
        ),
        'delete' => array(
          'runs when' => t('After deleting a comment')
        ),
        'view' => array(
          'runs when' => t('When a comment is being viewed by an
            authenticated user')
        ),
      ),
    ),
  );
}
```

If we had a module called `monitoring.module` installed that introduced a new hook to Drupal called the monitoring hook, it might describe its two operations (overheating and freezing) like this:

```
/**
 * Implementation of hook_hook_info().
 */
function monitoring_hook_info() {
  return array(
    'monitoring' => array(
      'monitoring' => array(
        'overheating' => array(
          'runs when' => t('When hardware is about to melt down'),
        ),
        'freezing' => array(
          'runs when' => t('When hardware is about to freeze up'),
        ),
      ),
    ),
  );
}
```

After enabling the monitoring module, Drupal would pick up the new implementation of hook_hook_info() and modify the triggers page to include a separate tab for the new hook, as shown in Figure 3-6. Of course, the module itself would still be responsible for firing the hooks using `module_invoke()` or `module_invoke_all()` and for firing the actions. In this example, the module would need to call `module_invoke_all('monitoring', 'overheating')`. It would then need to implement `hook_monitoring($op)` and fire the actions with `actions_do()`. See `trigger_cron()` in `modules/trigger/trigger.module` for a simple implementation.

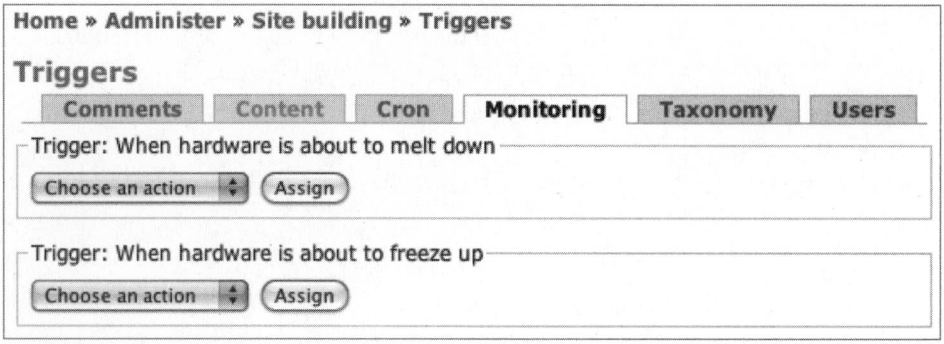

Figure 3-6. *The newly defined trigger appears as a tab in the triggers user interface.*

Although a module may define multiple new hooks, only the hook that matches the module name will create a new tab in the triggers interface. In our example, the monitoring module defined the monitoring hook. If it had also defined a different hook, that hook would not appear under the monitoring tab, nor would it have a tab of its own. However, a hook that does not match the module name is still accessible at `http://example.com/?q=admin/build/trigger/`*hookname*.

Adding Triggers to Existing Hooks

Sometimes, you may want to add triggers to an existing hook if your code is adding a new operation. For example, you might want to add an operation to the nodeapi hook. Suppose you have written a module that archives old nodes and moves them to a data warehouse. You could define an entirely new hook for this, and that would be perfectly appropriate. But since this operation is on a node, you might want to fire an `archive` operation in the nodeapi hook instead so that operations on content all appear under the same tab in the triggers interface. The following code adds an additional trigger:

```
/**
 * Declare a new trigger, to appear in the node tab.
 */
function archiveoffline_hook_info() {
  $info['archiveoffline'] = array(
    'nodeapi' => array(
      'archive' => array(
        'runs when' => t('When the post is about to be archived'),
```

```
        ),
      ),
   );

   return $info;
}
```

The new trigger is now available at the end of the list of triggers on the triggers administration page at Administer ➤ Site building ➤ Triggers, as shown in Figure 3-7.

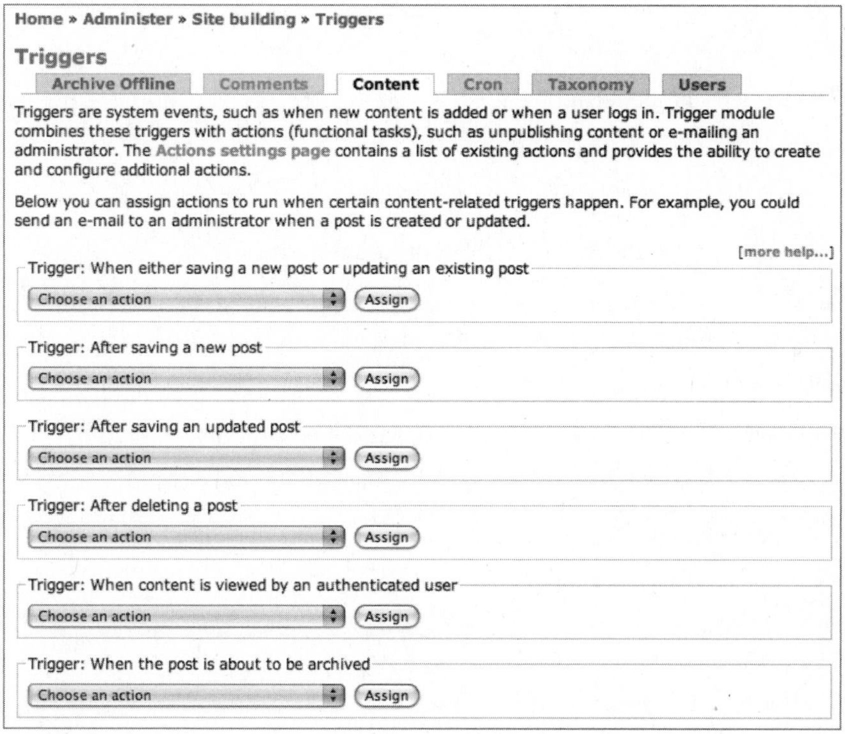

Figure 3-7. *The additional trigger ("When the post is about to be archived") appears in the user*
interface.

The first key in the hook_hook_info() implementation is used by Drupal's menu system
to automatically create a tab on the trigger administration page. Drupal names the tab with
the module's name as defined in the module's .info file (see the unused Archive Offline tab in
Figure 3-7). But our new trigger does not need to be placed under its own tab; we placed it
under the Content tab intentionally by adding our own operation to the nodeapi hook. We
can remove the unwanted tab using hook_menu_alter() (see Chapter 4 for more information
on how this hook works). The following code changes the automatically created tab from
type MENU_LOCAL_TASK (which Drupal renders as a tab by default) to type MENU_CALLBACK,
which Drupal does not render:

```
/**
 * Implementation of hook_menu_alter().
 */
function archiveoffline_menu_alter(&$items) {
  $items['admin/build/trigger/archiveoffline']['type'] = MENU_CALLBACK;
}
```

For the `archiveoffline_menu_alter()` function to take effect, you'll need to visit Administer ➤ Site building ➤ Modules so that menus will be rebuilt.

Summary

After reading this chapter, you should be able to

- Understand how to assign actions to triggers.

- Write a simple action.

- Write an advanced action and its associated configuration form.

- Create and rename instances of advanced actions using the actions administration page.

- Understand what a context is.

- Understand how actions can use the context to change their behavior.

- Understand how actions are stored, retrieved, and executed.

- Define your own hooks and have them displayed as triggers.

■■■

## CHAPTER 4

The Menu System

Drupal's menu system is complex but powerful. The term "menu system" is somewhat of a misnomer. It may be better to think of the menu system as having three primary responsibilities: callback mapping, access control, and menu customization. Essential code for the menu system is in `includes/menu.inc`, while optional code that enables such features as customizing menus is in `modules/menu`.

In this chapter, we'll explore what callback mapping is and how it works, see how to protect menu items with access control, learn to use menu wildcards, and inventory the various built-in types of menu items. The chapter finishes up by examining how to override, add, and delete existing menu items, so you can customize Drupal as nonintrusively as possible.

Callback Mapping

When a web browser makes a request to Drupal, it gives Drupal a URL. From this information, Drupal must figure out what code to run and how to handle the request. This is commonly known as *routing* or *dispatching*. Drupal trims off the base part of the URL and uses the latter part, called the *path*. For example, if the URL is `http://example.com/?q=node/3`, the *Drupal path* is `node/3`. If you are using Drupal's clean URLs feature, the URL in your browser would be `http://example.com/node/3` but your web server is quietly rewriting the URL to be `http://example.com/?q=node/3` before Drupal sees it; so Drupal always deals with the same Drupal path. In the preceding example, the Drupal path is `node/3` whether clean URLs are enabled or not. See "The Web Server's Role" in Chapter 1 for more detail on how this works.

Mapping URLs to Functions

The general approach taken is as follows: Drupal asks all enabled modules to provide an array of *menu items*. Each menu item consists of an array keyed by a path and containing some information about that path. One of the pieces of information a module must provide is a *page callback*. A callback in this context is simply the name of a PHP function that will be run when the browser requests a certain path. Drupal goes through the following steps when a request comes in:

1. Establish the Drupal path. If the path is an alias to a real path, Drupal finds the real path and uses it instead. For example, if an administrator has aliased `http://example.com/?q=about` to `http://example.com/?q=node/3` (using the path module, for example), Drupal uses `node/3` as the path.

2. Drupal keeps track of which paths map to which callbacks in the `menu_router` database table and keeps track of menu items that are links in the `menu_links` table. A check is made to see if the `menu_router` and `menu_links` tables need rebuilding, a rare occurrence that happens after Drupal installation or updating.

3. Figure out which entry in the `menu_router` table corresponds with the Drupal path and build a router item describing the callback to be called.

4. Load any objects necessary to pass to the callback.

5. Check whether the user is permitted to access the callback. If not, an "Access denied" message is returned.

6. Localize the menu item's title and description for the current language.

7. Load any necessary include files.

8. Call the callback and return the result, which `index.php` then passes through `theme_page()`, resulting in a finished web page.

A visual representation of this process is shown in Figures 4-1 and 4-2.

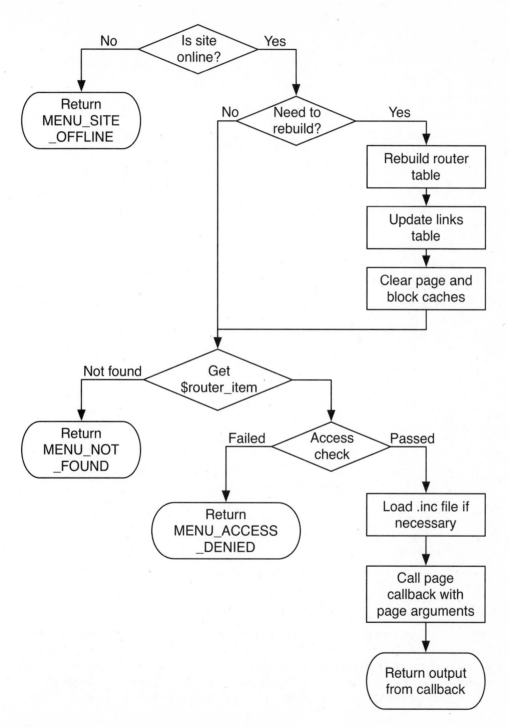

Figure 4-1. *Overview of the menu dispatching process*

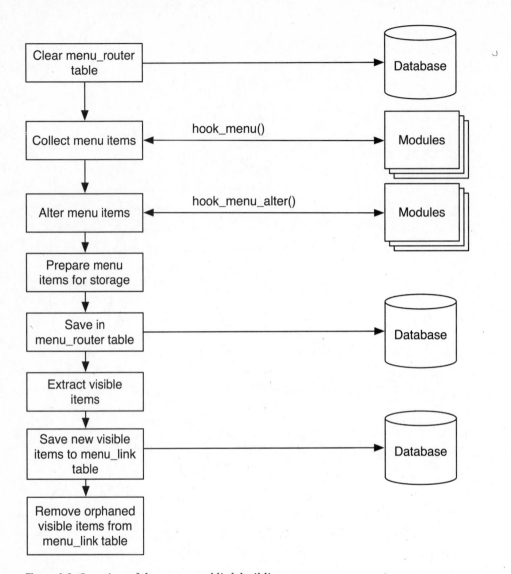

Figure 4-2. *Overview of the router and link building process*

Creating a Menu Item

The place to hook into the process is through the use of the menu hook in your module. This allows you to define menu items that will be included in the router table. Let's build an example module called menufun.module to experiment with the menu system. We'll map the Drupal path menufun to the PHP function that we'll write named menufun_hello(). First, we need a menufun.info file at sites/all/modules/custom/menufun/menufun.info:

```
; $Id$
name = Menu Fun
description = Learning about the menu system.
package = Pro Drupal Development
core = 6.x
```

Then we need to create the sites/all/modules/custom/menufun/menufun.module file, which contains our hook_menu() implementation and the function we want to run:

```php
<?php
// $Id$

/**
 * @file
 * Use this module to learn about Drupal's menu system.
 */

/**
 * Implementation of hook_menu().
 */
function menufun_menu() {
  $items['menufun'] = array(
    'page callback' => 'menufun_hello',
    'access callback' => TRUE,
    'type' => MENU_CALLBACK,
  );

  return $items;
}

/**
 * Page callback.
 */
function menufun_hello() {
  return t('Hello!');
}
```

Enabling the module at Administer ➤ Site building ➤ Modules causes the menu item to be inserted into the router table, so Drupal will now find and run our function when we go to http://example.com/?q=menufun, as shown in Figure 4-3.

The important thing to notice is that we are defining a path and mapping it to a function. The path is a Drupal path. We defined the path as the key of our $items array. We are using a path that is the same as the name of our module. This practice assures a pristine URL namespace. However, you can define any path.

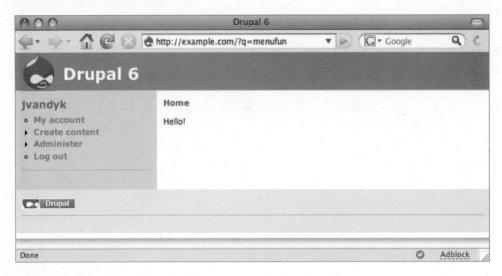

Figure 4-3. *The menu item has enabled Drupal to find and run the menufun_hello() function.*

Defining a Title

The implementation of hook_menu() written previously is as simple as possible. Let's add a few keys to make it more like an implementation you'd normally write.

```
function menufun_menu() {
  $items['menufun'] = array(
    'title' => 'Greeting',
    'page callback' => 'menufun_hello',
    'access callback' => TRUE,
    'type' => MENU_CALLBACK,
  );

  return $items;
}
```

We've given our menu item a title, which is automatically used as the page title when the page is displayed in the browser (if you want to override the page title during code execution later on, you can set it by using drupal_set_title()). After saving these changes, you would think that refreshing your browser should now display the title we've defined along with "Hello!" But it doesn't, because Drupal stores all of the menu items in the menu_router database table, and although our code has changed, the database has not. We have to tell Drupal to rebuild the menu_router table. There are two easy ways to do this. The easiest is to install the developer module (http://drupal.org/project/devel), and enable the devel block at Administer ➤ Site building ➤ Blocks. The devel block contains an item called Rebuild menus. Clicking this will rebuild the menu_router table. If you don't have the developer module handy, simply going to Administer ➤ Site building ➤ Modules will do the trick; as part of the preparation for displaying that page, Drupal rebuilds the menu tables. From here on, I'll assume that you know to rebuild the menu after each code change we make.

After the rebuild, our page looks like Figure 4-4.

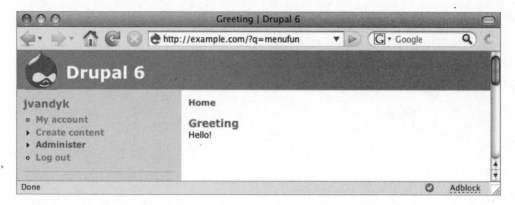

Figure 4-4. *The title of the menu item is shown in the page and browser title bar.*

Page Callback Arguments

Sometimes, you may wish to provide more information to the function that is mapped to the path. First of all, *any additional parts of the path are automatically passed along*. Let's change our function as follows:

```
function menufun_hello($first_name = '', $last_name = '') {
  return t('Hello @first_name @last_name',
    array('@first_name' => $first_name, '@last_name' => $last_name));
}
```

Now if we go to http://example.com/?q=menufun/John/Doe, we get the output shown in Figure 4-5.

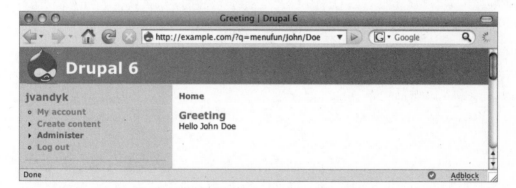

Figure 4-5. *Parts of the path are passed along to the callback function.*

Notice how each of the extra components of the URL was passed as a parameter to our callback function.

You can also define page callback arguments inside the menu hook by adding an optional page arguments key to the $items array. Defining page arguments is useful because you can call the same callback from different menu items and provide some hidden context for the callback through the page arguments. Let's define some page arguments for our menu item:

```
function menufun_menu() {
  $items['menufun'] = array(
    'title' => 'Greeting',
    'page callback' => 'menufun_hello',
    'page arguments' => array('Jane', 'Doe'),
    'access callback' => TRUE,
    'type' => MENU_CALLBACK,
  );

  return $items;
}
```

The callback arguments you define in page arguments will be passed to the callback function *before* (that is, placed first in the list of parameter values that are passed to the callback) any arguments generated from the path. The arguments from the URL are still available; to access them, you would change the function signature of your callback to add parameters from the URL. So with our revised menu item, the following function signature would result in $first_name being Jane (from the first item in the page arguments array), $last_name being Doe (from the second item in the page arguments array), $a being John (from the URL), and $b being Doe (from the URL).

```
function menufun_hello($first_name = '', $last_name = '', $a = '', $b = '') {...}
```

Let's test this by putting Jane Doe in the page arguments and John Doe in the URL and seeing which appears. Going to http://example.com/?q=John/Doe will now yield the results shown in Figure 4-6 (if you're not getting those results, you forgot to rebuild your menus).

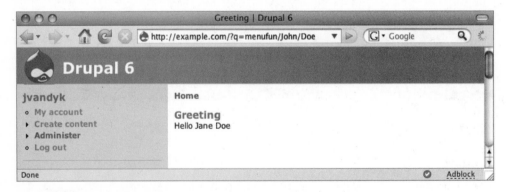

Figure 4-6. *Passing and displaying arguments to the callback function*

Keys in keyed arrays are ignored in page callback arguments, so you can't use keys to map to function parameters; only order is important. Callback arguments are usually variables and are often used in dynamic menu items.

Page Callbacks in Other Files

If you don't specify otherwise, Drupal assumes that your page callback can be found in your module. In Drupal 6, many modules have been split up so that a minimum amount of code is loaded on each page request. The `file` key of a menu item is used to specify which file contains the callback function if the function is not already in scope. We used the `file` key when writing the annotation module in Chapter 2.

If you define the `file` key, Drupal looks for that file in your module directory. If you are pointing to a page callback that is provided by another module and thus is not in your module directory, you'll need to tell Drupal the file path to use when looking for the file. That is easily accomplished with the `file path` key. We did that in "Defining Your Own Administration Section" in Chapter 2.

Adding a Link to the Navigation Block

We declared that our menu item was of type `MENU_CALLBACK`. By changing the type to `MENU_NORMAL_ITEM`, we indicate that we don't simply want to map the path to a callback function; we also want Drupal to include it in a menu.

Tip Because `MENU_NORMAL_ITEM` is Drupal's default menu item type, the `type` key could be omitted in the code snippet in this section. I shall omit it in further code examples.

```
function menufun_menu() {
  $items['menufun'] = array(
    'title' => 'Greeting',
    'page callback' => 'menufun_hello',
    'page arguments' => array('Jane', 'Doe'),
    'access callback' => TRUE,
    'type' => MENU_NORMAL_ITEM,
  );

  return $items;
}
```

The menu item would now show up in the navigation block, as shown in Figure 4-7.

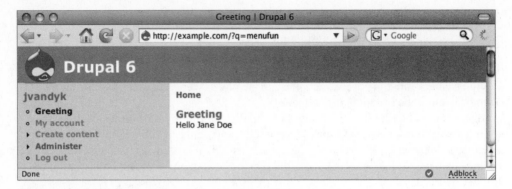

Figure 4-7. *The menu item appears in the navigation block.*

If we don't like where it is placed, we can move it down by increasing its weight. Weight is another key in the menu item definition:

```
function menufun_menu() {
  $items['menufun'] = array(
    'title' => 'Greeting',
    'page callback' => 'menufun_hello',
    'page arguments' => array('Jane', 'Doe'),
    'access callback' => TRUE,
    'weight' => 5,
  );

  return $items;
}
```

The effect of our weight increase is shown in Figure 4-8. Menu items can also be relocated without changing code by using the menu administration tools, located at Administer ➤ Site building ➤ Menus (the menu module must be enabled for these tools to appear).

Figure 4-8. *Heavier menu items sink down in the navigation block.*

Menu Nesting

So far, we've defined only a single static menu item. Let's add a second and another callback to go with it:

```
function menufun_menu() {
  $items['menufun'] = array(
    'title' => 'Greeting',
    'page callback' => 'menufun_hello',
    'access callback' => TRUE,
    'weight' => -10,
  );
  $items['menufun/farewell'] = array(
    'title' => 'Farewell',
    'page callback' => 'menufun_goodbye',
    'access callback' => TRUE,
  );

  return $items;
}


/**
 * Page callback.
 */
function menufun_hello() {
  return t('Hello!');
}


/**
 * Page callback.
 */
function menufun_goodbye() {
  return t('Goodbye!');
}
```

Drupal will notice that the path of the second menu item (menufun/farewell) is a child of the first menu item's path (menufun). Thus, when rendering (transforming to HTML) the menu, Drupal will indent the second menu as shown in Figure 4-9. It has also correctly set the breadcrumb trail at the top of the page to indicate the nesting. Of course, a theme may render menus or breadcrumb trails however the designer wishes.

Figure 4-9. *Nested menu*

Access Control

In our examples so far, we've simply set the access callback key of the menu item to TRUE, meaning that anyone can access our menu. Usually, menu access is controlled by defining permissions inside the module using hook_perm() and testing those permissions using a function. The name of the function to use is defined in the access callback key of the menu item and is typically user_access. Let's define a permission called *receive greeting*; if a user does not have a role that has been granted this permission, the user will receive an "Access denied" message if he or she tries to go to http://example.com/?q=menufun.

```
/**
 * Implementation of hook_perm().
 */
function menufun_perm() {
  return array('receive greeting');
}

/**
 * Implementation of hook_menu().
 */
function menufun_menu() {
  $items['menufun'] = array(
    'title' => 'Greeting',
    'page callback' => 'menufun_hello',
    'access callback' => 'user_access',
    'access arguments' => array('receive greeting'),
    'weight' => -10,
  );
  $items['menufun/farewell'] = array(
    'title' => 'Farewell',
    'page callback' => 'menufun_goodbye',
  );

  return $items;
}
```

In the preceding code, access will be determined by the result of a call to `user_access` (`'receive greeting'`). In this way, the menu system serves as a gatekeeper determining which paths may be accessed and which will be denied based on the user's role.

■Tip The `user_access()` function is the default access callback. If you do not define an access callback, your access arguments will be passed to `user_access()` by the menu system.

Child menu items do not inherit access callbacks and access arguments from their parents. The `access arguments` key must be defined for every menu item. The `access callback` key must only be defined if it differs from `user_access`. The exception to this is any menu item of type `MENU_DEFAULT_LOCAL_TASK`, which will inherit the parent `access callback` and `access arguments`, though for clarity it is best to explicitly define these keys even for default local tasks.

Title Localization and Customization

Drupal supports multiple languages. Translation of strings is done by the `t()` function. So you might think that defining a `title` key in a menu item should look like this:

```
'title' => t('Greeting') // No! don't use t() in menu item titles or descriptions.
```

However, menu title strings are stored in the `menu_router` table as original strings, and the translation of menu items is deferred until runtime. What's really happening is that Drupal has a default translation function (the `t()` function) that is being assigned to translate the title. You'll see later how to change the default translation function to a function of your choosing and how to pass arguments to that function. The function that does translation is called the *title callback*, and any arguments that are passed along are called *title arguments*.

Defining a Title Callback

If no title callback is defined in the menu item, Drupal will default to using the `t()` function. We can make the name of the callback function explicit by specifying it in the `title callback` key:

```
function menufun_menu() {
  $items['menufun'] = array(
    'title' => 'Greeting',
    'title callback' => 't',
    'description' => 'A salutation.',
    'page callback' => 'menufun_hello',
    'access arguments' => array('receive greeting'),
  );
}
```

■Note The description key is always translated using t(), no matter what the value of the title callback key. There is no description callback key.

Hmm. What would happen if we specified our own function for the title callback? Let's find out:

```
function menufun_menu() {
  $items['menufun'] = array(
    'title' => 'Greeting',
    'title callback' => 'menufun_title',
    'description' => 'A salutation.',
    'page callback' => 'menufun_hello',
    'access callback' => TRUE,
  );

  return $items;
}

/**
 * Page callback.
 */
function menufun_hello() {
  return t('Hello!');
}

/**
 * Title callback.
 */
function menufun_title() {
  $now = format_date(time());
  return t('It is now @time', array('@time' => $now));
}
```

As shown in Figure 4-10, setting of the menu item title at runtime can be achieved through the use of a custom title callback. But what if we want to decouple the menu item title from the title of the page? Easy. We set the page title using drupal_set_title():

```
function menufun_title() {
  drupal_set_title(t('The page title'));
  $now = format_date(time());
  return t('It is now @time', array('@time' => $now));
}
```

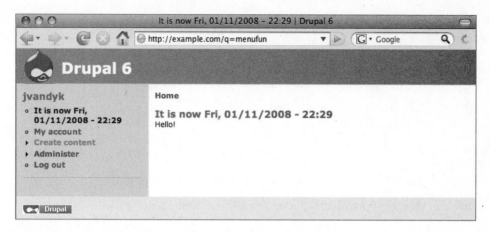

Figure 4-10. *Title callback setting the title of a menu item*

This results in one title for the page and another for the menu item, as shown in Figure 4-11.

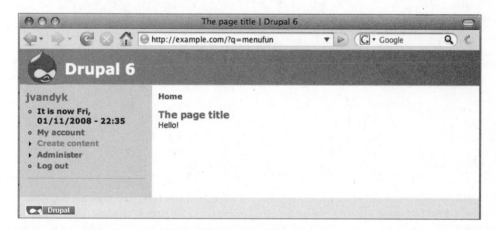

Figure 4-11. *Separate titles for the menu item and the page*

Title Arguments

Drupal's translation function accepts a string and a keyed array of replacements (for detailed information on how t() works, see Chapter 18), for example:

```
t($string, $keyed_array);
t('It is now @time', array('@time' => $now));
```

So if the title key in a menu item is the string that is to be passed through t(), where is the array of replacements? Good question. That's what the title arguments key is for:

```
function menufun_menu() {
  $items['menufun'] = array(
    'title' => 'Greeting for Dr. @name',
    'title callback' => 't',
    'title arguments' => array('@name' => 'Foo'),
    'page callback' => 'menufun_hello',
    'access callback' => TRUE,
  );

  return $items;
}
```

During runtime, the translation function runs and the placeholder is filled, as shown in Figure 4-12.

Figure 4-12. *Title arguments are passed to the title callback function.*

This kind of substitution has a flaw, though. Because items defined in the menu hook are saved into the database during the menu building process (see Figure 4-2), any code in title arguments is executed at menu-building time, not at runtime. If you need to modify your menu titles at runtime, it is best to define the title callback key; the function defined there *will* run at runtime.

■**Caution** The values of the title arguments key must be strings. Integers will be stripped out; thus 'title arguments' => array('@name' => 3) will not work but 'title arguments' => array('@name' => '3') will. This is because integers have special meaning, as you'll see shortly.

Wildcards in Menu Items

So far, we have been using regular Drupal path names in our menu items, names like menufun and menufun/farewell. But Drupal often uses paths like user/4/track or node/15/edit where part of the path is dynamic. Let's look at how that works.

Basic Wildcards

The % character is a special character in Drupal menu items. It means "any string up to the next / character." Here's a menu item that uses a wildcard:

```
function menufun_menu() {
  $items['menufun/%'] = array(
    'title' => 'Hi',
    'page callback' => 'menufun_hello',
    'access callback' => TRUE,
  );

  return $items;
}
```

This menu item will work for the Drupal paths menufun/hi, menufun/foo/bar, menufun/123, and menufun/file.html. It will *not* work for the path menufun; a separate menu item would have to be written for that path because it consists of only one part, and the wildcard menufun/% will only match a string with two parts. Note that although % is often used to designate a number (as in user/%/edit for user/2375/edit) it will match any text in that position.

Note A menu item with a wildcard in its path will no longer show up in navigation menus, even if the menu item's type is set to MENU_NORMAL_ITEM. It should be obvious why this is: since the path contains a wildcard, Drupal doesn't know how to construct the URL for the link. But see "Building Paths from Wildcards Using to_arg() Functions" later in this chapter to find out how you can tell Drupal what URL to use.

Wildcards and Page Callback Parameters

A wildcard at the end of the menu path does not interfere with the passing of additional parts of the URL to the page callback, because the wildcard matches only up to the next slash. Continuing with our example of the menufun/% path, the URL http://example.com/?q=menufun/foo/Fred would have the string foo matched by the wildcard, and the last portion of the path (Fred) would be passed as a parameter to the page callback.

Using the Value of a Wildcard

To use the part of the path that matched, specify the number of the path's part in the page arguments key:

```
function menufun_menu() {
  $items['menufun/%/bar/baz'] = array(
    'title' => 'Hi',
    'page callback' => 'menufun_hello',
    'page arguments' => array(1), // The matched wildcard.
    'access callback' => TRUE,
  );

  return $items;
}

/**
 * Page callback.
 */
function menufun_hello($a = NULL, $b = NULL) {
  return t('Hello. $a is @a and $b is @b', array('@a' => $a, '@b' => $b));
}
```

The parameters received by our page callback function menufun_hello() will be as shown in Figure 4-13.

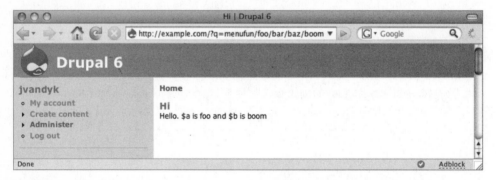

Figure 4-13. *The first parameter is from the matched wildcard, and the second is from the end of the URL.*

The first parameter, $a, is being passed via the page callback. The entry array(1) for the page callback means, "please pass part 1 of the path, whatever that is." We start counting at 0, so part 0 is 'menufun', part 1 is whatever the wildcard matched, part 2 would be 'bar', and so on. The second parameter, $b, is being passed because of Drupal's behavior of passing the portion of the path beyond the Drupal path as a parameter (see "Page Callback Arguments" earlier in this chapter).

Wildcards and Parameter Replacement

In practice, parts of a Drupal path are generally used to view or change an object, such as a node or a user. For example, the path node/%/edit is used to edit a node, and the path user/% is used to view information about a user by user ID. Let's take a look at the menu item for the latter, which can be found in the hook_menu() implementation in modules/user/user.module. The corresponding URL that this path matches would be something like http://example.com/?q=user/2375. That's the URL you would click to see the "My account" page on a Drupal site.

```
$items['user/%user_uid_optional'] = array(
  'title' => 'My account',
  'title callback' => 'user_page_title',
  'title arguments' => array(1),
  'page callback' => 'user_view',
  'page arguments' => array(1),
  'access callback' => 'user_view_access',
  'access arguments' => array(1),
  'file' => 'user_pages.inc',
);
```

Whoa! What kind of path is user/%user_uid_optional? It's shorthand for this:

1. Split the path into segments at each occurrence of a slash (/).

2. In the second segment, match the string after the % and before the next possible slash. In this case, the string would be user_uid_optional.

3. Append _load to the string to generate the name of a function. In this case, the name of the function is user_uid_optional_load.

4. Call the function and pass it, as a parameter, the value of the wildcard in the Drupal path. So if the URL is http://example.com/?q=user/2375, the Drupal path is user/2375, and the wildcard matches the second segment, which is 2375. So a call is made to user_uid_optional_load('2375').

5. The result of this call is then used *in place of* the wildcard. So when the title callback is called with the title arguments of array(1), instead of passing part 1 of the Drupal path (2375), we pass the result of the call to user_uid_optional_load('2375'), which is a user object. Think of it as a portion of the Drupal path being replaced by the object it represents.

6. Note that the page and access callbacks will also use the replacement object. So in the previous menu item, user_view_access() will be called for access and user_view() will be called to generate the page content, and both will be passed the user object for user 2375.

■**Tip** It is easier to think about object replacement in a Drupal path like node/%node/edit if you think about %node as being a wildcard with an annotation right there in the string. In other words, node/%node/edit is node/%/edit with the implicit instruction to run node_load() on the wildcard match.

Passing Additional Arguments to the Load Function

If additional arguments need to be passed to the load function, they can be defined in the load arguments key. Here's an example from the node module: the menu item for viewing a node revision. Both the node ID and the ID of the revision need to be passed to the load function, which is node_load().

```
$items['node/%node/revisions/%/view'] = array(
  'title' => 'Revisions',
  'load arguments' => array(3),
  'page callback' => 'node_show',
  'page arguments' => array(1, NULL, TRUE),
  'type' => MENU_CALLBACK,
);
```

The menu item specifies array(3) for the load arguments key. This means that in addition to the wildcard value for the node ID, which is passed automatically to the load function as outlined previously, a single additional parameter will be passed to the load function, since array(3) has one member; that is, the integer 3. As you saw in the "Using the Value of a Wild-card" section, this means that the part of the path in position 3 will be used. The position and path arguments for the example URL http://example.com/?q=node/56/revisions/4/view are shown in Table 4-2.

Table 4-2. *Position and Arguments for Drupal Path node/%node/revisions/%/view When Viewing the Page http://example.com/?q=node/56/revisions/4/view*

Position	Argument	Value from URL
0	node	node
1	%node	56
2	revisions	revisions
3	%	4
4	view	view

Thus, defining the load arguments key means that the call node_load('56', '4') will be made instead of node_load('56').

When the page callback runs, the load function will have replaced the value '56' with the loaded node object, so the page callback call will be node_show($node, NULL, TRUE).

Special, Predefined Load Arguments: %map and %index

There are two special load arguments. The %map token passes the current Drupal path as an array. In the preceding example, if %map were passed as a load argument its value would be array('node', '56', 'revisions', '4', 'view'). The values of the map can be manipulated by the load function if it declares the parameter as a reference. For example, user_category_load($uid, &$map, $index) in modules/user/user.module does this to handle slashes in category names.

The %index token is the position of the wildcard denoting the load function. So for the preceding example, the token's value would be 1 because the wildcard is at position 1, as shown in Table 4-2.

Building Paths from Wildcards Using to_arg() Functions

Recall that I said that Drupal cannot produce a valid link from a Drupal path that contains a wildcard, like user/% (after all, how would Drupal know what to replace the % with)? That's not strictly true. We can define a helper function that produces a replacement for the wildcard that Drupal can then use when building the link. In the "My account" menu item, the path for the "My account" link is produced with the following steps:

1. The Drupal path is originally user/%user_uid_optional.

2. When building the link, Drupal looks for a function with the name user_uid_optional_ to_arg(). If this function is not defined, Drupal cannot figure out how to build the path and does not display the link.

3. If the function is found, Drupal uses the result of the function as a replacement for the wildcard in the link. The user_uid_optional_to_arg() function returns the user ID of the current user, so if you are user 4, Drupal connects the "My account" link to http://example.com/?q=user/4.

The use of a to_arg() function is not specific to the execution of a given path. In other words, the to_arg() function is run during link building on any page, not the specific page that matches the Drupal path of a menu item. The "My account" link is shown on all pages, not just when the page http://example.com/?q=user/3 page is being viewed.

Special Cases for Wildcards and to_arg() Functions

The to_arg() function that Drupal will look for when building a link for a menu item is based on the string following the wildcard in the Drupal path. This can be any string, for example:

```
/**
 * Implementation of hook_menu().
 */
function_menufun_menu() {
  $items['menufun/%a_zoo_animal'] = array(
    'title' => 'Hi',
    'page callback' => 'menufun_hello',
    'page arguments' => array(1),
    'access callback' => TRUE,
    'type' => MENU_NORMAL_ITEM,
    'weight' => -10
  );
```

```
    return $items;
}

function a_zoo_animal_to_arg($arg) {
    // $arg is '%' since it is a wildcard
    // Let's replace it with a zoo animal.
    return 'tiger';
}
```

This causes the link "Hi" to appear in the navigation block. The URL for the link is http://
example.com/?q=menufun/tiger. Normally, you would not replace the wildcard with a static
string as in this simple example. Rather the to_arg() function would produce something
dynamic, like the uid of the current user or the nid of the current node.

Altering Menu Items from Other Modules

When Drupal rebuilds the menu_router table and updates the menu_link tables (for example,
when a new module is enabled), modules are given a chance to change any menu item by
implementing hook_menu_alter(). For example, the "Log off" menu item logs out the current user by calling user_logout(), which destroys the user's session and then redirects
the user to the site's home page. The user_logout() function lives in modules/user/
user.pages.inc, so the menu item for the Drupal path has a file key defined. So normally
Drupal loads the file modules/user/user.pages.inc and runs the user_logout() page callback when a user clicks the "Log out" link from the Navigation block. Let's change that to
redirect users who are logging out to drupal.org.

```
/**
 * Implementation of hook_menu_alter().
 *
 * @param array $items
 *    Menu items keyed by path.
 */
function menufun_menu_alter(&$items) {
    // Replace the page callback to 'user_logout' with a call to
    // our own page callback.
    $items['logout']['page callback'] = 'menufun_user_logout';
    // Drupal no longer has to load the user.pages.inc file
    // since it will be calling our menufun_user_logout(), which
    // is in our module -- and that's already in scope.
    unset($items['logout']['file']);
}
```

```
/**
 * Menu callback; logs the current user out, and redirects to drupal.org.
 * This is a modified version of user_logout().
 */
function menufun_user_logout() {
  global $user;

  watchdog('menufun', 'Session closed for %name.', array('%name' => $user->name));

  // Destroy the current session:
  session_destroy();
  // Run the 'logout' operation of the user hook so modules can respond
  // to the logout if they want to.
  module_invoke_all('user', 'logout', NULL, $user);

  // Load the anonymous user so the global $user object will be correct
  // on any hook_exit() implementations.
  $user = drupal_anonymous_user();

  drupal_goto('http://drupal.org/');
}
```

Before our hook_menu_alter() implementation ran, the menu item for the logout path looked like this:

```
array(
  'access callback' => 'user_is_logged_in',
  'file'            => 'user.pages.inc',
  'module'          => 'user',
  'page callback'   => 'user_logout',
  'title'           => 'Log out',
  'weight'          => 10,
)
```

and after we have altered it, it looks like this:

```
array(
  'access callback' => 'user_is_logged_in',
  'module'          => 'user',
  'page callback'   => 'menufun_user_logout',
  'title'           => 'Log out',
  'weight'          => 10,
)
```

Altering Menu Links from Other Modules

When Drupal saves a menu item to the menu_link table, modules are given a chance to change the link by implementing hook_menu_link_alter(). Here is how the "Log out" menu item could be changed to be titled "Sign off."

```
/**
 * Implementation of hook_link_alter().
 *
 *   @param $item
 *     Associative array defining a menu link as passed into menu_link_save().
 *   @param $menu
 *     Associative array containing the menu router returned from
 *     menu_router_build().
 */
function menufun_menu_link_alter(&$item, $menu) {
  if ($item['link_path'] == 'logout') {
    $item['link_title'] = 'Sign off';
  }
}
```

This hook should be used to modify the title or weight of a link. If you need to modify other properties of a menu item, such as the access callback, use hook_menu_alter() instead.

Note The changes made to a menu item in hook_menu_link_alter() are not overrideable by the user interface that menu.module presents at Administer ➤ Site building ➤ Menus.

Kinds of Menu Items

When you are adding a menu item in the menu hook, one of the possible keys you can use is the *type*. If you do not define a type, the default type MENU_NORMAL_ITEM will be used. Drupal will treat your menu item differently according to the type you assign. Each menu item type is composed of a series of *flags*, or attributes. Table 4-2 lists the menu item type flags.

Table 4-2. *Menu Item Type Flags*

Binary	Hexadecimal	Decimal	Constant
000000000001	0x0001	1	MENU_IS_ROOT
000000000010	0x0002	2	MENU_VISIBLE_IN_TREE
000000000100	0x0004	4	MENU_VISIBLE_IN_BREADCRUMB
000000001000	0x0008	8	MENU_LINKS_TO_PARENT
000000100000	0x0020	32	MENU_MODIFIED_BY_ADMIN
000001000000	0x0040	64	MENU_CREATED_BY_ADMIN
000010000000	0x0080	128	MENU_IS_LOCAL_TASK

For example, the constant MENU_NORMAL_ITEM has the flags MENU_VISIBLE_IN_TREE and MENU_VISIBLE_IN_BREADCRUMB, as shown in Table 4-3. Do you see how the separate flags can be expressed in a single constant?

Table 4-3. *Flags of the Menu Item Type MENU_NORMAL_ITEM*

Binary	Constant
000000000010	MENU_VISIBLE_IN_TREE
000000000100	MENU_VISIBLE_IN_BREADCRUMB
000000000110	MENU_NORMAL_ITEM

Therefore, MENU_NORMAL_ITEM has the following flags: 000000000110. Table 4-4 shows the available menu item types and the flags they express.

Table 4-4. *Flags Expressed by Menu Item Types*

Menu Flags	Menu Type Constants				
	MENU_NORMAL_ITEM	MENU_CALLBACK	MENU_SUGGESTED_ITEM*	MENU_LOCAL_TASK	MENU_DEFAULT_LOCAL_TASK
MENU_IS_ROOT					
MENU_VISIBLE_IN_TREE	X				
MENU_VISIBLE_IN_BREADCRUMB	X	X	X		
MENU_LINKS_TO_PARENT					X
MENU_MODIFIED_BY_ADMIN					
MENU_CREATED_BY_ADMIN					
MENU_IS_LOCAL_TASK				X	X

This constant is created with an additional bitwise OR with 0x0010.

So which constant should you use when defining the type of your menu item? Look at Table 4-4 and see which flags you want enabled, and use the constant that contains those flags. For a detailed description of each constant, see the comments in includes/menu.inc. The most commonly used are MENU_CALLBACK, MENU_LOCAL_TASK, and MENU_DEFAULT_LOCAL_TASK. Read on for details.

Common Tasks

This section lays out some typical approaches to common problems confronting developers when working with menus.

Assigning Callbacks Without Adding a Link to the Menu

Often, you may want to map a URL to a function without creating a visible menu item. For example, maybe you have a JavaScript function in a web form that needs to get a list of states from Drupal, so you need to wire up a URL to a PHP function but have no need of including this in any navigation menu. You can do this by assigning the MENU_CALLBACK type to your menu item, as in the first example in this chapter.

Displaying Menu Items As Tabs

In Drupal's admittedly obscure menu lingo, a callback that is displayed as a tab is known as a *local task* and has the type MENU_LOCAL_TASK or MENU_DEFAULT_LOCAL_TASK. The title of a local task should be a short verb, such as "add" or "list." Local tasks usually act on some kind of object, such as a node, or user. You can think of a local task as being a semantic declaration about a menu item, which is normally rendered as a tab—similar to the way that the <strong> tag is a semantic declaration and is usually rendered as boldfaced text.

Local tasks *must* have a parent item in order for the tabs to be rendered. A common practice is to assign a callback to a root path like milkshake, and then assign local tasks to paths that extend that path, like milkshake/prepare, milkshake/drink, and so forth. Drupal has built-in theming support for two levels of tabbed local tasks. (Additional levels are supported by the underlying system, but your theme would have to provide support for displaying these additional levels.)

The order in which tabs are rendered is determined by alphabetically sorting on the value of title for each menu item. If this order is not to your liking, you can add a weight key to your menu items, and they will be sorted by weight instead.

The following example shows code that results in two main tabs and two subtabs under the default local task. Create sites/all/modules/custom/milkshake/milkshake.info as follows:

```
; $Id$
name = Milkshake
description = Demonstrates menu local tasks.
package = Pro Drupal Development
core = 6.x
```

Then enter the following for sites/all/modules/custom/milkshake/milkshake.module:

```php
<?php
// $Id$

/**
 * @file
 * Use this module to learn about Drupal's menu system,
 * specifically how local tasks work.
 */

/**
 * Implementation of hook_perm().
 */
function milkshake_perm() {
  return array('list flavors', 'add flavor');
}
```

```
/**
 * Implementation of hook_menu().
 */
function milkshake_menu() {
  $items['milkshake'] = array(
    'title' => 'Milkshake flavors',
    'access arguments' => array('list flavors'),
    'page callback' => 'milkshake_overview',
    'type' => MENU_NORMAL_ITEM,
  );
  $items['milkshake/list'] = array(
    'title' => 'List flavors',
    'access arguments' => array('list flavors'),
    'type' => MENU_DEFAULT_LOCAL_TASK,
    'weight' => 0,
  );
  $items['milkshake/add'] = array(
    'title' => 'Add flavor',
    'access arguments' => array('add flavor'),
    'page callback' => 'milkshake_add',
    'type' => MENU_LOCAL_TASK,
    'weight' => 1,
  );
  $items['milkshake/list/fruity'] = array(
    'title' => 'Fruity flavors',
    'access arguments' => array('list flavors'),
    'page callback' => 'milkshake_list',
    'page arguments' => array(2), // Pass 'fruity'.
    'type' => MENU_LOCAL_TASK,
  );
  $items['milkshake/list/candy'] = array(
    'title' => 'Candy flavors',
    'access arguments' => array('list flavors'),
    'page callback' => 'milkshake_list',
    'page arguments' => array(2), // Pass 'candy'.
    'type' => MENU_LOCAL_TASK,
  );

  return $items;
}

function milkshake_overview() {
  $output = t('The following flavors are available...');
  // ... more code here
  return $output;
}
```

```
function milkshake_add() {
  return t('A handy form to add flavors might go here...');
}

function milkshake_list($type) {
  return t('List @type flavors', array('@type' => $type));
}
```

Figure 4-14 shows the result in the Bluemarine Drupal theme.

Figure 4-14. *Local tasks and tabbed menus*

Note that the title of the page is taken from the parent callback, not from the default local task. If you want a different title, you can use drupal_set_title() to set it.

Hiding Existing Menu Items

Existing menu items can be hidden by changing the hidden attribute of their link item. Suppose you want to remove the "Create content" menu item for some reason. Use our old friend hook_menu_link_alter():

```
/**
 * Implementation of hook_menu_link_alter().
 */
function menufun_menu_link_alter(&$item, $menu) {
  // Hide the Create content link.
  if ($item['link_path'] == 'node/add') {
    $item['hidden'] = 1;
  }
}
```

Using menu.module

Enabling Drupal's menu module provides a handy user interface for the site administrator to customize existing menus such as the navigation menu or primary/secondary links menus or to add new menus. When the `menu_rebuild()` function in `includes/menu.inc` is run, the data structure that represents the menu tree is stored in the database. This happens when you enable or disable modules or otherwise mess with things that affect the composition of the menu tree. The data is saved into the `menu_router` table of the database, and the information about links is stored in the `menu_links` table.

During the process of building the links for a page, Drupal first builds the tree based on path information received from modules' menu hook implementations and stored in the `menu_router` table, and then it overlays that information with the menu information from the database. This behavior is what allows you to use `menu.module` to change the parent, path, title, and description of the menu tree—you are not really changing the underlying tree; rather, you are creating data that is then overlaid on top of it.

■Note The menu item type, such as `MENU_CALLBACK` or `DEFAULT_LOCAL_TASK`, is represented in the database by its decimal equivalent.

`menu.module` also adds a section to the node form to add the current post as a menu item on the fly.

Common Mistakes

You've just implemented the menu hook in your module, but your callbacks aren't firing, your menus aren't showing up, or things just plain aren't working. Here are a few common things to check:

- Have you set an `access callback` key to a function that is returning `FALSE`?

- Did you forget to add the line `return $items;` at the end of your menu hook?

- Did you accidentally make the value of `access arguments` or `page arguments` a string instead of an array?

- Have you cleared your menu cache and rebuilt the menu?

- If you're trying to get menu items to show up as tabs by assigning the type as `MENU_LOCAL_TASK`, have you assigned a parent item that has a page callback?

- If you're working with local tasks, do you have at least two tabs on a page (this is required for them to appear)?

Summary

After reading this chapter, you should be able to

- Map URLs to functions in your module or other modules or .inc files.

- Understand how access control works.

- Understand how wildcards work in paths.

- Create pages with tabs (local tasks) that map to functions.

- Modify existing menu items and links programmatically.

For further reading, the comments in menu.inc are worth checking out. Also, see http://drupal.org/node/102338 and http://api.drupal.org/?q=api/group/menu/6.

CHAPTER 5

■■■

Working with Databases

Drupal depends on a database to function correctly. Inside Drupal, a lightweight database abstraction layer exists between your code and the database. In this chapter, you'll learn about how the database abstraction layer works and how to use it. You'll see how queries can be modified by modules. Then, you'll look at how to connect to additional databases (such as a legacy database). Finally, you'll examine how the queries necessary to create and update database tables can be included in your module's `.install` file by using Drupal's schema API.

Defining Database Parameters

Drupal knows which database to connect to and what username and password to issue when establishing the database connection by looking in the `settings.php` file for your site. This file typically lives at `sites/example.com/settings.php` or `sites/default/settings.php`. The line that defines the database connection looks like this:

```
$db_url = 'mysql://username:password@localhost/databasename';
```

This example is for connecting to a MySQL database. PostgreSQL users would prefix the connection string with `pgsql` instead of `mysql`. Obviously, the username and password used here must be valid for your database. They are database credentials, not Drupal credentials, and they are established when you set up the database account using your database's tools. Drupal's installer asks for the username and password so that it can build the `$db_url` string in your `settings.php` file.

Understanding the Database Abstraction Layer

Working with a database abstraction API is something you will not fully appreciate until you try to live without one again. Have you ever had a project where you needed to change database systems and you spent days sifting through your code to change database-specific function calls and queries? With an abstraction layer, you no longer have to keep track of nuances in function names for different database systems, and as long as your queries are American National Standards Institute (ANSI) SQL compliant, you will not need to write separate queries for different databases. For example, rather than calling `mysql_query()` or `pg_query()`, Drupal uses `db_query()`, which keeps the business logic database-agnostic.

Drupal's database abstraction layer is lightweight and serves two main purposes. The first is to keep your code from being tied to any one database. The second is to sanitize user-submitted data placed into queries to prevent SQL injection attacks. This layer was built on the principle that writing SQL is more convenient than learning a new abstraction layer language.

Drupal also has a schema API, which allows you to describe your database schema (that is, which tables and fields you will be using) to Drupal in a general manner and have Drupal translate that into specifics for the database you are using. We'll cover that in a bit when we talk about .install files.

Drupal determines the type of database to connect to by inspecting the $db_url variable inside your settings.php file. For example, if $db_url begins with mysql, then Drupal will include includes/database.mysql.inc. If it begins with pgsql, Drupal will include includes/database.pgsql.inc. This mechanism is shown in Figure 5-1.

As an example, compare the difference in db_fetch_object() between the MySQL and PostgreSQL abstraction layers:

```
// From database.mysqli.inc.
function db_fetch_object($result) {
  if ($result) {
    return mysql_fetch_object($result);
  }
}
```

```
// From database.pgsql.inc.
function db_fetch_object($result) {
  if ($result) {
    return pg_fetch_object($result);
  }
}
```

If you use a database that is not yet supported, you can write your own driver by implementing the wrapper functions for your database. For more information, see "Writing Your Own Database Driver" at the end of this chapter.

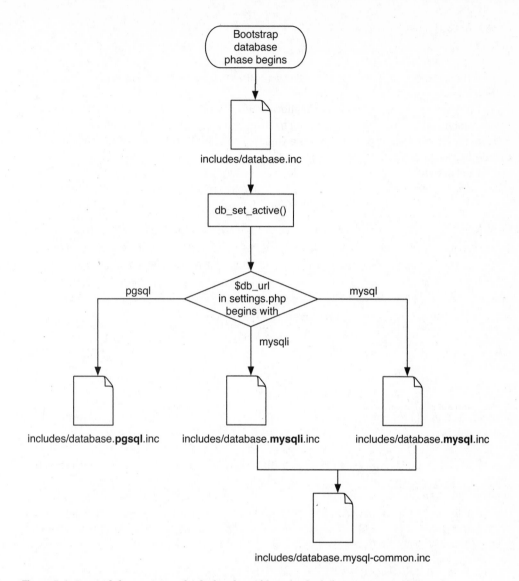

Figure 5-1. *Drupal determines which database file to include by examining $db_url.*

Connecting to the Database

Drupal automatically establishes a connection to the database as part of its normal bootstrap process, so you do not need to worry about doing that.

If you are working outside Drupal itself (for example, you're writing a stand-alone PHP script or have existing PHP code outside of Drupal that needs access to Drupal's database), you would use the following approach.

```
// Make Drupal PHP's current directory.
chdir('/full/path/to/your/drupal/installation');

// Bootstrap Drupal up through the database phase.
include_once('./includes/bootstrap.inc');
drupal_bootstrap(DRUPAL_BOOTSTRAP_DATABASE);

// Now you can run queries using db_query().
$result = db_query('SELECT title FROM {node}');
...
```

■**Caution** Drupal is often configured to have multiple folders in the sites directory so that the site can be moved from staging to production without changing database credentials. For example, you might have sites/staging.example.com/settings.php with database credentials for your testing database server and sites/www.example.com/settings.php with database credentials for your production database server. When establishing a database connection as shown in this section, Drupal will always use sites/default/settings.php, because there is no HTTP request involved.

Performing Simple Queries

Drupal's db_query() function is used to execute a query to the active database connection. These queries include SELECT, INSERT, UPDATE, and DELETE.

There is some Drupal-specific syntax you need to know when it comes to writing SQL statements. First, table names are enclosed within curly brackets so that table names can be prefixed to give them unique names, if necessary. This convention allows users who are restricted by their hosting provider in the number of databases they can create to install Drupal within an existing database and avoid table name collisions by specifying a database prefix in their settings.php file. Here is an example of a simple query to retrieve the name of role 2:

```
$result = db_query('SELECT name FROM {role} WHERE rid = %d', 2);
```

Notice the use of the %d placeholder. In Drupal, queries are always written using placeholders, with the actual value following as a parameter. The %d placeholder will automatically be replaced with the value of the parameter—in this case, 2. Additional placeholders mean additional parameters:

```
db_query('SELECT name FROM {role} WHERE rid > %d AND rid != %d', 1, 7);
```

The preceding line will become the following when it is actually executed by the database:

```
SELECT FROM role WHERE rid > 1 and rid != 7
```

User-submitted data must always be passed in as separate parameters so the values can be sanitized to avoid SQL injection attacks. Drupal uses the `printf` syntax (see `http://php.net/printf`) as placeholders for these values within queries. There are different % modifiers depending on the data type of the user-submitted information.

Table 5-1 lists the database query placeholders and their meaning.

Table 5-1. *Database Query Placeholders and Meanings*

Placeholder	Meaning
%s	String
%d	Integer
%f	Float
%b	Binary data; do not enclose in ' '
%%	Inserts a literal % sign (e.g., `SELECT * FROM {users} WHERE name LIKE '%%%s%%'`)

The first parameter for `db_query()` is always the query itself. The remaining parameters are the dynamic values to validate and insert into the query string. The values can be in an array, or each value can be its own parameter. The latter is the more common format.

We should note that using this syntax will typecast `TRUE`, `FALSE`, and `NULL` to their decimal equivalents (0 or 1). In most cases this should not cause problems.

Let's look at some examples. In these examples, we'll use a database table called `joke` that contains three fields: a node ID (integer), a version ID (integer), and a text field containing a punch line (for more information on the joke module, see Chapter 7).

Let's start with an easy query. Get all rows of all fields from the table named `joke` where the field `vid` has an integer value that is the same as the value of `$node->vid`:

```
db_query('SELECT * FROM {joke} WHERE vid = %d', $node->vid);
```

Insert a new row into the table named `joke`. The new row will contain two integers and a string value. Note the string value's placeholder is in single quotes; this helps prevent SQL injection vulnerabilities. Because we have single quotes in the query itself, we use double quotes to enclose the query:

```
db_query("INSERT INTO {joke} (nid, vid, punchline) VALUES (%d, %d, '%s')",
  $node->nid, $node->vid, $node->punchline);
```

Change all rows in the table named `joke` where the field `vid` has an integer value that is the same as the value of `$node->vid`. The rows will be changed by setting the `punchline` field equal to the string value contained in `$node->punchline`:

```
db_query("UPDATE {joke} SET punchline = '%s' WHERE vid = %d",
  $node->punchline, $node->vid);
```

Delete all rows from the table named `joke` where the `nid` column contains an integer value that is the same as the value of `$node->nid`:

```
db_query('DELETE FROM {joke} WHERE nid = %d', $node->nid);
```

Retrieving Query Results

There are various ways to retrieve query results depending on whether you need a single row or the whole result set or whether you are planning to get a range of results for internal use or for display as a paged result set.

Getting a Single Value

If all you need from the database is a single value, you can use db_result() to retrieve that value. Here is an example of retrieving the total number of users who have not been blocked by the administrator (excluding the anonymous user):

```
$count = db_result(db_query('SELECT COUNT(uid) FROM {users} WHERE status = 1
  AND uid != 0'));
```

Getting Multiple Rows

In most cases, you will want to return more than a single field from the database. Here is a typical iteration pattern for stepping through the result set:

```
$type = 'blog';
$status = 1; // In the node table, a status of 1 means published.
$sql = "SELECT * FROM {node} WHERE type = '%s' AND status = %d";
$result = db_query(db_rewrite_sql($sql), $type, $status);
while ($data = db_fetch_object($result)) {
  $node = node_load($data->nid);
  print node_view($node, TRUE);
}
```

The preceding code snippet will print out all published nodes that are of type blog (the status field in the node table is 0 for unpublished nodes and 1 for published nodes). We will cover db_rewrite_sql() shortly. The db_fetch_object() function grabs a row from the result set as an object. To retrieve the result as an array, use db_fetch_array(). The practice of retrieving rows as objects, as opposed to arrays, is common since most developers prefer its less verbose syntax.

Getting a Limited Range of Results

As you might guess, running the preceding query on a site with, say, 10,000 blog entries is a dangerous idea. We'll limit the result of this query to only the ten newest blog entries:

```
$type = 'blog';
$status = 1; // In the node table, a status of 1 means published.
$sql = "SELECT * FROM {node} n WHERE type = '%s' AND status = %d ORDER BY
  n.created DESC";
$result = db_query_range(db_rewrite_sql($sql), $type, $status, 0, 10);
while ($data = db_fetch_object($result)) {
  $node = node_load($data->nid);
  print node_view($node, TRUE);
}
```

Instead of passing the query to db_query() and using the LIMIT clause, we instead use db_query_range(). Why? Because not all databases agree on the format of the LIMIT syntax, so we need to use db_query_range() as a wrapper function.

Note that you pass the variables that will fill placeholders before the range (so the type and status are passed before 0 and 10 in the example just shown).

Getting Results for Paged Display

We can present these blog entries in a better way: as a page of formatted results with links to more results. We can do that using Drupal's pager (see Figure 5-2). Let's grab all of the blog entries again, only this time we'll display them as a paged result, with links to additional pages of results and "first" and "last" links at the bottom of the page.

```
$type = 'blog';
$status = 1;
$sql = "SELECT * FROM {node} n WHERE type = '%s' AND status = %d ORDER BY
  n.created DESC";
$pager_num = 0; // This is the first pager on this page. We number it 0.
$result = pager_query(db_rewrite_sql($sql), 10, $pager_num, NULL, $type,
  $status);
while ($data = db_fetch_object($result)) {
  $node = node_load($data->nid);
  print node_view($node, TRUE);
}
// Add links to remaining pages of results.
print theme('pager', NULL, 10, $pager_num);
```

Although pager_query() is not really part of the database abstraction layer, it is good to know when you need to create a paged result set with navigation. A call to theme('pager') at the end will display the navigation links to the other pages. You don't need to pass the total number of results to theme('pager'), because the number of results is remembered internally from the pager_query() call.

Figure 5-2. *Drupal's pager gives built-in navigation through a result set.*

The Schema API

Drupal supports multiple databases (MySQL, PostreSQL, etc.) through its database abstraction layer. Each module that wants to have a database table describes that table to Drupal using a schema definition. Drupal then translates the definition into syntax that is appropriate for the database.

Using Module .install Files

As shown in Chapter 2, when you write a module that needs to create one or more database tables for storage, the instructions to create and maintain the table structure go into an .install file that is distributed with the module.

Creating Tables

The install hook usually hands off the installation of the database tables to drupal_install_schema(), which gets the schema definition from the module's schema hook and modifies the database, as shown in Figure 5-3. Then the install hook does any other necessary installation chores. Here's an example from the modules/book/book.install file showing the handoff to drupal_install_schema(). Because the book module deals with the book node type, it creates that node type after the database installation is complete.

```
/**
 * Implementation of hook_install().
 */
function book_install() {
  // Create tables.
  drupal_install_schema('book');

  // Add the node type.
  _book_install_type_create();
}
```

The schema is defined in the following general way:

```
$schema['tablename'] = array(
  // Table description.
  'description' => t('Description of what the table is used for.'),
    'fields' => array(
      // Field definition.
      'field1' => array(
        'type' => 'int',
        'unsigned' => TRUE,
        'not null' => TRUE,
        'default' => 0,
        'description' => t('Description of what this field is used for.'),
      ),
    ),
    // Index declarations.
    'primary key' => array('field1'),
  );
```

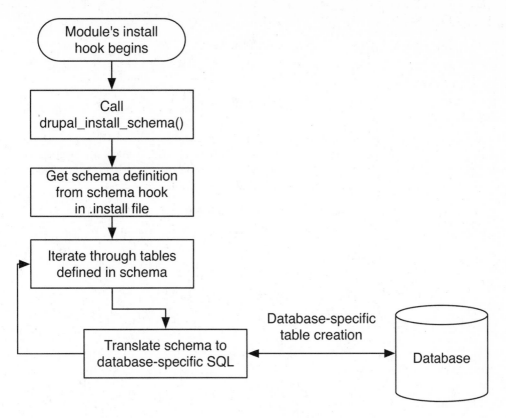

Figure 5-3. *The schema definition is used to create the database tables.*

Let's take a look at the schema definition for Drupal's book table, found in modules/book/book.install:

```
/**
 * Implementation of hook_schema().
 */
function book_schema() {
  $schema['book'] = array(
    'description' => t('Stores book outline information. Uniquely connects each node
                       in the outline to a link in {menu_links}'),
    'fields' => array(
      'mlid' => array(
        'type' => 'int',
        'unsigned' => TRUE,
        'not null' => TRUE,
        'default' => 0,
        'description' => t("The book page's {menu_links}.mlid."),
      ),
```

```
      'nid' => array(
        'type' => 'int',
        'unsigned' => TRUE,
        'not null' => TRUE,
        'default' => 0,
        'description' => t("The book page's {node}.nid."),
      ),
      'bid' => array(
        'type' => 'int',
        'unsigned' => TRUE,
        'not null' => TRUE,
        'default' => 0,
        'description' => t("The book ID is the {book}.nid of the top-level page."),
      ),
    ),
    'primary key' => array('mlid'),
    'unique keys' => array(
      'nid' => array('nid'),
    ),
    'indexes' => array(
      'bid' => array('bid'),
    ),
  );

  return $schema;
}
```

This schema definition describes the book table, which has three fields of type int. It also has a primary key, a unique index (which means all entries in that field are unique) and a regular index. Notice that when a field from another table is referred to in the field description curly brackets are used. That enables the schema module (see the next section) to build handy hyperlinks to table descriptions.

Using the Schema Module

At this point, you may be thinking, "What a pain! Building these big descriptive arrays to tell Drupal about my tables is going to be sheer drudgery." But do not fret. Simply download the schema module from http://drupal.org/project/schema and enable it on your site. Going to Administer ➤ Site building ➤ Schema will give you the ability to see a schema definition for any database table by clicking the Inspect tab. So if you have used SQL to create your table, you can get the schema definition by using the schema module, then copy and paste it into your .install file.

■**Tip** You should rarely have to write a schema from scratch. Instead, use your existing table(s) and the schema module's Inspect tab to have the schema module build the schema for you.

The schema module also allows you to view the schema of any module. For example, Figure 5-4 shows the schema module's display of the book module's schema. Note how the table names that were in curly brackets in the table and field descriptions have been turned into helpful links.

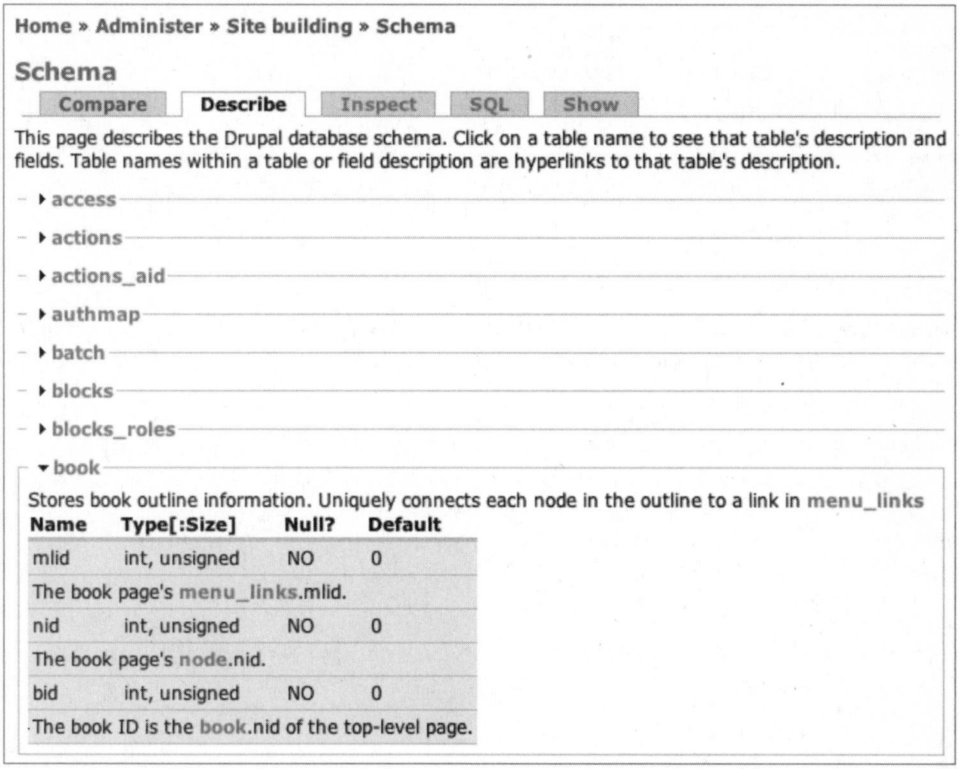

Home » Administer » Site building » Schema

Schema

| Compare | **Describe** | Inspect | SQL | Show |

This page describes the Drupal database schema. Click on a table name to see that table's description and fields. Table names within a table or field description are hyperlinks to that table's description.

- ▸ access
- ▸ actions
- ▸ actions_aid
- ▸ authmap
- ▸ batch
- ▸ blocks
- ▸ blocks_roles
- ▾ book

Stores book outline information. Uniquely connects each node in the outline to a link in `menu_links`

Name	Type[:Size]	Null?	Default
mlid	int, unsigned	NO	0
The book page's `menu_links`.mlid.			
nid	int, unsigned	NO	0
The book page's `node`.nid.			
bid	int, unsigned	NO	0
The book ID is the `book`.nid of the top-level page.			

Figure 5-4. *The schema module displays the schema of the book module.*

Field Type Mapping from Schema to Database

The field type that is declared in the schema definition maps to a native field type in the database. For example, an integer field with the declared size of `tiny` becomes a `TINYINT` field in MySQL but a `smallint` field in PostgreSQL. The actual map can be viewed in the `db_type_map()` function of the database driver file, such as `includes/database.pgsql.php` (see Table 5-2, later in this chapter).

Textual

Textual fields contain text.

Varchar

The varchar, or variable length character field, is the most frequently used field type for storing text less than 256 characters in length. A maximum length, in characters, is defined by the length key. MySQL varchar field lengths are 0–255 characters (MySQL 5.0.2 and earlier) and 0–65,535 characters (MySQL 5.0.3 and later); PostgreSQL varchar field lengths may be larger.

```
$field['fieldname'] = array(
  'type' => 'varchar',      // Required.
  'length' => 255,          // Required.
  'not null' => TRUE,       // Defaults to FALSE.
  'default' => 'chocolate', // See below.
  'description' => t('Always state the purpose of your field.'),
);
```

If the default key has not been set and the not null key has been set to FALSE, the default will be set to NULL.

Char

Char fields are fixed-length character fields. The length of the field, in characters, is defined by the length key. MySQL char field lengths are 0–255 characters.

```
$field['fieldname'] = array(
  'type' => 'char',         // Required.
  'length' => 64,           // Required.
  'not null' => TRUE,       // Defaults to FALSE.
  'default' => 'strawberry', // See below.
  'description' => t('Always state the purpose of your field.'),
);
```

If the default key has not been set and the not null key has been set to FALSE, the default will be set to NULL.

Text

Text fields are used for textual data that can be quite large. For example, the body field of the node_revisions table (where node body text is stored) is of this type. Default values may not be used for text fields.

```
$field['fieldname'] = array(
  'type' => 'text',  // Required.
  'size' => 'small', // tiny | small | normal | medium | big
  'not null' => TRUE, // Defaults to FALSE.
  'description' => t('Always state the purpose of your field.'),
);
```

Numerical

Numerical data types are used for storing numbers and include the integer, serial, float, and numeric types.

Integer

This field type is used for storing integers, such as node IDs. If the unsigned key is TRUE, negative integers will not be allowed.

```
$field['fieldname'] = array(
  'type' => 'int',    // Required.
  'unsigned' => TRUE, // Defaults to FALSE.
  'size' => 'small',  // tiny | small | medium | normal | big
  'not null' => TRUE, // Defaults to FALSE.
  'description' => t('Always state the purpose of your field.'),
);
```

Serial

A serial field keeps a number that increments. For example, when a node is added, the nid field of the node table is incremented. This is done by inserting a row and calling db_last_insert_id(). If a row is added by another thread between the insertion of a row and the retrieval of the last ID, the correct ID is still returned because it is tracked on a per-connection basis. A serial field must be indexed; it is usually indexed as the primary key.

```
$field['fieldname'] = array(
  'type' => 'serial',  // Required.
  'unsigned' => TRUE,  // Defaults to FALSE. Serial numbers are usually positive.
  'size' => 'small',   // tiny | small | medium | normal | big
  'not null' => TRUE,  // Defaults to FALSE. Typically TRUE for serial fields.
  'description' => t('Always state the purpose of your field.'),
);
```

Float

Floating point numbers are stored using the float data type. There is typically no difference between the tiny, small, medium, and normal sizes for a floating point number; in contrast, the big size specifies a double-precision field.

```
$field['fieldname'] = array(
  'type' => 'float',  // Required.
  'unsigned' => TRUE,  // Defaults to FALSE.
  'size' => 'normal',   // tiny | small | medium | normal | big
  'not null' => TRUE,  // Defaults to FALSE.
  'description' => t('Always state the purpose of your field.'),
);
```

Numeric

The numeric data type allows you to specify the precision and scale of a number. Precision is the total number of significant digits in the number; scale is the total number of digits to the right of the decimal point. For example, 123.45 has a precision of 5 and a scale of 2. The size key is not used. At the time of this writing, numeric fields are not used in the schema of the Drupal core.

```
$field['fieldname'] = array(
  'type' => 'numeric', // Required.
  'unsigned' => TRUE, // Defaults to FALSE.
  'precision' => 5,    // Significant digits.
  'scale' => 2,        // Digits to the right of the decimal.
  'not null' => TRUE, // Defaults to FALSE.
  'description' => t('Always state the purpose of your field.'),
);
```

Date and Time: Datetime

The Drupal core does not use this data type, preferring to use Unix timestamps in integer fields. The datetime format is a combined format containing both the date and the time.

```
$field['fieldname'] = array(
  'type' => 'datetime', // Required.
  'not null' => TRUE,   // Defaults to FALSE.
  'description' => t('Always state the purpose of your field.'),
);
```

Binary: Blob

The binary large object data (blob) type is used to store binary data (for example, Drupal's cache table to store the cached data). Binary data may include music, images, or video. Two sizes are available, normal and big.

```
$field['fieldname'] = array(
  'type' => 'blob',   // Required.
  'size' => 'normal'  // normal | big
  'not null' => TRUE, // Defaults to FALSE.
  'description' => t('Always state the purpose of your field.'),
);
```

Declaring a Specific Column Type with mysql_type

If you know the exact column type for your database engine, you can set the mysql_type (or pgsql_type) key in your schema definition. This will override the type and size keys for that database engine. For example, MySQL has a field type called TINYBLOB for small binary large objects. To specify that Drupal should use TINYBLOB if it is running on MySQL but fall back to using the regular BLOB type if it is running on a different database engine, the field could be declared like so:

```
$field['fieldname'] = array(
  'mysql_type' > 'TINYBLOB', // MySQL will use this.
  'type' => 'blob',          // Other databases will use this.
  'size' => 'normal',        // Other databases will use this.
  'not null' => TRUE,
  'description' => t('Wee little blobs.')
);
```

The native types for MySQL and PostgreSQL are shown in Table 5-2.

Table 5-2. *How Type and Size Keys in Schema Definitions Map to Native Database Types*

Schema Definition		Native Database Field Type	
Type	Size	MySQL	PostgreSQL
varchar	normal	VARCHAR	varchar
char	normal	CHAR	character
text	tiny	TINYTEXT	text
text	small	TINYTEXT	text
text	medium	MEDIUMTEXT	text
text	big	LONGTEXT	text
text	normal	TEXT	text
serial	tiny	TINYINT	serial
serial	small	SMALLINT	serial
serial	medium	MEDIUMINT	serial
serial	big	BIGINT	bigserial
serial	normal	INT	serial
int	tiny	TINYINT	smallint
int	small	SMALLINT	smallint
int	medium	MEDIUMINT	int
int	big	BIGINT	bigint
int	normal	INT	int
float	tiny	FLOAT	real
float	small	FLOAT	real
float	medium	FLOAT	real
float	big	DOUBLE	double precision
float	normal	FLOAT	real
numeric	normal	DECIMAL	numeric
blob	big	LONGBLOB	bytea
blob	normal	BLOB	bytea
datetime	normal	DATETIME	timestamp

Maintaining Tables

When you create a new version of a module, you might have to change the database schema. Perhaps you've added a column or added an index to a column. You can't just drop and re-create the table, because the table contains data. Here's how to ensure that the database is changed smoothly:

1. Update the hook_schema() implementation in your .install file so that new users who install your module will have the new schema installed. The schema definition in your .install file will always be the latest schema for your module's tables and fields.

2. Give existing users an upgrade path by writing an update function. Update functions are named sequentially, starting with a number that is based on the Drupal version. For example, the first update function for Drupal 6 would be modulename_update_6000() and the second would be modulename_update_6001(). Here's an example from modules/comment/comment.install where an index was added to the parent ID (pid) column of the comments table:

```
/**
 * Add index to parent ID field.
 */
function comment_update_6003() {
  $ret = array(); // Query results will be collected here.
  // $ret will be modified by reference.
  db_add_index($ret, 'comments', 'pid', array('pid'));
  return $ret;
}
```

This function will be run when the user runs http://example.com/update.php after upgrading the module.

Caution Because the schema definition found in your hook_schema() implementation changes every time you want a new table, field, or index, your update functions should never use the schema definition found there. Think of your hook_schema() implementation as being in the present and your update functions as being in the past. See http://drupal.org/node/150220.

A full list of functions for dealing with schemas can be found at http://api.drupal.org/api/group/schemaapi/6.

Tip Drupal keeps track of which schema version a module is currently using. This information is in the system table. After the update shown in this section has run, the row for the comment module will have a schema_version value of 6003. To make Drupal forget, use the Reinstall Modules option of the devel module, or delete the module's row from the system table.

Deleting Tables on Uninstall

When a module is disabled, any data that the module has stored in the database is left untouched, in case the administrator has a change of heart and reenables the module. The

Administer ➤ Site building ➤ Modules page has an Uninstall tab that removes the data from the database. If you want to enable the deletion of your module's tables on this page, implement the uninstall hook in your module's .install file. You might want to delete any variables you've defined at the same time. Here's an example for the annotation module we wrote in Chapter 2:

```
/**
 * Implementation of hook_uninstall().
 */
function annotate_uninstall() {
  // Use schema API to delete database table.
  drupal_uninstall_schema('annotate');

  // Clean up our entry in the variables table.
  variable_del('annotate_nodetypes');
}
```

Changing Existing Schemas with hook_schema_alter()

Generally modules create and use their own tables. But what if your module wants to alter an existing table? Suppose your module absolutely has to add a column to the node table. The simple way would be to go to your database and add the column. But then Drupal's schema definitions, which should reflect the actual database table, would be inconsistent. There is a better way: hook_schema_alter().

■**Caution** hook_schema_alter() is new to Drupal, and there is still some debate over what the best practices are for using this hook. Check http://api.drupal.org/api/group/hooks/6 for further details.

Suppose you have a module that marks nodes in some way, and for performance reasons, you are dead set on using the existing node table instead of using your own table and joining it using node IDs. Your module will have to do two things: alter the node table during your module's installation and modify the schema so that it actually reflects what is in the database. The former is accomplished with hook_install(), the latter with hook_schema_alter(). Assuming your module is called markednode.module, your markednode.install file would include the following functions:

```
/**
 * Implementation of hook_install().
 */
function markednode_install() {
  $field = array(
    'type' => 'int',
    'unsigned' => TRUE,
    'not null' => TRUE,
    'default' => 0,
```

```
      'initial' => 0, // Sets initial value for preexisting nodes.
      'description' => t('Whether the node has been marked by the
        markednode module.'),
  );

  // Create a regular index called 'marked' on the field named 'marked'.
  $keys['indexes'] = array(
    'marked' => array('marked')
  );

  $ret = array(); // Results of the SQL calls will be stored here.
  db_add_field($ret, 'node', 'marked', $field, $keys);
}

/**
 * Implementation of hook_schema_alter(). We alter $schema by reference.
 *
 * @param $schema
 *   The system-wide schema collected by drupal_get_schema().
 */
function markednode_schema_alter(&$schema) {
  // Add field to existing schema.
  $schema['node']['fields']['marked'] = array(
    'type' => 'int',
    'unsigned' => TRUE,
    'not null' => TRUE,
    'default' => 0,
    'description' => t('Whether the node has been marked by the
      markednode module.'),
  );
}
```

Inserts and Updates with drupal_write_record()

A common problem for programmers is handling inserts of new database rows and updates to existing rows. The code typically tests whether the operation is an insert or an update, then performs the appropriate operation.

Because each table that Drupal uses is described using a schema, Drupal knows what fields a table has and what the default values are for each field. By passing a keyed array of fields and values to drupal_write_record(), you can let Drupal generate and execute the SQL instead of writing it by hand.

Suppose you have a table that keeps track of your collection of giant bunnies. The schema hook for your module which describes the table looks like this:

```
/**
 * Implementation of hook_schema().
 */
function bunny_schema() {
  $schema['bunnies'] = array(
    'description' => t('Stores information about giant rabbits.'),
    'fields' => array(
      'bid' => array(
        'type' => 'serial',
        'unsigned' => TRUE,
        'not null' => TRUE,
        'description' => t("Primary key: A unique ID for each bunny."),
      ),
      'name' => array(
        'type' => 'varchar',
        'length' => 64,
        'not null' => TRUE,
        'description' => t("Each bunny gets a name."),
      ),
      'tons' => array(
        'type' => 'int',
        'unsigned' => TRUE,
        'not null' => TRUE,
        'description' => t('The weight of the bunny to the nearest ton.'),
      ),
    ),
    'primary key' => array('bid'),
    'indexes' => array(
      'tons' => array('tons'),
    ),
  );

  return $schema;
}
```

Inserting a new record is easy, as is updating a record:

```
$table = 'bunnies';
$record = new stdClass();
$record->name = t('Bortha');
$record->tons = 2;
drupal_write_record($table, $record);

// The new bunny ID, $record->bid, was set by drupal_write_record()
// since $record is passed by reference.
watchdog('bunny', 'Added bunny with id %id.', array('%id' => $record->bid));
```

```
// Change our mind about the name.
$record->name = t('Bertha');
// Now update the record in the database.
// For updates we pass in the name of the table's primary key.
drupal_write_record($table, $record, 'bid');

watchdog('bunny', 'Updated bunny with id %id.', array('%id' => $record->bid));
```

Array syntax is also supported, though if $record is an array drupal_write_record() will convert the array to an object internally.

Exposing Queries to Other Modules with hook_db_rewrite_sql()

This hook is used to modify queries created elsewhere in Drupal so that you do not have to hack modules directly. If you are sending a query to db_query() and you believe others may want to modify it, you should wrap it in the function db_rewrite_sql() to make the query accessible to other developers. When such a query is executed, it first checks for all modules that implement hook_db_rewrite_sql() and gives them a chance to modify the query. For example, the node module modifies queries for listings of nodes to exclude nodes that are protected by node access rules.

■Caution If you execute a node listing query (i.e., you are querying the node table for some subset of nodes) and you fail to wrap your query in db_rewrite_sql(), the node access rules will be bypassed because the node module will not have a chance to modify the query to exclude protected nodes. This may lead to nodes being shown to users who should not be allowed to see them.

If you are not the one issuing queries, but you want your module to have a chance to modify others' queries, implement hook_db_rewrite_sql() in your module.

Table 5-3 summarizes the two ways to use SQL rewriting.

Table 5-3. *Using the db_rewrite_sql() Function vs. Using the hook_db_rewrite_sql() Hook*

Name	When to Use
db_rewrite_sql()	When issuing node listing queries or other queries that you want others to be able to modify
hook_db_rewrite_sql()	When you want to modify queries that other modules have issued

Using hook_db_rewrite_sql()

Here's the function signature for hook_db_rewrite_sql():

```
function hook_db_rewrite_sql($query, $primary_table = 'n', $primary_field = 'nid',
  $args = array())
```

The parameters are as follows:

- $query: This is the SQL query available to be rewritten.

- $primary_table: This is the name or alias of the table that has the primary key field for this query. Example values are n for the node table or c for the comment table (e.g., for SELECT nid FROM {node} n, the value would be n). Common values are shown in Table 5-4.

- $primary_field: This is the name of the primary field in the query. Example values are nid, tid, vid, and cid (e.g., if you are querying to get a list of node IDs, the primary field would be nid).

- $args: This array of arguments is passed along to each module's implementation of hook_db_rewrite_sql().

Table 5-4. *Common Values of $primary_table Aliases*

Table	Alias
blocks	b
comments	c
forum	f
node	n
menu	m
term_data	t
vocabulary	v

Changing Other Modules' Queries

Let's take a look at an implementation of the hook_db_rewrite_sql(). The following example takes advantage of the moderate column in the node table to rewrite node queries. After we've modified the query, nodes that are in the moderated state (i.e., the moderate column is 1) will be hidden from users who do not have the "administer content" permission.

```
/**
 * Implementation of hook_db_rewrite_sql().
 */
function moderate_db_rewrite_sql($query, $primary_table, $primary_field, $args) {
  switch ($primary_field) {
    case 'nid':
      // Run only if the user does not already have full access.
      if (!user_access('administer content')) {
        $array = array();
```

```
        if ($primary_table == 'n') {
          // Node table is already present;
          // just add a WHERE to hide moderated nodes.
          $array['where'] = "(n.moderate = 0)";
        }
        // Test if node table is present but alias is not 'n'.
        elseif (preg_match('@{node} ([A-Za-z_]+)@', $query, $match)) {
          $node_table_alias = $match[1];

          // Add a JOIN so that the moderate column will be available.
          $array['join'] = "LEFT JOIN {node} n ON $node_table_alias.nid = n.nid";

          // Add a WHERE to hide moderated nodes.
          $array['where'] = "($node_table_alias.moderate = 0)";
        }

        return $array;
      }
    }
}
```

Notice that we are inspecting any query where nid is the primary key and inserting additional information into those queries. Let's take a look at this in action.

Here's the original query before moderate_db_rewrite_sql():

```
SELECT * FROM {node} n WHERE n.type = 'blog' AND n.status = 1
```

Here's the query after moderate_db_rewrite_sql():

```
SELECT * FROM {node} n WHERE n.type = 'blog' AND n.status = 1 AND n.moderate = 0
```

After moderate_db_rewrite_sql() was called, it appended AND n.moderate = 0 to the incoming query. Other uses of this hook usually relate to restricting access to viewing nodes, vocabularies, terms, or comments.

db_rewrite_sql() is limited in the SQL syntax it can understand. When joining tables you need to use the JOIN syntax rather than joining tables within the FROM clause.

The following is incorrect:

```
SELECT * FROM {node} AS n, {comment} AS c WHERE n.nid = c.nid
```

This is correct:

```
SELECT * FROM {node} n INNER JOIN {comment} c ON n.nid = c.nid
```

Connecting to Multiple Databases Within Drupal

While the database abstraction layer makes remembering function names easier, it also adds built-in security to queries. Sometimes, we need to connect to third-party or legacy databases, and it would be great to use Drupal's database API for this need as well and get the security benefits. The good news is that we can! For example, your module can open a connection to a non-Drupal database and retrieve data.

In the settings.php file, $db_url can be either a string (as it usually is) or an array composed of multiple database connection strings. Here's the default syntax, specifying a single connection string:

```
$db_url = 'mysql://username:password@localhost/databasename';
```

When using an array, the key is a shortcut name you will refer to while activating the database connection, and the value is the connection string itself. Here's an example where we specify two connection strings, default and legacy:

```
$db_url['default'] = 'mysql://user:password@localhost/drupal6';

$db_url['legacy'] = 'mysql://user:password@localhost/legacydatabase';
```

■**Note** The database that is used for your Drupal site should always be keyed as default.

When you need to connect to one of the other databases in Drupal, you activate it by its key name and switch back to the default connection when finished:

```
// Get some information from a non-Drupal database.
db_set_active('legacy');
$result = db_query("SELECT * FROM ldap_user WHERE uid = %d", $user->uid);

// Switch back to the default connection when finished.
db_set_active('default');
```

■**Note** Make sure to always switch back to the default connection, so Drupal can cleanly finish the request life cycle and write to its own tables.

Because the database abstraction layer is designed to use identical function names for each database, multiple kinds of database back-ends (e.g., both MySQL and PostgreSQL) cannot be used simultaneously. However, see http://drupal.org/node/19522 for more information on how to allow both MySQL and PostgreSQL connections from within the same site.

Using a Temporary Table

If you are doing a lot of processing, you may need to create a temporary table during the course of the request. You can do that using db_query_temporary() with a call of the following form:

```
$result = db_query_temporary($sql, $arguments, $temporary_table_name);
```

You can then query the temporary table using the temporary table name. It is good practice to build the temporary table name from "temp" plus the name of your module plus a specific name.

```
$final_result = db_query('SELECT foo FROM temp_mymodule_nids');
```

Notice how the temporary tables never require curly brackets for table prefixing, as a temporary table is short-lived and does not go through the table prefixing process. In contrast, names of permanent tables are always surrounded by curly brackets to support table prefixing.

Note Temporary tables are not used in the Drupal core, and the database user that Drupal is using to connect to the database may not have permission to create temporary tables. Thus, module authors should not assume that everyone running Drupal will have this permission.

Writing Your Own Database Driver

Suppose we want to write a database abstraction layer for a new, futuristic database system named DNAbase that uses molecular computing to increase performance. Rather than start from scratch, we'll copy an existing abstraction layer and modify it. We'll use the PostgreSQL implementation, since the MySQL driver is split up into includes/database.mysql-common.inc and a separate file for the mysql and mysqli drivers.

First, we make a copy of includes/database.pgsql.inc and rename it as includes/ database.dnabase.inc. Then we change the logic inside each wrapper function to map to DNAbase's functionality instead of PostgreSQL's functionality. When all is said and done, we have the following functions declared in our file:

```
_db_query($query, $debug = 0)
db_add_field(&$ret, $table, $field, $spec, $new_keys = array())
db_add_index(&$ret, $table, $name, $fields)
db_add_primary_key(&$ret, $table, $fields)
db_add_unique_key(&$ret, $table, $name, $fields)
db_affected_rows()
db_change_field(&$ret, $table, $field, $field_new, $spec, $new_keys = array())
db_check_setup()
```

```
db_column_exists($table, $column)
db_connect($url)
db_create_table_sql($name, $table)
db_decode_blob($data)
db_distinct_field($table, $field, $query)
db_drop_field(&$ret, $table, $field)
db_drop_index(&$ret, $table, $name)
db_drop_primary_key(&$ret, $table)
db_drop_table(&$ret, $table)
db_drop_unique_key(&$ret, $table, $name)
db_encode_blob($data)
db_error()
db_escape_string($text)
db_fetch_array($result)
db_fetch_object($result)
db_field_set_default(&$ret, $table, $field, $default)
db_field_set_no_default(&$ret, $table, $field)
db_last_insert_id($table, $field)
db_lock_table($table)
db_query_range($query)
db_query_temporary($query)
db_query($query)
db_rename_table(&$ret, $table, $new_name)
db_result($result)
db_status_report()
db_table_exists($table)
db_type_map()
db_unlock_tables()
db_version()
```

We test the system by connecting to the DNAbase database within Drupal by updating $db_url in settings.php. It looks something like this:

```
$db_url = 'dnabase://john:secret@localhost/mydnadatabase';
```

where john is the username; secret is the password; and mydnadatabase is the name of the database to which we will connect. You'll also want to create a test module that calls these functions directly to ensure that they work as expected.

Summary

After reading this chapter, you should be able to

- Understand Drupal's database abstraction layer.

- Perform basic queries.

- Get single and multiple results from the database.

- Get a limited range of results.

- Use the pager.

- Understand Drupal's schema API.

- Write queries so other developers can modify them.

- Cleanly modify the queries from other modules.

- Connect to multiple databases, including legacy databases.

- Write an abstraction layer driver.

## CHAPTER 6

Working with Users

Users are the reason for using Drupal. Drupal can help users create, collaborate, communicate, and form an online community. In this chapter, we look behind the scenes and see how users are authenticated, logged in, and represented internally. We start with an examination of what the $user object is and how it's constructed. Then we walk through the process of user registration, user login, and user authentication. We finish by examining how Drupal ties in with external authentication systems such as Lightweight Directory Access Protocol (LDAP) and Pubcookie.

The $user Object

Drupal requires that the user have cookies enabled in order to log in; a user with cookies turned off can still interact with Drupal as an *anonymous user*.

During the session phase of the bootstrap process, Drupal creates a global $user object that represents the identity of the current user. If the user is not logged in (and so does not have a session cookie), then he or she is treated as an anonymous user. The code that creates an anonymous user looks like this (and lives in includes/bootstrap.inc):

```
function drupal_anonymous_user($session = '') {
  $user = new stdClass();
  $user->uid = 0;
  $user->hostname = ip_address();
  $user->roles = array();
  $user->roles[DRUPAL_ANONYMOUS_RID] = 'anonymous user';
  $user->session = $session;
  $user->cache = 0;
  return $user;
}
```

On the other hand, if the user is currently logged in, the $user object is created by joining the users table and sessions table on the user's ID. Values of all fields in both tables are placed into the $user object.

Note The user's ID is an integer that is assigned when the user registers or the user account is created by the administrator. This ID is the primary key of the users table.

The $user object is easily inspected by adding global $user; print_r($user); to index.php. The following is what a $user object generally looks like for a logged-in user:

```
stdClass Object (
    [uid]        => 2
    [name]       => Joe Example
    [pass]       => 7701e9e11ac326e98a3191cd386a114b
    [mail]       => joe@example.com
    [mode]       => 0
    [sort]       => 0
    [threshold]  => 0
    [theme]      => bluemarine
    [signature]  => Drupal rocks!
    [created]    => 1201383973
    [access]     => 1201384439
    [login]      => 1201383989
    [status]     => 1
    [timezone]   => -21600
    [language]   =>
    [picture]    => sites/default/files/pictures/picture-1.jpg
    [init]       => joe@example.com
    [data]       =>
    [roles]      => Array ( [2] => authenticated user )
    [sid]        => fq5vvn5ajvj4sihli314ltsqe4
    [hostname]   => 127.0.0.1
    [timestamp]  => 1201383994
    [cache]      => 0
    [session]    => user_overview_filter|a:0:{}
)
```

In the $user object just displayed, italicized field names denote that the origin of the data is the sessions table. The components of the $user object are explained in Table 6-1.

Table 6-1. *Components of the $user Object*

Component	Description
Provided by the users Table	
uid	The user ID of this user. This is the primary key of the users table and is unique to this Drupal installation.
name	The user's username, typed by the user when logging in.
pass	An MD5 hash of the user's password, which is compared when the user logs in. Since the actual passwords aren't saved, they can only be reset and not restored.
mail	The user's current e-mail address.
mode, sort, and threshold	User-specific comment viewing preferences.
theme	If multiple themes are enabled, the user's chosen theme. If a user's theme is uninstalled, Drupal will revert to the site's default theme.

Component	Description
signature	The signature the user entered on his or her account page. Used when the user adds a comment and only visible when the comment module is enabled.
created	A Unix timestamp of when this user account was created.
access	A Unix timestamp denoting the user's last access time.
login	A Unix timestamp denoting the user's last successful login.
status	Contains 1 if the user is in good standing or 0 if the user has been blocked.
timezone	The number of seconds that the user's time zone is offset from GMT.
language	The user's default language. Empty unless multiple languages are enabled on a site and the user has chosen a language by editing account preferences.
picture	The path to the image file the user has associated with the account.
init	The initial e-mail address the user provided when registering.
data	Arbitrary data can be stored here by modules (see the next section, "Storing Data in the $user Object").
Provided by the user_roles Table	
roles	The roles currently assigned to this user.
Provided by the sessions Table	
sid	The session ID assigned to this user session by PHP.
hostname	The IP address from which the user is viewing the current page.
timestamp	A Unix timestamp representing time at which the user's browser last received a completed page.
cache	A timestamp used for per-user caching (see includes/cache.inc).
session	Arbitrary, transitory data stored for the duration of the user's session can be stored here by modules.

Storing Data in the $user Object

The users table contains a field called data that holds extra information in a serialized array. If you add your own data to the $user object, it will be stored in this field by user_save():

```
// Add user's disposition.
global $user;
$extra_data = array('disposition' => t('Grumpy'));
user_save($user, $extra_data);
```

The $user object now has a permanent attribute:

```
global $user;
print $user->disposition;
```

```
Grumpy
```

While this approach is convenient, it creates additional overhead when the user logs in and the $user object is instantiated, since any data stored in this way must be unserialized. Thus, throwing large amounts of data willy-nilly into the $user object can create a performance bottleneck. An alternate and preferred method, in which attributes are added to the $user object when the object is loaded, is discussed shortly in the section titled "Adding Data to the $user Object at Load Time."

Testing If a User Is Logged In

During a request, the standard way of testing if a user is logged in is to test whether $user->uid is 0. Drupal has a convenience function called user_is_logged_in() for this purpose (there is a corresponding user_is_anonymous() function):

```
if (user_is_logged_in()) {
  $output = t('User is logged in.');
else {
  $output = t('User is an anonymous user.');
}
```

Introduction to hook_user()

Implementing hook_user() gives your modules a chance to react to the different operations performed on a user account and to modify the $user object. Let's examine the function signature:

```
function hook_user($op, &$edit, &$account, $category = NULL)
```

The $op parameter is used to describe the current operation being performed on the user account and can have many different values:

- after_update: This is called after the $user object has been saved to the database.

- categories: This returns an array of categories that appear as Drupal menu local tasks (typically rendered as clickable tabs) when the user edits the user account. These are actually Drupal menu items. See profile_categories() in profile.module for a sample implementation.

- delete: A user has just been deleted from the database. This is an opportunity for the module to remove information related to the user from the database.

- form: Inject additional form field elements to the user edit form being displayed.

- insert: The row for the new user account has been inserted into the database; $user->data is about to be saved and roles assigned. After that, the finished $user object will be loaded.

- `load`: The user account was successfully loaded. The module may add additional information into the $user object (passed to the user hook by reference as the $account parameter).

- `login`: The user has successfully logged in.

- `logout`: The user just logged out and his or her session has been destroyed.

- `register`: The user account registration form is about to be displayed. The module may add additional form elements to the form.

- `submit`: The user edit form has been submitted. Modify the account information before it is sent to `user_save()`.

- `update`: The existing user account is about to be saved to the database.

- `validate`: The user account has been modified. The module should validate its custom data and raise any necessary errors.

- `view`: The user's account information is being displayed. The module should return its custom additions to the display as a structured element of $user->content. The view operation ultimately calls `theme_user_profile()` to format the user profile page (more details on this shortly).

The $edit parameter is an array of the form values submitted when a user account is being created or updated. Notice that it's passed by reference, so any changes you make will actually change the form values.

The $account object (which is really a $user object) is also passed by reference, so any changes you make will actually change the $user information.

The $category parameter is the active user account category being edited. Think of categories as separate groups of information that relate to the user. For example, if you go to your "My account" page while logged in to drupal.org and click the Edit tab, you'll see separate categories for account settings, personal information, newsletter subscriptions, and so on.

■Caution Don't confuse the $account parameter within hook_user() with the global $user object. The $account parameter is the user object for the account currently being manipulated. The global $user object is the user currently logged in. Often, but not always, they are the same.

Understanding hook_user('view')

hook_user('view') is used by modules to add information to user profile pages (e.g., what you see at http://example.com/?q=user/1; see Figure 6-1).

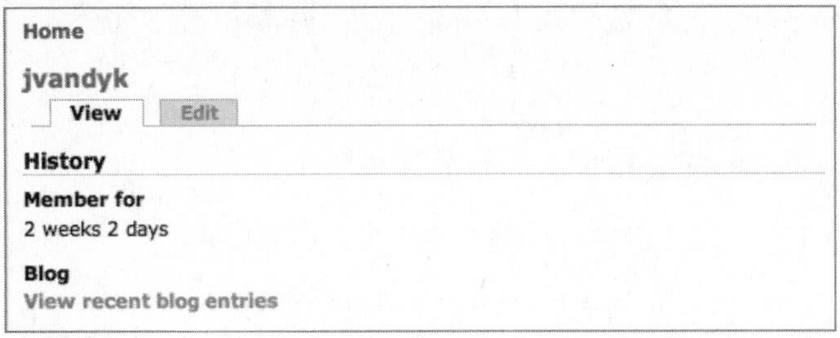

Figure 6-1. *The user profile page, with the blog module and the user module implementing hook_user('view') to add additional information*

Let's examine how the blog module added its information to this page:

```
/**
 * Implementation of hook_user().
 */
function blog_user($op, &$edit, &$user) {
  if ($op == 'view' && user_access('create blog entries', $user)) {
    $user->content['summary']['blog'] = array(
      '#type' => 'user_profile_item',
      '#title' => t('Blog'),
      '#value' => l(t('View recent blog entries'), "blog/$user->uid",
        array('title' => t("Read @username's latest blog entries.",
        array('@username' => $user->name)))),
      '#attributes' => array('class' => 'blog'),
    );
  }
}
```

The view operation stashes some information into $user->content. User profile information is organized into categories, with each category representing a page of information about a user. In Figure 6-1, there is just one category, called History. The outer array should be keyed by category name. In the preceding example, the name of the key is summary, which corresponds to the History category (admittedly, it would make more sense to name the key and the category the same thing). The interior array(s) should have a unique textual key (blog in this case) and have #type, #title, #value, and #attributes elements. The type user_profile_item points Drupal's theming layer to modules/user/user-profile-item.tpl.php. By comparing the code snippet with Figure 6-1, you can see how these elements are rendered. Figure 6-2 shows the contents of the $user->content array, which became the page shown in Figure 6-1.

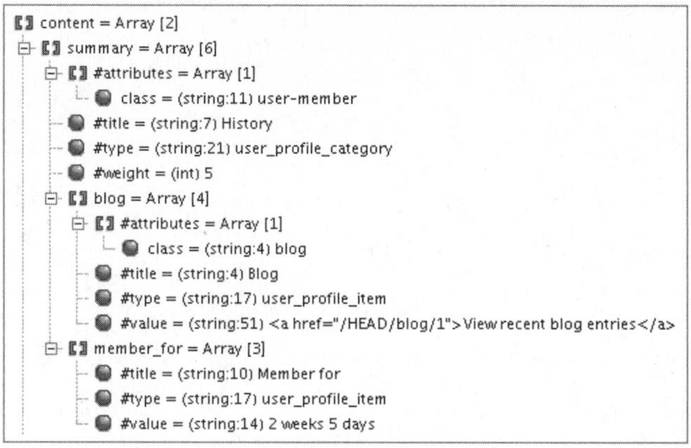

```
[] content = Array [2]
[] summary = Array [6]
    [] #attributes = Array [1]
        class = (string:11) user-member
    #title = (string:7) History
    #type = (string:21) user_profile_category
    #weight = (int) 5
    [] blog = Array [4]
        [] #attributes = Array [1]
            class = (string:4) blog
        #title = (string:4) Blog
        #type = (string:17) user_profile_item
        #value = (string:51) <a href="/HEAD/blog/1">View recent blog entries</a>
    [] member_for = Array [3]
        #title = (string:10) Member for
        #type = (string:17) user_profile_item
        #value = (string:14) 2 weeks 5 days
```

Figure 6-2. *The structure of $user->content*

Your module may also implement hook_profile_alter() to manipulate the profile items in the $user->content array before they are themed. The following is an example of simply removing the blog profile item from the user profile page. The function is named as if it were in the hypothetical hide.module:

```
/**
 * Implementation of hook_profile_alter().
 */
function hide_profile_alter(&$account) {
  unset($account->content['summary']['blog']);
}
```

The User Registration Process

By default, user registration on a Drupal site requires nothing more than a username and a valid e-mail address. Modules can add their own fields to the user registration form by implementing the user hook. Let's write a module called legalagree.module that provides a quick way to make your site play well in today's litigious society.

First, create a folder at sites/all/modules/custom/legalagree, and add the following files (see Listings 6-1 and 6-2) to the legalagree directory. Then, enable the module via Administer ➤ Site building ➤ Modules.

Listing 6-1. *legalagree.info*

```
; $Id$
name = Legal Agreement
description = Displays a dubious legal agreement during user registration.
package = Pro Drupal Development
core = 6.x
```

Listing 6-2. *legalagree.module*

```php
<?php
// $Id$

/**
 * @file
 * Support for dubious legal agreement during user registration.
 */

/**
 * Implementation of hook_user().
 */
function legalagree_user($op, &$edit, &$user, $category = NULL) {
  switch($op) {
    // User is registering.
    case 'register':
      // Add a fieldset containing radio buttons to the
      // user registration form.
      $fields['legal_agreement'] = array(
        '#type' => 'fieldset',
        '#title' => t('Legal Agreement')
      );
      $fields['legal_agreement']['decision'] = array(
        '#type' => 'radios',
        '#description' => t('By registering at %site-name, you agree that
at any time, we (or our surly, brutish henchmen) may enter your place of
residence and smash your belongings with a ball-peen hammer.',
array('%site-name' => variable_get('site_name', 'drupal'))),
        '#default_value' => 0,
        '#options' => array(t('I disagree'), t('I agree'))
      );
      return $fields;

    // Field values for registration are being checked.
    case 'validate':
      // Make sure the user selected radio button 1 ('I agree').
      // The validate op is reused when a user updates information on
      // the 'My account' page, so we use isset() to test whether we are
      // on the registration page where the decision field is present.
      if (isset($edit['decision']) && $edit['decision'] != '1') {
        form_set_error('decision', t('You must agree to the Legal Agreement
          before registration can be completed.'));
      }
      break;
```

```
    // New user has just been inserted into the database.
    case 'insert':
      // Record information for future lawsuit.
      watchdog('user', t('User %user agreed to legal terms',
        array('%user' => $user->name)));
      break;
  }
}
```

The user hook gets called during the creation of the registration form, during the validation of that form, and after the user record has been inserted into the database. Our brief module will result in a registration form similar to the one shown in Figure 6-3.

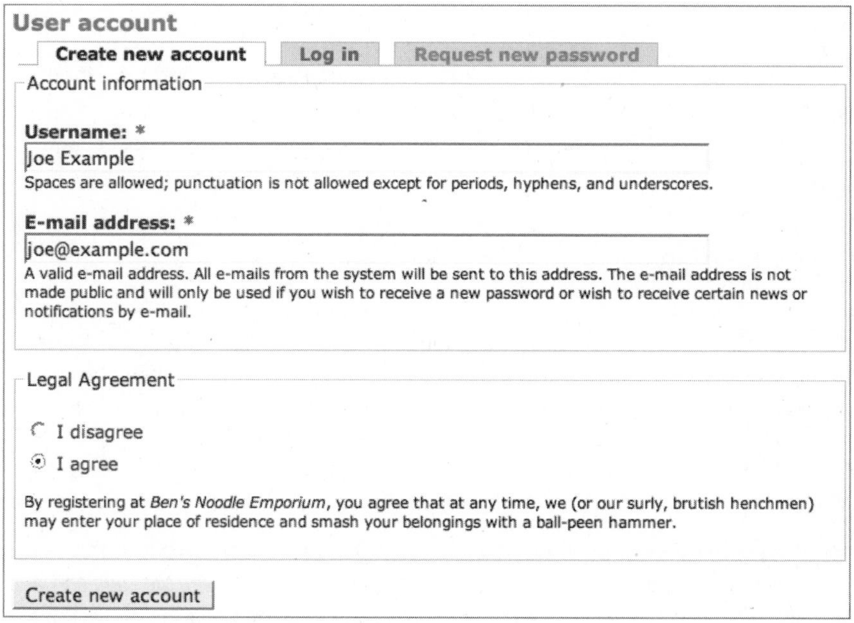

Figure 6-3. *A modified user registration form*

Using profile.module to Collect User Information

If you plan to extend the user registration form to collect information about users, you would do well to try out profile.module before writing your own module. It allows you to create arbitrary forms to collect data, define whether or not the information is required and/or collected on the user registration form, and designate whether the information is public or private. Additionally, it allows the administrator to define pages so that users can be viewed by their profile choices using a URL constructed from *site URL* plus *profile/* plus *name of profile field* plus *value*.

For example, if you define a textual profile field named `profile_color`, you could view all the users who chose black for their favorite color at `http://example.com/?q=profile/profile_color/black`. Or suppose you are creating a conference web site and are responsible for planning dinner for attendees. You could define a check box profile field named `profile_vegetarian` and view all users who are vegetarians at `http://example.com/?q=profile/profile_vegetarian` (note that for check box fields, the value is implicit and thus ignored; that is, there is no value appended to the URL like the value `black` was for the `profile_color` field).

As a real-world example, the list of users at `http://drupal.org` who attended the 2008 Drupal conference in Boston, Massachusetts, can be viewed at `http://drupal.org/profile/conference-boston-2008` (in this case, the name of the field is not prefixed with `profile_`).

■**Tip** Automatic creation of profile summary pages works only if the field Page title is filled out in the profile field settings and is not available for textarea, URL, or date fields.

The Login Process

The login process begins when a user fills out the login form (typically at `http://example.com/?q=user` or displayed in a block) and clicks the "Log in" button.

The validation routines of the login form check whether the username has been blocked, whether an access rule has denied access, and whether the user has entered an incorrect username or password. The user is duly notified of any of these conditions.

■**Note** Drupal has both local and external authentication. Examples of external authentication systems include OpenID, LDAP, Pubcookie, and others. One type of external authentication is *distributed authentication*, where users from one Drupal site are permitted to log on to another Drupal site (see the site_network module at `http://drupal.org/project/site_network`).

Drupal attempts to log in a user locally by searching for a row in the `users` table with the matching username and password hash. A successful login results in the firing of two user hooks (`load` and `login`), which your modules can implement, as shown in Figure 6-4.

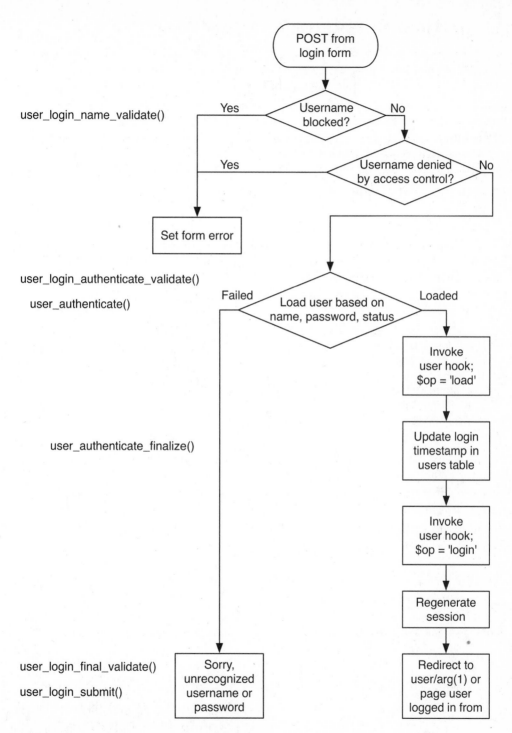

Figure 6-4. *Path of execution for a local user login*

Adding Data to the $user Object at Load Time

The load operation of the user hook is fired when a $user object is successfully loaded from the database in response to a call to user_load(). This happens when a user logs in, when authorship information is being retrieved for a node, and at several other points.

Note Because invoking the user hook is expensive, user_load() is *not* called when the current $user object is instantiated for a request (see the earlier "The $user Object" section). If you are writing your own module, always call user_load() before calling a function that expects a fully loaded $user object, unless you are sure this has already happened.

Let's write a module named loginhistory that keeps a history of when the user logged in. We'll display the number of times the user has logged in on the user's "My account" page. Create a folder named loginhistory in sites/all/modules/custom/, and add the files in Listings 6-3 through 6-5. First up is sites/all/modules/custom/loginhistory/loginhistory.info.

Listing 6-3. *loginhistory.info*

```
; $Id$
name = Login History
description = Keeps track of user logins.
package = Pro Drupal Development
core = 6.x
```

We need an .install file to create the database table to store the login information, so we create sites/all/modules/custom/loginhistory/loginhistory.install.

Listing 6-4. *loginhistory.install*

```php
<?php
// $Id$

/**
 * Implementation of hook_install().
 */
function loginhistory_install() {
  // Create tables.
  drupal_install_schema('loginhistory');
}
```

```php
/**
 * Implementation of hook_uninstall().
 */
function loginhistory_uninstall() {
  // Remove tables.
  drupal_uninstall_schema('loginhistory');
}

/**
 * Implementation of hook_schema().
 */
function loginhistory_schema() {
  $schema['login_history'] = array(
    'description' => t('Stores information about user logins.'),
    'fields' => array(
      'uid' => array(
        'type' => 'int',
        'unsigned' => TRUE,
        'not null' => TRUE,
        'description' => t('The {user}.uid of the user logging in.'),
      ),
      'login' => array(
        'type' => 'int',
        'unsigned' => TRUE,
        'not null' => TRUE,
        'description' => t('Unix timestamp denoting time of login.'),
      ),
    ),
    'index' => array('uid'),
  );

  return $schema;
}
```

Listing 6-5. *loginhistory.module*

```php
<?php
// $Id$

/**
 * @file
 * Keeps track of user logins.
 */
```

```
/**
 * Implementation of hook_user().
 */
function loginhistory_user($op, &$edit, &$account, $category = NULL) {
  switch($op) {
    // Successful login.
    case 'login':
      // Record timestamp in database.
      db_query("INSERT INTO {login_history} (uid, login) VALUES (%d, %d)",
        $account->uid, $account->login);
      break;

    // $user object has been created and is given to us as $account parameter.
    case 'load':
      // Add the number of times user has logged in.
      $account->loginhistory_count = db_result(db_query("SELECT COUNT(login) AS
        count FROM {login_history} WHERE uid = %d", $account->uid));
      break;

    // 'My account' page is being created.
    case 'view':
      // Add a field displaying number of logins.
      $account->content['summary']['login_history'] = array(
        '#type' => 'user_profile_item',
        '#title' => t('Number of Logins'),
        '#value' => $account->loginhistory_count,
        '#attributes' => array('class' => 'login-history'),
        '#weight' => 10,
      );
      break;
  }
}
```

After installing this module, each successful user login will fire the login operation of the user hook, which the module will respond to by inserting a record into the login_history table in the database. When the $user object is loaded, the user load hook will be fired, and the module will add the current number of logins for that user to $account->loginhistory_count. And when the user views the "My account" page, the login count will be displayed, as shown in Figure 6-5.

```
Home

jvandyk
  View        Edit

History

Blog
View recent blog entries

Member for
2 weeks 5 days

Number of Logins
3
```

Figure 6-5. *Login history tracking user logins*

■**Note** It's always a good idea to prefix any properties you are adding to objects like $user or $node with the name of your module to avoid namespace collisions. That's why the example used `$account->loginhistory_count` instead of `$account->count`.

Although we presented the extra information that we added to the $user object on the "My account" page, remember that because the $user object is global, any other module can access it. I leave it as a useful exercise for the reader to modify the preceding module to provide a nicely formatted list of past logins as a block in a sidebar for security purposes ("Hey! *I* didn't log in this morning at 3:00 a.m.!").

Providing User Information Categories

If you have an account on `http://drupal.org`, you can see the effects of providing categories of user information by logging in and clicking the "My account" link, and then selecting the Edit tab. In addition to editing your account information, such as your password, you can provide information about yourself in several other categories. At the time of this writing, `http://drupal.org` supported editing of CVS information, Drupal involvement, personal information, work information, and preferences for receiving newsletters.

You can add information categories like these by using `profile.module` or by responding to the `categories` operation of the user hook; see the implementation in `profile.module`.

External Login

Sometimes, you may not want to use Drupal's local `users` table. For example, maybe you already have a table of users in another database or in LDAP. Drupal makes it easy to integrate external authentication into the login process.

Simple External Authentication

Let's implement a very simple external authentication module to illustrate how external authentication works. Suppose your company only hires people named Dave, and usernames are assigned based on first and last names. This module authenticates anyone whose user-name begins with the string dave, so the users davebrown, davesmith, and davejones will all successfully log in. Our approach will be to use form_alter() to alter the user login validation handler so that it runs our own validation handler. Here is sites/all/modules/custom/authdave/authdave.info:

```
; $Id$
name = Authenticate Daves
description = External authentication for all Daves.
package = Pro Drupal Development
core = 6.x
```

And here is the actual authdave.module:

```php
<?php
// $Id$

/**
 * Implementation of hook_form_alter().
 * We replace the local login validation handler with our own.
 */
function authdave_form_alter(&$form, $form_state, $form_id) {
  // In this simple example we authenticate on username only,
  // so password is not a required field. But we leave it in
  // in case another module needs it.
  if ($form_id == 'user_login' || $form_id == 'user_login_block') {
    $form['pass']['#required'] = FALSE;


    // If the user login form is being submitted, add our validation handler.
    if (isset($form_state['post']['name'])) {
      // Find the local validation function's entry so we can replace it.
      $array_key = array_search('user_login_authenticate_validate',
        $form['#validate']);

      if ($array_key === FALSE) {
        // Could not find it. Some other module must have run form_alter().
        // We will simply add our validation just before the final validator.
        $final_validator = array_pop($form['#validate']);
        $form['#validate'][] = 'authdave_login_validate';
        $form['#validate'][] = $final_validator;
      }
```

```
      else {
        // Found the local validation function. Replace with ours.
        $form['#validate'][$array_key] = 'authdave_login_validate';
      }
    }
  }
}

/**
 * Form validation handler.
 */
function authdave_login_validate($form, &$form_state) {
  global $user;
  if (!empty($user->uid)) {
    // Another module has already handled authentication.
    return;
  }
  // Call our custom authentication function.
  if (!authdave_authenticate($form_state['values'])) {
    // Authentication failed; username did not begin with 'dave'.
    form_set_error('name', t('Unrecognized username.'));
  }
}

/**
 * Custom authentication function. This could be much more complicated,
 * checking an external database, LDAP, etc.
 */
function authdave_authenticate($form_values) {
  global $authdave_authenticated;
  $username = $form_values['name'];
  if (substr(drupal_strtolower($username), 0, 4) == 'dave') {
    // Log user in, or register new user if not already present.
    user_external_login_register($username, 'authdave');

    // Write session, update timestamp, run user 'login' hook.
    user_authenticate_finalize($form_state['values']);
    // Use a global variable to save the fact that we did authentication.
    // (See use of this global in hook_user() implementation of next
    // code listing.)
    $authdave_authenticated = TRUE;
    return TRUE;
  }
```

```
else {
  // Not a Dave.
  return FALSE;
  }
}
```

Figure 6-4 shows Drupal's local login process. It consists of three form validation handlers:

- `user_login_name_validate()`: Set a form error if the username has been blocked or if access rules (Administer ➤ User management ➤ Access rules) deny the username or host.

- `user_login_authenticate_validate()`: Set a form error if a search of the users table for a user with this username, password, and a status setting of 1 (that is, unblocked) fails.

- `user_login_final_validate()`: If the user has not been successfully loaded, set the error "Sorry, unrecognized username or password. Have you forgotten your password?" and write a watchdog entry: "Login attempt failed for user".

In the authdave module (see Figure 6-6), we simply swap out the second validation handler for our own. Compare Figure 6-6 with Figure 6-4, which shows the local user login process.

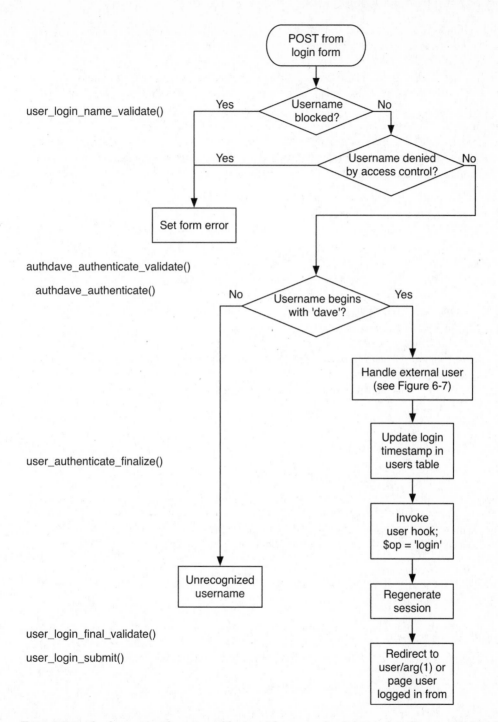

Figure 6-6. *Path of execution for external login with a second validation handler provided by the authdave module (compare with Figure 6-4)*

The function user_external_login_register() is a helper function that registers the user if this is the first login and then logs the user in. The path of execution is shown in Figure 6-7 for a hypothetical user davejones logging in for the first time.

If the username begins with "dave" and this is the first time this user has logged in, a row in the users table does not exist for this user, so one will be created. However, no e-mail address has been provided like it was for Drupal's default local user registration, so a module this simple is not a real solution if your site relies on sending e-mail to users. You'll want to set the mail column of the users table so you will have an e-mail address associated with the user. To do this, you can have your module respond to the insert operation of the user hook, which is fired whenever a new user is inserted:

```
/**
 * Implementation of hook_user().
 */
function authdave_user($op, &$edit, &$account, $category = NULL) {
  switch($op) {
    case 'insert':
      // New user was just added; if we did authentication,
      // look up e-mail address of user in a legacy database.
      global $authdave_authenticated;
      if ($authdave_authenticated) {
        $email = mycompany_email_lookup($account->name);
        // Set e-mail address in the users table for this user.
        db_query("UPDATE {users} SET mail = '%s' WHERE uid = %d", $email,
          $account->uid);
      }
      break;
    ...
  }
}
```

Savvy readers will notice that there is no way for the code running under the insert operation to tell whether the user is locally or externally authenticated, so we've cleverly saved a global indicating that our module did authentication. We could also have queried the authmap table like so:

```
db_query("SELECT uid FROM {authmap} WHERE uid = %d AND module = '%s'",
  $account->uid, 'authdave');
```

All users who were added via external authentication will have a row in the authmap table as well as the users table. However, in this case the authentication and the user hook run during the same request, so a global variable is a good alternative to a database query.

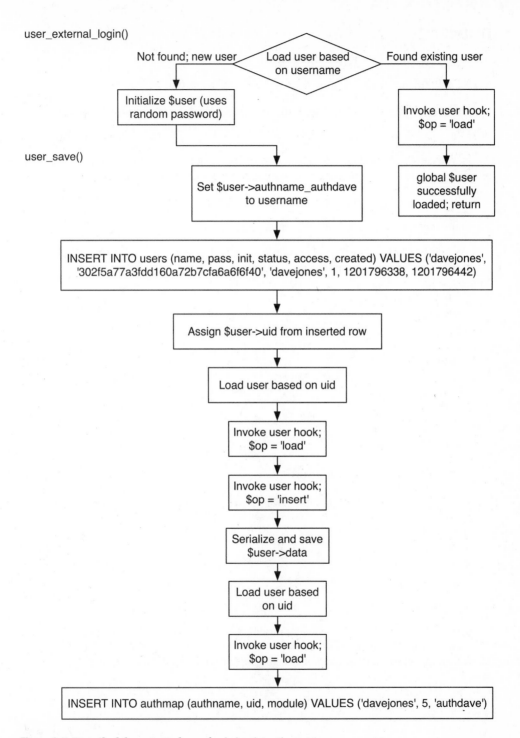

Figure 6-7. *Detail of the external user login/registration process*

Summary

After reading this chapter, you should be able to

- Understand how users are represented internally in Drupal.

- Understand how to store information associated with a user in several ways.

- Hook into the user registration process to obtain more information from a registering user.

- Hook into the user login process to run your own code at user login time.

- Understand how external user authentication works.

- Implement your own external authentication module.

For more information on external authentication, see the `openid.module` (part of the Drupal core) or the contributed `pubcookie.module`.

CHAPTER 7

■ ■ ■

Working with Nodes

This chapter will introduce nodes and node types. I'll show you how to create a node type in two different ways. I'll first show you the programmatic solution by writing a module that uses Drupal hooks. This approach allows for a greater degree of control and flexibility when defining what the node can and can't do. Then I'll show you how to build a node type from within the Drupal administrative interface and briefly discuss the Content Construction Kit (CCK), which is slowly making its way into the Drupal core distribution. Finally, we'll investigate Drupal's node access control mechanism.

■**Tip** Developers often use the terms *node* and *node type*. In Drupal's user interface, they are referred to as *posts* and *content types,* respectively, in an effort to use terms that will resonate with site administrators.

So What Exactly Is a Node?

One of the first questions asked by those new to Drupal development is, "What is a node?" A node is a piece of content. Drupal assigns each piece of content an ID number called a *node ID* (abbreviated in the code as $nid). Generally each node has a title also, to allow an administrator to view a list of nodes by title.

■**Note** If you're familiar with object orientation, think of a node type as a class and an individual node as an object instance. However, Drupal's code is not 100 percent object oriented, and there's good reason for this (see http://api.drupal.org/api/HEAD/file/developer/topics/oop.html). Future versions of Drupal promise to become more object oriented when the need is justified, since PHP 4 (with its poor object support) will no longer be supported.

There are many different kinds of nodes, or *node types*. Some common node types are "blog entry," "poll," and "book page." Often the term *content type* is used as a synonym for *node type*, although a node type is really a more abstract concept and can be thought of as a derivation of a base node, as Figure 7-1 represents.

The beauty of all content types being nodes is that they're based on the same underlying data structure. For developers, this means that for many operations you can treat all content the same programmatically. It's easy to perform batch operations on nodes, and you also get a lot of functionality for custom content types out of the box. Searching, creating, editing, and managing content are supported natively by Drupal because of the underlying node data structure and behavior. This uniformity is apparent to end users too. The forms for creating, editing, and deleting nodes have a similar look and feel, leading to a consistent and thus easier-to-use interface.

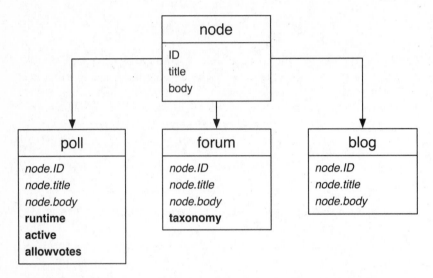

Figure 7-1. *Node types are derived from a basic node and may add fields.*

Node types extend the base node, usually by adding their own data attributes. A node of type poll stores voting options such as the duration of the poll, whether the poll is currently active and whether the user is allowed to vote. A node of type forum loads the taxonomy term for each node so it will know where it fits in the forums defined by the administrator. blog nodes, on the other hand, don't add any other data. Instead, they just add different views into the data by creating blogs for each user and RSS feeds for each blog. All nodes have the following attributes stored within the node and node_revisions database table:

- nid: A unique ID for the node.

- vid: A unique revision ID for the node, needed because Drupal can store content revisions for each node. The vid is unique across all nodes and node revisions.

- type: Every node has a node type; for example, blog, story, article, image, and so on.

- language: The language for the node. Out of the box, this column is empty, indicating language-neutral nodes.

- title: A short 255-character string used as the node's title, unless the node type declares that it does not have a title, indicated by a 0 in the has_title field of the node_type table.

- uid: The user ID of the author. By default, nodes have a single author.

- status: A value of 0 means unpublished; that is, content is hidden from those who don't have the "administer nodes" permission. A value of 1 means the node is published and the content is visible to those users with the "access content" permission. The display of a published node may be vetoed by Drupal's node-level access control system (see the "Limiting Access to a Node Type with hook_access()" and "Restricting Access to Nodes" sections later in this chapter). A published node will be indexed by the search module if the search module is enabled.

- created: A Unix timestamp of when the node was created.

- changed: A Unix timestamp of when the node was last modified. If you're using the node revisions system, the same value is used for the timestamp field in the node_revisions table.

- comment: An integer field describing the status of the node's comments, with three possible values:

    - 0: Comments have been disabled for the current node. This is the default value for existing nodes when the comment module is disabled. In the user interface of the node editing form's "Comment settings" section, this is referred to as Disabled.

    - 1: No more comments are allowed for the current node. In the user interface of the node editing form's "Comment settings" section, this is referred to as "Read only."

    - 2: Comments can be viewed, and users can create new comments. Controlling who can create comments and how comments appear visually is the responsibility of the comment module. In the user interface of the node editing form's "Comment settings" section, this is referred to as Read/Write.

- promote: An integer field to determine whether to show the node on the front page, with two values:

    - 1: Promoted to the front page. The node is promoted to the default front page of your site. The node will still appear at its normal page, for example, http://example.com/?q=node/3. It should be noted here that, because you can change which page is considered the front page of your site at Administer ➤ Site configuration ➤ Site information, "front page" can be a misnomer. It's actually more accurate to say the http://example.com/?q=node page will contain all nodes whose promote field is 1. The URL http://example.com/?q=node is the front page by default.

    - 0: Node isn't shown on http://example.com/?q=node.

- moderate: An integer field where a 0 value means moderation is disabled and a value of 1 enables moderation. And now the caveat: there is no interface in the core Drupal installation for this field. In other words, you can change the value back and forth, and it does absolutely nothing by default. So it's up to the developer to program any functionality he or she desires into this field. Contributed modules, such as http://drupal.org/project/modr8 and http://drupal.org/project/revision_moderation, use this field.

- `sticky`: When Drupal displays a listing of nodes on a page, the default behavior is to list first those nodes marked as `sticky`, and then list the remaining unsticky nodes in the list by date created. In other words, sticky nodes stick to the top of node listings. A value of 1 means `sticky`, and a value of 0 means, well, unsticky. You can have multiple `sticky` nodes within the same list.

- `tnid`: When a node serves as the translated version of another node, the `nid` of the source node being translated is stored here. For example, if node 3 is in English and node 5 is the same content as node 3 but in Swedish, the `tnid` field of node 5 will be 3.

- `translate`: A value of 1 indicates that the translation needs to be updated; a value of 0 means translation is up to date.

If you're using the node revisions system, Drupal will create a revision of the content as well as track who made the last edit.

Not Everything Is a Node

Users, blocks, and comments are not nodes. Each of these specialized data structures has its own hook system geared towards its intended purpose. Nodes (usually) have title and body content, and a data structure representing a user doesn't need that. Rather, users need an e-mail address, a username, and a safe way to store passwords. Blocks are lightweight storage solutions for smaller pieces of content such as menu navigation, a search box, a list of recent comments, and so on. Comments aren't nodes either, which keeps them lightweight as well. It's quite possible to have 100 or more comments per page, and if each of those comments had to go through the node hook system when being loaded, that would be a tremendous performance hit.

In the past, there have been great debates about whether users or comments should be nodes, and some contributed modules actually implement this. Be warned that raising this argument is like shouting "Emacs is better!" at a programming convention.

Creating a Node Module

Traditionally, when you wanted to create a new content type in Drupal, you would write a *node module* that took responsibility for providing the new and interesting things your content type needed. We say "traditionally" because recent advents within the Drupal framework allow you to create content types within the administrative interface and extend their functionality with contributed modules rather than writing a node module from scratch. We'll cover both solutions within this chapter.

Let's write a node module that lets users add jokes to a site. Each joke will have a title, the joke itself, and a punch line. You should easily be able to use the built-in node `title` attribute for your joke titles and the node `body` for the joke contents, but you'll need to make a new database table to store the punch lines. We'll do that by using a `.install` file.

Start by creating a folder a named `joke` in your `sites/all/modules/custom` directory.

Creating the .install File

You will need to store some information in your database table. First, you'll need the node ID, so you can associate the data stored here with a node in the node_revisions table, which stores the title and body. Second, you'll need to store the revision ID of the node so that your module will work with Drupal's built-in revision control. And of course, you'll store the punch line. Because you now know the database schema, let's go ahead and create the joke.install file and place it inside the sites/all/modules/custom/joke directory. See Chapter 2 for more information on creating install files.

```php
<?php
// $Id$

/**
 * Implementation of hook_install().
 */
function joke_install() {
  drupal_install_schema('joke');
}

/**
 * Implementation of hook_uninstall().
 */
function joke_uninstall() {
  drupal_uninstall_schema('joke');
}

/**
 * Implementation of hook_schema().
 */
function joke_schema() {
  $schema['joke'] = array(
    'description' => t("Stores punch lines for nodes of type 'joke'."),
    'fields' => array(
      'nid' => array(
        'type' => 'int',
        'unsigned' => TRUE,
        'not null' => TRUE,
        'default' => 0,
        'description' => t("The joke's {node}.nid."),
      ),
      'vid' => array(
        'type' => 'int',
        'unsigned' => TRUE,
        'not null' => TRUE,
        'default' => 0,
        'description' => t("The joke's {node_revisions}.vid."),
      ),
```

```
          'punchline' => array(
            'type' => 'text',
            'not null' => TRUE,
            'description' => t('Text of the punchline.'),
            ),
          ),
      'primary key' => array('nid', 'vid'),
      'unique keys' => array(
          'vid' => array('vid')
      ),
      'indexes' => array(
          'nid' => array('nid')
      ),
  );

  return $schema;
}
```

Creating the .info File

Let's also create the joke.info file and add it to the joke folder.

```
; $Id$
name = Joke
description = A content type for jokes.
package = Pro Drupal Development
core = 6.x
```

Creating the .module File

Last, you need the module file itself. Create a file named joke.module, and place it inside sites/all/modules/custom/joke. After you've completed the module, you can enable the module on the module listings page (Administer ➤ Site building ➤ Modules). You begin with the opening PHP tag, CVS placeholder, and Doxygen comments.

```php
<?php
// $Id$

/**
 * @file
 * Provides a "joke" node type.
 */
```

Providing Information About Our Node Type

Now you're ready to add hooks to joke.module. The first hook you'll want to implement is hook_node_info(). Drupal calls this hook when it's discovering which node types are available. You'll provide some metadata about your custom node.

```
/**
 * Implementation of hook_node_info().
 */
function joke_node_info() {
  // We return an array since a module can define multiple node types.
  // We're only defining one node type, type 'joke'.
  return array(
    'joke' => array(
      'name' => t('Joke'), // Required.
      'module' => 'joke',  // Required.
      'description' => t('Tell us your favorite joke!'), // Required.
      'has_title' => TRUE,
      'title_label' => t('Title'),
      'has_body' => TRUE,
      'body_label' => t('Joke'),
      'min_word_count' => 2,
      'locked' => TRUE
    )
  );
}
```

A single module can define multiple node types, so the return value should be an array. Here's the breakdown of metadata values that may be provided in the node_info() hook:

- name *(required)*: The name of the node type to display on the site. For example, if the value is 'Joke', Drupal will use this when titling the node submission form.

- module *(required)*: The name of the prefix of the callback functions Drupal will look for. We used 'joke', so Drupal will look for callback functions named joke_validate(), joke_insert(), joke_delete(), and so on.

- description: This is generally used to add a brief description about what this content type is used for. This text will be displayed as part of the list on the "Create content" page (http://example.com/?q=node/add).

- has_title: Boolean value indicating whether or not this content type will use the title field. The default value is TRUE.

- title_label: The text label for the title field in the node editing form. The text label is only visible when has_title is TRUE. The default value is Title.

- has_body: Boolean value that indicates whether or not this content type will use the body textarea field. The default value is TRUE.

- `body_label`: The form field text label for the body textarea field. The label is only visible when `has_body` is TRUE. The default value is `Body`.

- `min_word_count`: The minimum number of words the body textarea field needs to pass validation. The default is `0`. (We set it to `2` in our module to avoid one-word jokes.)

- `locked`: Boolean value indicating whether the internal name of this content type is locked from being changed by a site administrator editing the content type's options at Administer ➤ Content management ➤ Content types. The default value for `locked` is TRUE, meaning the name is locked and therefore *not* editable.

Note The internal `name` field mentioned in the preceding list is used for constructing the URL of the "Create content" links. For example, we're using `joke` as the internal name of our node type (it's the key to the array we're returning), so to create a new joke users will go to `http://example.com/?q=node/add/joke`. Usually it's not a good idea to make this modifiable by setting `locked` to FALSE. The internal name is stored in the `type` column of the `node` and `node_revisions` tables.

Modifying the Menu Callback

Having a link on the "Create content" page isn't necessary for implementing `hook_menu()`. Drupal will automatically discover your new content type and add its entry to the `http://example.com/?q=node/add` page, as shown in Figure 7-2. A direct link to the node submission form will be at `http://example.com/?q=node/add/joke`. The name and description are taken from the values you defined in `joke_node_info()`.

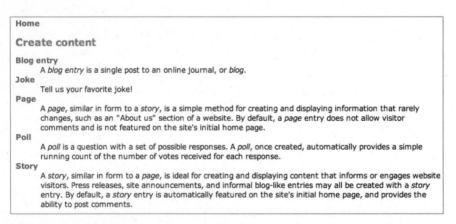

Figure 7-2. *The content type appears on the page at http://example.com/node/add.*

If you do not wish to have the direct link added, you could remove it by using `hook_menu_alter()`. For example, the following code would remove the page for anyone who does not have "administer nodes" permission.

```
/**
 * Implementation of hook_menu_alter().
 */
function joke_menu_alter(&$callbacks) {
  // If the user does not have 'administer nodes' permission,
  // disable the joke menu item by setting its access callback to FALSE.
  if (!user_access('administer nodes')) {
    $callbacks['node/add/joke']['access callback'] = FALSE;
    // Must unset access arguments or Drupal will use user_access()
    // as a default access callback.
    unset($callbacks['node/add/joke']['access arguments']);
  }
}
```

Defining Node-Type–Specific Permissions with hook_perm()

Typically the permissions for module-defined node types include the ability to create a node of that type, edit a node you have created, and edit any node of that type. These are defined in hook_perm() as create joke, edit own joke, and edit any joke, and so on. You've yet to define these permissions within your module. Let's create them now using hook_perm():

```
/**
 * Implementation of hook_perm().
 */
function joke_perm() {
  return array('create joke', 'edit own joke', 'edit any joke', 'delete own joke',
    'delete any joke');
}
```

Now if you navigate over to Administer ➤ User management ➤ Permissions, the new permissions you defined are there and ready to be assigned to user roles.

Limiting Access to a Node Type with hook_access()

You defined permissions in hook_perm(), but how are they enforced? Node modules can limit access to the node types they define using hook_access(). The superuser (user ID 1) will always bypass any access check, so this hook isn't called in that case. If this hook isn't defined for your node type, all access checks will fail, so only the superuser and those with "administer nodes" permissions will be able to create, edit, or delete content of that type.

```
/**
 * Implementation of hook_access().
 */
function joke_access($op, $node, $account) {
  $is_author = $account->uid == $node->uid;
  switch ($op) {
    case 'create':
      // Allow if user's role has 'create joke' permission.
      return user_access('create joke', $account);
```

```
  case 'update':
    // Allow if user's role has 'edit own joke' permission and user is
    // the author; or if the user's role has 'edit any joke' permission.
    return user_access('edit own joke', $account) && $is_author ||
      user_access('edit any joke', $account);

  case 'delete':
    // Allow if user's role has 'delete own joke' permission and user is
    // the author; or if the user's role has 'delete any joke' permission.
    return user_access('delete own joke', $account) && $is_author ||
      user_access('delete any joke', $account);
  }
}
```

The preceding function allows users to create a joke node if their role has the "create joke" permission. They can also update a joke if their role has the "edit own joke" permission and they're the node author, or if they have the "edit any joke" permission. Those with "delete own joke" permission can delete their own jokes, and those with "delete any joke" permission can delete any node of type joke.

One other $op value that's passed into hook_access() is view, allowing you to control who views this node. A word of warning, however: hook_access() is only called for single node view pages. hook_access() will not prevent someone from viewing a node when it's in teaser view, such as a multinode listing page. You could get creative with other hooks and manipulate the value of $node->teaser directly to overcome this, but that's a little hackish. A better solution is to use hook_node_grants() and hook_db_rewrite_sql(), which we'll discuss shortly.

Customizing the Node Form for Our Node Type

So far, you've got the metadata defined for your new node type and the access permissions defined. Next, you need to build the node form so that users can enter jokes. You do that by implementing hook_form():

```
/**
 * Implementation of hook_form().
 */
function joke_form($node) {
  // Get metadata for this node type
  // (we use it for labeling title and body fields).
  // We defined this in joke_node_info().
  $type = node_get_types('type', $node);
```

```
  $form['title'] = array(
    '#type' => 'textfield',
    '#title' => check_plain($type->title_label),
    '#required' => TRUE,
    '#default_value' => $node->title,
    '#weight' => -5,
    '#maxlength' => 255,
  );
  $form['body_filter']['body'] = array(
    '#type' => 'textarea',
    '#title' => check_plain($type->body_label),
    '#default_value' => $node->body,
    '#rows' => 7,
    '#required' => TRUE,
  );
  $form['body_filter']['filter'] = filter_form($node->format);
  $form['punchline'] = array(
    '#type' => 'textfield',
    '#title' => t('Punchline'),
    '#required' => TRUE,
    '#default_value' => isset($node->punchline) ? $node->punchline : '',
    '#weight' => 5
  );
  return $form;
}
```

■**Note** If you are unfamiliar with the form API, see Chapter 10.

As the site administrator, if you've enabled your module you can now navigate to Create content ➤ Joke and view the newly created form. The first line inside the preceding function returns the metadata information for this node type. node_get_types() will inspect $node->type to determine the type of node to return metadata for (in our case, the value of $node->type will be joke). Again, the node metadata is set within hook_node_info(), and you set it earlier in joke_node_info().

The rest of the function contains three form fields to collect the title, body, and punch line (see Figure 7-3). An important point here is how the #title keys of title and body are dynamic. Their values are inherited from hook_node_info() but can also be changed by the site administrators at http://example.com/?q=admin/content/types/joke as long as the locked attribute defined in hook_node_info() is FALSE.

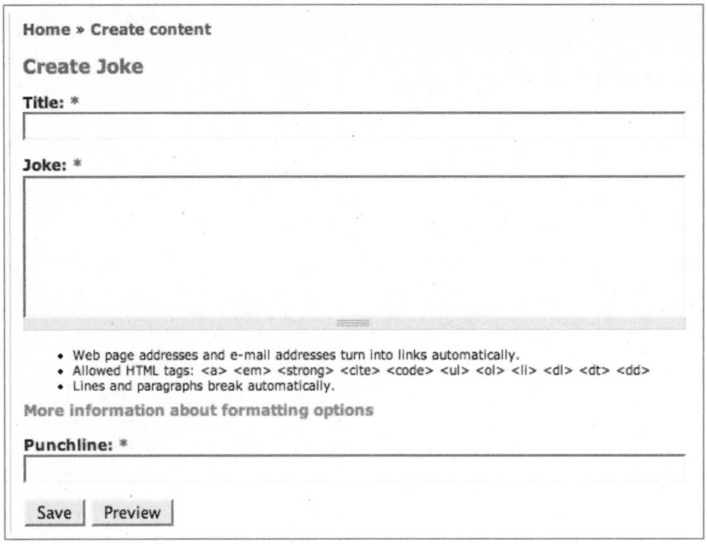

Figure 7-3. *The form for submission of a joke*

Adding Filter Format Support

Because the body field is a textarea, and node body fields are aware of filter formats, the form included Drupal's standard content filter with the following line (filters transform text; see Chapter 11 for more on using filters):

```
$form['body_filter']['filter'] = filter_form($node->format);
```

The $node->format property denotes the ID of the filter format being used for this node's body field. The value of this property is stored in the node_revisions table. If you wanted the punchline field to also be able to use input filter formats, you'd need somewhere to store the information about which filter that field is using. A good solution would be to add an integer column named punchline_format to your joke database table to store the input filter format setting per punch line.

Then you'd change your last form field definition to something similar to the following:

```
$form['punchline']['field'] = array(
    '#type' => 'textarea',
    '#title' => t('Punchline'),
    '#required' => TRUE,
    '#default_value' => $node->punchline,
    '#weight' => 5
  );
// Add filter support.
$form['punchline']['filter'] = filter_form($node->punchline_format);
```

When you're working with a node form and not a generic form, the node module handles validating and storing all the default fields it knows about within the node form (such as the title and body fields—we named the latter Joke but the node module still handles it as the node body) and provides you, the developer, with hooks to validate and store your custom fields. We'll cover those next.

Validating Fields with hook_validate()

When a node of your node type is submitted, your module will be called via hook_validate(). Thus, when the user submits the form to create or edit a joke, the invocation of hook_validate() will look for the function joke_validate() so that you can validate the input in your custom field(s). You can make changes to the data after submission—see form_set_value(). Errors should be set with form_set_error(), as follows:

```
/**
 * Implementation of hook_validate().
 */
function joke_validate($node) {
  // Enforce a minimum word length of 3 on punch lines.
  if (isset($node->punchline) && str_word_count($node->punchline) < 3) {
    $type = node_get_types('type', $node);
    form_set_error('punchline', t('The punch line of your @type is too short. You
      need at least three words.', array('@type' => $type->name)));
  }
}
```

Notice that you already defined a minimum word count for the body field in hook_node_info(), and Drupal will validate that for you automatically. However, the punchline field is an extra field you added to the node type form, so you are responsible for validating (and loading and saving) it.

Saving Our Data with hook_insert()

When a new node is saved, hook_insert() is called. This is the place to handle storing custom data to related tables. *This hook is only called for the module that is defined in the node type metadata.* This information is defined in the module key of hook_node_info() (see the "Providing Information About Our Node Type" section). For example, if the module key is joke, then joke_insert() is called. If you enabled the book module and created a new node of type book, joke_insert() would *not* be called; book_insert() would be called instead because book.module defines its node type with a module key of book.

Note If you need to do something with a node of a different type when it's inserted, use hook_nodeapi() to hook into the general node submittal process. See the "Manipulating Nodes That Are Not Our Type with hook_nodeapi()" section.

Here's the `hook_insert()` function for `joke.module`:

```
/**
 * Implementation of hook_insert().
 */
function joke_insert($node) {
  db_query("INSERT INTO {joke} (nid, vid, punchline) VALUES (%d, %d, '%s')",
    $node->nid, $node->vid, $node->punchline);
}
```

Keeping Data Current with hook_update()

The `update()` hook is called when a node has been edited and the core node data has already been written to the database. This is the place to write database updates for related tables. Like `hook_insert()`, this hook is only called for the current node type. For example, if the node type's `module` key in `hook_node_info()` is `joke`, then `joke_update()` is called.

```
/**
 * Implementation of hook_update().
 */
function joke_update($node) {
  if ($node->revision) {
    // New revision; treat it as a new record.
    joke_insert($node);
  }
  else {
    db_query("UPDATE {joke} SET punchline = '%s' WHERE vid = %d",
      $node->punchline, $node->vid);
  }
}
```

In this case, you check if the node revision flag is set, and if so, you create a new copy of the punch line to preserve the old one.

Cleaning Up with hook_delete()

Just after a node is deleted from the database, Drupal lets modules know what has happened via `hook_delete()`. This hook is typically used to delete related information from the database. This hook is only called for the current node type being deleted. If the node type's `module` key in `hook_node_info()` is `joke`, then `joke_delete()` is called.

```
/**
 * Implementation of hook_delete().
 */
function joke_delete(&$node) {
  // Delete the related information we were saving for this node.
  db_query('DELETE FROM {joke} WHERE nid = %d', $node->nid);
}
```

■**Note** When a revision rather than the entire node is deleted, Drupal fires hook_nodeapi() with the $op set to delete revision, and the entire node object is passed in. Your module is then able to delete its data for that revision using $node->vid as the key.

Modifying Nodes of Our Type with hook_load()

Another hook you need for your joke module is the ability to add your custom node attributes into the node object as it's constructed. We need to inject the punch line into the node loading process so it's available to other modules and the theme layer. For that you use hook_load().

This hook is called just after the core node object has been built and is only called for the current node type being loaded. If the node type's module key in hook_node_info() is joke, then joke_load() is called.

```
/**
 * Implementation of hook_load().
 */
function joke_load($node) {
  return db_fetch_object(db_query('SELECT punchline FROM {joke} WHERE vid = %d',
    $node->vid));
}
```

The punchline: hook_view()

Now you have a complete system to enter and edit jokes. However, your users will be frustrated, because although punch lines can be entered on the node submission form, you haven't provided a way to make your module-provided punchline field visible when viewing the joke! Let's do that now with hook_view():

```
/**
 * Implementation of hook_view().
 */
function joke_view($node, $teaser = FALSE, $page = FALSE) {
  // If $teaser is FALSE, the entire node is being displayed.
  if (!$teaser) {
    // Use Drupal's default node view.
    $node = node_prepare($node, $teaser);

    // Add a random number of Ha's to simulate a laugh track.
    $node->guffaw = str_repeat(t('Ha!'), mt_rand(0, 10));

    // Now add the punch line.
    $node->content['punchline'] = array(
      '#value' => theme('joke_punchline', $node),
      '#weight' => 2
      );
  }
```

```
  // If $teaser is TRUE, node is being displayed as a teaser,
  // such as on a node listing page. We omit the punch line in this case.
  if ($teaser) {
    // Use Drupal's default node view.
    $node = node_prepare($node, $teaser);
  }

  return $node;
}
```

This code includes the punch line for the joke only if the node is not being rendered as a teaser (that is, $teaser is FALSE). You've broken the formatting of the punch line out into a separate theme function so that it can be easily overridden. This is a courtesy to the overworked system administrators who will be using your module but who want to customize the look and feel of the output. You declare to Drupal that you will be using the joke_punchline theme function by implementing hook_theme() and provide a default implementation of the theme function:

```
/**
 * Implementation of hook_theme().
 * We declare joke_punchline so Drupal will look for a function
 * named theme_joke_punchline().
 */
function joke_theme() {
  return array(
    'joke_punchline' => array(
      'arguments' => array('node'),
    ),
  );
}

function theme_joke_punchline($node) {
  $output = '<div class="joke-punchline">'.
    check_markup($node->punchline). '</div><br />';
  $output .= '<div class="joke-guffaw">'.
    $node->guffaw .'</div>';
  return $output;
}
```

You will need to clear the cached theme registry so that Drupal will look at your theme hook. You can clear the cache using devel.module or by simply visiting the Administer ➤ Site building ➤ Modules page. You should now have a fully functioning joke entry and viewing system. Go ahead and enter some jokes and try things out. You should see your joke in a plain and simple format, as in Figures 7-4 and 7-5.

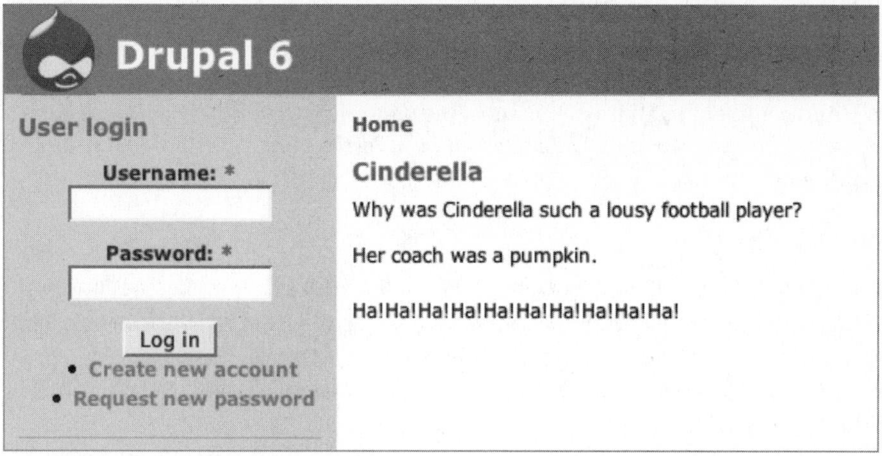

Figure 7-4. *Simple theme of joke node*

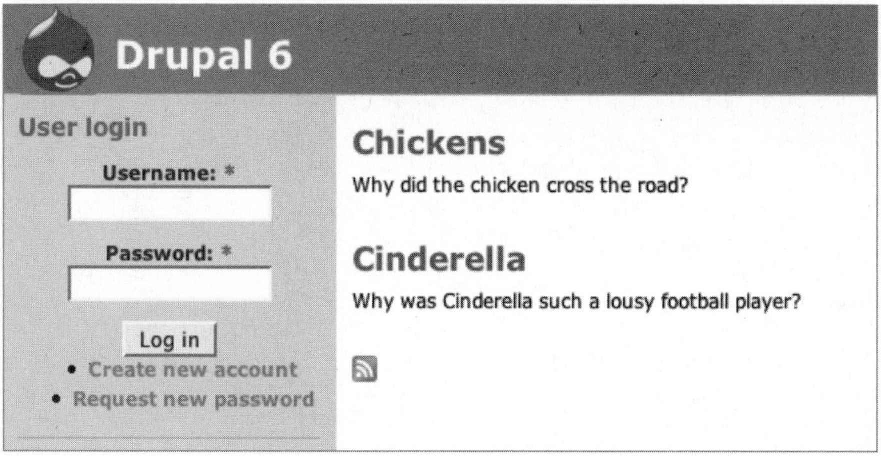

Figure 7-5. *The punch line is not added when the node is shown in teaser view*

Although this works, there's a good chance the user will read the punch line right away when viewing the node in full page view. What we'd really like to do is to have a collapsible field that the user can click to display the punch line. The collapsible fieldset functionality already exists within Drupal, so you'll use that rather than create your own JavaScript file. Adding this interaction is better done in a template file in your site's theme instead of a theme function, as it depends on markup and CSS classes. Your designers will love you if you use a template file instead of a theme function, because to change the look and feel of joke nodes, they'll be able simply to edit a file.

Here's what you'll put into a file called node-joke.tpl.php in the directory containing the theme you're currently using. If you're using the Bluemarine theme, then node-joke.tpl.php would be placed in themes/bluemarine. Because we're going to use a template file, the hook_theme() implementation and the theme_joke_punchline() function are no longer needed, so go ahead and comment them out in your module file. Remember to clear the cached theme registry as we did before so that Drupal will no longer look for theme_joke_ punchline(). And comment out the assignment of the punch line to $node->content in joke_view(), since the template file will take care of printing the punch line (otherwise, the punch line will show up twice).

Note After you visit Administer ➤ Site building ➤ Modules (which automatically rebuilds the theme registry), node-joke.tpl.php will automatically be discovered by the theme system, and Drupal will use that file to change the look and feel of jokes rather than use the default node template, usually node.tpl.php. To learn more about how the theme system makes these decisions, please see Chapter 8.

```
<div class="node<?php if ($sticky) { print " sticky"; } ?>
  <?php if (!$status) { print " node-unpublished"; } ?>">
    <?php if ($picture) {
      print $picture;
    }?>
    <?php if ($page == 0) { ?><h2 class="title"><a href="<?php
      print $node_url?>"><?php print $title?></a></h2><?php }; ?>
    <span class="submitted"><?php print $submitted?></span>
    <span class="taxonomy"><?php print $terms?></span>
    <div class="content">
      <?php print $content?>
      <fieldset class="collapsible collapsed">
        <legend>Punchline</legend>
          <div class="form-item">
            <label><?php if (isset($node->punchline)) print
              check_markup($node->punchline)?></label>
            <label><?php if (isset($node->guffaw)) print $node->guffaw?></label>
          </div>
        </legend>
      </fieldset>
    </div>
  <?php if ($links) { ?><div class="links">&raquo; <?php print $links?></div>
    <?php }; ?>
</div>
```

The JavaScript in misc/collapsible.js looks for collapsible CSS selectors for a fieldset and knows how to take over from there, as shown in Figure 7-6. Thus, in node-joke.tpl.php it sees the following and activates itself:

```
<fieldset class="collapsible collapsed">
```

This results in the kind of interactive joke experience that we were aiming for.

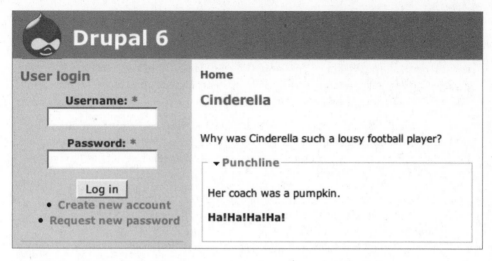

Figure 7-6. *Using Drupal's collapsible CSS support to hide the punch line*

Manipulating Nodes That Are Not Our Type with hook_nodeapi()

The preceding hooks are only invoked based on the module key of the module's hook_node_info() implementation. When Drupal sees a blog node type, blog_load() is called. What if you want to add some information to every node, regardless of its type? The hooks we've reviewed so far aren't going to cut it; for that, we need an exceptionally powerful hook: hook_nodeapi().

This hook creates an opportunity for modules to react to the different operations during the life cycle of any node. The nodeapi() hook is usually called by node.module just after the node-type–specific callback is invoked. For example, first joke_insert() might be called, then immediately the nodeapi hook would be called with $op set to insert. Here's the function signature:

```
hook_nodeapi(&$node, $op, $a3 = NULL, $a4 = NULL)
```

The $node object is passed by reference, so any changes you make will actually change the node. The $op parameter is used to describe the current operation being performed on the node, and can have many different values:

- prepare: The node form is about to be shown. This applies to both the node Add and Edit forms.

- validate: The user has just finished editing the node and is trying to preview or submit it. Here, your code should check to make sure the data is what you expect and should call form_set_error() if something is wrong; that will return an error message to the user. You can use this hook to check or even modify the data, though modifying data in the validation hook is considered bad style.

- presave: The node passed validation and will soon be saved to the database.

- insert: A new node has just been inserted into the database.

- `update`: The node has just been updated in the database.

- `delete`: The node was deleted.

- `delete revision`: A revision of a node was deleted. Modules will respond to this if they are keeping data related to the revision. The node ID can be found at $node->nid, and the revision ID can be found at $node->vid.

- `load`: The basic node object has been loaded from the database, plus the additional node properties set by the node type (in response to hook_load(), which has already been run; see "Modifying Nodes of Our Type with hook_load()" earlier in this chapter). You can add new properties or manipulate node properties.

- `alter`: The node's content has gone through drupal_render() and been saved in $node->body (if the node is being built for full view) or $node->teaser (if the node is being built for teaser view), and the node is about to be passed to the theme layer. Modules may modify the fully built node. Changes to fields in $node->content should be done in the view operation, not this operation.

- `view`: The node is about to be presented to the user. This action is called after hook_view(), so the module may assume the node is filtered and now contains HTML. Additional items may be added to $node->content (see how we added a joke punch line previously, for example).

- `search result`: The node is about to be displayed as a search result item.

- `update index`: The node is being indexed by the search module. If you want additional information to be indexed that isn't already visible through the nodeapi view operation, you should return it here (see Chapter 12).

- `prepare translation`: The node is being prepared for translation by the translation module. Modules may add custom translated fields.

- `rss item`: The node is being included as part of an RSS feed.

The last two parameters to a hook_nodeapi() function are variables whose values change depending on which operation is being performed. When a node is being displayed and $op is alter or view, $a3 will be $teaser, and $a4 will be $page (see node_view() in node.module). See Table 7-1 for an overview.

Table 7-1. *The Meaning of the $a3 and $a4 Parameters in hook_nodeapi() When $op Is alter or view*

Parameter	Meaning
$teaser	Whether to display the teaser only, such as on http://example.com/?q=node
$page	True if the node is being displayed as a page by itself (e.g., at http://example.com/?q=node/2)

When a node is being validated, the $a3 parameter is the $form parameter from node_validate() (that is, the form definition array).

The order in which hooks are fired when displaying a node page such as `http://example.com/?q=node/3` is shown in Figure 7-7.

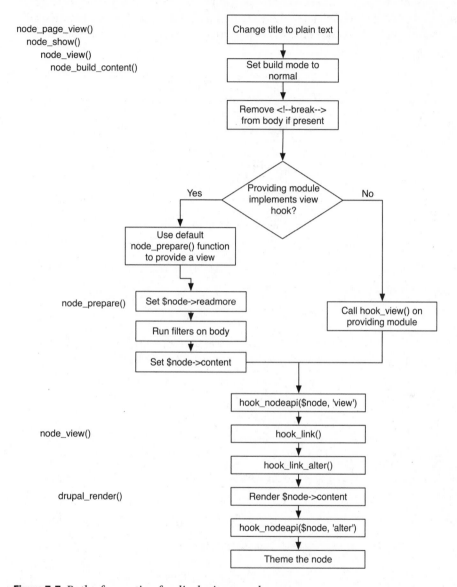

Figure 7-7. *Path of execution for displaying a node page*

How Nodes Are Stored

Nodes live in the database as separate parts. The node table contains most of the metadata describing the node. The node_revisions table contains the node's body and teaser, along with revision-specific information. And as you've seen in the joke.module example, other nodes are free to add data to the node at node load time and store whatever data they want in their own tables.

A node object containing the most common attributes is pictured in Figure 7-8. Note that the table you created to store punch lines is used to populate the node. Depending on which other modules are enabled, the node objects in your Drupal installation might contain more or fewer properties.

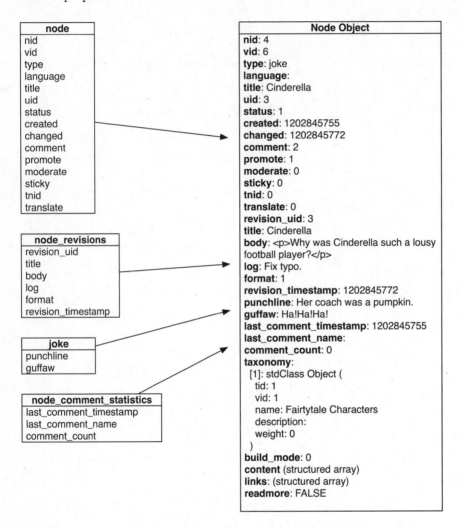

Figure 7-8. *The node object*

Creating a Node Type with CCK

Although creating a node module like you did with the joke.module offers exceptional control and performance, it's also a bit tedious. Wouldn't it be nice to be able to assemble a new node type without doing any programming? That's what the CCK modules provide.

■**Note** For more information about CCK, visit the CCK project at `http://drupal.org/project/cck`.

You can add new content types (such as a joke content type) through the administrative interface at Administer ➤ Content management ➤ Content types. Make sure to use a different name for the node type if you have `joke.module` enabled to prevent a namespace collision. The part of CCK that is still being sorted out for core is the ability to add fields beyond `title` and `body` to these new content types. In the `joke.module` example, you needed three fields: `title`, `joke`, and `punchline`. You used Drupal's `hook_node_info()` to relabel the `body` field as `Joke` and provided the `punchline` field by implementing several hooks and creating your own table for punch line storage. In CCK, you simply create a new text field called `punchline` and add it to your content type. CCK takes care of storing, retrieving, and deleting the data for you.

■**Note** The Drupal contributions repository is full of CCK field modules for adding images, dates, e-mail addresses, and so on. Visit `http://drupal.org/project/Modules/category/88` to see all CCK-related contributed modules.

Because CCK is under heavy development at the time of this writing, I won't go into more detail. However, it seems clear that in the future, writing a module to create a new node type will become rarer, while the CCK approach of assembling content types through the web will become more common.

Restricting Access to Nodes

There are several ways to restrict access to nodes. You have already seen how to restrict access to a node type using `hook_access()` and permissions defined using `hook_perm()`. But Drupal provides a much richer set of access controls using the `node_access` table and two more access hooks: `hook_node_grants()` and `hook_node_access_records()`.

When Drupal is first installed, a single record is written to the `node_access` table, which effectively turns off the node access mechanism. Only when a module that uses the node access mechanism is enabled does this part of Drupal kick in. The function `node_access_rebuild()` in `modules/node/node.module` keeps track of which node access modules are enabled, and if they are all disabled this function will restore the default record, which is shown in Table 7-2.

Table 7-2. *The Default Record for the node_access Table*

nid	gid	realm	grant_view	grant_update	grant_delete
0	0	all	1	0	0

In general, if a node access module is being used (that is, one that modifies the node_access table), Drupal will deny access to a node unless the node access module has inserted a row into the node_access table defining how access should be treated.

Defining Node Grants

There are three basic permissions for operations on nodes: view, update, and delete. When one of these operations is about to take place, the module providing the node type gets first say with its hook_access() implementation. If that module doesn't take a position on whether the access is allowed (that is, it returns NULL instead of TRUE or FALSE), Drupal asks all modules that are interested in node access to respond to the question of whether the operation ought to be allowed. They do this by responding to hook_node_grants() with a list of grant IDs for each realm for the current user.

What Is a Realm?

A realm is an arbitrary string that allows multiple node access modules to share the node_access table. For example, acl.module is a contributed module that manages node access via access control lists (ACLs). Its realm is acl. Another contributed module is taxonomy_access.module, which restricts access to nodes based on taxonomy terms. It uses the term_access realm. So, the realm is something that identifies your module's space in the node_access table; it's like a namespace. When your module is asked to return grant IDs, you'll do so for the realm your module defines.

What Is a Grant ID?

A grant ID is an identifier that provides information about node access permissions for a given realm. For example, a node access module—such as forum_access.module, which manages access to nodes of type forum by user role—may use role IDs as grant IDs. A node access module that manages access to nodes by US ZIP code could use ZIP codes as grant IDs. In each case, it will be something that is determined about the user: Has the user been assigned to this role? Or is this user in the ZIP code 12345? Or is the user on this access control list? Or is this user's subscription older than 1 year?

Although each grant ID means something special to the node access module that provides grant IDs for the realm containing the grant ID, *the mere presence of a row containing the grant ID in the* node_access *table enables access*, with the type of access being determined by the presence of a 1 in the grant_view, grant_update, or grant_delete column.

Grant IDs get inserted into the node_access table when a node is being saved. Each module that implements hook_node_access_records() is passed the node object. The module is expected to examine the node and either simply return (if it won't be handling access for this node) or return an array of grants for insertion into the node_access table. The grants are batch-inserted by node_access_acquire_grants(). The following is an example from forum_access.module.

```
/**
 * Implementation of hook_node_access_records().
 *
 * Returns a list of grant records for the passed in node object.
 */
function forum_access_node_access_records($node) {
  ...

  if ($node->type == 'forum') {
    $result = db_query('SELECT * FROM {forum_access} WHERE tid = %d', $node->tid);
    while ($grant = db_fetch_object($result)) {
      $grants[] = array(
        'realm'        => 'forum_access',
        'gid'          => $grant->rid,
        'grant_view'   => $grant->grant_view,
        'grant_update' => $grant->grant_update,
        'grant_delete' => $grant->grant_delete
      );
    }
    return $grants;
  }
}
```

The Node Access Process

When an operation is about to be performed on a node, Drupal goes through the process outlined in Figure 7-9.

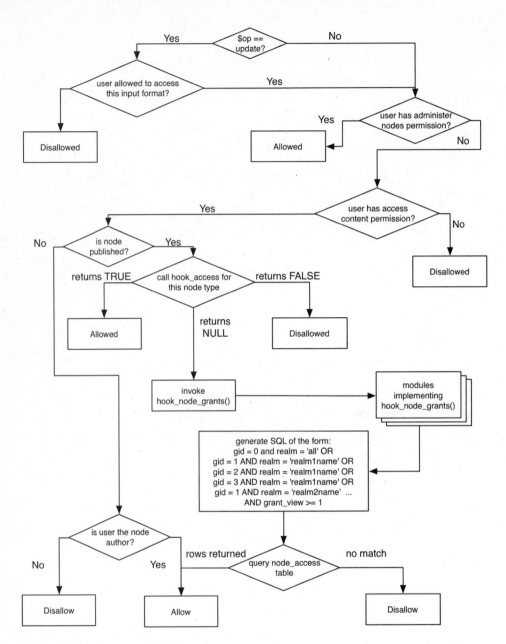

Figure 7-9. *Determining node access for a given node*

Summary

After reading this chapter, you should be able to

- Understand what a node is and what node types are.

- Write modules that create node types.

- Understand how to hook into node creation, saving, loading, and so on.

- Understand how access to nodes is determined.

■ ■ ■

## CHAPTER 8

The Theme System

Changing the HTML or other markup that Drupal produces requires knowledge of the layers that make up the theme system. The theme system is an elegant architecture that'll keep you from hacking core code, but it does have a learning curve, especially when you're trying to make your Drupal site look different from other Drupal sites. I'll teach you how the theme system works and reveal some of the best practices hiding within the Drupal core. Here's the first one: you don't need to (nor should you) edit the HTML within module files to change the look and feel of your site. By doing that, you've just created your own proprietary content management system and have thus lost one the biggest advantages of using a community-supported open source software system to begin with. Override, don't change!

Theme System Components

The theme system comprises several levels of abstraction: template languages, theme engines, and themes.

Template Languages and Theme Engines

The theme system is abstracted to work with most templating languages. Smarty, PHPTAL, and PHPTemplate can all be used to fill template files with dynamic data within Drupal. To use these languages, a wrapper, called a *theme engine*, is needed to interface Drupal with the corresponding template language. You can find theme engines for the most popular templating languages at `http://drupal.org/project/Theme+engines`. You install theme engines by placing the respective theme engine directory inside the engines directory for your site at `sites/`*sitename*`/themes/engines`. To have the theme engine accessible to all sites in a multisite setup, place the theme engine directory inside `sites/all/themes/engines` as shown in Figure 8-1.

The Drupal community has created its own theme engine, optimized for Drupal. It's called PHPTemplate, and it relies on PHP to function as the templating language, which removes the intermediary parsing step other template languages usually go through. This is the most widely supported template engine for Drupal and ships with the core distribution. It's located at `themes/engines/phptemplate`, as shown in Figure 8-2.

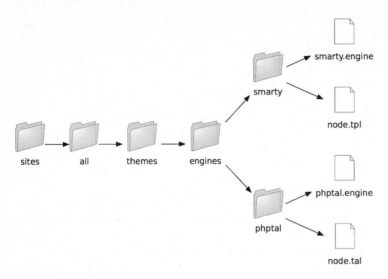

Figure 8-1. *Directory structure for adding custom theme engines to Drupal*

Figure 8-2. *Directory structure for Drupal core theme engines. This location is reserved for core theme engines.*

■Note It's entirely possible to skip using a templating language altogether and simply use pure PHP template files. If you're a speed freak or maybe just want to torture your designers, you can skip using a theme engine and just wrap your entire theme inside PHP functions, using functions like `themename_page()` and `themename_node()` instead of template files. For an example of a PHP-based theme, see `themes/chameleon/chameleon.theme`.

Don't expect to see any change to your site after dropping in a new theme engine. Because a theme engine is only an interface library, you'll also need to install a Drupal theme that depends on that engine before the theme engine will be used.

Which template language should you use? If you're converting a legacy site, perhaps it's easier to use the previous template language, or maybe your design team is more comfortable working within WYSIWYG editors, in which case PHPTAL is a good choice because it prevents templates from being mangled within those editors. You'll find the most documentation and support for PHPTemplate, and if you're building a new site it's probably your best bet in terms of long-term maintenance and community support.

Themes

In Drupal-speak, themes are a collection of files that make up the look and feel of your site. You can download preconstructed themes from `http://drupal.org/project/Themes`, or you can roll your own, which is what you'll learn to do in this chapter. Themes are made up of most of the things you'd expect to see as a web designer: style sheets, images, JavaScript files, and so on. The difference you'll find between a Drupal theme and a plain HTML site is targeted template files. These files typically contain large sections of HTML and smaller special snippets that are replaced by dynamic content. They are responsible for the look-and-feel of one specific component of your site. The syntax of a template file depends on the theme engine that is being used. For example, take the template file snippets in Listings 8-1, 8-2, and 8-3, which output the exact same HTML but contain radically different template file content.

Listing 8-1. *Smarty*

```
<div id="top-nav">
  {if count($secondary_links)}
    <ul id="secondary">
    {foreach from=$secondary_links item=link}
      <li>{$link}</li>
    {/foreach}
    </ul>
  {/if}

  {if count($primary_links)}
    <ul id="primary">
    {foreach from=$primary_links item=link}
      <li>{$link}</li>
    {/foreach}
    </ul>
  {/if}
</div>
```

Listing 8-2. *PHPTAL*

```
<div id="top-nav">
  <ul tal:condition="php:is_array(secondary_links)" id="secondary">
    <li tal:repeat="link secondary_links" tal:content="link">secondary link</li>
  </ul>

  <ul tal:condition="php:is_array(primary_links)" id="primary">
    <li tal:repeat="link primary_links" tal:content="link">primary link</li>
  </ul>
</div>
```

Listing 8-3. *PHPTemplate*

```
<div id="top-nav">
  <?php if (count($secondary_links)) : ?>
    <ul id="secondary">
    <?php foreach ($secondary_links as $link): ?>
      <li><?php print $link?></li>
    <?php endforeach; ?>
    </ul>
  <?php endif; ?>
  <?php if (count($primary_links)) : ?>
    <ul id="primary">
    <?php foreach ($primary_links as $link): ?>
      <li><?php print $link?></li>
    <?php endforeach; ?>
    </ul>
  <?php endif; ?>
</div>
```

Each template file will look different based on the template language in use. The file extension of a template file denotes the template language, and thus the theme engine it depends on (see Table 8-1).

Table 8-1. *Template File Extensions Indicate the Template Language They Depend On*

Template File Extension	Theme Engine
.theme	PHP
.tpl.php	PHPTemplate*
.tal	PHPTAL
.tpl	Smarty

* PHPTemplate is Drupal's default theme engine.

Installing a Theme

To have a new theme show up within the Drupal administrative interface, place the theme in sites/all/themes. This makes the theme accessible to your Drupal site and to all sites on a multisite setup. If you wish the theme to be used for a specific site only and you are using a multisite setup, you should place it in sites/*sitename*/themes. You can install as many themes as you want on your site, and themes are installed in much the same way modules are. Once the theme files are in place, navigate to the administrative interface via Administer ➤ Site building ➤ Themes. You can install multiple themes. You can even enable multiple themes at once. What does that mean? By enabling multiple themes, users who have been given the select different theme permission will be able to select any one of the enabled themes from within their profile. Their chosen theme will be used when they are browsing the site.

When downloading or creating a new theme, it's a best practice to keep the new theme separate from the rest of the core and contributed themes. You can do this by creating another level of folders inside your themes folder. Place custom themes inside a folder named custom, and themes downloaded from the Drupal contributions repository inside a folder named drupal-contrib. This practice is not as important to follow as with custom and contributed modules, as you are unlikely to have many themes on one site but very likely to have many modules.

Building a PHPTemplate Theme

There are several ways to create a theme, depending on your starting materials. Suppose your designer has already given you the HTML and CSS for the site. How easy is it to take the designer's design and convert it into a Drupal theme? It's actually not that bad, and you can probably get 80 percent of the way there in short order. The other 20 percent—the final nips and tucks—are what set apart Drupal theming ninjas from lackeys. So let's knock out the easy parts first. Here's an overview:

1. Create or modify an HTML file for the site.

2. Create or modify a CSS file for the site.

3. Create a .info file to describe your new theme to Drupal.

4. Standardize the filenames according to what Drupal expects.

5. Insert available variables into your template.

6. Create additional files for individual node types, blocks, and so on.

■**Note** If you're starting your design from scratch, there are many great designs at the Open Source Web Design site at http://www.oswd.org/. (Note that these are HTML and CSS designs, not Drupal themes.)

Using Existing HTML and CSS Files

Let's assume you're given the HTML page and style sheet in Listings 8-4 and 8-5 to convert to a Drupal theme. Obviously, the files you'd receive in a real project would be more detailed than these, but you get the idea.

Listing 8-4. *page.html*

```
<html>
<head>
  <title>Page Title</title>
  <link rel="stylesheet" href="global.css" type="text/css" />
</head>
```

```html
<body>
  <div id="container">
    <div id="header">
      <h1>Header</h1>
    </div>

    <div id="sidebar-left">
      <p>
        Lorem ipsum dolor sit amet, consectetuer adipiscing elit, sed diam
        nonummy nibh euismod tincidunt ut.
      </p>
    </div>

    <div id="main">
      <h2>Subheading</h2>
      <p>
        Lorem ipsum dolor sit amet, consectetuer adipiscing elit, sed diam
        nonummy nibh euismod tincidunt ut.
      </p>
    </div>

    <div id="footer">
      Footer
    </div>
  </div>
</body>
</html>
```

Listing 8-5. *global.css*

```css
#container {
  width: 90%;
  margin: 10px auto;
  background-color: #fff;
  color: #333;
  border: 1px solid gray;
  line-height: 130%;
}
#header {
  padding: .5em;
  background-color: #ddd;
  border-bottom: 1px solid gray;
}
#header h1 {
  padding: 0;
  margin: 0;
}
```

```css
#sidebar-left {
  float: left;
  width: 160px;
  margin: 0;
  padding: 1em;
}
#main {
  margin-left: 200px;
  border-left: 1px solid gray;
  padding: 1em;
  max-width: 36em;
}
#footer {
  clear: both;
  margin: 0;
  padding: .5em;
  color: #333;
  background-color: #ddd;
  border-top: 1px solid gray;
}
#sidebar-left p {
  margin: 0 0 1em 0;
}
#main h2 {
  margin: 0 0 .5em 0;
}
```

The design is shown in Figure 8-3.

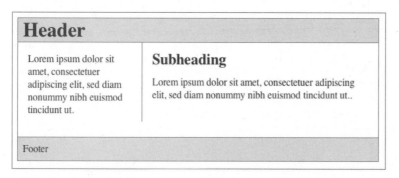

Figure 8-3. *Design before it has been converted to a Drupal theme*

Let's call this new theme greyscale, so make a folder at sites/all/themes/custom/ greyscale. You might need to create the themes/custom folders if you haven't already. Copy page.html and global.css into the greyscale folder. Next, rename page.html to page.tpl.php so it serves as the new page template for every Drupal page.

Creating a .info File for Your Theme

Each theme needs to include a file that describes the capabilities of the theme to Drupal. This file is the theme's .info file. Because we called our theme greyscale, our .info file will be named greyscale.info. Create the file at sites/all/themes/custom/greyscale/greyscale.info, and enter the ten lines shown in Listing 8-6.

Listing 8-6. *.info File for the Greyscale Theme*

```
; $Id$
name = Greyscale
core = 6.x
engine = phptemplate
regions[left] = Left sidebar
; We do not have a right sidebar.
; regions[right] = Right sidebar
regions[content] = Content
regions[header] = Header
regions[footer] = Footer
```

If we wanted to get more complicated, we could give Drupal a lot more information in our .info file. Let's take a moment to see what information can be included, which is shown in Listing 8-7.

Listing 8-7. *.info File with More Information*

```
; $Id$
; Name and core are required; all else is optional.
name = Greyscale
description = Demurely grey tableless theme.
screenshot = screenshot.png
core = 6.x
engine = phptemplate

regions[left] = Left sidebar
; We do not have a right sidebar
; regions[right] = Right sidebar
regions[content] = Content
regions[header] = Header
regions[footer] = Footer

; Features not commented out here appear as checkboxes
; on the theme configuration page for this theme.
features[] = logo
features[] = name
features[] = slogan
features[] = mission
```

```
features[] = node_user_picture
features[] = comment_user_picture
features[] = search
features[] = favicon
features[] = primary_links
features[] = secondary_links

; Stylesheets can be declared here or, for more
; control, be added by drupal_add_css() in template.php.
; Add a stylesheet for media="all":
stylesheets[all][] = mystylesheet.css
; Add a stylesheet for media="print":
stylesheets[print][] = printable.css
; Add a stylesheet for media="handheld":
stylesheets[handheld][] = smallscreen.css
; Add a stylesheet for media="screen, projection, tv":
stylesheets[screen, projection, tv][] = screen.css
; Override an existing Drupal stylesheet with our own
; (in this case the forum module's stylesheet):
stylesheets[all][] = forum.css

; JavaScript files can be declared here or, for more
; control, be added by drupal_add_js() in template.php.
; scripts.js is added automatically (just like style.css
; is added automatically to stylesheets[]).
scripts[] = custom.js

; PHP version is rarely used; you might need it if your
; templates have code that uses very new PHP features.
php = 5.2.0

; Themes may be based on other themes; for example, they
; may simply override some of the parent theme's CSS.
; See the Minnelli theme at themes/garland/minnelli for
; an example of a theme that does this in Drupal core.
base theme = garland
```

Because the Greyscale theme now has a .info file (the simple one in Listing 8-6) and a page.tpl.php file, you can enable it within the administrative interface. Go to Administer ➤ Site building ➤ Themes and make it the default theme.

Congratulations! You should now see your design in action. The external style sheet won't yet load (we'll address that later), and any page you navigate to within your site will be the same HTML over and over again, but this is a great start! Any page you navigate to within your site will just serve the static contents of page.tpl.php, so there's no way to get to Drupal's administrative interface. We've just locked you out of your Drupal site! Whoops. Getting locked out is bound to happen, and I'll show you now how to recover from this situation. One solution is to rename the folder of the theme currently enabled. In this case, you can simply rename greyscale to greyscale_, and you'll be able to get back into the site. That's a quick fix, but because you know what the real problem is (that is, that we're not including dynamic content yet), instead you'll add the proper variables to page.tpl.php so that the dynamic Drupal content is displayed rather than the static content.

Every PHPTemplate template file—such as page.tpl.php, node.tpl.php, block.tpl.php, and so on—is passed a different set of dynamic content variables to use within the files. Open page.tpl.php, and start replacing the static content with corresponding Drupal variables. Don't worry; I'll cover what these variables actually do soon.

```
<html>
<head>
  <title><?php print $head_title ?></title>
  <link rel="stylesheet" href="global.css" type="text/css" />
</head>

<body>
  <div id="container">
    <div id="header">
      <h1><?php print $site_name ?></h1>
      <?php print $header ?>
    </div>

    <?php if ($left): ?>
      <div id="sidebar-left">
        <?php print $left ?>
      </div>
    <?php endif; ?>

    <div id="main">
      <?php print $breadcrumb ?>
      <h2><?php print $title ?></h2>
      <?php print $content ?>
    </div>

    <div id="footer">
      <?php print $footer_message ?>
      <?php print $footer ?>
    </div>
  </div>
<?php print $closure ?>
</body>
</html>
```

Reload your site, and you'll notice that the variables are being replaced with the content from Drupal. Yay! You'll notice that the global.css style sheet isn't loading because the path to the file is no longer correct. You could manually adjust the path, or you could do this the Drupal way and gain some flexibility and benefits.

The first step is to rename global.css to style.css. By convention, Drupal automatically looks for a style.css file for every theme. Once found, it adds this information into the $styles variable that's passed into page.tpl.php. So let's update page.tpl.php with this information:

```
<html>
<head>
  <title><?php print $head_title ?></title>
  <?php print $styles ?>
</head>
...
```

Save your changes and reload the page. Voilà! You'll also notice that if you view the source code of the page, other style sheets from enabled modules have also been added, thanks to the addition of this $styles variable:

```
<html>
<head>
  <title>Example | Drupal 6</title>
  <link type="text/css" rel="stylesheet" media="all"
    href="modules/node/node.css?f" />
  <link type="text/css" rel="stylesheet" media="all"
    href="modules/system/defaults.css?f" />
  <link type="text/css" rel="stylesheet" media="all"
    href="modules/system/system.css?f" />
  <link type="text/css" rel="stylesheet" media="all"
    href="modules/system/system-menus.css?f" />
  <link type="text/css" rel="stylesheet" media="all"
    href="modules/user/user.css?f" />
  <link type="text/css" rel="stylesheet" media="all"
    href="sites/all/themes/greyscale/style.css?f" />
</head>
...
```

By naming your CSS file style.css, you also allow Drupal to apply its CSS preprocessing engine to it to remove all line breaks and spaces from all CSS files, and instead of serving multiple style sheets, Drupal can now serve them as a single file. To learn more about this feature, see Chapter 22.

■**Note** Drupal adds a dummy query string (?f in the preceding examples) to the end of the style sheet URLs so that it can control caching. It changes the string when needed, such as after running update.php or after a full cache clear from the Administer ➤ Site configuration ➤ Performance page.

When you refresh your browser after renaming global.css to style.css, you should see a theme similar to that in Figure 8-3, with a header, footer, and left sidebar. Try going to Administer ➤ Site building ➤ Blocks and assigning the "Who's online" block to the left sidebar.

There are plenty more variables to add to page.tpl.php and the other template files. So let's dive in! If you have not already done so, browse through the existing themes in your Drupal installation's themes directory to get a feel for how the variables are used.

Understanding Template Files

Some themes have all sorts of template files, while others only have page.tpl.php. So how do you know which template files you can create that Drupal will recognize? What naming conventions surround the creation of template files? You'll learn the ins and outs of working with template files in the following sections.

The Big Picture

page.tpl.php is the granddaddy of all template files, and provides the overall page layout for the site. Other template files are inserted into page.tpl.php, as the diagram in Figure 8-4 illustrates.

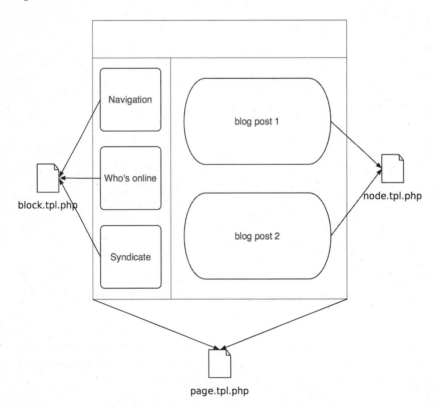

Figure 8-4. *Other templates are inserted within the encompassing page.tpl.php file.*

The insertion of block.tpl.php and node.tpl.php in Figure 8-4 happens automatically by the theme system during page building. Remember when you created your own page.tpl.php file in the previous example? Well, the $content variable contained the output of the node.tpl.php calls, and $left contained the output from the block.tpl.php calls. Let's examine how this works.

Let's add a node template file to our Greyscale theme. Rather than writing it from scratch, we'll copy Drupal's default node template file; that is, the node template that is used if node.tpl.php cannot be found in a theme. Copy modules/node/node.tpl.php to sites/all/themes/custom/greyscale/node.tpl.php. Then visit Administer ➤ Site building ➤ Modules so that the theme registry will be rebuilt. Drupal will find sites/all/themes/custom/greyscale/node.tpl.php during the rebuilding process, and from now on, it will use this file as the node template. Create a node using Create content ➤ Page (fill out just the Title and Body fields). Now change your node.tpl.php file slightly (maybe add "Hello world!" to the end of it). The display of your node should change to use the new template with your modifications.

You could do the same thing with block.tpl.php (you can find the default block template file at modules/system/block.tpl.php) or with any other template file that you find in Drupal.

Introducing the theme() Function

When Drupal wants to generate some HTML output for a themable item (like a node, a block, a breadcrumb trail, a comment, or a user signature), it looks for a theme function or template file that will generate HTML for that item. Almost all parts of Drupal are themable, which means you can override the actual HTML that is generated for that item. We'll look at some examples soon.

Tip For a list of themable items in Drupal, see http://api.drupal.org/api/group/themeable/6.

An Overview of How theme() Works

Here's a high-level overview of what happens when a simple node page, such as http://example.com/?q=node/3 is displayed:

1. Drupal's menu system receives the request and hands off control to the node module.

2. After building the node data structure, theme('node', $node, $teaser, $page) is called. This finds the correct theme function or template file, defines lots of variables that the template may use, and applies the template, resulting in finished HTML for the node. (If multiple nodes are being displayed, as happens with a blog, this process happens for each node.)

3. If the comment module is enabled, any comments are changed into HTML and appended to the node's HTML.

4. This whole glob of HTML is returned (you can see it as the $return variable in index.php) and passed to the theme() function again as theme('page', $return).

5. Before processing the page template, Drupal does some preprocessing, such as discovering which regions are available and which blocks should be shown in each region. Each block is turned into HTML by calling theme('blocks', $region), which defines variables and applies a block template. You should be starting to see a pattern here.

6. Finally, Drupal defines lots of variables for the page template to use and applies the page template.

You should be able to discern from the preceding list that the theme() function is very important to Drupal. It is in charge of running preprocessing functions to set variables that will be used in templates and dispatching a theme call to the correct function or finding the appropriate template file. The result is HTML. The process is shown graphically in Figure 8-5. We will take an in-depth look at how this function works later. Right now, it is enough to understand that when Drupal wants to turn a node into HTML, theme('node') is called. Depending on which theme is enabled, the theme_node() function will generate the HTML or a template file named node.tpl.php will do it.

This process can be overridden at many levels. For example, themes can override built-in theme functions, so when theme('node') is called a function called greyscale_node() might handle it instead of theme_node(). Template files have naming conventions that we'll explore later too, so that a node-story.tpl.php template file would target only nodes of type Story.

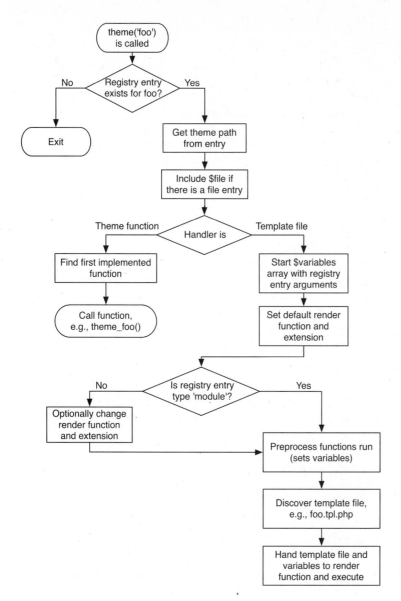

Figure 8-5. *Flow of execution for a call to the theme() function*

Overriding Themable Items

The core philosophy behind Drupal's theme system is similar to that of the hook system. By adhering to a naming convention, functions can identify themselves as theme-related functions that are responsible for formatting and returning your site's content or template files containing PHP can be used.

Overriding with Theme Functions

As you've seen, themable items are identifiable by their function names, which all begin with theme_, or by the presence of a template file. This naming convention gives Drupal the ability to create a function-override mechanism for all themable functions. Designers can instruct Drupal to execute an alternative function, which takes precedence over the theme functions that module developers expose or over Drupal's default template files. For example, let's examine how this process works when building the site's breadcrumb trail.

Open includes/theme.inc, and examine the functions inside that file. Many functions in there begin with theme_, which is the telltale sign that they can be overridden. In particular, let's examine theme_breadcrumb():

```
/**
 * Return a themed breadcrumb trail.
 *
 * @param $breadcrumb .
 *   An array containing the breadcrumb links.
 * @return a string containing the breadcrumb output.
 */
function theme_breadcrumb($breadcrumb) {
  if (!empty($breadcrumb)) {
    return '<div class="breadcrumb">'. implode(' » ', $breadcrumb) .'</div>';
  }
}
```

This function controls the HTML for the breadcrumb navigation within Drupal. Currently, it adds a right-pointing double-arrow separator between each item of the trail. Suppose you want to change the div tag to a span and use an asterisk (*) instead of a double arrow. How should you go about it? One solution would be to edit this function within theme.inc, save it, and call it good. (No! No! Do *not* do this!) There are better ways.

Have you ever seen how these theme functions are invoked within core? You'll never see theme_breadcrumb() called directly. Instead, it's always wrapped inside the theme() helper function. You'd expect the function to be called as follows:

```
theme_breadcrumb($breadcrumb)
```

But it's not. Instead, you'll see developers use the following invocation:

```
theme('breadcrumb', $breadcrumb);
```

This generic theme() function is responsible for initializing the theme layer and dispatching of function calls to the appropriate places, bringing us to the more elegant solution to our problem. The call to theme() instructs Drupal to look for the breadcrumb functions shown in Figure 8-5, in the following order.

Assuming the theme you're using is Greyscale, which is a PHPTemplate-based theme, Drupal would look for the following (we'll ignore breadcrumb.tpl.php for a moment):

```
greyscale_breadcrumb()
phptemplate_breadcrumb()
sites/all/themes/custom/greyscale/breadcrumb.tpl.php
theme_breadcrumb()
```

Where would you put a function like `phptemplate_breadcrumb()` to override the built-in breadcrumb function?

Easy—your theme's `template.php` file is the place to override Drupal's default theme functions, and intercept and create custom variables to pass along to template files.

Note Don't use Garland as the active theme when doing these exercises, since Garland already has a `template.php` file. Use Greyscale (or Bluemarine) instead.

To tweak the Drupal breadcrumbs, create `sites/all/themes/custom/greyscale/template.php` file and copy and paste the `theme_breadcrumb()` function in there from `theme.inc`. Be sure to include the starting `<?php` tag. Also, rename the function from `theme_breadcrumb` to `phptemplate_breadcrumb`. Next, visit Administer ➤ Site building ➤ Modules to rebuild the theme registry so Drupal will detect your new function.

```php
<?php
/**
 * Return a themed breadcrumb trail.
 *
 * @param $breadcrumb
 *   An array containing the breadcrumb links.
 * @return a string containing the breadcrumb output.
 */
function phptemplate_breadcrumb($breadcrumb) {
  if (!empty($breadcrumb)) {
    return '<span class="breadcrumb">'. implode(' * ', $breadcrumb) .'</span>';
  }
}
```

The next time Drupal is asked to format the breadcrumb trail, it'll find your function first and use it instead of the default `theme_breadcrumb()` function, and breadcrumbs will contain your asterisks instead of Drupal's double arrows. Pretty slick, eh? By passing all theme function calls through the `theme()` function, Drupal will always check if the current theme has overridden any of the `theme_` functions and call those instead. Developers, take note: any parts of your modules that output HTML or XML should only be done within theme functions so they become accessible for themers to override.

Overriding with Template Files

If you're working with a designer, telling him or her to "just go in the code and find the themable functions to override" is out of the question. Fortunately, there's another way to make this more accessible to designer types. You can instead map themable items to their own template files. I'll demonstrate with our handy breadcrumb example.

Before we begin, make sure that no theme function is overriding `theme_breadcrumb()`. So if you created a `phptemplate_breadcrumb()` function in your theme's `template.php` file in the preceding section, comment it out. Then, create a file at `sites/all/themes/custom/greyscale/breadcrumb.tpl.php`. This is the new template file for breadcrumbs. Because we wanted to change the `<div>` tag to a `<span>` tag, go ahead and populate the file with the following:

```
<?php if (!empty($breadcrumb)): ?>
  <span class="breadcrumb"><?php print implode(' ! ', $breadcrumb) ?></span>
<?php endif; ?>
```

That's easy enough for a designer to edit. Now you need to let Drupal know to call this template file when looking to render its breadcrumbs. To do that, rebuild the theme registry by visiting Administer ➤ Site building ➤ Modules. While rebuilding the theme registry, Drupal will discover your `breadcrumb.tpl.php` file and map the breadcrumb themable item to that template file.

Now you know how to override any themable item in Drupal in a way that will make your designers happy.

Adding and Manipulating Template Variables

The question becomes this: if you can make your own template files and control the variables being sent to them, how can you manipulate or add variables being passed into page and node templates?

■**Note** Variables are only aggregated and passed into themable items that are implemented as template files. Variables are not passed into themable items implemented as theme functions.

Every call to load a template file passes through a series of preprocess functions. These functions are responsible for aggregating the variables to pass along to the correct template file. Let's continue with our example of using the breadcrumb trail. First, let's modify `sites/all/themes/custom/greyscale/breadcrumb.tpl.php` to use a variable called `$breadcrumb_delimiter` for the breadcrumb delimiter:

```
<?php if (!empty($breadcrumb)): ?>
  <span class="breadcrumb">
    <?php print implode(' '. $breadcrumb_delimiter .' ', $breadcrumb) ?>
  </span>
<?php endif; ?>
```

How are we going to set the value of `$breadcrumb_delimiter`? One option would be in a module. We could create `sites/all/modules/custom/crumbpicker.info`:

```
; $Id$
name = Breadcrumb Picker
description = Provide a character for the breadcrumb trail delimiter.
package = Pro Drupal Development
core = 6.x
```

The module at sites/all/modules/custom/crumbpicker.module would be tiny:

```php
<?php
// $Id$

/**
 * @file
 * Provide a character for the breadcrumb trail delimiter.
 */

/**
 * Implementation of $modulename_preprocess_$hook().
 */
function crumbpicker_preprocess_breadcrumb(&$variables) {
  $variables['breadcrumb_delimiter'] = '/';
}
```

After enabling the module at Administer ➤ Site building ➤ Modules, your breadcrumb trail should look like Home / Administer / Site building.

The preceding example illustrates a module setting a variable for a template file to use. But there must be an easier way than creating a module every time a variable needs to be set. Sure enough, it's template.php to the rescue. Let's write a function to set the breadcrumb delimiter. Add the following to your theme's template.php file:

```php
/**
 * Implementation of $themeenginename_preprocess_$hook().
 * Variables we set here will be available to the breadcrumb template file.
 */
function phptemplate_preprocess_breadcrumb(&$variables) {
  $variables['breadcrumb_delimiter'] = '#';
}
```

That's easier than creating a module, and frankly, the module approach is usually best for existing modules to provide variables to templates; modules are not generally written solely for this purpose. Now, we have a module providing a variable and a function in template.php providing a variable. Which one will actually be used?

Actually, a whole hierarchy of preprocess functions run in a certain order, each one with the potential to overwrite variables that have been defined by previous preprocess functions. In the preceding example, the breadcrumb delimiter will be # because phptemplate_ preprocess_breadcrumb() will be executed after crumbpicker_preprocess_breadcrumb(), and thus its variable assignment will override any previous variable assignment for $breadcrumb_ delimiter. The order of execution of preprocess functions is shown in Figure 8-6.

For the theming of a breadcrumb trail using the Greyscale theme, the actual order of precedence (from first called to last called) would be:

```
template_preprocess()
template_preprocess_breadcrumb()
crumbpicker_preprocess()
crumbpicker_preprocess_breadcrumb()
phptemplate_preprocess()
phptemplate_preprocess_breadcrumb()
greyscale_preprocess()
greyscale_preprocess_breadcrumb()
```

Thus `greyscale_preprocess_breadcrumb()` can override any variable that has been set; it's called last before the variables are handed to the template file. Calling all those functions when only some of them are implemented may seem to you like a waste of time. If so, you are correct, and when the theme registry is built, Drupal determines which functions are implemented and calls only those.

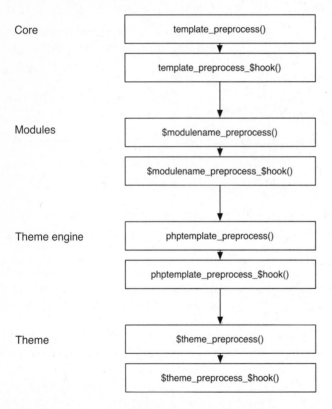

Figure 8-6. *Order of execution of preprocess functions*

___

■**Note** One of the variables you can change within a preprocess function is `$variables`
`['template_file']`, which is the name of the template file Drupal is about to call. If you need to
load an alternate template file based on a more complex condition, this is the place to do it.

___

Variables for All Templates

Drupal prepopulates the following general variables before setting variables for specific templates:

- $zebra: This value is either odd or even, and it toggles with each call to theme('node') to allow for easy theming of node listings.

- $id: This integer is incremented with each call to this themable item. For example, each time theme('node') is called, $id is incremented. So in a page that lists many node teasers, the $id variable available to the node template that themes node teasers will increment with each node teaser.

- $directory: This is the path to the theme, such as themes/bluemarine (or if a theme is not providing a template file, the path to the module that is providing one, e.g., modules/node).

The following will be set if the database is active and the site is not in maintenance mode, which is most of the time:

- $is_admin: The result of user_access('access administration pages')

- $is_front: TRUE if the front page is being built; FALSE otherwise

- $logged_in: TRUE if the current user is logged in; FALSE otherwise

- $user: The global $user object (do not use properties from this object directly in themes without sanitizing them; see Chapter 20)

page.tpl.php

If you need to make a custom page template, you can start by cloning page.tpl.php from an existing theme or from modules/system/page.tpl.php and then tweak it as needed. In fact, all that is needed for a minimal theme is a .info file and a style.css file; Drupal will use modules/system/page.tpl.php if no page.tpl.php file exists in your theme. For basic themes, this may be all you need.

The following variables are passed into page templates:

- $base_path: The base path of the Drupal installation. At the very least, this will always default to / if Drupal is installed in a root directory.

- $body_classes: A space-delimited string of CSS class names that will be used in the body element. These classes can then be used to create smarter themes. For example, the value of $body_classes for a page node type viewed at http://example.com/?q=node/3 will be not-front logged-in page-node node-type-page one-sidebar sidebar-left.

- $breadcrumb: Returns the HTML for displaying the navigational breadcrumbs on the page.

- $closure: Returns the output of hook_footer() and thus is usually displayed at the bottom of the page, just before the close of the body tag. hook_footer() is used to allow modules to insert HTML or JavaScript at the end of a page. Note that drupal_add_js() will not work in hook_footer().

Caution $closure is an essential variable and should be included in all page.tpl.php files, since various modules depend on it being there. If it is not included, these modules may not work correctly, because they will not be able to insert their HTML or JavaScript.

- $content: Returns the HTML content to be displayed. Examples include a node, an aggregation of nodes, the content of the administrative interface, and so on.

- $css: Returns an array structure of all the CSS files to be added to the page. Use $styles if you are looking for the HTML version of the $css array.

- $directory: The relative path to the directory the theme is located in; for example, themes/bluemarine or sites/all/themes/custom/greyscale. You'll commonly use this variable in conjunction with the $base_path variable to build the absolute path to your site's theme:

```php
<?php print $base_path . $directory ?>
```

will resolve to

```php
<?php print '/' . 'sites/all/themes/custom/greyscale' ?>
```

- $feed_icons: Returns RSS feed links for the page. RSS feed links are added via drupal_add_feed().

- $footer: Returns the HTML for the footer region, including the HTML for blocks belonging to this region. Do not confuse this with hook_footer(), which is a Drupal hook that lets modules add HTML or JavaScript that will appear in the $closure variable just before the closing body tag.

- $footer_message: Returns the text of the footer message that was entered at Administer ➤ Site configuration ➤ Site information.

- $front_page: The output of url() with no parameters; for example, /drupal/. Use $front_page instead of $base_path when linking to the front page of a site, because $front_page will include the language domain and prefix when applicable.

- $head: Returns the HTML to be placed within the <head></head> section. Modules append to $head by calling drupal_set_html_head() to add additional markup.

- $head_title: The text to be displayed in the page title, between the HTML <title></title> tags. It is retrieved using drupal_get_title().

- $header: Returns the HTML for the header region, including the HTML for blocks belonging to this region.

- `$help`: Help text, mostly for administrative pages. Modules can populate this variable by implementing `hook_help()`.

- `$is_front`: `TRUE` if the front page is currently being displayed.

- `$language`: An object containing the properties of the language in which the site is being displayed. For example, `$language->language` may be en, and `$language->name` may be `English`.

- `$layout`: This variable allows you to style different types of layouts, and the value for `$layout` depends on the number of sidebars enabled. Possible values include `none`, `left`, `right`, and `both`.

- `$left`: Returns the HTML for the left sidebar, including the HTML for blocks belonging to this region.

- `$logged_in`: `TRUE` if the current user is logged in; `FALSE` otherwise.

- `$logo`: The path to the logo image, as defined in the theme configuration page of enabled themes. It's used as follows in Drupal's default page template:

```
<img src="<?php print $logo; ?>" alt="<?php print t('Home'); ?>" />
```

- `$messages`: This variable returns the HTML for validation errors, success notices for forms, and other messages as well. It's usually displayed at the top of the page.

- `$mission`: Returns the text of the site mission that was entered at Administer ➤ Site configuration ➤ Site information. This variable is only populated when `$is_front` is `TRUE`.

- `$node`: The entire node object, available when viewing a single node page.

- `$primary_links`: An array containing the primary links as they have been defined at Administer ➤ Site building ➤ Menus. Usually `$primary_links` is styled through the `theme('links')` function as follows:

```
<?php
  print theme('links', $primary_links, array('class' => ➥
    'links primary-links'))
?>
```

- `$right`: Returns the HTML for the right sidebar, including the HTML for blocks belonging to this region.

- `$scripts`: Returns the HTML for adding the `<script>` tags to the page. This is also how jQuery is loaded (see Chapter 17 for more on jQuery).

- `$search_box`: Returns the HTML for the search form. `$search_box` is empty when the administrator has disabled the display on the theme configuration page of enabled themes or if the search module is disabled.

- `$secondary_links`: An array containing the secondary links as they have been defined at Administer ➤ Site building ➤ Menus. Usually `$secondary_links` is styled through the `theme('links')` function as follows:

```
<?php
  print theme('links', $secondary_links, array('class' => ➥
    'links primary-links'))
?>
```

- $show_blocks: This is an argument to the theme call theme('page', $content, $show_blocks, $show_messages). It defaults to TRUE; when $show_blocks is FALSE the $blocks variable which populates the left and right sidebars is set to the empty string, suppressing block display.

- $show_messages: This is an argument to the theme call theme('page', $content, $show_blocks, $show_messages). It defaults to TRUE; when $show_messages is FALSE the $messages variable (see the $messages bullet point) is set to the empty string, suppressing message display.

- $site_name: The name of the site, which is set at Administer ➤ Site configuration ➤ Site information. $site_name is empty when the administrator has disabled the display on the theme configuration page of enabled themes.

- $site_slogan: The slogan of the site, which is set at Administer ➤ Site configuration ➤ Site information. $site_slogan is empty when the administrator has disabled the display of the slogan on the theme configuration page of enabled themes.

- $styles: Returns the HTML for linking to the necessary CSS files to the page. CSS files are added to the $styles variable through drupal_add_css().

- $tabs: Returns the HTML for displaying tabs such as the View/Edit tabs for nodes. Tabs are usually at the top of the page in Drupal's core themes.

- $template_files: Suggestions of the names of template files that might be available to theme the page being displayed. The names lack file extensions, for example, page-node, page-front. See the "Multiple Page Templates" section for the default order in which template files are searched for.

- $title: The main content title, different from $head_title. When on a single node view page $title is the title of the node. When viewing Drupal's administration pages, $title is usually set by the menu item that corresponds to the page being viewed (see Chapter 4 for more on menu items).

■**Caution** Even if you don't output the region variables ($header, $footer, $left, $right) within page.tpl.php, they are still being built. This is a performance issue because Drupal is doing all that block building only to throw them away for a given page view. If custom page templates don't require blocks, a better approach than excluding the variable from the template file is to head over to the block administration interface and disable those blocks from showing on your custom pages. See Chapter 9 for more details on disabling blocks on certain pages.

---

node.tpl.php

Node templates are responsible for controlling individual pieces of content displayed within a page. Rather than affecting the entire page, node templates only affect the $content variable within page.tpl.php. They're responsible for the presentation of nodes in teaser view (when multiple nodes are listed on a single page) and also in body view (when the node fills the entire $content variable in page.tpl.php and stands alone on its own page). The $page variable within a node template file will be TRUE when you're in body view or FALSE if you're in teaser view.

The node.tpl.php file is the generic template that handles the view of all nodes. What if you want a different template for, say, blogs than forum posts? How can you make node templates for a specific node type rather than just a generic catch-all template file?

The good news is that node templates offer a refreshing level of granularity that's not entirely obvious out of the box. Simply cloning node.tpl.php and renaming the new file to node-*nodetype*.tpl.php is enough for PHPTemplate to choose this template over the generic one. So theming blog entries is as simple as creating node-blog.tpl.php. Any node type you create via Administer ➤ Content management ➤ Content types can have a corresponding node template file in the same fashion. You can use the following variables in node templates:

- $build_mode: Some information about the context in which the node is being built. The value will be one of the following constants: NODE_BUILD_NORMAL, NODE_BUILD_PREVIEW, NODE_BUILD_SEARCH_INDEX, NODE_BUILD_SEARCH_RESULT, or NODE_BUILD_RSS.

- $content: The body of the node or the teaser if it's a paged result view.

- $date: The formatted date the node was created. You can choose a different format by using $created, for example, format_date($created, 'large').

- $links: The links associated with a node, such as "Read more" and "Add new comment." Modules add additional links by implementing hook_link(). The links have already gone through theme_links().

- $name: Formatted name of the user who authored the page, linked to his or her profile.

- $node: The entire node object and all its properties.

- $node_url: The URL path to this node; for example, for http://example.com/?q=node/3, the value would be /node/3.

- $page: TRUE if the node is being displayed by itself as a page. FALSE if it is on a multiple node listing view.

- $picture: If the "User pictures in posts" option has been chosen at Administer ➤ Site building ➤ Themes ➤ Configure and the "Display post information on" option for this node type has been chosen in the global theme settings, the output of theme('user_picture', $node) will be in $picture.

- $taxonomy: An array of the node's taxonomy terms in a format suitable for passing to theme_links(). In fact, the output of theme_links() is available in the $terms variable.

- $teaser: Boolean to determine whether or not the teaser is displayed. This variable can be used to indicate whether $content consists of the node body (FALSE) or teaser (TRUE).

- $terms: HTML containing the taxonomy terms associated with this node. Each term is also linked to its own taxonomy term pages.

- $title: Title of the node. Will also be a link to the node's body view when on a multiple node listing page. The text of the title has been passed through check_plain().

- $submitted: "Submitted by" text from theme('node_submitted', $node). The administrator can configure display of this information in the theme configuration page on a per-node-type basis.

- $picture: HTML for the user picture, if pictures are enabled and the user picture is set.

■**Note** Because node properties are merged with the variables that are passed to node templates, node properties are available as variables. For a list of node properties, see Chapter 7. Using node properties directly may be a security risk; see Chapter 20 for how to minimize risk.

Often the $content variable within node template files doesn't structure the data the way you'd like it to. This is especially true when using contributed modules that extend a node's attributes, such as Content Construction Kit (CCK) field-related modules.

Luckily, PHPTemplate passes the entire node object to the node template files. If you write the following debug statement at the top of your node template file and reload a page containing a node, you'll discover all the properties that make up the node. It's probably easier to read if you view the source of the page you browse to.

```
<pre>
  <?php print_r($node) ?>
</pre>
```

Now you can see all the components that make up a node, access their properties directly, and thus mark them up as desired, rather than work with an aggregated $content variable.

■**Caution** When formatting a node object directly, you also become responsible for the security of your site. Please see Chapter 20 to learn how to wrap user-submitted data in the appropriate functions to prevent XSS attacks.

---

block.tpl.php

Blocks are listed on Administer ➤ Site building ➤ Blocks and are wrapped in the markup provided by block.tpl.php. If you're not familiar with blocks, please see Chapter 9 for more details. Like the page template and node template files, the block system uses a suggestion hierarchy to find the template file to wrap blocks in. The hierarchy is as follows:

```
block-modulename-delta.tpl.php
block-modulename.tpl.php
block-region.tpl.php
block.tpl.php
```

In the preceding sequence, *modulename* is the name of the module that implements the block. For example, here's the sequence for the "Who's Online" block, which is implemented by user.module (assume the block's delta is 1):

```
block-user-1.tpl.php
block-user.tpl.php
block-left.tpl.php
block.tpl.php
```

Blocks created by the site administrator are always tied to the block module, so the value for *modulename* in the preceding suggestion hierarchy will be block for administrator-created blocks. If you don't know the module that implemented a given block, you can find all the juicy details by doing some PHP debugging. By typing in the following one-liner at the top of your block.tpl.php file, you print out the entire block object for each block that's enabled on the current page:

```
<pre>
  <?php print_r($block); ?>
</pre>
```

This is easier to read if you view the source code of the web browser page. Here's what it looks like for the "Who's online" block:

```
stdClass Object
(
  [bid] => 42
  [module] => user
  [delta] => 3
  [theme] => bluemarine
  [status] => 1
  [weight] => 0
  [region] => footer
  [custom] => 0
  [throttle] => 0
  [visibility] => 0
  [pages] =>
  [title] =>
  [cache] => -1
  [subject] => Who's online
  [content] => There are currently ...
)
```

Now that you have all the details of this block, you can easily construct one or more of the following block template files, depending on the scope of what you want to target:

```
block-user-3.tpl.php // Target just the Who's online block.
block-user.tpl.php   // Target all block output by user module.
block-footer.tpl.php // Target all blocks in the footer region.
block.tpl.php        // Target all blocks on any page.
```

Here's a list of the default variables you can access within block template files:

- $block: The entire block object. Generally, you will use $block->subject and $block->content; see block.tpl.php in core themes for examples.

- $block_id: An integer that increments each time a block is generated and the block template file is invoked.

- $block_zebra: Whenever $block_id is incremented, it toggles this variable back and forth between odd and even.

comment.tpl.php

The comment.tpl.php template file adds markup to comments. The following variables are passed into the comment template:

- $author: Hyperlink author name to the author's profile page, if he or she has one.

- $comment: Comment object containing all comment attributes.

- $content: The body of the comment.

- $date: Formatted creation date of the post. A different format can be used by calling format_date(), for example, format_date($comment->timestamp, 'large').

- $links: HTML for contextual links related to the comment such as "edit, "reply," and "delete."

- $new: Returns "new" for a comment yet to be viewed by the currently logged in user and "updated" for an updated comment. You can change the text returned from $new by overriding theme_mark() in includes/theme.inc. Drupal doesn't track which comments have been read or updated for anonymous users.

- $node: The entire node object for the node to which this comment applies.

- $picture: HTML for the user picture. You must enable picture support at Administer ➤ User management ➤ User settings, and you must check "User pictures in comments" on each theme's configuration page for enabled themes. Finally, either the site administrator must provide a default picture or the user must upload a picture so there is an image to display.

- $signature: Filtered HTML of the user's signature. Signature support must be enabled at Administer ➤ User management ➤ User settings for this variable to be useful.

- $status: Reflects the comment's status with one of the following values: `comment-preview`, `comment-unpublished`, and `comment-published`.

- $submitted: "Submitted by" string with username and date, output from `theme('comment_submitted', $comment)`.

- $title: Hyperlinked title to this comment, including URL fragment.

box.tpl.php

The `box.tpl.php` template file is one of the more obscure template files within Drupal. It's used in the Drupal core to wrap the comment submission form and search results. Other than that, it doesn't have much use. It serves no function for blocks, as one might erroneously think (because blocks created by the administrator are stored in a database table named `boxes`). You have access to the following default variables within the box template:

- $content: The content of a box.

- $region: The region in which the box should be displayed. Examples include `header`, `left`, and `main`.

- $title: The title of a box.

Other .tpl.php Files

The templates we've examined so far are the most commonly used templates. But there are many other templates available. To view them, browse through the `modules` directory, and look for files that end in `.tpl.php`. For example, `modules/forum` contains six such files. These files are nicely documented and can be copied directly into your custom theme's directory and modified as needed. This is much more efficient than starting from scratch!

Multiple Page Templates

What if you want to create different layouts for different pages on your site, and a single page layout isn't going to cut it? Here is a best practice for creating additional page templates.

You can create additional page templates within Drupal based on the current system URL of the site. For example, if you were to visit `http://example.com/?q=user/1`, PHPTemplate would look for the following page templates in this order, assuming you were using the Greyscale theme:

```
sites/all/themes/custom/greyscale/page-user-1.tpl.php
modules/system/page-user-1.tpl.php
sites/all/themes/custom/greyscale/page-user.tpl.php
modules/system/page-user.tpl.php
sites/all/themes/custom/greyscale/page.tpl.php
modules/system/page.tpl.php
```

PHPTemplate stops looking for a page template as soon as it finds a template file to include. The `page-user.tpl.php` file would execute for all user pages, whereas page-user-1.tpl.php would only execute for the URLs of user/1, user/1/edit, and so on. If Drupal cannot find a page template anywhere in the theme, it will fall back to its own plain vanilla built-in template at modules/system/page.tpl.php.

Note Drupal looks at the internal system URL only, so if you're using the path or pathauto modules, which allow you to alias URLs, the page templates will still need to reference Drupal's system URL and not the alias.

Let's use the node editing page at http://example.com/?q=node/1/edit as an example. Here's the order of template files PHPTemplate would look for:

```
sites/all/themes/custom/greyscale/page-node-edit.tpl.php
modules/system/page-node-edit.tpl.php
sites/all/themes/custom/greyscale/page-node-1.tpl.php
modules/system/page-node-1.tpl.php
sites/all/themes/custom/greyscale/page-node.tpl.php
modules/system/page-node.tpl.php
sites/all/themes/custom/greyscale/page.tpl.php
modules/system/page.tpl.php
```

By looking at the preceding paths, you can see that if you are a module writer you can easily provide default templates with your module; browse through the modules directory of your Drupal installation for examples.

Tip To create a custom page template for the front page of your site, simply create a template file named page-front.tpl.php.

Advanced Drupal Theming

If you would like to fully understand how theming works in Drupal, there are two essential areas to understand. You'll start by learning about the engine that drives the theme system: the theme registry. Then, you'll follow a detailed walkthrough of the theme() function so that you know how it works and where it can be tweaked.

The Theme Registry

The theme registry is where Drupal keeps track of all theming functions and templates. Each themable item in Drupal is themed by either a function or a template. When Drupal builds the theme registry, it discovers and maps information about each item. This means the process does not have to occur at runtime, making Drupal faster.

How the Registry Is Built

When the theme registry is built, such as when a new theme is enabled, it looks around for theme hooks in the following order:

1. First, it looks for hook_theme() implementations in modules to discover theme functions and template files provided by modules.

2. If the theme is based on another theme, the hook_theme() implementation in the base theme engine is called first. For example, Minnelli is a theme based on Garland. The theme engine for the base theme is PHPTemplate. So phptemplate_theme() is called to discover theme functions prefixed with phptemplate_ or garland_ and template files named in a specific way in the base theme directory. For example, the template file themes/garland/node.tpl.php is added here.

3. The hook_theme() implementation for the theme is called. So in the case of Minnelli, phptemplate_theme() is called to discover theme functions prefixed with phptemplate_ or minnelli_ and template files in the theme directory. So if Minnelli provided a node template at themes/garland/minnelli/node.tpl.php, it would be discovered.

Notice that at each step, newly discovered theme functions and template files override those already in the registry. This is the mechanism for inheritance that allows you to override any theme function or template file.

Let's examine a hook_theme() implementation in a module more closely. The job of the theme hook is to return an array of themable items. When an item is being themed by a theme function, the arguments of the function are included. For example, the breadcrumb trail is themed by the function theme_breadcrumb($breadcrumb). So in the theme hook of a hypothetical foo.module, the fact that breadcrumbs are themable is stated this way:

```
/**
 * Implementation of hook_theme().
 */
foo_theme() {
  return array(
    'breadcrumb' => array(
      'arguments' => array('breadcrumb' => NULL),
    ),
  );
}
```

The NULL here is the default value to use if the parameter that will be passed is empty. So you're really describing the item's name and its parameters, complete with their default values. If there is a file that needs to be included to bring the theme function or template preprocess function into scope you can specify it using the file key:

```
/**
 * Implementation of hook_theme().
 */
function user_theme() {
  return array(
    'user_filter_form' => array(
      'arguments' => array('form' => NULL),
      'file' => 'user.admin.inc',
    ),
    ...
  );
}
```

If you would like to declare that a themable item will utilize a template file instead of a theme function, you define the name of the template file (without the .tpl.php ending) in the theme hook:

```
/**
 * Implementation of hook_theme().
 */
function user_theme() {
  return array(
    'user_profile_item' => array(
      'arguments' => array('element' => NULL),
      'template' => 'user-profile-item',
      'file' => 'user.pages.inc',
    ),
    ...
  );
}
```

In the preceding user_profile_item example, the template file that is referred to in the template key can be inspected at modules/user/user-profile-item.tpl.php. The template preprocess function can be found in modules/user/user.pages.inc and is called template_ preprocess_user_profile_item(). That preprocess function is passed the variables that were defined by template_preprocess() as well as the $element variable defined in the arguments key. The value of the $element variable is assigned during rendering.

A Detailed Walkthrough of theme()

In this section, we'll go behind the scenes, so you can learn how the theme() function actually works. Let's walk through the details of the path of execution when the following theme call is made and Drupal's core Bluemarine theme is the active theme:

```
theme('node', $node, $teaser, $page)
```

First, Drupal looks at the first argument to find out what is being themed. In this, case it's node, so Drupal looks in the theme registry for an entry for node. The registry entry it finds looks something like Figure 8-7.

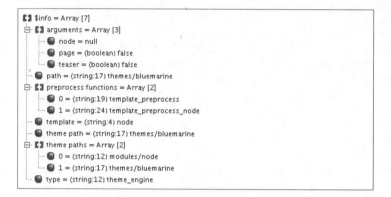

```
[ ] $info = Array [7]
 └─[ ] arguments = Array [3]
      ├─● node = null
      ├─● page = (boolean) false
      └─● teaser = (boolean) false
    ─● path = (string:17) themes/bluemarine
 └─[ ] preprocess functions = Array [2]
      ├─● 0 = (string:19) template_preprocess
      └─● 1 = (string:24) template_preprocess_node
    ─● template = (string:4) node
    ─● theme path = (string:17) themes/bluemarine
 └─[ ] theme paths = Array [2]
      ├─● 0 = (string:12) modules/node
      └─● 1 = (string:17) themes/bluemarine
    ─● type = (string:12) theme_engine
```

Figure 8-7. *Registry entry for node when the Bluemarine theme is chosen*

If the registry path had a file entry, Drupal would run include_once() for the file to get any necessary theme functions in scope, but in this case, there is no such entry.

Drupal checks to see if this theme call will be handled by a function or a template file. If the call will be handled by a function, Drupal simply calls the function and returns the output. But since no function is defined in the registry entry for this call, Drupal will prepare some variables in order to hand them over to a template file.

To start with, the arguments that were passed in to the theme() function are made available. The arguments passed in this case were $node, $teaser, and $page. So for each argument listed in the arguments registry entry, Drupal assigns a corresponding variable:

```
$variables['node']   = $node;
$variables['teaser'] = $teaser;
$variables['page']   = $page;
```

Next, the default render function is set to theme_render_template(), and the default extension is set to .tpl.php (the standard file extension for PHPTemplate templates). The render function is in charge of handing over the variables to the template file, as you'll see in a moment.

The rest of the variables that the template will use are provided by template preprocess functions. The first, template_preprocess(), is always called for every themed item, whether that item is a node, block, breadcrumb trail, or what have you. The second is specific to the item being rendered (in this case, a node). Figure 8-7 shows the two preprocess functions defined for node, and they are called as follows:

```
template_preprocess($variables, 'node');
template_preprocess_node($variables, 'node');
```

The first function is `template_preprocess()`. You can see the code for the function at `http://api.drupal.org/api/function/template_preprocess/6` or by looking in `includes/theme.inc`. This function sets the variables that are available to all templates (see the "Variables for All Templates" section).

Preprocess functions come in pairs. The end of the name of the second preprocess function corresponds with the thing being themed. So while `template_preprocess()` has just run, `template_preprocess_node()` now runs. It adds the following variables: `$taxonomy`, `$content`, `$date`, `$links`, `$name`, `$node_url`, `$terms`, and `$title`. This is shown in the code for `template_preprocess_node()`. Note that each entry in the `$variables` array will become a stand-alone variable for the template file to use. For example, `$variables['date']` will be usable as simply `$date` in the template file:

```
**
 * Process variables for node.tpl.php
 *
 * Most themes utilize their own copy of node.tpl.php. The default is located
 * inside "modules/node/node.tpl.php". Look in there for the full list of
 * variables.
 *
 * The $variables array contains the following arguments:
 *    $node, $teaser, $page
 */
function template_preprocess_node(&$variables) {
  $node = $variables['node'];
  if (module_exists('taxonomy')) {
    $variables['taxonomy'] = taxonomy_link('taxonomy terms', $node);
  }
  else {
    $variables['taxonomy'] = array();
  }

  if ($variables['teaser'] && $node->teaser) {
    $variables['content'] = $node->teaser;
  }
  elseif (isset($node->body)) {
    $variables['content'] = $node->body;
  }
  else {
    $variables['content'] = '';
  }

  $variables['date']       = format_date($node->created);
  $variables['links']      = !empty($node->links) ?
    theme('links', $node->links, array('class' => 'links inline')) : '';
  $variables['name']       = theme('username', $node);
```

```
$variables['node_url']   = url('node/'. $node->nid);
$variables['terms']      = theme('links', $variables['taxonomy'],
  array('class' => 'links inline'));
$variables['title']      = check_plain($node->title);

// Flatten the node object's member fields.
$variables = array_merge((array)$node, $variables);
...
}
```

Details on what these variables mean have been provided earlier in this chapter.

After the assignment of variables, something crazy happens. The node itself is converted from an object to an array and is merged with the variables we already have. So any node property is available to the template file merely by prefixing the name of the property with a dollar sign. For example, $node->nid is available as $nid. If a node property and a variable have the same name, the variable takes precedence. For example, the $title variable contains a plain text version of $node->title. When the merge happens, the plain text version survives and is available to the template file. Note the original title is still accessible at $variables['node']->title, though it should not be used without being passed through a filter for security reasons (see Chapter 20).

OK, Drupal has run the preprocess functions. Now a decision needs to be made: which template file is going to receive all these variables and be used as a template for the node? To decide that, Drupal examines the following:

1. Are any template files defined in $variables['template_files']? The entries here are names of the template files that will be looked for by Drupal. In our example, the node is of type story, so node-story is defined there; Drupal attempts to match a content-type-specific template before a general node template. See http://drupal.org/node/190815 for more details.

2. Is $variables['template_file'] set? If so, that takes precedence.

The drupal_discover_template() function decides which template to use. It does so by looking for the template files in theme paths that are defined in the theme registry entry. In our case, it looks for themes/bluemarine/node-story.tpl.php and then modules/node/node-story.tpl.php. If neither file exists (and in this example, neither does: the node module does not provide per-node-type template files in its directory and the Bluemarine theme does not provide a template for story nodes by default—just a general node template), then the first round of template discovery has failed. Next, Drupal checks a concatenation of the path, template file, and extension: themes/bluemarine/node.tpl.php. Satisfied that this file exists, it calls the render function (remember, that's theme_render_template()) and passes in the template file choice and the variables' array.

The render function hands the variables to the template and executes it, returning the results. In this example, the result is the HTML from the execution of themes/bluemarine/node.tpl.php.

Defining New Block Regions

Regions in Drupal are areas in themes where blocks can be placed. You assign blocks to regions and organize them within the Drupal administrative interface at Administer ➤ Site building ➤ Blocks.

The default regions used in themes are `left`, `right`, `content`, `header`, and `footer`, although you can create as many regions as you want. Once declared, they're made available to your page template files (for example, `page.tpl.php`) as a variable. For instance, use `<?php print $header ?>` for the placement of the `header` region. You create additional regions by defining them within your theme's `.info` file.

Theming Drupal's Forms

Changing the markup within Drupal forms isn't as easy as creating a template file, because forms within Drupal are dependent on their own API. Chapter 10 covers how to map theme functions to forms in detail.

Using the Theme Developer Module

An invaluable resource for working with Drupal themes is the theme developer module. It is part of `devel.module` and can be downloaded at `http://drupal.org/project/devel`. The theme developer module lets you point to an element on a page and discover which templates or theme functions were involved in creating that element as well as the variables (and their values) available to that element. Figure 8-8 gives an example of the information provided to you.

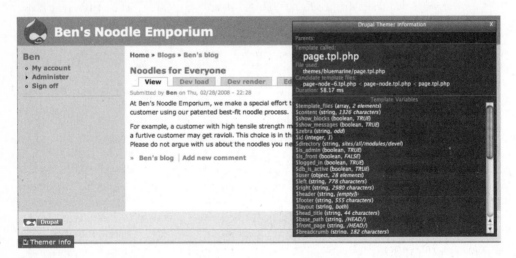

Figure 8-8. *The theme developer module*

Summary

After reading this chapter you should be able to

- Understand what theme engines and themes are.
- Understand how PHPTemplate works within Drupal.
- Create template files.
- Override theme functions.
- Manipulate template variables.
- Create new page regions for blocks.

## CHAPTER 9

Working with Blocks

B*locks* are snippets of text or functionality that usually live outside the main content area of a web site, such as in the left or right sidebars, in the header, in the footer, and so on. If you've ever logged in to a Drupal site or navigated to a Drupal administrative interface, then you've used a block. Block permissions and placement are controlled within the administrative interface, simplifying the work of developers when creating blocks. The block configuration page is located at Administer ➤ Site building ➤ Blocks (`http://example.com/?q=admin/build/block`).

What Is a Block?

Blocks have a title and a description and are used mostly for advertising, code snippets, and status indicators, not for full-fledged pieces of content; thus, blocks aren't nodes and don't follow the same rules nodes do. Nodes have revision control, fine-grained permissions, the ability to have comments attached to them, RSS feeds, and taxonomy terms; they are usually reserved for the beefier content portions of a site.

Regions are sections of the site where blocks are placed. Regions are created and exposed by themes (in the theme's `.info` file) and aren't defined by the block API. Blocks with no regions assigned to them aren't displayed.

Blocks have options to control who can see them and on which pages of the site they should appear. If the throttle module is enabled, nonessential blocks can also be set to turn off automatically during times of high traffic. The block overview page is shown in Figure 9-1.

Blocks are defined either through Drupal's web interface (custom blocks) or programmatically through the block API (module-provided blocks). How do you know which method to use when creating a block? A one-off block such as a bit of static HTML related to the site is a good candidate for a custom block. Blocks that are dynamic in nature, related to a module you've written, or that consist of mostly PHP code are excellent candidates for using the block API and for being implemented within a module. Try to avoid storing PHP code in custom blocks, as code in the database is harder to maintain than code written in a module. A site editor can come along and accidentally delete all that hard work too easily. Rather, if it doesn't make sense to create a block at the module level, just call a custom function from within the block and store all that PHP code elsewhere.

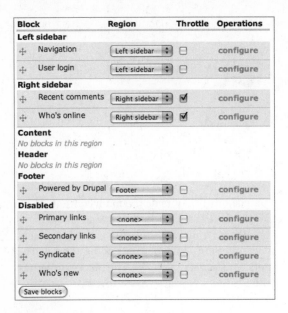

Figure 9-1. *The block overview page showing throttle options when the throttle module is enabled*

■**Tip** A common practice for blocks and other components that are site-specific is to create a site-specific module and place the custom functionality for the site inside that module. For example, the developer of a web site for the Jones Pies and Soda Company may create a jonespiesandsoda module.

Although the block API is simple and driven by a single function, hook_block(), don't disregard the complexity of what you can do within that framework. Blocks can display just about anything you want (that is, they are written in PHP and thus are not limited in what they can do), but they usually play a supporting role to the main content of the site. For example, you could create a custom navigation block for each user role, or you could expose a block that lists comments pending approval.

Block Configuration Options

Developers usually don't need to worry about block visibility, as most of it can be handled from the block administration pages at Administer ➤ Site building ➤ Blocks. Clicking the "configure" link for a block (see Figure 9-1) will reveal the configuration page for the block. Using the interface shown in Figure 9-2, you can control the following options:

- *User-specific visibility settings*: Administrators can allow individual users to customize the visibility of a given block for that user within their account settings. Users would click on their "My account" link to modify block visibility.

- *Role-specific visibility settings*: Administrators can choose to make a block be visible to only those users within certain roles.

- *Page-specific visibility settings*: Administrators can choose to make a block be visible or hidden on a certain page or range of pages or when your custom PHP code determines that certain conditions are true.

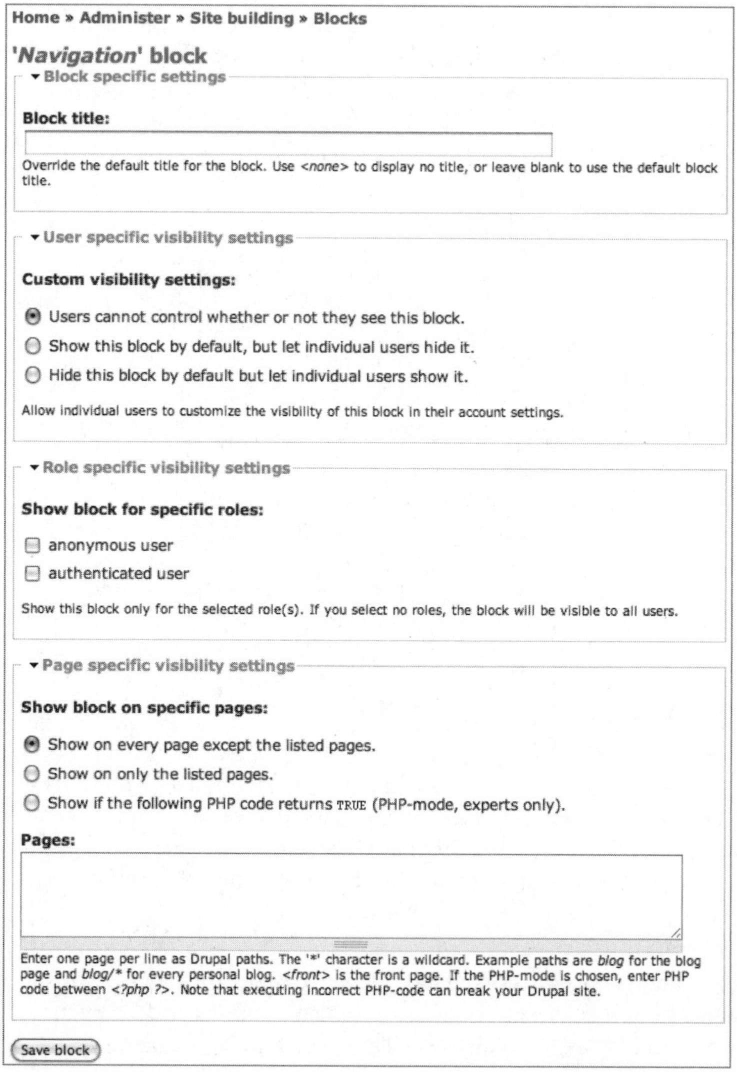

Home » Administer » Site building » Blocks

'Navigation' block
▾ Block specific settings

Block title:

Override the default title for the block. Use *<none>* to display no title, or leave blank to use the default block title.

▾ User specific visibility settings

Custom visibility settings:

◉ Users cannot control whether or not they see this block.

○ Show this block by default, but let individual users hide it.

○ Hide this block by default but let individual users show it.

Allow individual users to customize the visibility of this block in their account settings.

▾ Role specific visibility settings

Show block for specific roles:

☐ anonymous user

☐ authenticated user

Show this block only for the selected role(s). If you select no roles, the block will be visible to all users.

▾ Page specific visibility settings

Show block on specific pages:

◉ Show on every page except the listed pages.

○ Show on only the listed pages.

○ Show if the following PHP code returns TRUE (PHP-mode, experts only).

Pages:

Enter one page per line as Drupal paths. The '*' character is a wildcard. Example paths are *blog* for the blog page and *blog/** for every personal blog. *<front>* is the front page. If the PHP-mode is chosen, enter PHP code between *<?php ?>*. Note that executing incorrect PHP-code can break your Drupal site.

(Save block)

Figure 9-2. *Configuration screen of a block in the administrative interface*

Block Placement

I mentioned previously that the block administration page gives site administrators a choice of regions where blocks can appear. On the same page, they can also choose in what order the blocks are displayed within a region, as shown in Figure 9-1. Regions are defined by the theme layer in the theme's .info file, rather than through the block API, and different themes may expose different regions. Please see Chapter 8 for more information on creating regions.

Defining a Block

Blocks are defined within modules by using hook_block(), and a module can implement multiple blocks within this single hook. Once a block is defined, it will be shown on the block administration page. Additionally, a site administrator can manually create custom blocks through the web interface. In this section, we'll mostly focus on programmatically creating blocks. Let's take a look at the database schema for blocks, shown in Figure 9-3.

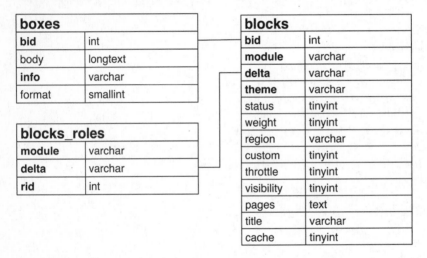

Figure 9-3. *Database schema for blocks*

Block properties for every block are stored in the blocks table. Additional data for blocks created from within the block configuration interface, such as their content and input format type, are stored in the boxes table. Lastly, blocks_roles stores the role-based permissions for each block. The following properties are defined within the columns of the blocks table:

- bid: This is the unique ID of each block.

- module: This column contains the name of the module that defined the block. The user login block was created by the user module, and so on. Custom blocks created by the administrator at Administer ➤ Site building ➤ Blocks are considered to have been created by the block module.

- delta: Because modules can define multiple blocks within hook_block(), the delta column stores a key for each block that's unique only for each implementation of hook_block(), and not for all blocks across the board. A delta can be an integer or a string.

- theme: Blocks can be defined for multiple themes. Drupal therefore needs to store the name of the theme for which the block is enabled. Every theme for which the block is enabled will have its own row in the database. Configuration options are not shared across themes.

- status: This tracks whether the block is enabled. A value of 1 means that it's enabled, while 0 means it's disabled. When a block doesn't have a region associated with it, Drupal sets the status flag to 0.

- weight: The weight of the block determines its position relative to other blocks within a region.

- region: This is the name of the region in which the block will appear, for example, footer.

- custom: This is the value of the user-specific visibility settings for this block (see Figure 9-2). A value of 0 means that users cannot control the visibility of this block; a value of 1 means that the block is shown by default but users can hide it; and a value of 2 means that the block is hidden by default but users can choose to display it.

- throttle: When the throttle module is enabled, this column tracks which blocks should be throttled. A value of 0 indicates that throttling is disabled, and 1 that it is eligible to be throttled. The throttle module is used to automatically detect a surge in incoming traffic and temporarily disable certain processor-intensive parts of a site (see Chapter 22 for more about the throttle module).

- visibility: This value represents how the block's visibility is determined. A value of 0 means the block will be shown on all pages except listed pages; a value of 1 means the block will be shown only on listed pages; and a value of 2 means that Drupal will execute custom PHP code defined by the administrator to determine visibility.

- pages: The contents of this field depend on the setting in the visibility field. If the value of the visibility field is 0 or 1, this field will contain a list of Drupal paths. If the value of the visibility field is 2, the pages field will contain custom PHP code to be evaluated to determine whether or not to display the block.

- title: This is a custom title for the block. If this field is empty, the block's default title (provided by the module that provides the block) will be used. If the field contains <none>, no title will be displayed for the block. Otherwise, text in this field is used for the block's title.

- cache: This value determines how Drupal will cache this block. A value of –1 means the block will not be cached. A value of 1 means that the block will be cached for each role, and this is Drupal's default setting for blocks that do not specify a cache setting. A value of 2 means the block will be cached for each user. A value of 4 means that the block will be cached for each page. A value of 8 means that the block will be cached but will be cached the same way for everyone regardless of role, user, or page.

Understanding How Blocks Are Themed

During a page request, the theme system will ask the block system to return a list of blocks for each region. It does this when generating the variables to send to the page template (usually page.tpl.php). To gather the themed blocks for each region (such as the footer region), Drupal executes something like this:

```
$variables['footer']  = theme('blocks', 'footer');
```

You might remember from Chapter 8 that theme('blocks') is actually a call to theme_blocks(). Here's what theme_blocks() actually does:

```
/**
 * Return a set of blocks available for the current user.
 *
 * @param $region
 *   Which set of blocks to retrieve.
 * @return
 *   A string containing the themed blocks for this region.
 */
function theme_blocks($region) {
  $output = '';

  if ($list = block_list($region)) {
    foreach ($list as $key => $block) {
      $output .= theme('block', $block);
    }
  }

  // Add any content assigned to this region through drupal_set_content() calls.
  $output .= drupal_get_content($region);

  return $output;
}
```

In the preceding code snippet, we iterate through each block for the given region and execute a theme function call for each block, which will usually result in a block.tpl.php file being run. For details on how this works and how to override the look and feel of individual blocks, see Chapter 8. Finally, we return all the themed blocks for that region back to the calling code.

Using the Block Hook

The block hook, hook_block(), handles all the logic for programmatic block creation. Using this hook, you can declare a single block or a set of blocks. Any module can implement hook_block() to create blocks. Let's take a look at the function signature:

```
function hook_block($op = 'list', $delta = 0, $edit = array())
```

Parameter List

The block hook takes the parameters discussed in the sections that follow.

$op

This parameter defines the phases a block passes through. The model of passing an $op parameter to define a phase of operation is common within the Drupal framework—for example, hook_nodeapi() and hook_user() also use this model. Possible values for $op follow:

- list: Return an array of all blocks defined by the module. Array keys are the delta (the unique identifier for this block among all the blocks defined by this module). Each array value is, in turn, a keyed array that provides vital data about the block. Possible list values, and their defaults, follow:

  - info: This value is *required*. A translatable string (i.e., wrapping the string in the t() function) provides a description of the block suitable for site administrators.

  - cache: How should the block be cached? Possible values are BLOCK_NO_CACHE (do not cache the block), BLOCK_CACHE_PER_ROLE (cache the block for each role), BLOCK_CACHE_PER_USER (cache the block for each user—not a good idea on a site with lots of users!), BLOCK_CACHE_PER_PAGE (cache the block for each page), and BLOCK_CACHE_GLOBAL (cache the block just once for everyone).

  - status: Should the block be enabled by default—TRUE or FALSE? The default is FALSE.

  - region: The default region may be set by the block. Of course, the block can be moved by the administrator to a different region. The region value only has an effect if the status value is TRUE; if the block is not enabled the region is set to None.

  - weight: This controls the arrangement of a block when displayed within its region. A block with lighter weight will rise to the top of the region vertically and left of the region horizontally. A block with a heavy weight will sink to the bottom or to the right of the region. The default weight is 0.

  - pages: Defines the default pages on which the block should be visible. Default is an empty string. The value of pages consists of Drupal paths separated by line breaks. The * character is a wildcard. Example paths are blog for the blog page and blog/* for every personal blog. <front> is the front page.

  - custom: TRUE means this is a custom block, and FALSE means that it's a block implemented by a module.

  - title: The default block title.

- configure: Return a form definition array of fields for block-specific settings. This is merged with the overall form on the block configuration page, allowing you to extend the ways in which the block can be configured. If you implement this, you also need to implement the save operation (see the next list item).

- save: The save operation happens when the configuration form is submitted. This is when your module can save custom block configuration information that you collected in the configure operation. The data that you want to save is contained in the $edit parameter. No return value is needed.

- view: The block is being displayed. Return an array containing the block's title and content.

$delta

This is ID of the block to return. You can use an integer or a string value for $delta. Note that $delta is ignored when the $op parameter is list because it is in the list operation that deltas are defined.

$edit

When $op is save, $edit contains the submitted form data from the block configuration form.

Building a Block

For this example, you'll create two blocks that make content moderation easier to manage. First, you'll create a block to list comments being held pending approval, then you'll create a block to list unpublished nodes. Both blocks will also provide links to the edit form for each piece of moderated content.

Let's create a new module named approval.module to hold our block code. Create a new folder named approval within sites/all/modules/custom (you might need to create the modules and custom folders if they don't exist).

Next, add approval.info to the folder:

```
; $Id$
name = Approval
description = Blocks for facilitating pending content workflow.
package = Pro Drupal Development
core = 6.x
```

Then, add approval.module as well:

```
<?php
// $Id$

/**
 * @file
 * Implements various blocks to improve pending content workflow.
 */
```

Once you've created these files, enable the module via Administer ➤ Site building ➤ Modules. You'll continue to work within approval.module, so keep your text editor open.

Let's add our block hook and implement the list operation, so our block appears in the list of blocks on the block administration page (see Figure 9-4):

```
/**
 * Implementation of hook_block().
 */
function approval_block($op = 'list', $delta = 0, $edit = array()) {
  switch ($op) {
    case 'list':
      $blocks[0]['info'] = t('Pending comments');
      $blocks[0]['cache'] = BLOCK_NO_CACHE;
      return $blocks;
  }
}
```

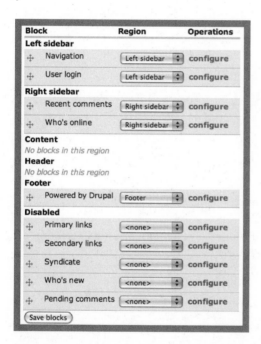

Figure 9-4. *"Pending comments" is now a block listed on the block overview page under the Disabled heading. It can now be assigned to a region.*

Note that the value of info isn't the title of the block that shows up to users once the block is enabled; rather, info is a description that only appears in the list of blocks the administrator can configure. You'll implement the actual block title later in the view case. First, though, you're going to set up additional configuration options. To do this, implement the configure case as shown in the following code snippet. You create a new form field that's visible after clicking the configure link next to the block on the block administration page, shown in Figure 9-5.

```
function approval_block($op = 'list', $delta = 0, $edit = array()) {
  switch ($op) {
    case 'list':
      $blocks[0]['info'] = t('Pending comments');
      $blocks[0]['cache'] = BLOCK_NO_CACHE;
      return $blocks;

    case 'configure':
      $form['approval_block_num_posts'] = array(
        '#type' => 'textfield',
        '#title' => t('Number of pending comments to display'),
        '#default_value' => variable_get('approval_block_num_posts', 5),
      );
      return $form;
  }
}
```

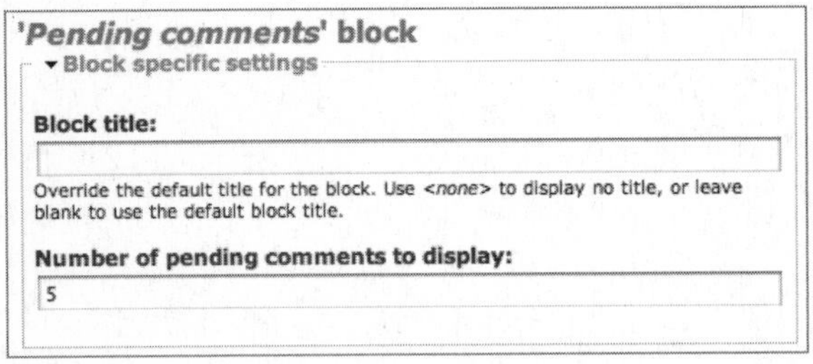

Figure 9-5. *Block configuration form with the block's custom fields*

When the block configuration form shown in Figure 9-6 is submitted, it will trigger the next $op, which is save. You'll use this next phase to save the value of the form field:

```
function approval_block($op = 'list', $delta = 0, $edit = array()) {
  switch ($op) {
    case 'list':
      $blocks[0]['info'] = t('Pending comments');
      $blocks[0]['cache'] = BLOCK_NO_CACHE;
      return $blocks;

    case 'configure':
      $form['approval_block_num_posts'] = array(
        '#type' => 'textfield',
        '#title' => t('Number of pending comments to display'),
        '#default_value' => variable_get('approval_block_num_posts', 5),
      );
      return $form;
```

```
    case 'save':
      variable_set('approval_block_num_posts',
        (int)$edit['approval_block_num_posts']);
      break;
  }
}
```

You save the number of pending comments to display using Drupal's built-in variable system with variable_set(). Note how we typecast the value to an integer as a sanity check. Finally, add the view operation and return a list of pending comments when the block is viewed:

```
function approval_block($op = 'list', $delta = 0, $edit = array()) {
  switch ($op) {
    case 'list':
      $blocks[0]['info'] = t('Pending comments');
      return $blocks;

    case 'configure':
      $form['approval_block_num_posts'] = array(
        '#type' => 'textfield',
        '#title' => t('Number of pending comments to display'),
        '#default_value' => variable_get('approval_block_num_posts', 5),
      );
      return $form;

    case 'save':
      variable_set('approval_block_num_posts',
        (int)$edit['approval_block_num_posts']);
      break;

    case 'view':
      if (user_access('administer comments')) {
        // Retrieve the number of pending comments to display that
        // we saved earlier in the 'save' op, defaulting to 5.
        $num_posts = variable_get('approval_block_num_posts', 5);

        // Query the database for unpublished comments.
        $result = db_query_range('SELECT c.* FROM {comments} c WHERE
          c.status = %d ORDER BY c.timestamp', COMMENT_NOT_PUBLISHED, 0,
          $num_posts);

        // Preserve our current location so user can return after editing.
        $destination = drupal_get_destination();
```

```
        $items = array();
        while ($comment = db_fetch_object($result)) {
          $items[] = l($comment->subject, 'node/'. $comment->nid,
                      array('fragment' => 'comment-'. $comment->cid)) .' '.
                    l(t('[edit]'), 'comment/edit/'. $comment->cid,
                      array('query' => $destination));
        }

        $block['subject'] = t('Pending comments');
        // We theme our array of links as an unordered list.
        $block['content'] = theme('item_list', $items);
      }
      return $block;
  }
}
```

Here, we're querying the database for the comments that need approval and displaying the comment titles as links, along with an edit link for each comment, as shown in Figure 9-6.

Take note of how we used drupal_get_destination() in the preceding code. This function remembers the page you were on before you submitted a form, so after you update the comment form to publish or delete a comment, you'll be automatically redirected from whence you came.

You also set the title of the block with the following line:

```
$block['subject'] = t('Pending comments');
```

Pending comments
- **Great job [edit]**
- **Question or two [edit]**

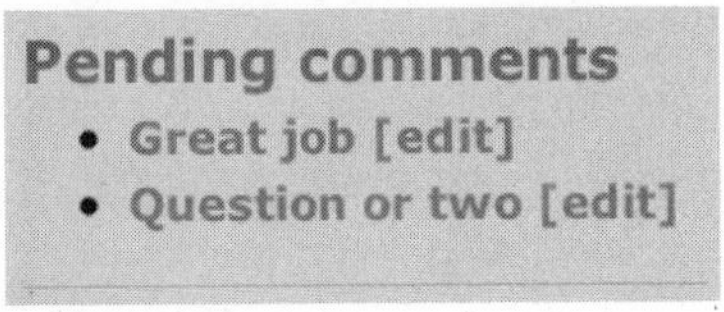

Figure 9-6. *The "Pending comments" listing block after it has been enabled. It shows two pending comments.*

Now that the "Pending comments" block is finished, let's define another block within this approval_block() function—one that lists all unpublished nodes and provides a link to their edit page:

```
function approval_block($op = 'list', $delta = 0, $edit = array()) {
  switch ($op) {
    case 'list':
      $blocks[0]['info'] = t('Pending comments');
      $blocks[0]['cache'] = BLOCK_NO_CACHE;
```

```
      $blocks[1]['info'] = t('Unpublished nodes');
      $blocks[1]['cache'] = BLOCK_NO_CACHE;
      return $blocks;
  }
}
```

Notice how the blocks are each assigned a key ($blocks[0], $blocks[1], ... $blocks[n]). The block module will subsequently use these keys as the $delta parameter. Here, we've defined the $delta IDs to be 0 for the "Pending comments" block and 1 for the "Unpublished nodes" block. These could just as easily have been pending and unpublished. It's at the programmer's discretion to decide which keys to use, and the keys need not be numeric.

Here's the complete function; our new block is shown in Figure 9-7:

```
function approval_block($op = 'list', $delta = 0, $edit = array()) {
  switch ($op) {
    case 'list':
      $blocks[0]['info'] = t('Pending comments');
      $blocks[0]['cache'] = BLOCK_NO_CACHE;

      $blocks[1]['info'] = t('Unpublished nodes');
      $blocks[1]['cache'] = BLOCK_NO_CACHE;
      return $blocks;

    case 'configure':
      // Only in block 0 (the Pending comments block) can one
      // set the number of comments to display.
      $form = array();
      if ($delta == 0) {
        $form['approval_block_num_posts'] = array(
          '#type' => 'textfield',
          '#title' => t('Number of pending comments to display'),
          '#default_value' => variable_get('approval_block_num_posts', 5),
        );
      }
      return $form;

    case 'save':
      if ($delta == 0) {
        variable_set('approval_block_num_posts', (int)
          $edit['approval_block_num_posts']);
      }
      break;
```

```
    case 'view':
      if ($delta == 0 && user_access('administer comments')) {
        // Retrieve the number of pending comments to display that
        // we saved earlier in the 'save' op, defaulting to 5.
        $num_posts = variable_get('approval_block_num_posts', 5);
        // Query the database for unpublished comments.
        $result = db_query_range('SELECT c.* FROM {comments} c WHERE c.status = %d
          ORDER BY c.timestamp', COMMENT_NOT_PUBLISHED, 0, $num_posts);

        $destination = drupal_get_destination();
        $items = array();
        while ($comment = db_fetch_object($result)) {
          $items[] = l($comment->subject, 'node/'. $comment->nid,
                        array('fragment' => 'comment-'. $comment->cid)) .' '.
                     l(t('[edit]'), 'comment/edit/'. $comment->cid,
                        array('query' => $destination));
        }

        $block['subject'] = t('Pending Comments');
        // We theme our array of links as an unordered list.
        $block['content'] = theme('item_list', $items);
      }
      elseif ($delta == 1 && user_access('administer nodes')) {
        // Query the database for the 5 most recent unpublished nodes.
        // Unpublished nodes have their status column set to 0.
        $result = db_query_range('SELECT title, nid FROM {node} WHERE
          status = 0 ORDER BY changed DESC', 0, 5);
        $destination = drupal_get_destination();
        while ($node = db_fetch_object($result)) {
          $items[] = l($node->title, 'node/'. $node->nid). ' '.
                     l(t('[edit]'), 'node/'. $node->nid .'/edit',
                        array('query' => $destination));
        }

        $block['subject'] = t('Unpublished nodes');
        // We theme our array of links as an unordered list.
        $block['content'] = theme('item_list', $items);
      }
      return $block;
  }
}
```

Because you have multiple blocks, you use the if ... elseif construct under the view op. In each case you check the $delta of the block being viewed to see if you should run the code. In a nutshell, it looks like this:

```
if ($delta == 0) {
  // Do something to block 0
}
elseif ($delta == 1) {
  // Do something to block 1
}
elseif ($delta == 2) {
  // Do something to block 2
}
return $block;
```

The result of your new unpublished nodes block is shown in Figure 9-7.

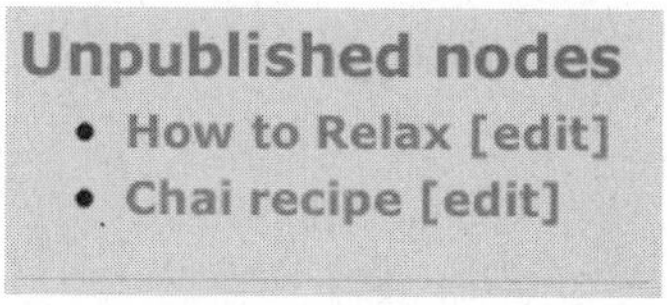

Unpublished nodes
- **How to Relax [edit]**
- **Chai recipe [edit]**

Figure 9-7. *A block listing unpublished nodes*

Bonus Example: Adding a Pending Users Block

If you'd like to extend `approval.module`, you could add another block that displays a list of user accounts that are pending administrative approval. It's left as an exercise for you to add this to the existing `approval.module`. Here it's shown as a block in a hypothetical `userapproval.module`.

```
function userapproval_block($op = 'list', $delta = 0, $edit = array()) {
  switch ($op) {
    case 'list':
      $blocks[0]['info'] = t('Pending users');
      return $blocks;

    case 'view':
      if (user_access('administer users')) {
        $result = db_query_range('SELECT uid, name, created FROM {users}
          WHERE uid != 0 AND status = 0 ORDER BY created DESC', 0, 5);
        $destination = drupal_get_destination();
        // Defensive coding: we use $u instead of $user to avoid potential namespace
        // collision with global $user variable should this code be added to later.
        while ($u = db_fetch_object($result)) {
          $items[] = theme('username', $u). ' '.
            l('[edit]', 'user/'. $u->uid. '/edit', array('query' => $destination));
        }
```

```
      $block['subject'] = t('Pending users');
      $block['content'] = theme('item_list', $items);
    }
    return $block;
  }
}
```

Enabling a Block When a Module Is Installed

Sometimes, you want a block to show up automatically when a module is installed. This is fairly straightforward, and is done through a query that inserts the block settings directly into the blocks table. The query goes within hook_install(), located in your module's .install file. Here's an example of the user module enabling the user login block when Drupal is being installed (see modules/system/system.install):

```
db_query("INSERT INTO {blocks} (module, delta, theme, status, weight, region,
  pages, cache) VALUES ('%s', '%s', '%s', %d, %d, '%s', '%s', %d)",
  'user', '0', 'garland', 1, 0, 'left', '', -1);
```

The preceding database query inserts the block into the blocks table and sets its status to 1 so it is enabled. It is assigned to the left region; that is, the left sidebar.

Block Visibility Examples

Within the block administrative interface, you can enter snippets of PHP code in the "Page visibility settings" section of the block configuration page. When a page is being built, Drupal will run the PHP snippet to determine whether a block will be displayed. Examples of some of the most common snippets follow; each snippet should return TRUE or FALSE to indicate whether the block should be visible for that particular request.

Displaying a Block to Logged-In Users Only

Only return TRUE when $user->uid is not 0.

```
<?php
  global $user;
  return (bool) $user->uid;
?>
```

Displaying a Block to Anonymous Users Only

Only return TRUE when $user->uid is 0.

```
<?php
  global $user;
  return !(bool) $user->uid;
?>
```

Summary

In this chapter, you learned the following:

- What blocks are and how they differ from nodes

- How block visibility and placement settings work

- How to define a block or multiple blocks

- How to enable a block by default

■ ■ ■

## CHAPTER 10

The Form API

Drupal features an application programming interface (API) for generating, validating, and processing HTML forms. The form API abstracts forms into a nested array of properties and values. The array is then rendered by the form rendering engine at the appropriate time while a page is being generated. There are several implications of this approach:

- Rather than output HTML, we create an array and let the engine generate the HTML.

- Since we are dealing with a representation of the form as structured data, we can add, delete, reorder, and change forms. This is especially handy when you want to modify a form created by a different module in a clean and unobtrusive way.

- Any form element can be mapped to any theme function.

- Additional form validation or processing can be added to any form.

- Operations with forms are protected against form injection attacks, where a user modifies a form and then tries to submit it.

- The learning curve for using forms is a little steeper!

In this chapter, we'll face the learning curve head on. You'll learn how the forms engine works; how to create forms, validate them, process them; and how to pummel the rendering engine into submission when you want to make an exception to the rule. This chapter covers the form API as implemented in Drupal 6. We will start by examining how the form processing engine works. If you are just starting out with forms in Drupal and want to start with an example, you might want to jump ahead to the section titled "Creating Basic Forms." If you are looking for details about individual form properties, you'll find it in the last part of the chapter in the section titled "Form API Properties."

Understanding Form Processing

Figure 10-1 shows an overview of the form building, validation, and submission process. In the following sections, we'll be using this figure as a guide and describing what happens along the way.

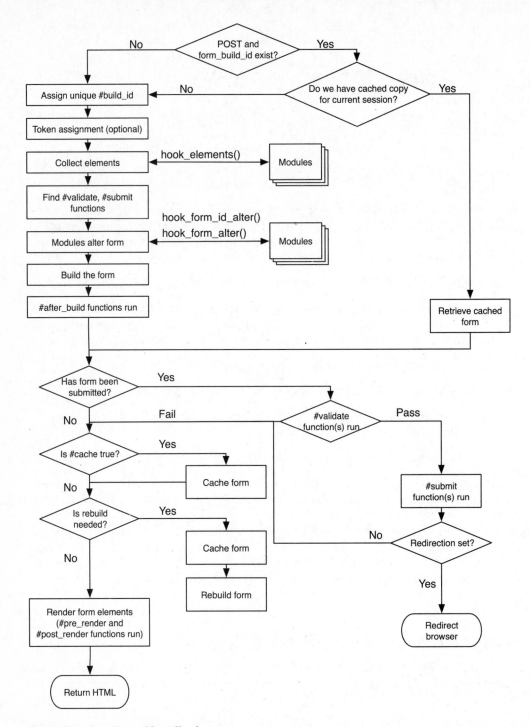

Figure 10-1. *How Drupal handles forms*

In order to interact with the forms API intelligently, it's helpful to know how the engine behind the API works. Modules describe forms to Drupal using associative arrays. Drupal's form engine takes care of generating HTML for the forms to be displayed and securely processing submitted forms using three phases: validation, submission, and redirection. The following sections explain what happens when you call `drupal_get_form()`.

Initializing the Process

There are three variables that are very important when dealing with forms. The first, `$form_id`, contains a string identifying the form. The second, `$form`, is a structured array describing the form. And the third, `$form_state`, contains information about the form, such as the form's values and what should happen when form processing is finished. `drupal_get_form()` begins by initializing `$form_state`.

Setting a Token

One of the form system's advantages is that it strives to guarantee that the form being submitted is actually the form that Drupal created, for security and to counteract spammers or would-be site attackers. To do this, Drupal sets a private key for each Drupal installation. The key is generated randomly during the installation process and distinguishes this particular Drupal installation from other installations of Drupal. Once the key is generated, it's stored in the `variables` table as `drupal_private_key`. A pseudorandom token based on the private key is sent out in the form in a hidden field and tested when the form is submitted. See http://drupal.org/node/28420 for background information. Tokens are used for logged-in users only, as pages for anonymous users are usually cached, resulting in a nonunique token.

Setting an ID

A hidden field containing the form ID of the current form is sent to the browser as part of the form. This ID usually corresponds with the function that defines the form and is sent as the first parameter of `drupal_get_form()`. For example, the function `user_register()` defines the user registration form and is called this way:

```
$output = drupal_get_form('user_register');
```

Collecting All Possible Form Element Definitions

Next, `_element_info()` is called. This invokes `hook_elements()` on all modules that implement it. Within Drupal core, the standard elements, such as radio buttons and check boxes, are defined by `modules/system/system.module`'s implementation of `hook_elements()` (see `system_elements()`). Modules implement this hook if they want to define their own element types. You might implement `hook_elements()` in your module because you want a special kind of form element, like an image upload button that shows you a thumbnail during node preview, or because you want to extend an existing form element by defining more properties.

For example, the contributed fivestar module defines its own element type:

```
/**
 * Implementation of hook_elements().
 *
 * Defines 'fivestar' form element type.
 */
function fivestar_elements() {
  $type['fivestar'] = array(
    '#input' => TRUE,
    '#stars' => 5,
    '#widget' => 'stars',
    '#allow_clear' => FALSE,
    '#auto_submit' => FALSE,
    '#auto_submit_path' => '',
    '#labels_enable' => TRUE,
    '#process' => array('fivestar_expand'),
  );
  return $type;
}
```

And the TinyMCE module uses hook_elements() to potentially modify the default properties of an existing type. TinyMCE adds a #process property to the textarea element type so that when the form is being built it will call tinymce_process_textarea(), which may modify the element. The #process property is an array of function names to call.

```
/**
 * Implementation of hook_elements().
 */
function tinymce_elements() {
  $type = array();

  if (user_access('access tinymce')) {
    // Let TinyMCE potentially process each textarea.
    $type['textarea'] = array(
      '#process' => array('tinymce_process_textarea'),
    );
  }

  return $type;
}
```

The _element_info() hook collects all the default properties for all form elements and keeps them in a local cache. Any default properties that are not yet present in the form definition are added before continuing to the next step—looking for a validator for the form.

Looking for a Validation Function

A validation function for a form can be assigned by setting the #validate property in the form to an array with the function name as the value. Multiple validators may be defined in this way:

```
// We want foo_validate() and bar_validate() to be called during form validation.
$form['#validate'][] = 'foo_validate';
$form['#validate'][] = 'bar_validate';

// Optionally stash a value in the form that the validator will need
// by creating a unique key in the form.
$form['#value_for_foo_validate'] = 'baz';
```

If there is no property named #validate in the form, the next step is to look for a function with the name of the form ID plus _validate. So if the form ID is user_register, the form's #validate property will be set to user_register_validate.

Looking for a Submit Function

The function that handles form submission can be assigned by setting the #submit property in the form to an array with the name of the function that will handle form submission:

```
// Call my_special_submit_function() on form submission.
$form['#submit'][] = 'my_special_submit_function';
// Also call my_second_submit_function().
$form['#submit'][] = 'my_second_submit_function';
```

If there is no property named #submit, Drupal tests to see if a function named with the form ID plus _submit exists. So if the form ID is user_register, Drupal sets the #submit property to the form processor function it found; that is, user_register_submit.

Allowing Modules to Alter the Form Before It's Built

Before building the form, modules have two chances to alter the form. Modules can implement a function named from the form_id plus _alter, or they may simply implement hook_form_alter(). Any module that implements either of these can modify anything in the form. This is the primary way to change, override, and munge forms that are created by modules other than your own.

Building the Form

The form is now passed to form_builder(), which processes through the form tree recursively and adds standard required values. This function also checks the #access key for each element and denies access to form elements and their children if #access is FALSE for the element.

Allowing Functions to Alter the Form After It's Built

Each time `form_builder()` encounters a new branch in the $form tree (for example, a new fieldset or form element), it looks for a property called #after_build. This is an optional array of functions to be called once the current form element has been built. When the entire form has been built, a final call is made to the optional functions whose names may be defined in $form['#after_build']. All #after_build functions receive $form and $form_state as parameters. An example of its use in core is during the display of the file system path at Administer ➤ Site configuration ➤ File system. An #after_build function (in this case `system_check_directory()`) runs to determine if the directory does not exist or is not writable and sets an error against the form element if problems are encountered.

Checking If the Form Has Been Submitted

If you've been following along in Figure 10-1, you'll see that we have come to a branch point. If the form is being displayed for the first time, Drupal will go on to create the HTML for the form. If the form is being submitted, Drupal will go on to process the data that was entered in the form; we'll come back to that case in a moment (see the "Validating the Form" section later in the chapter). We'll assume for now the form is being displayed for the first time. It is important to realize that Drupal does all of the work described previously both when a form is being displayed for the first time *and* when a form is being submitted.

Finding a Theme Function for the Form

If $form['#theme'] has been set to an existing function, Drupal simply uses that function to theme the form. If not, the theme registry is checked for an entry that corresponds with the form ID of this form. If such an entry is found, the form ID is assigned to $form['#theme'], so later when Drupal renders the form, it will look for a theme function based on the form ID. For example, if the form ID is `taxonomy_overview_terms`, Drupal will call the corresponding theme function `theme_taxonomy_overview_terms()`. Of course, that theme function could be overridden by a theme function or template file in a custom theme; see Chapter 8 for details on how themable items are themed.

Allowing Modules to Modify the Form Before It's Rendered

The only thing left to do is to transform the form from a data structure to HTML. But just before that happens, modules have a last chance to tweak things. This can be useful for multi-page form wizards or other approaches that need to modify the form at the last minute. Any function defined in the $form['#pre_render'] property is called and passed the form being rendered.

Rendering the Form

To convert the form tree from a nested array to HTML code, the form builder calls `drupal_render()`. This recursive function goes through each level of the form tree, and with each, it performs the following actions:

1. Determine if the #children element has been defined (synonymous with content having been generated for this element); if not, render the children of this tree node as follows:

   • Determine if a #theme function has been defined for this element.

   • If so, temporarily set the #type of this element to markup. Next, pass this element to the theme function, and reset the element back to what it was.

   • If no content was generated (either because no #theme function was defined for this element or because the call to the #theme function was not found in the theme registry or returned nothing), each of the children of this element are rendered in turn (i.e., by passing the child element to drupal_render()).

   • On the other hand, if content *was* generated by the #theme function, store the content in the #children property of this element.

2. If the element itself has not yet been rendered, call the default theme function for the #type of this element. For example, if this element is a text field in a form (i.e., the #type property has been set to textfield in the form definition), the default theme function will be theme_textfield(). If the #type of this element has not been set, default to markup. Default theme functions for core elements such as text fields are found in includes/form.inc.

3. If content was generated for this element and one or more function names are found in the #post_render property, call each of them, and pass the content and the element. The #post_render function(s) must return the final content.

4. Prepend #prefix and append #suffix to the content, and return it from the function.

The effect of this recursive iteration is that HTML is generated for every level of the form tree. For example, in a form with a fieldset with two fields, the #children element of the fieldset will contain HTML for the fields inside it, and the #children element of the form will contain all of the HTML for the form (including the fieldset's HTML).

This generated HTML is then returned to the caller of drupal_get_form(). That's all it takes! We've reached the "Return HTML" endpoint in Figure 10-1.

Validating the Form

Now let's go back in Figure 10-1, to the place where we branched off in "Checking if the Form has been Submitted." Let's assume that the form has been submitted and contains some data; we'll take the other branch and look at that case. Drupal's form processing engine determines whether a form has been submitted is based on $_POST being nonempty and the presence of a string at $_POST['form_id'] that matches the ID of the form definition that was just built (see the "Setting an ID" section). When a match is found, Drupal validates the form.

The purpose of validation is to check that the values that are being submitted are reasonable. Validation will either pass or fail. If validation fails at any point, the form will be redisplayed with the validation errors shown to the user. If all validation passes, Drupal will move on to the actual processing of the submitted values.

Token Validation

The first check in validation is to determine whether this form uses Drupal's token mechanism (see the "Setting a Token" section). All Drupal forms that use tokens have a unique token that is sent out with the form and expected to be submitted along with other form values. If the token in the submitted data does not match the token that was set when the form was built, or if the token is absent, validation fails (though the rest of validation is still carried out so that other validation errors can also be flagged).

Built-in Validation

Next, required fields are checked to see if the user left them empty. Fields with a `#maxlength` property are checked to make sure the maximum number of characters has not been exceeded. Elements with options (check boxes, radio buttons, and drop-down selection fields) are examined to see if the selected value is actually in the original list of options present when the form was built.

Element-Specific Validation

If there is an `#element_validate` property defined for an individual form element, the functions defined in the property are called and passed the `$form_state` and `$element`.

Validation Callbacks

Finally, the form ID and form values are handed over to the validator function(s) specified for the form (usually the name of the form ID plus `_validate`).

Submitting the Form

If validation passes, it's time to pass the form and its values to a function that will finally do something as a result of the form's submission. Actually, more than one function could process the form, since the `#submit` property can contain an array of function names. Each function is called and passed `$form` and `$form_state`.

Redirecting the User

The function that processes the form should set `$form_state['redirect']` to a Drupal path to which the user will be redirected, such as `node/1234`. If there are multiple functions in the `#submit` property, the last function to set `$form_state['redirect']` will win. If no function sets `$form_state['redirect']` to a Drupal path, the user is returned to the same page (that is, the value of `$_GET['q']`). Returning `FALSE` from the final submit function avoids redirection.

The redirect set in `$form_state['redirect']` by a submit function can be overridden by defining a `#redirect` property in the form, such as

```
$form['#redirect'] = 'node/1'
```

or

```
$form['#redirect'] = array('node/1', $query_string, $named_anchor)
```

Using the parameter terms used in drupal_goto(), the last example could be written as

```
$form['#redirect'] = array('node/1', $query, $fragment)
```

Determination of form redirection is carried out by drupal_redirect_form() in includes/form.inc. The actual redirection is carried out by drupal_goto(), which returns a Location header to the web server. The parameters that drupal_goto() takes correspond to the members of the array in the latter example: drupal_goto($path = '', $query = NULL, $fragment = NULL).

Creating Basic Forms

If you come from a background where you have created your own forms directly in HTML, you may find Drupal's approach a bit baffling at first. The examples in this section are intended to get you started quickly with your own forms. To begin, we'll write a simple module that asks you for your name and prints it on the screen. We'll put it in our own module, so we don't have to modify any existing code. Our form will have only two elements: the text input field and a submit button. We'll start by creating a .info file at sites/all/modules/custom/formexample/formexample.info and entering the following:

```
; $Id$
name = Form example
description = Shows how to build a Drupal form.
package = Pro Drupal Development
core = 6.x
```

Next, we'll put the actual module into sites/all/modules/custom/formexample/formexample.module:

```php
<?php
// $Id$

/**
 * @file
 * Play with the Form API.
 */

/**
 * Implementation of hook_menu().
 */
function formexample_menu() {
  $items['formexample'] = array(
    'title' => 'View the form',
    'page callback' => 'formexample_page',
    'access arguments' => array('access content'),
  );
  return $items;
}
```

```
/**
 * Menu callback.
 * Called when user goes to http://example.com/?q=formexample
 */
function formexample_page() {
  $output = t('This page contains our example form.');

  // Return the HTML generated from the $form data structure.
  $output .= drupal_get_form('formexample_nameform');
  return $output;
}

/**
 * Define a form.
 */
function formexample_nameform() {
  $form['user_name'] = array(
    '#title' => t('Your Name'),
    '#type' => 'textfield',
    '#description' => t('Please enter your name.'),
  );
  $form['submit'] = array(
    '#type' => 'submit',
    '#value' => t('Submit')
  );
  return $form;
}

/**
 * Validate the form.
 */
function formexample_nameform_validate($form, &$form_state) {
  if ($form_state['values']['user_name'] == 'King Kong') {
    // We notify the form API that this field has failed validation.
    form_set_error('user_name',
      t('King Kong is not allowed to use this form.'));
  }
}

/**
 * Handle post-validation form submission.
 */
function formexample_nameform_submit($form, &$form_state) {
  $name = $form_state['values']['user_name'];
  drupal_set_message(t('Thanks for filling out the form, %name',
    array('%name' => $name)));
}
```

We've implemented the basic functions you need to handle forms: one function to define the form, one to validate it, and one to handle form submission. Additionally, we implemented a menu hook and a function so that a URL could be associated with our function. Our simple form should look like the one shown in Figure 10-2.

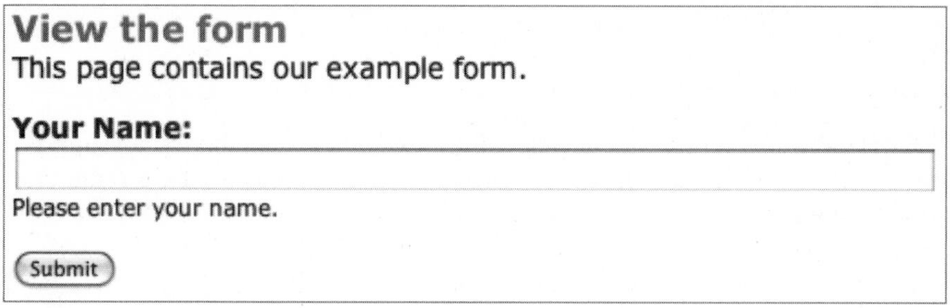

View the form
This page contains our example form.

Your Name:

Please enter your name.

(Submit)

Figure 10-2. *A basic form for text input with a submit button*

The bulk of the work goes into populating the form's data structure, that is, describing the form to Drupal. This information is contained in a nested array that describes the elements and properties of the form and is typically contained in a variable called $form.

The important task of defining a form happens in formexample_nameform() in the preceding example, where we're providing the minimum amount of information needed for Drupal to display the form.

■**Note** What is the difference between a property and an element? The basic difference is that properties cannot have properties, while elements can. An example of an element is the submit button. An example of a property is the #type property of the submit button element. You can always recognize properties, because they are prefixed with the # character. We sometimes call properties keys, because they have a value, and to get to the value, you have to know the name of the key. A common beginner's mistake is to forget the # before a property name. Drupal, and you, will be very confused if you do this. If you see the error "Cannot use string offset as an array in form.inc" you probably forgot the leading # character.

Form Properties

Some properties can be used anywhere, and some can be used only in a given context, like within a button. For a complete list of properties, see the end of this chapter. Here's a more complex version of a form than that given in our previous example:

```
$form['#method'] = 'post';
$form['#action'] = 'http://example.com/?q=foo/bar';
$form['#attributes'] = array(
  'enctype' => 'multipart/form-data',
  'target' => 'name_of_target_frame'
);
$form['#prefix'] = '<div class="my-form-class">';
$form['#suffix'] = '</div>';
```

The #method property defaults to post and can be omitted. The get method is not supported by the forms API and is not usually used in Drupal, because it's easy to use the automatic parsing of arguments from the path by the menu routing mechanism. The #action property is defined in system_elements() and defaults to the result of the function request_uri(). This is typically the same URL that displayed the form.

Form IDs

Drupal needs to have some way of uniquely identifying forms, so it can determine which form is submitted when there are multiple forms on a page and can associate forms with the functions that should process that particular form. To uniquely identify a form, we assign each form a form ID. The ID is defined in the call to drupal_get_form(), like this:

```
drupal_get_form('mymodulename_identifier');
```

For most forms, the ID is created by the convention "module name" plus an identifier describing what the form does. For example, the user login form is created by the user module and has the ID user_login.

Drupal uses the form ID to determine the names of the default validation, submission, and theme functions for the form. Additionally, Drupal uses the form ID as a basis for generating an HTML ID attribute in the <form> tag for that specific form, so forms in Drupal always have a unique ID. You can override the ID by setting the #id property:

```
$form['#id'] = 'my-special-css-identifier';
```

The resulting HTML tag will look something like this:

```
<form action="/path" "accept-charset="UTF-8" method="post"
  id="my-special-css-identifier">
```

The form ID is also embedded into the form as a hidden field named form_id. In our example, we chose formexample_nameform as the form ID because it describes our form. That is, the purpose of our form is for the user to enter his or her name. We could have just used formexample_form, but that's not very descriptive—and later we might want to add another form to our module.

Fieldsets

Often, you want to split your form up into different fieldsets—the form API makes this easy. Each fieldset is defined in the data structure and has fields defined as children. Let's add a favorite color field to our example:

```
function formexample_nameform() {
  $form['name'] = array(
    '#title' => t('Your Name'),
    '#type' => 'fieldset',
    '#description' => t('What people call you.')
  );
  $form['name']['user_name'] = array(
    '#title' => t('Your Name'),
    '#type' => 'textfield',
    '#description' => t('Please enter your name.')
  );
  $form['color'] = array(
    '#title' => t('Color'),
    '#type' => 'fieldset',
    '#description' => t('This fieldset contains the Color field.'),
    '#collapsible' => TRUE,
    '#collapsed' => FALSE
  );
  $form['color_options'] = array(
    '#type' => 'value',
    '#value' => array(t('red'), t('green'), t('blue'))
  );
  $form['color']['favorite_color'] = array(
    '#title' => t('Favorite Color'),
    '#type' => 'select',
    '#description' => t('Please select your favorite color.'),
    '#options' => $form['color_options']['#value']
  );
  $form['submit'] = array(
    '#type' => 'submit',
    '#value' => t('Submit')
  );
  return $form;
}
```

The resulting form looks like the one shown in Figure 10-3.

View the form

This page contains our example form.

┌─Your Name───┐
│ What people call you.   │
│   │
│ **Your Name:**   │
│ ┌───┐ │
│ │   │ │
│ └───┘ │
│ Please enter your name.   │
│   │
└───┘

┌─ ▾ Color──┐
│ This fieldset contains the Color field.   │
│   │
│ **Favorite Color:**   │
│ ┌──────────┐   │
│ │ red   ▲▼│   │
│ └──────────┘   │
│ Please select your favorite color.   │
│   │
└───┘

(Submit)

Figure 10-3. *A simple form with fieldsets*

We used the optional #collapsible and #collapsed properties to tell Drupal to make the second fieldset collapsible using JavaScript by clicking on the fieldset title.

Here's a question for thought: when $form_state['values'] gets passed to the validate and submit functions, will the color field be $form_state['values']['color'] ['favorite_color'] or $form_state['values']['favorite_color']? In other words, will the value be nested inside the fieldset or not? The answer: it depends. By default, the form processor flattens the form values, so that the following function would work correctly:

```
function formexample_nameform_submit($form_id, $form_state) {
  $name =      $form_state['values']['user_name'];
  $color_key = $form_state['values']['favorite_color'];
  $color =     $form_state['values']['color_options'][$color_key];

  drupal_set_message(t('%name loves the color %color!',
    array('%name' => $name, '%color' => $color)));
}
```

The message set by the updated submit handler can be seen in Figure 10-4.

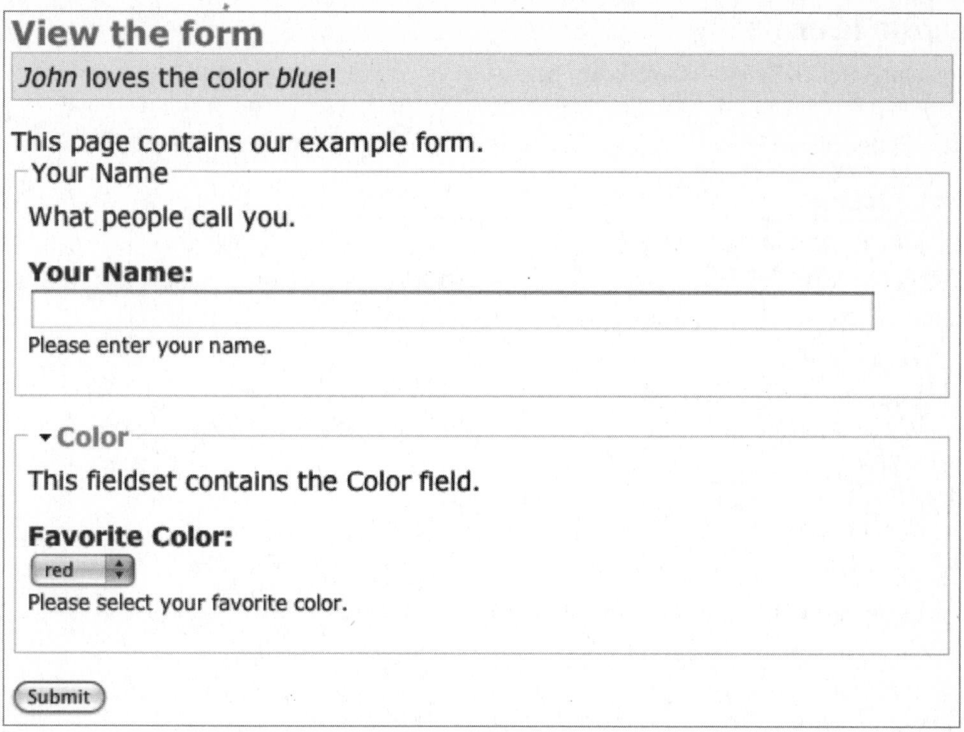

View the form

John loves the color *blue*!

This page contains our example form.

┌─ Your Name ───┐
│   │
│ What people call you.   │
│   │
│ **Your Name:**   │
│ ┌───┐ │
│ │   │ │
│ └───┘ │
│ Please enter your name.   │
│   │
└───┘

┌─ ▼ Color ───┐
│   │
│ This fieldset contains the Color field.   │
│   │
│ **Favorite Color:**   │
│ [red   ▲▼]   │
│ Please select your favorite color.   │
│   │
└───┘

(Submit)

Figure 10-4. *Message from the submit handler for the form*

If, however, the #tree property is set to TRUE, the data structure of the form will be reflected in the names of the form values. So, if in our form declaration we had said

```
$form['#tree'] = TRUE;
```

then we would access the data in the following way:

```
function formexample_nameform_submit($form, $form_state) {
  $name =      $form_state['values']['name']['user_name'];
  $color_key = $form_state['values']['color']['favorite_color'];
  $color =     $form_state['values']['color_options'][$color_key];
  drupal_set_message(t('%name loves the color %color!',
    array('%name' => $name, '%color' => $color)));
}
```

■Tip Setting #tree to TRUE gives you a nested array of fields with their values. When #tree is set to FALSE (the default), you get a flattened representation of fieldnames and values.

Theming Forms

Drupal has built-in functions to take the form data structure that you define and transform, or *render*, it into HTML. However, often you may need to change the output that Drupal generates, or you may need fine-grained control over the process. Fortunately, Drupal makes this easy.

Using #prefix, #suffix, and #markup

If your theming needs are very simple, you can get by with using the #prefix and #suffix attributes to add HTML before and/or after form elements:

```
$form['color'] = array(
  '#prefix' => '<hr />',
  '#title' => t('Color'),
  '#type' => 'fieldset',
  '#suffix' => '<div class="privacy-warning">' .
    t('This information will be displayed publicly!') . '</div>',
);
```

This code would add a horizontal rule above the Color fieldset and a privacy message below it, as shown in Figure 10-5.

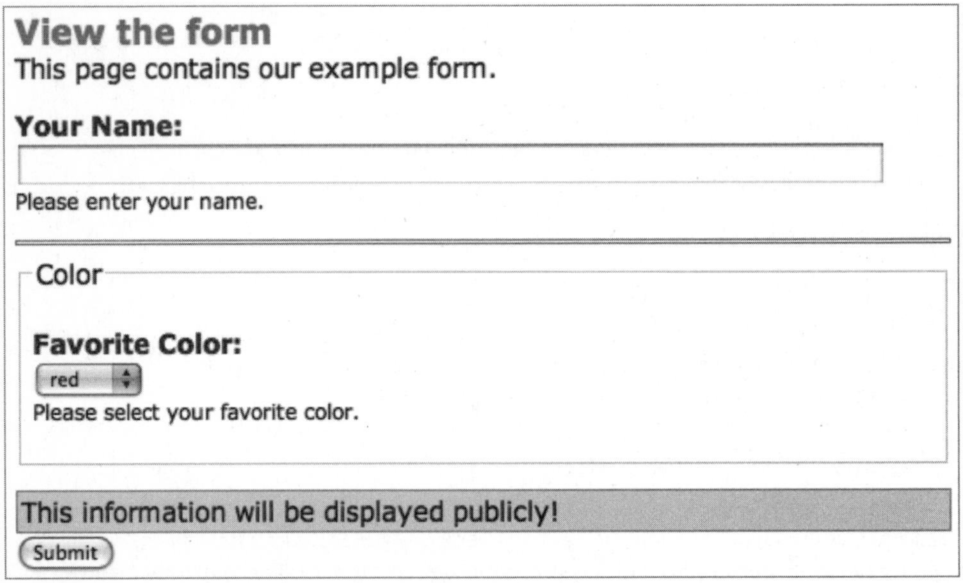

Figure 10-5. *The #prefix and #suffix properties add content before and after an element.*

You can even declare HTML markup as type #markup in your form (though this is not widely used). Any form element without a #type property defaults to markup.

```
$form['blinky'] = array(
  '#type' = 'markup',
  '#value' = '<blink>Hello!</blink>'
);
```

■**Note** This method of introducing HTML markup into your forms is generally considered to be as good an idea as using the `<blink>` tag. It is not as clean as writing a theme function and usually makes it more difficult for designers to work with your site.

Using a Theme Function

The most flexible way to theme forms is to use a theme function specifically for that form or form element. There are two steps involved. First, Drupal needs to be informed of which theme functions our module will be implementing. This is done through hook_theme() (see Chapter 8 for details). Here's a quick implementation of hook_theme() for our module, which basically says "Our module provides two theme functions and they can be called with no extra arguments":

```
/**
 * Implementation of hook_theme().
 */
function formexample_theme() {
  return array(
    'formexample_nameform' => array(
      'arguments' => array(),
    ),
    'formexample_alternate_nameform' => array(
      'arguments' => array(),
    )
  );
}
```

By default, Drupal looks for a function named theme_ plus the name of your form ID. In our example, Drupal would look for a theme_formexample_nameform entry in the theme registry and would find ours because we defined it in formexample_theme(). The following theme function would be called and would render the exact same output as Drupal's default theming:

```
function theme_formexample_nameform($form) {
  $output = drupal_render($form);
  return $output;
}
```

The benefits to having our own theme function are that we're able to parse, munge, and add to $output as we please. We could quickly make a certain element appear first in the form, as in the following code, where we put the color fieldset at the top:

```
function theme_formexample_nameform($form) {
  // Always put the the color selection at the top.
  $output = drupal_render($form['color']);

  // Then add the rest of the form.
  $output .= drupal_render($form);

  return $output;
}
```

Telling Drupal Which Theme Function to Use

You can direct Drupal to use a function that does not match the formula "theme_ plus form ID name" by specifying a #theme property for a form:

```
// Now our form will be themed by the function
// theme_formexample_alternate_nameform().
$form['#theme'] = 'formexample_alternate_nameform';
```

Or you can tell Drupal to use a special theme function for just one element of a form:

```
// Theme this fieldset element with theme_formexample_coloredfieldset().
$form['color'] = array(
  '#title' => t('Color'),
  '#type' => 'fieldset',
  '#theme' => 'formexample_coloredfieldset'
);
```

Note that, in both cases, the function you are defining in the #theme property must be known by the theme registry; that is, it must be declared in a hook_theme() implementation somewhere.

■Note Drupal will prefix the string you give for #theme with theme_, so we set #theme to formexample_coloredfieldset and not theme_formexample_coloredfieldset, even though the name of the theme function that will be called is the latter. See Chapter 8 to learn why this is so.

Specifying Validation and Submission Functions with hook_forms()

Sometimes, you have a special case where you want to have many different forms but only a single validation or submit function. This is called *code reuse*, and it's a good idea in that kind of a situation. The node module, for example, runs all kinds of node types through its validation and submission functions. So we need a way to map multiple form IDs to validation and submission functions. Enter hook_forms().

When Drupal is retrieving the form, it first looks for a function that defines the form based on the form ID (in our code, we used the formexample_nameform() function for this purpose). If it doesn't find that function, it invokes hook_forms(), which queries all modules for a mapping of form IDs to callbacks. For example, node.module uses the following code to map all different kinds of node form IDs to one handler:

```
/**
 * Implementation of hook_forms(). All node forms share the same form handler.
 */
function node_forms() {
  $forms = array();
  if ($types = node_get_types()) {
    foreach (array_keys($types) as $type) {
      $forms[$type .'_node_form']['callback'] = 'node_form';
    }
  }
  return $forms;
}
```

In our form example, we could implement hook_forms() to map another form ID to our existing code.

```
/**
 * Implementation of hook_forms().
 */
function formexample_forms($form_id, $args) {
  $forms['formexample_special'] = array(
    'callback' => 'formexample_nameform');
  return $forms;
}
```

Now, if we call drupal_get_form('formexample_special'), Drupal will first check for a function named formexample_special() that defines the form. If it cannot find this function, hook_forms() will be called, and Drupal will see that we have mapped the form ID formexample_special to formexample_nameform. Drupal will call formexample_nameform() to get the form definition, then attempt to call formexample_special_validate() and formexample_special_submit() for validation and submission, respectively.

Call Order of Theme, Validation, and Submission Functions

As you've seen, there are several places to give Drupal information about where your theme, validation, and submission functions are. Having so many options can be confusing, so here's a summary of where Drupal looks, in order, for a theme function, assuming you are using a PHPTemplate-based theme named `bluemarine`, and you're calling `drupal_get_form('formexample_nameform')`. This is, however, dependent upon your `hook_theme()` implementation.

First, if `$form['#theme']` has been set to `'foo'` in the form definition:

```
1. themes/bluemarine/foo.tpl.php // Template file provided by theme.
2. formexample/foo.tpl.php // Template file provided by module.
3. bluemarine_foo() // Function provided theme.
4. phptemplate_foo() // Theme function provided by theme engine.
5. theme_foo() // 'theme_' plus the value of $form['#theme'].
```

However, if `$form['#theme']` has not been set in the form definition:

```
1. themes/bluemarine/formexample-nameform.tpl.php // Template provided by theme.
2. formexample/formexample-nameform.tpl.php // Template file provided by module.
3. bluemarine_formexample_nameform() // Theme function provided by theme.
4. phptemplate_formexample_nameform() // Theme function provided by theme engine.
5. theme_formexample_nameform() // 'theme_' plus the form ID.
```

During form validation, a validator for the form is set in this order:

```
1. A function defined by $form['#validate']
2. formexample_nameform_validate // Form ID plus 'validate'.
```

And when it's time to look for a function to handle form submittal, Drupal looks for the following:

```
1. A function defined by $form['#submit']
2. formexample_nameform_submit // Form ID plus 'submit'.
```

Remember that forms can have multiple validation and submission functions.

Writing a Validation Function

Drupal has a built-in mechanism for highlighting form elements that fail validation and displaying an error message to the user. Examine the validation function in our example to see it at work:

```
/**
 * Validate the form.
 */
function formexample_nameform_validate($form, $form_state) {
  if ($form_state['values']['user_name'] == 'King Kong') {
    // We notify the form API that this field has failed validation.
```

```
    form_set_error('user_name',
      t('King Kong is not allowed to use this form.'));
  }
}
```

Note the use of form_set_error(). When King Kong visits our form and types in his name on his giant gorilla keyboard, he sees an error message at the top of the page and the field that contains the error has its contents highlighted in red, as shown in Figure 10-6.

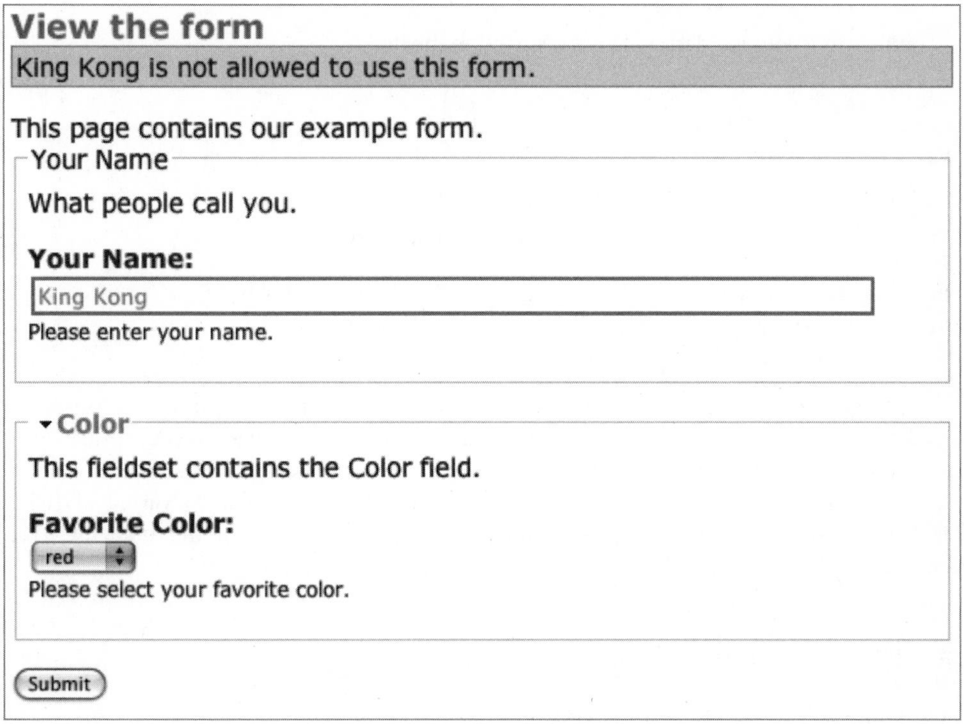

Figure 10-6. *Validation failures are indicated to the user.*

Perhaps he should have used his given name, Kong, instead. Anyway, the point is that form_set_error() files an error against our form and will cause validation to fail.

Validation functions should do just that—validate. They should not, as a general rule, change data. However, they may add information to the $form_state array, as shown in the next section.

Passing Data Along from Validation Functions

If your validation function does a lot of processing and you want to store the result to be used in your submit function, you have two different options. You could use form_set_value() or use $form_state.

Using form_set_value() to Pass Data

The most formal option is to create a form element to stash the data when you create your form in your form definition function, and then use form_set_value() to store the data. First, you create a placeholder form element:

```
$form['my_placeholder'] = array(
  '#type' => 'value',
  '#value' => array()
);
```

Then, during your validation routine, you store the data:

```
// Lots of work here to generate $my_data as part of validation.
...
// Now save our work.
form_set_value($form['my_placeholder'], $my_data, $form_state);
```

And you can then access the data in your submit function:

```
// Instead of repeating the work we did in the validation function,
// we can just use the data that we stored.
$my_data = $form_values['my_placeholder'];
```

Or suppose you need to transform data to a standard representation. For example, you have a list of country codes in the database that you will validate against, but your unreasonable boss insists that users be able to type in their country names in text fields. You would need to create a placeholder in your form and validate the user's input using a variety of trickery so you can recognize both "The Netherlands" and "Nederland" as mapping to the ISO 3166 country code "NL."

```
$form['country'] = array(
  '#title' => t('Country'),
  '#type' => 'textfield',
  '#description' => t('Enter your country.')
);
```

```
// Create a placeholder. Will be filled in during validation.
$form['country_code'] = array(
  '#type' => 'value',
  '#value' => ''
);
```

Inside the validation function, you'd save the country code inside the placeholder.

```
// Find out if we have a match.
$country_code = formexample_find_country_code($form_state['values']['country']);
if ($country_code) {
  // Found one. Save it so that the submit handler can see it.
  form_set_value($form['country_code'], $country_code, $form_state);
}
```

```
else {
  form_set_error('country', t('Your country was not recognized. Please use
    a standard name or country code.'));
}
```

Now, the submit handler can access the country code in $form_values['country_code'].

Using $form_state to Pass Data

A simpler approach is to use $form_state to store the value. Since $form_state is passed to both validation and submission functions by reference, validation functions can store data there for submission functions to see. It is a good idea to use your module's namespace within $form_state instead of just making up a key.

```
// Lots of work here to generate $weather_data from slow web service
// as part of validation.
...
// Now save our work in $form_state.
$form_state['mymodulename']['weather'] = $weather_data
```

And you can then access the data in your submit function:

```
// Instead of repeating the work we did in the validation function,
// we can just use the data that we stored.
$weather_data = $form_state['mymodulename']['weather'];
```

You may be asking, "Why not store the value in $form_state['values'] along with the rest of the form field values?" That will work too, but keep in mind that $form_state['values'] is the place for form field values, not random data stored by modules. Remember that because Drupal allows any module to attach validation and submission functions to any form, you cannot make the assumption that your module will be the only one working with the form state, and thus data should be stored in a consistent and predictable way.

Element-Specific Validation

Typically, one validation function is used for a form. But it is possible to set validators for individual form elements as well as for the entire form. To do that, set the #element_validate property for the element to an array containing the names of the validation functions. A full copy of the element's branch of the form data structure will be sent as the first parameter. Here's a contrived example where we force the user to enter **spicy** or **sweet** into a text field:

```
// Store the allowed choices in the form definition.
$allowed_flavors = array(t('spicy'), t('sweet'));
$form['flavor'] = array(
  '#type' => 'textfield',
  '#title' => 'flavor',
  '#allowed_flavors' => $allowed_flavors,
  '#element_validate' => array('formexample_flavor_validate')
);
```

Then your element validation function would look like this:

```
function formexample_flavor_validate($element, $form_state) {
  if (!in_array($form_state['values']['flavor'], $element['#allowed_flavors'])) {
    form_error($element, t('You must enter spicy or sweet.'));
  }
}
```

The validation function for the form will still be called after all element validation functions have been called.

Tip Use `form_set_error()` when you have the name of the form element you wish to file an error against and `form_error()` when you have the element itself. The latter is simply a wrapper for the former.

Form Rebuilding

During validation, you may decide that you do not have enough information from the user. For example, you might run the form values through a textual analysis engine and determine that there is a high probability that this content is spam. As a result, you want to display the form again (complete with the values the user entered) but add a CAPTCHA to disprove your suspicion that this user is a robot. You can signal to Drupal that a rebuild is needed by setting `$form_state['rebuild']` inside your validation function, like so:

```
$spam_score = spamservice($form_state['values']['my_textarea']);
if ($spam_score > 70) {
  $form_state['rebuild'] = TRUE;
  $form_state['formexample']['spam_score'] = $spam_score;
}
```

In your form definition function, you would have something like this:

```
function formexample_nameform($form_state) {
  // Normal form definition happens.
  ...
  if (isset($form_state['formexample']['spam_score'])) {
    // If this is set, we are rebuilding the form;
    // add the captcha form element to the form.
    ...
  }
  ...
}
```

Writing a Submit Function

The submit function is the function that takes care of actual form processing after the form has been validated. It only executes if form validation passed completely and the form has not been flagged for rebuilding. The submit function is expected to modify $form_state ['redirect'].

If you want the user to continue to a different page when the form has been submitted, return the Drupal path that you want the user to land on next:

```
function formexample_form_submit($form, &$form_state) {
  // Do some stuff.
  ...
  // Now send user to node number 3.
  $form_state['redirect'] = 'node/3';
}
```

If you have multiple functions handling form submittal (see the "Submitting the Form" section earlier in this chapter), the last function to set $form_state['redirect'] will have the last word. The redirection of the submit function can be overridden by defining a #redirect property in the form (see the "Redirecting the User" section earlier in this chapter). This is often done by using hook_form_alter().

Tip The $form_state['rebuild'] flag can be set in submit functions too, just like in validation functions. If set, all submit functions will run but any redirect value will be ignored and the form will be rebuilt using the submitted values. This can be useful for adding optional fields to a form.

Changing Forms with hook_form_alter()

Using hook_form_alter(), you can change any form. All you need to know is the form's ID. There are two approaches to altering forms.

Altering Any Form

Let's change the login form that is shown on the user login block and the user login page.

```
function formexample_form_alter(&$form, &$form_state, $form_id) {
  // This code gets called for every form Drupal builds; use an if statement
  // to respond only to the user login block and user login forms.
  if ($form_id == 'user_login_block' || $form_id == 'user_login') {
    // Add a dire warning to the top of the login form.
    $form['warning'] = array(
      '#value' => t('We log all login attempts!'),
      '#weight' => -5
      );
```

```
    // Change 'Log in' to 'Sign in'.
    $form['submit']['#value'] = t('Sign in');
  }
}
```

Since $form is passed by reference, we have complete access to the form definition here and can make any changes we want. In the example, we added some text using the default form element (see "Markup" later in this chapter) and then reached in and changed the value of the Submit button.

Altering a Specific Form

The previous approach works, but if lots of modules are altering forms and every form is passed to every hook_form_alter() implementation, alarm bells may be going off in your head. "This is wasteful," you're probably thinking. "Why not just construct a function from the form ID and call that?" You are on the right track. Drupal does exactly that. So the following function will change the user login form too:

```
function formexample_form_user_login_alter(&$form, &$form_state) {
  $form['warning'] = array(
     '#value' => t('We log all login attempts!'),
     '#weight' => -5
  );

  // Change 'Log in' to 'Sign in'.
  $form['submit']['#value'] = t('Sign in');
}
```

The function name is constructed from this:

```
modulename + 'form' + form ID + 'alter'
```

For example

```
'formexample' + 'form' + 'user_login' + 'alter'
```

results in

```
formexample_form_user_login_alter
```

In this particular case, the first form of hook_form_alter() is preferred, because two form IDs are involved (user_login for the form at http://example.com/?q=user and user_login_block for the form that appears in the user block).

Submitting Forms Programmatically with drupal_execute()

Any form that is displayed in a web browser can also be filled out programmatically. Let's fill out our name and favorite color programmatically:

```
$form_id = 'formexample_nameform';
$form_state['values'] = array(
  'user_name' => t('Marvin'),
  'favorite_color' => t('green')
);
// Submit the form using these values.
drupal_execute($form_id, $form_state);
```

That's all there is to it! Simply supply the form ID and the values for the form, and call drupal_execute().

■**Caution** Many submit functions assume that the user making the request is the user submitting the form. When submitting forms programmatically, you will need to be very aware of this, as the users are not necessarily the same.

Multipage Forms

We've been looking at simple one-page forms. But you may need to have users fill out a form that spans several pages or has several different steps for data entry. Let's build a short module that demonstrates the multipage form technique by collecting three ingredients from the user in three separate steps. Our approach will be to pass values forward in Drupal's built-in form storage bin. We'll call the module formwizard.module. Of course, we'll need a sites/all/modules/custom/formwizard.info file:

```
; $Id$
name = Form Wizard Example
description = An example of a multistep form.
package = Pro Drupal Development
core = 6.x
```

Next, we'll write the actual module. The module will display two pages: one page on which data is entered (which we'll use repeatedly) and a final page on which we'll display what the user entered and thank them for their input. Here is sites/all/modules/custom/formwizard.module:

```php
<?php
// $Id$

/**
 * @file
 * Example of a multistep form.
 */
```

```php
/**
 * Implementation of hook_menu().
 */
function formwizard_menu() {
  $items['formwizard'] = array(
    'title' => t('Form Wizard'),
    'page callback' => 'drupal_get_form',
    'page arguments' => array('formwizard_multiform'),
    'type' => MENU_NORMAL_ITEM,
    'access arguments' => array('access content'),
  );
  $items['formwizard/thanks'] = array(
    'title' => t('Thanks!'),
    'page callback' => 'formwizard_thanks',
    'type' => MENU_CALLBACK,
    'access arguments' => array('access_content'),
  );

  return $items;
}

/**
 * Form definition. We build the form differently depending on
 * which step we're on.
 */
function formwizard_multiform(&$form_state) {
  // Find out which step we are on. If $form_state is not set,
  // that means we are beginning. Since the form is rebuilt, we
  // start at 0 in that case and the step is 1 during rebuild.
  $step = isset($form_state['values']) ? (int)$form_state['storage']['step'] : 0;

  // Store next step.
  $form_state['storage']['step'] = $step + 1;

  // Customize the fieldset title to indicate the current step to the user.
  $form['indicator'] = array(
    '#type' => 'fieldset',
    '#title' => t('Step @number', array('@number' => $step))
  );

  // The name of our ingredient form element is unique for
  // each step, e.g. ingredient_1, ingredient_2...
  $form['indicator']['ingredient_' . $step] = array(
    '#type' => 'textfield',
    '#title' => t('Ingredient'),
    '#description' => t('Enter ingredient @number of 3.', array('@number' => $step))
  );
```

```
  // The button will say Next until the last step, when it will say Submit.
  $button_name = t('Submit');
  if ($step < 3) {
    $button_name = t('Next');
  }
  $form['submit'] = array(
    '#type' => 'submit',
    '#value' => $button_name
  );

  switch($step) {
    case 2:
      // Save ingredient in storage bin.
      $form_state['storage']['ingredient_1'] =
        $form_state['values']['ingredient_1'];
      break;
    case 3:
      // Add ingredient to storage bin.
      $form_state['storage']['ingredient_2'] =
        $form_state['values']['ingredient_2'];
  }

  return $form;
}

/**
 * Validate handler for form ID 'formwizard_multiform'.
 */
function formwizard_multiform_validate($form, &$form_state) {
  // Show user which step we are on.
  drupal_set_message(t('Validation called for step @step',
    array('@step' => $form_state['storage']['step'] - 1)));
}

/**
 * Submit handler for form ID 'formwizard_multiform'.
 */
function formwizard_multiform_submit($form, &$form_state) {
  if ($form_state['storage']['step'] < 4) {
    return;
  }
```

```
drupal_set_message(t('Your three ingredients were %ingredient_1, %ingredient_2,
  and %ingredient_3.', array(
    '%ingredient_1' => $form_state['storage']['ingredient_1'],
    '%ingredient_2' => $form_state['storage']['ingredient_2'],
    '%ingredient_3' => $form_state['values']['ingredient_3']
    )
  )
);
// Clear storage bin to avoid automatic form rebuild that overrides our redirect.
unset($form_state['storage']);

// Redirect to a thank-you page.
$form_state['redirect'] = 'formwizard/thanks';
}

function formwizard_thanks() {
  return t('Thanks, and have a nice day.');
}
```

There are a few things to notice about this simple module. In our form building function, `formwizard_multiform()`, we have one parameter, `$form_state`, which gives information about the state of the form. Let's walk through the process. If we go to `http://example.com/?q=formwizard`, we get the initial form, as shown in Figure 10-7.

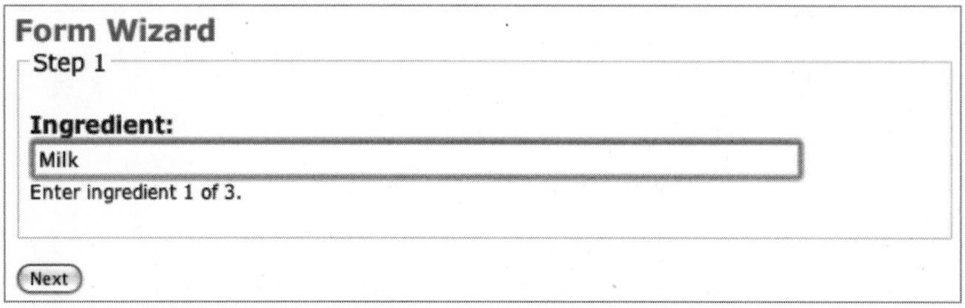

Figure 10-7. *The initial step of the multistep form*

When we click the Next button, Drupal will process this form just like any other form: the form will be built; the validate function will be called, and the submit function will be called. But if we are not on the final step of the form, the submit function will simply return. Drupal will notice that there are values in the storage bin at `$form_state['storage']`, so it calls the form building function again, this time with a copy of `$form_state`. (We could also have set `$form_state['rebuild']` to cause the rebuild to happen, but that is not necessary when `$form_state['storage']` is populated.) Calling the form building function again and passing `$form_state` allows `formwizard_multiform()` in our module to look at `$form_state['storage']['step']` to determine which step we are on and build the form accordingly. We end up with the form shown in Figure 10-8.

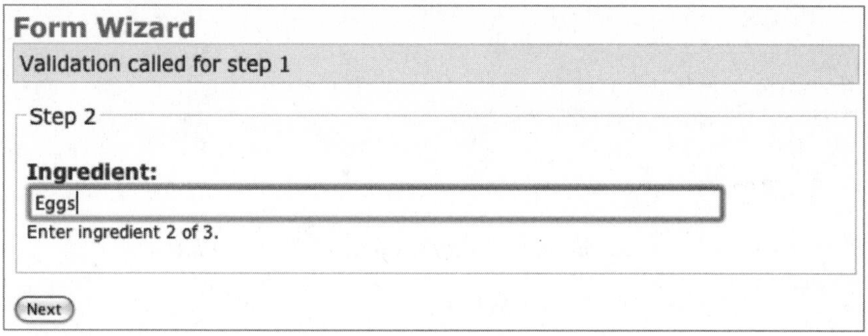

Figure 10-8. *The second step of the multistep form*

We have evidence that our validation function ran, because it has placed a message on the screen by calling drupal_set_message(). And our fieldset title and text field descriptions have been properly set, indicating that the user is on step 2. We'll fill in the last ingredient, as shown in Figure 10-9.

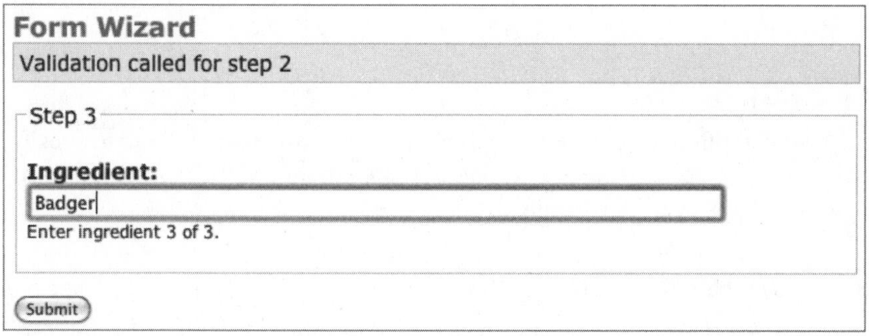

Figure 10-9. *The last step of the multistep form*

Notice that, on the third step, we changed the button to read Submit instead of Next. Also, the submit handler can send the user to a new page when processing is finished. Now, when we press the Submit button, our submit handler will recognize that this is step four and instead of bailing out, as previously, it will process the data. In this example, we just call drupal_set_message(), which will display information on the next page Drupal serves and redirect the user to formwizard/thankyou. The result is shown in Figure 10-10.

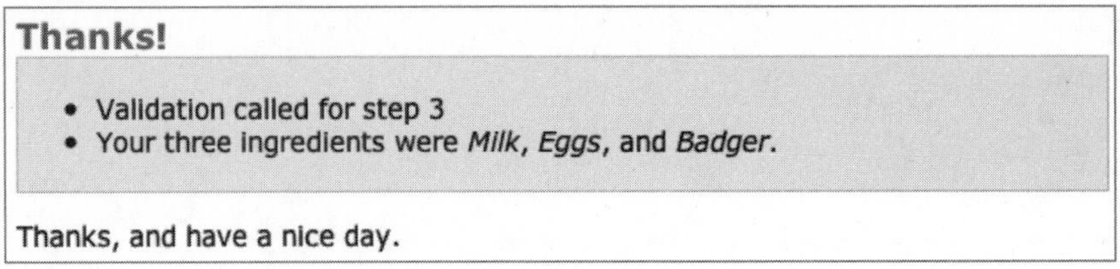

> **Thanks!**
>
> - Validation called for step 3
> - Your three ingredients were *Milk*, *Eggs*, and *Badger*.
>
> Thanks, and have a nice day.

Figure 10-10. *The submit handler for the multistep form has run, and the user has been redirected to formwizard/thankyou.*

The preceding example is intended to give you the basic outline of how multistep forms work. Instead of using the storage bin in $form_state, your module could store data in hidden fields and pass them along to the next step, or you could modify your submit handler to store it in the database or in the $_SESSION superglobal using the form ID as a key. The important part to understand is that the form building function continues to be called because $form_state['storage'] is populated and that, by using the preceding approach to increment $form_state['storage']['step'], validation and submission functions can make intelligent decisions about what to do.

Form API Properties

When building a form definition in your form building function, array keys are used to specify information about the form. The most common keys are listed in the following sections. Some keys are added automatically by the form builder.

Properties for the Root of the Form

The properties in the following sections are specific to the form root. In other words, you can set $form['#programmed'] = TRUE, but setting $form['myfieldset']['mytextfield'] [#programmed'] = TRUE will not make sense to the form builder.

#parameters

This property is an array of original arguments that were passed in to drupal_get_form(). It is added by drupal_retrieve_form().

#programmed

This Boolean property indicates that a form is being submitted programmatically, for example, by drupal_execute(). Its value is set by drupal_prepare_form() if #post has been set prior to form processing.

#build_id

This property is a string (an MD5 hash). The #build_id identifies a specific instance of a form. Sent along as a hidden field, this form element is set by drupal_prepare_form(), as shown in the following snippet:

```
$form['form_build_id'] = array(
    '#type' => 'hidden',
    '#value' => $form['#build_id'],
    '#id' => $form['#build_id'],
    '#name' => 'form_build_id',
);
```

#token

This string (MD5 hash) is a unique token that is sent out with every form, so Drupal can determine that the form is actually a Drupal form and not being sent by a malicious user.

#id

This property is a string that is the result of form_clean_id($form_id), and it is an HTML ID attribute. Any reversed bracket pair (][), underscore (_), or space(' ') characters in the $form_id are replaced by hyphens to create consistent IDs for CSS usage. Drupal will enforce the requirement that IDs be unique on a page. If the same ID is encountered twice (for example, the same form twice on a page), a hyphen and an incremented integer will be appended, for example, foo-form, foo-form-1, and foo-form-2.

#action

This string property is the action attribute for the HTML form tag. By default, it is the return value of request_uri().

#method

This string property is the form submission method—normally post. The form API is built around the POST method and will not process forms using the GET method. See the HTML specifications regarding the difference between GET and POST. If you are in a situation where you are trying to use GET, you probably need Drupal's menu API, not the form API.

#redirect

This property's type is a string or array. If set to a string, the string is the Drupal path that the user is redirected to after form submission. If set to an array, the array is passed as parameters to drupal_goto() with the first element of the array being the destination path (this construct allows additional parameters such as a query string to be passed to drupal_goto()).

#pre_render

This property is an array of functions to call just before the form will be rendered. Each function is called and passed the element for which #pre_render is set. For example, setting $form['#pre_render'] = array('foo', 'bar') will cause Drupal to call foo(&$form) and then bar(&$form). If set on an element of the form, such as $form['mytextfield']['#pre_render'] = array('foo'), Drupal will call foo(&$element) where $element is $form['mytextfield']. This is useful if you want to hook into form processing to modify the structure of the form after validation has run but before the form is rendered. To modify the form before validation has been run, use hook_form_alter().

#post_render

This property allows you to provide an array of functions that may modify the content that has just been rendered. If you set `$form['mytextfield']['#post_render'] = array('bar')`, you could modify the content that was created like this:

```
function bar($content, $element) {
  $new_content = t('This element (ID %id) has the following content:',
    array('%id' => $element['#id'])) . $content;
  return $new_content;
}
```

#cache

This property controls whether or not the form will be cached by Drupal's general caching system. Caching the form means it will not have to be rebuilt when it is submitted. You might want to set `$form['#cache'] = FALSE` if you want to force the form to be built every time.

Properties Added to All Elements

When the form builder goes through the form definition, it ensures that each element has some default values set. The default values are set in `_element_info()` in `includes/form.inc` but can be overridden by an element's definition in `hook_elements()`.

#description

This string property is added to all elements and defaults to `NULL`. It's rendered by the element's theme function. For example, a text field's description is rendered underneath the textfield as shown in Figure 10-2.

#required

This Boolean property is added to all elements and defaults to `FALSE`. Setting this to `TRUE` will cause Drupal's built-in form validation to throw an error if the form is submitted but the field has not been completed. Also, if set to `TRUE`, a CSS class is set for this element (see `theme_form_element()` in `includes/form.inc`).

#tree

This Boolean property is added to all elements and defaults to `FALSE`. If set to `TRUE`, the `$form_state['values']` array resulting from a form submission will not be flattened. This affects how you access submitted values (see the "Fieldsets" section of this chapter).

#post

This array property is a copy of the original `$_POST` data and is added to each form element by the form builder. That way, the functions defined in `#process` and `#after_build` can make intelligent decisions based on the contents of `#post`.

#parents

This array property is added to all elements and defaults to an empty array. It is used internally by the form builder to identify parent elements of the form tree. For more information, see `http://drupal.org/node/48643`.

#attributes

This associative array is added to all elements and defaults to an empty array, but theme functions generally populate it. Members of this array will be added as HTML attributes, for example, `$form['#attributes'] = array('enctype' => 'multipart/form-data')`.

Properties Allowed in All Elements

The properties explained in the sections that follow are allowed in all elements.

#type

This string declares the type of an element. For example, `#type = 'textfield'`. The root of the form must contain the declaration `#type = 'form'`.

#access

This Boolean property determines whether or not the element is shown to the user. If the element has children, the children will not be shown if the parent's `#access` property is `FALSE`. For example, if the element is a fieldset, none of the fields included in the fieldset will be shown if `#access` is `FALSE`.

The `#access` property can be set to `TRUE` or `FALSE` directly, or the value can be set to a function that returns `TRUE` or `FALSE` when executed. Execution will happen when the form definition is retrieved. Here's an example from Drupal's default node form:

```
$form['revision_information']['revision'] = array(
  '#access' => user_access('administer nodes'),
  '#type' => 'checkbox',
  '#title' => t('Create new revision'),
  '#default_value' => $node->revision,
);
```

#process

This property is an associative array. Each array entry consists of a function name as a key and any arguments that need to be passed as the values. These functions are called when an element is being built and allow additional manipulation of the element at form building time. For example, in `modules/system/system.module` where the `checkboxes` type is defined, the function `expand_checkboxes()` in `includes/form.inc` is set to be called during form building:

```
$type['checkboxes'] = array(
    '#input' => TRUE,
    '#process' => array('expand_checkboxes'),
    '#tree' => TRUE
);
```

See also the example in this chapter in the "Collecting All Possible Form Element Definitions" section. After all functions in the #process array have been called, a #processed property is added to each element.

#after_build

This property is an array of functions that will be called immediately after the element has been built. Each function will be called with two parameters: $form and $form_state. For example, if $form['#after_build'] = array('foo', 'bar'), then Drupal will call foo($form, $form_state) and bar($form, $form_state) after the form is built. Once the function has been called, Drupal internally adds the #after_build_done property to the element.

#theme

This optional property defines a string that will be used when Drupal looks for a theme function for this element. For example, setting #theme = 'foo' will cause Drupal to check the theme registry for an entry that corresponds with foo. See the "Finding a Theme Function for the Form" section earlier in this chapter.

#prefix

The string defined in this property will be added to the output when the element is rendered, just before the rendered element.

#suffix

The string defined in this property will be added to the output when the element is rendered, just after the rendered element.

#title

This string is the title of the element.

#weight

This property can be an integer or a decimal number. When form elements are rendered, they are sorted by their weight. Those with smaller weights "float up" and appear higher; those with larger weights "sink down" and appear lower on the rendered page.

#default_value

The type for this property is mixed. For input elements, this is the value to use in the field if the form has not yet been submitted. Do not confuse this with the #value element, which defines an internal form value that is never given to the user but is defined in the form and appears in $form_state['values'].

Form Elements

In this section, we'll present examples of the built-in Drupal form elements.

Textfield

An example of a textfield element follows:

```
$form['pet_name'] = array(
  '#title' => t('Name'),
  '#type' => 'textfield',
  '#description' => t('Enter the name of your pet.'),
  '#default_value' => $user->pet_name,
  '#maxlength' => 32,
  '#required' => TRUE,
  '#size' => 15,
  '#weight' => 5,
  '#autocomplete_path' => 'pet/common_pet_names',
  );

$form['pet_weight'] = array(
  '#title' => t('Weight'),
  '#type' => 'textfield',
  '#description' => t('Enter the weight of your pet in kilograms.'),
  '#field_suffix' => t('kilograms'),
  '#default_value' => $user->pet_weight,
  '#size' => 4,
  '#weight' => 10,
  );
```

This results in the form element shown in Figure 10-11.

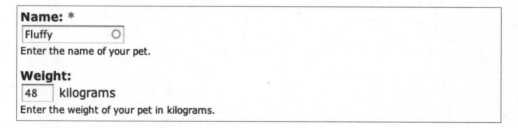

Figure 10-11. *The textfield element*

The #field_prefix and #field_suffix properties are specific to text fields and place a string immediately before or after the textfield input.

The #autocomplete property defines a path where Drupal's automatically included JavaScript will send HTTP requests using JQuery. In the preceding example, it will query http://example.com/?q=pet/common_pet_names. See the user_autocomplete() function in modules/user/user.pages.inc for a working example.

Properties commonly used with the textfield element follow: #attributes, #autocomplete_path (the default is FALSE), #default_value, #description, #field_prefix, #field_suffix, #maxlength (the default is 128), #prefix, #required, #size (the default is 60), #suffix, #title, #process (the default is form_expand_ahah), and #weight.

Password

This element creates an HTML password field, where input entered by the user is not shown (usually bullet characters are echoed to the screen instead). An example from user_login_block() follows:

```
$form['pass'] = array('#type' => 'password',
  '#title' => t('Password'),
  '#maxlength' => 60,
  '#size' => 15,
  '#required' => TRUE,
);
```

Properties commonly used with the password element are #attributes, #description, #maxlength, #prefix, #required, #size (the default is 60), #suffix, #title, #process (the default is form_expand_ahah), and #weight. The #default_value property is not used with the password element for security reasons.

Password with Confirmation

This element creates two HTML password fields and attaches a validator that checks if the two passwords match. For example, this element is used by the user module when a user changes his or her password.

```
$form['account']['pass'] = array(
  '#type' => 'password_confirm',
  '#description' => t('To change the current user password, enter the new
    password in both fields.'),
  '#size' => 25,
);
```

Textarea

An example of the textarea element follows:

```
$form['pet_habits'] = array(
  '#title' => t('Habits'),
  '#type' => 'textarea',
  '#description' => t('Describe the habits of your pet.'),
  '#default_value' => $user->pet_habits,
  '#cols' => 40,
  '#rows' => 3,
  '#resizable' => FALSE,
  '#weight' => 15,
);
```

Properties commonly used with the textarea element are #attributes, #cols (the default is 60), #default_value, #description, #prefix, #required, #resizable, #suffix, #title, #rows (the default is 5), #process (the default is form_expand_ahah), and #weight.

The #cols setting may not be effective if the dynamic text area resizer is enabled by setting #resizable to TRUE.

Select

A select element example from modules/statistics/statistics.admin.inc follows:

```
$period = drupal_map_assoc(array(3600, 10800, 21600, 32400, 43200, 86400, 172800,
  259200, 604800, 1209600, 2419200, 4838400, 9676800), 'format_interval');

/* Period now looks like this:
  Array (
    [3600] => 1 hour
    [10800] => 3 hours
    [21600] => 6 hours
    [32400] => 9 hours
    [43200] => 12 hours
    [86400] => 1 day
    [172800] => 2 days
    [259200] => 3 days
    [604800] => 1 week
    [1209600] => 2 weeks
    [2419200] => 4 weeks
    [4838400] => 8 weeks
    [9676800] => 16 weeks )
*/
```

```
$form['access']['statistics_flush_accesslog_timer'] = array(
  '#type' => 'select',
  '#title' => t('Discard access logs older than'),
  '#default_value' => variable_get('statistics_flush_accesslog_timer', 259200),
  '#options' => $period,
  '#description' => t('Older access log entries (including referrer statistics)
    will be automatically discarded. (Requires a correctly configured
    <a href="@cron">cron maintenance task</a>.)', array('@cron' =>
    url('admin/reports/status'))),
);
```

Drupal supports grouping in the selection options by defining the #options property to be an associative array of submenu choices as shown in Figure 10-12.

```
$options = array(
  array(
    t('Healthy') => array(
      1 => t('wagging'),
      2 => t('upright'),
      3 => t('no tail')
    ),
  ),
  array(
    t('Unhealthy') => array(
      4 => t('bleeding'),
      5 => t('oozing'),
    ),
  ),
);
$form['pet_tail'] = array(
  '#title' => t('Tail demeanor'),
  '#type' => 'select',
  '#description' => t('Pick the closest match that describes the tail
    of your pet.'),
  '#options' => $options,
  '#multiple' => FALSE,
  '#weight' => 20,
);
```

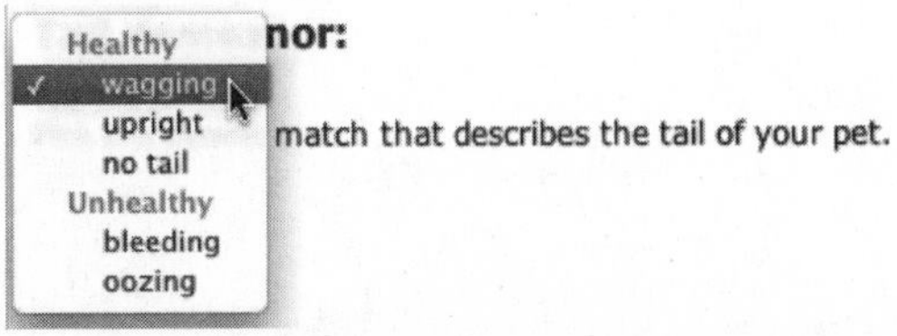

Figure 10-12. *A select field using choice grouping*

Selection of multiple choices is enabled by setting the #multiple property to TRUE. This also changes the value in $form_state['values'] from a string (e.g., 'pet_tail' = '2', assuming upright is selected in the preceding example) to an array of values (e.g., pet_tail = array(1 => '1', 2 => '2') assuming wagging and upright are both chosen in the preceding example).

Properties commonly used with the select element are #attributes, #default_value, #description, #multiple, #options, #prefix, #required, #suffix, #title, #process (the default is form_expand_ahah), and #weight.

Radio Buttons

A radio button example from modules/block/block.admin.inc follows:

```
$form['user_vis_settings']['custom'] = array(
  '#type' => 'radios',
  '#title' => t('Custom visibility settings'),
  '#options' => array(
    t('Users cannot control whether or not they see this block.'),
    t('Show this block by default, but let individual users hide it.'),
    t('Hide this block by default but let individual users show it.')
  ),
  '#description' =>  t('Allow individual users to customize the visibility of
    this block in their account settings.'),
  '#default_value' => $edit['custom'],
);
```

Properties commonly used with this element are #attributes, #default_value, #description, #options, #prefix, #required, #suffix, #title, and #weight. Note that the #process property is set to expand_radios() (see includes/form.inc) by default.

Check Boxes

An example of the check boxes element follows. The rendered version of this element is shown in Figure 10-13.

```
$options = array(
  'poison' => t('Sprays deadly poison'),
  'metal' => t('Can bite/claw through metal'),
  'deadly' => t('Killed previous owner')  );
$form['danger'] = array(
  '#title' => t('Special conditions'),
  '#type' => 'checkboxes',
  '#description' => (t('Please note if any of these conditions apply to your
    pet.')),
  '#options' => $options,
  '#weight' => 25,
);
```

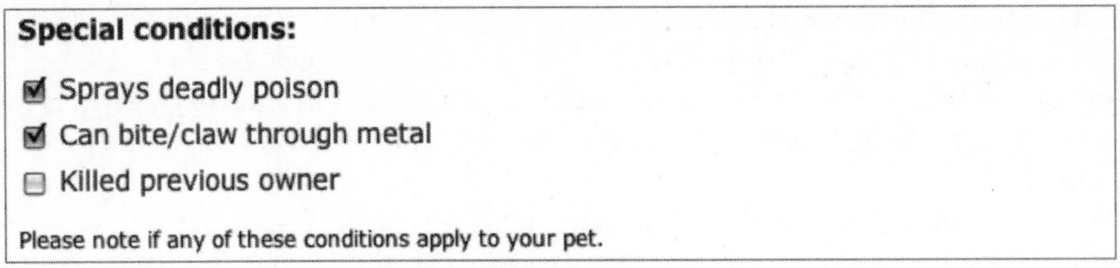

Special conditions:

☑ Sprays deadly poison

☑ Can bite/claw through metal

☐ Killed previous owner

Please note if any of these conditions apply to your pet.

Figure 10-13. *An example using the check boxes element*

The `array_filter()` function is often used in validation and submission functions to get the keys of the checked boxes. For example, if the first two check boxes are checked in Figure 10-13, `$form_state['values']['danger']` would contain the following:

```
array(
  'poison' => 'poison',
  'metal' => 'metal',
  deadly' => 0,
)
```

Running `array_filter($form_state['values']['danger'])` results in an array containing only the keys of the checked boxes: `array('poison', 'metal')`.

Properties commonly used with the check boxes element are #attributes, #default_value, #description, #options, #prefix, #required, #suffix, #title, #tree (the default is TRUE), and #weight. Note that the #process property is set to `expand_checkboxes()` (see `includes/form.inc`) by default.

Value

The value element is used to pass values internally from $form to `$form_state['values']` without ever being sent to the browser, for example:

```
$form['pid'] = array(
  '#type' => 'value',
  '#value' => 123,
);
```

When the form is submitted, `$form_state['values']['pid']` will be 123.

Do not confuse #type => 'value' and #value => 123. The first declares what kind of element is being described, and the second declares the value of the element. Only #type and #value properties may be used with the value element.

Hidden

This element is used to pass a hidden value into a form using an HTML input field of type hidden, as in the following example.

```
$form['my_hidden_field'] = array(
  '#type' => 'hidden',
  '#value' => t('I am a hidden field value'),
);
```

If you want to send a hidden value along through the form, it's usually a better idea to use the value element for this, and use the hidden element only when the value element does not suffice. That's because the user can view the hidden element in the HTML source of a web form, but the value element is internal to Drupal and not included in the HTML.

Only the #prefix, #suffix, #process (the default is form_expand_ahah), and #value properties are used with the hidden element.

Date

The date element, as shown in Figure 10-14, is a combination element with three select boxes:

```
$form['deadline'] = array(
  '#title' => t('Deadline'),
  '#type' => 'date',
  '#description' => t('Set the deadline.'),
  '#default_value' => array(
    'month' => format_date(time(), 'custom', 'n'),
    'day' => format_date(time(), 'custom', 'j'),
    'year' => format_date(time(), 'custom', 'Y'),
  ),
);
```

Figure 10-14. *A date field*

Properties commonly used by the date element are #attributes, #default_value, #description, #prefix, #required, #suffix, #title, and #weight. The #process property defaults to call expand_date(), in which the year selector is hard coded to the years 1900 to 2050. The #element_validate property defaults to date_validate() (both functions can be found in includes/form.inc). You can define these properties when defining the date element in your form to use your own code instead.

Weight

The weight element (not to be confused with the #weight property) is a drop-down used to specify weights:

```
$form['weight'] = array(
  '#type' => 'weight',
  '#title' => t('Weight'),
  '#default_value' => $edit['weight'],
  '#delta' => 10,
  '#description' => t('In listings, the heavier vocabularies will sink and the
    lighter vocabularies will be positioned nearer the top.'),
);
```

The preceding code will be rendered as shown in Figure 10-15.

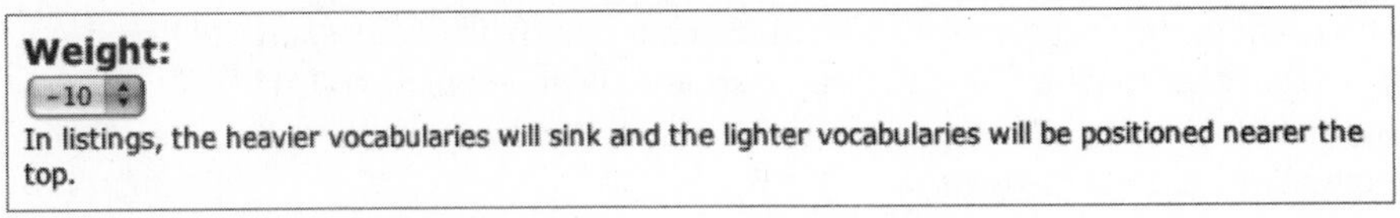

Weight:
-10 ⬍
In listings, the heavier vocabularies will sink and the lighter vocabularies will be positioned nearer the top.

Figure 10-15. *The weight element*

The #delta property determines the range of weights to choose from and defaults to 10. For example, if you set #delta to 50 the range of weights would be from -50 to 50. Properties commonly used with the weight element are #attributes, #delta (the default is 10), #default_value, #description, #prefix, #required, #suffix, #title, and #weight. The #process property defaults to array('process_weight', 'form_expand_ahah').

File Upload

The file element creates a file upload interface. Here's an example from modules/user/user.module:

```
$form['picture']['picture_upload'] = array(
  '#type' => 'file',
  '#title' => t('Upload picture'),
  '#size' => 48,
  '#description' => t('Your virtual face or picture.')
);
```

The way this element is rendered is shown in Figure 10-16.

Upload picture:
(Choose File) no file selected
Your virtual face or picture.

Figure 10-16. *A file upload element*

Note that if you use the file element, you'll need to set the enctype property at the root of your form:

```
$form['#attributes']['enctype'] = 'multipart/form-data';
```

Properties commonly used with the file element are #attributes, #default_value, #description, #prefix, #required, #size (the default is 60), #suffix, #title, and #weight.

Fieldset

A fieldset element is used to group elements together. It can be declared collapsible, which means JavaScript automatically provided by Drupal is used to open and close the fieldset dynamically with a click while a user is viewing the form. Note the use of the #access property in this example to allow or deny access to all fields within the fieldset:

```
// Node author information for administrators.
$form['author'] = array(
  '#type' => 'fieldset',
  '#access' => user_access('administer nodes'),
  '#title' => t('Authoring information'),
  '#collapsible' => TRUE,
  '#collapsed' => TRUE,
  '#weight' => 20,
);
```

Properties commonly used with the fieldset element are #attributes, #collapsed (the default is FALSE), #collapsible (the default is FALSE), #description, #prefix, #suffix, #title, #process (the default is form_expand_ahah), and #weight.

Submit

The submit element is used to submit the form. The word displayed inside the button defaults to "Submit" but can be changed using the #value property:

```
$form['submit'] = array(
  '#type' => 'submit',
  '#value' => t('Continue'),
);
```

Properties commonly used with the submit element are #attributes, #button_type (the default is 'submit'), #executes_submit_callback (the default is TRUE), #name (the default is 'op'), #prefix, #suffix, #value, #process (the default is form_expand_ahah), and #weight.

Additionally, the #validate and #submit properties may be assigned directly to the submit element. For example, if #submit is set to array('my_special_form_submit'), the function my_special_form_submit() will be used instead of the form's defined submit handler(s).

Button

The button element is the same as the submit element except that the #executes_submit_ callback property defaults to FALSE. This property tells Drupal whether to process the form (when TRUE) or simply re-render the form (if FALSE). Like the submit button, specific validation and submit functions can be assigned directly to a button.

Image Button

The image button element is the same as the submit element with two exceptions. First, it has a #src property that has the URL of an image as its value. Secondly, it sets the internal form property #has_garbage_value to TRUE, which prevents #default_value from being used due to a bug in Microsoft Internet Explorer. Do not use #default_value with image buttons. Here is an image button that uses the built-in Powered by Drupal image as the button:

```
$form['my_image_button'] = array(
  '#type' => 'image_button',
  '#src' => 'misc/powered-blue-80x15.png',
  '#value' => 'foo',
);
```

The value of the button can be safely retrieved by looking in $form_state['clicked_button']['#value'].

Markup

The markup element is the default element type if no #type property has been used. It is used to introduce text or HTML into the middle of a form.

```
$form['disclaimer'] = array(
  '#prefix' => '<div>',
  '#value' => t('The information below is entirely optional.'),
  '#suffix' => '</div>',
);
```

Properties commonly used with the markup element are #attributes, #prefix (the default is the empty string ''), #suffix (the default is the empty string ''), #value, and #weight.

■**Caution** If you are outputting text inside a collapsible fieldset, wrap it in <div> tags, as shown in the example, so that when the fieldset is collapsed, your text will collapse within it.

Item

The item element is formatted in the same way as other input element types like textfield or select field, but it lacks the input field.

```
$form['removed'] = array(
  '#title' => t('Shoe size'),
  '#type' => 'item',
  '#description' => t('This question has been removed because the law prohibits us
    from asking your shoe size.'),
);
```

The preceding element is rendered as shown in Figure 10-17.

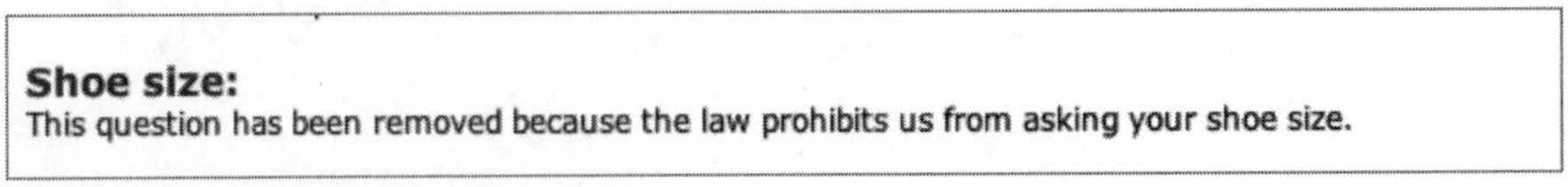

Shoe size:
This question has been removed because the law prohibits us from asking your shoe size.

Figure 10-17. *An item element*

Properties commonly used with the item element are #attributes, #description, #prefix (the default is an empty string, ''), #required, #suffix (the default is an empty string, ''), #title, #value, and #weight.

#ahah Property

The #ahah element property gives information to Drupal's implementation of Asynchronous HTML and HTTP (AHAH), which allows form elements to be changed using JavaScript.

Tip You may have noticed that in many of the form elements we've described, the default value for #process is form_expand_ahah. The presence of an #ahah property in the element indicates to Drupal that AHAH will be used with this element. The form_expand_ahah() function makes sure that the #ahah values have reasonable defaults.

Here is an example of its use in the Attach button provided by the upload module for file uploading:

```
$form['new']['attach'] = array(
  '#type' => 'submit',
  '#value' => t('Attach'),
  '#name' => 'attach',
  '#ahah' => array(
    'path' => 'upload/js',
    'wrapper' => 'attach-wrapper',
    'progress' => array(
      'type' => 'bar',
      'message' => t('Please wait...'),
    ),
  ),
  '#submit' => array('node_form_submit_build_node'),
);
```

The value of an #ahah property is a keyed array. The following keys are required:

- path: The Drupal path of the menu item that the JavaScript will request. The callback for the menu item and the path of the menu item end in js to indicate that the item is called by JavaScript. In the preceding example, the Drupal path is upload/js, and the corresponding callback is upload_js() (you can verify this by inspecting upload_menu() in modules/upload/upload.module).

- wrapper: Corresponds with the id attribute of an HTML element (usually <div>). In the preceding example, the upload module is referring to the following element: <div id= "attach-wrapper">.

The following keys are optional:

- effect: The visual effect to use when replacing the element. Possible values are none, fade, and slide. The default value is none.

- event: The event that will trigger the browser's execution of a JavaScript HTTP request. Drupal sets default values based on element type. These values are shown in Table 10-1.

Table 10-1. *Default Names of Events That Will Trigger AHAH in Form Elements*

Element	Default Event
submit	mousedown*
button	mousedown*
image_button	mousedown*
password	blur
textfield	blur
textarea	blur
radio	change
checkbox	change
select	change

The keypress event is also added.

- method: The JQuery method that will be used to change the existing HTML when the response from the JavaScript HTTP request comes back. Possible values are after, append, before, prepend, and replace. The default method is replace. This value will be used in the following JavaScript (see misc/ahah.js):

```
if (this.method == 'replace') {
  wrapper.empty().append(new_content);
}
else {
  wrapper[this.method](new_content);
}
```

- progress: The way that Drupal will signal to the user that a JavaScript event is happening. The value of this property is an array with the following keys: type and message, for example:

```
$form['submit'] = array(
  '#type' => 'submit',
  '#value' => t('Click Me'),
  '#ahah' => array(
    'event' => 'click',
    'path' => 'poof/message_js',
    'wrapper' => 'target',
    'effect' => 'fade',
```

```
      'progress' => array(
        'type' => 'throbber',
        'message' => t('One moment...'),
      ),
    )
  );
```

The default value of type is throbber, which is a circular animated icon that displays an optional message while the JavaScript HTTP request is running. The other choice is bar, which is a progress bar (a separate JavaScript file, misc/progress.js, will be added if bar is specified). If type is set to bar, the following optional keys are available: url and interval. The url key specifies a URL for the progress bar to call to determine its percentage as an integer from 0 to 100, and the interval key specifies how frequently the progress should be checked (in seconds).

- selector: Specifying a selector is a way to attach the result of the JavaScript HTTP request to multiple elements on the page (not just the form element).

Here is a brief example of a form that allows dynamic replacement of some text using AHAH. The button uses the throbber to indicate that the user should wait, as shown in Figure 10-18. Here is sites/all/modules/custom/poof/poof.info:

```
; $Id$
name = Poof
description = Demonstrates AHAH forms.
package = Pro Drupal Development
core = 6.x
```

And here is sites/all/modules/custom/poof/poof.module:

```php
<?php

/**
 * Implementation of hook_menu().
 */
function poof_menu() {
  $items['poof'] = array(
    'title' => 'Ahah!',
    'page callback' => 'drupal_get_form',
    'page arguments' => array('poof_form'),
    'access arguments' => array('access content'),
  );
  $items['poof/message_js'] = array(
    'page callback' => 'poof_message_js',
    'type' => MENU_CALLBACK,
    'access arguments' => array('access content'),
  );
  return $items;
}
```

```
/**
 * Form definition.
 */
function poof_form() {
  $form['target'] = array(
    '#type' => 'markup',
    '#prefix' => '<div id="target">',
    '#value' => t('Click the button below. I dare you.'),
    '#suffix' => '</div>',
  );
  $form['submit'] = array(
    '#type' => 'submit',
    '#value' => t('Click Me'),
    '#ahah' => array(
      'event' => 'click',
      'path' => 'poof/message_js',
      'wrapper' => 'target',
      'effect' => 'fade',
    )
  );

  return $form;
}

/**
 * Menu callback for AHAH additions.
 */
function poof_message_js() {
  $output = t('POOF!');
  drupal_json(array('status' => TRUE, 'data' => $output));
}
```

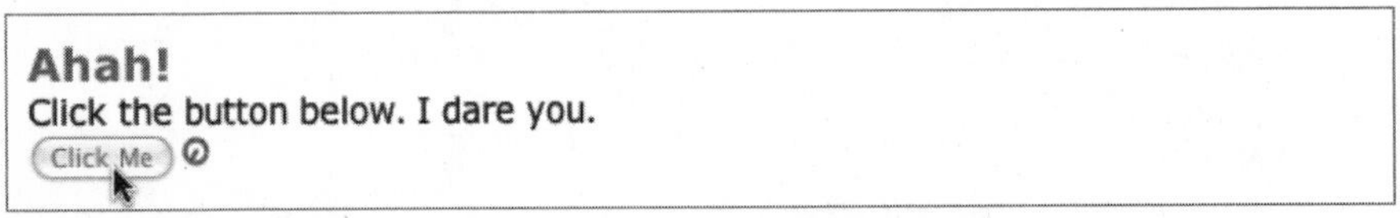

Figure 10-18. *Clicking the button will result in AHAH-based text replacement after display of circular animated throbber icon.*

The same module follows, this time implemented so that a progress bar is used and is updated every two seconds (see Figure 10-19).

■**Caution** This module simply demonstrates how to interact with the progress bar; in a real module, you would report on the percentage completion of an actual task. In particular, you would not use Drupal's persistent variable system to store and read progress like the example does, as multiple users running the form simultaneously would confuse the values. Instead, you might do a database query to see what percentage of rows have been inserted.

```php
<?php

/**
 * Implementation of hook_menu().
 */
function poof_menu() {
  $items['poof'] = array(
    'title' => 'Ahah!',
    'page callback' => 'drupal_get_form',
    'page arguments' => array('poof_form'),
    'access arguments' => array('access content'),
  );
  $items['poof/message_js'] = array(
    'page callback' => 'poof_message_js',
    'type' => MENU_CALLBACK,
    'access arguments' => array('access content'),
  );
  $items['poof/interval_js'] = array(
    'page callback' => 'poof_interval_js',
    'type' => MENU_CALLBACK,
    'access arguments' => array('access content'),
  );
  return $items;
}

/**
 * Form definition.
 */
function poof_form() {
  $form['target'] = array(
    '#type' => 'markup',
    '#prefix' => '<div id="target">',
    '#value' => t('Click the button below. I dare you.'),
    '#suffix' => '</div>',
  );
```

```php
  $form['submit'] = array(
    '#type' => 'submit',
    '#value' => t('Click Me'),
    '#ahah' => array(
      'event' => 'click',
      'path' => 'poof/message_js',
      'wrapper' => 'target',
      'effect' => 'fade',
      'progress' => array(
        'type' => 'bar',
        'message' => t('One moment...'),
        'interval' => 2,
        'url' => 'poof/interval_js',
      ),
    )
  );

  return $form;
}

/**
 * Menu callback for AHAH additions.
 */
function poof_message_js() {
  $output = t('POOF!');
  for ($i = 0; $i < 100; $i = $i + 20) {
    // Record how far we are.
    variable_set('poof_percentage', $i);
    // Simulate performing a task by waiting 2 seconds.
    sleep(2);
  }
  drupal_json(array('status' => TRUE, 'data' => $output));
}

/**
 * Menu callback for AHAH progress bar intervals.
 */
function poof_interval_js() {
  // Read how far we are.
  $percentage = variable_get('poof_percentage', 0);
  // Return the value to the JavaScript progress bar.
  drupal_json(array('percentage' => $percentage));
}
```

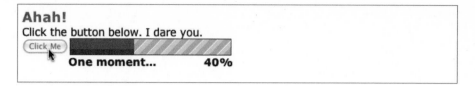

Figure 10-19. *The progress bar shows the percentage completion.*

Summary

After reading this chapter, you should understand the following concepts:

- How the form API works

- Creating simple forms

- Changing the rendered form using theme functions

- Writing a validation function for a form or for individual elements

- Writing a submit function and do redirection after form processing

- Altering existing forms

- Writing multistep forms

- The form definition properties you can use and what they mean

- The form elements (text fields, select fields, radios, and so on) that are available in Drupal

- How AHAH-based text replacement works with forms

For more information about forms, including tips and tricks, see the *Drupal Handbook* at http://drupal.org/node/37775.

■ ■ ■

## CHAPTER 11

Manipulating User Input: The Filter System

Adding content to a web site can be quite a chore when you have to format the information by hand. Conversely, making textual content look good on a web site requires knowledge of HTML—knowledge most users don't want to be bothered with. For those of us who are HTML-savvy, it's still a pain to stop and insert tags into our posts during the middle of a brainstorm or literary breakthrough. Paragraph tags, link tags, break tags . . . yuck. The good news is that Drupal uses prebuilt routines called *filters* to make data entry easy and efficient. Filters perform text manipulations such as making URLs clickable, converting line breaks to `<p>` and `<br />` tags, and even stripping out malicious HTML. `hook_filter()` is the mechanism behind filter creation and manipulation of user-submitted data.

Filters

Filters are almost always a single action such as "strip out all hyperlinks," "add a random image to this post," or even "translate this into pirate-speak" (see `pirate.module` at `http://drupal.org/project/pirate`). As shown in Figure 11-1, they take some kind of textual input, manipulate it, and return output.

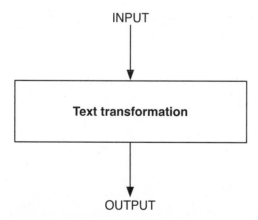

INPUT

Text transformation

OUTPUT

Figure 11-1. *A filter transforms text in some way and returns the transformed text.*

A common use for a filter is to remove unwanted markup from user-submitted input. Figure 11-2 shows Drupal's HTML filter at work.

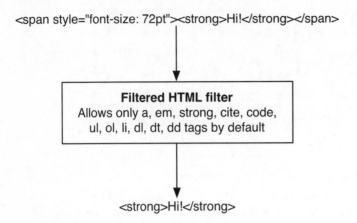

```
<span style="font-size: 72pt"><strong>Hi!</strong></span>
```

Filtered HTML filter
Allows only a, em, strong, cite, code,
ul, ol, li, dl, dt, dd tags by default

```
<strong>Hi!</strong>
```

Figure 11-2. *The HTML filter allows only certain tags through. This filter is essential to prevent cross-site scripting attacks.*

Filters and Input Formats

Trying to find a list of installed filters within the administrative interface isn't intuitive and assumes you already understand what filters do to know what to look for. For filters to perform their job, you must assign them to a Drupal *input format* as shown in Figure 11-3. Input formats group filters together so they can run as a batch when processing content. This is much easier than checking off a handful of filters for each submission. To view a list of installed filters, either configure an existing input format or create a new one at Administer ➤ Site configuration ➤ Input formats.

■**Tip** A Drupal input format is made up of a collection of filters.

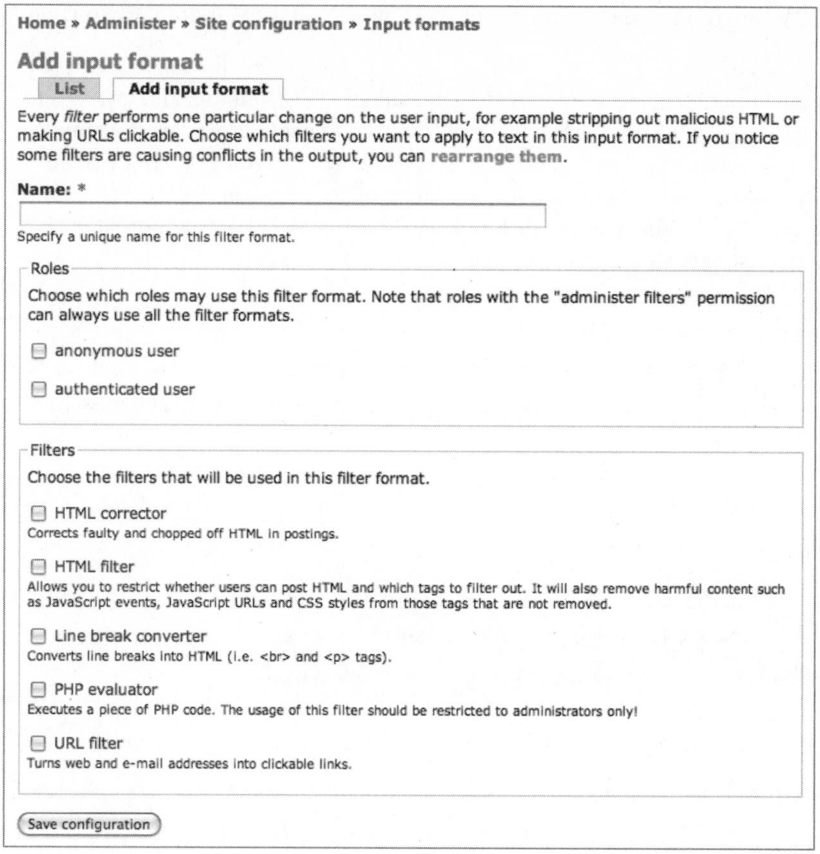

Home » Administer » Site configuration » Input formats

Add input format

| List | **Add input format** |

Every *filter* performs one particular change on the user input, for example stripping out malicious HTML or making URLs clickable. Choose which filters you want to apply to text in this input format. If you notice some filters are causing conflicts in the output, you can rearrange them.

Name: *

Specify a unique name for this filter format.

┌─ Roles ──
│ Choose which roles may use this filter format. Note that roles with the "administer filters" permission
│ can always use all the filter formats.
│
│ ☐ anonymous user
│
│ ☐ authenticated user
│
└──

┌─ Filters ──
│ Choose the filters that will be used in this filter format.
│
│ ☐ HTML corrector
│ Corrects faulty and chopped off HTML in postings.
│
│ ☐ HTML filter
│ Allows you to restrict whether users can post HTML and which tags to filter out. It will also remove harmful content such
│ as JavaScript events, JavaScript URLs and CSS styles from those tags that are not removed.
│
│ ☐ Line break converter
│ Converts line breaks into HTML (i.e.
 and <p> tags).
│
│ ☐ PHP evaluator
│ Executes a piece of PHP code. The usage of this filter should be restricted to administrators only!
│
│ ☐ URL filter
│ Turns web and e-mail addresses into clickable links.
│
└──

(Save configuration)

Figure 11-3. *Installed filters are listed on the "Add input format" form.*

Drupal ships with three input formats (see Figure 11-4):

- The *Filtered HTML* input format is made up of four filters:

  - The *HTML corrector* filter, which makes sure that all HTML tags are properly closed and nested;

  - The *HTML filter*, which restricts HTML tags and attempts to prevent cross-site scripting (usually referred to as XSS) attacks;

  - The *line break converter*, which converts carriage returns to their HTML counterparts; and

  - The *URL filter*, which transforms web and e-mail addresses into hyperlinks.

- The *Full HTML* input format doesn't restrict HTML in any way, but it does use the line break converter filter.

- The *PHP Code* input format is made up of a filter called PHP evaluator, and its job is to execute any PHP within a post. A good rule of thumb is never to give users the ability to execute an input format that uses PHP evaluator. If they can run PHP, they can do anything PHP can do, including taking down your site, or worse yet, deleting all your data. To protect against this possibility, Drupal ships with the PHP evaluator filter disabled. If you must make it available, enable the PHP filter module.

■Caution Enabling the PHP Code input format for any user on your site is a security issue. Best practice is to not use this input format. If you must use it, use it sparingly, and only for the superuser (the user with user ID 1).

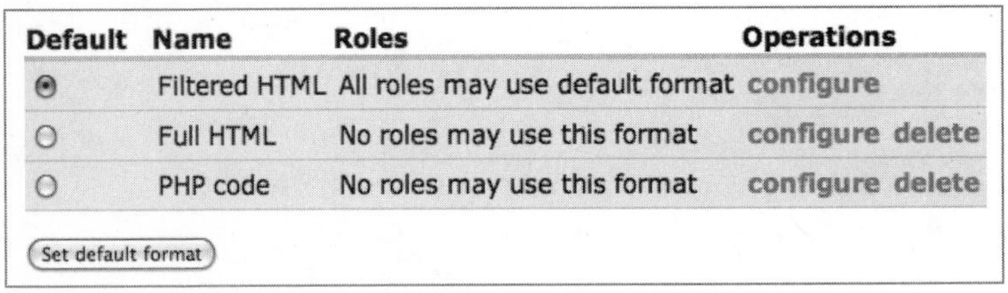

Default	Name	Roles	Operations
⊙	Filtered HTML	All roles may use default format	configure
○	Full HTML	No roles may use this format	configure delete
○	PHP code	No roles may use this format	configure delete

(Set default format)

Figure 11-4. *Drupal installs with three configurable input formats by default.*

Because input formats are collections of filters, they are extensible. You can add and remove filters, as shown in Figure 11-5. You can change the input format's name, add a filter, remove a filter, or even rearrange the order in which an input format's filters are executed to avoid conflicts. For example, you might want to run the URL filter before the HTML filter runs so the HTML filter can inspect the anchor tags created by the URL filter.

■Note Input formats (groups of filters) are controlled at the interface level. Developers don't need to worry about input formats when defining a new filter. That work is left to the Drupal site administrator.

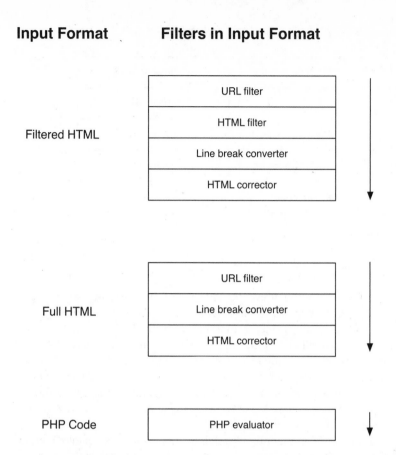

Figure 11-5. *Input formats are made up of a collection of filters. Shown in this figure are Drupal's three default input formats. The direction of execution is shown by arrows.*

Installing a Filter

Installing a filter follows the same procedure as installing a module, because filters live within module files. Making a filter available to use is therefore as easy as enabling or disabling the corresponding module at Administer ➤ Site building ➤ Modules. Once installed, navigate to Administer ➤ Site configuration ➤ Input formats to assign the new filter to the input format(s) of your choosing. Figure 11-6 shows the relationship between filters and modules.

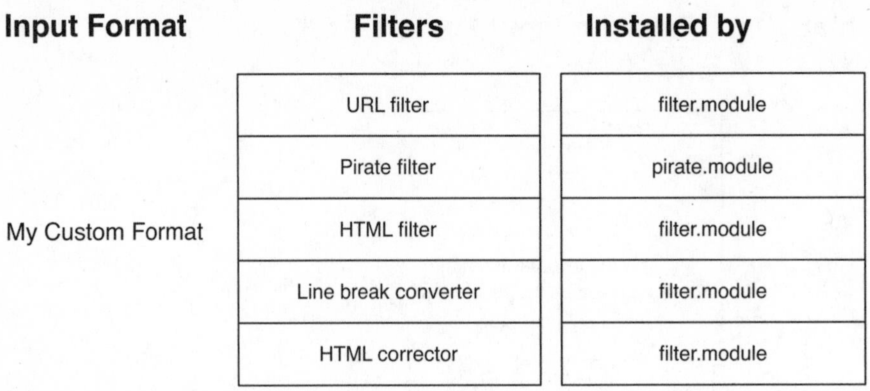

Input Format	Filters	Installed by
	URL filter	filter.module
	Pirate filter	pirate.module
My Custom Format	HTML filter	filter.module
	Line break converter	filter.module
	HTML corrector	filter.module

Figure 11-6. *Filters are created as part of modules.*

Know When to Use Filters

You might be wondering why a filter system is even needed when you can easily manipulate text using existing hooks found elsewhere. For example, it would be just as easy to use hook_nodeapi() to convert URLs to clickable links rather than using the URL filter. But consider the case in which you have five different filters that need to be run on the body field of nodes. Now suppose you're viewing the default http://example.com/?q=node page, which displays ten nodes at a time. That means 50 filters need to be run to generate a single page view, and filtering text can be an expensive operation. It would also mean that whenever a node is called it has to run through the filters, even if the text that's being filtered is unchanged. You'd be running this operation over and over again unnecessarily.

The filter system has a caching layer that provides significant performance gains. Once all filters have run on a given piece of text, the filtered version of that text is stored in the cache_filter table, and it stays cached until the text is once again modified (modification is detected using an MD5 hash of the filtered contents). To go back to our example, loading ten nodes could effectively bypass all filters and just load their data straight from the cache table when that text hasn't changed—much faster! See Figure 11-7 for an overview of the filter system process.

Tip MD5 is an algorithm for computing the hash value of a string of text. Drupal uses this as an efficient index column in the database for finding the filtered data of a node.

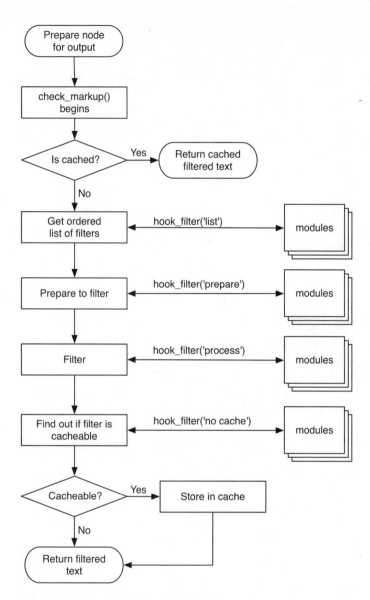

Figure 11-7. *Life cycle of the text-filtering system*

■**Tip** For sites with lots of content, stunning performance gains can be had by moving filter caching to an in-memory cache like memcached.

Now you could get really clever and say, "Well, what if we resave the filtered text back to the node table in our nodeapi hook? Then it would behave the same as the filter system." Although that certainly addresses the performance issue, you'd be breaking a fundamental concept of the Drupal architecture: *never alter a user's original data*. Imagine that one of your novice users goes back to edit a post only to find it smothered in HTML angle brackets. You'll most certainly be getting a tech support call on that one. The goal of the filter system is to leave the original data untouched while making cached copies of the filtered data available to the rest of the Drupal framework. You'll see this principle over and over again with other Drupal APIs.

■**Note** The filter system will cache its data even when caching is disabled at the page level in Drupal. If you're seeing stale, filtered data, try emptying the `cache_filter` table by clicking the "Clear cached data" button at the bottom of the Administer ➤ Site configuration ➤ Performance page.

Creating a Custom Filter

Sure, Drupal filters can make links, format your content, and transform text to pirate-speak on the fly, but what'd be really slick would be for it to write our blog entries for us, or at least help us get our creative juices flowing. Sure, it can do that too! Let's build a module with a filter to insert random sentences into a blog entry. We'll set it up so that when you run out of juice in your post and need a creative spurt, you can simply type **[juice!]** while writing, and when you save your entry, it'll be replaced with a randomly generated sentence. We'll also make it so that if you need lots of creative juice, you can use the [juice!] tag multiple times per post.

Create a folder named creativejuice located in sites/all/modules/custom/. First, add the creativejuice.info file to the creativejuice folder:

```
; $Id$
name = Creative Juice
description = Adds a random sentence filter to content.
package = Pro Drupal Development
core = 6.x
```

Next, create the creativejuice.module file and add it, too:

```php
<?php
// $Id$

/**
 * @file
 * A silly module to assist whizbang novelists who are in a rut by providing a
 * random sentence generator for their posts.
 */
```

Implementing hook_filter()

Now that the basics of the module are in place, let's add our implementation of hook_filter() to creativejuice.module:

```
/**
 * Implementation of hook_filter().
 */
function creativejuice_filter($op, $delta = 0, $format = -1, $text = '') {
  switch ($op) {
    case 'list':
      return array(
        0 => t('Creative Juice filter')
      );

    case 'description':
      return t('Enables users to insert random sentences into their posts.');

    case 'settings':
      // No settings user interface for this filter.
      break;

    case 'no cache':
      // It's OK to cache this filter's output.
      return FALSE;

    case 'prepare':
      // We're a simple filter and have no preparatory needs.
      return $text;

    case 'process':
      return preg_replace_callback("|\[juice!\]|i",
        'creativejuice_sentence', $text);

    default:
      return $text;
  }
}
```

The filter API passes through several stages, from collecting the name of the filter, to caching, to a processing stage where actual manipulation is formed. Let's take a look at those stages or operations by examining creativejuice_filter(). Here's a breakdown of the parameters passed into this hook:

- $op: The operation to be performed. We'll cover this in more detail in the following section.

- $delta: A module that implements hook_filter() can provide multiple filters. You use $delta to track the ID of the currently executing filter. $delta is an integer. Because the creativejuice module provides only one filter, we can ignore it.

- $format: An integer representing which input format is being used. Drupal keeps track of these in the filter_formats database table.

- $text: The content to be filtered.

Depending on the $op parameter, different operations are performed.

The list Operation

It's possible to declare multiple filters when using a single instance of hook_filter(), which explains why the list operation returns an associative array of filter names with numerical keys. These keys are used for subsequent operations and passed back to the hook through the $delta parameter.

```
case 'list':
    return array(
      0 => t('Creative Juice filter'),
      1 => t('The name of my second filter'),
    );
```

The description Operation

This returns a short description of what the filter does. This is only visible to users with the "administer filters" permission.

```
case 'description':
  switch ($delta) {
    case 0:
      return t('Enables users to insert random sentences into their posts.');
    case 1:
      return t('If this module provided a second filter, the description
        for that second filter would go here.');

    // Should never reach default case as value of $delta never exceeds
    // the last index of the 'list' array.
    default:
      return;
  }
```

The settings Operation

Used when a filter needs a form interface for configuration, this operation returns a form definition. Values are automatically saved using `variable_set()` when the form is submitted. This means values are retrieved with `variable_get()`. For a usage example, see `filter_filter()` in `modules/filter/filter.module`.

The no cache Operation

Should the filter system bypass its caching mechanism for filtered text when using this filter? The code should return `TRUE` if caching should be disabled. You'll want to disable caching when developing filters, to make debugging easier. If you change the Boolean return value of the `no cache` operation, you'll need to edit an input format that uses your filter before the changes take effect, since editing the input format will update the `filter_formats` table with the caching setting for the filter.

■**Caution** Disabling the cache for a single filter removes the caching for any input format that uses the filter.

The prepare Operation

The actual filtering of content is a two-step process. First, filters are allowed to prepare text for processing. The main goal of this step is to convert HTML to corresponding entities. For example, take a filter that allows users to paste code snippets. The "prepare" step would convert this code to HTML entities to prevent the filters that follow from interpreting it as HTML. The *HTML filter* would strip out this HTML if it weren't for this step. An example of a filter that uses `prepare` can be found in `codefilter.module`, a module that handles `<code></code>` and `<?php ?>` tags, to let users post code without having to worry about escaping HTML entities. The module can be downloaded from `http://drupal.org/project/codefilter`.

The process Operation

The results from the `prepare` step are passed back through `hook_filter()` during the `process` operation. It's here that the actual text manipulation takes place: converting URLs to clickable links, removing bad words, adding word definitions, and so on. The `prepare` and `process` operations should always return `$text`.

The default Operation

It's important to include the default case. This will be called if your module doesn't implement some of the operations, and ensures that `$text` (the text given to your module to filter) will always be returned.

Helper Function

When $op is process, you execute a helper function named creativejuice_sentence() for every occurrence of the [juiçe!] tag. Add this to creativejuice.module as well.

```
/**
 * Generate a random sentence.
 */
function creativejuice_sentence() {
  $phrase[0][] = t('A majority of us believe');
  $phrase[0][] = t('Generally speaking,');
  $phrase[0][] = t('As times carry on');
  $phrase[0][] = t('Barren in intellect,');
  $phrase[0][] = t('Deficient in insight,');
  $phrase[0][] = t('As blazing blue sky poured down torrents of light,');
  $phrase[0][] = t('Aloof from the motley throng,');

  $phrase[1][] = t('life flowed in its accustomed stream');
  $phrase[1][] = t('he ransacked the vocabulary');
  $phrase[1][] = t('the grimaces and caperings of buffoonery');
  $phrase[1][] = t('the mind freezes at the thought');
  $phrase[1][] = t('reverting to another matter');
  $phrase[1][] = t('he lived as modestly as a hermit');

  $phrase[2][] = t('through the red tape of officialdom.');
  $phrase[2][] = t('as it set anew in some fresh and appealing form.');
  $phrase[2][] = t('supported by evidence.');
  $phrase[2][] = t('as fatal as the fang of the most venomous snake.');
  $phrase[2][] = t('as full of spirit as a gray squirrel.');
  $phrase[2][] = t('as dumb as a fish.');
  $phrase[2][] = t('like a damp-handed auctioneer.');
  $phrase[2][] = t('like a bald ferret.');

  foreach ($phrase as $key => $value) {
    $rand_key = array_rand($phrase[$key]);
    $sentence[] = $phrase[$key][$rand_key];
  }

  return implode(' ', $sentence);
}
```

hook_filter_tips()

You use `creativejuice_filter_tips()` to display help text to the end user. By default, a short message is shown with a link to `http://example.com/?q=filter/tips`, where more detailed instructions are given for each filter.

```
/**
 * Implementation of hook_filter_tips().
 */
function creativejuice_filter_tips($delta, $format, $long = FALSE) {
  return t('Insert a random sentence into your post with the [juice!] tag.');
}
```

In the preceding code, you return the same text for either the brief or long help text page, but if you wanted to return a longer explanation of the text, you'd check the $long parameter as follows:

```
/**
 * Implementation of hook_filter_tips().
 */
function creativejuice_filter_tips($delta, $format, $long = FALSE) {
  if ($long) {
    // Detailed explanation for http://example.com/?q=filter/tips page.
    return t('The Creative Juice filter is for those times when your
      brain is incapable of being creative. These times come for everyone,
      when even strong coffee and a barrel of jelly beans do not
      create the desired effect. When that happens, you can simply enter
      the [juice!] tag into your posts...'
    );
  }
  else {
    // Short explanation for underneath a post's textarea.
    return t('Insert a random sentence into your post with the [juice!] tag.');
  }
}
```

Once this module is enabled on the modules page, the creativejuice filter will be available to be enabled for either an existing input format or a new input format. For example, Figure 11-8 shows what the "Input format" section of the node editing form looks like after the creativejuice filter has been added to the Filtered HTML input format.

┌─ ▾Input format ──┐
│   │
│ ⦿ Filtered HTML   │
│   • Web page addresses and e-mail addresses turn into links automatically. │
│   • Insert a random sentence into your post with the [juice!] tag. │
│   • Allowed HTML tags: <a> <em> <strong> <cite> <code> <ul> <ol> <li> <dl> <dt> │
│   <dd>   │
│   • Lines and paragraphs break automatically.   │
│   │
│ ◯ Full HTML   │
│   • Web page addresses and e-mail addresses turn into links automatically. │
│   • Lines and paragraphs break automatically.   │
│   │
│ More information about formatting options   │
│   │
└──┘

Figure 11-8. *The Filtered HTML input format now contains the creativejuice filter, as indicated by the preceding section of the node editing form.*

You can create a new blog entry with the correct input format and submit text that uses the [juice!] tag:

```
Today was a crazy day. [juice!] Even if that sounds a little odd,
it still doesn't beat what I heard on the radio. [juice!]
```

This is converted upon submission to something like the following:

```
Today was a crazy day! Generally speaking, life flowed in its accustomed stream
through the red tape of officialdom. Even if that sounds a little odd, it still
doesn't beat what I heard on the radio. Barren in intellect, reverting to another
matter like a damp-handed auctioneer.
```

Protecting Against Malicious Data

If you want to protect against malicious HTML, run everything through the Filtered HTML filter, which checks against XSS attacks. If you're in a situation where the Filtered HTML filter can't be used, you could manually filter XSS in the following manner:

```
function mymodule_filter($op, $delta = 0, $format = -1, $text = '') {
  switch ($op) {
    case 'process':
      // Decide which tags are allowed.
      $allowed_tags = '<a> <em> <strong> <cite> <code> <ul> <ol> <li>';
      return filter_xss($text, $allowed_tags);
    default:
      return $text;
      break;
  }
}
```

Summary

After reading this chapter you should be able to

- Understand what a filter and an input format are and how they are used to transform text.

- Understand why the filter system is more efficient than performing text manipulations in other hooks.

- Understand how input formats and filters behave.

- Create a custom filter.

- Understand how the various filter operations function.

■ ■ ■

## CHAPTER 12

Searching and Indexing Content

Both MySQL and PostgreSQL have built-in full-text search capabilities. While it's very easy to use these database-specific solutions to build a search engine, you sacrifice control over the mechanics and lose the ability to fine-tune the system according to the behavior of your application. What the database sees as a high-ranking word might actually be considered a "noise" word by the application if it had a say.

The Drupal community decided to build a custom search engine in order to implement Drupal-specific indexing and page-ranking algorithms. The result is a search engine that walks, talks, and quacks like the rest of the Drupal framework with a standardized configuration and user interface—no matter which database back-end is used.

In this chapter we discuss how modules can hook into the search API and build custom search forms. We also look at how Drupal parses and indexes content and how you can hook into the indexer.

Tip Drupal understands complicated search queries containing Boolean AND/OR operators, exact phrases, or even negative words. An example of all these in action is as follows: `Beatles OR John Lennon "Penny Lane" -insect`.

Building a Custom Search Page

Drupal has the ability to search nodes and usernames out of the box. Even when you develop your own custom node types, Drupal's search system indexes the content that's rendered to the node view. For example, suppose you have a `recipe` node type with the fields `ingredients` and `instructions`, and you create a new recipe node whose node ID is 22. As long as those fields are viewable by the administrator when you visit `http://example.com/?q=node/22`, the search module will index the recipe node and its additional metadata during the next `cron` run.

While it would appear at first glance that node searching and user searching would use the same underlying mechanism, they're actually two separate ways of extending search functionality. Rather than querying the `node` table directly for every search, node searching uses the help of an indexer to process the content ahead of time in a structured format. When a node search is performed, the structured data is queried, yielding noticeably faster and more accurate results. We'll get to know the indexer later in this chapter.

Username searches are not nearly as complex, because usernames are a single field in the database that the search query checks. Also, usernames are not allowed to contain HTML, so there's no need to use the HTML indexer. Instead, you can query the users table directly with just a few lines of code.

In both of the preceding cases, Drupal's search module delegates the actual search to the appropriate module. The simple username search can be found in the user_search() function of modules/user/user.module, while the more complex node search is performed by node_search() in modules/node/node.module. The important point here is that the search module orchestrates the search but delegates the implementation to the modules that know the searchable content best.

The Default Search Form

You'll be glad to know the search API has a default search form ready to use (see Figure 12-1). If that interface works for your needs, then all you need to do is write the logic that finds the hits for the search requested. This search logic is usually a query to the database.

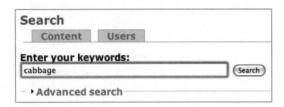

Figure 12-1. *The default user interface for searching with the search API*

While it appears simple, the default content search form is actually wired up to query against all the visible elements of the node content of your site. This means a node's title, body, additional custom attributes, comments, and taxonomy terms are searched from this interface.

The Advanced Search Form

The advanced search feature, shown in Figure 12-2, is yet another way to filter search results. The category selections come from any vocabularies that have been defined on the site (see Chapter 14). The types consist of any content types that are enabled on the site.

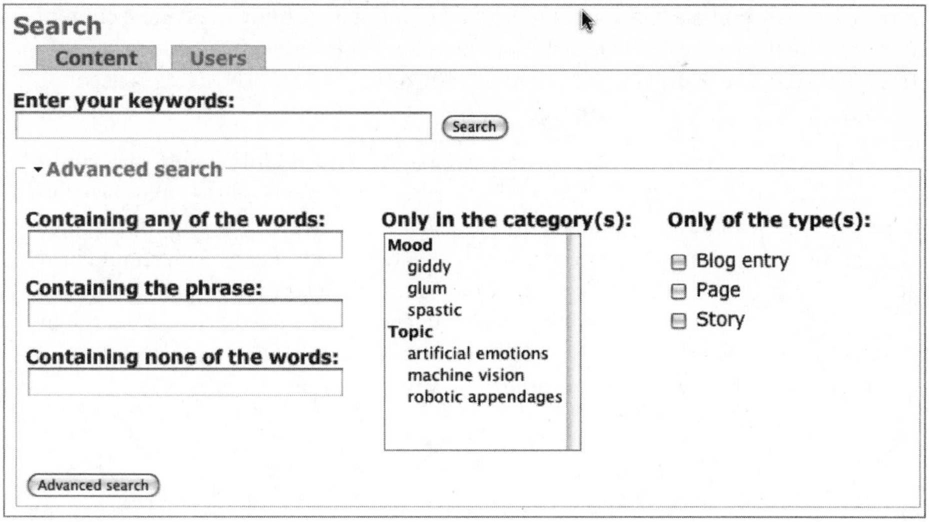

Figure 12-2. *The advanced search options provided by the default search form*

The default search form can be changed by implementing the search hook in a module, then using `hook_form_alter()` on the form ID `search_form` (see Chapter 10) to provide an interface for the user. In Figure 12-2, both of these are happening. The node module is implementing the search hook to make nodes searchable (see `node_search()` in `modules/node/node.module`) and is extending the form to provide an interface (see `node_form_alter()` in `modules/node/node.module`).

Adding to the Search Form

Let's look at an example. Suppose we are using `path.module` and want to enable searching of URL aliases on our site. We'll write a short module that will implement `hook_search()` to make the aliases searchable and provide an additional tab in Drupal's search interface.

Introducing hook_search()

Let's start out by examining the search hook we'll be implementing. The function signature of `hook_search()` looks like this:

```
function hook_search($op = 'search', $keys = NULL)
```

The `$op` parameter is used to describe the current operation being performed and can have the following values:

- name: The caller expects to receive a translated name representing the type of content this implementation of hook_search() will provide. For example, the node module returns t('Content'), and the user module returns t('Users'). The name is used to build the tabs on the search form (see Figure 12-1).

- search: A search on this type of content is happening. The module should perform a search and return results. The $keys parameter will contain the string that the user entered in the search form. Note that this is a string, not an array. After performing a search, your module should return an array of search results. Each result should have, at a minimum, link and title keys. Optional additional keys to return are type, user, date, snippet, and extra. Here is the part of implementing hook_search('search') in node.module where the results array is built (see comment_nodeapi() in modules/comment/comment.module for an example of how the extra key is used):

```
$extra = node_invoke_nodeapi($node, 'search result');
$results[] = array(
  'link' => url('node/'. $item->sid, array('absolute' => TRUE)),
  'type' => check_plain(node_get_types('name', $node)),
  'title' => $node->title,
  'user' => theme('username', $node),
  'date' => $node->changed,
  'node' => $node,
  'extra' => $extra,
  'score' => $item->score / $total,
  'snippet' => search_excerpt($keys, $node->body),
);
```

- reset: The search index is about to be rebuilt. Used by modules that also implement hook_update_index(). If your module is keeping track of how much of its data has been indexed, it should reset its counters in preparation for reindexing.

- status: The user wants to know how much of the content provided by this module has been indexed. This operation is used by modules that also implement hook_update_index(). Return an array with the keys remaining and total, with their values being the number of items that remain to be indexed and the total number of items that will be indexed when indexing is complete.

- admin: The page at Administer ➤ Site configuration ➤ Search settings is about to be displayed. Return a form definition array containing any elements you wish to add to this page. This form uses the system_settings_form() approach, so the names of element keys must match the names of persistent variables used for default values. See "Adding Module-Specific Settings" in Chapter 2 if you need a refresher on how system_settings_form() works.

The name and search operations are the only ones that are required, and the only ones we'll be implementing in our path aliasing search.

Formatting Search Results with hook_search_page()

If you have written a module that provides search results, you might want to take over the look and feel of the results page by implementing hook_search_page(). If you do not implement this hook, the results will be formatted by a call to theme('search_results', $results, $type), which has its default implementation in modules/search/search-results.tpl.php. Do not confuse this with theme('search_result', $result, $type), which formats a single search result and has its default implementation in modules/search/search-result.tpl.php.

Making Path Aliases Searchable

Let's begin our example. We'll be implementing the name and search operations of hook_search().

■**Note** For the following examples to work, you'll need to have the path module enabled and some paths assigned to nodes (so there is something to search). You'll also need to rebuild your search index data before testing these examples. You can do so by selecting Administer ➤ Site configuration ➤ Search settings and clicking the "Re-index site" button and then visiting Administer ➤ Reports ➤ Status report to run cron manually. The search module does indexing when cron runs.

Create a new folder named pathfinder at sites/all/modules/custom, and create the files shown in Listings 12-1 and 12-2 with the new directory.

Listing 12-1. *pathfinder.info*

```
; $Id$
name = Pathfinder
description = Gives administrators the ability to search URL aliases.
package = Pro Drupal Development
core = 6.x
```

Listing 12-2. *pathfinder.module*

```
<?php
// $Id$

/**
 * @file
 * Search interface for URL aliases.
 */
```

Leave pathfinder.module open in your text editor; you'll continue to work with it. The next function to implement is hook_search($op, $keys). This hook returns different information based on the value of the operation ($op) parameter.

```
/**
 * Implementation of hook_search().
 */
function pathfinder_search($op = 'search', $keys = null) {
  switch ($op) {
    case 'name':
      if (user_access('administer url aliases')) {
        return t('URL aliases');
      }
      break;

    case 'search':
      if (user_access('administer url aliases')) {
        $found = array();
        // Replace wildcards with MySQL/PostgreSQL wildcards.
        $keys = preg_replace('!\*+!', '%', $keys);
        $sql = "SELECT * FROM {url_alias} WHERE LOWER(dst) LIKE LOWER('%%%s%%')";
        $result = pager_query($sql, 50, 0, NULL, $keys);
        while ($path = db_fetch_object($result)) {
          $found[] = array('title' => $path->dst,
            'link' => url("admin/build/path/edit/$path->pid"));
        }

        return $found;
      }
  }
}
```

When the search API invokes hook_search('name'), it's looking for the name the menu tab should display on the generic search page (see Figure 12-3). In our case, we're returning "URL aliases." By returning the name of the menu tab, the search API wires up the link of the menu tab to a new search form.

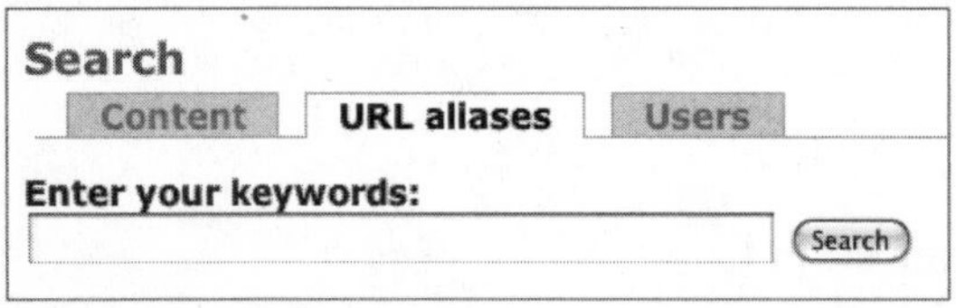

Search

| Content | **URL aliases** | Users |

Enter your keywords:

[   ] (Search)

Figure 12-3. *By returning the name of the menu tab from hook_search(), the search form becomes accessible.*

hook_search('search') is the workhorse part of hook_search(). It is invoked when the search form is submitted, and its job is to collect and return the search results. In the preceding code, we query the url_alias table, using the search terms submitted from the form. We then collect the results of the query and send them back in an array. The results are formatted by the search module and displayed to the user, as shown in Figure 12-4.

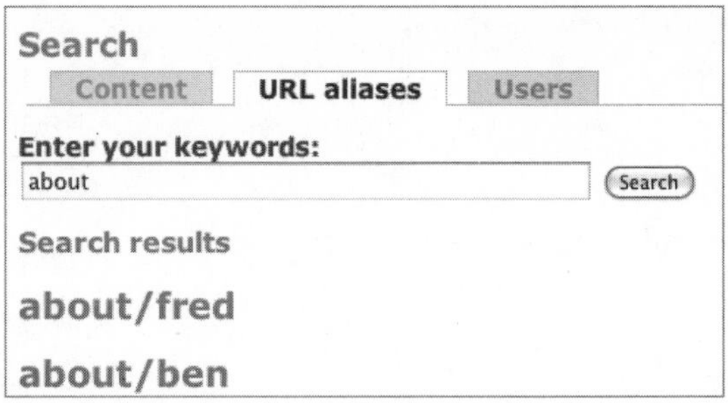

Figure 12-4. *Search results are formatted by the search module.*

Let's move on to the search results page. If the default search results page isn't as robust as you'd like it to be, you can override the default view. In our case, rather than showing just a list of matching aliases, let's make a sortable table of search results with individual "edit" links for each matching alias. With a couple of adjustments to the return value of hook_search ('search') and by implementing hook_search_page(), we're set.

```
/**
 * Implementation of hook_search().
 */
function pathfinder_search($op = 'search', $keys = null) {
  switch ($op) {
    case 'name':
      if (user_access('administer url aliases')) {
        return t('URL aliases');
      }
      break;

    case 'search':
      if (user_access('administer url aliases')) {
        $header = array(
          array('data' => t('Alias'), 'field' => 'dst'),
          t('Operations'),
        );

        // Return to this page after an 'edit' operation.
        $destination = drupal_get_destination();
        // Replace wildcards with MySQL/PostgreSQL wildcards.
        $keys = preg_replace('!\*+!', '%', $keys);
        $sql = "SELECT * FROM {url_alias} WHERE LOWER(dst) LIKE LOWER('%%%s%%')" .
          tablesort_sql($header);
        $result = pager_query($sql, 50, 0, NULL, $keys);
        while ($path = db_fetch_object($result)) {
          $rows[] = array(
            l($path->dst, $path->dst),
```

```
            l(t('edit'), "admin/build/path/edit/$path->pid",
                array('query' => $destination))
          );
        }
        if (!$rows) {
          $rows[] = array(array('data' => t('No URL aliases found.'),
              'colspan' => '2'));
        }

        return $rows;
      }
    }
}

/**
 * Implementation of hook_search_page().
 */
function pathfinder_search_page($rows) {
  $header = array(
      array('data' => t('Alias'), 'field' => 'dst'), ('Operations'));
  $output = theme('table', $header, $rows);
  $output .= theme('pager', NULL, 50, 0);
  return $output;
}
```

In the preceding code, we use drupal_get_destination() to retrieve the current location of the page we're on, and if we click and edit a URL alias, we'll automatically be taken back to this search results page. The path editing form knows where to return to because that information is passed in as part of the edit link. You'll see an additional parameter in the URL called destination, which contains the URL to return to once the form is saved.

For sorting of the results table, we append the tablesort_sql() function to the search query string to make sure the correct SQL ORDER BY clauses are appended to the query. Finally, pathfinder_search_page() is an implementation of hook_search_page() and allows us to control the output of the search results page. Figure 12-5 shows the final search results page.

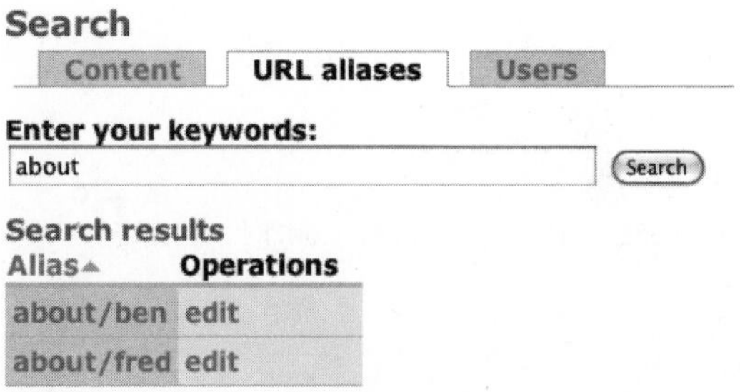

Figure 12-5. *The search results page now presents results as a sortable table.*

Using the Search HTML Indexer

So far, we've examined how to interact with the default search form by providing a simple implementation of hook_search('search'). However, when we move from searching a simple VARCHAR database column with LIKE to seriously indexing web site content, it's time to outsource the task to Drupal's built-in HTML indexer.

The goal of the indexer is to efficiently search large chunks of HTML. It does this by processing content when cron is called (via http://example.com/cron.php). As such, there is a lag time between when new content is searchable and how often cron is scheduled to run. The indexer parses data and splits text into words (called *tokenization*), assigning scores to each token based on a rule set, which can be extended with the search API. It then stores this data in the database, and when a search is requested it uses these indexed tables instead of the node tables directly.

■**Note** Because searching and indexing happens with cron, there is a lag time between when new content is searchable and how often cron is scheduled to run. Also, indexing is an intensive task. If you have a busy Drupal site where hundreds of new nodes are added between cron runs, it might be time to move to a search solution that works alongside Drupal, such as Solr (see http://drupal.org/project/apachesolr).

When to Use the Indexer

Indexers are generally used when implementing search engines that evaluate more than the standard "most words matched" approach. Search *relevancy* refers to content passing through a (usually complex) rule set to determine ranking within an index.

You'll want to harness the power of the indexer if you need to search a large bulk of HTML content. One of the greatest benefits in Drupal is that blogs, forums, pages, and so forth are all nodes. Their base data structures are identical, and this common bond means they also share basic functionality. One such common feature is that all nodes are automatically indexed if a search module is enabled; no extra programming is needed. Even if you create a custom node type, searching of that content is already built in, provided that the modifications you make show up in the node when it is rendered.

How the Indexer Works

The indexer has a preprocessing mode where text is filtered through a set of rules to assign scores. Such rules include dealing with acronyms, URLs, and numerical data. During the preprocessing phase, other modules have a chance to add logic to this process in order to perform their own data manipulations. This comes in handy during language-specific tweaking, as shown here using the contributed Porter-Stemmer module:

- resumé ➤ resume (accent removal)

- skipping ➤ skip (stemming)

- skips ➤ skip (stemming)

Another such language preprocessing example is word splitting for the Chinese, Japanese, and Korean languages to ensure the character text is correctly indexed.

■Tip The Porter-Stemmer module (`http://drupal.org/project/porterstemmer`) is an example of a module that provides word stemming to improve English language searching. Likewise, the Chinese Word Splitter module (`http://drupal.org/project/csplitter`) is an enhanced preprocessor for improving Chinese, Japanese, and Korean searching. A simplified Chinese word splitter is included with the search module and can be enabled on the search settings page.

After the preprocessing phase, the indexer uses HTML tags to find more important words (called *tokens*) and assigns them adjusted scores based on the default score of the HTML tags and the number of occurrences of each token. These scores will be used to determine the ultimate relevancy of the token. Here's the full list of the default HTML tag scores (they are defined in `search_index()`):

```
<h1> = 25
<h2> = 18
<h3> = 15
<h4> = 12
<a> = 10
<h5> = 9
<h6> = 6
<b> = 3
<strong> = 3
<i> = 3
<em> = 3
<u> = 3
```

Let's grab a chunk of HTML and run it through the indexer to better understand how it works. Figure 12-6 shows an overview of the HTML indexer parsing content, assigning scores to tokens, and storing that information in the database.

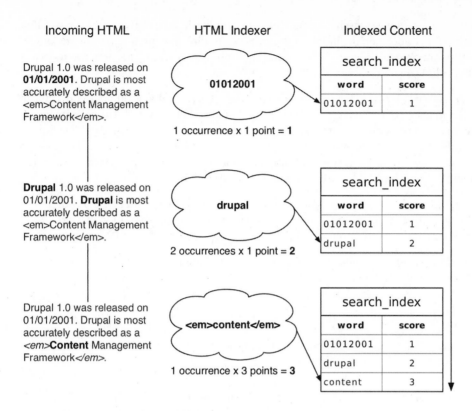

Figure 12-6. *Indexing a chunk of HTML and assigning token scores*

When the indexer encounters numerical data separated by punctuation, the punctuation is removed and numbers alone are indexed. This makes elements such as dates, version numbers, and IP addresses easier to search for. The middle process in Figure 12-6 shows how a word token is processed when it's not surrounded by HTML. These tokens have a weight of 1. The last row shows content that is wrapped in an emphasis (<em>) tag. The formula for determining the overall score of a token is as follows:

```
Number of matches x Weight of the HTML tag
```

It should also be noted that Drupal indexes the filtered output of nodes so, for example, if you have an input filter set to automatically convert URLs to hyperlinks, or another filter to convert line breaks to HTML breaks and paragraph tags, the indexer sees this content with all the markup in place and can take the markup into consideration and assign scores accordingly. A greater impact of indexing filtered output is seen with a node that uses the PHP evaluator filter to generate dynamic content. Indexing dynamic content could be a real hassle, but because Drupal's indexer sees only the output of content generated by the PHP code, dynamic content is automatically fully searchable.

When the indexer encounters internal links, they too are handled in a special way. If a link points to another node, then the link's words are added to the target node's content, making answers to common questions and relevant information easier to find. There are two ways to hook into the indexer:

- hook_nodeapi('update index'): You can add data to a node that is otherwise invisible in order to tweak search relevancy. You can see this in action within the Drupal core for taxonomy terms and comments, which technically aren't part of the node object but should influence the search results. These items are added to nodes during the indexing phase using the taxonomy module's implementation of the nodeapi('update index') hook. You may recall that hook_nodeapi() only deals with nodes.

- hook_update_index(): You can use the indexer to index HTML content that is not part of a node using hook_update_index(). For a Drupal core implementation of hook_update_index(), see node_update_index() in modules/node/node.module.

Both of these hooks are called during cron runs in order to index new data. Figure 12-7 shows the order in which these hooks run.

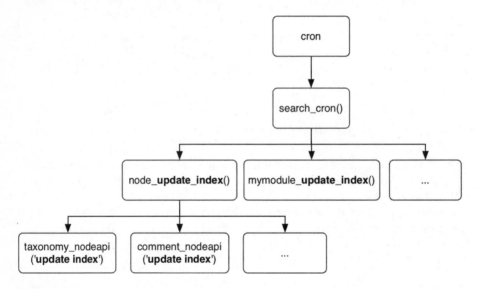

Figure 12-7. *Overview of HTML indexing hooks*

We'll look at these hooks in more detail in the sections that follow.

Adding Metadata to Nodes: hook_nodeapi('update_index')

When Drupal indexes a node for searching, it first runs the node through node_view() to generate the same output anonymous users would see in their web browser. This means any parts of the node that are visible will be indexed. For example, assume we have a node with an ID of 26. The parts of the node that are visible when viewing the URL http://example.com/ ?q=node/26 are what the indexer also sees.

What if we have a custom node type that contains hidden data that needs to influence search results? A good example of where we might want to do this is with `book.module`. We could index the chapter headings along with each child page to boost the relevancy of those children pages.

```
/**
 * Implementation of hook_nodeapi().
 */
function book_boost_nodeapi($node, $op) {
  switch ($op) {
    case 'update index':
      // Book nodes have a parent link ID attribute.
      // If it's nonzero we can have the menu system retrieve
      // the parent's menu item which gives us the title.
      if ($node->type == 'book' && $node->book['plid']) {
        $item = menu_link_load($node->book['plid']);
        return '<h2>'. $item['title'] .'</h2>';
      }
  }
}
```

Notice that we wrapped the title in HTML heading tags to inform the indexer of a higher relative score value for this text.

Note The nodeapi hook is only for appending metadata to nodes. To index elements that aren't nodes, use `hook_update_index()`.

Indexing Content That Isn't a Node: hook_update_index()

If you need to wrap the search engine around content that isn't made up of Drupal nodes, you can hook right into the indexer and feed it any textual data you need, thus making it searchable within Drupal. Suppose your group supports a legacy application that has been used for entering and viewing technical notes about products for the last several years. For political reasons, you cannot yet replace it with a Drupal solution, but you'd love to be able to search those technical notes from within Drupal. No problem. Let's assume the legacy application keeps its data in a database table called `technote`. We'll create a short module that will send the information in this database to Drupal's indexer using `hook_update_index()` and present search results using `hook_search()`.

Note If you'd like to index content from a non-Drupal database, take a look at Chapter 5 for more information on connecting to multiple databases.

Create a folder named `legacysearch` inside `sites/all/modules/custom`. If you want to have a legacy database to play with, create a file named `legacysearch.install`, and add the following contents:

```php
<?php
// $Id$

/**
 * Implementation of hook_install().
 */
function legacysearch_install() {
  // Create table.
  drupal_install_schema('legacysearch');
  // Insert some data.
  db_query("INSERT INTO technote VALUES (1, 'Web 1.0 Emulator',
    '<p>This handy product lets you emulate the blink tag but in
    hardware...a perfect gift.</p>', 1172542517)");
  db_query("INSERT INTO technote VALUES (2, 'Squishy Debugger',
    '<p>Fully functional debugger inside a squishy gel case.
    The embedded ARM processor heats up...</p>', 1172502517)");
}

/**
 * Implementation of hook_uninstall().
 */
function legacysearch_uninstall() {
  drupal_uninstall_schema('legacysearch');
}

/**
 * Implementation of hook_schema().
 */
function legacysearch_schema() {
  $schema['technote'] = array(
    'description' => t('A database with some example records.'),
    'fields' => array(
      'id' => array(
        'type' => 'serial',
        'not null' => TRUE,
        'description' => t("The tech note's primary ID."),
      ),
      'title' => array(
        'type' => 'varchar',
        'length' => 255,
        'description' => t("The tech note's title."),
      ),
```

```
      'note' => array(
        'type' => 'text',
        'description' => t('Actual text of tech note.'),
      ),
      'last_modified' => array(
        'type' => 'int',
        'unsigned' => TRUE,
        'description' => t('Unix timestamp of last modification.'),
      ),
    ),
    'primary key' => array('id'),
  );
  return $schema;
}
```

This module typically wouldn't need this install file, since the legacy database would already exist; we're just using it to make sure we have a legacy table and data to work with. You would instead adjust the queries within the module to connect to your existing non-Drupal table. The following queries assume the data is in a non-Drupal database with the database connection defined by $db_url['legacy'] in settings.php.

Next, add sites/all/modules/custom/legacysearch/legacysearch.info with the following content:

```
; $Id$
name = Legacy Search
description = Example of indexing/searching external content with Drupal.
package = Pro Drupal Development
core = 6.x
```

Finally, add sites/all/modules/custom/legacysearch/legacysearch.module along with the following code:

```php
<?php
// $Id$

/**
 * @file
 * Enables searching of non-Drupal content.
 */
```

Go ahead and keep legacysearch.module open in your text editor, and we'll add hook_update_index(), which feeds the legacy data to the HTML indexer. You can now safely enable your module after creating these files.

```php
/**
 * Implementation of hook_update_index().
 */
function legacysearch_update_index() {
```

```
  // We define these variables as global so our shutdown function can
  // access them.
  global $last_change, $last_id;

  // If PHP times out while indexing, run a function to save
  // information about how far we got so we can continue at next cron run.
  register_shutdown_function('legacysearch_update_shutdown');

  $last_id = variable_get('legacysearch_cron_last_id', 0);
  $last_change = variable_get('legacysearch_cron_last_change', 0);

  // Switch database connection to legacy database.
  db_set_active('legacy');
  $result = db_query("SELECT id, title, note, last_modified
                      FROM {technote}
                      WHERE (id > %d) OR (last_modified > %d)
                      ORDER BY last_modified ASC", $last_id, $last_change);

  // Switch database connection back to Drupal database.
  db_set_active('default');

  // Feed the external information to the search indexer.
  while ($data = db_fetch_object($result)) {
    $last_change = $data->last_modified;
    $last_id = $data->id;

    $text = '<h1>' . check_plain($data->title) . '</h1>' . $data->note;

    search_index($data->id, 'technote', $text);
  }
}
```

Each piece of content is passed to search_index() along with an identifier (in this case the value from the ID column of the legacy database), the type of content (I made up the type technote; when indexing Drupal content it's typically node or user), and the text to be indexed.

register_shutdown_function() assigns a function that's executed after the PHP script execution is complete for a request. This is to keep track of the ID of the last indexed item, because PHP may time out before all content has been indexed.

```
/**
 * Shutdown function to make sure we remember the last element processed.
 */
function legacysearch_update_shutdown() {
  global $last_change, $last_id;

  if ($last_change && $last_id) {
    variable_set('legacysearch_cron_last', $last_change);
    variable_set('legacysearch_cron_last_id', $last_id);
  }
}
```

The last function we need for this module is an implementation of hook_search(), which lets us use the built-in search interface for our legacy information.

```php
/**
 * Implementation of hook_search().
 */
function legacysearch_search($op = 'search', $keys = NULL) {
  switch ($op) {
    case 'name':
      return t('Tech Notes'); // Used on search tab.

    case 'reset':
      variable_del('legacysearch_cron_last');
      variable_del('legacysearch_cron_last_id');
      return;

    case 'search':
      // Search the index for the keywords that were entered.
      $hits = do_search($keys, 'technote');

      $results = array();

      // Prepend URL of legacy system to each result. Assume a legacy URL
      // for a given tech note is http://technotes.example.com/note.pl?3
      $legacy_url = 'http://technotes.example.com/';

      // We now have the IDs of the results. Pull each result
      // from the legacy database.
      foreach ($hits as $item) {
        db_set_active('legacy');
        $note = db_fetch_object(db_query("SELECT * FROM {technote} WHERE
          id = %d", $item->sid));
        db_set_active('default');

        $results[] = array(
          'link' => url($legacy_url . 'note.pl', array('query' => $item->sid,
            'absolute' => TRUE)),
          'type' => t('Note'),
          'title' => $note->title,
          'date' => $note->last_modified,
          'score' => $item->score,
          'snippet' => search_excerpt($keys, $note->note));
      }
      return $results;
  }
}
```

After cron has run and the information has been indexed, the technical notes will be available to search, as shown in Figure 12-8. They will be indexed inside Drupal, but legacysearch_search() will return search results that are built from (and point to) the legacy system.

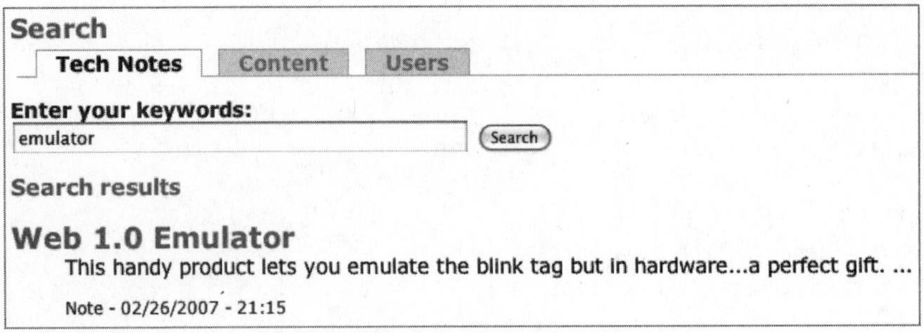

Figure 12-8. *Searching an external legacy database*

Summary

After reading this chapter, you should be able to

- Customize the search form.

- Understand how to use the search hook.

- Understand how the HTML indexer works.

- Hook into the indexer for any kind of content.

■ ■ ■

## CHAPTER 13

Working with Files

Drupal has the ability to upload and download files in a variety of ways. In this chapter, you'll learn about public and private files and how they're served, deal briefly with the handling of media files, and look at Drupal's file authentication hook.

How Drupal Serves Files

Drupal provides two mutually exclusive modes for managing file download security: public mode and private mode. In private mode, it is possible to check user permissions when a download is requested, and the download is denied if the user doesn't have proper access. In public mode, any user who can access a file's URL may download the file. This setting is applied on a site-wide basis rather than module by module or file by file, so the decision to use privately or publicly served files is usually made during initial site setup and affects all modules using Drupal's file API.

■**Caution** Because public and private file storage methods result in different URLs being generated for file downloads, it's important to choose the option that will work best for your site before you start uploading files, and stick to the method you choose.

To set up the file system paths and specify which download method to use, navigate to Administer ➤ Site configuration ➤ File system.

As shown in Figure 13-1, Drupal will warn you if the directory you have specified doesn't exist, or if PHP doesn't have write permission to it.

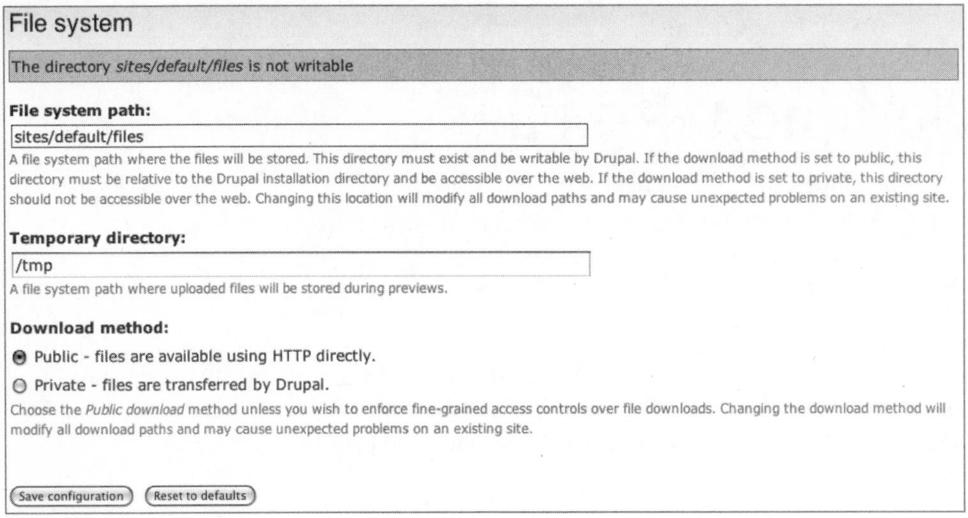

File system

The directory *sites/default/files* is not writable

File system path:

```
sites/default/files
```

A file system path where the files will be stored. This directory must exist and be writable by Drupal. If the download method is set to public, this directory must be relative to the Drupal installation directory and be accessible over the web. If the download method is set to private, this directory should not be accessible over the web. Changing this location will modify all download paths and may cause unexpected problems on an existing site.

Temporary directory:

```
/tmp
```

A file system path where uploaded files will be stored during previews.

Download method:

◉ Public - files are available using HTTP directly.

◯ Private - files are transferred by Drupal.

Choose the *Public download* method unless you wish to enforce fine-grained access controls over file downloads. Changing the download method will modify all download paths and may cause unexpected problems on an existing site.

(Save configuration)   (Reset to defaults)

Figure 13-1. *The interface for specifying file-related settings in Drupal. In this case, Drupal is warning that the file system path that has been specified does not have the proper permissions; the directory specified by the file system path must be created and given appropriate permissions.*

Public Files

The most straightforward configuration is the public file download method, in which Drupal stays out of the download process. When files are uploaded, Drupal simply saves them in the directory you've specified in Administer ➤ Site configuration ➤ File system and keeps track of the URLs of the files in a database table (so Drupal knows which files are available, who uploaded them, and so on). When a file is requested, it's transferred directly by the web server over HTTP as a static file and Drupal isn't involved at all. This has the advantage of being very fast, because no PHP needs to be executed. However, no Drupal user permissions are checked.

When specifying the file system path, the folder must exist and be writable by PHP. Usually the user (on the operating system) that is running the web server is also the same user running PHP. Thus, giving that user write permission to the `files` folder allows Drupal to upload files. With that done, be sure to specify the file system path at Administer ➤ Site configuration ➤ File system. Once these changes are saved, Drupal automatically creates an `.htaccess` file inside your `files` folder. This is necessary to protect your server from a known Apache security exploit allowing users to upload and execute scripts embedded in uploaded files (see `http://drupal.org/node/66763`). Check to make sure your `files` folder contains an `.htaccess` file containing the following information:

```
SetHandler Drupal_Security_Do_Not_Remove_See_SA_2006_006
Options None
Options +FollowSymLinks
```

■**Tip** When running Drupal on a web server cluster, the location of the temporary files directory needs to be shared by all web servers. Because Drupal may use one request to upload the file and a second to change its status from temporary to permanent, many load-balancing schemes will result in the temp file going to one server while the second request goes to another. When this happens, files will appear to upload properly, but will never appear in the nodes or content to which they're attached. Ensure that all your web servers are using the same shared `temp` directory, and use a sessions-based load balancer. Your files directory, like your database, should be global to your web servers.

Private Files

In private download mode, the `files` folder can be located anywhere PHP may read and write, and need not be (and in most cases ought not be) directly accessible by the web server itself.

The security of private files comes at a performance cost. Rather than delegating the work of file serving to the web server, Drupal takes on the responsibility of checking access permissions and serving out the files, and Drupal is fully bootstrapped on every file request.

PHP Settings

A number of settings in `php.ini` are easy to overlook but are important for file uploads. The first is `post_max_size` under the Data Handling section of `php.ini`. Because files are uploaded by an HTTP POST request, attempts to upload files of a size greater than `post_max_size` will fail due to the amount of POST data being sent.

```
; Maximum size of POST data that PHP will accept.
post_max_size = 8M
```

The File Uploads section of `php.ini` contains several more important settings. Here you can determine whether file uploads are allowed and what the maximum file size for uploaded files should be.

```
;;;;;;;;;;;;;;;;
; File Uploads ;
;;;;;;;;;;;;;;;;

; Whether to allow HTTP file uploads.
file_uploads = On

; Temporary directory for HTTP uploaded files (will use system default if not
; specified).
;upload_tmp_dir =

; Maximum allowed size for uploaded files.
upload_max_filesize = 20M
```

If file uploads seem to be failing, check that these settings are not at fault. Also, note that upload_max_filesize should be less than post_max_size, which should be less than memory_limit:

```
upload_max_filesize < post_max_size < memory_limit
```

Two final settings that can leave you stumped are max_execution_time and max_input_time. If your script exceeds these limits while uploading a file, PHP will terminate your script. Check these settings if you see uploads from slow Internet connections failing.

```
;;;;;;;;;;;;;;;;;;;
; Resource Limits ;
;;;;;;;;;;;;;;;;;;;

max_execution_time = 60     ; Maximum execution time of each script, in seconds
                            ; xdebug uses this, so set it very high for debugging
max_input_time = 60         ; Maximum amount of time each script may spend
                            ; parsing request data
```

When debugging, you'll want to have max_execution_time set at a high value (e.g., 1600) so the debugger does not time out. Bear in mind, however, that if your server is very busy, it is possible to tie up Apache processes for a long time while the files are uploaded, raising a potential scalability concern.

Media Handling

The file API (found in includes/file.inc) doesn't provide a generic user interface for uploading files. To fill that gap for most end users, upload.module exists in Drupal core, and several contributed modules offer alternatives.

Upload Module

The upload module adds an upload field to the node types of your choice. The upload field is shown in Figure 13-2.

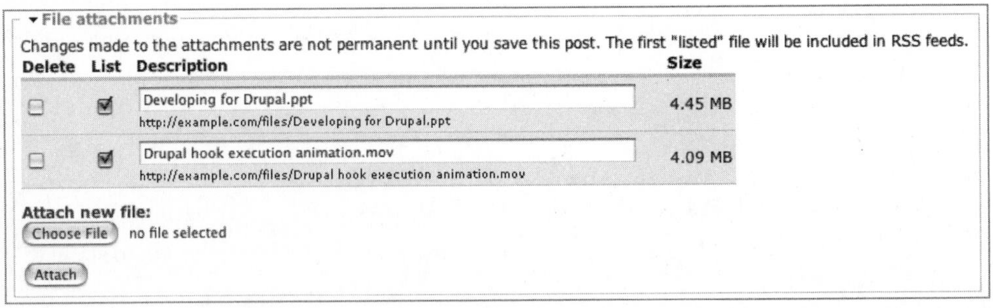

Figure 13-2. *The "File attachments" field is added to the node form when the upload module is enabled and the user has "upload files" permission.*

After a file has been uploaded on the node edit form, `upload.module` can add download links to uploaded files underneath the node body. The links are visible to those who have "view uploaded files" permission, as shown in Figure 13-3.

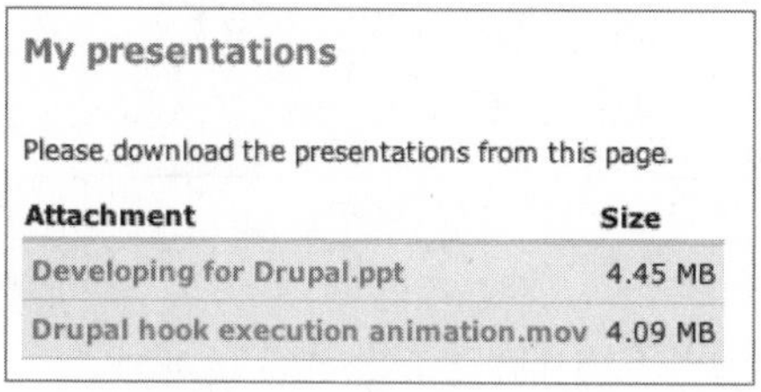

My presentations

Please download the presentations from this page.

Attachment	Size
Developing for Drupal.ppt	4.45 MB
Drupal hook execution animation.mov	4.09 MB

Figure 13-3. *A generic list view of files uploaded to a node using the core upload module*

This generic solution probably isn't robust enough for most people, so let's see some specific examples in the following section.

Other Generic File-Handling Modules

Alternatives to `upload.module` for file uploading can be viewed at `http://drupal.org/project/Modules/category/62`. Another option for file uploads is to use the CCK module with one of its contributed file-handling fields, such as imagefield or filefield. See `http://drupal.org/project/Modules/category/88` for more CCK field types.

Images and Image Galleries

Need to create an image gallery? The image module (`http://drupal.org/project/image`) is a good place to start. It handles image resizing and gallery creation. There are also some very nice solutions when using CCK for displaying images inline. Imagecache (`http://drupal.org/project/imagecache`) handles on-the-fly creation of image derivatives (additional modified copies of the uploaded image, such as thumbnails), while imagefield (`http://drupal.org/project/imagefield`) creates image upload fields within node forms.

Video and Audio

Numerous modules that help to manage media such as video files, Flash content, slideshows, and so on can be found at `http://drupal.org/project/Modules/category/67`.

File API

The file API lives in `includes/file.inc`. We'll cover some of the commonly used functions in this section. For more, the interested reader is directed to the API documentation to study the API in its current form at `http://api.drupal.org/api/6/group/file/6`.

Database Schema

Although Drupal stores files on disk, it still uses the database to store a fair amount of metadata about the files. In addition to authorship, MIME type, and location, it maintains revision information for uploaded files. The schema for the `files` table is shown in Table 13-1.

Table 13-1. *The files Table*

Field*	Type	Default	Description
fid	serial		Primary key
uid	int	0	User ID of the user associated with the file
filename	varchar(255)	' '	Name of the file
filepath	varchar(255)	' '	Path of the file relative to the Drupal root
filemime	varchar(255)	' '	The MIME type of the file
filesize	int	0	Size of the file in bytes
status	int	0	Flag indicating whether files is temporary (1) or permanent (0)
timestamp	int	0	Unix timestamp indicating when file was added

* Bold indicates a primary key; italics indicate an indexed field

Modules that enable file management keep their own data in their own table(s). For example, since the upload module associates files with nodes, it keeps track of that information in the `upload` table. The schema of the core upload module's table is shown in Table 13-2.

Table 13-2. *The upload Table Used by the Upload Module*

Field*	Type	Default	Description
fid	int	0	Primary key (the fid of the file in the files table)
nid	int	0	The nid associated with the uploaded file
vid	int	0	The node revision ID associated with the uploaded file
description	varchar(255)	' '	Description of the uploaded file
list	int	0	Flag indicating whether the file should be listed (1) or not (0) on the node
weight	int	0	Weight of this upload in relation to others on this node

* Bold indicates a primary key; italics indicate an indexed field

Common Tasks and Functions

If you want to do something with a file, chances are that the File API already has a convenient function for you to use. Let's look at some of these.

Finding the File System Path

The file system path is the path to the directory where Drupal will write files, such as those that have been uploaded. This directory is called "File system path" in Drupal's administrative user interface at Administer ➤ Site configuration ➤ File system, and corresponds with the Drupal variable file_directory_path.

file_directory_path()

This function is really just a wrapper for variable_get('file_directory_path', conf_path() .'/files'). In a new Drupal installation, the return value is sites/default/files.

Saving Data to a File

Sometimes you just want to save data in a file. That's what the following function does.

file_save_data($data, $dest, $replace = FILE_EXISTS_RENAME)

The $data parameter will become the contents of the file. The $dest parameter is the file path of the destination. The $replace parameter determines Drupal's behavior if a file of the same name already exists at the destination. Possible values are shown in Table 13-3.

Table 13-3. *Constants That Determine Drupal's Behavior When a File of the Same Name Exists at the Destination*

Name	Meaning
FILE_EXISTS_REPLACE	Replace the existing file with the current file.
FILE_EXISTS_RENAME	Append an underscore and integer to make the new filename unique.
FILE_EXISTS_ERROR	Abort and return FALSE.

Here's a quick example that puts a short string into a file in Drupal's file system directory:

```
$filename = 'myfile.txt';
$dest= file_directory_path() .'/'. $filename;
file_save_data('My data', $dest);
```

The file is at a location like sites/default/files/myfile.txt and contains the string My data.

Copying and Moving Files

The following functions help you work with files that are already on the file system.

file_copy(&$source, $dest = 0, $replace = FILE_EXISTS_RENAME)

The file_copy() function copies files into Drupal's file system path (typically sites/default/files). The $source parameter is a string specifying the location of the original file, though the function will also handle a file object that has $source->filepath and optionally

`$source->filename` defined (e.g., the upload module uses a file object). Note that because the `$source` parameter is passed by reference, it must be a variable, not a string literal. Listings 13-1 and 13-2 show a file being copied to Drupal's default `files` directory (thus, the lack of a defined destination) incorrectly and correctly, respectively.

Listing 13-1. *Incorrect Way to Copy File to Drupal's Default files Directory (A String Cannot Be Passed by Reference)*

```
file_copy('/path/to/file.pdf');
```

Listing 13-2. *Correct Way to Copy File to Drupal's Default files Directory*

```
$source = '/path/to/file.pdf';
file_copy($source);
```

The `$dest` parameter is a string specifying the destination of the newly copied file inside Drupal's file system path. If the `$dest` parameter is not specified, the default file system path is used. The copy will fail if `$dest` is outside of Drupal's file system path (other than Drupal's temporary directory) or if the directory specified by the file system path is not writable.

The `$replace` parameter determines Drupal's behavior when the file already exists at the destination. Table 13-3 summarizes the constants that may be used for the `$replace` parameter.

file_move(&$source, $dest = 0, $replace = FILE_EXISTS_RENAME)

The `file_move()` function works just like the `file_copy()` function (in fact, it calls `file_copy()`), but also removes the original file by calling `file_delete()`.

Checking Directories, Paths, and Locations

When you work with files, you often need to stop and determine whether things are okay. For example, maybe a directory does not exist or is not writable. The following functions will help with those sorts of problems.

file_create_path($dest = 0)

This function is used to get the path of items within Drupal's file system path. For example, when Drupal creates the `css` subdirectory where aggregated and compressed CSS files are stored when CSS optimization is enabled, it does this:

```
// Create the css/ within the files folder.
$csspath = file_create_path('css');
file_check_directory($csspath, FILE_CREATE_DIRECTORY);
```

Some examples follow:

```
$path = file_create_path('foo');     // returns 'sites/default/files/foo'
$path = file_create_path('foo.txt'); // returns 'sites/default/files/foo.txt'
$path = file_create_path('sites/default/files/bar/baz')
                                     // returns 'sites/default/files/bar/baz'
$path = file_create_path('/usr/local/') // returns FALSE
```

file_check_directory(&$directory, $mode = 0, $form_item = NULL)

This function checks that a given directory exists and is writable. The $directory parameter is the path to a directory and must be passed as a variable, since it is passed by reference. The $mode parameter determines what Drupal should do if the directory does not exist or is not writable. Modes are shown in Table 13-4.

Table 13-4. *Possible Values of the $mode Parameter for file_check_directory()*

Value	Meaning
0	Do not create the directory if it does not exist.
FILE_CREATE_DIRECTORY	Create the directory if it does not exist.
FILE_MODIFY_PERMISSIONS	Create the directory if it does not exist. If the directory already exists, attempt to make it writable.

The $form_item parameter is the name of a form item against which errors should be set if, for example, directory creation fails. The $form_item parameter is optional.

This function also tests whether the directory being checked is the file system path or the temporary directory, and if so, adds an .htaccess file for security (see Chapter 20).

file_check_path(&$path)

If you have a file path that you'd like to split into filename and base name components, use file_check_path(). The $path parameter must be in a variable; the variable will be modified to contain the base name. Here are some examples:

```
$path = 'sites/default/files/foo.txt';
$filename = file_check_path($path);
```

$path now contains sites/default/files and $filename now contains foo.txt.

```
$path = 'sites/default/files/css'; // Where Drupal stores optimized CSS files.
$filename = file_check_path($path);
```

$path now contains sites/default/files and $filename now contains css if the css directory does not exist or an empty string if the css directory exists.

```
$path = '/etc/bar/baz.pdf';
$filename = file_check_path($path);
```

$path now contains /etc/bar and $filename now contains FALSE (since /etc/bar does not exist or is not writable).

file_check_location($source, $directory = '')

Sometimes you have a file path, but you don't trust it. Maybe a user entered it and is trying to exploit your site by getting creative with dots (e.g., providing files/../../../etc/passwd instead of a filename). Calling this function answers the question "Is this file really in this directory?" For example, the following will return 0 if the file's real location is not inside Drupal's file system path:

```
$real_path = file_check_location($path, file_directory_path());
```

If the file *is* inside the file system path, the real path of the file will be returned.

Uploading Files

Although the upload module offers a full-fledged implementation of file uploading for nodes, sometimes you just want to be able to upload a file that is not associated with a node. The following functions can help in that situation.

file_save_upload($source, $validators = array(), $dest = FALSE, $replace = FILE_EXISTS_RENAME)

The $source parameter tells the function which uploaded file is to be saved. $source corresponds with the name of the file input field in a web form. For example, the name of the form's file field on the "My account" page that allows you to upload your image (if this capability has been enabled at Administer ➤ User settings) is picture_upload. The form, as it appears in the web browser, is shown in Figure 13-4. The resulting $_FILES superglobal variable, as it exists when the user has clicked the Save button, is shown in Figure 13-5. Note that information in $_FILES is keyed by the name of the form's file field (that way, multiple file fields in a single form can be supported). The $_FILES superglobal is defined by PHP itself, not by Drupal.

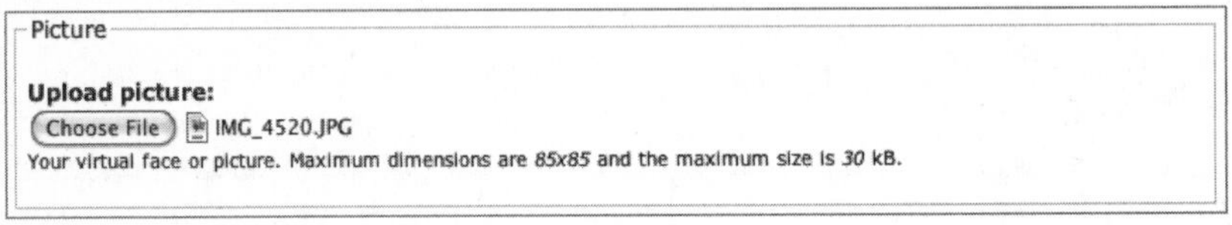

Figure 13-4. *File field for user_picture form element as it appears on the "My account" page*

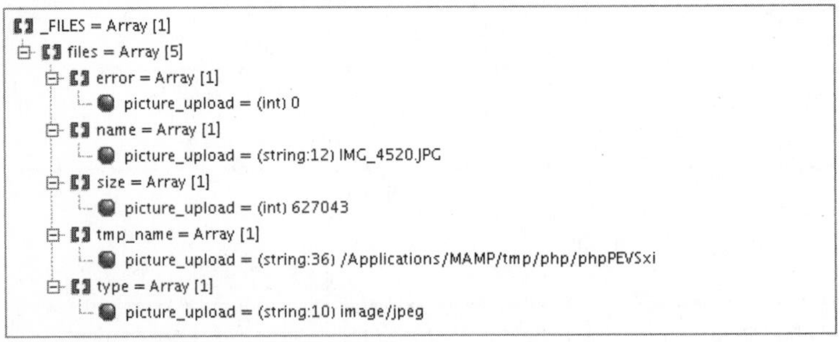

Figure 13-5. *Resulting $_FILES global variable settings after HTTP POST*

The $validators parameter contains an array of function names that will be called if the file is successfully uploaded. For example, the user_validate_picture() function, which is a form validation function that is called after a user edits his or her "My account" page, adds three validators before calling file_save_upload(). If a parameter is to be passed to the validation function, it is defined in an array. For example, in the following code, when the validators are run, the call to file_validate_image_resolution() will look something like file_validate_image_resolution('85x85'):

```
/**
 * Validates uploaded picture on user account page.
 */
function user_validate_picture(&$form, &$form_state) {
  $validators = array(
    'file_validate_is_image' => array(),
    'file_validate_image_resolution' =>
      array(variable_get('user_picture_dimensions', '85x85')),
    'file_validate_size' => array(variable_get('user_picture_file_size', '30')
      * 1024),
  );
  if ($file = file_save_upload('picture_upload', $validators)) {
    ...
  }
  ...
}
```

The $dest parameter in the file_save_upload() function is optional and may contain the directory to which the file will be copied. For example, when processing files attached to a node, the upload module uses file_directory_path() (which defaults to sites/default/files) as the value for $dest (see Figure 13-6). If $dest is not provided, the temporary directory will be used.

The $replace parameter defines what Drupal should do if a file with the same name already exists. Possible values are listed in Table 13-3.

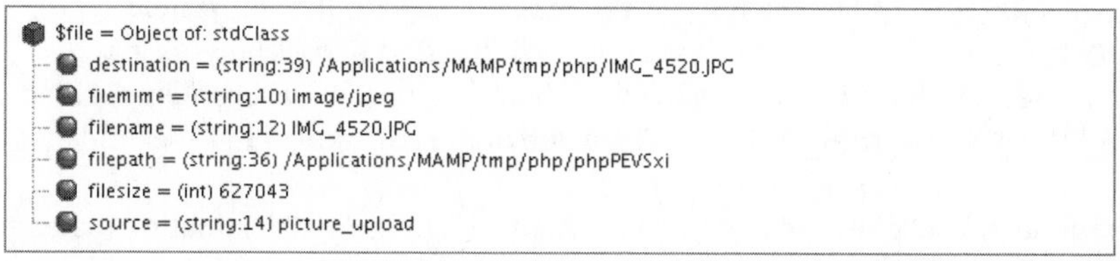

Figure 13-6. *The file object as it exists when passed to file_save_upload() validators*

The return value for file_save_upload() is a fully populated file object (as shown in Figure 13-7), or 0 if something went wrong.

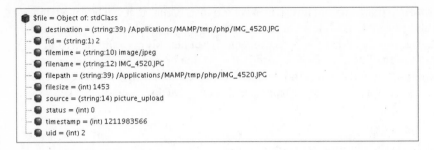

```
$file = Object of: stdClass
  destination = (string:39) /Applications/MAMP/tmp/php/IMG_4520.JPG
  fid = (string:1) 2
  filemime = (string:10) image/jpeg
  filename = (string:12) IMG_4520.JPG
  filepath = (string:39) /Applications/MAMP/tmp/php/IMG_4520.JPG
  filesize = (int) 1453
  source = (string:14) picture_upload
  status = (int) 0
  timestamp = (int) 1211983566
  uid = (int) 2
```

Figure 13-7. *The file object as it exists when returned from a successful call to file_save_upload()*

After calling file_save_upload(), a new file exists in Drupal's temporary directory and a new record is written to the files table. The record contains the same values as the file object shown in Figure 13-7.

Notice that the status field is set to 0. That means that as far as Drupal is concerned, this is still a temporary file. It is the caller's responsibility to make the file permanent. Continuing with our example of uploading a user picture, we see that the user module takes the approach of copying this file to the directory defined in Drupal's user_picture_path variable and renaming it using the user's ID:

```
// The image was saved using file_save_upload() and was added to the
// files table as a temporary file. We'll make a copy and let the garbage
// collector delete the original upload.
$info = image_get_info($file->filepath);
$destination = variable_get('user_picture_path', 'pictures') .
  '/picture-'. $form['#uid'] .'.'. $info['extension'];
file_copy($file, $destination, FILE_EXISTS_REPLACE));
...
```

This moves the uploaded image to sites/default/files/pictures/picture-2.jpg.

The garbage collector that is referred to in the preceding code comment is responsible for cleaning up temporary files that are languishing in the temporary directory. Drupal knows about them because it has a record for each file in the files table with the status field set to 0. The garbage collector can be found in the system_cron() function in modules/system/system.module. It deletes temporary files that are older than the number of seconds specified by the constant DRUPAL_MAXIMUM_TEMP_FILE_AGE. The value of the constant is 1440 seconds, or 24 minutes.

If the $dest parameter was provided and the file was moved to its final destination instead of the temporary directory, the caller can change the status of the record in the files table to permanent by calling file_set_status(&$file, $status), with $file set to the full file object (as shown in Figure 13-7) and $status set to FILE_STATUS_PERMANENT. According to includes/file.inc, if you plan to use additional status constants in your own modules, you must start with 256, as 0, 1, 2, 4, 8, 16, 32, 64, and 128 are reserved for core.

Validation functions that may be used with file_save_upload() follow.

file_validate_extensions($file, $extensions)

The $file parameter is the name of a file. The $extensions parameter is a string of space-delimited file extensions. The function will return an empty array if the file extension is allowed, and an array of error messages like `Only files with the following extensions are allowed: jpg jpeg gif png txt doc xls pdf ppt pps odt ods odp` if the file extension is disallowed. This function is a possible validator for `file_save_upload()`.

file_validate_is_image(&$file)

This function takes a file object and attempts to pass $file->filepath to `image_get_info()`. The function will return an empty array if `image_get_info()` was able to extract information from the file, or an array containing the error message `Only JPEG, PNG and GIF images are allowed` if the process failed. This function is a possible validator for `file_save_upload()`.

file_validate_image_resolution(&$file, $maximum_dimensions = 0, $minimum_dimensions = 0)

This function takes a file object and uses $file->filepath in several operations. If the file is an image, the function will check if the image exceeds $maximum_dimensions and attempt to resize it if possible. If everything goes well, an empty array will be returned and the $file object, which was passed by reference, will have $file->filesize set to the new size if the image was resized. Otherwise, the array will contain an error message, such as `The image is too small; the minimum dimensions are 320x240 pixels`. The $maximum_dimensions and $minimum_dimensions parameters are strings made up of width and height in pixels with a lowercase x separating them (e.g., 640x480 or 85x85). The default value of 0 indicates no restriction on size. This function is a possible validator for `file_save_upload()`.

file_validate_name_length($file)

The $file parameter is a file object. It returns an empty array if $file->filename exceeds 255 characters. Otherwise, it returns an array containing an error message instructing the user to use a shorter name. This function is a possible validator for `file_save_upload()`.

file_validate_size($file, $file_limit = 0, $user_limit = 0)

This function checks that a file is below a maximum limit for the file or a cumulative limit for a user. The $file parameter is a file object that must contain $file->filesize, which is the size of the file in bytes. The $file_limit parameter is an integer representing the maximum file size in bytes. The $user_limit parameter is an integer representing the maximum cumulative number of bytes that the current user is allowed to use. A 0 means "no limit." If validation passes, an empty array will be returned; otherwise, an array containing an error will be returned. This function is a possible validator for `file_save_upload()`.

Getting the URL for a File

If you know the name of a file that has been uploaded and want to tell a client what the URL for that file is, the following function will help.

file_create_url($path)

This function will return the correct URL for a file no matter whether Drupal is running in public or private download mode. The $path parameter is the path to the file (e.g., sites/ default/files/pictures/picture-1.jpg or pictures/picture-1.jpg). The resulting URL might be http://example.com/sites/default/files/pictures/picture-1.jpg. Note that the absolute path name to the file is not used. This makes it easier to move a Drupal site from one location (or server) to another.

Finding Files in a Directory

Drupal provides a powerful function called file_scan_directory(). It looks through a directory for files that match a given pattern.

file_scan_directory($dir, $mask, $nomask = array('.', '..', 'CVS'), $callback = 0, $recurse = TRUE, $key = 'filename', $min_depth = 0)

Let's walk through the function signature:

- $dir is the path of the directory in which to search. Do not include a trailing slash.

- $mask is the pattern to apply to the files that are contained in the directory. This is a regular expression.

- $nomask is an array of regular expression patterns. Any matches to the $nomask patterns will be ignored. The default array contains . (the current directory), .. (the parent directory), and CVS.

- $callback is the name of a function to be called for each match. The callback function will be passed one parameter: the path of the file.

- $recurse is a Boolean indicating whether the search should descend into subdirectories.

- $key determines what the array returned by file_scan_directory() should be keyed by. Possible values are filename (full path of matched files), basename (filename without path), and name (filename without path and without file suffix).

- $min_depth is the minimum depth of directories to return files from.

The return value is an associative array of objects. The key to the array depends on what is passed in the $key parameter, and defaults to filename. Following are some examples. Scan the themes/bluemarine directory for any files ending with .css:

```
$found = file_scan_directory('themes/bluemarine', '\.css$');
```

The resulting array of objects is shown in Figure 13-8.

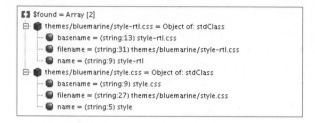

Figure 13-8. *The default result from file_scan_directory() is an array of objects keyed by the full filename.*

Changing the $key parameter to basename changes the keys of the resulting array, as shown in the following code and Figure 13-9.

```
$found = file_scan_directory('themes/bluemarine', '\.css$', array('.', '..', 'CVS'),
  0, TRUE, 'basename');
```

```
[] $found = Array [2]
  style-rtl.css = Object of: stdClass
      basename = (string:13) style-rtl.css
      filename = (string:31) themes/bluemarine/style-rtl.css
      name = (string:9) style-rtl
  style.css = Object of: stdClass
      basename = (string:9) style.css
      filename = (string:27) themes/bluemarine/style.css
      name = (string:5) style
```

Figure 13-9. *The result is now keyed by the filename with the full file path omitted.*

The use of the $callback parameter is what makes it easy for Drupal to clear the optimized CSS file cache, typically found in sites/default/files/css. The drupal_clear_css_cache() function passes in file_delete as the callback:

```
file_scan_directory(file_create_path('css'), '.*', array('.', '..', 'CVS'),
  'file_delete', TRUE);
```

Finding the Temp Directory

The following function reports the location of the temporary directory, often called the "temp" directory.

file_directory_temp()

The function first checks the file_directory_temp Drupal variable. If that's not set, it looks for the /tmp directory on Unix or the c:\\windows\temp and c:\\winnt\temp directories on Windows. If none of those succeed, it sets the temporary directory to a directory named tmp inside the file system path (e.g., sites/default/files/tmp). It returns whatever the final location of the temporary directory is and sets the file_directory_temp variable to that value.

Neutralizing Dangerous Files

Suppose you are using the public file download method and you have file uploads enabled. What will happen when someone uploads a file named `bad_exploit.php`? Will it run when the attacker hits `http://example.com/sites/default/files/bad_exploit.php`? Hopefully not, for three reasons. The first is that `.php` should never be in the list of allowed extensions for uploaded files. The second is the `.htaccess` file, which should be in `sites/default/files/` `.htaccess` (see Chapter 20). However, in several common Apache configurations, uploading the file `exploit.php.txt` may result in code execution of the file as PHP code (see `http://drupal.org/files/sa-2006-007/advisory.txt`). That brings us to the third reason: file name munging to render the file harmless. As a defense against uploaded executable files, the following function is used.

file_munge_filename($filename, $extensions, $alerts = TRUE)

The `$filename` parameter is the name of the file to modify. The `$extensions` parameter is a space-separated string containing file extensions. The `$alerts` parameter is a Boolean value that defaults to `TRUE` and results in the user being alerted through `drupal_set_message()` that the name of the file has been changed. The filename, with underscores inserted to disable potential execution, is returned.

```
$extensions = variable_get('upload_extensions_default', 'jpg jpeg gif png txt
  doc xls pdf ppt pps odt ods odp');
$filename = file_munge_filename($filename, $extensions, FALSE);
```

```
$filename is now exploit.php_.txt.
```

You can prevent filename munging by defining the Drupal variable `allow_insecure_uploads` to be 1 in `settings.php`. But this is usually a bad idea given the security implications.

file_unmunge_filename($filename)

This function attempts to undo the effects of `file_munge_filename()` by replacing an underscore followed by a dot with a dot:

```
$original = file_unmunge_filename('exploit.php_.txt');
```

```
$original is now exploit.php.txt.
```

Note that this will also replace any intentional occurrences of `_.` in the original filename.

Checking Disk Space

The following function reports on space used by files.

file_space_used($uid = NULL)

This function returns total disk space used by files. It does not actually check the file system, but rather reports the sum of the `filesize` field in the `files` table in the database. If a user ID is passed to this function, the query is restricted to files that match that user's ID in the `files` table. The upload module wraps this function with `upload_space_used()`. Call `file_space_used()` directly, as `upload_space_used()` is only available when the upload module is enabled.

Authentication Hooks for Downloading

Module developers can implement `hook_file_download()` to set access permissions surrounding the download of private files. The hook is used to determine the conditions on which a file will be sent to the browser, and returns additional headers for Drupal to append in response to the file HTTP request. Note that this hook will have no effect if your Drupal installation is using the public file download setting. Figure 13-10 shows an overview of the download process using the implementation of `hook_file_download()` found in the user module as an example.

Because Drupal invokes all modules with a `hook_file_download()` function for each download, it's important to specify the scope of your hook. For example, take `user_file_download()`, which only responds to file downloads if the file to be downloaded is within the `pictures` directory. If that's true, it appends headers to the request.

```
function user_file_download($file) {
  $picture_path = variable_get('user_picture_path', 'pictures');
  if (strpos($file, $picture_path .'/picture-') === 0) {
    $info = image_get_info(file_create_path($file));
    return array('Content-type: '. $info['mime_type']);
  }
}
```

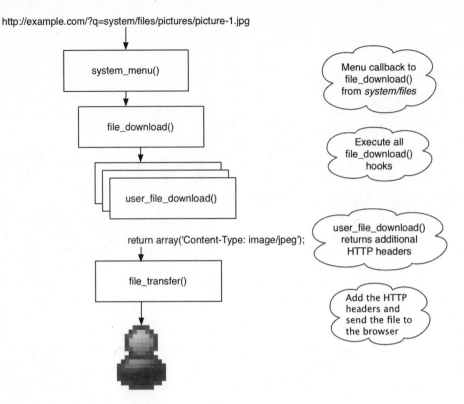

Figure 13-10. *Life cycle of a private file download request*

Implementations of hook_file_download() should return an array of headers if the request should be granted, or -1 to state that access to the file is denied. If no modules respond to the hook, then Drupal will return a 404 Not Found error to the browser.

Summary

In this chapter, you learned

- The difference between public and private files

- Contributed modules to use for image, video, and audio handling

- The database schema for file storage

- Common functions for manipulating files

- Authentication hooks for private file downloading

CHAPTER 14

■ ■ ■

Working with Taxonomy

Taxonomy is the classification of things. Drupal comes with a taxonomy module that allows you to classify nodes (which are, essentially, "things"). In this chapter, you'll look at the different kinds of taxonomies Drupal supports. You'll also see how the data is stored and how to write queries against the taxonomy database tables for incorporation into your own modules. Finally, you'll see how your modules can be notified of changes to taxonomies, and we'll go over some common taxonomy-related tasks.

What Is Taxonomy?

Taxonomy involves putting things into categories. You'll find Drupal's taxonomy support under Administer ➤ Content Management ➤ Taxonomy (if it doesn't appear there, make sure the taxonomy module is enabled). It's important to be precise when using words that involve Drupal's taxonomy system. Let's go through some of the common words you'll encounter.

Terms

A *term* is the actual label that will be applied to the node. For example, suppose you have a web site containing product reviews. You could label each review with the terms "Bad," "OK," or "Excellent." Terms are sometimes called *tags*, and the action of assigning terms to an object (such as a product review node) is sometimes called *tagging*.

A Level of Abstraction

As you'll see in a moment when you look at the data structures, Drupal adds a level of abstraction to all terms that are entered, and refers to them internally by a numeric ID, not by name. For example, if you enter the previous terms, but your manager decides that the word "Poor" is a better word than "Bad," there's no problem. You simply edit term number 1, and change "Bad" to "Poor." Everything inside Drupal will keep working, because Drupal thinks of it internally as term number 1.

Synonyms

When defining a term, you can enter *synonyms* of the term; a synonym is another term with the same semantic meaning. The taxonomy functionality included in Drupal allows you to enter synonyms and provides the database tables for storage and some utility functions like taxonomy_get_synonyms($tid) and taxonomy_get_synonym_root($synonym), but the implementation of the user interface for these functions is left up to contributed modules, such as the glossary module (http://drupal.org/project/glossary).

Vocabularies

A *vocabulary* consists of a collection of terms. Drupal allows you to associate a vocabulary with one or more node types. This loose association is very helpful for categorizing across node type boundaries. For example, if you had a web site where users could submit stories and pictures about travel, you could have a vocabulary containing country names as terms; this would allow you to see all stories *and* pictures tagged with "Belgium" easily. The vocabulary editing interface is shown in Figure 14-1.

Required Vocabularies

Vocabularies may be required or not required. If a vocabulary is required, the user must associate a term with a node before that node will be accepted for submittal. If a vocabulary is not required, the user may choose the default term "None selected" when submitting a node.

Controlled Vocabularies

When a vocabulary has a finite number of terms (that is, users cannot add new terms) it is said to be a *controlled vocabulary*. In a controlled vocabulary, terms are typically presented to the user inside a drop-down selection field. Of course, the administrator or a user who has been given administer taxonomy permission may add, delete, or modify terms.

Tags

A *tag* is the same thing as a *term*. However, the word "tagging" generally implies that the users of the web site create the tags. This is the opposite of a controlled vocabulary. Instead, users may enter their own term(s) when they submit a node. If a term is not already part of the vocabulary, it will be added. When the Tags check box on the vocabulary editing interface is checked (see Figure 14-1), the user interface to the vocabulary is presented as a text field (with JavaScript autocomplete enabled), rather than the drop-down selection field of a controlled vocabulary.

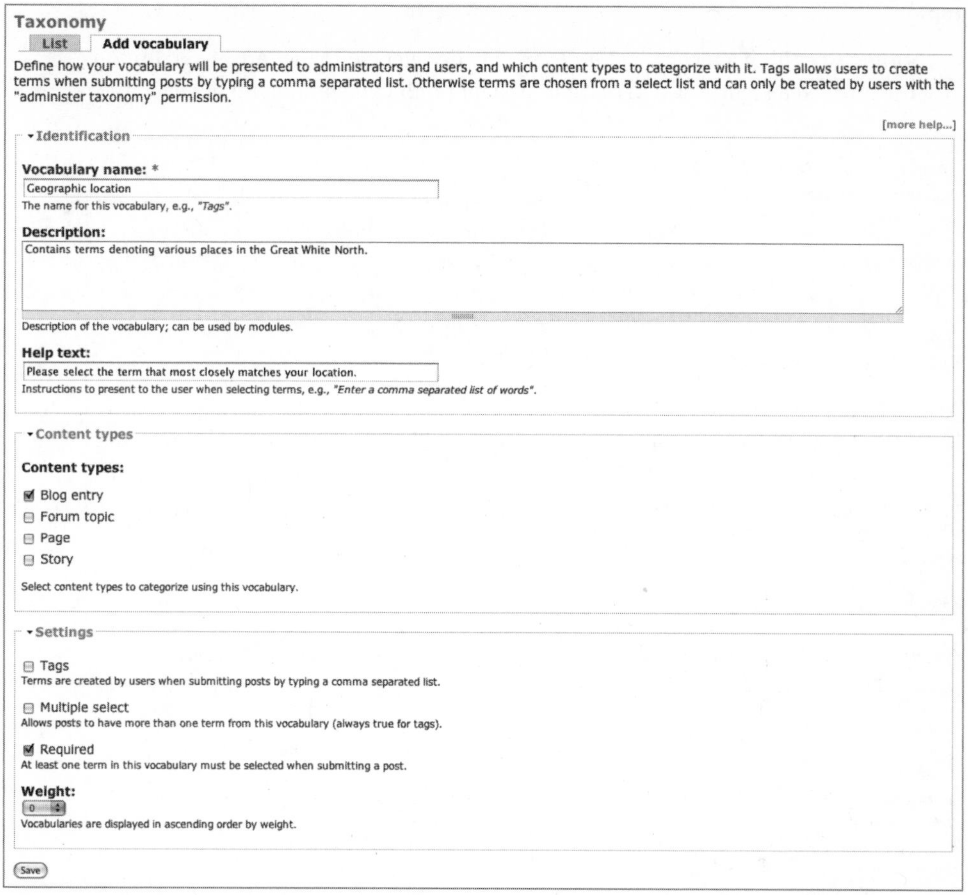

Taxonomy

| List | Add vocabulary |

Define how your vocabulary will be presented to administrators and users, and which content types to categorize with it. Tags allows users to create terms when submitting posts by typing a comma separated list. Otherwise terms are chosen from a select list and can only be created by users with the "administer taxonomy" permission.

[more help...]

┌─ ▾ **Identification** ───

Vocabulary name: *

| Geographic location |

The name for this vocabulary, e.g., *"Tags"*.

Description:

| Contains terms denoting various places in the Great White North. |

Description of the vocabulary; can be used by modules.

Help text:

| Please select the term that most closely matches your location. |

Instructions to present to the user when selecting terms, e.g., *"Enter a comma separated list of words"*.

┌─ ▾ **Content types** ──

Content types:

☑ Blog entry
☐ Forum topic
☐ Page
☐ Story

Select content types to categorize using this vocabulary.

┌─ ▾ **Settings** ───

☐ Tags
Terms are created by users when submitting posts by typing a comma separated list.

☐ Multiple select
Allows posts to have more than one term from this vocabulary (always true for tags).

☑ Required
At least one term in this vocabulary must be selected when submitting a post.

Weight:
| 0 ⬍ |
Vocabularies are displayed in ascending order by weight.

(Save)

Figure 14-1. *The form for adding a vocabulary*

Single vs. Multiple Terms

Drupal allows you to specify whether a single term or multiple terms can be selected for a given node by using the "Multiple select" check box on the vocabulary editing interface. Specifying multiple terms changes the user interface on the node submission form from a simple drop-down selection field to a multiple-selection drop-down field.

■**Tip** The "Multiple select" option only applies to controlled vocabularies, not to vocabularies with Tags enabled.

Parents

When adding or editing a term, a *parent term* may be selected in the "Advanced options" section of the form (see Figure 14-2). This defines a hierarchical relationship between the terms.

```
Add term to Geographic location
   List      Add term
 ┌─ ▾ Identification ──────────────────────────────────────────────
 │  Term name: *
 │  ┌──────────────────────────────────────────────┐
 │  │ British Columbia                               │
 │  └──────────────────────────────────────────────┘
 │  The name of this term.
 │  Description:
 │  ┌──────────────────────────────────────────────┐
 │  │ A western province of stunning beauty.        │
 │  │                                                │
 │  │                                                │
 │  └──────────────────────────────────────────────┘
 │  A description of the term. To be displayed on taxonomy/term pages and RSS feeds.
 └─────────────────────────────────────────────────────────────────

 ┌─ ▾ Advanced options ────────────────────────────────────────────
 │  Parents:
 │  ┌──────────┐
 │  │ <root>   │
 │  │ Canada   │
 │  │          │
 │  └──────────┘
 │  Parent terms.
 │  Related terms:
 │  ┌──────────┐
 │  │ <none>   │
 │  │ Canada   │
 │  │          │
 │  └──────────┘
 │  Synonyms:
 │  ┌──────────────────────────────────────────────┐
 │  │ The Pacific Province                           │
 │  │                                                │
 │  │                                                │
 │  └──────────────────────────────────────────────┘
 │  Synonyms of this term, one synonym per line.
 │  Weight: *
 │  ┌──────┐
 │  │ 0    │
 │  └──────┘
 │  Terms are displayed in ascending order by weight.
 └─────────────────────────────────────────────────────────────────
 ( Save )
```

Figure 14-2. *The form for adding a term*

Related Terms

If a vocabulary allows related terms, a multiple-selection field will be presented when you define a new term or edit an existing term so that you can choose the existing terms to which the term is related. The field appears in the "Advanced options" section of the form (see Figure 14-2).

Weights

Each vocabulary has a weight from –10 to 10 (see Figure 14-1). This controls the arrangement of the vocabularies when displayed to the user on the node submission form. A vocabulary with a light weight will rise to the top of the Vocabularies fieldset and be presented first; a vocabulary with a heavy weight will sink to the bottom of the fieldset.

   Each term has a weight, too. The position of a term when displayed to the user in the drop-down selection field is determined by the weight of the term. This order is the same as that displayed at Administer ➤ Content management ➤ Taxonomy ➤ List terms.

Kinds of Taxonomy

There are several kinds of taxonomy. The simplest is a list of terms, and the most complex has multiple hierarchical relationships. Additionally, terms may be synonyms of or related to other terms. Let's start with the simplest first.

Flat

A vocabulary that consists of only a list of terms is straightforward. Table 14-1 shows how you can classify some programming languages in a simple, flat vocabulary that we'll call Programming Languages.

Table 14-1. *Simple Terms in a Vocabulary*

Term ID	Term Name
1	C
2	C++
3	Cobol

Hierarchical

Now, let's introduce the concept of *hierarchy*, where each term may have a relationship to another term; see Table 14-2.

Table 14-2. *Hierarchical Terms in a Vocabulary (Child Terms Are Indented Below Their Parent)*

Term ID	Term Name
1	Object-Oriented
2	C++
3	Smalltalk
4	Procedural
5	C
6	Cobol

Figure 14-3 shows the hierarchical relationships explicitly. In this example, Procedural is a parent and Cobol is a child. Notice that each term has its own ID, no matter whether it's a parent or a child.

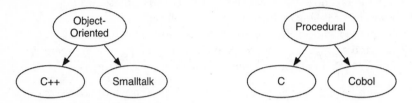

Figure 14-3. *A hierarchical vocabulary has parent-child relationships between terms.*

You can arrange terms into hierarchies when the term is created by selecting a parent term from the Parent field in the "Advanced options" section of the "Add term" form or by using drag and drop to position terms. After more than one term has been added, the drag-and-drop interface becomes available at Administer ➤ Content management ➤ Taxonomy by clicking the "list terms" link for the vocabulary you are working with. The drag-and-drop interface is shown in Figure 14-4.

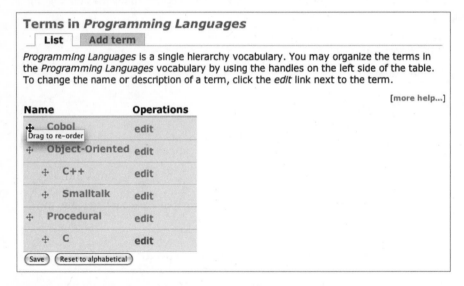

Figure 14-4. *Terms can be arranged into a hierarchy using the drag-and-drop interface.*

Multiple Hierarchical

A vocabulary may have multiple hierarchies instead of a single hierarchy. This simply means that a term may have more than one parent. For example, suppose you add PHP to your vocabulary of programming languages. PHP can be written procedurally, but in recent versions, object-oriented capabilities have been introduced. Should you classify it under Object-Oriented or Procedural? With multiple hierarchical relationships, you can do both, as shown in Figure 14-5.

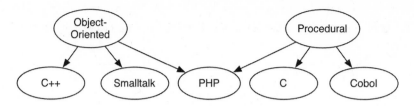

Figure 14-5. *In a multiple hierarchical vocabulary, terms can have more than one parent.*

It's worthwhile to spend a significant amount of time thinking through use cases for taxonomy when in the planning stage of a web site to determine what kind of vocabulary you need.

Because a multiple hierarchy vocabulary cannot easily be shown in a user interface, Drupal warns you that the drag-and-drop interface (shown in Figure 14-4) will be disabled if you select multiple parents for a term. The warning is shown in Figure 14-6.

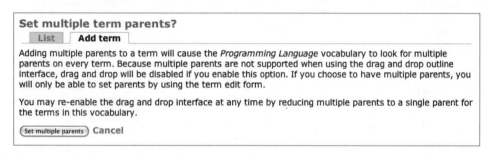

Figure 14-6. *Selecting multiple parents for a term will disable the drag-and-drop interface.*

Viewing Content by Term

You can always view the nodes associated with a given term by going to the term's URL, unless a module has overridden this view. For example, in http://example.com/?q=taxonomy/term/5, the 5 is the term ID of the term you wish to view. The result will be a list containing titles and teasers of each node tagged with that term.

Using AND and OR in URLs

The syntax for constructing taxonomy URLs supports AND and OR by use of the comma (,) and plus sign (+) characters, respectively. Some examples follow.

To show all nodes that have been assigned term IDs 5 and 6, use the following URL:

http://example.com/?q=taxonomy/term/5,6

Use the following URL to show all nodes that have been assigned term IDs 1, 2, or 3:

http://example.com/?q=taxonomy/term/1+2+3

Mixed AND and OR are not currently supported using taxonomy.module.

■**Tip** Use the path module to set friendly URL aliases for the taxonomy URLs you use so they won't have all those scary numbers at the end.

Specifying Depth for Hierarchical Vocabularies

In the previous examples, we've been using an implied parameter. For example, the URL

```
http://example.com/?q=taxonomy/term/5
```

is really

```
http://example.com/?q=taxonomy/term/5/0
```

where the trailing 0 is the number of levels of hierarchy to search when preparing the result set for display; all would designate that all levels should be included. Suppose you had the hierarchical vocabulary shown in Table 14-3.

Table 14-3. *A Geographical Hierarchical Vocabulary (Child Terms Are Indented Below Their Parent)*

Term ID	Name
1	Canada
2	British Columbia
3	Vancouver
4	Ontario
5	Toronto

The first level of hierarchy is the country, Canada; it has two children, the provinces British Columbia and Ontario. Each province has one child, a major Canadian city where Drupal development is rampant. Here's the effect of changing the depth parameter of the URL.

All nodes tagged with Vancouver will share the following URL:

```
http://example.com?q=taxonomy/term/3 or http://example.com?q=taxonomy/term/3/0
```

To display all nodes tagged with British Columbia (but none tagged with Vancouver), use this URL:

```
http://example.com?q=taxonomy/term/2
```

The following URL applies to all nodes tagged with British Columbia and any British Columbian city (note that we're setting the depth to one level of hierarchy):

```
http://example.com?q=taxonomy/term/2/1
```

All nodes tagged with Canada or with any Canadian province or city will be displayed if you use this one:

```
http://example.com?q=taxonomy/term/1/all
```

■Note The result set is displayed as a regular node listing. If you want to have the node titles and/or teasers *displayed* hierarchically, you'd need to write a custom theme function that does this or use the views module (`http://drupal.org/project/views`).

Automatic RSS Feeds

Each term has an automatic RSS feed that displays the latest nodes tagged with that term. For example, the feed for term ID 3 is at

```
http://example.com/?q=taxonomy/term/3/0/feed
```

Note that the depth parameter (0 in this case) is required. As expected, you can combine terms using AND or OR to make a combined feed. For example, here's a feed for terms 2 or 4, including all immediate child terms:

```
http://example.com/?q=taxonomy/term/2+4/1/feed
```

Here's one that contains all child terms:

```
http://example.com/?q=taxonomy/term/2+4/all/feed
```

Storing Taxonomies

If you're going to go beyond the built-in taxonomy capabilities, it's imperative that you understand how taxonomies are stored in the database. In a typical non-Drupal database, you might create a flat taxonomy by simply adding a column to a database table. As you've seen, Drupal adds a taxonomy through normalized database tables. Figure 14-7 shows the table structures.

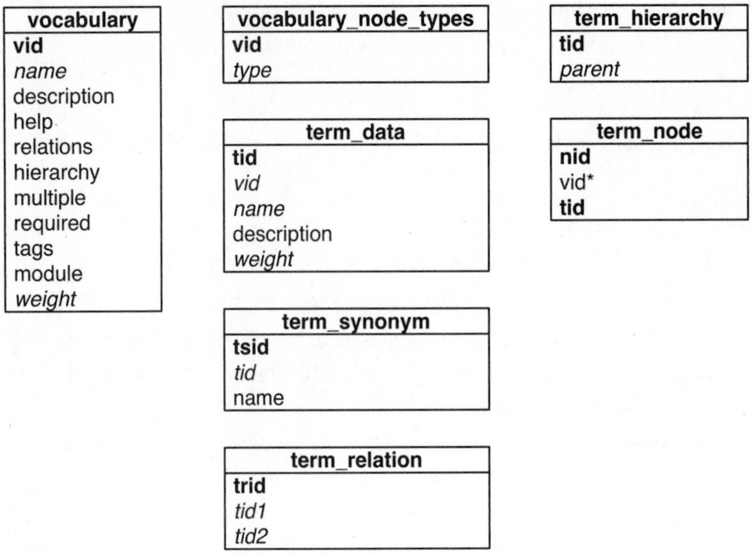

vocabulary
vid
name
description
help
relations
hierarchy
multiple
required
tags
module
weight

vocabulary_node_types
vid
type

term_data
tid
vid
name
description
weight

term_synonym
tsid
tid
name

term_relation
trid
tid1
tid2

term_hierarchy
tid
parent

term_node
nid
vid*
tid

Figure 14-7. *Drupal's taxonomy tables: Primary keys are in bold; indexed fields are in italics. *vid in the term_node table refers to the version ID in the node_revisions table, not to vocabulary ID.*

The following tables make up Drupal's taxonomy storage system:

- vocabulary: This table stores the information about a vocabulary that's editable through Drupal's Taxonomy interface.

- vocabulary_node_types: This table keeps track of which vocabularies may be used with which node types. The type is Drupal's internal node type name (for example, blog) and is matched with the node table's type column.

- term_data: This table contains the actual name of the term, which vocabulary it's in, its optional description, and the weight that determines its position in lists of terms presented to the user for term selection (for example, on the node submit form).

- term_synonym: Synonyms for a given term ID are contained in this table.

- term_relation: This match table contains the term IDs of terms that have been selected as related when defining a term.

- term_hierarchy: The term_hierarchy table contains the term ID of a term as well as the term ID of its parent. If a term is at the root (that is, it has no parent), the ID of the parent is 0.

- term_node: This table is used to match terms with the node that has been tagged with the term.

Module-Based Vocabularies

In addition to the vocabularies that can be created using Administer ➤ Content ➤ Categories, modules can use the taxonomy tables to store their own vocabularies. For example, the forum module uses the taxonomy tables to keep a vocabulary of containers and forums. The image module uses the taxonomy tables to organize image galleries. Any time you find yourself implementing hierarchical terms, ask yourself if you're not better off using the taxonomy module and a module-based vocabulary.

The module that owns a vocabulary is identified in the `module` column of the `vocabulary` table. Normally, this column will contain `taxonomy`, because the taxonomy module manages most vocabularies.

Creating a Module-Based Vocabulary

Let's look at an example of a module-based vocabulary. The contributed image gallery module (included with the image module; see `http://drupal.org/project/image`) uses taxonomy to organize different image galleries. It creates its vocabulary programmatically, as shown in the following example, and assumes ownership of the vocabulary by setting the module key of the `$vocabulary` array to the module name (without `.module`).

```
/**
 * Returns (and possibly creates) a new vocabulary for Image galleries.
 */
function _image_gallery_get_vid() {
  $vid = variable_get('image_gallery_nav_vocabulary', '');
  if (empty($vid) || is_null(taxonomy_vocabulary_load($vid))) {
    // Check to see if an image gallery vocabulary exists.
    $vid = db_result(db_query("SELECT vid FROM {vocabulary} WHERE
      module='image_gallery'"));
    if (!$vid) {
      $vocabulary = array(
        'name' => t('Image Galleries'),
        'multiple' => '0',
        'required' => '0',
        'hierarchy' => '1',
        'relations' => '0',
        'module' => 'image_gallery',
        'nodes' => array(
          'image' => 1
        )
      );
```

```
      taxonomy_save_vocabulary($vocabulary);
      $vid = $vocabulary['vid'];
    }
    variable_set('image_gallery_nav_vocabulary', $vid);
  }

  return $vid;
}
```

Providing Custom Paths for Terms

If your module is in charge of maintaining a vocabulary, it might want to provide custom paths for terms under its control, instead of using the default taxonomy/term/[term id] provided by taxonomy.module. When generating a link for a term, the taxonomy_term_path() function in taxonomy.module is called. (You should always call this function instead of generating links to taxonomy terms yourself; don't assume that the taxonomy module maintains the taxonomy.) Note how it checks with the module that owns the vocabulary in the following code:

```
/**
 * For vocabularies not maintained by taxonomy.module, give the maintaining
 * module a chance to provide a path for terms in that vocabulary.
 *
 * @param $term
 *    A term object.
 * @return
 *    An internal Drupal path.
 */

function taxonomy_term_path($term) {
  $vocabulary = taxonomy_get_vocabulary($term->vid);
  if ($vocabulary->module != 'taxonomy' &&
    $path = module_invoke($vocabulary->module, 'term_path', $term)) {
      return $path;
  }
  return 'taxonomy/term/'. $term->tid;
}
```

For example, image_gallery.module redirects paths to image/tid/[term id]:

```
function image_gallery_term_path($term) {
  return 'image/tid/'. $term->tid;
}
```

Keeping Informed of Vocabulary Changes with hook_taxonomy()

If you do keep a vocabulary for your own module, you'll want to be informed of any changes that are made to the vocabulary through the standard Taxonomy user interface. You might also want to be informed when a change is made to an existing vocabulary maintained by taxonomy.module. In either case, you can be informed of changes to vocabularies by implementing hook_taxonomy(). The following module has an implementation of hook_taxonomy() that keeps you informed of vocabulary changes by e-mail. Here's the taxonomymonitor.info file:

```
; $Id$
name = Taxonomy Monitor
description = Sends email to notify of changes to taxonomy vocabularies.
package = Pro Drupal Development
dependencies[] = taxonomy
core = 6.x
```

Here's taxonomymonitor.module:

```php
<?php
// $Id$

/**
 * Implementation of hook_taxonomy().
 *
 * Sends email when changes to vocabularies or terms occur.
 */
function taxonomymonitor_taxonomy($op, $type, $array = array()) {
  $to = 'me@example.com';
  $name = check_plain($array['name']);

  // $type is either 'vocabulary' or 'term'.
  switch ($type) {
    case 'vocabulary':
      switch($op) {
        case 'insert':
          $subject = t('Vocabulary @voc was added.', array('@voc' => $name));
          break;
        case 'update':
          $subject = t('Vocabulary @voc was changed.', array('@voc' => $name));
          break;
        case 'delete':
          $subject = t('Vocabulary @voc was deleted.', array('@voc' => $name));
          break;
      }
```

```
        break;
    case 'term':
      switch($op) {
        case 'insert':
          $subject = t('Term @term was added.', array('@term' => $name));
          break;
        case 'update':
          $subject = t('Term @term was changed.', array('@term' => $name));
          break;
        case 'delete':
          $subject = t('Term @term was deleted.', array('@term' => $name));
          break;
      }
  }

  // Dump the vocabulary or term information out and send it along.
  $body = print_r($array, TRUE);

  // Send the email.
  watchdog('taxonomymonitor', 'Sending email for @type @op',
    array('@type' => $type, '@op' => $op));
  hook_mail('taxonomymonitor-notify', $to, $subject, $body);
}
```

For extra bonus points, you could modify the module to include the name of the user who made the change.

Common Tasks

Here are some common tasks you may encounter when working with taxonomies.

Finding Taxonomy Terms in a Node Object

Taxonomy terms are loaded into a node during node_load() via the implementation of hook_nodeapi() in taxonomy.module. The taxonomy_node_get_terms() function does the actual work of retrieving the terms from the database. This results in an array of term objects inside the taxonomy key of the node:

```
print_r($node->taxonomy);
```

```
Array (
  [3] => stdClass Object (
     [tid]  => 3
     [vid]  => 1
     [name] => Vancouver
     [description] => By Land, Sea, and Air we Prosper.
     [weight] => 0 )
 )
```

Drupal supports node revisions. Because the taxonomy terms associated with a node can change from one revision of the node to the next, terms kept in the term_node table are associated with revisions by use of the revision id (dubbed vid for "version ID" in that table) as shown in Figure 14-7.

Building Your Own Taxonomy Queries

If you need to generate a node listing of some sort, you might end up wishing that things were simpler; you might wish that Drupal kept taxonomy terms in the node table, so you could say the following:

```
SELECT * FROM node WHERE vocabulary = 1 and term = 'cheeseburger'
```

The cost of flexibility is a bit more work for the Drupal developer. Instead of making simple queries such as this, you must learn to query the taxonomy tables using JOINs.

Using taxonomy_select_nodes()

Before you start writing a query, consider whether you can get what you want using an existing function. For example, if you want titles of nodes tagged by term IDs 5 and 6, you can use taxonomy_select_nodes():

```
$tids = array(5, 6);
$result = taxonomy_select_nodes($tids, 'and');
$titles = array();
while ($data = db_fetch_object($result)) {
  $titles[] = $data->title;
}
```

Taxonomy Functions

The following sections explain functions that might be useful for your module.

Retrieving Information About Vocabularies

The built-in functions in the following sections retrieve information about vocabularies, as vocabulary data objects or as an array of such objects.

taxonomy_ vocabulary_load($vid)

This function retrieves a single vocabulary (the $vid parameter is the vocabulary ID) and returns a vocabulary object. It also caches vocabulary objects internally, so multiple calls for the same vocabulary aren't expensive. This function is also a special load function from the point of view of Drupal's menu system (see Chapter 4 for details).

taxonomy_get_vocabularies($type)

The taxonomy_get_vocabularies($type) function retrieves all vocabulary objects. The $type parameter restricts the vocabularies retrieved to a given node type; for example, blog. This function returns an array of vocabulary objects.

Adding, Modifying, and Deleting Vocabularies

The following functions create, modify, and delete vocabularies. They return a status code that's one of the Drupal constants SAVED_UPDATED, SAVED_NEW, or SAVED_DELETED.

taxonomy_save_vocabulary(&$vocabulary)

This function creates a new vocabulary or updates an existing one. The $vocabulary parameter is an associative array (note that it is *not* a vocabulary object!) containing the following keys:

- name: The name of the vocabulary.

- description: The description of the vocabulary.

- help: Any help text that will be displayed underneath the field for this vocabulary in the node creation form.

- nodes: An array of node types to which this vocabulary applies.

- hierarchy: Set to 0 for no hierarchy, 1 for single hierarchy, and 2 for multiple hierarchy.

- relations: Set to 0 to disallow related terms or 1 to allow related terms.

- tags: Set to 0 to disable free tagging, or 1 to enable free tagging.

- multiple: Set to 0 to disable multiple selection of terms or 1 to enable multiple selection.

- required: Set to 0 to make the selection of a term prior to node submission optional (introduces a default "None selected" term) or 1 to make term selection required.

- weight: The weight of the vocabulary; it affects the placement of the node submission form in the Vocabularies fieldset.

- module: The name of the module that's responsible for this vocabulary. If this key is not passed, the value will default to taxonomy.

- vid: The vocabulary ID. If this key is not passed, a new vocabulary will be created.

The taxonomy_save_vocabulary(&$vocabulary) function returns SAVED_NEW or SAVED_UPDATED.

taxonomy_del_vocabulary($vid)

The $vid parameter of this function is the ID of the vocabulary. Deleting a vocabulary deletes all its terms by calling taxonomy_del_term() for each term. The taxonomy_del_vocabulary($vid) function returns SAVED_DELETED.

Retrieving Information About Terms

The built-in functions in the following sections retrieve information about terms, typically as objects or as an array of objects.

taxonomy_get_term($tid)

This function retrieves a term (the $tid parameter is the term ID) and returns a term object. It caches term objects internally, so multiple calls for the same term aren't expensive. The structure of the term object looks like this:

```
$term = taxonomy_get_term(5);
var_dump($term);
```

```
object(stdClass)#6 (5) {
  ["tid"] => string(1) "3"
  ["vid"] => string(1) "1"
  ["name"]=> string(9) "Vancouver"
  ["description"]=> string(32) "By Land, Sea, and Air we Prosper"
  ["weight"]=> string(1) "0"
}
```

taxonomy_get_term_by_name($text)

The taxonomy_get_term_by_name($text) function searches for terms matching a string (the $text parameter is a string). Whitespace is stripped from $text, and matches are found the query WHERE LOWER(t.name) = LOWER($text). This function returns an array of term objects.

taxonomy_node_get_terms($node, $key)

This function finds all terms associated with a node. The $node parameter is the node ID for which to retrieve terms, and the $key parameter defaults to tid and is a bit tricky. It affects the way results are returned. The taxonomy_node_get_terms($node, $key) function returns an array of arrays, keyed by $key. Therefore, the array of results will, by default, be keyed by term ID, but you can substitute any column of the term_data table (tid, vid, name, description, weight). This function caches results internally for each node.

■Tip The only property used from the node that is passed in is $node->vid. So if you know the version ID of the node for which you are trying to retrieve terms, you can avoid doing an expensive node_load() by passing in a fake node object with a $vid property, for example, $fake_node = new stdClass(); $fake_node->$vid = 12; $terms = taxonomy_node_get_terms($fake_node);.

---

taxonomy_node_get_terms_by_vocabulary($node, $vid, $key)

This function finds all terms within one vocabulary ($vid) that are associated with a node ($node). See the description of the $key parameter under taxonomy_node_get_terms($node, $key) for more information.

Adding, Modifying, and Deleting Terms

The following functions create, modify, and delete terms. They return a status code that is one of the Drupal constants SAVED_UPDATED, SAVED_NEW, or SAVED_DELETED.

taxonomy_save_term(&$term)

This function creates a new term or updates an existing term. The $term parameter is an associative array (note that it is *not* a term object!) consisting of the following keys:

- name: The name of the term.

- description: The description of the term. This value is unused by Drupal's default user interface, but might be used by your module or other third-party modules.

- vid: The ID of the vocabulary to which this term belongs.

- weight: The weight of this term. It affects the order in which terms are shown in term selection fields.

- relations: An optional array of term IDs to which this term is related.

- parent: Can be a string representing the term ID of the parent term, an array containing either strings representing the term IDs of the parent terms, or a subarray containing strings representing the term IDs of the parent terms. Optional.

- synonyms: An optional string containing synonyms delimited by line break (\n) characters.

- tid: The term ID. If this key isn't passed, a new term will be created.

This function returns SAVED_NEW or SAVED_UPDATED.

taxonomy_del_term($tid)

The taxonomy_del_term($tid) function deletes a term; the $tid parameter is the term ID. If a term is in a hierarchical vocabulary and has children, the children will be deleted as well, unless a child term has multiple parents.

Retrieving Information About Term Hierarchy

When working with hierarchical vocabularies, the functions in the following sections can come in handy.

taxonomy_get_parents($tid, $key)

This function finds the immediate parents of a term; the $tid parameter is the term ID. The $key parameter defaults to tid and is a column of the term_data table (tid, vid, name, description, weight). taxonomy_get_parents($tid, $key) returns an associative array of term objects, keyed by $key.

taxonomy_get_parents_all($tid)

This function finds all ancestors of a term; the $tid parameter is the term ID. The function returns an array of term objects.

taxonomy_get_children($tid, $vid, $key)

The taxonomy_get_children($tid, $vid, $key) function finds all children of a term. The $tid parameter is the term ID. The $vid parameter is optional; if a vocabulary ID is passed, the children of the term will be restricted to that vocabulary (note that this is only important for terms that have multiple parents in different vocabularies, a rare occurrence). The $key parameter defaults to tid and is a column of the term_data table (tid, vid, name, description, weight). This function returns an associative array of term objects, keyed by $key.

taxonomy_get_tree($vid, $parent, $depth, $max_depth)

This function generates a hierarchical representation of a vocabulary. The $vid parameter is the vocabulary ID of the vocabulary for which to generate the tree. You can specify the $parent parameter if you don't want the entire tree for a vocabulary and want only that part of the tree that exists under the term ID specified by $parent. The $depth parameter is for internal use and defaults to -1. The $max_depth parameter is an integer indicating the number of levels of the tree to return, and it defaults to NULL, indicating all levels. This function returns an array of term objects with depth and parent keys added. The depth key is an integer indicating the level of hierarchy at which the term exists in the tree, and the parents key is an array of term IDs of a term's parents. For example, let's get the results for the vocabulary shown in Table 14-3, which happens to be vocabulary ID 2:

```
$vid = 2;
print_r($taxonomy_get_tree($vid));
```

The results follow:

```
Array (
  [0] => stdClass Object (
    [tid] => 1
    [vid] => 2
    [name] => Canada
    [description] => A mari usque ad mare.
    [weight] => 0
    [depth] => 0
    [parents] => Array (
      [0] => 0 )
    )
  [1] => stdClass Object (
    [tid] => 4
    [vid] => 2
    [name] => Ontario
    [description] => Ut incepit fidelis sic permanet.
    [weight] => 0
    [depth] => 1
    [parents] => Array (
      [0] => 1 )
    )
  [2] => stdClass Object (
    [tid] => 5
    [vid] => 2
    [name] => Toronto
    [description] => Diversity Our Strength.
    [weight] => 0
    [depth] => 2
    [parents] => Array (
      [0] => 4 )
    )
  [3] => stdClass Object (
    [tid] => 2
    [vid] => 2
    [name] => British Columbia
    [description] => Splendor sine occasu.
```

```
      [weight] => 0
      [depth] => 1
      [parents] => Array (
        [0] => 1 )
      )
  [4] => stdClass Object (
    [tid] => 3
    [vid] => 2
    [name] => Vancouver
    [description] => By Land, Sea and Air We Prosper.
    [weight] => 0
    [depth] => 2
    [parents] => Array (
      [0] => 2 )
    )
)
```

Retrieving Information About Term Synonyms

The functions in the following sections might help you if your module implements support for synonyms.

taxonomy_get_synonyms($tid)

Use this function to retrieve an array of synonyms for a given term. The $tid parameter is the term ID. The function returns an array of strings; each string is a synonym of the term.

taxonomy_get_synonym_root($synonym)

Given a string in the $synonym parameter, this function executes an exact match search in the term_synonym table. It returns a single term object representing the first term found with that synonym.

Finding Nodes with Certain Terms

Sometimes, you want to have an easy way to query which nodes have certain terms or output the results of such a query. The following functions will help you with that.

taxonomy_select_nodes($tids, $operator, $depth, $pager, $order)

This function finds nodes that match conditions by building and executing a database query based on given parameters. It returns a resource identifier pointing to the query results. The $tids parameter is an array of term IDs. The $operator parameter is or (default) or and, and it specifies how to interpret the array of $tids. The $depth parameter indicates how many levels deep to traverse the taxonomy tree and defaults to 0, meaning "don't search for any children of the terms specified in $tid." Setting $depth to 1 would search for all nodes in which the terms specified in $tids *and their immediate children* occurred. Setting $depth to all searches the entire hierarchy below the terms specified in $tid. The $pager parameter is a Boolean value indicating whether resulting nodes will be used with a pager, and it defaults to TRUE. You might set $pager to FALSE if you were generating an XML feed. The $order parameter contains a literal order clause that will be used in the query's SQL and defaults to n.sticky DESC, n.created DESC.

If you're searching for many terms, this function can be database intensive.

taxonomy_render_nodes($result)

If you're using taxonomy_select_nodes() to query for nodes that match certain taxonomy conditions, it can be helpful to look at taxonomy_render_nodes() as a starting point for creating simple output from your query.

Additional Resources

Many modules use taxonomy for everything from adding access control (http://drupal.org/project/taxonomy_access), to dynamic category browsing (http://drupal.org/project/taxonomy_browser), to showing nodes that are related via taxonomy terms in a block (http://drupal.org/project/similarterms). The *Drupal Handbook* has more information about taxonomy at http://drupal.org/handbook/modules/taxonomy. See also the list of taxonomy-related modules at http://drupal.org/project/Modules/category/71.

You're encouraged to try the views module, especially for theming of taxonomy listings (http://drupal.org/project/views).

Summary

After reading this chapter, you should be able to

- Understand what taxonomy is.

- Understand terms, vocabularies, and their different options.

- Differentiate between flat, hierarchical, and multiple hierarchical vocabularies.

- Construct URLs to do AND and OR searches of taxonomy terms.

- Construct URLs for RSS feeds of taxonomy terms and term combinations.

- Understand how taxonomies are stored.

- Know how to use vocabularies within your own module.

- Set up your module to receive notification of changes to taxonomies.

■ ■ ■

## CHAPTER 15

Caching

Building pages for dynamic web sites requires numerous trips to the database to retrieve information about saved content, site settings, the current user, and so on. Saving the results of these expensive operations for later use is one of the easiest ways within the application layer to speed up a sluggish site. And it's not just database calls that are saved: the processing of the retrieved information in PHP is avoided too. Drupal's built-in cache API does this automatically for most core data and provides a number of tools for Drupal developers who want to leverage the API for their own purposes. For example, the memcache module (`http://drupal.org/project/memcache`) is an example of memory-based caching that makes use of the cache API.

▊Note This chapter covers caching within the Drupal application. Other layers of caching, such as the database's internal caching (e.g., MySQL's query cache), can also have a significant effect on performance. These are mentioned in Chapter 22).

Knowing When to Cache

It's important to remember that caching is a trade-off. Caching large chunks of data will boost performance quite a bit, but only in cases where that specific chunk of data is needed a second or third time. That's why Drupal's built-in full-page caching is only used for anonymous visitors—registered users often require customized versions of pages, and the caching would be much less effective. Caching smaller chunks of data (e.g., the list of today's popular articles) means less dramatic performance gains but still helps to speed up your site.

Caching works best on data that doesn't change rapidly. A list of the week's top stories works well. Caching a list of the last five comments posted on a busy forum is less helpful, because that information will become out of date so quickly that few visitors will be able to use the cached list before it needs to be updated. In the worst case, a bad caching strategy (e.g., caching data that changes too often) will add overhead to a site rather than reduce it.

How Caching Works

Modules often have to make expensive database queries or calls to remote web services. Rather than using resources for those operations every time they occur, modules can store a cache of their data into one of the database tables reserved for caching within the Drupal database, or they can create their own table and store the data there. The next time the data is needed, it can be quickly retrieved with a single query. As you'll see later in the chapter, Drupal's caching back-end is pluggable, so although we refer to database tables here, in reality the back-end may be some other storage such as flat files or a memory-based cache.

The default table to which your module can write cached information is named cache. Using this table is the best option when storing only a couple rows of cached information. If you're caching information for every node, menu, or user, you'll want your module to have its own dedicated cache table. This will improve performance by minimizing the number of rows in Drupal's cache table and reducing write contention. When defining a new cache table for your module to use, it must be structurally identical to the default cache table while having a different table name. It's a good idea to prepend cache_ to the table name for consistency. Let's take a look at the database structure of the cache table; see Table 15-1.

■**Note** When defining a new cache table for your module, it must be structurally identical to the default cache table.

Table 15-1. *cache Table Schema*

Field*	Type	Null	Default
cid	varchar(255)	NO	—
data	longblob	YES	—
expire	int	NO	0
created	int	NO	0
headers	text	YES	NULL
serialized	smallint	NO	0

Bold indicates a primary key; italics indicate an indexed field.

The cid column stores the primary cache ID for quick retrieval. Examples of cache IDs used within the Drupal core are the URL of the page for page caching (e.g., http://example.com/?q=node/1), a string and a theme name for caching the theme registry (e.g., theme_registry:garland), or even regular strings (e.g., the contents of the variables table are cached with the primary cache ID set to variables). The important point is that the cache ID must be a unique identifier for the item being cached.

The data column stores the information you wish to cache. Complex data types such as arrays or objects need to be serialized using PHP's serialize() function to preserve their data structure within the database (Drupal does this automatically).

The expire column takes one of the three following values:

- CACHE_PERMANENT: Indicates that the item should not be removed until cache_clear_all() has been called with the cache ID of the permanent item to wipe.

- CACHE_TEMPORARY: Indicates that the item should be removed the next time cache_clear_all() is called for a "general" wipe, with no minimum time enforcement imposed. Items marked CACHE_PERMANENT will not be removed from the cache.

- *A Unix timestamp*: Indicates that the item should be kept at least until the time provided, after which it will behave like an item marked CACHE_TEMPORARY and become eligible for deletion.

The created column is a Unix timestamp indicating the date the cache entry was created.

The headers column is for storing HTTP header responses when the cache data is an entire Drupal page request. Most of the time, you won't use the headers field, as you'll be caching data that doesn't rely on headers, such as parts of the page rather than the entire page itself. Bear in mind, though, that your custom cache table structure must still be identical to the default cache table, so keep the headers column around even if it isn't being used.

The serialized column indicates whether the data in the data column is in serialized form. A 0 indicates unserialized data while a 1 indicates serialized data. If the data is serialized and the value of the serialized column is 1, the cache system will unserialize the data before returning it to the caller. The cache system automatically serializes object and array data and sets the serialized column to 1 when this type of data is cached.

How Caching Is Used Within Drupal Core

Drupal ships with six cache tables by default: cache stores a copy of the variables table and the database schema and theme registry; cache_block stores cached copies of blocks; cache_menu stores cached copies of the navigational menus; cache_filter stores cached copies of each node's content after it has been parsed by the filter system; cache_form is used by the form API to avoid form building when possible; and cache_page stores cached copies of pages for anonymous users. We'll look at each of these caches in the following sections. It should be noted that the "Page cache" and "Block cache" settings at Administer ➤ Site configuration ➤ Performance only affect the page cache and block cache tables, not the other cache components within Drupal. In other words, filters, menus, and module settings are always cached.

Menu System

The menu system caches the router information that connects Drupal paths to callbacks. Any menu created by the menu module is cached, whether or not Drupal's page caching is enabled. So to clear the menu cache, use the "Clear cached data" button on the Administer ➤ Site configuration ➤ Performance page, or call menu_cache_clear_all(). If you've made changes to the menus that will affect blocks, you might want to call the more aggressive menu_rebuild() function instead; the menu cache is cleared when menus are rebuilt. Examples of menus include Drupal's Primary and Secondary links as well as the user navigation block. Menus are cached on a per-user, per-locale basis. See Chapter 4 for more information on the menu system.

Filtered Input Formats

When a node is created or edited, its content is run through the various filters associated with its input format. For example, the HTML Filter format converts line breaks to HTML <p> and <br /> tags, and also strips out malicious HTML. It would be an expensive operation to do this for every single view of a node. Therefore, the filters are applied to the node just after it has been created or edited, and that content is cached to the cache_filter database table, whether or not Drupal's page caching is enabled. See Chapter 11 for more information on input formats.

■**Tip** The filter cache is the reason that changes to the default length of node teasers within the adminis-trative interface take effect only after you resave each node. A quick workaround for this problem is to empty the cache_filter table so all node content is parsed and teasers built again. Or, if you are willing to have all caches cleared (including the filter cache), click the "Clear cached data" button on the Administer ➤ Site configuration ➤ Performance page.

Administration Variables and Module Settings

Drupal stores most administrative settings in the variables table, and caches that data in the cache table to speed the lookup of configuration data. Examples of such variables include the name of your site, settings for comments and users, and the location of the files directory. These variables are cached to a single row in the cache table, so they can be quickly retrieved, rather than making a database query for each variable value as it is needed. They are stored as a PHP array, so the cache value is serialized to preserve its structure. Any variable that uses variable_set() and variable_get() as its setter and getter functions will be stored and cached in this manner.

Pages

We have been discussing the bits and pieces that Drupal caches to optimize the more resource-heavy components of a site, but the biggest optimization Drupal makes is to cache an entire page view. For anonymous users, this is easily accomplished, since all pages look the same to all anonymous users. For logged-in users, however, every page is different and customized to each of their profiles. A different caching strategy is needed to cope with this situation.

For anonymous users, Drupal can retrieve the cached page content in a single query, although it takes a couple of other queries to load Drupal itself. You can choose one of two caching strategies for the anonymous user page cache: Normal or Aggressive. You can also disable caching. Normal and Aggressive strategies can be further modified by setting a minimum cache lifetime. These settings are found in the Drupal administration interface at Administer ➤ Site configuration ➤ Performance. The interface is shown in Figure 15-1. Let's look at each setting in the following sections.

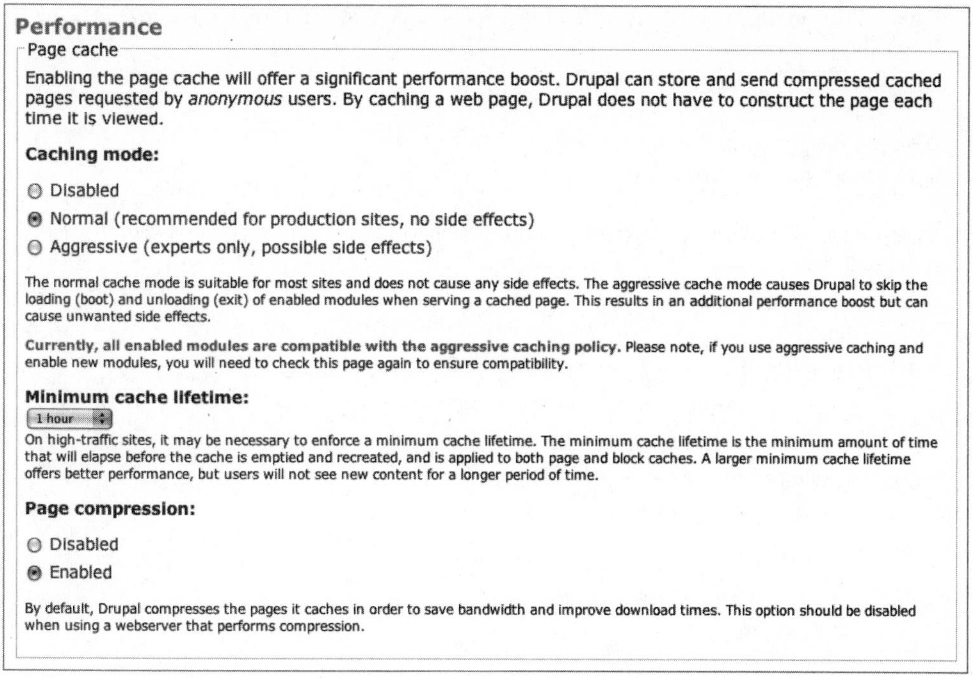

Performance

┌─ Page cache ──

Enabling the page cache will offer a significant performance boost. Drupal can store and send compressed cached pages requested by *anonymous* users. By caching a web page, Drupal does not have to construct the page each time it is viewed.

Caching mode:

○ Disabled

◉ Normal (recommended for production sites, no side effects)

○ Aggressive (experts only, possible side effects)

The normal cache mode is suitable for most sites and does not cause any side effects. The aggressive cache mode causes Drupal to skip the loading (boot) and unloading (exit) of enabled modules when serving a cached page. This results in an additional performance boost but can cause unwanted side effects.

Currently, all enabled modules are compatible with the aggressive caching policy. Please note, if you use aggressive caching and enable new modules, you will need to check this page again to ensure compatibility.

Minimum cache lifetime:

[1 hour ⬍]

On high-traffic sites, it may be necessary to enforce a minimum cache lifetime. The minimum cache lifetime is the minimum amount of time that will elapse before the cache is emptied and recreated, and is applied to both page and block caches. A larger minimum cache lifetime offers better performance, but users will not see new content for a longer period of time.

Page compression:

○ Disabled

◉ Enabled

By default, Drupal compresses the pages it caches in order to save bandwidth and improve download times. This option should be disabled when using a webserver that performs compression.

Figure 15-1. *The administrative interface for the control of page-caching behavior*

Disabled

This completely disables page caching. It is most useful when debugging a site. Generally, you will want to enable caching.

■**Note** Even with page caching disabled, Drupal will still cache user menus, filter content, the theme registry, the database schema, and system variables. These component-level caches cannot be disabled.

Normal

Normal page caching offers a huge performance boost over no caching at all, and is one of the easiest ways to speed up a slow Drupal site. Let's walk through the request life cycle when the Normal cache system is enabled.

To understand Normal page caching, you need to first make sense of Drupal's bootstrapping process. The bootstrapping process is made up of small, isolated steps called *phases*. Drupal takes advantage of this phased bootstrapping system to load and parse only the amount of code necessary to serve a cached page, and to keep database queries to a minimum.

Figure 15-2 details the process of serving a cached page request to an anonymous user.

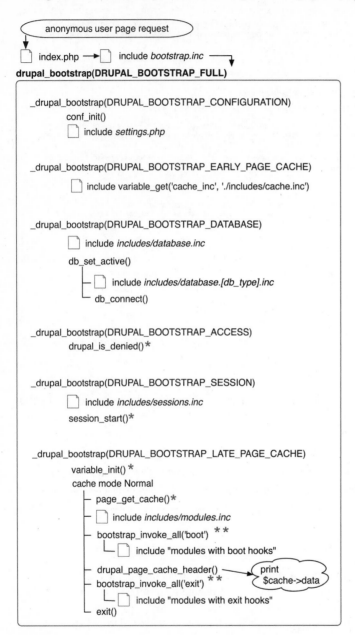

Figure 15-2. *This chart shows the request life cycle of anonymous user page caching under Drupal's Normal cache setting. The first five phases of the bootstrap process are not cache-specific and were added to this diagram for the sake of completeness. * indicates a database query; ** indicates that an unknown number of queries can be generated at this point.*

To begin, a request causes the web server to execute index.php. The first line of PHP code inside index.php is to include includes/bootstrap.inc, which contains the core functions for bootstrap loading. Next, index.php makes a call to drupal_bootstrap().

drupal_bootstrap() is in charge of executing each bootstrap phase. For normal caching, we only need to concern ourselves with the DRUPAL_BOOTSTRAP_LATE_PAGE_CACHE bootstrap phase. This phase begins with retrieving the system variables from the database. Assuming the cache strategy is Normal, the next step is to include includes/module.inc. Within module.inc are the functions allowing Drupal to bring the module system online. Drupal will then initialize modules that implement hook_boot() or hook_exit(). The activation of these hooks is accomplished with bootstrap_invoke_all('boot') and bootstrap_invoke_all('exit'), respectively. The statistics module, for example, uses the statistics_exit() function to track page visits. The throttle module uses the throttle_exit() function to alter the throttle level based on current traffic levels.

■**Note** Using hook_boot() or hook_exit() within a module comes at a performance price to the overall site, since your module will then be loaded for every cached page served to a visitor when running in Normal cache mode. You are also limited to the functions available to you when implementing these hooks, since includes/common.inc is not loaded. Common functions such as t(), l(), url(), and pager_query() are thus inaccessible.

---

drupal_page_cache_header() prepares the cache data by setting HTTP headers. Drupal will set Etag and 304 headers as appropriate, so browsers can use their own internal caching mechanisms and avoid unnecessary HTTP round-trips when applicable. The cached data is then sent to the browser if the headers sent by the browser have requested it.

Aggressive

Aggressive caching completely bypasses the loading of all modules (see Figure 15-3). This means the boot and exit hooks are never called for cached pages. The end result is less PHP code to parse, since no modules are loaded. There are also fewer database queries to execute. If you have modules enabled that use these hooks (such as the statistics module and the throttle module), they may not work correctly when Aggressive caching is enabled. Drupal will warn you about modules that may be affected on the administrative page at Administer ➤ Site configuration ➤ Performance.

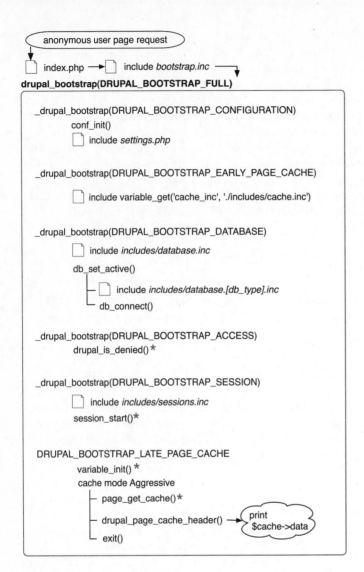

Figure 15-3. *The request life cycle of anonymous user page caching under Drupal's Aggressive cache setting. * indicates a database query.*

Minimum Cache Lifetime

This setting controls the lifetime of expired cache content on your site. When a user submits new content, he or she will always see the changes immediately; however, all other users will need to wait until the minimum cache lifetime expires in order to see new content. Of course, if the minimum cache lifetime is set to "none," everyone will always see new content immediately.

fastpath: The Hidden Cache Setting

The fastpath cache setting is not configurable from within the Drupal administration interface because of its highly advanced nature; fastpath gives developers the ability to bypass
Drupal to implement a highly customized cache solution, such as memory or file-based
caching (see Figure 15-4).

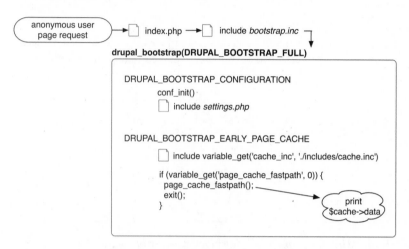

Figure 15-4. *The request life cycle of anonymous user page caching under Drupal's fastpath
cache setting*

The cacherouter contributed module (http://drupal.org/project/cacherouter) is one
module that takes advantage of fastpath mode. Suppose you have installed the module in
sites/all/modules/contrib.

Since fastpath doesn't make a database connection by default, all configuration options
reside within your settings.php file:

```
$conf = array(
  'page_cache_fastpath'  => TRUE,
  'cache_inc' => './sites/all/modules/contrib/cacherouter/cacherouter.inc',
  ... // More settings here.
);
```

The first item of the array enables fastpath mode by setting fastpath to TRUE. That's all
there is to enabling it! The second specifies the file that Drupal will load instead of loading
includes/cache.inc. In this case, the file specified is the custom-caching library that the
cacherouter module will use. The cacherouter module needs a bit more configuration; see
http://drupal.org/project/cacherouter for details.

When you load your own custom-caching library instead of the includes/cache.inc
library that Drupal uses by default, you'll need to write your own cache_set(), cache_get(),
and cache_clear_all() functions.

> **Note** Once `fastpath` caching is enabled, it overrides any caching options set within Drupal's administrative interface.

Blocks

Depending on their content, blocks may be cachable. Drupal's block caching can be enabled or disabled using the administrative interface at Administer ➤ Site configuration ➤ Performance (see Figure 15-5).

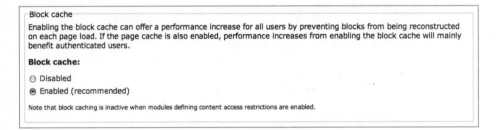

Figure 15-5. *The administrative interface for controlling block-caching behavior*

Block caching is accomplished when a module that provides a block declares the cachability of that block when responding to the list operation of hook_block(). For example, here is part of the hook_block() implementation of modules/user/user.module:

```
function user_block($op = 'list', $delta = 0, $edit = array()) {
  global $user;

  if ($op == 'list') {
    $blocks[0]['info'] = t('User login');
    // Not worth caching.
    $blocks[0]['cache'] = BLOCK_NO_CACHE;

    $blocks[1]['info'] = t('Navigation');
    // Menu blocks can't be cached because each menu item can have
    // a custom access callback. menu.inc manages its own caching.
    $blocks[1]['cache'] = BLOCK_NO_CACHE;

    $blocks[2]['info'] = t('Who\'s new');

    // Too dynamic to cache.
    $blocks[3]['info'] = t('Who\'s online');
    $blocks[3]['cache'] = BLOCK_NO_CACHE;
    return $blocks;
  }
...
}
```

In the preceding example, all the blocks provided by the user module declare that they should not be cached, with one exception. The "Who's new" block does not declare a cache preference, which means that if the administrator has enabled block caching and then enables the "Who's new" block, it will receive the default caching setting of BLOCK_CACHE_PER_ROLE. That means that a separate cached version of the block will be stored for each role. To be more precise, a separate cached version will be stored for each combination of roles; the cache ID is created by concatenating the current user's role IDs (see _block_get_cache_id() in modules/block/block.module). The possible constants for block caching are shown in Table 15-2.

Table 15-2. *Possible Constants for Block Caching*

Constant	Value	Meaning
BLOCK_NO_CACHE	-1	Do not cache this block.
BLOCK_CACHE_PER_ROLE	1	Each role sees a separate cached block.*
BLOCK_CACHE_PER_USER	2	Each user sees a separate cached block.
BLOCK_CACHE_PER_PAGE	4	Each page has its own cached block.
BLOCK_CACHE_GLOBAL	8	Blocks are cached once for all users.

* Default for blocks that do not declare a cache setting

All blocks that are cached are cached on a per-theme and per-language basis. This prevents users from seeing a block that is themed by a theme other than the one the user is viewing when multiple themes are enabled, and it prevents blocks from showing up in the wrong language when multiple languages are enabled.

■**Note** Blocks are never cached for the superuser (user 1).

The block constants (like menu constants) can be used together using PHP bitwise operators. For example, the "Book navigation" block provided by the book module's implementation of hook_block() uses both BLOCK_CACHE_PER_ROLE and BLOCK_CACHE_PER_PAGE:

```
function book_block($op = 'list', $delta = 0, $edit = array()) {
  $block = array();
  switch ($op) {
    case 'list':
      $block[0]['info'] = t('Book navigation');
      $block[0]['cache'] = BLOCK_CACHE_PER_PAGE | BLOCK_CACHE_PER_ROLE;
      return $block;
...
}
```

The BLOCK_CACHE_PER_ROLE and BLOCK_CACHE_PER_USER constants should not be combined with the bitwise OR operator (|), as the two caching modes are mutually exclusive.

Per-Request Caching with Static Variables

Many Drupal functions use a static variable to cache data. Within the lifetime of the HTTP request, a second call to the function will return the data instantly. Here is an example from the node module:

```
function node_get_types($op = 'types', $node = NULL, $reset = FALSE) {
  static $_node_types, $_node_names;

  if ($reset || !isset($_node_types)) {
    list($_node_types, $_node_names) = _node_types_build();
  }
  ...
}
```

Caching is never without cost. The cost for static variable caches is memory. Luckily, memory is usually more abundant than database CPU cycles.

Using the Cache API

Module developers looking to take advantage of the cache API have two functions they need to know: cache_set() and cache_get().

Caching Data with cache_set()

cache_set() is used for writing data to the cache. The function signature follows:

```
cache_set($cid, &data, $table = 'cache', $expire = CACHE_PERMANENT, $headers = NULL)
```

and the function parameters are

- $cid: A unique cache ID string that acts as a key to the data. Colons are used to delimit the hierarchy of possibilities.

- $table: The name of the table to store the data in. You can create your own table or use cache, cache_block, cache_filter, cache_form, cache_menu, or cache_page. The cache table is used by default.

- $data: The data to store in the cache. PHP objects and arrays will be automatically serialized.

- $expire: The length of time for which the cached data is valid. Possible values are CACHE_PERMANENT, CACHE_TEMPORARY, or a Unix timestamp. If a Unix timestamp is given, the data will be treated as if it were marked CACHE_TEMPORARY after the current time exceeds the Unix timestamp.

- $headers: For cached pages, a string of HTTP headers to pass along to the browser.

A common iteration pattern for cache_set() can be seen in modules/filter/filter.module:

```
// Store in cache with a minimum expiration time of 1 day.
if ($cache) {
  cache_set($cid, $text, 'cache_filter', time() + (60 * 60 * 24));
}
```

Retrieving Cached Data with cache_get()

cache_get() is for retrieving the cached data. The function signature follows:

```
cache_get($cid, $table = 'cache')
```

and the function parameters are

- $cid: The cache ID of the data to retrieve.

- $table: The name of the table from which to retrieve the data. This might be a table you created or one of the tables provided by Drupal: cache, cache_block, cache_filter, cache_form, cache_menu, or cache_page. The cache table is used by default.

A common pattern for cache_get() can be seen in modules/filter/filter.module.

```
// Check for a cached version of this piece of text.
if ($cached = cache_get($cid, 'cache_filter')) {
  return $cached->data;
}
```

Clearing Caches

If your module knows best when its data becomes stale, it should take responsibility for clearing caches at an appropriate time. Two guiding principles should be applied to cache clearing:

- Clear the most specific cache possible. Do not broadly wipe all Drupal's caches just because a bit of module-specific data has changed! It's the equivalent of ripping out and replacing all the carpeting in the house because the kitchen floor needs sweeping.

- Use cached data as long as you can. Although the point of caching is to increase responsiveness by decreasing the amount of work that needs to be done, there is significant work involved in clearing cached data, especially if there is a lot of it.

The following subsections describe some ways of clearing cached data.

Using the $reset Parameter

Many Drupal functions that do internal caching with static variables have an optional $reset parameter that instructs the function to clear its internal cache. For example, here's our old friend node_load():

```
function node_load($param = array(), $revision = NULL, $reset = NULL) {
  static $nodes = array();

  if ($reset) {
    $nodes = array();
  }
  ...
}
```

Using cache_clear_all()

The main function for clearing cached data is cache_clear_all() in includes/cache.inc. The function signature is as follows:

```
function cache_clear_all($cid = NULL, $table = NULL, $wildcard = FALSE) {...}
```

The $cid and $table parameters have the same meaning as they do for cache_set() and cache_get(). The $wildcard parameter is used to indicate that the $cid being passed should be treated as a substring with any right-hand matches being cleared. Some examples follow.

Clear the specific entry foo:bar from the cache table:

```
$cid = 'foo:bar';
cache_clear_all($cid, 'cache');
```

Clear any expirable entry in the cache table that was set by the foo module (and thus has a $cid that begins with the foo: prefix):

```
$cid = 'foo:'; // Will match cache keys foo:bar, foo:baz, etc.
cache_clear_all($cid, 'cache', TRUE);
```

The actual database query that is run in the preceding case is

```
db_query("DELETE FROM {". $table ."} WHERE cid LIKE '%s%%'", $cid);
```

If the foo module keeps its data in its own cache table named cache_foo, that table needs to be specified so cache_clear_all() knows which to clear:

```
$cid = 'foo:bar';
cache_clear_all($cid, 'cache_foo');
```

If you want to completely empty a cache table, pass * as the $cid and set the $wildcard parameter to TRUE. This example clears the entire cache_foo table:

```
cache_clear_all('*', 'cache_foo', TRUE);
```

Clear any expirable entries from the page and block caches (i.e., the cache_page and cache_block tables):

```
cache_clear_all();
```

Using hook_flush_caches()

Drupal has a central function that flushes all the caches, including the JavaScript and CSS caches. Here is the `drupal_flush_all_caches()` function from `includes/common.inc`:

```
/**
 * Flush all cached data on the site.
 *
 * Empties cache tables, rebuilds the menu cache and theme registries, and
 * exposes a hook for other modules to clear their own cache data as well.
 */
function drupal_flush_all_caches() {
  // Change query-strings on css/js files to enforce reload for all users.
  _drupal_flush_css_js();

  drupal_clear_css_cache();
  drupal_clear_js_cache();
  system_theme_data();
  drupal_rebuild_theme_registry();
  menu_rebuild();
  node_types_rebuild();
  // Don't clear cache_form - in-progress form submissions may break.
  // Ordered so clearing the page cache will always be the last action.
  $core = array('cache', 'cache_block', 'cache_filter', 'cache_page');
  $cache_tables = array_merge(module_invoke_all('flush_caches'), $core);
  foreach ($cache_tables as $table) {
    cache_clear_all('*', $table, TRUE);
  }
}
```

Notice the line that includes `module_invoke_all('flush_caches')`. This is the invocation of `hook_flush_caches()`. If you are using your own cache tables, the hook gives your module a chance to clear its caches when the "Clear cached data" button is clicked on the Administer ➤ Site configuration ➤ Performance page. The submit handler for that button calls `drupal_flush_all_caches()`. An implementation of `hook_flush_caches()` is simple to write; your module should simply return the names of any cache tables that should be flushed. Here's an example from the update status module:

```
/**
 * Implementation of hook_flush_caches().
 */
function update_flush_caches() {
  return array('cache_update');
}
```

Summary

In this chapter, you learned about

- The various types of caching Drupal provides: page, block, menu, variable, and filter caching

- How the page-caching systems work

- The differences among Normal, Aggressive, and `fastpath` caching

- How the block-caching system works

- The cache API functions

## CHAPTER 16

Sessions

HTTP is a stateless protocol, which means that each interaction between the web browser and server stands alone. So how do you track a user as he or she navigates through a series of web pages on a web site? You use sessions. Starting with version 4, PHP offers built-in support for sessions via the session family of functions. In this chapter, you'll see how Drupal uses PHP's sessions.

What Are Sessions?

When a browser first requests a page from a Drupal site, PHP issues the browser a cookie containing a randomly generated 32-character ID, called PHPSESSID by default. This is done by the inclusion of one line in the HTTP response headers sent to the browser the first time it visits the site:

```
HTTP/1.1 200 OK
Date: Thu, 17 Apr 2008 20:24:58 GMT
Server: Apache
Set-Cookie: PHPSESSID=3sulj1mainvme55r8udcc6j2a4; expires=Sat, 10 May 2008 23:58:19
  GMT; path=/
Last-Modified: Thu, 17 Apr 2008 20:24:59 GMT
Cache-Control: store, no-cache, must-revalidate
Cache-Control: post-check=0, pre-check=0
Content-Type: text/html; charset=utf-8
```

On subsequent visits to the site, the browser presents the cookie to the server by including it in each HTTP request:

```
GET / HTTP/1.1
User-Agent=Mozilla/5.0 (Macintosh; U; Intel Mac OS X; en-US; rv:1.8.1.14)
  Gecko/20080404 Firefox/2.0.0.14
Cookie: PHPSESSID=3sulj1mainvme55r8udcc6j2a4
```

This allows PHP to keep track of a single browser as it visits the web site. The 32-character ID, known as the *session ID*, is used as the key to the information Drupal stores about the session and allows Drupal to associate sessions with individual users.

Usage

Drupal uses sessions for several important functions internally to store transient information regarding an individual user's state or preferences. For example, drupal_set_message() needs to carry over a status message or an error message for the user from the page on which the error occurred to the next page. This is done by storing the messages in an array named messages inside the user's session:

```
/**
 * Set a message which reflects the status of the performed operation.
 *
 * If the function is called with no arguments, this function returns all set
 * messages without clearing them.
 *
 * @param $message
 *   The message should begin with a capital letter and always ends with a
 *   period '.'.
 * @param $type
 *   The type of the message. One of the following values are possible:
 *   'status', 'warning', 'error'
 * @param $repeat
 *   If this is FALSE and the message is already set, then the message won't
 *   be repeated.
 */
function drupal_set_message($message = NULL, $type = 'status', $repeat = TRUE) {
  if ($message) {
    if (!isset($_SESSION['messages'])) {
      $_SESSION['messages'] = array();
    }

    if (!isset($_SESSION['messages'][$type])) {
      $_SESSION['messages'][$type] = array();
    }

    if ($repeat || !in_array($message, $_SESSION['messages'][$type])) {
      $_SESSION['messages'][$type][] = $message;
    }
  }

  // Messages not set when DB connection fails.
  return isset($_SESSION['messages']) ? $_SESSION['messages'] : NULL;
}
```

Another example is from comment.module, where the session is used to store viewing preferences for anonymous users:

```
$_SESSION['comment_mode'] = $mode;
$_SESSION['comment_sort'] = $order;
$_SESSION['comment_comments_per_page'] = $comments_per_page;
```

Drupal also uses sessions to keep a handle on file uploads when a node is being previewed, to remember viewing preferences when filtering the list of site content at Administer ➤ Content management ➤ Content or the list of recent log entries at Administer ➤ Reports ➤ Recent log entries, and for the installation and update systems (install. php and update.php).

Drupal creates sessions for both users that are logged into a site (authenticated users) and are not logged in (anonymous users). In the row of the sessions table representing an anonymous user, the uid column is set to 0. Because sessions are browser specific (they're tied to the browser's cookie), having multiple browsers open on a single computer results in multiple sessions.

■**Caution** Drupal doesn't store session information the first time an anonymous user visits a site. This is to keep evil web crawlers and robots from flooding the sessions table with data. As a developer, this means you cannot store session information for the first visit from an anonymous user.

The actual data stored in a session is stored as serialized data in the session column of the sessions table. Three rows of a typical sessions table are shown in Table 16-1. The table shows records for the superuser (uid 1), an authenticated user (uid 3), and an anonymous user (uid 0). The superuser has watchdog filtering settings (used by the dblog module) stored in the session.

Table 16-1. *Example Rows from the Sessions*

uid	sid	hostname	timestamp	cache	session
1	f5268d678333a1a7cce27e7e42b0c2e1	1.2.3.4	1208464106	0	dblog_overview_filter|a:0:{}
3	be312e7b35562322f3ee98ccb9ce8490	5.6.7.8	1208460845	0	--
0	5718d73975456111b268ed06233d36de	127.0.0.1	1208461007	0	--

The sessions table is cleaned when PHP's session garbage collection routine runs. The length of time a row remains in the table is determined by the session.gc_maxlifetime setting in settings.php. If a user logs out, the row for that session is removed from the database immediately. Note that if a user is logged in via multiple browsers (not browser windows) or multiple IP addresses at the same time, each browser has a session; therefore, logging out from one browser doesn't log the user out from the other browsers.

Session-Related Settings

There are three places where Drupal modifies session-handling settings: in the .htaccess file, in the settings.php file, and in the bootstrap code in the includes/bootstrap.inc file.

In .htaccess

Drupal ensures that it has full control over when sessions start by turning off PHP's `session.auto_start` functionality in the Drupal installation's default `.htaccess` file with the following line:

```
php_value session.auto_start              0
```

`session.auto_start` is a configuration option that PHP cannot change at runtime, which is why it lives in the `.htaccess` file instead of `settings.php`.

In settings.php

You'll set most session settings within the `settings.php` file, located at `sites/default/settings.php` or `sites/example.com/settings.php`.

```
ini_set('session.cache_expire',     200000);  // 138.9 days.
ini_set('session.cache_limiter',    'none');  // Cache control is done elsewhere.
ini_set('session.cookie_lifetime',  2000000); // 23.1 days.
ini_set('session.gc_maxlifetime',   200000);  // 55 hours.
ini_set('session.save_handler',     'user');  // Use user-defined session handling.
ini_set('session.use_only_cookies', 1);       // Require cookies.
ini_set('session.use_trans_sid',    0);       // Don't use URL-based sessions.
```

Having these settings in `settings.php` instead of `.htaccess` allows subsites to have different settings and allows Drupal to modify the session settings on hosts running PHP as a CGI (PHP directives in `.htaccess` don't work in such a configuration).

Drupal uses the `ini_set('session.save_handler', 'user');` function to override the default session handling provided by PHP and implement its own session management; *user-defined* in this context means "defined by Drupal" (see `http://www.php.net/manual/en/function.session-set-save-handler.php`).

In bootstrap.inc

PHP provides built-in session-handling functions but allows you to override those functions if you want to implement your own handlers. PHP continues to handle the cookie management, while Drupal's implementation does the back-end handling of session storage.

The following call during the `DRUPAL_BOOTSTRAP_SESSION` phase of bootstrapping sets the handlers to functions in `includes/sessions.inc` and starts session handling:

```
require_once variable_get('session_inc', './includes/session.inc');
session_set_save_handler('sess_open', 'sess_close', 'sess_read', 'sess_write',
  'sess_destroy_sid', 'sess_gc');
session_start();
```

This is one of the few cases where the names of the functions inside a file don't match the file's name. You would expect the preceding function names to be `session_open`, `session_close`, and so on. However, because PHP already has built-in functions in that namespace, the shorter prefix `sess_` is used.

Notice that the file being included is defined by a Drupal variable. This means that you can cleanly implement your own session handling and plug in that instead of using Drupal's default session handling. For example, the memcache module (drupal.org/project/memcache) implements the sess_open(), sess_close(), sess_read(), sess_write(), sess_destroy_sid(), and sess_gc() functions. Setting the session_inc Drupal variable causes Drupal to use this code for sessions instead of using default session handling:

```php
<?php
  variable_set('session_inc', './sites/all/modules/memcache/memcache-session.inc');
?>
```

You could also override the variable by setting it in your settings.php file:

```php
$conf = array(
  'session_inc' => './sites/all/modules/memcache/memcache-session.inc,
  ...
);
```

Requiring Cookies

If the browser doesn't accept cookies, a session cannot be established because the PHP directive sessions_use_only_cookies has been set to 1 and the alternative (passing the PHPSESSID in the query string of the URL) has been disabled by setting sessions.use_trans_sid to 0. This is a best practice, as recommended by Zend (see http://php.net/session.configuration):

> *URL based session management has additional security risks compared to cookie-based session management. Users may send a URL that contains an active session ID to their friends by e-mail or users may save a URL that contains a session ID to their bookmarks and access your site with the same session ID always, for example.*

When PHPSESSID appears in the query string of a site, it's typically a sign that the hosting provider has locked down PHP and doesn't allow the ini_set() function to set PHP directives at runtime. Alternatives are to move the settings into the .htaccess file (if the host is running PHP as an Apache module) or into a local php.ini file (if the host is running PHP as a CGI executable).

To discourage session hijacking, the session ID is regenerated when a user logs in (see the user_authenticate_finalize() function in modules/user/user.module). The session is also regenerated when a user changes his or her password.

Storage

Session information is stored in the sessions table, which associates session IDs with Drupal user IDs during the DRUPAL_BOOTSTRAP_SESSION phase of bootstrapping (see Chapter 15 to learn more about Drupal's bootstrapping process). In fact, the $user object, which is used extensively throughout Drupal, is first built during this phase by sess_read() in includes/sessions.inc (see Chapter 6 to see how the $user object is built).

Table 16-2 shows the table structure in which sessions are stored.

Table 16-2. *The Structure of the Sessions Table*

Field	Type	Length	Description
uid	int		User ID of authenticated user (0 for anonymous user)
sid	int	64	Session ID generated by PHP
hostname	varchar	128	IP address that last used this session ID
timestamp	int		Unix timestamp of last page request
cache	int		Time of user's last post, which is used to enforce minimum cache lifetime
session	text	big	Serialized contents of data stored in $_SESSION

When Drupal serves a page, the last task completed is to write the session to the sessions table (see sess_write() in includes/session.inc). This is only done if the browser has presented a valid cookie to avoid bloating the sessions table with sessions for web crawlers.

Session Life Cycle

The session life cycle is shown in Figure 16-1. It begins when a browser makes a request to the server. During the DRUPAL_BOOTSTRAP_SESSION phase of Drupal's bootstrap routines (see includes/bootstrap.inc) the session code begins. If the browser doesn't present a cookie that it had previously received from the site, PHP's session management system will give the browser a new cookie with a new PHP session ID. This ID is usually a 32-character representation of a unique MD5 hash, though PHP 5 allows you to set the configuration directive session.hash_function to 1, optionally giving you SHA-1 hashes that are represented by 40-character strings.

■**Note** MD5 is an algorithm for computing the hash value of a string of text and is the algorithm of choice for computing hashes within Drupal. For information on MD5 and other hash algorithms, see http:// en.wikipedia.org/wiki/Cryptographic_hash_functions.

Drupal then checks the sessions table for the existence of a row with the session ID as the key. If found, the sess_read() function in includes/sessions.inc retrieves the session data and performs an SQL JOIN on the row from the sessions table and on the corresponding row from the users table. The result of this join is an object containing all fields and values from both rows. This is the global $user object that's used throughout the rest of Drupal (see Chapter 6). Thus, session data is also available by looking in the $user object, specifically in $user->session, $user->sid, $user->hostname, $user->timestamp, and $user->cache. Roles for the current user are looked up and assigned to $user->roles in sess_read() as well.

But what happens if there's no user in the users table with a user ID that matches the user ID in the session? This is a trick question. Because Drupal's installer creates a row in the users table with the user ID of 0, and because unauthenticated (anonymous) users are assigned the uid of 0 in the sessions table, the join always works.

Caution Never delete all rows from the users table of your Drupal installation. The row containing user ID 0 is needed for Drupal to function properly.

If you want to find out the last time the user accessed a page, you could either look at $user->timestamp (remember, that comes from the sessions table) or at $user->access, which is kept in the users table. Of the two, $user->timestamp will give you more accurate results if it is present, because updating of $user->access in the users table is subject to throttling so that writes do not happen more often than every 180 seconds by default. This value can be changed by setting the Drupal variable session_write_interval. From sess_write() in includes/session.inc:

```
// Last access time is updated no more frequently than once every 180 seconds.
// This reduces contention in the users table.
$session_write_interval = variable_get('session_write_interval', 180);
if ($user->uid && time() - $user->access > $session_write_interval) {
  db_query("UPDATE {users} SET access = %d WHERE uid = %d", time(), $user->uid);
}
```

Of course, neither $user->timestamp nor $user->access will be present for users visiting for the first time, as no timestamp has been saved yet.

When the web page has been delivered to the browser, the last step is to close the session. PHP invokes the sess_write() function in includes/session.inc, which writes anything that was stashed in $_SESSION (during the request) to the sessions table. It is a good idea to only store data in $_SESSION if you absolutely need to, and even then only when you are sure that the user has authenticated. The reason for this is to prevent the table from bloating up with rows generated by web crawlers, as the size of the table can impact performance.

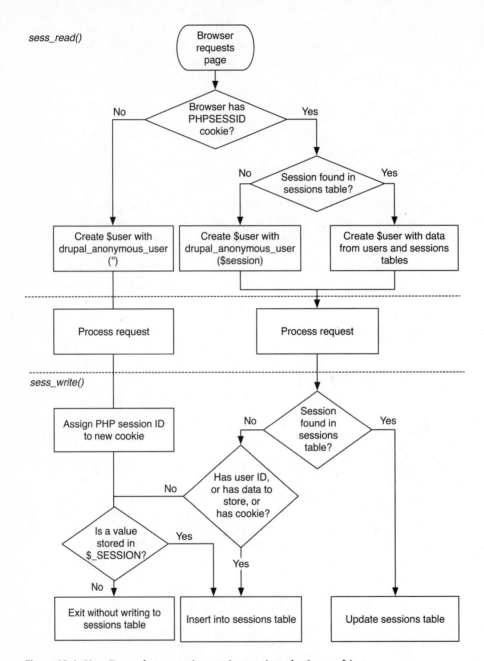

Figure 16-1. *How Drupal uses sessions to instantiate the $user object*

Session Conversations

Here are some examples of what happens when you visit Drupal in your browser, from a sessions perspective.

First Visit

Browser: Hi, I'd like a page, please.

Drupal: May I see your cookie?

Browser: Sorry, I don't have a cookie; this is my first time here.

Drupal: OK, here's one.

Second Visit

Browser: May I have another page, please?

Drupal: May I see your cookie?

Browser: Right here. It says session number 6tc47s8jd6rls9cugkdrrjm8h5.

Drupal: Hmm, I can't find you in my records. But here's your page anyway. I'll make a note of you in case you visit again.

User with an Account

[The user has created an account and clicked the Log In button.]

Browser: Hi, I'd like a page, please.

Drupal: May I see your cookie?

Browser: Right here. It says session number 31bfa29408ebb23239042ca8f0f77652.

Drupal: Hi, Joe! [Mumbling] You're user ID 384, and you like your comments nested and your coffee black. Here's a new cookie so your session doesn't get hijacked. I'll make a note that you visited. Have a nice day.

Common Tasks

Here are some common ways in which you might want to use sessions or tweak session settings.

Changing the Length of Time Before a Cookie Expires

The length of time before the cookie containing the session ID expires is controlled by `session.cookie_lifetime` in `settings.php` and set by default to 2,000,000 seconds (about 23 days). Modifying this value to 0 causes the cookie to be destroyed when the user closes the browser.

Changing the Name of the Session

A common problem with sessions arises when deploying web sites on multiple subdomains. Because each site uses the same default value for `session.cookie_domain` and the same `session.name` of `PHPSESSID` by default, users find themselves able to log into only one site at any given time. Drupal solves this problem by creating a unique session name for each site. The session name is based on a MD5 hash, with some modifications, of the base URL for the site. See `conf_init()` in `includes/bootstrap.inc` for details.

The automatic generation of the session name can be bypassed by uncommenting a line in `settings.php` and specifying the value of the `$cookie_domain` variable. The value should contain alphanumeric characters only. Here is the relevant section of `settings.php`:

```
/**
 * Drupal automatically generates a unique session cookie name for each site
 * based on on its full domain name. If you have multiple domains pointing at
 * the same Drupal site, you can either redirect them all to a single domain
 * (see comment in .htaccess), or uncomment the line below and specify their
 * shared base domain. Doing so assures that users remain logged in as they
 * cross between your various domains.
 */
# $cookie_domain = 'example.com';
```

■**Note**   The only time Perl-style comment characters (#) are used in Drupal are in `settings.php`, `.htaccess`, `robots.txt`, and the actual Perl and shell scripts in the `scripts` directory.

Storing Data in the Session

Storing data in a user's session is convenient, because the data is automatically stored by the sessions system. Whenever you want to store data that you want to associate with a user during a visit (or multiple visits up to `session.cookie_lifetime`), use the `$_SESSION` superglobal:

```
$_SESSION['favorite_color'] = $favorite_color;
```

Later, on a subsequent request, do the following to retrieve the value:

```
$favorite_color = $_SESSION['favorite_color'];
```

If you know the user's `uid` and you want to persist some data about the user, it's usually more practical to store it in the `$user` object as a unique attribute such as `$user->foo = $bar` by calling `user_save($user, array('foo' => $bar))`, which serializes the data to the `users` table's data column. Here's a good rule of thumb to use: If the information is transient and you don't mind if it's lost, or if you need to store short-term data for anonymous users, you can store it in the session. If you want to tie a preference permanently to a user's identity, store it in the `$user` object.

■**Caution**   `$user` should not be used to store information for anonymous users.

Summary

After reading this chapter, you should be able to

- Understand how Drupal modifies PHP's session handling.

- Understand which files contain session configuration settings.

- Understand the session life cycle and how Drupal's $user object is created during a request.

- Store data in and retrieve data from a user's session.

## CHAPTER 17

Using jQuery

JavaScript is ubiquitous. Every mainstream web browser ships with a JavaScript interpreter. Apple's Dashboard widgets are written with JavaScript. Mozilla Firefox uses JavaScript to implement its user interface. Adobe Photoshop can be scripted with JavaScript. It's everywhere.

It's easy to be embittered by the clunky JavaScript of yesteryear. If you've had a bad run-in with JavaScript, it's time to let bygones be bygones and say hello to jQuery. jQuery makes writing JavaScript intuitive and fun, and it's also part of Drupal! In this chapter, you'll find out what jQuery is and how it works with Drupal. Then you'll work through a practical example.

What Is jQuery?

jQuery, created by John Resig, responds to the common frustrations and limitations that developers might have with JavaScript. JavaScript code is cumbersome to write and verbose, and it can be difficult to target the specific HTML or CSS elements you wish to manipulate. jQuery gives you a way to find these elements quickly and easily within your document.

The technical name for targeting an object is *DOM traversal*. DOM stands for Document Object Model. The model provides a tree-like way to access page elements through their tags and other elements through JavaScript, as shown in Figure 17-1.

■Note You can learn more about jQuery from the official jQuery web site at http://jquery.com/, and from http://visualjquery.com/.

When writing JavaScript code, you usually have to spend time dealing with browser and operating system incompatibilities. jQuery handles this for you. Also, there aren't many high-level functions within JavaScript. Common tasks such as animating parts of a page, dragging things around, or having sortable elements don't exist. jQuery overcomes these limitations as well.

Like Drupal, jQuery has a small and efficient codebase, weighing in at just under 30 kilobytes. At the heart of jQuery is an extensible framework that JavaScript developers can hook into, and hundreds of jQuery plug-ins are already available at http://plugins.jquery.com/.

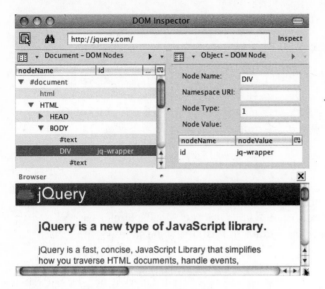

Figure 17-1. *The DOM representation of http://jquery.com, using the Mozilla DOM Inspector tool, which installs with the Firefox browser*

The Old Way

Let's first do a quick review of the pure JavaScript way of DOM traversal. The following code shows how Drupal used to find elements within a page (in this case the legend element within all collapsible fieldsets) before jQuery came along:

```
var fieldsets = document.getElementsByTagName('fieldset');
var legend, fieldset;
for (var i = 0; fieldset = fieldsets[i]; i++) {
  if (!hasClass(fieldset, 'collapsible')) {
    continue;
  }
  legend = fieldset.getElementsByTagName('legend');
  if (legend.length == 0) {
    continue;
  }
  legend = legend[0];
  ...
}
```

And here's the updated code within Drupal after jQuery entered the scene:

```
$('fieldset.collapsible > legend:not(.collapse-processed)', context).each(
  function() { ... });
```

As you can see, jQuery lives up to its tagline of "Write Less, Do More." jQuery takes the common, repetitive tasks of manipulating the DOM using JavaScript and encapsulates them behind a concise and intuitive syntax. The end result is code that's short, smart, and easy to read.

How jQuery Works

jQuery is a tool for finding things in a structured document. Elements from the document can be selected by using CSS selectors or jQuery's own custom selectors (a jQuery plug-in supports the use of XPath selectors as well). The use of CSS selectors for DOM traversal is helpful to the developer, because most developers are already familiar with CSS syntax. jQuery has full support of CSS 1 to 3. Let's go through some very basic examples of jQuery syntax before we dive into using jQuery with Drupal.

Using a CSS ID Selector

Let's a do a quick review of basic CSS syntax. Suppose the HTML you want to manipulate is the following:

```
<p id="intro">Welcome to the World of Widgets.</p>
```

If you want to set the background color of the paragraph to blue, you use CSS to target this specific paragraph in your style sheet using the #intro CSS ID selector. According to the HTML specification, IDs must be unique within a given document, so we are assured that no other element has this ID. Within the style sheet that will be applied to your document, the following entry will make your paragraph blue:

```
#intro {
  background-color: blue;
}
```

Note that there are essentially two tasks here: find the element that has the #intro ID, and set the background color of that element to blue.

You can accomplish the same thing using jQuery. But first, a word about jQuery syntax: in order to keep the code short and simple, jQuery maps the jQuery namespace onto the dollar sign character ($) using this line in the jQuery JavaScript code:

```
var jQuery = window.jQuery = function( selector, context ) {...};
...
// Map the jQuery namespace to the '$' one
window.$ = jQuery;
```

Note If you're interested in how the jQuery engine works, you can download the entire uncompressed jQuery JavaScript file from http://jquery.com/. The version included with Drupal is a compressed version to keep the amount of data that browsers must download from your site small.

Here's how you can select your paragraph and turn the background color to blue using jQuery:

```
$("#intro").css("background-color", "blue");
```

You could even add a little jQuery pizzazz, and slowly fade in the paragraph text:

```
$("#intro").css("background-color", "blue").fadeIn("slow");
```

Using a CSS Class Selector

Here's a similar example using a CSS class selector instead of using a CSS ID as we did in the preceding section. The HTML would be as follows:

```
<p class="intro">Welcome to the World of Widgets.</p>
<p class="intro">Widgets are available in many sizes.</p>
```

Our CSS would look like this:

```
.intro {
  background-color: blue;
}
```

The following would also work, and is a slightly more specific rule:

```
p.intro {
  background-color: blue;
}
```

Here's how the CSS translates to jQuery code:

```
$(".intro").css("background-color", "blue").fadeIn("slow");
```

or

```
$("p.intro").css("background-color", "blue").fadeIn("slow");
```

In the first of the preceding examples, you're asking jQuery to find any HTML element that has the intro class, while the second example is subtly different. You instead ask for any paragraph tag with an intro class. Note that the last example will be slightly faster because there's less HTML for jQuery to search through, given the example's restriction to just the paragraph tags using p.intro.

Tip In CSS, the dot is a class selector that can be reused within a document, and the hash refers to a unique ID selector whose name can only occur once per page.

Now that you've had a taste of how jQuery works, let's see it in action within Drupal.

jQuery Within Drupal

Using jQuery within Drupal is easy because jQuery is preinstalled and is automatically made available when JavaScript is added. In Drupal, JavaScript files are added via the `drupal_add_js()` function. In this section, you'll investigate some basic jQuery functionality within Drupal.

Your First jQuery Code

Let's get set up to play with jQuery.

1. Log into your Drupal site as user 1 (the administrative account).

2. At Administer ➤ Site building ➤ Modules, enable the PHP filter module.

3. Create a new node of type Page, but on the node creation form, be sure to select "PHP code" under the "Input formats" section, as shown in Figure 17-2. Enter Testing jQuery as the title, and add the following to the body section of the form:

```php
<?php
  drupal_add_js(
    '$(document).ready(function(){
      // Hide all the paragraphs.
      $("p").hide();
      // Fade them into visibility.
      $("p").fadeIn("slow");
    });',
    'inline'
  );
?>

<p id="one">Paragraph one</p>
<p>Paragraph two</p>
<p>Paragraph three</p>
```

Click Submit, and reload the page. The three paragraphs you created will slowly fade in. Cool, eh? Refresh the page to see it again. Let's study this example a little more.

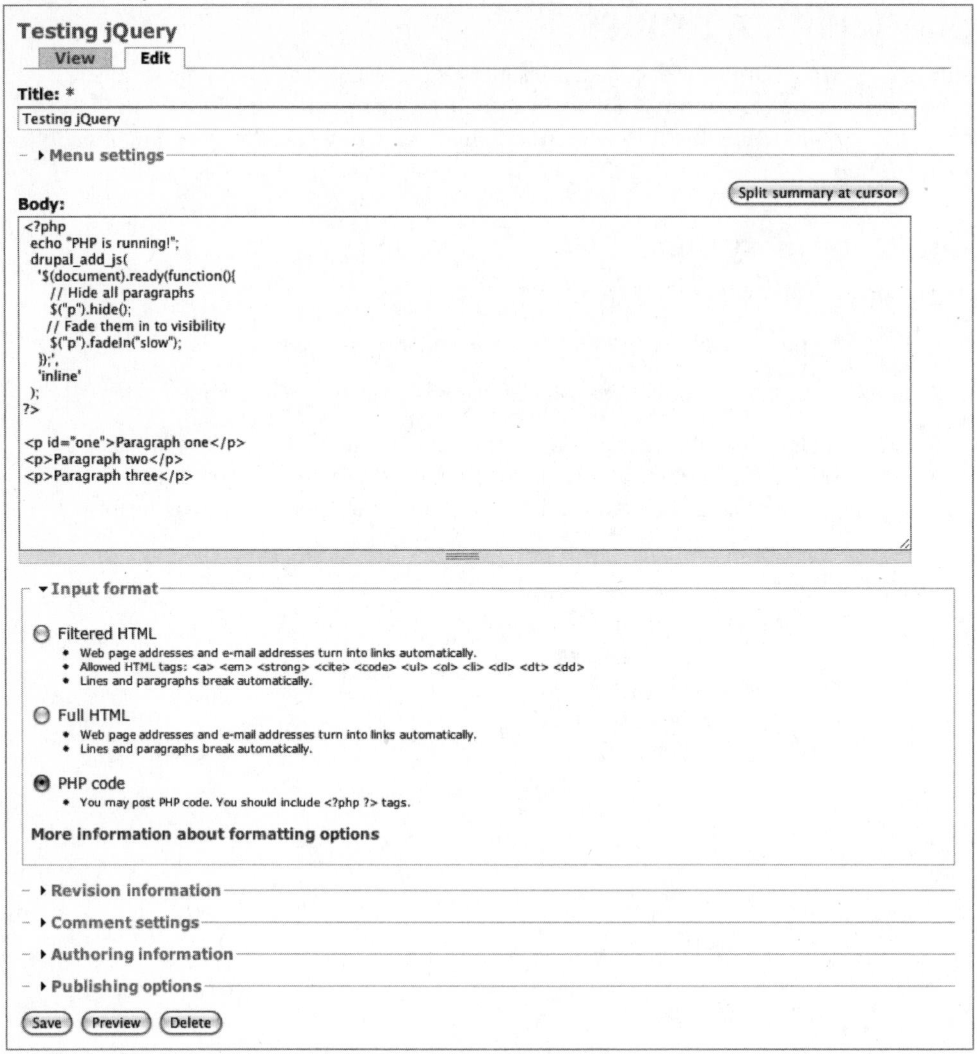

Testing jQuery

| View | **Edit** |

Title: *

Testing jQuery

– ▸ Menu settings

Body: (Split summary at cursor)

```
<?php
  echo "PHP is running!";
  drupal_add_js(
    '$(document).ready(function(){
      // Hide all paragraphs
      $("p").hide();
      // Fade them in to visibility
      $("p").fadeIn("slow");
    });',
    'inline'
  );
?>

<p id="one">Paragraph one</p>
<p>Paragraph two</p>
<p>Paragraph three</p>
```

– ▾ Input format

◯ Filtered HTML
  • Web page addresses and e-mail addresses turn into links automatically.
  • Allowed HTML tags: <a> <em> <strong> <cite> <code> <ul> <ol> <li> <dl> <dt> <dd>
  • Lines and paragraphs break automatically.

◯ Full HTML
  • Web page addresses and e-mail addresses turn into links automatically.
  • Lines and paragraphs break automatically.

◉ PHP code
  • You may post PHP code. You should include <?php ?> tags.

More information about formatting options

– ▸ Revision information
– ▸ Comment settings
– ▸ Authoring information
– ▸ Publishing options

(Save) (Preview) (Delete)

Figure 17-2. *Experimenting with jQuery using the PHP filter*

The jQuery code is contained in a file, misc/jquery.js. This file is not loaded for every page within Drupal. Instead, anytime a drupal_add_js() call is made, jquery.js is loaded. Two parameters are passed into drupal_add_js(). The first parameter is the JavaScript code you wish to have executed, and the second parameter (inline) tells Drupal to write the code inside a pair of <script></script> tags within the document's <head> element.

■**Note** We're using drupal_add_js() quite simply here, but it has many more possibilities which you can discover at http://api.drupal.org/api/function/drupal_add_js/6.

Let's look at the JavaScript jQuery code in more detail.

```
$(document).ready(function(){
  // Hide all the paragraphs.
  $("p").hide();
  // Fade them into visibility.
  $("p").fadeIn("slow");
});
```

The first line needs a little more explaining. When the browser is rendering a page, it gets to a point where it has received the HTML and fully parsed the DOM structure of the page. The next step is to render that DOM, which includes loading additional local—and possibly even remote—files. If you try to execute JavaScript code before the DOM has been generated, the code may throw errors and not run because the objects it wants to manipulate are not there yet. JavaScript programmers used to get around this by using some variation of the following code snippet:

```
window.onload = function(){ ... }
```

The difficulty with using `window.onload` is that it has to wait for the additional files to also load, which is too long of a wait. Additionally, the `window.onload` approach allows the assignment of only a single function. To circumvent both problems, jQuery has a simple statement that you can use:

```
$(document).ready(function(){
  // Your code here.
});
```

`$(document).ready()` is executed just after the DOM is generated. You'll always want to wrap jQuery code in the preceding statement for the reasons listed earlier. The `function()` call defines an anonymous function in JavaScript—in this case, containing the code you want to execute.

That leaves us with the actual meat of the code, which ought to be self-explanatory at this point:

```
// Hide all the paragraphs.
$("p").hide();
// Fade them into visibility.
$("p").fadeIn("slow");
```

The preceding code finds all paragraph tags, hides them, and then slowly reveals them within the page. In jQuery lingo, the `fadeIn()` part is referred to as a *method*.

> **■Note** We're changing all the paragraph tags, so if you visit a node listing page such as `http://example.com/?q=node`, you'll find that *all* paragraph tags, not just the ones in the teaser from your test page, are affected! In our example, we could limit the set of p tags being selected by changing our `node.tpl.php` template file to surround the content with `<div class='standalone'>` when the node is being displayed on a page by itself and starting the example with `$(".standalone > p")`. This query selects only the p elements that are descendents of elements within the `.standalone` class.

Targeting an Element by ID

Let's repeat our experiment, but this time target only the first paragraph, which we've identified with the ID of one:

```php
<?php
  drupal_add_js(
    '$(document).ready(function(){
      // Hide paragraph with ID "one".
      $("#one").hide();
      // Fade it into visibility.
      $("#one").fadeIn("slow");
    });',
    'inline'
  );
?>

<p id="one">Paragraph one</p>
<p>Paragraph two</p>
<p>Paragraph three</p>
```

> **■Note** Accessing an element by ID is one of the fastest selector methods within jQuery because it translates to the native JavaScript: `document.getElementById("one")`. The alternative, `$("p#one")`, would be slower because jQuery needs to find all paragraph tags and then look for an `intro` ID. The slowest selector method in jQuery is the class selector `$(".foo")`, because a search would have to be made through all elements with the `.foo` selector class. (It would be faster to do `$("p.foo")` in that case.)

Method Chaining

We can concatenate a series of jQuery methods because most methods within jQuery return a jQuery object. Let's chain some methods together in a single jQuery command:

```
// Hide all the p tags, fade them in to visibility, then slide them up and down.
$("p").hide().fadeIn("slow").slideUp("slow").slideDown("slow");
```

jQuery calls are invoked from left to right. The preceding snippet finds all the paragraph tags, fades them in, and then uses a sliding effect to move the paragraphs up and then down. Because each of these methods returns the jQuery wrapper object containing the same set it was given (all the p elements), we can manipulate the same set of elements over and over again until the final effect is achieved.

Adding or Removing a Class

jQuery can dynamically change the CSS class of an element. Here, we turn the first paragraph of our example red by selecting it by ID and then assigning Drupal's error class to it:

```
$("#one").addClass("error");
```

The counterpart to the addClass() method is the removeClass() method. The following snippet will remove the error class we just added:

```
$("#one").removeClass("error");
```

And then there's the toggleClass() method, which adds or removes a class each time it is called:

```
$("#one").toggleClass("error"); // Adds class "error".
$("#one").toggleClass("error"); // Removes class "error".
$("#one").toggleClass("error"); // Adds class "error" again.
```

Wrapping Existing Elements

Instead of just adding an error class to the <p id="one"> element, let's wrap that element in a div so that the red will show up better. The following jQuery snippet will do that:

```
<?php
  drupal_add_js(
    '$(document).ready(function(){
      $("#one").wrap("<div class=\'error\'></div>");
    });',
    'inline'
  );
?>

<p id="one">Paragraph one</p>
<p>Paragraph two</p>
<p>Paragraph three</p>
```

Note the escaping of the single quotes, which is necessary because we already have open single quotes inside the drupal_add_js() function. The result of the div wrapping is shown in Figure 17-3.

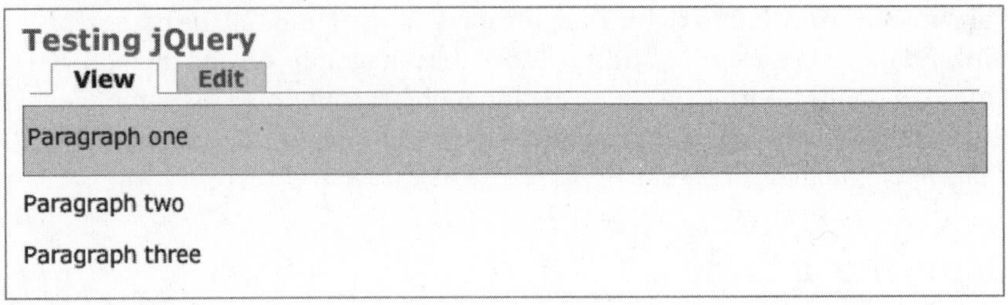

Testing jQuery

View | Edit

Paragraph one

Paragraph two

Paragraph three

Figure 17-3. *The paragraph with ID "one" is wrapped in a div tag of class "error".*

Changing Values of CSS Elements

jQuery can be used to assign (or reassign) values to CSS elements. Let's set the border surrounding the first paragraph to solid (see Figure 7-4):

```
$("#one").wrap("<div class=\'error\'></div>").css("border", "solid");
```

Notice that the css method is still acting on the p element, not on the div element, because the wrap method returned the targeted p element after wrapping it.

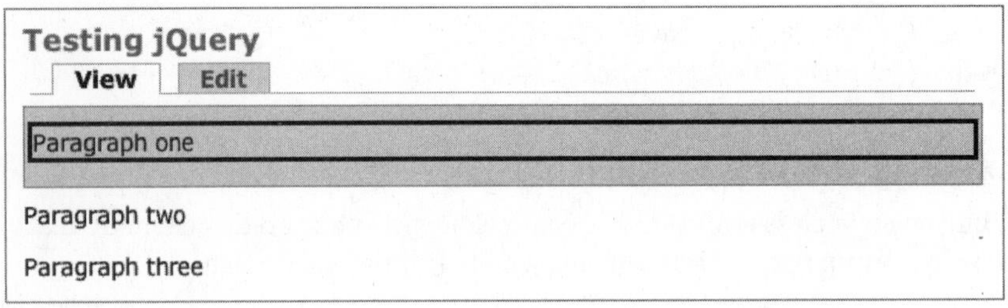

Testing jQuery

View | Edit

Paragraph one

Paragraph two

Paragraph three

Figure 17-4. *The border property of the target element is changed.*

The preceding examples have demonstrated some basic tasks that barely scratched the surface of what jQuery can do. You are urged to learn more at http://jquery.com/ or by picking up a good book on the subject.

Where to Put JavaScript

In the preceding examples, you have been testing jQuery by writing JavaScript in a node with the PHP filter enabled. While this is handy for testing, that's not a good approach for a production site, where best practices dictate that the PHP filter be unavailable if at all possible. There are several different options for including JavaScript files in your Drupal site. For example, you can add them to your theme, include them from a module, or even include them but give others the option of modifying or overriding your code.

Adding JavaScript via a Theme .info File

The most convenient but least flexible way to include JavaScript files is to include a line in your theme's `.info` file. Let's add an effect to your site that emphasizes the logo of your site by making it fade out and then fade in again when a page is loaded. Place the following JavaScript code in a file called `logofade.js` in your current theme. For example, if you are using the Garland theme, it would be at `themes/garland/logofade.js`.

```
// $Id$


// Selects the theme element with the id "logo", fades it out,
// then fades it in slowly.
if (Drupal.jsEnabled) {
  $(document).ready(function(){
    $("#logo").fadeOut("fast").fadeIn("slow");
  });
}
```

The JavaScript file is in place; now we just have to tell Drupal to load it. Add the following line to your current theme's `.info` file:

```
scripts[] = logofade.js
```

The last step is to make Drupal reread the `.info` file so that it will see that it needs to load `logofade.js`. To do that, go to Administer ➤ Site building ➤ Themes, temporarily switch to a different theme, and then switch back.

This method of adding JavaScript is useful if the JavaScript will be loaded on every single page of your web site. In the next section, you'll see how to add JavaScript only when a module that uses it is enabled.

A Module That Uses jQuery

Let's build a small module that includes some jQuery functions in a JavaScript file. First, we'll need a use case. Hmm, how about some JavaScript code that controls blocks? Blocks can be helpful in Drupal: they can show you your login status, tell you who's new on the site or who's online, and provide helpful navigation. But sometimes you just want to focus on the content of the page! Wouldn't it be nice to hide blocks by default and show them only if you want to see them? The following module does just that, using jQuery to identify and hide the blocks in the left and right sidebar regions and providing a helpful button that will bring the blocks back. Here's `sites/all/modules/custom/blockaway.info`:

```
; $Id$
name = Block-Away
description = Uses jQuery to hide blocks until a button is clicked.
package = Pro Drupal Development
core = 6.x
```

And here's sites/all/modules/custom/blockaway.module:

```php
<?php
// $Id$

/**
 * @file
 * Use this module to learn about jQuery.
 */

/**
 * Implementation of hook_init().
 */
function blockaway_init() {
  drupal_add_js(drupal_get_path('module', 'blockaway') .'/blockaway.js');
}
```

All the module does is include the following JavaScript file, which you can put at sites/all/modules/custom/blockaway/blockaway.js:

```javascript
// $Id$

/**
 * Hide blocks in sidebars, then make them visible at the click of a button.
 */
if (Drupal.jsEnabled) {
  $(document).ready(function() {
    // Get all div elements of class 'block' inside the left sidebar.
    // Add to that all div elements of class 'block' inside the
    // right sidebar.
    var blocks = $('#sidebar-left div.block, #sidebar-right div.block');

    // Hide them.
    blocks.hide();

    // Add a button that, when clicked, will make them reappear.
    $('#sidebar-left').prepend('<div id="collapsibutton">Show Blocks</div>');
    $('#collapsibutton').css({
      'width': '90px',
      'border': 'solid',
      'border-width': '1px',
      'padding': '5px',
      'background-color': '#fff'
    });
```

```
  // Add a handler that runs once when the button is clicked.
  $('#collapsibutton').one('click', function() {
    // Button clicked! Get rid of the button.
    $('#collapsibutton').remove();
    // Display all our hidden blocks using an effect.
    blocks.slideDown("slow");
  });
  });
}
```

When you enable the module at Administer ➤ Site building ➤ Modules, any blocks you have visible should disappear and be replaced with a plain button as shown in Figure 17-5.

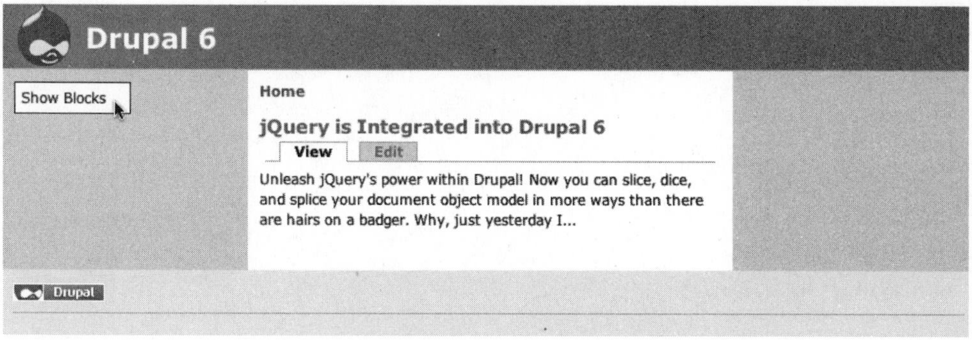

Figure 17-5. *A node being viewed with blockaway.module enabled*

After clicking the button, the blocks should appear using a sliding effect, becoming visible as shown in Figure 17-6.

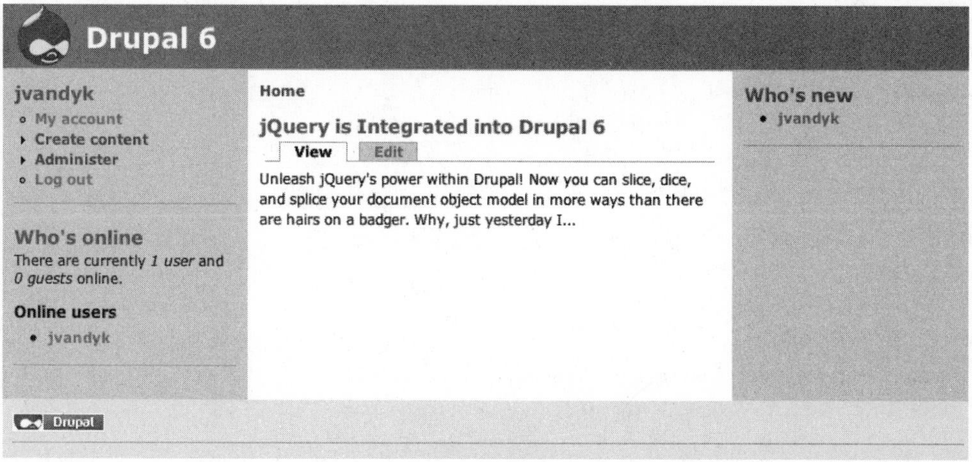

Figure 17-6. *After clicking the Show Blocks button, blocks become visible.*

Overridable JavaScript

The code in `blockaway.module` is simple and easy to understand. It just makes sure the `blockaway.js` file is included. However, if the module were more complicated, it would be friendlier to others to put the `drupal_add_js()` function call in a theme function instead of in `hook_init()`. That way, those who wanted to use your module but customize the JavaScript code in some way could do so without touching your module code at all (see Chapter 8 for how the theme system works its magic). The code that follows is a revised version of `blockaway.module` that declares a theme function using `hook_theme()`, moves the `drupal_add_js()` call into the theme function, and calls the theme function from `hook_init()`. The functionality is the same, but the `blockaway.js` file can now be overridden by savvy developers.

```php
<?php
// $Id$

/**
 * @file
 * Use this module to learn about jQuery.
 */

/**
 * Implementation of hook_init().
 */
function blockaway_init() {
  theme('blockaway_javascript');
}

/**
 * Implementation of hook_theme().
 * Register our theme function.
 */
function blockaway_theme() {
  return array(
    'blockaway_javascript' => array(
      'arguments' => array(),
    ),
  );
}

/**
 * Theme function that just makes sure our JavaScript file
 * gets included.
 */
function theme_blockaway_javascript() {
  drupal_add_js(drupal_get_path('module', 'blockaway') .'/blockaway.js');
}
```

Let's go ahead and see if this approach works. We're going to override the JavaScript provided by the module with JavaScript provided by the theme. Copy sites/all/modules/custom/blockaway/blockaway.js to your current theme—for example, themes/garland/blockaway.js. Let's change the JavaScript file slightly so that we'll know which JavaScript file is being used. Change the effect from slideDown("slow") to fadeIn(5000); this will fade in the blocks over a period of 5 seconds. Here is the new file:

```
// $Id$

/**
 * Hide blocks in sidebars, then make them visible at the click of a button.
 */
if (Drupal.jsEnabled) {
  $(document).ready(function() {
    // Get all div elements of class 'block' inside the left sidebar.
    // Add to that all div elements of class 'block' inside the
    // right sidebar.
    var blocks = $('#sidebar-left div.block, #sidebar-right div.block');

    // Hide them.
    blocks.hide();

    // Add a button that, when clicked, will make them reappear.
    // Translate strings with Drupal.t(), just like t() in PHP code.
    var text = Drupal.t('Show Blocks');
    $('#sidebar-left').prepend('<div id="collapsibutton">' + text + '</div>');
    $('#collapsibutton').css({
      'width': '90px',
      'border': 'solid',
      'border-width': '1px',
      'padding': '5px',
      'background-color': '#fff'
    });

    // Add a handler that runs once when the button is clicked.
    $('#collapsibutton').one('click', function() {
      // Button clicked! Get rid of the button.
      $('#collapsibutton').remove();
      // Display all our hidden blocks using an effect.
      blocks.fadeIn(5000);
    });
  });
}
```

The last change we need to make is to tell Drupal to load this new JavaScript file instead of the one in sites/all/modules/custom/blockaway. We do that by overriding the theme function. Add the following function to the template.php file of your theme (if your theme doesn't have a template.php file, it's okay to create one):

```php
<?php
// $Id$

/**
 * Override theme_blockaway_javascript() with the
 * following function.
 */
function phptemplate_blockaway_javascript() {
  drupal_add_js(path_to_theme() . '/blockaway.js');
}
```

Now when you visit a page in your web browser, you should see the Show Blocks button, and clicking it should reveal the blocks via a gradual fade-in effect instead of the slide effect we were using earlier. Congratulations! You've learned how to use jQuery in your module, how to write it in a way that is friendly to themers and other developers, and coincidentally, how to cleanly override or enhance JavaScript files provided by other module developers who have been equally courteous.

Before we leave this example, let me demonstrate how to override a template file. First, remove the phptemplate_blockaway_javascript() function that you added to the template.php file. Next, in your current theme, create an empty file called blockaway-javascript.tpl.php. For example, if you are using the Garland theme, create themes/garland/blockaway-javascript.tpl.php. *Don't put anything inside this file.* Now visit Administer ➤ Site building ➤ Modules. The act of visiting this page will rebuild the theme registry. Drupal will find the template file and use it instead of the theme function in your module. The result is that blockaway.js will never be loaded; you've essentially commented out the theme function by creating an empty template file (recall from Chapter 8 that, when building the theme registry, Drupal will look for a template file and then for theme functions).

Now, add the following to your blockaway-javascript.tpl.php file:

```php
<?php drupal_add_js(path_to_theme() . '/blockaway.js'); ?>
```

When you reload your page, you should see that the JavaScript file is now loading. Do you see how these techniques can be useful for substituting your own enhanced JavaScript file in a third-party module or for preventing some JavaScript from loading?

■**Note** You cannot call drupal_add_js() from inside page.tpl.php or any theme functions that are called in its preprocessing (such as blocks), because they are executed too late in the page building process. See modules/block/block-admin-display-form.tpl.php for an example of a core template file that adds JavaScript.

Building a jQuery Voting Widget

Let's write a slightly more complicated jQuery-enabled Drupal module. We'll build an AJAX voting widget as shown in Figure 17-7, which lets users add a single point to a post they like. We'll use jQuery to cast the vote and change the total vote score without reloading the entire page. We'll also add a role-based permission so only users with the "rate content" permission are allowed to vote. Because users can only add one point per vote, let's name the module plusone.

Figure 17-7. *The voting widget*

We'll have to get some basic module building out of the way before we can get to the actual jQuery part of plusone. Please see Chapter 2 if you've never built a module before. Otherwise, let's get to it!

Create a directory in sites/all/modules/custom, and name it plusone (you might need to create the sites/all/modules/custom directory). Inside the plusone directory, create the file plus1.info, which contains the following lines:

```
; $Id$
name = Plus One
description = "A +1 voting widget for nodes. "
package = Pro Drupal Development
core = 6.x
```

This file registers the module with Drupal so it can be enabled or disabled within the administrative interface.

Next, you'll create the plusone.install file. The functions within this PHP file are invoked when the module is enabled, disabled, installed, or uninstalled; usually to create or delete tables from the database. In this case, we'll want to keep track of who voted on which node:

```php
<?php
// $Id$

/**
 * Implementation of hook_install().
 */
function plusone_install() {
  // Create tables.
  drupal_install_schema('plusone');
}
```

```php
/**
 * Implementation of hook_uninstall().
 */
function plusone_uninstall() {
  // Remove tables.
  drupal_uninstall_schema('plusone');
}

/**
 * Implementation of hook_schema().
 */
function plusone_schema() {
  $schema['plusone_votes'] = array(
    'description' => t('Stores votes from the plusone module.'),
    'fields' => array(
      'uid'  => array(
        'type' => 'int',
        'not null' => TRUE,
        'default' => 0,
        'description' => t('The {user}.uid of the user casting the vote.'),
      ),
      'nid'  => array(
        'type' => 'int',
        'not null' => TRUE,
        'default' => 0,
        'description' => t('The {node}.nid of the node being voted on.'),
      ),
      'vote_count'  => array(
        'type' => 'int',
        'not null' => TRUE,
        'default' => 0,
        'description' => t('The number of votes cast.'),
      ),
    ),
    'primary key' => array('uid', 'nid'),
    'indexes' => array(
      'nid' => array('nid'),
      'uid' => array('uid'),
    ),
  );
  return $schema;
}
```

Also, add the file sites/all/modules/custom/plusone/plusone.css. This file isn't strictly needed, but it makes the voting widget a little prettier for viewing, as shown in Figure 17-8.

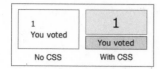

Figure 17-8. *Comparison of voting widget with and without CSS*

Add the following content to `plusone.css`:

```css
div.plusone-widget {
  width: 100px;
  margin-bottom: 5px;
  text-align: center;
}
div.plusone-widget .score {
  padding: 10px;
  border: 1px solid #999;
  background-color: #eee;
  font-size: 175%;
}
div.plusone-widget .vote {
  padding: 1px 5px;
  margin-top: 2px;
  border: 1px solid #666;
  background-color: #ddd;
}
```

Now that you have the supporting files created, let's focus on the module file and the jQuery JavaScript file. Create two empty files: `sites/all/modules/custom/plusone/plusone.js` and `sites/all/modules/custom/plusone/plusone.module`. You'll be gradually adding code to these files in the next few steps. To summarize, you should have the following files:

```
sites/
  all/
    modules/
      custom/
        plusone/
          plusone.js
          plusone.css
          plusone.info
          plusone.install
          plusone.module
```

Building the Module

Open up the empty `plusone.module` in a text editor and add the standard Drupal header documentation:

```php
<?php
// $Id$

/**
 * @file
 * A simple +1 voting widget.
 */
```

Next you'll start knocking off the Drupal hooks you're going to use. An easy one is hook_perm(), which lets you add the "rate content" permission to Drupal's role-based access control page. You'll use this permission to prevent anonymous users from voting without first creating an account or logging in.

```php
/**
 * Implementation of hook_perm().
 */
function plusone_perm() {
  return array('rate content');
}
```

Now you'll begin to implement some AJAX functionality. One of the great features of jQuery is its ability to submit its own HTTP GET or POST requests, which is how you'll submit the vote to Drupal without refreshing the entire page. jQuery will intercept the clicking on the Vote link and will send a request to Drupal to save the vote and return the updated total. jQuery will use the new value to update the score on the page. Figure 17-9 shows a "big picture" overview of where we're going.

Once jQuery intercepts the clicking of the Vote link, it needs to be able to call a Drupal function via a URL. We'll use hook_menu() to map the vote URL submitted by jQuery to a Drupal PHP function. The PHP function saves the vote to the database and returns the new score to jQuery in JavaScript Object Notation (JSON) (OK, so we're not using XML and thus it's not strictly AJAX).

```php
/**
 * Implementation of hook_menu().
 */
function plusone_menu() {
  $items['plusone/vote'] = array(
    'page callback' => 'plusone_vote',
    'access arguments' => array('rate content'),
    'type'   => MENU_CALLBACK,
  );
  return $items;
}
```

In the preceding function, whenever a request for the path plusone/vote comes in, the function plusone_vote() handles it when the user requesting the path has the "rate content" permission.

Figure 17-9. *Overview of the vote updating process*

■Note If the user making the call does not have the "rate content" permission, Drupal will return an Access Denied page. However, we'll be sure to build our voting widget dynamically so that those ineligible to vote do not see a vote link. But note how Drupal's permission system is protecting us from those nefarious people who might want to bypass our widget and hit the URL `http://example.com/?q=plusone/vote` directly.

The path `plusone/vote/3` translates into the PHP function call `plusone_vote(3)` (see Chapter 4, about Drupal's menu/callback system, for more details).

```php
/**
 * Called by jQuery, or by browser if JavaScript is disabled.
 * Submits the vote request. If called by jQuery, returns JSON.
 * If called by the browser, returns page with updated vote total.
 */
function plusone_vote($nid) {
  global $user;
  $nid = (int)$nid;

  // Authors may not vote on their own posts. We check the node table
  // to see if this user is the author of the post.
  $is_author = db_result(db_query('SELECT uid FROM {node} WHERE nid = %d AND
    uid = %d', $nid, $user->uid));

  if ($nid > 0 && !$is_author) {
    // Get current vote count for this user.
    $vote_count = plusone_get_vote($nid, $user->uid);
    if (!$vote_count) {
      // Delete existing vote count for this user.
      db_query('DELETE FROM {plusone_votes} WHERE uid = %d AND nid = %d',
        $user->uid, $nid);
      db_query('INSERT INTO {plusone_votes} (uid, nid, vote_count) VALUES
        (%d, %d, %d)', $user->uid, $nid, $vote_count + 1);
      watchdog('plusone', 'Vote by @user on node @nid.', array(
        '@user' => $user->name, '@nid' => $nid));
    }
  }
  // Get new total to display in the widget.
  $total_votes = plusone_get_total($nid);
```

```
  // Check to see if jQuery made the call. The AJAX call used
  // the POST method and passed in the key/value pair js = 1.
  if (!empty($_POST['js'])) {
    // jQuery made the call.
    // This will return results to jQuery's request.
    drupal_json(array(
      'total_votes' => $total_votes,
      'voted' => t('You voted')
      )
    );
    exit();
  }


  // It was a non-JavaScript call. Redisplay the entire page
  // with the updated vote total by redirecting to node/$nid
  // (or any URL alias that has been set for node/$nid).
  $path = drupal_get_path_alias('node/'. $nid);
  drupal_goto($path);
}
```

The preceding `plusone_vote()` function saves the current vote and returns information to jQuery in the form of an associative array containing the new total and the string You voted, which replaces the Vote text underneath the voting widget. This array is passed into `drupal_json()`, which converts PHP variables into their JavaScript equivalents, in this case converting a PHP associative array to a JavaScript object, and sets the HTTP header to `Content-type: text/javascript`. For more on how JSON works, see http://en.wikipedia.org/wiki/JSON.

Notice that we've written the preceding function to degrade gracefully. When we write the jQuery code, we'll make sure that the AJAX call from jQuery will pass along a parameter called js and will use the POST method. If the js parameter isn't there, we'll know that the user clicked on the Vote link and the browser itself is requesting the path—for example, plusone/vote/3. In that case, we don't return JSON, because the browser is expecting a regular HTML page. Instead, we update the vote total to reflect the fact that the user voted, and then we redirect the browser back to the original page, which will be rebuilt by Drupal and will show the new vote total.

We called `plusone_get_vote()` and `plusone_get_total()` in the preceding code, so let's create those:

```
/**
 * Return the number of votes for a given node ID/user ID pair.
 */
function plusone_get_vote($nid, $uid) {
  return (int)db_result(db_query('SELECT vote_count FROM {plusone_votes} WHERE
    nid = %d AND uid = %d', $nid, $uid));
}
```

```
/**
 * Return the total vote count for a node.
 */
function plusone_get_total($nid) {
  return (int)db_result(db_query('SELECT SUM(vote_count) FROM {plusone_votes}
    WHERE nid = %d', $nid));
}
```

Now, let's focus on getting the voting widget to display alongside the posts. There are two parts to this. First, we'll define some variables inside a plusone_widget() function. Then we'll pass those variables to a theme function. Here's the first part:

```
/**
 * Create voting widget to display on the web page.
 */
function plusone_widget($nid) {
  global $user;

  $total   = plusone_get_total($nid);
  $is_author = db_result(db_query('SELECT uid FROM {node} WHERE nid = %d
    AND uid = %d', $nid, $user->uid));
  $voted = plusone_get_vote($nid, $user->uid);

  return theme('plusone_widget', $nid, $total, $is_author, $voted);
}
```

Remember that if we are going to have a themable item we will need to declare it to Drupal using hook_theme() so it gets included in the theme registry. Here we go:

```
/**
 * Implementation of hook_theme().
 * Let Drupal know about our theme function.
 */
function plusone_theme() {
  return array(
    'plusone_widget' => array(
      'arguments' => array('nid', 'total', 'is_author', 'voted'),
    ),
  );
}
```

And then we need the actual theme function. Notice that this is where we include our JavaScript and CSS files.

```
/**
 * Theme for the voting widget.
 */
function theme_plusone_widget($nid, $total, $is_author, $voted) {
  // Load the JavaScript and CSS files.
  drupal_add_js(drupal_get_path('module', 'plusone') .'/plusone.js');
  drupal_add_css(drupal_get_path('module', 'plusone') .'/plusone.css');

  $output = '<div class="plusone-widget">';
  $output .= '<div class="score">'. $total .'</div>';

  $output .= '<div class="vote">';
  if ($is_author) {
    // User is author; not allowed to vote.
    $output .= t('Votes');
  }
  elseif ($voted) {
    // User already voted; not allowed to vote again.
    $output .= t('You voted');
  }
  else {
    // User is eligible to vote.
    $output .= l(t('Vote'), "plusone/vote/$nid", array(
      'attributes' => array('class' => 'plusone-link')
      ));
  }
  $output .= '</div>'; // Close div with class "vote".
  $output .= '</div>'; // Close div with class "plusone-widget".

  return $output;
}
```

In `plusone_widget()` in the preceding code, we set some variables and then hand off the theming of the widget to a custom theme function we created called `theme_plusone_widget()`. Keep in mind that `theme('plusone_widget')` actually calls `theme_plusone_widget()` (see Chapter 8 for how that works). Creating a separate theme function rather than building the HTML inside the `plusone_widget()` function allows designers to override this function if they want to change the markup.

Our theme function, `theme_plusone_widget()`, makes sure to add class attributes for the key HTML elements to make targeting these elements within jQuery really easy. Also, take a look at the URL of the link. It's pointing to `plusone/vote/$nid`, where `$nid` is the current node ID of the post. When the user clicks on the link, it will be intercepted and processed by jQuery instead of Drupal. This happens because we'll wire jQuery up to watch for the `onClick` event for that link. See how we defined the `plusone-link` CSS selector when building the link? Look for that selector to appear in our JavaScript later on as `a.plusone-link`. That is, an anchor (`<a>`) HTML element with the CSS class `plusone-link`.

The HTML of the widget that would appear on the page `http://example.com/?q=node/4` would look like this:

```
<div class="plusone-widget">
  <div class="score">0</div>
  <div class="vote">
    <a class="plusone-link" href="/plusone/vote/4">Vote</a>
  </div>
</div>
```

The `theme_plusone_widget()` function is what generates the voting widget to be sent to the browser. You want this widget to appear in node views so that users can use it to vote on the node they're looking at. Can you guess which Drupal hook would be a good one to use? It's our old friend `hook_nodeapi()`, which allows us to modify any node as it's being built.

```
/**
 * Implementation of hook_nodeapi().
 */
function plusone_nodeapi(&$node, $op, $teaser, $page) {
  switch ($op) {
    case 'view':
      // Show the widget, but only if the full node is being displayed.
      if (!$teaser) {
        $node->content['plusone_widget'] = array(
            '#value' => plusone_widget($node->nid),
            '#weight' => 100,
          );
      }
      break;

    case 'delete':
      // Node is being deleted; delete associated vote data.
      db_query('DELETE FROM {plusone_vote} WHERE nid = %d', $node->nid);
      break;
  }
}
```

We set the `weight` element to a large (or "heavy") number so that it shows at the bottom rather than the top of the post. We sneak a `delete` case in to remove voting records for a node when that node is deleted.

That's it for the content of `plusone.module`. All that's left until our module is complete is filling out `plusone.js`, with the jQuery code that will make the AJAX call, update the vote total, and change the `Vote` string to `You voted`.

```
// $Id$

// Only run if we are in a supported browser.
if (Drupal.jsEnabled) {
  // Run the following code when the DOM has been fully loaded.
  $(document).ready(function () {
    // Attach some code to the click event for the
    // link with class "plusone-link".
    $('a.plusone-link').click(function () {
      // When clicked, first define an anonymous function
      // to the variable voteSaved.
      var voteSaved = function (data) {
        // Update the number of votes.
        $('div.score').html(data.total_votes);
        // Update the "Vote" string to "You voted".
        $('div.vote').html(data.voted);
      }
      // Make the AJAX call; if successful the
      // anonymous function in voteSaved is run.
      $.ajax({
        type: 'POST',        // Use the POST method.
        url: this.href,
        dataType: 'json',
        success: voteSaved,
        data: 'js=1'         // Pass a key/value pair.
      });
      // Prevent the browser from handling the click.
      return false;
    });
  });
}
```

You should wrap all your jQuery code in a `Drupal.jsEnabled` test. This test makes sure certain DOM methods are supported within the current browser (if they're not, there's no point in our JavaScript being run).

This JavaScript adds an event listener to `a.plusone-link` (remember we defined `plusone-link` as a CSS class selector?) so that when users click the link it fires off an HTTP POST request to the URL it's pointing to. The preceding code also demonstrates how jQuery can pass data back into Drupal. After the AJAX request is completed, the return value (sent over from Drupal) is passed as the `data` parameter into the anonymous function that's assigned to the variable `voteSaved`. The array is referenced by the associative array keys that were initially built in the `plusone_vote()` function inside Drupal. Finally, the JavaScript updates the score and changes the `Vote` text to `You voted`.

To prevent the entire page from reloading (because the JavaScript handled the click), use a return value of `false` from the JavaScript jQuery function.

Using Drupal.behaviors

JavaScript interaction works by attaching behaviors (i.e., actions triggered by events such as a mouse click) to elements in the DOM. A change in the DOM can result in this binding being lost. So while the plusone.js file we used previously will work fine for a basic Drupal site, it might have trouble if other JavaScript files manipulate the DOM. Drupal provides a central object called Drupal.behaviors with which JavaScript functions may register to ensure that rebinding of behaviors takes place when necessary. The following version of plusone.js allows voting via AJAX just like the previous version but safeguards our bindings by registering with Drupal.behaviors:

```
// $Id$

Drupal.behaviors.plusone = function (context) {
  $('a.plusone-link:not(.plusone-processed)', context)
  .click(function () {
    var voteSaved = function (data) {
      $('div.score').html(data.total_votes);
      $('div.vote').html(data.voted);
    }
    $.ajax({
      type: 'POST',
      url: this.href,
      dataType: 'json',
      success: voteSaved,
      data: 'js=1'
    });
    return false;
  })
  .addClass('plusone-processed');
}
```

Note that we don't even have to test for Drupal.jsEnabled, since Drupal now takes care of that for us. For more details on Drupal.behaviors, see misc/drupal.js.

Ways to Extend This Module

A nice extension to this module would be to allow the site administrator to enable the voting widget for only certain node types. You could do that the same way we did for the node annotation module we built in Chapter 2. Then you would need to check whether or not voting was enabled for a given node type inside hook_nodeapi('view') before adding the widget. There are plenty of other possible enhancements, like weighting votes based on roles or limiting a user to a certain number of votes per 24-hour period. Our purpose here was to keep the module simple to emphasize the interactions between Drupal and jQuery.

Compatibility

jQuery compatibility, as well as a wealth of information about jQuery, can be found at `http://docs.jquery.com/`. In short, jQuery supports the following browsers:

- Internet Explorer 6.0 and greater

- Mozilla Firefox 1.5 and greater

- Apple Safari 2.0.2 and greater

- Opera 9.0 and greater

More detailed information on browser compatibility can be found at `http://docs.jquery.com/Browser_Compatibility`.

Next Steps

To learn more about how Drupal leverages jQuery, take a look at the `misc` directory of your Drupal installation. There, you'll find the JavaScript files responsible for form field automatic completion, batch processing, fieldset collapsibility, progress bar creation, draggable table rows, and more. See also the Drupal JavaScript Group at `http://groups.drupal.org/javascript`.

Summary

In this chapter, you learned

- What jQuery is

- The general concepts of how jQuery works

- How to include JavaScript files with your module

- How jQuery and Drupal interact to pass requests and data back and forth

- How to build a simple voting widget

CHAPTER 18

■ ■ ■

Localization and Translation

Localization is the replacement of strings in the user interface with translated strings appropriate for the user's locale. Drupal is developed and used by an international community. Therefore, it supports localization by default, as well as offering theming support for right-to-left languages such as Arabic and Hebrew. In this chapter, you'll see how to enable localization and how to use interface translation to selectively replace Drupal's built-in strings with strings of your own. Then, we'll look at full-fledged translations and learn how to create, import, and export them. Finally, we'll examine Drupal's ability to present the same content in multiple languages (such as a Canadian web site that presents content in English and French) and learn how Drupal selects the appropriate language to display.

Enabling the Locale Module

The locale module, which provides language handling functionality and user interface translation for Drupal, is not enabled when you install Drupal. This is in accordance with Drupal's philosophy of enabling functionality only when needed. You can enable the locale module at Administer ➤ Site building ➤ Modules. If Drupal has been installed using a language translation other than English, the locale module is enabled as part of the installation process. The examples in this chapter assume the locale module is enabled.

User Interface Translation

The interface for Drupal is made up of words, phrases, and sentences that communicate with the user. In the following sections, you'll see how they can be changed. Our examples will focus on string replacement, with the understanding that translation has its foundation in string replacement.

Strings

From a programming perspective, a string is a series of characters, such as the five-character string `Hello`. The translation of strings forms the basis of user interface translation in Drupal. When Drupal prepares a string for output, it checks if the string needs to be translated so that if the English language is enabled the word "Hello" is displayed, while if the French language is enabled the word "Bonjour" is displayed. Let's examine how that happens.

Translating Strings with t()

All strings that will be shown to the end user in Drupal should be run through the t() function; this is Drupal's *translate* function, with the function name shortened to "t" for convenience because of its frequent use.

■Note Some places in Drupal run t() implicitly, such as strings passed to watchdog() or titles and descriptions in the menu hook. Plurals are translated with format_plural(), which takes care of calling t() (see http://api.drupal.org/api/function/format_plural/6).

The locale-specific part of the t() function looks like this:

```
function t($string, $args = array(), $langcode = NULL) {
  global $language;
  static $custom_strings;

  $langcode = isset($langcode) ? $langcode : $language->language;

  // First, check for an array of customized strings. If present, use the array
  // *instead of* database lookups. This is a high performance way to provide a
  // handful of string replacements. See settings.php for examples.
  // Cache the $custom_strings variable to improve performance.
  if (!isset($custom_strings[$langcode])) {
    $custom_strings[$langcode] = variable_get('locale_custom_strings_'.
      $langcode, array());
  }
  // Custom strings work for English too, even if locale module is disabled.
  if (isset($custom_strings[$langcode][$string])) {
    $string = $custom_strings[$langcode][$string];
  }
  // Translate with locale module if enabled.
  elseif (function_exists('locale') && $langcode != 'en') {
    $string = locale($string, $langcode);
  }
  if (empty($args)) {
    return $string;
  }
  ...
}
```

In addition to translation, the t() function also handles insertion of values into placeholders in strings. The values are typically user-supplied input, which must be run through a text transformation before being displayed.

```
t('Hello, my name is %name.', array('%name' => 'John');
```

Hello, my name is *John*.

The placement of the text to be inserted is denoted by placeholders, and the text to be inserted is in a keyed array. This text transformation process is critical to Drupal security (see Chapter 20 for more information). Figure 18-1 shows you how t() handles translation; see Figure 20-1 to see how t() handles placeholders.

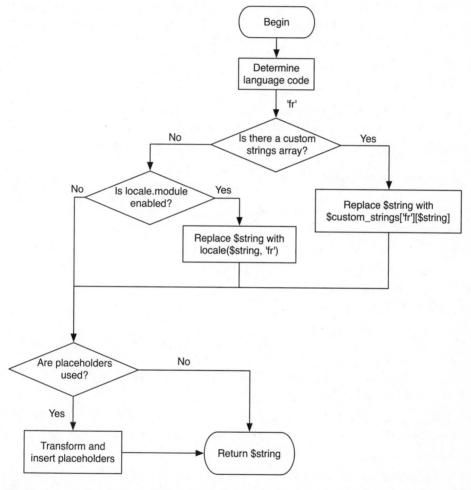

Figure 18-1. *How t() does translation and placeholder insertion, assuming the current language is set to French*

Replacing Built-In Strings with Custom Strings

Translating the user interface is essentially replacing one string with another. Let's start small, choosing just a few strings to change. There are a couple of possible solutions to the translation problem. We'll approach them from the simplest to the most complex. The first involves editing your settings file, and the second involves the locale module. Let's start by doing a simple string replacement in the breadcrumb trail and move on to replacing Blog with Journal.

String Overrides in settings.php

Find your settings.php file (typically at sites/default/settings.php). You may need to make the file writable before making changes, as Drupal tries its best to keep this file read-only. Scroll to the end of settings.php. We'll add the following custom string array:

```
/**
 * String overrides:
 *
 * To override specific strings on your site with or without enabling locale
 * module, add an entry to this list. This functionality allows you to change
 * a small number of your site's default English language interface strings.
 *
 * Remove the leading hash signs to enable.
 */
# $conf['locale_custom_strings_en'] = array(
#   'forum'       => 'Discussion board',
#   '@count min' => '@count minutes',
# );

$conf['locale_custom_strings_en'] = array(
  'Home' => 'Sweet Home',
);
```

If you visit your site, you'll notice that in the breadcrumb trail, Home has been changed to Sweet Home, as shown in Figure 18-2.

Now that you know how to do string overrides, let's go ahead and replace the word Blog with the word Journal:

```
$conf['locale_custom_strings_en'] = array(
  'Blog' => 'Journal',
);
```

Then enable the blog module at Administer ➤ Site building ➤ Modules. Go to Create content ➤ Blog entry, and you should see a screen like the one shown in Figure 18-3.

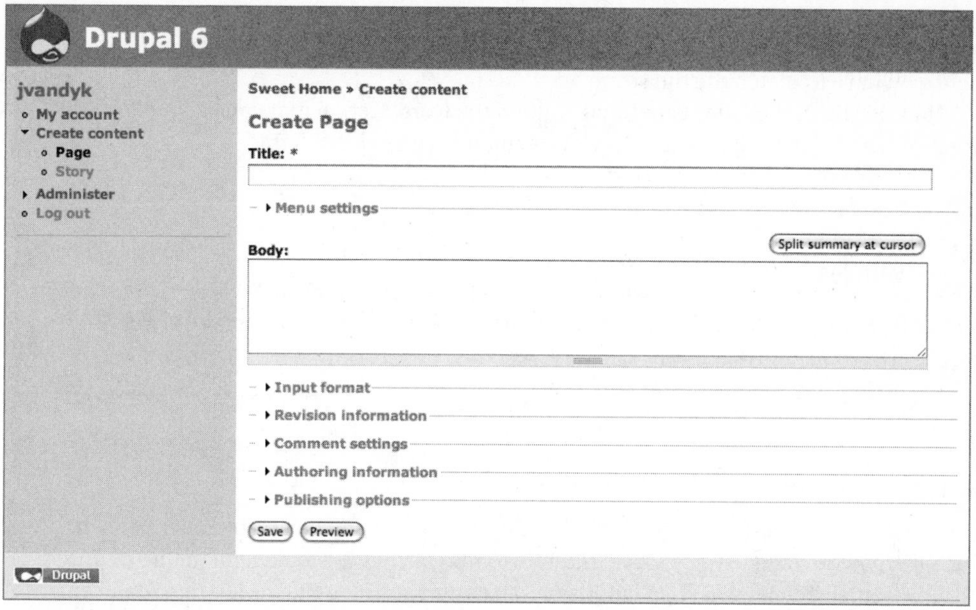

Figure 18-2. *The string Home is replaced with Sweet Home in the breadcrumb trail.*

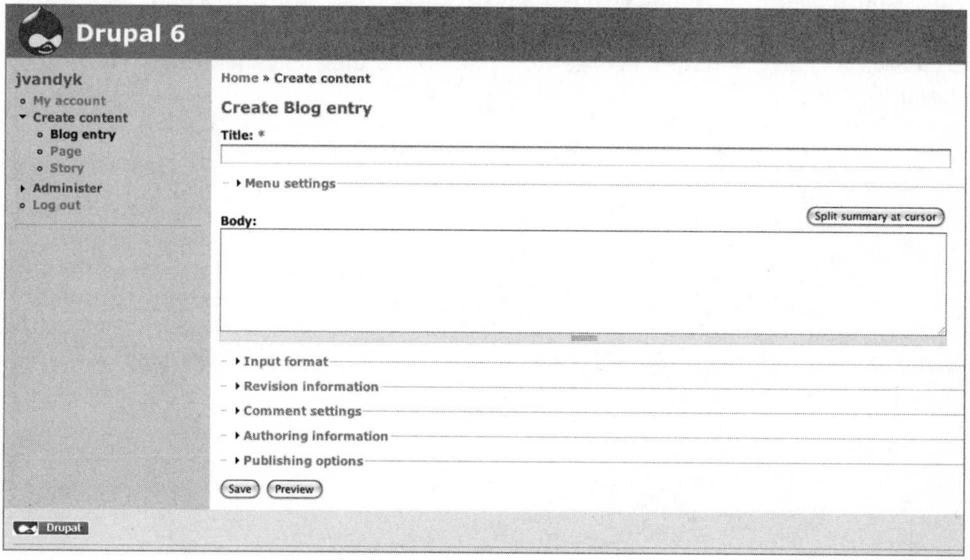

Figure 18-3. *The string Blog entry has not become Journal entry.*

What's wrong? Why was your custom string replacement array ignored? It's because the string Blog entry is not the same as the string Blog. You can't just pick substrings for replacement; you have to match the full string.

How do you find all the strings that contain the word Blog so that you can replace each string with its Journal equivalent? The locale module can help with this.

Tip Using string overrides in settings.php is highly performant (for small sets of strings only) because no database call is needed; the replacement string is simply looked up in an array. You don't even have to have the locale module enabled for string overrides to work. See also the string overrides module at http://drupal.org/project/stringoverrides.

Replacing Strings with the Locale Module

Instead of using string replacement by defining a list of custom string replacements in settings.php, you can use the locale module to find strings for replacement and define what the replacements will be. A language translation is a set of custom string replacements for Drupal. When Drupal prepares to display a string, it will run the string through the t() function as outlined previously. If it finds a replacement in the current language translation, it will use the replacement; if not, it will simply use the original string. This process, which is what the locale() function does, is shown in a simplified form in Figure 18-4. The approach is to create a language with the language code en-US containing only the string(s) we want replaced.

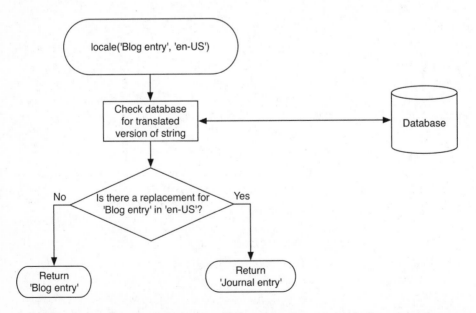

Figure 18-4. *If the locale module does not find a replacement string in the current language translation, it will fall back to using the original string.*

Okay, let's begin the process of changing any strings containing "blog" to strings containing "journal." Because Drupal will fall back to using the original string if no translation is found, we only need to provide the strings we want to change. We can put the strings into a custom language and let Drupal fall back to original strings for any strings we don't provide. First, let's add a custom language to hold our custom strings. The interface for doing that is shown in Figure 18-5. We'll call it English-custom and use en-US for the language code and path prefix.

Home » Administer » Site configuration » Languages

Languages

| List | **Add language** | Configure |

Add all languages to be supported by your site. If your desired language is not available in the *Language name* drop-down, click *Custom language* and provide a language code and other details manually. When providing a language code manually, be sure to enter a standardized language code, since this code may be used by browsers to determine an appropriate display language.

▼ Predefined language

Language name:

Abkhazian (аҧсуа бызшәа) ▼

Select the desired language and click the *Add language* button. (Use the *Custom language* options if your desired language does not appear in this list.)

[Add language]

▼ Custom language

Language code: *

en-US

RFC 4646 compliant language identifier. Language codes typically use a country code, and optionally, a script or regional variant name. *Examples: "en", "en-US" and "zh-Hant".*

Language name in English: *

English-custom

Name of the language in English. Will be available for translation in all languages.

Native language name: *

English-custom

Name of the language in the language being added.

Path prefix:

en-US

Language code or other custom string for pattern matching within the path. With language negotiation set to *Path prefix only* or *Path prefix with language fallback*, this site is presented in this language when the Path prefix value matches an element in the path. For the default language, this value may be left blank. **Modifying this value will break existing URLs and should be used with caution in a production environment.** *Example: Specifying "deutsch" as the path prefix for German results in URLs in the form "www.example.com/deutsch/node".*

Language domain:

Language-specific URL, with protocol. With language negotiation set to *Domain name only*, the site is presented in this language when the URL accessing the site references this domain. For the default language, this value may be left blank. **This value must include a protocol as part of the string.** *Example: Specifying "http://example.de" or "http://de.example.com" as language domains for German results in URLs in the forms "http://example.de/node" and "http://de.example.com/node", respectively.*

Direction: *

◉ Left to right

○ Right to left

Direction that text in this language is presented.

[Add custom language]

Figure 18-5. *Adding a custom language for targeted string translation*

Now, enable your new language, and make it the default, as shown in Figure 18-6. Click "Save configuration," uncheck the Enabled check box next to English, and click "Save configuration" again, as shown in Figure 18-7. With only one language enabled, users will not be presented with the somewhat confusing "Language settings" choice shown in Figure 18-8 when editing their user accounts.

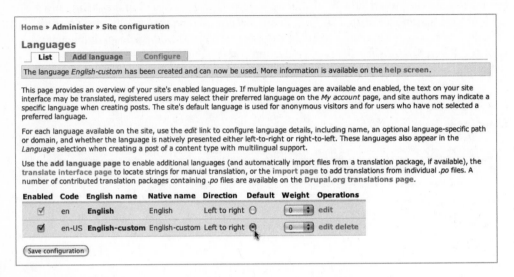

Figure 18-6. *Enabling the new language and selecting it as the default*

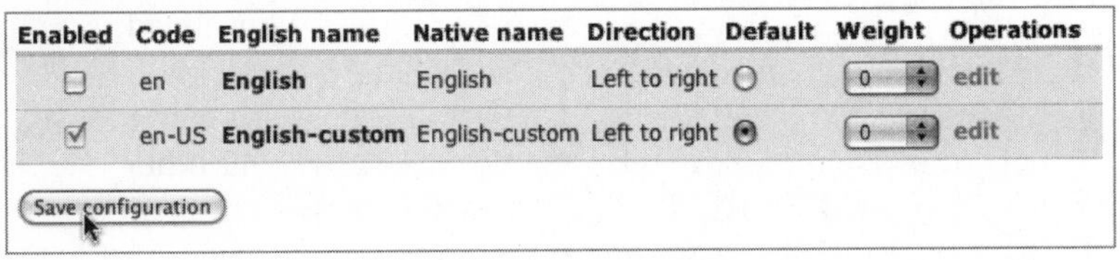

Enabled	Code	English name	Native name	Direction	Default	Weight	Operations
☐	en	**English**	English	Left to right ○		0	edit
☑	en-US	**English-custom**	English-custom	Left to right ●		0	edit

Save configuration

Figure 18-7. *Disabling English so that English-custom will be the only enabled language*

┌─ Language settings ───

Language:

○ English
● English-custom

This account's default language for e-mails.

Figure 18-8. *The user interface on the "My account" page, where a user may select the preferred language for e-mail sent by the site. (The interface only appears if multiple languages are enabled.)*

Okay, you've got a single language translation called English-custom enabled. It is currently empty, since we haven't added any string replacements yet. So for every string, Drupal will go through the process shown in Figure 18-4, fail to find a string replacement in English-custom, and fall back to returning the original English string from the English language. Let's set up some string replacements. Navigate to Administer ➤ Site building ➤ Translate interface, which is shown in Figure 18-9.

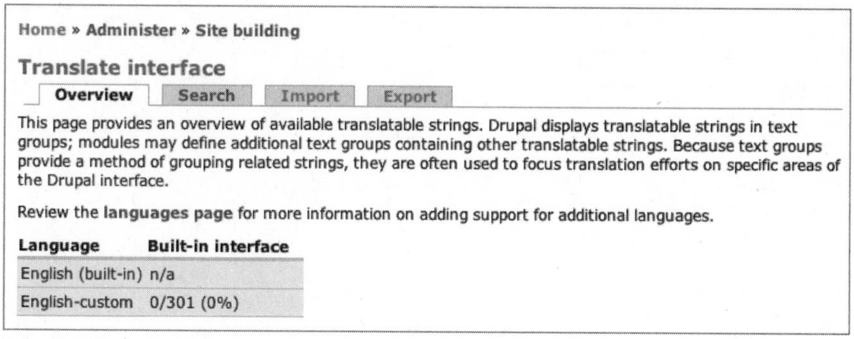

```
Home » Administer » Site building

Translate interface
  Overview      Search      Import      Export

This page provides an overview of available translatable strings. Drupal displays translatable strings in text
groups; modules may define additional text groups containing other translatable strings. Because text groups
provide a method of grouping related strings, they are often used to focus translation efforts on specific areas of
the Drupal interface.

Review the languages page for more information on adding support for additional languages.

Language          Built-in interface
English (built-in) n/a
English-custom    0/301 (0%)
```

Figure 18-9. *The overview page of the "Translate interface" screen*

Drupal uses just-in-time translation. When a page is loaded, each string is passed through the t() function and on through the locale() function where, if the string is not already present in the locales_source and locales_target database tables, it is added to those tables. So the values in the "Built-in interface" column in Figure 18-9 show that 301 strings have passed through t() and are available for translation. Go ahead and click around to some other pages in Drupal and then return to this one. You should see that the number of strings has increased as Drupal encounters more and more parts of the interface that will need translation. We'll now use the locale module's web interface to translate some strings.

After clicking on the Search tab, we are presented with a search interface that allows us to find strings for translation. Let's search for all of those 301 or more strings that are available to us so far. The search interface is shown in Figure 18-10.

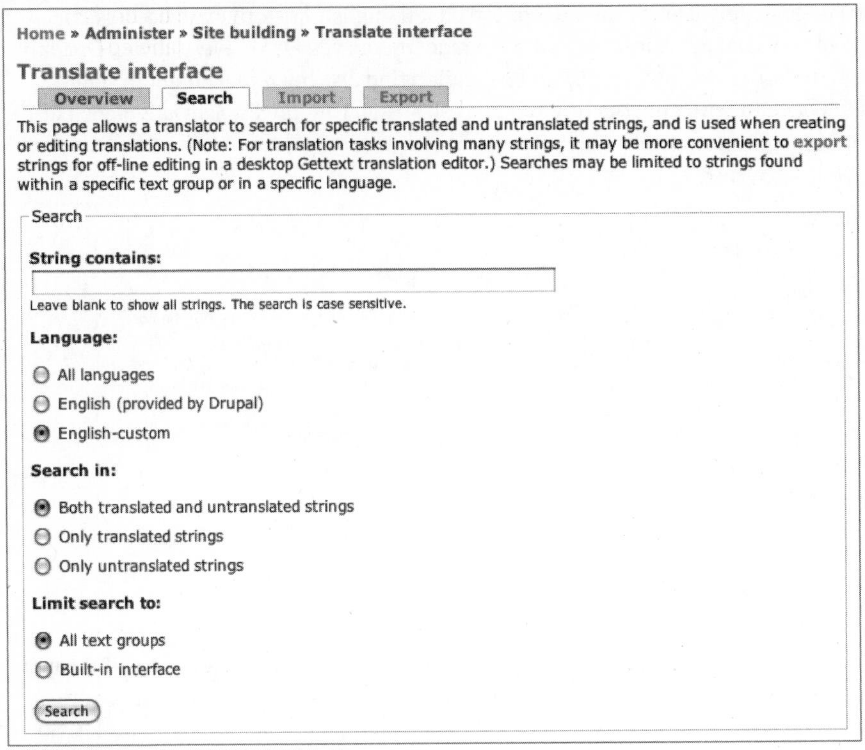

Home » Administer » Site building » Translate interface

Translate interface

| Overview | **Search** | Import | Export |

This page allows a translator to search for specific translated and untranslated strings, and is used when creating or editing translations. (Note: For translation tasks involving many strings, it may be more convenient to export strings for off-line editing in a desktop Gettext translation editor.) Searches may be limited to strings found within a specific text group or in a specific language.

Search

String contains:

Leave blank to show all strings. The search is case sensitive.

Language:

○ All languages

○ English (provided by Drupal)

◉ English-custom

Search in:

◉ Both translated and untranslated strings

○ Only translated strings

○ Only untranslated strings

Limit search to:

◉ All text groups

○ Built-in interface

(Search)

Figure 18-10. *The search interface for showing translatable strings*

Selecting our language (English-custom), searching for all strings, and leaving the search box blank will show us all translatable strings. Each string has an "edit" link next to it. After the list of strings, the search interface is shown again at the bottom of the page. Since the list of strings is quite long, let's reduce it to only the strings that contain the word "Search." Type the word **Search** in the "String contains" field, and click the Search button. The result should be a list of strings that contain the word "Search," as shown in Figure 18-11. Let's change the string Search to Search now by clicking the "edit" link.

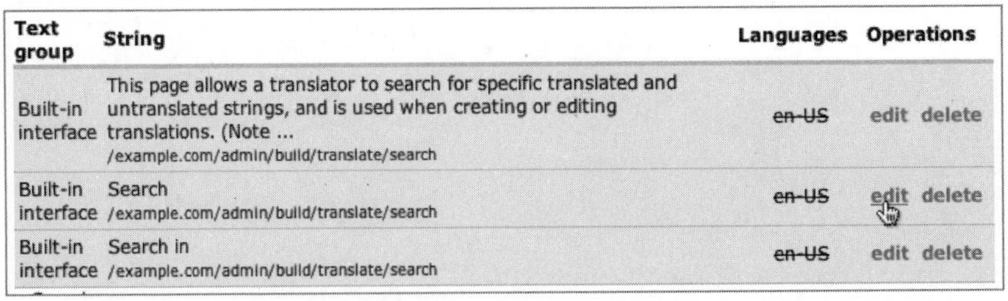

Text group	String	Languages	Operations
Built-in interface	This page allows a translator to search for specific translated and untranslated strings, and is used when creating or editing translations. (Note ... /example.com/admin/build/translate/search	en-US	edit delete
Built-in interface	Search /example.com/admin/build/translate/search	en-US	edit delete
Built-in interface	Search in /example.com/admin/build/translate/search	en-US	edit delete

Figure 18-11. *A list of translatable strings containing the word "search" and their statuses*

After you've edited the string, you are returned to the Search tab. But wait! It's now called the "Search now" tab! And the button at the bottom of the search form is now labeled "Search now" instead of "Search," as shown in Figure 18-12. In fact, in *every place* the word "Search" occurred, it is replaced with "Search now."

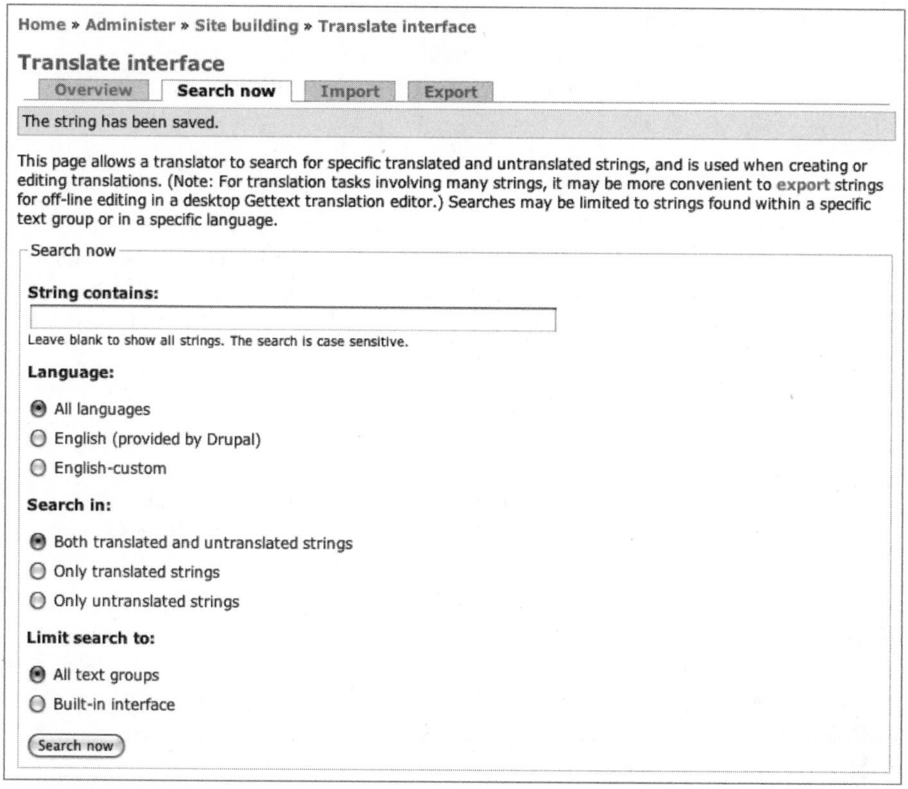

Figure 18-12. *The string Search is now replaced by the string Search now.*

Go ahead and search for the string Search again. You should see in the resulting list of strings that the strikethrough is removed from the Languages column for this entry, indicating that the string has been translated, as shown in Figure 18-13.

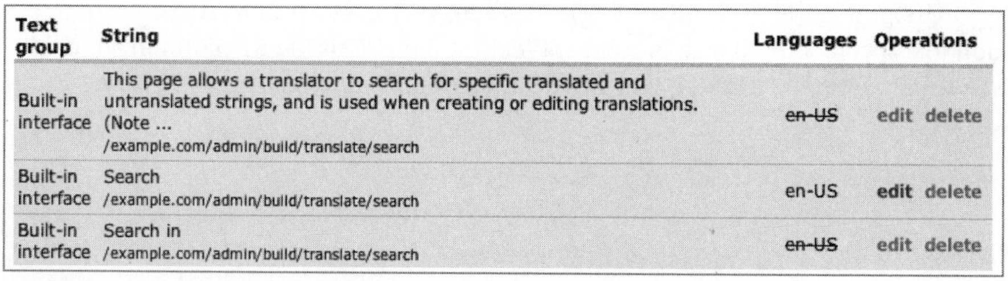

Figure 18-13. *The list of translatable strings after editing "Search"*

Note that the original string is shown, not the translation. If you return to the Overview tab, you will see that English-custom now has one replacement string available.

Now that you've learned how to change strings, we can get on to the business of changing all occurrences of "blog" to "journal." After enabling the blog module and visiting the blog-related pages (such as /node/add/blog and blog/1), the translatable strings should be available for us to translate. The search at Administer ➤ Site building ➤ Translate interface is case-sensitive, so one search for "blog" and another for "Blog" will show us all the occurrences and let us change them to equivalent replacement strings using our preferred words "journal" and "Journal."

Caution The method we are introducing here is for touching up Drupal sites and targeting certain interface elements for string replacement, and it is not complete. For example, if a module containing the word "blog" were not enabled, we would miss the translation of those strings. A more complete method is introduced in the "Starting a New Translation" section of this chapter.

That change is all well and good, but it's still bothersome that the URL for creating a new journal entry is still http://example.com/?q=node/add/blog; shouldn't it be http://example.com/?q=node/add/journal instead? Sure, it should. We can fix that quickly by enabling the path module and adding an alias with node/add/blog as the existing system path and node/add/journal as the alias. Presto! All references to "blog" have disappeared, and you can use the site without shuddering at seeing the word "blog".

Tip A third-party module that will make string translation easier is the Localization client module, available at http://drupal.org/project/l10n_client. The module provides an on-page localization editor interface and makes extensive use of AJAX.

Exporting Your Translation

After you've gone through the work of selecting and translating the strings you want to change, it would be a shame to have to do it all over again when you set up your next Drupal site. By using the Export tab at Administer ➤ Site building ➤ Translate interface, you can save the translation to a special file called a portable object (.po) file. This file will contain all of the strings that Drupal has passed through t(), as well as any replacement strings you have defined.

Portable Object Files

The first few lines of the file that results from exporting our English-custom translation follow:

```
# English-custom translation of Drupal 6
# Copyright (c) 2007 drupalusername <me@example.com>
#
msgid ""
msgstr ""
"Project-Id-Version: PROJECT VERSION\n"
"POT-Creation-Date: 2008-05-09 12:46-0500\n"
"PO-Revision-Date: 2008-05-09 12:46-0500\n"
"Last-Translator: drupalusername <me@example.com>\n"
"Language-Team: English-custom <me@example.com>\n"
"MIME-Version: 1.0\n"
"Content-Type: text/plain; charset=utf-8\n"
"Content-Transfer-Encoding: 8bit\n"

#: /example.com/?q=admin/build/translate/search
msgid "Search"
msgstr "Search now"

#: /example.com/?q=node/add/blog
msgid "blog"
msgstr "journal"

#: /example.com/?q=admin/build/modules/list/confirm
msgid "Blog entry"
msgstr "Journal entry"

#: /example.com/?q=admin/build/translate/search
msgid ""
"A <em>blog entry</em> is a single post to an online journal, or "
"<em>blog</em>."
msgstr "A <em>journal entry</em> is a single post to an online journal."
...
```

The `.po` file consists of some metadata headers followed by the translated strings. Each string has three components: a comment that shows where the string first occurred, a `msgid` denoting the original string, and a `msgstr` denoting the translated string to use. For a full description of the `.po` file format, see `http://www.gnu.org/software/gettext/manual/gettext.html#PO-Files`.

The `en-US.po` file can now be imported into another Drupal site (that has the locale module enabled) using the import tab at Administer ➤ Site building ➤ Translate interface.

Portable Object Templates

While a translation consists of some metadata and a lot of original and translated strings, a portable object template (.pot) file contains all the strings available for translation, without any translated strings. This is useful if you are starting a language translation from scratch or want to determine whether any new strings were added to Drupal since the last version before modifying your site (another way to find this out would be to upgrade a copy of your Drupal site and search for untranslated strings as shown in the "Replacing Built-In Strings with Custom Strings" section).

Starting a New Translation

Drupal's user interface has been translated into many languages. If you'd like to volunteer to assist in translating, chances are you will be warmly welcomed. Each existing language translation has a project page where development is tracked. For example, the French translation is at http://drupal.org/project/fr. Assistance for translation in general can be found in the translations forum at http://drupal.org/forum/30.

■**Note** Serious translators working with languages other than English do not use the string replacement methods first introduced in this chapter. They become comfortable working with .pot and .po files, often using special software to help them manage translations (see http://drupal.org/node/11131). See also the project to create a web-based tool for translators at http://drupal.org/project/l10n_server.

Getting .pot Files for Drupal

The definitive .pot files for Drupal can be downloaded from http://drupal.org/project/drupal-pot. After downloading and extracting the .tar.gz file for the branch of Drupal you are interested in, you should have a directory full of .pot files corresponding to Drupal files. For example, modules-aggregator.pot contains the translatable strings from Drupal's aggregator module.

```
$ gunzip drupal-pot-6.x-1.0.tar.gz
$ tar -xf drupal-pot-6.x-1.0.tar
$ ls drupal-pot
LICENSE.txt              modules-dblog.pot        modules-statistics.pot
README.txt               modules-filter.pot       modules-syslog.pot
general.pot              modules-forum.pot        modules-system.pot
includes.pot             modules-help.pot         modules-taxonomy.pot
installer.pot            modules-locale.pot       modules-throttle.pot
misc.pot                 modules-menu.pot         modules-tracker.pot
modules-aggregator.pot   modules-node.pot         modules-translation.pot
modules-block.pot        modules-openid.pot       modules-trigger.pot
modules-blog.pot         modules-path.pot         modules-update.pot
modules-blogapi.pot      modules-php.pot          modules-upload.pot
```

```
modules-book.pot          modules-ping.pot      modules-user.pot
modules-color.pot         modules-poll.pot      themes-chameleon.pot
modules-comment.pot       modules-profile.pot   themes-garland.pot
modules-contact.pot       modules-search.pot    themes-pushbutton.pot
```

You'll notice a few other files in the distribution as well. There's an informative README.txt file (read it!), a file named general.pot, and a file named installer.pot. The general.pot file is the place to start when translating, as it contains strings that occur in more than one place. The installer.pot contains the strings that must be translated if you want to create a translation of the installer interface.

Generating .pot Files with Translation Template Extractor

The contributed translation template extractor module (see http://drupal.org/project/potx) can generate .pot files for you. This is useful if you've written your own module or downloaded a contributed module for which there is no existing translation. The translation template extractor module contains both a command-line version and a web-based version of the extractor. If you are familiar with the xgettext program for Unix, think of this module as a Drupal-savvy version of that program.

Creating a .pot File for Your Module

Let's generate a .pot file for the annotation module we created in Chapter 2.

First, we'll need to download the translation template extractor module from http://drupal.org/project/potx, and place the resulting folder at sites/all/modules/potx.

Using the Command Line

Copy potx.inc and potx-cli.php into the annotate module's directory at sites/all/modules/custom/annotate. Next, we need to run the extractor, so it can create the .pot files.

■**Caution** You're adding to your Drupal site an executable PHP script that needs write privileges to the directory it runs in (so it can write the .pot file). Always do template extraction on a copy of your site on your development machine, never on a live site.

Here are the results from running the extractor:

```
$ cd sites/all/modules/custom/annotate
$ php potx-cli.php
Processing annotate.admin.inc...
Processing annotate.module...
Processing annotate.install...
Processing annotate.info...

Done.
```

Let's see what was generated:

```
annotate.admin.inc     general.pot
annotate.info          potx-cli.php
annotate.install       potx.inc
annotate.module
```

Running the extractor script resulted in a new file called `general.pot`, which contains the strings from `annotate.module`, `annotate.info`, and `annotate.install`. The script placed all the strings into `general.pot` by default but can generate separate files if you'd prefer. Run

```
$ php potx-cli.php --help
```

to see the various options offered by the extractor script. In the present case, it's handy to have all of the strings in one file. If we were to share this translation template with others, we'd create a `translations` subdirectory inside the `annotate` directory, move the `general.pot` into the translations directory and rename it `annotate.pot`. If we then made a French translation by opening the combined `.pot` file, translating the strings, and saving it as `fr.po`, our module directory would look like this:

```
annotate.admin.inc
annotate.info
annotate.install
annotate.module
translations/
  annotate.pot
  fr.po
```

Using the Web-Based Extractor

Instead of using the command line, you can extract strings from your module using the web-based user interface provided by the translation template extractor module. After making sure that you have downloaded the module and moved it to `sites/all/modules/potx` as described previously, go to Administer ➤ Site building ➤ Modules, and enable both the annotate and translation template extractor modules. Next, go to Administer ➤ Site building ➤ Translate interface, and notice the new Extract tab. Click it, and you'll be able to generate a `.pot` file by choosing "Language independent template" and clicking the Extract button, as shown in Figure 18-14. The `.pot` file will be downloaded via your web browser. You can then place it in `sites/all/custom/annotate/translations` as we did with the command-line extractor.

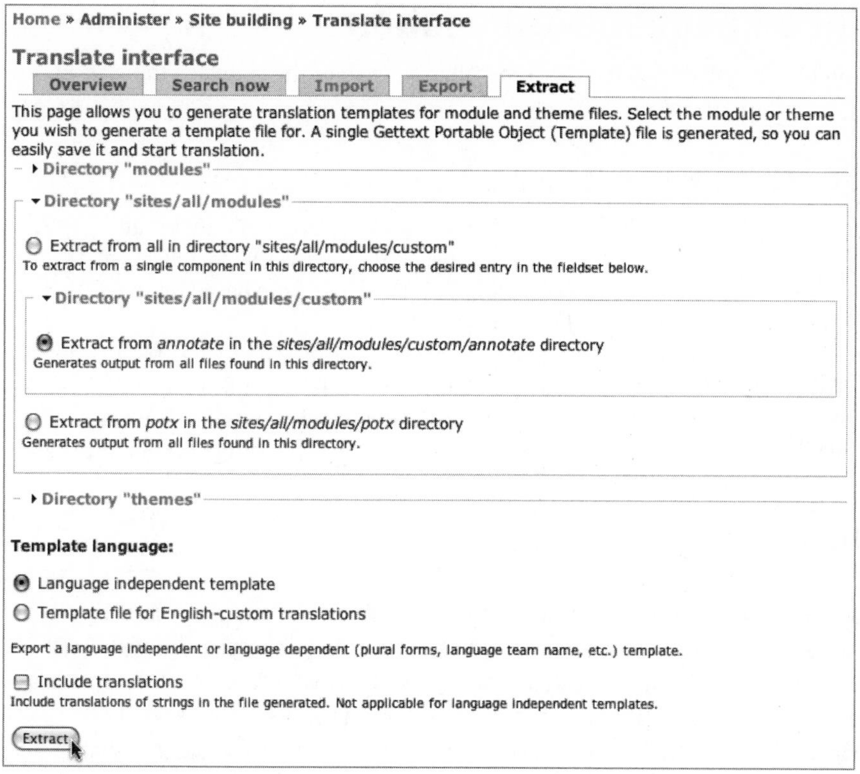

Figure 18-14. *Extracting a .pot file for the annotate module using the web-based user interface of the translation template extractor module*

Creating .pot Files for an Entire Site

If you wish to create .pot files for all translatable strings in your site, place the potx.inc and potx-cli.php files at the root of your site, ensure you have write access to that current directory, and run potx-cli.php. You would run the script from the command line with the mode parameter set to core if you want to generate .pot files with the same layout as those available at http://drupal.org/project/Translations:

```
$ php potx-cli.php --mode=core
```

The script always outputs .pot files in the same directory the script is in; for example, modules-aggregator.pot will be created in the root directory of your site, not in modules/aggregator/. The name of the .pot file reflects where it was found. So in the previous example, a sites-all-modules-custom-annotate.pot file would be generated.

Installing a Language Translation

Drupal can either be installed in a language other than English or the language translation can be added later. Let's cover both possibilities.

Setting Up a Translation at Install Time

Drupal's installer recognizes installer translations with the st() function rather than t(), which isn't available to the installer at runtime because, well, Drupal isn't installed yet. Installer translations are offered as a choice during installation and are based on the installer.pot file (see the "Getting .pot Files for Drupal" section).

To view the installer's translation capabilities in action, let's download the French translation of Drupal from http://drupal.org/project/Translations. This results in the file fr-6.x-1.x.tar.gz. You can tell from the .tar.gz ending that this is a .tar file that has been compressed with GZIP compression. One way to extract the file is by using the Unix tar utility:

```
$ tar -xzvf fr-6.x-1.x.tar.gz
```

■**Caution** The file contains a directory structure that mirrors the directory structure of Drupal. When extracting it, be careful to use an extraction method that merges the directory structure in the tarball with your existing Drupal directory structure. The default extractor in Mac OS X will not do it correctly. If you end up with a folder called fr-6.x-1.x-dev after extraction, the merge did not take place. See http://www.lullabot.com/videocast/installing-drupal-translation for a screencast demonstrating the proper way to do the extraction.

After successful extraction of the translation, additional folders called translations should be found in your Drupal directories. For example, the profiles/default folder (where Drupal's default installation profile lives) now has a translations subfolder containing a fr.po file. That's the French translation of the installer. When Drupal's installer runs, you can see the new choice presented, as shown in Figure 18-15.

If you choose French, the installation will proceed in French, and the default language for the site will be set to French.

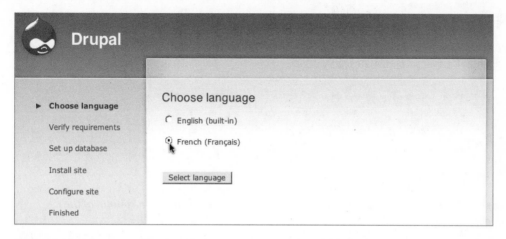

Figure 18-15. *When a .po file exists in the installation profile's translations subdirectory, Drupal's installer allows you to choose a language for the installer.*

Installing a Translation on an Existing Site

To install a language translation on an existing site, the same extraction steps outlined in the previous section need to be followed. When the translation files have been properly extracted (you can check by looking for the new `translations` subdirectories), you can add the language by navigating to Administer ➤ Site configuration ➤ Languages and clicking the "Add language" tab. Next, simply choose the language that corresponds with the language translation files you have extracted, and click "Add language," as shown in Figure 18-16. If you have correctly extracted the translation files, Drupal will show a progress bar as it installs them. The new language will then be shown in the table at Administer ➤ Site configuration ➤ Languages.

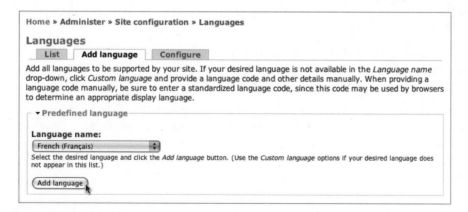

Figure 18-16. *Installing a language. (Translation files must be properly extracted prior to clicking the Add language button.)*

Right-to-Left Language Support

The directionality of a language is displayed in the list of language translations that have been added to Drupal, as shown in Figure 18-17.

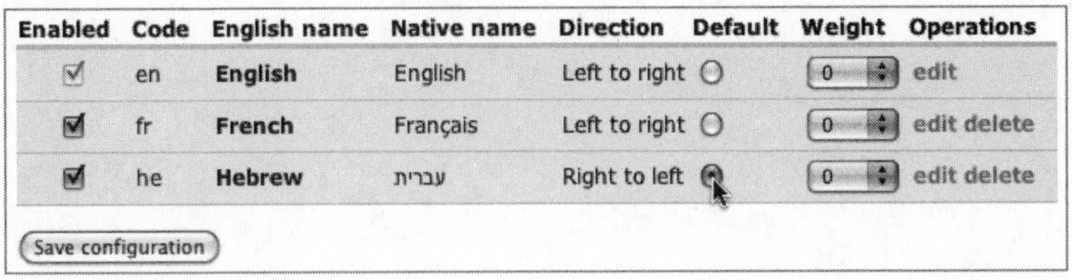

Enabled	Code	English name	Native name	Direction	Default	Weight	Operations
☑	en	**English**	English	Left to right ○	0 ▲▼	edit
☑	fr	**French**	Français	Left to right ○	0 ▲▼	edit delete
☑	he	**Hebrew**	עברית	Right to left ◉	0 ▲▼	edit delete

(Save configuration)

Figure 18-17. *Right-to-left languages can be identified using the Direction column of the language table.*

Drupal's support for right-to-left languages such as Hebrew is at the theming layer. When Drupal is informed that a style sheet should be included in the current page, and the current language is a right-to-left language, Drupal will check for a corresponding style sheet name that ends in `-rtl.css`. If that style sheet exists, it will be loaded *in addition to* the requested style sheet. The logic is shown in Figure 18-18. Thus, themes that support right-to-left languages generally have the styles defined in the main style sheet, and CSS overrides defined in the corresponding right-to-left style sheet.

For example, if the current language is Hebrew and the theme is set to Bluemarine, when Drupal adds the `themes/bluemarine/style.css` style sheet, the `themes/bluemarine/style-rtl.css` file is included as well. Check out the right-to-left style sheets in Drupal's default themes to see what kind of CSS elements are overridden.

The direction of a language can be changed by going to Administer ➤ Site configuration ➤ Languages and clicking the "edit" link for the language in question.

Testing for the directionality of the current language can be done in code using the following approach:

```
if (defined('LANGUAGE_RTL') && $language->direction == LANGUAGE_RTL) {
  // Do something.
}
```

The reason this works is that the constant `LANGUAGE_RTL` is defined by the locale module, so if the locale module is not loaded, right-to-left language support is not available.

drupal_add_css('style.css', 'theme')
Add style.css
Is current language right-to-left?
No
Yes
Does style-rtl.css exist?
No
Yes
Add style-rtl.css
Done

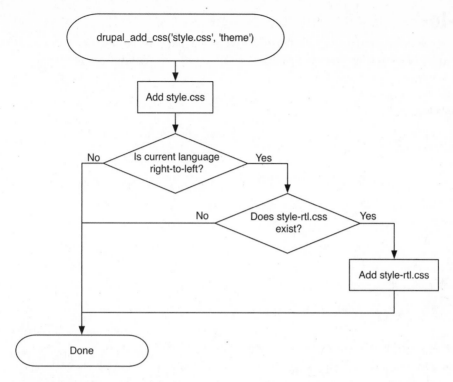

Figure 18-18. *If the current language is a right-to-left language, an additional style sheet will be included if the additional style sheet exists.*

Language Negotiation

Drupal implements most of the common ways of determining a user's language so that when multiple languages are enabled on a Drupal site, the user's preferred language is used. In the following sections we will assume that the French translation of Drupal has been installed as described in the previous section. The way that Drupal determines the language setting is configured at Administer ➤ Site configuration ➤ Languages under the Configure tab. The relevant user interface is shown in Figure 18-19. Let's examine each of these options.

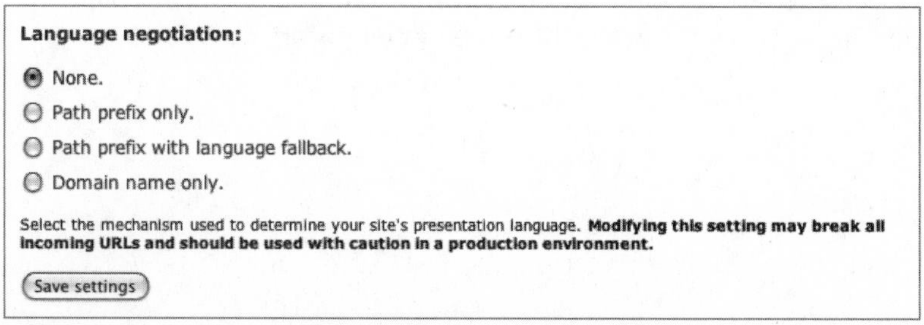

Language negotiation:
None.
Path prefix only.
Path prefix with language fallback.
Domain name only.
Select the mechanism used to determine your site's presentation language. Modifying this setting may break all incoming URLs and should be used with caution in a production environment.
Save settings

Figure 18-19. *The possible settings for language negotiation*

None

This is the default option and the simplest one. The language that is set as the default language is used for all users when displaying pages. See Figure 18-17 to see the user interface in which the default language is specified.

User-Preferred Language

If more than one language is enabled, users will see the fieldset shown in Figure 18-20 when they edit their "My account" pages.

```
┌─Language settings──────────────────────────────────────────┐
│                                                             │
│  Language:                                                  │
│                                                             │
│  ◉ English                                                  │
│  ○ French (Français)                                        │
│  ○ Hebrew (עברית)                                           │
│  This account's default language for e-mails.               │
│                                                             │
└─────────────────────────────────────────────────────────────┘
```

Figure 18-20. *Choosing a user-specific language for e-mail messages*

The language that a user has chosen can be retrieved as follows:

```
// Retrieve user 3's preferred language.
$account = user_load(array('uid' => 3));
$language = user_preferred_language($account);
```

If the user has not set a preferred language, the default language for the site will be returned. The result will be a language object (see the next section for more about the language object). When the "Language negotiation" setting is set to None, the user's preferred language is used *only* for determining which language should be used for e-mail sent from the site. The user's preferred language has no effect on the language used for page display when the "Language negotiation" setting is set to None.

The Global $language Object

You can determine the current language programmatically by looking at the global $language variable, which is an object. The variable is initialized during the DRUPAL_BOOTSTRAP_LANGUAGE portion of bootstrap. You can see what the object looks like by doing a var_dump():

```
global $language;
var_dump($language);
```

Results are shown here:

```
object(stdClass) (11) {
  ["language"]  =>  string(2) "fr"
  ["name"]      =>  string(6) "French"
  ["native"]    =>  string(9) "Français"
  ["direction"] =>  string(1) "0"
  ["enabled"]   =>  int(1)
  ["plurals"]   =>  string(1) "2"
  ["formula"]   =>  string(6) "($n>1)"
  ["domain"]    =>  string(0) ""
  ["prefix"]    =>  string(2) "fr"
  ["weight"]    =>  string(1) "0"
  ["javascript"]=>  string(0) ""
}
```

The RFC 4646 language identifier (such as fr in the previous example) can be retrieved by getting the language property of the $language object:

```
global $language;
$lang = $language->language;
```

Path Prefix Only

When language negotiation is set to Path Prefix Only, there are only two possibilities. Either a language path prefix is found in the path, or the default language is used. For example, suppose you are creating a site that supports users in both English and French. English is the default language for the site, but the French translation has also been installed and enabled. Going to Administer ➤ Site configuration ➤ Languages and clicking the "edit" link next to the French language will show you the user interface shown in Figure 18-21. Notice that the "Path prefix" field is set to fr. This value could be changed to any string.

With the path prefix set to fr, Drupal will determine the current language by looking at the requested URL. The process is shown in Figure 18-22.

Home » Administer » Site configuration

Edit language

Language code:
fr

Language name in English: *

French

Name of the language in English. Will be available for translation in all languages.

Native language name: *

Français

Name of the language in the language being added.

Path prefix:

fr

Language code or other custom string for pattern matching within the path. With language negotiation set to *Path prefix only* or *Path prefix with language fallback*, this site is presented in this language when the Path prefix value matches an element in the path. For the default language, this value may be left blank. **Modifying this value will break existing URLs and should be used with caution in a production environment.** *Example: Specifying "deutsch" as the path prefix for German results in URLs in the form "www.example.com/deutsch/node".*

Language domain:

Language-specific URL, with protocol. With language negotiation set to *Domain name only*, the site is presented in this language when the URL accessing the site references this domain. For the default language, this value may be left blank. **This value must include a protocol as part of the string.** *Example: Specifying "http://example.de" or "http://de.example.com" as language domains for German results in URLs in the forms "http://example.de/node" and "http://de.example.com/node", respectively.*

Direction: *

◉ Left to right

◯ Right to left

Direction that text in this language is presented.

(Save language)

Figure 18-21. *User interface for the Edit language screen showing the "Path prefix" field*

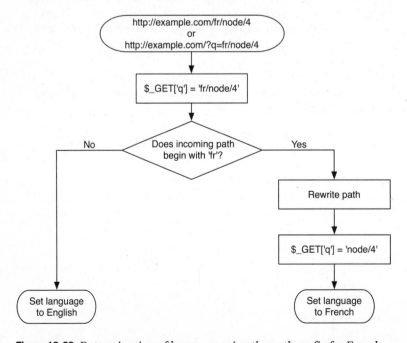

Figure 18-22. *Determination of language using the path prefix for French*

Path Prefix with Language Fallback

When language negotiation is set to this setting, Drupal will first look at the path prefix. If a match is not made, the user's preferred language is checked by examining $user->language. If the user has not selected a preferred language, Drupal next tries to determine the user's preferred language by looking at the Accept-language HTTP header in the browser's HTTP request. If the browser does not specify a preferred language, the default language for the site is used. Assuming that English is the default language for the site, and both French and Hebrew are enabled, the process of language determination is shown in Figure 18-23.

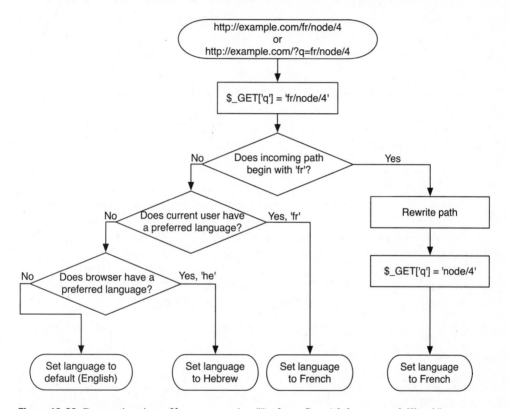

Figure 18-23. *Determination of language using "Path prefix with language fallback"*

Domain Name Only

When language negotiation is set to this setting, Drupal will determine the current language by attempting to match the domain of the current URL with the language domain specified in the "Language domain" field of the "Edit language" page of a language (see Figure 18-21). For example, with English as the default language, specifying http://fr.example.com as the language domain for the French language would set the current language to French for users visiting http://fr.example.com/?q=node/2 and English for users visiting http://example.com/?q=node/2.

■**Note** A user's preferred language setting from the "My account" page and the client browser settings are ignored when "Language negotiation" is set to Domain Name Only.

Content Translation

So far, we've been focusing on the translation of Drupal's user interface. But what about the content? Once the current language setting has been determined, there's a good chance that the user wants to see the site content in that language! Let's find out how content translation works.

Introducing the Content Translation Module

Drupal comes with a built-in way to manage translation of content: the content translation module. This module adds additional multilingual support and translation management options to Drupal content types.

Multilingual Support

After going to Administer ➤ Site building ➤ Modules and enabling the locale and content translation modules, "Multilingual support" options will show up in the "Workflow settings" fieldset of each content type. To see the settings, go to Administer ➤ Content management ➤ Content types, and click the "edit" link for the Page content type. Expanding the "Workflow settings" fieldset should reveal the new settings for "Multilingual support," as shown in Figure 18-24. The locale module provides the Disabled and Enabled settings while the content translation module provides the "Enabled, with translation" setting.

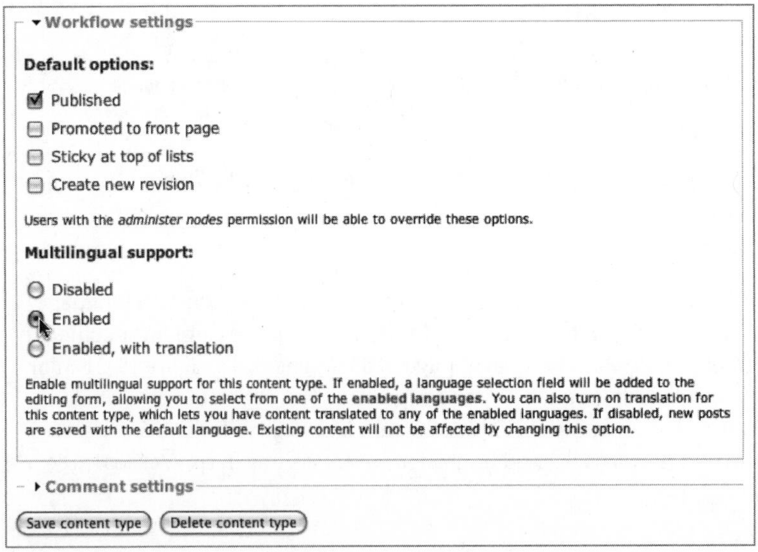

Figure 18-24. *The multilingual settings for a content type*

Now if you go to Create content ➤ Page, you will see a new dropdown field on the content creation form that allows you to select which language the content will be written in or whether the content is "Language neutral." The field is shown in Figure 18-25.

Figure 18-25. *The language selection field on the content creation form*

After creating a few pages in different languages, you can see that the administration page for content at Administer ➤ Content management ➤ Content has changed to display the language of the post. Also, an option to filter content by language has been added, as shown in Figure 18-26.

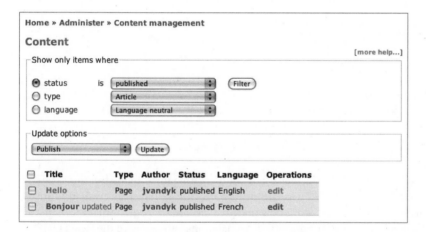

Figure 18-26. *The content administration page with multilingual support enabled*

Multilingual Support with Translation

Having the ability to create content in multiple languages is good. However, most sites do not have one piece of content in English and another unrelated piece of content in French. Instead, the French content is usually a translation of the English content (or vice versa). When "Multilingual support" for a content type is set to "Enabled, with translation" (see Figure 18-24) that becomes possible. It involves the following approach:

1. A post is created in one language. This is the source post.

2. Translations of the post are created.

Let's step through these tasks with an example. First, make sure that the current "Multilingual support" setting for the Page content type is set to "Enabled, with translation." Next, we'll create a simple page in English. Go to Create content ➤ Page, and type **Hello** for the title and **Have a nice day.** for the body. Set the language selection to English, and click the Save button. You should now see a Translate tab in addition to the usual View and Edit tabs (see Figure 18-27).

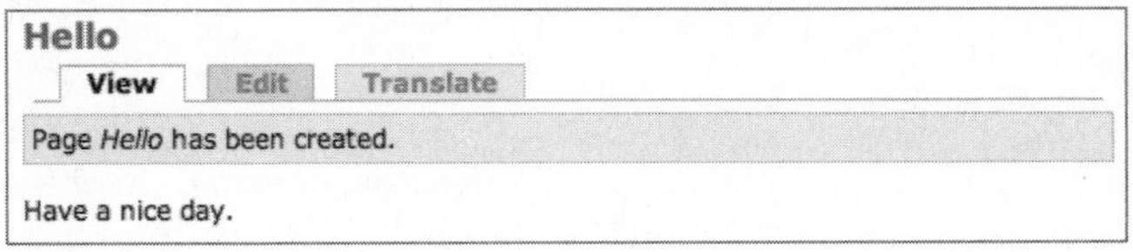

Hello

| View | Edit | Translate |

Page *Hello* has been created.

Have a nice day.

Figure 18-27. *The node now has a tab for translation.*

Clicking the Translate tab reveals a summary of the post's translation status. As shown in Figure 18-28, a source post exists in English, but that's all. Let's create a French translation by clicking the "add translation" link.

Translations of *Hello*

| View | Edit | **Translate** |

Translations of a piece of content are managed with translation sets. Each translation set has one source post and any number of translations in any of the **enabled languages**. All translations are tracked to be up to date or outdated based on whether the source post was modified significantly.

Language	Title	Status	Operations
English (source)	Hello	Published	edit
French	n/a	Not translated	add translation
Hebrew	n/a	Not translated	add translation

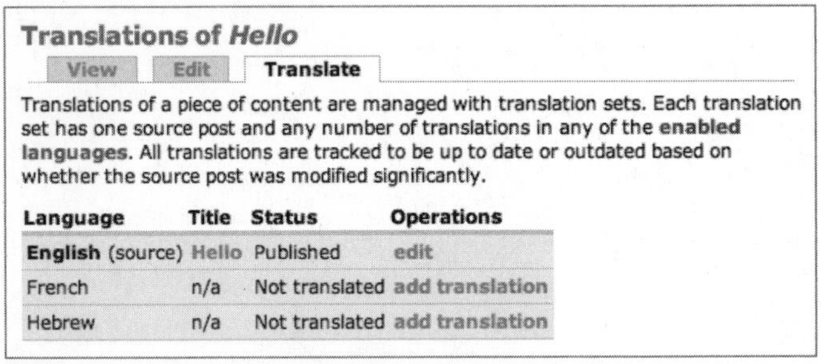

Figure 18-28. *Clicking the translate tab shows a summary of the translation status.*

Clicking the "add translation" link brings up the node editing form again, but this time, the language selection is set to French. Type **Bonjour** for the title and **Ayez un beau jour.** for the body. When the Save button is clicked, a new node will be added. Drupal will automatically create links between the source node and the translations, labeled with the language. Figure 18-29 shows how the French translation of the source node looks when the source node is in English and an additional translation exists in Hebrew.

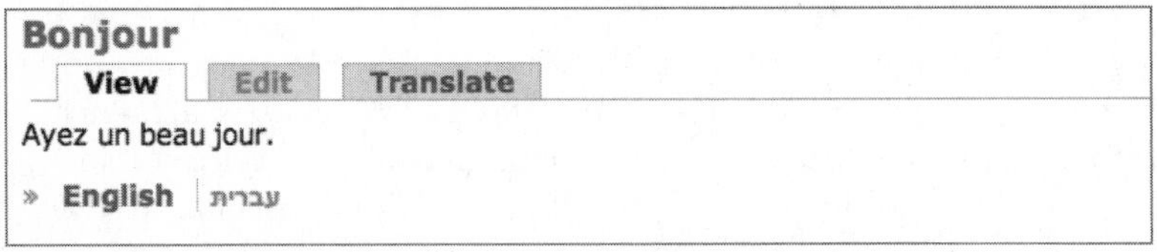

Bonjour

| View | Edit | Translate |

Ayez un beau jour.

» **English** | עברית

Figure 18-29. *The French translation of the source node has links to English and Hebrew versions.*

The links are built by the implementation of `hook_link()` in `modules/translation/translation.module`:

```
/**
 * Implementation of hook_link().
 *
 * Display translation links with native language names, if this node
 * is part of a translation set.
 */
function translation_link($type, $node = NULL, $teaser = FALSE) {
  $links = array();
  if ($type == 'node' && ($node->tnid) &&
    $translations = translation_node_get_translations($node->tnid)) {
    // Do not show link to the same node.
    unset($translations[$node->language]);
    $languages = language_list();
    foreach ($translations as $language => $translation) {
      $links["node_translation_$language"] = array(
        'title'      => $languages[$language]->native,
        'href'       => "node/$translation->nid",
        'language'   => $languages[$language],
        'attributes' => array(
          'title' => $translation->title,
          'class' => 'translation-link'
        )
      );
    }
  }
  return $links;
}
```

In addition to the links that are generated, the locale module provides a language switcher block that can be enabled under Administer ➤ Site building ➤ Blocks. The language switcher block will only show up if multiple languages are enabled and the "Language negotiation" setting is set to something other than None. The language switcher block is shown in Figure 18-30.

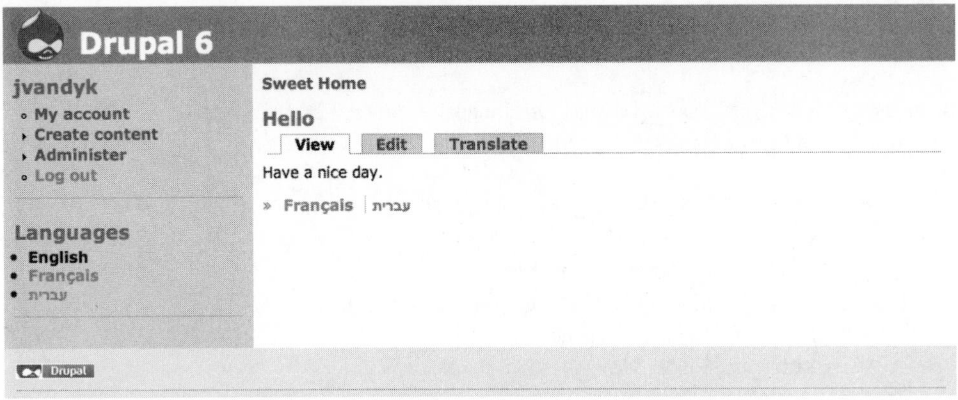

Figure 18-30. *The language switcher block*

Let's get back to our discussion of source nodes and their translations. If a node is a source node, editing it will show an additional fieldset called "Translation settings" in the node editing form. This fieldset contains a single check box labeled "Flag translations as outdated," as shown in Figure 18-31.

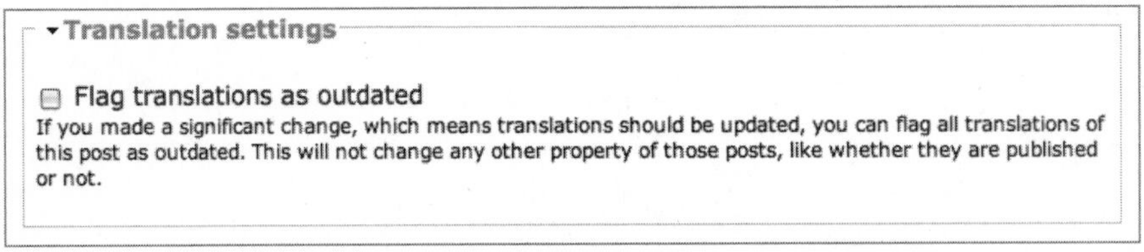

Figure 18-31. *The "Translation settings" fieldset in the node editing form of a source node*

The check box is used to indicate that edits to the source node have been major enough to require retranslation. Checking the box to flag translations as outdated simply causes the word "outdated" to be displayed when viewing the translation status of a node. Compare Figure 18-28 with Figure 18-32.

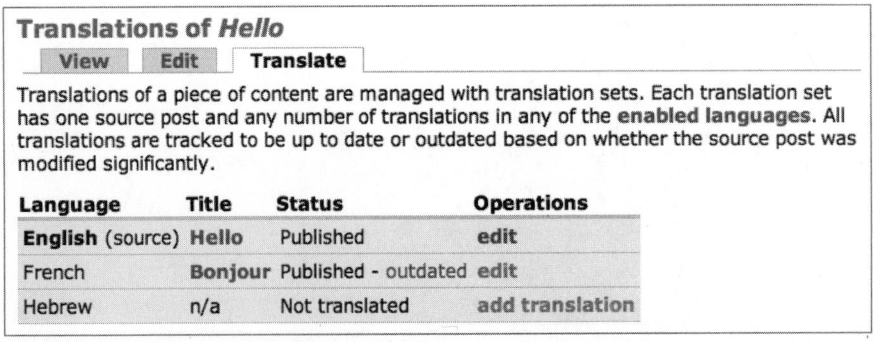

Figure 18-32. *The source post has been edited, and the translated post is flagged as outdated.*

A source node and translations of the source node have separate node numbers and, in fact, exist as completely separate nodes in the database. They are related to each other by the tnid column of the node table, which has as its value the node ID of the source node. Assuming that the English version is the source node and is the first node on the site and the French and Hebrew translations are the next two nodes added, the node table will look like Figure 18-33.

nid	vid	type	language	title	uid	status	created	changed	comment	promote	moderate	sticky	tnid	translate
1	1	page	en	Hello	1	1	1210468998	1210470183	0	0	0	0	1	0
2	2	page	fr	Bonjour	1	1	1210469820	1210469820	0	0	0	0	1	1
3	3	page	he	שלום	1	1	1210470544	1210471153	0	0	0	0	1	0

Figure 18-33. *The tnid column tracks relationships between source nodes and their translations.*

Notice that the 1 in the translate column indicates an outdated translation.

Localization- and Translation-Related Files

Sometimes, knowing which parts of Drupal are responsible for which localization or translation functions is difficult. Table 18-1 shows these files and their responsibilities.

Table 18-1. *Files Related to Localization and Translation Within Drupal*

File	Responsibility
includes/bootstrap.inc	Runs the DRUPAL_BOOTSTRAP_LANGUAGE phase that determines the current language.
includes/language.inc	Included by bootstrap if multiple languages are enabled. Provides code for choosing a language and rewriting internal URLs to be language-specific.
includes/common.inc	t() is found here, as is drupal_add_css(), which supports right-to-left languages.
includes/locale.inc	Contains user interfaces and functions for managing language translations.
modules/locale/locale.module	Provides string replacement and translation imports when modules or themes are installed or enabled. Adds language settings interface to path, node, and node type forms.
modules/translation/translation.module	Manages source nodes and translations thereof.
modules/translation/translation.admin.inc	Provides the translation overview shown when the Translate tab is clicked (see Figure 18-31).

Additional Resources

Internationalization support is very important to the Drupal project. To follow the progress of this effort or to get involved, see http://groups.drupal.org/i18n.

Summary

In this chapter, you've learned the following:

- How the t() function works

- How to customize built-in Drupal strings

- How to export your customizations

- What portable object and portable object template files are

- How to download portable object template files and generate your own

- How to import an existing Drupal translation

- How to use style sheets for right-to-left language support

- How language negotiation settings affect Drupal

- How content translation works

## CHAPTER 19

XML-RPC

Drupal "plays well with others." That is, if there's an open standard out there, chances are that Drupal supports it either natively or through a contributed module. XML-RPC is no exception; Drupal supports it natively. In this chapter, you'll learn how to take advantage of Drupal's ability both to send and receive XML-RPC calls.

What Is XML-RPC?

A *remote procedure call* is when one program asks another program to execute a function. XML-RPC is a standard for remote procedure calls where the call is encoded with XML and sent over HTTP. The XML-RPC protocol was created by Dave Winer of UserLand Software in collaboration with Microsoft. It's specifically targeted at distributed web-based systems talking to each other, as when one Drupal site asks another Drupal site for some information.

There are two players when XML-RPC happens. One is the site from which the request originates, known as the *client*. The site that receives the request is the *server*.

Prerequisites for XML-RPC

If your site will be acting only as a server, there's nothing to worry about because incoming XML-RPC requests use the standard web port (usually port 80). The file `xmlrpc.php` in your Drupal installation contains the code that's run for an incoming XML-RPC request. It's known as the XML-RPC endpoint.

Note Some people add security through obscurity by renaming the `xmlrpc.php` file to change their XML- RPC endpoint. This prevents evil wandering robots from probing the server's XML-RPC interfaces. Others delete it altogether if the site isn't accepting XML-RPC requests.

For your Drupal site to act as a client, it must have the ability to send outgoing HTTP requests. Some hosting companies don't allow this for security reasons, and your attempts won't get past their firewall.

XML-RPC Clients

The client is the computer that will be sending the request. It sends a standard HTTP POST request to the server. The body of this request is composed of XML and contains a single tag named <methodCall>. Two tags, <methodName> and <params>, are nested inside the <methodCall> tag. Let's see how this works using a practical example.

■ Note The remote procedure being called is referred to as a *method*. That's why the XML encoding of an XML-RPC call wraps the name of the remote procedure in a <methodName> tag.

XML-RPC Client Example: Getting the Time

The site that hosts the XML-RPC specification (http://www.xmlrpc.com/) also hosts some test implementations. In our first example, let's ask the site for the current time via XML-RPC:

```
$time = xmlrpc('http://time.xmlrpc.com/RPC2', 'currentTime.getCurrentTime');
```

You're calling Drupal's xmlrpc() function, telling it to contact the server time.xmlrpc.com with the path RPC2, and to ask that server to execute a method called currentTime.getCurrentTime(). You're not sending any parameters along with the call. Drupal turns this into an HTTP request that looks like this:

```
POST /RPC2 HTTP/1.0
Host: time.xmlrpc.com
User-Agent: Drupal (+http://drupal.org/)
Content-Length: 118
Content-Type: text/xml

<?xml version="1.0"?>
<methodCall>
  <methodName>currentTime.getCurrentTime</methodName>
  <params></params>
</methodCall>
```

The server time.xmlrpc.com happily executes the function and returns the following response to you:

```
HTTP/1.1 200 OK
Connection: close
Content-Length: 183
Content-Type: text/xml
Date: Wed, 23 Apr 2008 16:14:30 GMT
Server: UserLand Frontier/9.0.1-WinNT
```

```
<?xml version="1.0"?>
<methodResponse>
  <params>
    <param>
      <value>
        <dateTime.iso8601>20080423T09:14:30</dateTime.iso8601>
      </value>
    </param>
  </params>
</methodResponse>
```

When the response comes back, Drupal parses it and recognizes it as a single value in ISO 8601 international date format. Drupal then helpfully returns not only the ISO 8601 representation of the time but also the year, month, day, hour, minute, and second components of the time. The object with these properties is assigned to the $time variable, as shown in Figure 19-1.

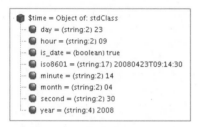

Figure 19-1. *Result of XML-RPC call to get the current time*

The important lessons here are as follows:

- You called a remote server and it answered you.

- The request and response were represented in XML.

- You used the xmlrpc() function and included a URL and the name of the remote procedure to call.

- The value returned to you was tagged as a certain data type.

- Drupal recognized the data type and parsed the response automatically.

- You did this all with one line of code.

XML-RPC Client Example: Getting the Name of a State

Let's try a slightly more complicated example. It's only more complicated because you're sending a parameter along with the name of the remote method you're calling. UserLand Software runs a web service at betty.userland.com that has the 50 United States listed in alphabetical order. So if you ask for state 1, it returns Alabama; state 50 is Wyoming. The name of the method is examples.getStateName. Let's ask it for state number 3 in the list:

```
$state_name = xmlrpc('http://betty.userland.com/RPC2', 'examples.getStateName', 3);
```

This sets $state_name to Arizona. Here's the XML Drupal sends (we'll ignore the HTTP headers for clarity from now on):

```
<?xml version="1.0"?>
<methodCall>
  <methodName>examples.getStateName</methodName>
    <params>
      <param>
        <value>
          <int>3</int>
        </value>
      </param>
    </params>
</methodCall>
```

Here's the response you get from betty.userland.com:

```
<?xml version="1.0"?>
<methodResponse>
  <params>
    <param>
      <value>Arizona</value>
    </param>
  </params>
</methodResponse>
```

Notice that Drupal automatically saw that the parameter you sent was an integer and encoded it as such in your request. But what's happening in the response? The value doesn't have any type tags around it! Shouldn't that be <value><string>Arizona</string></value>? Well, yes, that would work as well; but in XML-RPC a value without a type is assumed to be a string, so this is less verbose.

That's how simple it is to make an XML-RPC client call in Drupal. One line:

```
$result = xmlrpc($url, $method, $param_1, $param_2, $param_3...)
```

Handling XML-RPC Client Errors

When dealing with remote servers, much can go wrong. For example, you could get the syntax wrong; the server could be offline; or the network could be down. Let's take a look at what Drupal does in each of these situations.

Network Errors

Drupal uses the `drupal_http_request()` function in `includes/common.inc` to issue outgoing HTTP requests, including XML-RPC requests. Inside that function, the PHP function `fsockopen` is used to open a socket to the remote server. If the socket cannot be opened, Drupal will either set a negative error code or a code of 0, depending on which platform PHP is running on and at what point in opening the socket that the error occurs. Let's misspell the name of the server when getting the state name:

```
$state_name = xmlrpc('http://betty.userland.comm/RPC2', 'examples.getStateName', 3);
if ($error = xmlrpc_error()) {
  if ($error->code <= 0) {
    $error->message = t('Outgoing HTTP request failed because the socket could
      not be opened.');
  }
  drupal_set_message(t('Could not get state name because the remote site gave
    an error: %message (@code).', array(
      '%message' => $error->message,
      '@code' => $error->code
    )
  )
);
```

This will result in the following message being displayed:

Could not get state name because the remote site gave an error: *Outgoing HTTP request failed because the socket could not be opened.* (-19891355).

HTTP Errors

The preceding code will work for HTTP errors, such as when a server is up but no web service is running at that path. Here, we ask drupal.org to run the web service, and drupal.org points out that there is nothing at `http://drupal.org/RPC2`:

```
$state = xmlrpc('http://drupal.org/RPC2', 'examples.getStateName');
if ($error = xmlrpc_error()) {
  if ($error->code <= 0) {
    $error->message = t('Outgoing HTTP request failed because the socket could
      not be opened.');
  }
  drupal_set_message(t('Could not get state name because the remote site gave
    an error: %message (@code).', array(
      '%message' => $error->message,
      '@code' => $error->code
    )
  )
);
```

This will result in the following message being displayed:

Could not get state name because the remote site gave an error: *Not Found* (404).

Call Syntax Errors

Here's what is returned if you can successfully reach the server but try to get a state name from betty.userland.com without giving the state number, which is a required parameter:

```
$state_name = xmlrpc('http://betty.userland.com/RPC2', 'examples.getStateName');
```

The remote server returns the following:

```xml
<?xml version="1.0"?>
<methodResponse>
  <fault>
    <value>
      <struct>
        <member>
          <name>faultCode</name>
          <value>
            <int>4</int>
          </value>
        </member>
        <member>
          <name>faultString</name>
          <value>
            <string>Can't call "getStateName" because there aren't enough
              parameters.</string>
          </value>
        </member>
      </struct>
    </value>
  </fault>
</methodResponse>
```

The server was up and our communication with it is fine; the preceding code is returned with an HTTP response code of 200 OK. The error is identified by a fault code and a string describing the error in the XML response. Your error-handling code would be the same:

```
$state_name = xmlrpc('http://betty.userland.com/RPC2', 'examples.getStateName');
if ($error = xmlrpc_error()) {
  if ($error->code <= 0) {
    $error->message = t('Outgoing HTTP request failed because the socket could
      not be opened.');
  }
```

```
drupal_set_message(t('Could not get state name because the remote site gave
  an error: %message (@code).', array(
    '%message' => $error->message,
    '@code' => $error->code
  )
 )
);
```

This code results in the following message being displayed to the user:

Could not get state name because the remote site gave an error: *Can't call*
"getStateName" because there aren't enough parameters. (4)

Note that when you report errors, you should tell three things: what you were trying to do, why you can't do it, and additional information to which you have access. Often a friendlier error is displayed using `drupal_set_message()` to notify the user, and a more detailed error is written to the watchdog and is viewable at Administer ➤ Reports ➤ Recent log entries.

Casting Parameter Types

Often the remote procedure that you're calling requires that parameters be in certain XML-RPC types, such as integers or arrays. One way to ensure this is to send your parameters using PHP typecasting:

```
$state_name = xmlrpc('http://betty.userland.com/RPC2', 'examples.getStateName',
  (int)$state_num);
```

A better way to do it is to ensure that elsewhere in your code when the variable is assigned that the variable is already set to the correct type.

A Simple XML-RPC Server

As you've seen in the XML-RPC client examples, Drupal does most of the heavy lifting for you. Let's go through a simple server example. You need to do three things to set up your server:

1. Define the function you want to execute when a client request arrives.

2. Map that function to a public method name.

3. Optionally define a method signature.

As usual with Drupal, you want to keep your code separate from the core system and just plug it in as a module. So here's a brief module that says "hello" via XML-RPC. Create the `sites/all/modules/custom/remotehello/remotehello.info` file:

```
; $Id$
name = Remote Hello
description = Greets XML-RPC clients by name.
package = Pro Drupal Development
core = 6.x
```

Here's remotehello.module:

```php
<?php
// $Id$

/**
 * Implementation of hook_xmlrpc().
 * Map external names of XML-RPC methods to PHP callback functions.
 */
function remotehello_xmlrpc() {
  $methods['remoteHello.hello'] = 'xmls_remotehello_hello';
  return $methods;
}

/**
 * Greet a user.
 */
function xmls_remotehello_hello($name) {
  if (!$name) {
    return xmlrpc_error(1, t('I cannot greet you by name if you do not
      provide one.'));
  }
  return t('Hello, @name!', array('@name' => $name));
}
```

Mapping Your Method with hook_xmlrpc()

The xmlrpc hook describes external XML-RPC methods provided by the module. In our example we're only providing one method. In this case the method name is remoteHello.hello. This is the name that requestors will use, and it's completely arbitrary. A good practice is to build the name as a dot-delimited string using your module name as the first part and a descriptive verb as the latter part.

■**Note** Although camelCase is generally shunned in Drupal, external XML-RPC method names are the exception.

The second part of the array is the name of the function that will be called when a request for remoteHello.hello comes in. In our example, we'll call the PHP function xmls_remotehello_hello(). As you develop modules, you'll be writing many functions.

By including "xmls" (shorthand for XML-RPC Server) in the function name, you'll be able to tell at a glance that this function talks to the outside world. Similarly, you can use "xmlc" for functions that call out to other sites. This is particularly good practice when you're writing a module that essentially calls itself, though on another web site, because otherwise debugging can be very confusing.

When your module determines that an error has been encountered, use xmlrpc_error() to define an error code and a helpful string describing what went wrong to the client. Numeric error codes are arbitrary and application-specific.

Assuming the site with this module lives at example.com, you're now able to send your name from a separate Drupal installation (say, at example2.com) using the following code:

```
$url = 'http://example.com/xmlrpc.php';
$method_name = 'remoteHello.hello';
$name = t('Joe');
$result = xmlrpc($url, $method_name, $name);
```

```
$result is now "Hello, Joe."
```

Automatic Parameter Type Validation with hook_xmlrpc()

The xmlrpc hook has two forms. In the simpler form, shown in our remotehello.module example, it simply maps an external method name to a PHP function name. In the more advanced form, it describes the method signature of the method; that is, what XML-RPC type it returns and what the type of each parameter is (see http://www.xmlrpc.com/spec for a list of types). Here's the more complex form of the xmlrpc hook for remotehello.module:

```
/**
 * Implementation of hook_xmlrpc().
 * Map external names of XML-RPC methods to callback functions.
 * Verbose syntax, specifying data types of return value and parameters.
 */
function remotehello_xmlrpc() {
  $methods = array();
  $methods[] = array(
    'remoteHello.hello',        // External method name.
    'xmls_remotehello_hello',   // PHP function to run.
    array('string', 'string'),  // The return value's type,
                                // then any parameter types.
    t('Greets XML-RPC clients by name.')  // Description.
  );
  return $methods;
}
```

Figure 19-2 shows the XML-RPC request life cycle of a request from an XML-RPC client to our module. If you implement the xmlrpc hook for your module using the more complex form, you'll get several benefits. First, Drupal will validate incoming types against your method signature automatically and return -32602: Server error. Invalid method

parameters to the client if validation fails. (This also means that your function will be pick-
ier. No more automatic type coercion, like accepting the string '3' if the integer 3 is meant!)
Also, if you use the more complex form of the xmlrpc hook, Drupal's built-in XML-RPC
methods system.methodSignature and system.methodHelp will return information about
your method. Note that the description you provide in your xmlrpc hook implementation
will be returned as the help text in the system.methodHelp method, so take care to write a
useful description.

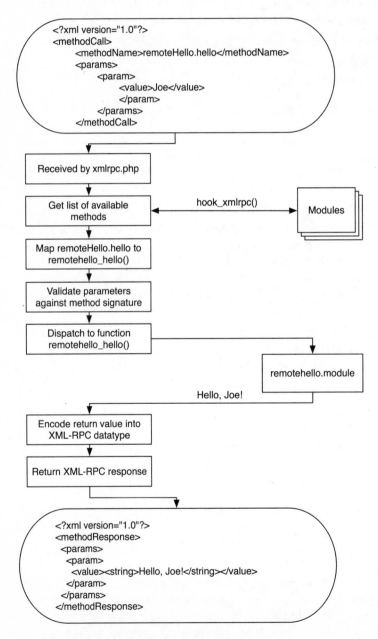

Figure 19-2. *Processing of an incoming XML-RPC request*

Built-In XML-RPC Methods

Drupal comes with several XML-RPC methods enabled out of the box. The following sections describe these built-in methods.

system.listMethods

The system.listMethods method lists which XML-RPC methods are available. This is the response a Drupal site will give when queried for which methods it provides:

```php
// Get an array of all the XML-RPC methods available on this server.
$url = 'http://example.com/xmlrpc.php';
$methods = xmlrpc($url, 'system.listMethods');
```

The response from the server follows:

```xml
<?xml version="1.0"?>
<methodResponse>
  <params>
    <param>
      <value>
        <array>
          <data>
            <value>
              <string>system.multicall</string>
            </value>
            <value>
              <string>system.methodSignature</string>
            </value>
            <value>
              <string>system.getCapabilities</string>
            </value>
            <value>
              <string>system.listMethods</string>
            </value>
            <value>
              <string>system.methodHelp</string>
            </value>
            <value>
              <string>remoteHello.hello</string>
            </value>
          </data>
        </array>
      </value>
    </param>
  </params>
</methodResponse>
```

The content of $methods is now an array of method names available on the server: ('system.multicall', 'system.methodSignature', 'system.getCapabilities', 'system.listMethods', 'system.methodHelp', 'remoteHello.hello').

system.methodSignature

This built-in Drupal XML-RPC method returns an array of data types. Listed first is the data type of the return value of the function; next come any parameters that a given method expects. For example, the remoteHello.hello method returns a string and expects one parameter: a string containing the name of the client. Let's call system.methodSignature to see if Drupal agrees:

```
// Get the method signature for our example method.
$url = 'http://example.com/xmlrpc.php';
$signature = xmlrpc($url, 'system.methodSignature', 'remoteHello.hello');
```

Sure enough, the value of $signature becomes an array: ('string', 'string').

system.methodHelp

This built-in Drupal XML-RPC method returns the description of the method that is defined in the xmlrpc hook implementation of the module providing the method.

```
// Get the help string for our example method.
$url = 'http://example.com/xmlrpc.php';
$help = xmlrpc($url, 'system.methodHelp', 'remoteHello.hello');
```

The value of $help is now a string: Greets XML-RPC clients by name.

system.getCapabilities

This built-in Drupal XML-RPC method describes the capabilities of Drupal's XML-RPC server in terms of which specifications are implemented. Drupal implements the following specifications:

```
xmlrpc:
specURL        http://www.xmlrpc.com/spec
specVersion    1


faults_interop:
specURL        http://xmlrpc-epi.sourceforge.net/specs/rfc.fault_codes.php
specVersion    20010516


system.multicall
specURL        http://www.xmlrpc.com/discuss/msgReader$1208
specVerson     1


introspection
specURL        http://scripts.incutio.com/xmlrpc/introspection.html
specVersion    1
```

system.multiCall

The other built-in method worth mentioning is `system.multiCall`, which allows you to make more than one XML-RPC method call per HTTP request. For more information on this convention (which isn't in the XML-RPC spec) see the following URL (note that it is one continuous string): `http://web.archive.org/web/20060502175739/http://www.xmlrpc.com/discuss/msgReader$1208`.

Summary

After reading this chapter, you should

- Be able to send XML-RPC calls from a Drupal site to a different server

- Be able to implement a basic XML-RPC server

- Understand how Drupal maps XML-RPC methods to PHP functions

- Be able to implement simple and complex versions of the xmlrpc hook

- Know Drupal's built-in XML-RPC methods

CHAPTER 20

■ ■ ■

Writing Secure Code

It seems that almost daily we see headlines about this or that type of software having a security flaw. Keeping unwanted guests out of your web application and server should be a high priority for any serious developer.

There are many ways in which a user with harmful intent can attempt to compromise your Drupal site. Some of these include slipping code into your system and getting it to execute, manipulating data in your database, viewing materials to which the user should not have access, and sending unwanted e-mail through your Drupal installation. In this chapter, you'll learn how to program defensively to ward off these kinds of attacks.

Fortunately, Drupal provides some tools that make it easy to eliminate the most common causes of security breaches.

Handling User Input

When users interact with Drupal, it is typically through a series of forms, such as the node submission form or the comment submission form. Users might also post remotely to a Drupal-based blog via XML-RPC using the blogapi module. Drupal's approach to user input can be summarized as *store the original; filter on output*. The database should always contain an accurate representation of what the user entered. As user input is being prepared to be incorporated into a web page, it is sanitized (i.e., potentially executable code is neutralized).

Security breaches can be caused when text entered by a user is *not* sanitized and is executed inside your program. This can happen when you don't think about the full range of possibilities when you write your program. You might expect users to enter only standard characters, when in fact they could enter nonstandard strings or encoded characters, such as control characters. You might have seen URLs with the string %20 in them; for example, http://example.com/my%20document.html. This is a space character that has been encoded in compliance with the URL specification (see http://www.w3.org/Addressing/URL/url-spec.html). When someone saves a file named my document.html and it's served by a web server, the space is encoded. The % denotes an encoded character, and the 20 shows that this is ASCII character 32 (20 is the hexadecimal representation of 32). Tricky use of encoded characters by nefarious users can be problematic, as you'll see later in this chapter.

Thinking About Data Types

When dealing with text in a system such as Drupal where user input is displayed as part of a web site, it's helpful to think of the user input as a typed variable. If you've programmed in a strongly typed language such as Java, you'll be familiar with typed variables. For example, an integer in Java is really an integer, and will not be treated as a string unless the programmer explicitly makes the conversion. In PHP (a weakly typed language), you're usually fine treating an integer as a string or an integer, depending on the context, due to PHP's automatic type conversion. But good PHP programmers think carefully about types and use automatic type conversion to their advantage. In the same way, even though user input from, say, the Body field of a node submission form can be treated as text, it's much better to think of it as *a certain type of text*. Is the user entering plain text? Or is the user entering HTML tags and expecting that they'll be rendered? If so, could these tags include harmful tags, such as JavaScript that replaces your page with an advertisement for cell phone ringtones? A page that will be displayed to a user is in HTML format; user input is in a variety of "types" of textual formats and must be securely converted to HTML before being displayed. Thinking about user input in this way helps you to understand how Drupal's text conversion functions work. Common types of textual input, along with functions to convert the text to another format, are shown in Table 20-1.

Table 20-1. *Secure Conversions from One Text Type to Another*

Source Format	Target Format	Drupal Function	What It Does
Plain text	HTML	check_plain()	Encodes special characters into HTML entities
HTML text	HTML	filter_xss()	Checks and cleans HTML using a tag whitelist
Rich text	HTML	check_markup()	Runs text through filters
Plain text	URL	drupal_urlencode()	Encodes special characters into %0x
URL	HTML	check_url()	Strips out harmful protocols, such as javascript:
Plain text	MIME	mime_header_encode()	Encodes non-ASCII, UTF-8 encoded characters

Plain Text

Plain text is text that is supposed to contain only, well, plain text. For example, if you ask a user to type in his or her favorite color in a form, you expect the user to answer "green" or "purple," without markup of any kind. Including this input in another web page without checking to make sure that it really does contain only plain text is a gaping security hole. For example, the user might enter the following instead of entering a color:

```
<img src="javascript:window.location ='<a
href="http://evil.example.com/133/index.php?s=11&">
http://evil.example.com/133/index.php?s=11&</a>;ce_cid=38181161'">
```

Thus, we have the function check_plain() available to enforce that all other characters are neutralized by encoding them as HTML entities. The text that is returned from check_plain() will have no HTML tags of any kind, as they've all been converted to entities. If a user enters the evil JavaScript in the preceding code, the check_plain() function will turn it into the following text, which will be harmless when rendered in HTML:

```
&lt;img src=&quot;javascript:window.location =&#039;&lt;a
href=&quot;http://evil.example.com/133/index.php?s=11&amp;&quot;&gt;http://evil.
example.com/133/index.php?s=11&amp;&lt;/a&gt;;;ce_cid=38181161&#039;&quot;&gt;
```

HTML Text

HTML text can contain HTML markup. However, you can never blindly trust that the user has entered only "safe" HTML; generally you want to restrict users to using a subset of the available HTML tags. For example, the <script> tag is not one that you generally want to allow because it permits users to run scripts of their choice on your site. Likewise, you don't want users using the <form> tag to set up forms on your site.

Rich Text

Rich text is text that contains more information than plain text but is not necessarily in HTML. It may contain wiki markup, or Bulletin Board Code (BBCode), or some other markup language. Such text must be run through a filter to convert the markup to HTML before display.

■**Note** For more information on filters, see Chapter 11.

URL

URL is a URL that has been built from user input or from another untrusted source. You might have expected the user to enter `http://example.com`, but the user entered `javascript:runevilJS()` instead. Before displaying the URL in an HTML page, you must run it through `check_url()` to make sure it is well formed and does not contain attacks.

Using check_plain() and t() to Sanitize Output

Use `check_plain()` any time you have text that you don't trust and in which you do not want any markup.

Here is a naïve way of using user input, assuming the user has just entered a favorite color in a text field:

The following code is insecure:

```
drupal_set_message("Your favorite color is $color!"); // No input checking!
```

The following is secure but bad coding practice:

```
drupal_set_message('Your favorite color is ' . check_plain($color));
```

This is bad code because we have a text string (namely the implicit result of the `check_plain()` function), but it isn't inside the `t()` function, which should always be used for text strings. If you write code like the preceding, be prepared for complaints from angry translators, who will be unable to translate your phrase because it doesn't pass through `t()`.

You cannot just place variables inside double quotes and give them to `t()`.

The following code is still insecure because no placeholder is being used:

```
drupal_set_message(t("Your favorite color is $color!")); // No input checking!
```

The t() function provides a built-in way of making your strings secure by using a place-holding token with a one-character prefix, as follows.

The following is secure and in good form:

```
drupal_set_message(t('Your favorite color is @color', array('@color' => $color));
```

Note that the key in the array (@color) is the same as the replacement token in the string. This results in a message like the following:

```
Your favorite color is brown.
```

The @ prefix tells t() to run the value that is replacing the token through check_plain().

■**Note** When running a translation of Drupal, the token is run through check_plain(), but the translated string is not. So you need to trust your translators.

In this case, we probably want to emphasize the user's choice of color by changing the style of the color value. This is done using the % prefix, which means "execute theme ('placeholder', $value) on the value." This passes the value through check_plain() indirectly, as shown in Figure 20-1. The % prefix is the most commonly used prefix.

The following is secure and good form:

```
drupal_set_message(t('Your favorite color is %color', array('%color' => $color));
```

This results in a message like the following. In addition to escaping the value, theme_ placeholder() has wrapped the value in <em></em> tags.

```
Your favorite color is brown.
```

If you have text that has been previously sanitized, you can disable checks in t() by using the ! prefix. For example, the l() function builds a link, and for convenience, it runs the text of the link through check_plain() while building the link. So in the following example, the ! prefix can be safely used:

```
// The l() function runs text through check_plain() and returns sanitized text
// so no need for us to do check_plain($link) or to have t() do it for us.
$link = l($user_supplied_text, $path);
drupal_set_message(t('Go to the website !website', array('!website' => $link));
```

■**Note** The l() function passes the text of the link through check_plain() unless you have indicated to l() that the text is already in HTML format by setting html to TRUE in the options parameter. See http://api.drupal.org/api/function/l/6.

The effect of the @, %, and ! placeholders on string replacement in t() is shown in Figure 20-1. Although for simplicity's sake it isn't shown in the figure, remember that you may use multiple placeholders by defining them in the string and adding members to the array, for example:

```
drupal_set_message(t('Your favorite color is %color and you like %food',
  array('%color' => $color, '%food' => $food)));
```

Be especially cautious with the use of the ! prefix, since that means the string will not be run through check_plain().

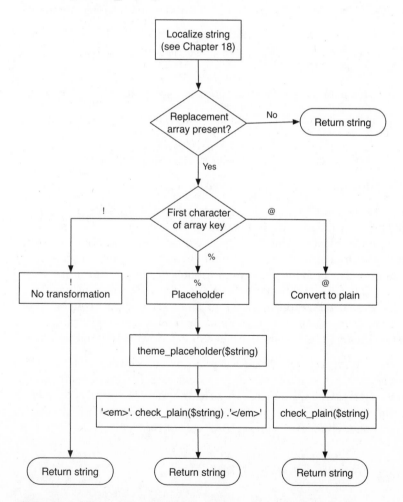

Figure 20-1. *Effect of the placeholder prefixes on string replacement*

Using filter_xss() to Prevent Cross-Site Scripting Attacks

Cross-site scripting (XSS) is a common form of attack on a web site where the attacker is able to insert his or her own code into a web page, which can then be used for all sorts of mischief.

Note For examples of XSS attacks, see `http://ha.ckers.org/xss.html`.

Suppose that you allow users to enter HTML on your web site, expecting them to enter

```
<em>Hi!</em> My name is Sally, and I...
```

but instead they enter

```
<script src=http://evil.example.com/xss.js"></script>
```

Whoops! Again, the lesson is to never trust user input. Here is the function signature of `filter_xss()`:

```
filter_xss($string, $allowed_tags = array('a', 'em', 'strong', 'cite', 'code',
  'ul', 'ol', 'li', 'dl', 'dt', 'dd'))
```

The `filter_xss()` function performs the following operations on the text string it is given:

1. It checks to make sure that the text being filtered is valid UTF-8 to avoid a bug with Internet Explorer 6.

2. It removes odd characters such as `NULL` and Netscape 4 JavaScript entities.

3. It ensures that HTML entities such as `&amp;` are well formed.

4. It ensures that HTML tags and tag attributes are well formed. During this process, tags that are not on the whitelist—that is, the second parameter for `filter_xss()`— are removed. The `style` attribute is removed, too, because that can interfere with the layout of a page by overriding CSS or hiding content by setting a spammer's link color to the background color of the page. Any attributes that begin with `on` are removed (e.g., `onclick` or `onfocus`) because they represent JavaScript event-handler definitions. If you write regular expressions for fun and can name character codes for HTML entities from memory, you'll enjoy stepping through `filter_xss()` (found in `modules/filter/filter.module`) and its associated functions with a debugger.

5. It ensures that no HTML tags contain disallowed protocols. Allowed protocols are `http`, `https`, `ftp`, `news`, `nntp`, `telnet`, `mailto`, `irc`, `ssh`, `sftp`, and `webcal`. You can modify this list by setting the `filter_allowed_protocols` variable. For example, you could restrict the protocols to `http` and `https` by adding the following line to your `settings.php` file (see the comment about variable overrides in the `settings.php` file):

```
$conf = array(
  'filter_allowed_protocols' => array('http', 'https')
);
```

Here's an example of the use of `filter_xss()` from `modules/aggregator/aggregator.pages.inc`. The aggregator module deals with potentially dangerous RSS or Atom feeds. Here the module is preparing variables for use in the template file that will display a feed item:

```
/**
 * Process variables for aggregator-item.tpl.php.
 *
 * @see aggregator-item.tpl.php
 */
function template_preprocess_aggregator_item(&$variables) {
  $item = $variables['item'];

  $variables['feed_url'] = check_url($item->link);
  $variables['feed_title'] = check_plain($item->title);
  $variables['content'] = aggregator_filter_xss($item->description);
    ...
}
```

Note the call to `aggregator_filter_xss()`, which is a wrapper for `filter_xss()` and provides an array of acceptable HTML tags. I have slightly simplified the function in the following code:

```
/**
 * Safely render HTML content, as allowed.
 */
function aggregator_filter_xss($value) {
  $tags = variable_get("aggregator_allowed_html_tags",
      '<a> <b> <br> <dd> <dl> <dt> <em> <i> <li> <ol> <p> <strong> <u> <ul>');
  // Turn tag list into an array so we can pass it as a parameter.
  $allowed_tags = preg_split('/\s+|<|>/', $tags, -1, PREG_SPLIT_NO_EMPTY));
  return filter_xss($value, $allowed_tags);
}
```

■**Note** As a security exercise, you might want to take any custom modules you have and trace user input as it comes into the system, is stored, and goes out to ensure that the text is being sanitized somewhere along the way.

Using filter_xss_admin()

Sometimes you want your module to produce HTML for administrative pages. Because administrative pages should be protected by access controls, it's assumed that users given access to administrative screens can be trusted more than regular users. You could set up a special filter for administrative pages and use the filter system, but that would be cumbersome. For these reasons, the function `filter_xss_admin()` is provided. It is simply a wrapper for `filter_xss()` with a liberal list of allowed tags, including everything except the `<script>`, `<object>`, and `<style>` tags. An example of its use is in the display of the site mission in a theme:

```
if (drupal_is_front_page()) {
  $mission = filter_xss_admin(theme_get_setting('mission'));
}
```

The site's mission can only be set from the Administer ➤ Site configuration ➤ "Site information" page, to which only the superuser and users with the "administer site configuration" permission have access, so this is a situation in which the use of `filter_xss_admin()` is appropriate.

Handling URLs Securely

Often modules take user-submitted URLs and display them. Some mechanism is needed to make sure that the value the user has given is indeed a legitimate URL. Drupal provides the `check_url()` function, which is really just a wrapper for `filter_xss_bad_protocol()`. It checks to make sure that the protocol in the URL is among the allowed protocols on the Drupal site (see step 5 in the earlier section "Using filter_xss() to Prevent Cross-Site Scripting Attacks") and runs the URL through `check_plain()`.

If you want to determine whether a URL is in valid form, you can call `valid_url()`. It will check the syntax for `http`, `https`, and `ftp` URLs and check for illegal characters; it returns `TRUE` if the URL passes the test. This is a quick way to make sure that users aren't submitting URLs with the `javascript` protocol.

■**Caution** Just because a URL passes a syntax check does *not* mean the URL is safe!

If you're passing on some information via a URL—for example, in a query string—you can use `drupal_urlencode()` to pass along escaped characters. Calling `drupal_urlencode()` does some encoding of slashes, hashes, and ampersands for compatibility with Drupal's clean URLs and then calls PHP's `rawurlencode()` function. The `drupal_urlencode()` function is not more secure than calling `rawurlencode()` directly, but it is handy for making encoded strings that will work well with Apache's `mod_rewrite` module.

■**Tip** The `drupal_urlencode()` function is an example of a wrapped PHP function—you could call PHP's `rawurlencode()` directly, but then you wouldn't get the benefit of Drupal taking care of the function's eccentricities for you. See `includes/unicode.inc` for similar wrapped string functions; for example, `drupal_strlen()` instead of the PHP function `strlen()`.

Making Queries Secure with db_query()

A common way of exploiting web sites is called *SQL injection*. Let's examine a module written by someone not thinking about security. This person just wants a simple way to list titles of all nodes of a certain type:

```
/*
 * Implementation of hook_menu().
 */
function insecure_menu() {
  $items['insecure'] = array(
    'title' => 'Insecure Module',
    'description' => 'Example of how not to do things.',
    'page callback' => 'insecure_code',
    'access arguments' => array('access content'),
  );
  return $items;
}


/*
 * Menu callback, called when user goes to http://example.com/?q=insecure
 */
function insecure_code($type = 'story') {
  // SQL statement where variable is embedded directly into the statement.
  $sql = "SELECT title FROM {node} WHERE type = '$type'"; // Never do this!
  $result = db_query($sql);
  $titles = array();
  while ($data = db_fetch_object($result)) {
    $titles[] = $data->title;
  }
  // For debugging, output the SQL statement to the screen.
  $output = $sql;

  $output .= theme('item_list', $titles);
  return $output;
}
```

Going to http://example.com/?q=insecure works as expected. We get the SQL and then a list of stories, as shown in Figure 20-2.

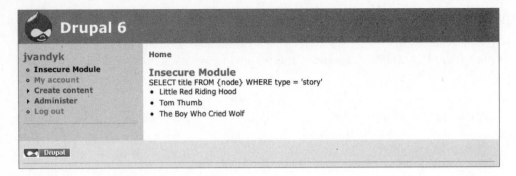

Figure 20-2. *Simple listing of story node titles*

Note how the programmer cleverly gave the insecure_code() function a $type parameter that defaults to 'story'. This programmer is taking advantage of the fact that Drupal's menu system forwards additional path arguments automatically as parameters to callbacks, so http://example.com/?q=insecure/page will get us all titles of nodes of type 'page', as shown in Figure 20-3.

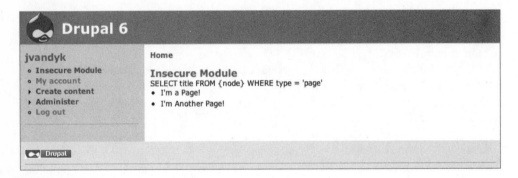

Figure 20-3. *Simple listing of page node titles*

However, the programmer has made a potentially fatal error. By coding the variable $type directly into the SQL and relying on PHP's variable expansion, the web site is entirely compromisable. Let's go to http://example.com/?q=insecure/page'%20OR%20type%20=%20'story (see Figure 20-4).

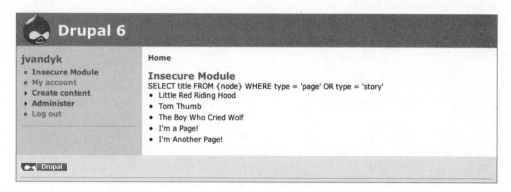

Figure 20-4. *SQL injection caused by not using placeholders in db_query()*

Whoops! We were able to enter SQL into the URL and have it executed! How did this happen? Recall that earlier I mentioned that %20 was the encoded version of a space? We simply entered the encoded version of the following text:

```
page' OR type = 'story
```

Remember our insecure assignment of SQL to the $sql variable? Look what happens when the encoded text we entered gets unencoded and becomes part of the statement.

Here's the code before:

```
SELECT title FROM {node} WHERE type = '$type'
```

Substituting in $type, which is now set to page' OR type = 'story, we now have

```
SELECT title from {node} WHERE type = 'page' OR type = 'story'
```

Once a user is able to change the SQL you're sending to your database, your site is easy to compromise (see http://xkcd.com/327/). Here's an improvement:

```
function insecure_code($type = 'story') {
  // SQL now protected by using a quoted placeholder.
  $sql = "SELECT title FROM {node} WHERE type = '%s'";
  $result = db_query($sql, $type);
  $titles = array();
  while ($data = db_fetch_object($result)) {
    $titles[] = $data->title;
  }
  // For debugging, output the SQL statement to the screen.
  $output = $sql;

  $output .= theme('item_list', $titles);
  return $output;
}
```

Now when we try to manipulate the URL by going to http://example.com/?q=insecure/ page'%20OR%20type%20=%20'story, the db_query() function sanitizes the value by escaping the embedded single quotes. The query becomes the following:

```
SELECT title FROM node WHERE type = 'page\' OR type = \'story'
```

This query will clearly fail because we have no node type named "page\' OR type = \'story".

The situation can still be improved, however. In this case, the URL should contain only members of a finite set; that is, the node types on our site. We know what those are, so we should always confirm that the user-supplied value is in our list of known values. For example, if we have only the page and story node types enabled, we should only attempt to proceed if we have been given those types in the URL. Let's add some code to check for that:

```php
function insecure_code($type = 'story') {
  // Check to make sure $type is in our list of known content types.
  $types = node_get_types();
  if (!isset($types[$type])) {
    watchdog('security', 'Possible SQL injection attempt!', array(),
      WATCHDOG_ALERT);
    return t('Unable to process request.');
  }

  // SQL now protected by using a placeholder.
  $sql = "SELECT title FROM {node} WHERE type = '%s'";
  $result = db_query($sql, $type);
  $titles = array();
  while ($data = db_fetch_object($result)) {
    $titles[] = $data->title;
  }
  // For debugging, output the SQL statement to the screen.
  $output = $sql;

  $output .= theme('item_list', $titles);
  return $output;
}
```

Here we've added a check to make sure that $type is one of our existing node types, and if the check fails, a handy warning will be recorded for system administrators. There are more problems, though. The SQL does not distinguish between published and unpublished nodes, so even titles of unpublished nodes will show up. Plus, node titles are user-submitted data, so they need to be sanitized before output. But as the code currently stands, it just gets the titles from the database and displays them. Let's fix these problems.

```
function insecure_code($type = 'story') {
  // Check to make sure $type is in our list of known content types.
  $types = node_get_types();
  if (!isset($types[$type])) {
    watchdog('security', 'Possible SQL injection attempt!', array(),
      WATCHDOG_ALERT);
    return t('Unable to process request.');
  }

  // SQL now protected by using a placeholder.
  $sql = "SELECT title FROM {node} WHERE type = '%s' AND status = 1";
  $result = db_query($sql, $type);
  $titles = array();
  while ($data = db_fetch_object($result)) {
    $titles[] = $data->title;
  }

  // Pass all array members through check_plain().
  $titles = array_map('check_plain', $titles);
  $output = theme('item_list', $titles);
  return $output;
}
```

Now only unpublished nodes will show up, and all the titles are run through check_plain() before being displayed. We've also removed the debugging code. This module has come a long way! But there's still a security flaw. Can you see it? If not, read on.

Keeping Private Data Private with db_rewrite_sql()

The preceding example of listing nodes is a common task for contributed modules (though less so now that the views module makes it so easy to define node listings through the Web). Question: If a node access control module is enabled on the site, where is the code in the preceding example that makes sure our user sees only the subset of nodes that is allowed? You're right . . . it's completely absent. The preceding code will show all nodes of a given type, *even those protected by node access modules*. It's arrogant code that doesn't care what other modules think! Let's change that.

Before:

```
$sql = "SELECT title FROM {node} WHERE type = '%s' AND status = 1";
$result = db_query($sql, $type);
```

After:

```
$sql = "SELECT n.nid, title FROM {node} n WHERE type = '%s' AND status = 1";
$result = db_query(db_rewrite_sql($sql), $type); // Respect node access rules.
```

We've wrapped the $sql parameter for db_query() in a call to db_rewrite_sql(), a function that allows other modules to modify the SQL. Queries that pass through db_rewrite_sql() need to have their primary field (n.nid) and table alias (n) stated in the query, so we've added them to the SQL. A significant example of a module that rewrites queries against the node table is the node module. It checks to see if there are entries in the node_access table that might restrict a user's access to nodes and inserts query fragments to check against these permissions. In our case, the node module will modify the SQL to include an AND in the WHERE clause that will filter out results to which the user does not have access. See Chapter 5 to see how this is done and for more about db_rewrite_sql().

Dynamic Queries

If you have a varying number of values in your SQL that cannot be determined until runtime, it doesn't excuse you from using placeholders. You'll need to create your SQL programmatically using placeholder strings such as '%s' or %d, and then pass along an array of values to fill these placeholders. If you're calling db_escape_string() yourself, you're doing something wrong. Here's an example showing the generation of placeholders, supposing that we want to retrieve a list of published node IDs and titles from nodes matching certain node types:

```
// $node_types is an array containing one or more node type names
// such as page, story, blog, etc.
$node_types = array('page', 'story', 'blog');
// Generate an appropriate number of placeholders of the appropriate type.
$placeholders = db_placeholders($node_types, 'text');
// $placeholders is now a string that looks like '%s', '%s', '%s'
$sql = "SELECT n.nid, n.title from {node} n WHERE n.type IN ($placeholders)
  AND status = 1";
// Let db_query() fill in the placeholders with values.
$result = db_query(db_rewrite_sql($sql), $node_types);
```

After db_rewrite_sql() is evaluated in the preceding code, the db_query() call looks like this:

```
db_query("SELECT DISTINCT(n.nid), n.title from {node} n WHERE n.type IN
  ('%s','%s','%s') AND status = 1", array('page', 'story', 'blog'));
```

Now the node type names will be sanitized when db_query() executes. See db_query_callback() in includes/database.inc if you are curious about how this happens.

Here's another example. Sometimes you're in the situation where you want to restrict a query by adding some number of AND restrictions to the WHERE clause of a query. You need to be careful to use placeholders in that case, too. In the following code, assume any sane value for $uid and $type (e.g., 3 and page).

```
$sql = "SELECT n.nid, n.title FROM {node} n WHERE status = 1";
$where = array();
$where_values = array();
```

```
$where[] = "AND n.uid = %d";
$where_values[] = $uid;

$where[] = "AND n.type = '%s'";
$where_values[] = $type;

$sql = $sql . ' ' . implode(' ', $where) ;
// $sql is now SELECT n.nid, n.title
//               FROM {node} n
//               WHERE status = 1 AND n.uid = %d AND n.type = '%s'

// The values will now be securely inserted into the placeholders.
$result = db_query(db_rewrite_sql($sql), $where_values));
```

Permissions and Page Callbacks

Another aspect to keep in mind when writing your own modules is the access arguments key of each menu item you define in the menu hook. In the earlier example demonstrating insecure code, we used the following access arguments:

```
/*
 * Implementation of hook_menu().
 */
function insecure_menu() {
  $items['insecure'] = array(
    'title' => 'Insecure Module',
    'description' => 'Example of how not to do things.',
    'page callback' => 'insecure_code',
    'access arguments' => array('access content'),
  );
  return $items;
}
```

It's important to question who is allowed to access this callback. The "access content" permission is a very general permission. You probably want to define your own permissions, using hook_perm(), and use those to protect your menu callbacks. Permissions are unique strings describing the permission being granted (see the section "Access Control" in Chapter 4 for more details).

Because your implementation of the menu hook is the gatekeeper that allows or denies a user from reaching the code behind it (through the callback), it's especially important to give some thought to the permissions you use here.

Cross-Site Request Forgeries (CSRF)

Suppose that you have logged into `drupal.org` and are browsing the forums there. Then you get off on a tangent and end up browsing at another web site. Someone evil at that web site has crafted an image tag like this:

```
<img src="http://drupal.org/some/path">
```

When your web browser loads the image, it will request that path from `drupal.org`. Because you are currently logged in to `drupal.org`, your browser will send your cookie along with the request. Here's a question to ponder: when `drupal.org` receives the request, will it consider you a logged-in user with all the access privileges you've been given? You bet it will! The evil person's image tag has essentially made your user click a link on `drupal.org`.

The first defense against this type of attack is to never use `GET` requests to actually change things on the server; that way, any requests generated this way will be harmless. The Drupal form API follows the `HTTP/1.1` convention that the `GET` method should not take any action other than data retrieval. Drupal uses `POST` exclusively for actions that make changes to the server (see `http://www.w3.org/Protocols/rfc2616/rfc2616-sec9.html#sec9.1`).

Second, the form API uses tokens and unique IDs to make sure that submitted form values from `POST` requests are coming from a form that Drupal sent out (for more on this, see Chapter 10). When you are writing modules, be sure to use the form API for your forms and you will gain this protection automatically. Any action that your module takes as a result of form input should happen *in the submit function* for the form. That way, you are assured that the form API has protected you.

Finally, you can also protect `GET` requests if necessary by using a token (generated by `drupal_get_token()`) in the URL and verifying the token with `drupal_valid_token()`.

File Security

The dangers faced by Drupal when handling files and file paths are the same as with other web applications.

File Permissions

File permissions should be set in such a way that the user cannot manipulate (add, rename, or delete) files. The web server should have read-only access to Drupal files and directories. The exception is the file system path. Clearly, the web server must have access to that directory so it can write uploaded files.

Protected Files

The `.htaccess` file that ships with Drupal has the following lines:

```
# Protect files and directories from prying eyes.
<FilesMatch "\.(engine|inc|info|install|module|profile|po
  |sh|.*sql|theme|tpl(\.php)?|xtmpl)$|^(code-style\.pl
  |Entries.*|Repository|Root|Tag|Template)$">
  Order allow,deny
</FilesMatch>
```

The `Order` directive is set to `allow,deny` but no `Allow` or `Deny` directives are included. This means that the implicit behavior is to deny. In other words, reject all requests for the files shown in Table 20-2.

Table 20-2. *Files Rejected by the FilesMatch Directive's Regular Expression in Drupal's .htaccess File*

Files Matched	Description
Ends with `.engine`	Template engines
Ends with `.inc`	Library files
Ends with `.info`	Module and theme `.info` files
Ends with `.install`	Module `.install` files
Ends with `.module`	Module files
Ends with `.profile`	Installation profiles
Ends with `.po`	Portable object files (translations)
Ends with `.sh`	Shell scripts
Ends with `.*sql`	SQL files
Ends with `.theme`	PHP themes
Ends with `.tpl.php`	PHPTemplate template files
Ends with `.tpl.php4`	PHPTemplate template files
Ends with `.tpl.php5`	PHPTemplate template files
Ends with `.xtmpl`	XTemplate files
Named `code-style.pl`	Syntax-checking script
Begins with `Entries.`	CVS file
Named `Repository`	CVS file
Named `Root`	CVS file
Named `Tag`	CVS file
Named `Template`	CVS file

File Uploads

If a module is enabled to allow file uploading, the files should be placed in a specific directory, and access should be enforced by the code.

If file uploads are enabled and the private download method is chosen at Administer ➤ Site configuration ➤ File system, the file system path on that same screen must be *outside* of the web root. In other words, trying to enforce application-specific user permissions on files within the web root is counterproductive.

The big danger with file uploads is that if someone were to be able to upload an executable file, that file could be used to gain access to your server. Drupal protects against that on two fronts. First, the following `.htaccess` file is written to the directory specified by the file system path:

```
SetHandler Drupal_Security_Do_Not_Remove_See_SA_2006_006
Options None
Options +FollowSymLinks
```

The `SetHandler` directive tells Apache that any execution of any files in this directory should be handled by the handler `Drupal_Security_Do_Not_Remove_See_SA_2006_006` (which does not exist). Thus, the handler overrides any handlers defined by Apache, such as

```
AddHandler application/x-httpd-php .php
```

Drupal's upload module also implements file renaming for files with multiple extensions. Thus, `evilfile.php.txt` becomes `evilfile.php_.txt` upon upload. See `http://drupal.org/node/65409` and `http://drupal.org/node/66763` for details.

■**Note** The preceding solution is Apache-specific. If you are running Drupal on a different web server, you should be cognizant of the security issues surrounding the possibility of users uploading executable files.

Filenames and Paths

No filename or file path information from the user can be trusted! When you are writing a module and your code expects to receive `somefile.txt`, realize that it may get something else instead, like

```
../somefile.txt // File in a parent directory.
```

```
../settings.php // Targeted file.
```

```
somefile.txt; cp ../settings.php ../settings.txt // Hoping this runs in shell.
```

The first two examples try to manipulate the file path by including the two dots that indicate a parent directory to the underlying operating system. The last example hopes that the programmer will execute a shell command and has included a semicolon so that after the shell command runs, an additional command will run that will make `settings.php` readable and thus reveal the database username and password. All of the preceding examples are hoping that file permissions are set incorrectly, and that the web server actually has write access to directories other than the file system path.

Whenever you are using file paths, a call to `file_check_location()` is in order, like this:

```
if (!file_check_location($path, 'mydirectory') {
  // Abort! File path is not what was expected!
}
```

The `file_check_location()` function will find out the real location of the file and compare it to the directory you expect it to be in. If the file path is OK, the real path of the file is returned; if not, `0` is returned.

In general, you probably don't want the Next Great File Management Module to be your first Drupal project. Instead, study existing file-related modules that have been around for a while.

Encoding Mail Headers

When writing any code that takes user input and builds it into an e-mail message, consider the following two facts:

1. E-mail headers are separated by line feeds (only line feeds that aren't followed by a space or tab are treated as header separators).

2. Users can inject their own headers in the body of the e-mail if you don't check that their input is free of line feeds.

For example, say you expect the user to enter a subject for his or her message and the user enters a string interspersed by escaped line feed (%0A) and space (%20) characters:

```
Have a nice day%0ABcc:spamtarget@example.com%0A%0ALOw%20cOst%20mortgage!
```

The result would be as follows:

```
Subject: Have a nice day
Bcc: spamtarget@example.com

LOw cOst mortgage!
...
```

For that reason, Drupal's built-in mail function `drupal_mail()` in `includes/mail.inc` runs all headers through `mime_header_encode()` to sanitize headers. Any nonprintable characters will be encoded into ASCII printable characters according to RFC 2047, and thus neutralized. This involves prefixing the character with `=?UTF-8?B?` and then printing the Base64-encoded character plus `?=`.

You're encouraged to use `drupal_mail()`; if you choose not to, you'll have to make the `mime_header_encode()` calls yourself.

Files for Production Environments

Not all files included in the distribution of Drupal are necessary for production sites. For example, making the `CHANGELOG.txt` file available on a production site means that anyone on the Web can see what version of Drupal you are running (of course, the black hats have other ways of detecting that you are running Drupal; see `http://www.lullabot.com/articles/is-site-running-drupal`). Table 20-3 lists the files and/or directories that are necessary for Drupal to function after it has been installed; the others can be removed from a production site (keep a copy, though!). Alternatively, read access can be denied to the web server.

Table 20-3. *Files and Directories That Are Necessary for Drupal to Function*

File/Directory	Purpose
.htaccess	Security, clean URL, and caching support on Apache
cron.php	Allows regularly scheduled tasks to run
includes/	Function libraries
index.php	Main entry point for Drupal requests
misc/	JavaScript and graphics
modules/	Core modules
robots.txt	Prevents well-behaved robots from hammering your site
sites/	Site-specific modules, themes, and files
themes/	Core themes
xmlrpc.php	XML-RPC endpoint; only necessary if your site will receive incoming XML-RPC requests

Protecting cron.php

Drupal has regularly scheduled tasks that must be executed, such as pruning log files, updating statistics, and so forth. This is accomplished by running the file cron.php either from a regularly scheduled cron task on a Unix machine or from the task scheduler on Windows. The file may be run either from the command line or through the web server. The execution of this file simply does a full Drupal bootstrap and then invokes the drupal_cron_run() function in includes/common.inc. This function uses a semaphore to prevent multiple overlapping cron runs; however, the paranoid may want to prevent just anyone from going to http://example.com/cron.php. You can do that by adding the following lines to the .htaccess file in Drupal's root directory:

```
<Files cron.php>
  Order deny,allow
  Deny from all
  Allow from example.com
  Allow from 1.2.3.4
  Allow from 127.0.0.1
</Files>
```

The preceding directives tell Apache to deny access to all clients except those in the example.com domain, the computer with IP address 1.2.3.4, and the local machine.

Some administrators simply rename the cron.php file.

SSL Support

By default, Drupal handles user logins in plain text over HTTP. However, Drupal will happily run over HTTPS if your web server supports it. No modification to Drupal is required.

Stand-Alone PHP

Occasionally, you might need to write a stand-alone .php file instead of incorporating the code into a Drupal module. When you do, be sure to keep security implications in mind. Suppose, when you were testing your web site, you wrote some quick and dirty code to insert users into the database so you could test performance with many users. Perhaps you called it testing.php and put it at the root of your Drupal site, next to index.php. Then you bookmarked it in your browser, and every time you wanted a fresh user table, you selected the bookmark:

```php
<?php
/**
 * This script generates users for testing purposes.
 */
// These lines are all that is needed to have full
// access to Drupal's functionality.
include_once 'includes/bootstrap.inc';
drupal_bootstrap(DRUPAL_BOOTSTRAP_FULL);

db_query('DELETE FROM {users} WHERE uid > 1'); // Whoa!
for ($i = 2; $i <= 5000; $i++) {
  $name = md5($i);
  $pass = md5(user_password());
  $mail = $name .'@localhost';
  $status = 1;
  db_query("INSERT INTO {users} (name, pass, mail, status, created, access)
    VALUES ('%s', '%s', '%s', %d, %d, %d)", $name, $pass, $mail, $status,
    time(), time());
}
print t('Users have been created.');
```

That's useful for testing, but imagine what would happen if you forgot that the script was there and the script made it onto your production site! Anyone who found the URL to your script (http://example.com/testing.php) could delete your users with a single request. That's why it's important, even in quick one-off scripts, to include a security check, as follows:

```php
<?php
/**
 * This script generates users for testing purposes.
 */
// These lines are all that is needed to have full
// access to Drupal's functionality.
include_once 'includes/bootstrap.inc';
drupal_bootstrap(DRUPAL_BOOTSTRAP_FULL);
```

```
// Security check; only superuser may execute this.
if ($user->uid != 1) {
  print t('Not authorized.');
  exit();
}

db_query('DELETE FROM {users} WHERE uid > 1'); // Whoa!
for ($i = 2; $i <= 5000; $i++) {
  $name = md5($i);
  $pass = md5(user_password());
  $mail = $name .'@localhost';
  $status = 1;
  db_query("INSERT INTO {users} (name, pass, mail, status, created, access)
    VALUES ('%s', '%s', '%s', %d, %d, %d)", $name, $pass, $mail, $status, time(),
    time());
}
print t('Users have been created.');
```

Here are two take-home lessons:

1. Write security checking even into quickly written scripts, preferably working from a template that includes the necessary code.

2. Remember that an important part of deployment is to remove or disable testing code.

AJAX Security

The main thing to remember about security in connection with AJAX capabilities such as jQuery is that although you usually develop the server side of the AJAX under the assumption that it will be called from JavaScript, there's nothing to prevent a malicious user from making AJAX calls directly (e.g., from command-line tools like curl or wget, or even just by typing the URL into a web browser). Be sure to test your code from both positions.

Form API Security

One of the benefits of using the form API is that much of the security is handled for you. For example, Drupal checks to make sure that the value the user chose from a drop-down selection field was actually a choice that Drupal presented. The form API uses a set sequence of events, such as form building, validation, and execution. You should not use user input before the validation phase because, well, it hasn't been validated. For example, if you're using a value from $_POST, you have no guarantee that the user hasn't manipulated that value. Also, use the #value element to pass information along in the form instead of using hidden fields whenever possible, as malicious users can manipulate hidden fields but have no access to #value elements.

Any user-submitted data that is used to build a form must be properly sanitized like any other user-submitted data, as in the following example.

Unsafe:

```
$form['foo'] = array(
  '#type' => 'textfield',
  '#title' => $node->title, // XSS vulnerability!
  '#description' => 'Teaser is: '. $node->teaser, // XSS vulnerability!
  '#default_value' => check_plain($node->title), // Unnecessary.
);
```

Safe:

```
$form['foo'] = array(
  '#type' => 'textfield',
  '#title' => check_plain($node->title),
  '#description' => t('Teaser is: @teaser', array('@teaser' => $node->teaser)),
  '#default_value' => $node->title,
};
```

It is not necessary to run the default value through check_plain() because the theme function for the form element type (in this case, theme_textfield() in includes/form.inc) does that.

■**Caution** If you are writing your own theme functions or overriding Drupal's default theme functions, always make a point to ask yourself if any user input is being sanitized, and to duplicate that in your code.

See Chapter 10 for more about the form API.

Protecting the Superuser Account

The easiest way to obtain credentials for a Drupal web site is probably to call a naïve secretary somewhere and say, "Hi, this is Joe. <Insert small talk here.> I'm with the computer support team, and we're having some problems with the web site. What is the username and password you usually log in with?" Sadly, many people will simply give out such information when asked. While technology can help, user education is the best defense against such attacks.

This is why it is a good idea to never assign user 1 (the superuser) to anyone as a matter of course. Instead, each person who will be maintaining a web site should be given only the permissions needed to perform the tasks for which he or she is authorized. That way, if a security breach happens, damage may be contained.

Using eval()

Don't. You might come up with a splendid way to do metaprogramming or eliminate many lines of code by using the PHP eval() function, which takes a string of text as input and evaluates it using the PHP interpreter. This is almost always a mistake. If there's any way for the input to eval() to be manipulated by a user, you risk exposing the power of the PHP interpreter to the user. How long will it be before that power is used to display the username and password for your database?

This is also why you should only use the PHP code filter in Drupal and its associated permissions in the most desperate of circumstances. To sleep soundly at night, shun eval() and the PHP code filter. Drupal does use eval() in the core Drupal installation, but it occurs rarely and is wrapped by drupal_eval(), which prevents the code being evaluated from overwriting variables in the code that called it. drupal_eval() is in includes/common.inc.

Summary

After reading this chapter, you should know

- That you should never, ever trust input from the user

- How you can transform user input to make it safe for display

- How to avoid XSS attacks

- How to avoid SQL injection attacks

- How to write code that respects node access modules

- How to avoid CSRF attacks

- How Drupal protects uploaded files

- How to avoid e-mail header injections

■ ■ ■

## CHAPTER 21

Development Best Practices

In this chapter, you'll find all the little coding tips and best practices that'll make you an upstanding Drupal citizen and help keep your forehead separated from the keyboard. I'll begin by introducing Drupal's coding standards, then show you how to create documentation that will help other developers understand your code. I will help you find things quickly in Drupal's codebase, introduce version control, walk you through module maintenance, and wrap up by discussing debugging and profiling your code.

Coding Standards

The Drupal community has agreed that its codebase must have a standardized look and feel to improve readability and make diving in easier for budding developers. Developers of contributed modules are encouraged to adopt these standards as well. Actually, let me be frank: your modules will not be taken seriously unless you follow the coding standards. I'll cover the standards first and then introduce a few automated tools to help you check your code (and even correct it for you!).

Line Indention

Drupal code uses two spaces for indentation—not tabs. In most editors, you can set a preference to automatically replace tabs with spaces, so you can still use the Tab key to indent if you're working against the force of habit.

PHP Opening and Closing Tags

Files that contain code, such as `.module` or `.inc` files, use an opening PHP code tag as follows:

```
<?php
...
```

The shorter opening tag form, `<?`, is never used.

The closing `?>` tag is not necessary and is not used in Drupal code. In fact, it can cause problems if used. The exception is that the closing tag is used in template files that exit out of PHP and go back into HTML, for example, in `themes/bluemarine/block.tpl.php`:

```php
<?php
// $Id: block.tpl.php,v 1.3 2007/08/07 08:39:36 goba Exp $
?>
  <div class="block block-<?php print $block->module; ?>" id="block-<?php
    print $block->module; ?>-<?php print $block->delta; ?>">
    <h2 class="title"><?php print $block->subject; ?></h2>
    <div class="content"><?php print $block->content; ?></div>
  </div>
```

Control Structures

Control structures are instructions that control the flow of execution in a program, like conditional statements and loops. *Conditional statements* are if, else, elseif, and switch statements. *Control loops* are while, do-while, for, and foreach.

Control structures should have a single space between the control keyword (if, elseif, while, for, etc.) and the opening parenthesis to visually distinguish them from function calls (which also use parentheses but have no space). Opening braces should be on the same line as the keyword (not on their own line). Ending function braces should be on their own line.

Incorrect

```php
if ($a && $b)
{
  sink();
}
```

Correct

```php
if ($a && $b) {
  sink();
}
elseif ($a || $b) {
  swim();
}
else {
  fly();
}
```

Braces should typically be used, even when they're not necessarily needed, to promote readability and reduce the chance of errors.

Incorrect

```php
while ($a < 10)
  $a++;
```

Correct

```
while ($a < 10) {
  $a++;
}
```

Switch statements should be formatted as follows (notice that a `break;` statement is not necessary in the default case):

```
switch ($a) {
  case 1:
    red();
    break;

  case 2:
    blue();
    break;

  case 3:
    purple();
    // Fall through to default case.

  default:
    green();
}
```

If the `break;` statement is omitted because execution is intended to fall through to the next case, note that decision in a code comment.

Function Calls

In function calls, there should be a single space surrounding the operator (=, <, >, etc.) and no spaces between the name of the function and the function's opening parenthesis. There is also no space between a function's opening parenthesis and its first parameter. Middle function parameters are separated with a comma and a space, and the last parameter has no space between it and the closing parenthesis. The following examples illustrate these points:

Incorrect

```
$var=foo ($bar,$baz);
```

Correct

```
$var = foo($bar, $baz);
```

There's one exception to the rule. In a block of related assignments, more space may be inserted between assignment operators if it promotes readability:

```
$a_value        = foo($b);
$another_value = bar();
$third_value    = baz();
```

Function Declarations

There should be no space between a function's name and its opening parenthesis. When writing a function that uses default values for some of its parameters, list those parameters last. Also, if your function generates any data that may be useful, returning that data in case the caller wants to use it is a good practice. Some function declaration examples follow:

Incorrect

```
function foo ($bar = 'baz', $qux){
  $value = $qux + some_function($bar);
}
```

Correct

```
function foo($qux, $bar = 'baz') {
  $value = $qux + some_function($bar);
  return $value;
}
```

Function Names

Function names in Drupal are in lowercase and based on the name of the module or system they are part of. This convention avoids namespace collisions. Underscores are used to separate descriptive parts of the function name. After the module name, the function should be named with the verb and the object of that verb: `modulename_verb_object()`. In the first following example, the incorrectly named function has no module prefix, and the verb and its object are reversed. The subsequent example, obviously, corrects these errors.

Incorrect

```
function some_text_munge() {
  ...
}
```

Correct

```
function mymodule_munge_some_text() {
  ...
}
```

Private functions follow the same conventions as other functions but are prefixed with an underscore.

Arrays

Arrays are formatted with spaces separating each element and each assignment operator. If an array block spans more than 80 characters, each element should be moved to its own line. It's good practice to put each element on its own line anyway for readability and maintainability. This allows you to easily add or remove array elements.

Incorrect

```
$fruit['basket'] = array('apple'=>TRUE, 'orange'=>FALSE, 'banana'=>TRUE,
  'peach'=>FALSE);
```

Correct

```
$fruit['basket'] = array(
  'apple'  => TRUE,
  'orange' => FALSE,
  'banana' => TRUE,
  'peach'  => FALSE,
);
```

Note The comma at the end of the last array element is not an error, and PHP allows this syntax. It's there to err on the side of caution, in case a developer bops along and decides to add or remove an element at the end of the array list. This convention is allowed and encouraged but not required.

When creating internal Drupal arrays, such as menu items or form definitions, always list only one element on each line:

```
$form['flavors'] = array(
  '#type' => 'select',
  '#title' => t('Flavors'),
  '#description' => t('Choose a flavor.'),
  '#options' => $flavors,
);
```

Constants

PHP constants should be in all capital letters, with underscores separating proper words:

```
/**
 * First bootstrap phase: initialize configuration.
 */
define('DRUPAL_BOOTSTRAP_CONFIGURATION', 0);
```

Names of constants should be prefixed by the module that uses them to avoid namespace collisions between constants. For example, if you are writing `tiger.module`, use `TIGER_STRIPED` instead of `STRIPED`.

Global Variables

The use of global variables is strongly discouraged. If you must use global variables, they should be named with a single underscore followed by your namespace (that is, the name of your module or theme) followed by an underscore and a descriptive name.

Incorrect
```
global $records;
```

Correct
```
global $_mymodulename_access_records;
```

Module Names

Module names should never include an underscore. To understand why, think of the following scenario:

1. A developer creates `node_list.module` that contains a function called `node_list_all()`.

2. In the next version of Drupal, the core node module adds a function called `node_list_all()`—namespace conflict!

The preceding conflict could be avoided if the developer follows the convention of naming the module with no underscores: `nodelist_all()` will never conflict with core code.

The easiest way of thinking about this is to recognize that anything to the left of the first underscore is owned by the module with that name. For example, the node module in core owns all of the `node_` namespace. If you are writing functions that begin with `node_`, `user_`, `filter_`, or any other core namespace, you are asking for trouble. A namespace conflict in a contributed module means extra work for you and for anyone who has written code that depends on your module.

Filenames

Filenames should be lowercase. The exception is documentation files, which are named in uppercase with the `.txt` suffix, for example:

```
CHANGELOG.txt
INSTALL.txt
README.txt
```

It is best to follow the conventions that core uses when naming files. The files from the book module in core are shown in Table 21-1.

Table 21-1. *File Names Used in the book Module and Module-Related Files*

Filename	Description
book.info	Module name, description, core compatibility, dependencies
book.install	Schema definition; includes hooks that run when the module is installed, uninstalled, enabled, or disabled
book.module	Code
book.admin.inc	Code included when accessing administrative pages
book.pages.inc	Code for user-specific (rarely used) functions
book.css	Default CSS for book-related classes and IDs
book-rtl.css	CSS overrides for right-to-left languages
book-all-books-block.tpl.php	Default template file
book-export-html.tpl.php	Default template file
book-navigation.tpl.php	Default template file
book-node-export-html.tpl.php	Default template file

PHP Comments

Drupal follows most of the Doxygen comment style guidelines. All documentation blocks must use the following syntax:

```
/**
 * Documentation here.
 */
```

The leading spaces that appear before the asterisks (*) on lines after the first one are required.

■**Note** Doxygen is a PHP-friendly documentation generator. It extracts PHP comments from the code and generates human-friendly documentation. For more information, visit http://www.doxygen.org.

When documenting a function, the documentation block must immediately precede the function it documents, with no intervening blank lines.

Drupal understands the Doxygen constructs in the following list; although I'll cover the most commons ones, please refer to the Doxygen site for more information on how to use them:

- @mainpage

- @file

- @defgroup

- `@ingroup`

- `@addtogroup` (as a synonym of `@ingroup`)

- `@param`

- `@return`

- `@link`

- `@see`

- `@{`

- `@}`

The beauty of adhering to these standards is that you can automatically generate documentation for your modules using the API contributed module. The API module is an implementation of a subset of the Doxygen documentation generator specification, tuned to produce output that best benefits a Drupal codebase. You can see this module in action by visiting `http://api.drupal.org` as well as learn more about the API module at `http://drupal.org/project/api`.

Documentation Examples

Let's walk through the skeleton of a module from top to bottom and highlight the different types of documentation along the way.

The second line of a module (after the opening `<?php` tag) should contain a concurrent versions system (CVS) tag to keep track of the file's revision number:

```
// $Id$
```

This tag is automatically parsed and expanded when the code is checked into CVS and updated subsequently by CVS following any CVS commit. Afterward, it will automatically look similar to this:

```
// $Id: comment.module,v 1.617.2.2 2008/04/25 20:58:46 goba Exp $
```

You'll learn more about how to use CVS shortly.

Before declaring functions, take a moment to document what the module does using the following format:

```
/**
 * @file
 * One-line description/summary of what your module does goes here.
 *
 * A paragraph or two in broad strokes about your module and how it behaves.
 */
```

Documenting Constants

PHP constants should be in all capital letters, with underscores separating proper words. When defining PHP constants, it's a good idea to explain what they're going to be used for, as shown in the following code snippet:

```
/**
 * Role ID for authenticated users; should match what's in the "role" table.
 */
define('DRUPAL_AUTHENTICATED_RID', 2);
```

Documenting Functions

Function documentation should use the following syntax:

```
/**
 * Short description, beginning with a verb.
 *
 * Longer description goes here.
 *
 * @param $foo
 *   A description of what $foo is.
 * @param $bar
 *   A description of what $bar is.
 * @return
 *   A description of what this function will return.
 */
function name_of_function($foo, $bar) {
  ...
  return $baz;
}
```

The short description should begin with an imperative verb in the present tense, such as "Munge form data" or "Do remote address lookups" (not "Munges form data" or "Does remote address lookups"). Let's take a look at an example from Drupal core that is found within system.module:

```
/**
 * Add default buttons to a form and set its prefix.
 *
 * @ingroup forms
 * @see system_settings_form_submit()
 * @param $form
 *   An associative array containing the structure of the form.
 * @return
 *   The form structure.
 */
function system_settings_form($form) {
  ...
}
```

There are a couple of new Doxygen constructs in the preceding example:

- `@see` tells you what other functions to reference. The preceding code is a form definition, so `@see` points to the submit handler for the form. When the API module parses this to produce documentation (such as that available at `http://api.drupal.org`), it will turn the function name that follows `@see` into a clickable link.

- `@ingroup` links a set of related functions together. In this example, it creates a group of functions that provide form definitions. You can create any group name you wish. Possible core values are: `batch`, `database`, `file`, `format`, `forms`, `hooks`, `image`, `menu`, `node_access`, `node_content`, `schemaapi`, `search`, `themeable`, and `validation`.

■**Tip** You can view all functions in a given group at `http://api.drupal.org`. For example, form builder functions are listed at `http://api.drupal.org/api/group/forms/6`, and themable functions are listed at `http://api.drupal.org/api/group/themeable/6`.

Functions that implement common Drupal constructs, such as hooks or form validation/submission functions, may omit the full `@param` and `@return` syntax but should still contain a one-line description of what the function does, as in this example:

```
/**
 * Validate the book settings form.
 *
 * @see book_admin_settings()
 */
function book_admin_settings_validate($form, &$form_state) {
   ...
   }
}
```

It is useful to know if a function is a menu callback (that is, mapped to a URL using `hook_menu()`):

```
/**
 * Menu callback; print a listing of all books.
 */
function book_render() {
   ...
}
```

Documenting Hook Implementations

When a function is a hook implementation, there is no need to document the hook. Simply state which hook is being implemented, for example:

```
/**
 * Implementation of hook_block().
 */
function statistics_block($op = 'list', $delta = 0, $edit = array() {
  ...
}
```

Checking Your Coding Style Programmatically

There are two main approaches to checking that your coding style matches the Drupal coding standards: one uses a Perl script and the other, a contributed module.

Using code-style.pl

Inside the scripts directory of your Drupal root directory, you'll find a Perl script named code-style.pl, which checks your Drupal coding style. Here's how to use it.

First, change the permissions in order to make the file executable; otherwise, you'll get a "Permission denied" error. This can be done from the command line using chmod as follows:

```
$ cd scripts
$ ls -l | grep code-style
-rw-r--r--  1 jvandyk  jvandyk  4946 Feb 15  2007 code-style.pl

$ chmod u+x code-style.pl
$ ls -l | grep code-style
-rwxr--r--  1 jvandyk  jvandyk  4946 Feb 15  2007 code-style.pl
```

Windows users don't need to worry about changing file permissions, but you may need to make sure that Perl is installed to run code-style.pl. Information about Perl can be found at http://www.perl.org.

Now you can execute code-style.pl by passing in the location of the module or other file to evaluate. The following example illustrates how this might be written:

```
$ ./code-style.pl ../modules/node/node.module
```

The output of the program will usually be in the following format:

```
line number : 'error' -> 'correction' : content of line
```

For example, the following script is telling us we need spaces around the assignment operator (=) on line 30 of foo.module, which currently contains the code $a=1;:

```
foo.module30: '=' -> ' = ' : $a=1;
```

■Note Beware of false positives. While this script does a pretty good job, it's not perfect, and you'll need to carefully evaluate each report.

Using the Coder Module

At `http://drupal.org/project/coder`, you'll find a treasure that will save you a lot of time and aggravation. It's the coder module: a module that reviews the code in other modules.

Download the latest version, place it in `sites/all/modules/contrib/`, and then enable it at Administer ➤ Site building ➤ Modules as you would any other module.

To have the coder module review your module, click the new "Code review" link in your site navigation, and select the kind of review you want and the module or theme you would like to have reviewed. Or use the handy Code Review link that this module provides on the list of modules at Administer ➤ Site building ➤ Modules.

■Tip Use of the coder module should be considered mandatory if you are serious about getting up to speed with Drupal's coding conventions.

You can even go a step further and use the `coder_format.php` script that comes with the coder module. The script actually fixes your code formatting errors. Here is how to have `coder_format.php` check the annotate module we wrote in Chapter 2:

```
$ cd sites/all/modules
$ php contrib/coder/scripts/coder_format/coder_format.php \
  custom/annotate/annotate.module
```

The script modifies the file `annotate.module` in place and saves the original as `annotate.module.coder.orig`. To see what the script did, use `diff`:

```
$ diff custom/annotate/annotate.module custom/annotate/annotate.module.coder.orig
```

Finding Your Way Around Code with egrep

egrep is a Unix command that searches through files looking for lines that match a supplied regular expression. No, it's not a bird (that's an egret). If you're a Windows user and would like to follow along with these examples, you can use egrep by installing a precompiled version (see `http://unxutils.sourceforge.net`) or by installing the Cygwin environment (`http://cygwin.com`). Otherwise, you can just use the built-in search functionality of the operating system rather than egrep.

egrep is a handy tool when looking for the implementation of hooks within Drupal core, finding the place where error messages are being built, and so on. Let's look at some examples of using egrep from within the Drupal root directory:

```
$ egrep -rl 'hook_init' .
./includes/bootstrap.inc
./includes/path.inc
./modules/aggregator/aggregator.module
./modules/book/book.module
./modules/forum/forum.module
./modules/node/node.module
./modules/poll/poll.module
./modules/system/system.module
./update.php
```

In the preceding case, we are recursively searching (-r) our Drupal files for instances of hook_init starting at the current directory (.) and printing out the filenames (-1) of the matching instances. Now look at this example:

```
$ egrep -rn 'hook_init' .
./includes/bootstrap.inc:1011:      // Initialize $_GET['q'] prior to loading
  modules and invoking hook_init().
./includes/path.inc:9: * to use them in hook_init() or hook exit() can make
  them available, by
./modules/aggregator/aggregator.module:261: * Implementation of hook_init().
./modules/book/book.module:164: * Implementation of hook_init(). Adds the
  book module's CSS.
./modules/forum/forum.module:160: * Implementation of hook_init().
./modules/node/node.module:1596: * Implementation of hook_init().
./modules/poll/poll.module:24: * Implementation of hook_init().
./modules/system/system.module:538: * Implementation of hook_init().
./update.php:18: * operations, such as hook_init() and hook_exit() invokes,
  css/js preprocessing
```

Here, we are recursively searching (-r) our Drupal files for instances of the string hook_init and printing out the actual lines and line numbers (-n) where they occur. We could further refine our search by piping results into another search. In the following example, we search for occurrences of the word poll in the previous example's search result set:

```
$ egrep -rn 'hook_init' . | egrep 'poll'
./modules/poll/poll.module:24: * Implementation of hook_init().
```

Another way to refine your search is by using the -v flag for egrep, which means "invert this match;" that is, let matches through that do *not* match the string. Let's find all the occurrences of the word lock without matching the words block or Block:

```
$ egrep -rn 'lock' . | egrep -v '[B|b]lock'
./includes/common.inc:2548:   // See if the semaphore is still locked.
./includes/database.mysql.inc:327:function db_lock_table($table) {
./includes/database.mysql.inc:332: * Unlock all locked tables.
...
```

Taking Advantage of Version Control

Version control is a must for any software project, and Drupal is no exception. Version control tracks all changes made to every file within Drupal. It keeps a history of all revisions as well as the author of each revision. You can literally get a line-by-line report of who made changes as well as when and why they were made. Version control also simplifies the process of rolling out new versions of Drupal to the public. The Drupal community uses the tried and true CVS software to maintain its revision history.

■**Tip** Discussion of the pros and cons of various version control systems (Bazaar, CVS, Git, Subversion, etc.) breaks out regularly on the Drupal development mailing list. Before starting a new thread on this topic, visit the archives to get familiar with previous discussions.

The benefits of revision control aren't reserved exclusively for managing the Drupal project. You can take advantage of Drupal's CVS to help maintain your own Drupal-based projects and dramatically reduce your own maintenance overhead. First though, you need to change the way you install Drupal.

Installing CVS-Aware Drupal

When you download the compressed Drupal package from the drupal.org downloads page, that copy of the code is devoid of any of the rich revision information used to inform you of the current state of your codebase.

Developers who are using CVS can quickly get answers to versioning questions and apply the updates while everyone else is still downloading the new version.

■**Note** The only visual difference between the two ways of downloading Drupal is that the CVS checkout contains an extra folder labeled CVS, where CVS information is kept, for every directory found within Drupal. Drupal's .htaccess file contains rules that automatically protect these folders if you are using Apache (some CVS clients such as TortoiseCVS hide CVS folders by default).

You may have had folks tell you that the CVS version of Drupal isn't safe to use and that CVS is the bleeding-edge code that's unstable. This is a common misconception and a confusion of two ideas. These people are referring to the "HEAD" version of a project; that is, the version of Drupal (or any project under CVS) where new features are currently being tested in preparation for the next release. CVS, however, is used to maintain the "HEAD" version *and* the stable versions of software.

Using CVS-Aware Drupal

So what are some of the things you can do with this fancy CVS checkout of Drupal?

- *You can apply security updates to the Drupal codebase* even before the official security announcements are released. Did I mention it's really easy to do? Rather than downloading an entirely new version of Drupal, you simply run a single CVS command.

- *You can maintain custom modifications to Drupal code.* Hacking Drupal core is a cardinal sin, but if you must do it, do it with CVS. CVS will intelligently attempt to upgrade even your modified core files, so you no longer inadvertently overwrite your custom changes during an upgrade process.

- *You can also use CVS to discover hacks made by other developers* to Drupal's core files. With a single command, you can generate a line-by-line list of any code on your working copy of Drupal that is different from the central Drupal server's pristine codebase.

Installing a CVS Client

Run the following command from the command line to test if a CVS client is installed:

```
$ cvs
```

If you receive a "Command not found" error, you probably need to install a CVS client. Windows users might want to take a look at TortoiseCVS (`http://tortoisecvs.sourceforge.net/`). Mac users should take a look at the following article: `http://developer.apple.com/internet/opensource/cvsoverview.html`. Linux users, you ought to know what to do.

If you see the following CVS documentation listed as the output of the cvs command, you're ready to go!

```
Usage: cvs [cvs-options] command [command-options-and-arguments]
```

Checking Out Drupal from CVS

I'll cover how to use CVS from the command line. There are plenty of graphical CVS applications out there, and you should be able to figure out how to use a GUI-based one once you understand how the command line works. Windows users can use the CVS command line by installing the Cygwin environment (see `http://drupal.org/node/150036`). It is almost always easier to get help with CVS from the community if you are using a command-line CVS client.

In CVS lingo, you will be doing a *checkout* of a working copy of Drupal from the central CVS repository. That might be a little wordy, but it's important to use the correct terms. Here's the command that grabs Drupal 6.2 from the CVS server:

```
cvs -d:pserver:anonymous:anonymous@cvs.drupal.org:/cvs/drupal checkout -d
~/www/drupal6 -r DRUPAL-6-2 drupal
```

Let's break that down. cvs executes the CVS client; that is, it runs a program named cvs on your computer:

```
cvs -d:pserver:anonymous:anonymous@cvs.drupal.org:/cvs/drupal checkout -d
~/www/drupal6 -r DRUPAL-6-2 drupal
```

The -d option for the cvs command stands for "directory" and is used for specifying the location of the CVS repository:

```
cvs -d:pserver:anonymous:anonymous@cvs.drupal.org:/cvs/drupal checkout -d
~/www/drupal6 -r DRUPAL-6-2 drupal
```

A *repository*, in CVS speak, is the location of the file tree of CVS-maintained files. Now, the -d option can be as simple as cvs -d /usr/local/myrepository, if the repository is on the same machine. However, the Drupal repository is located on a remote server, so we'll need to specify more connection parameters. Let's go deeper into this command.

Each parameter for the -d option is separated by a colon. pserver stands for "password-authenticated server" and is the connection method Drupal uses for connecting to the repository. However, CVS can connect via other protocols, such as SSH.

Next, the username and password are specified. For the Drupal CVS repository they are both the same: anonymous. Following the at symbol (@) is the hostname to connect to: cvs.drupal.org. And, finally, we need to specify the path to the repository on the remote host: /cvs/drupal.

■**Note** After you authenticate once to a CVS server, you shouldn't need to authenticate again, because a file named .cvspass is created in your home directory and stores the login information. Subsequent CVS commands applied to this repository shouldn't need the -d global option parameter.

Now that the connection parameters are established we can send along the actual command for cvs to execute, in this case the checkout command to grab a working copy of the Drupal repository:

```
cvs -d:pserver:anonymous:anonymous@cvs.drupal.org:/cvs/drupal checkout -d
~/www/drupal6 -r DRUPAL-6-2 drupal
```

Don't confuse the following -d with the global option -d that's passed to the cvs part of the command:

```
cvs -d:pserver:anonymous:anonymous@cvs.drupal.org:/cvs/drupal checkout -d
~/www/drupal6 -r DRUPAL-6-2 drupal
```

This -d is used to put a working copy of the repository in a directory called drupal6 in the www directory of your home directory on your computer. This is an optional parameter, and if it's not used, the repository will be copied to a folder with the same name of the repository itself. So, in this case, it would create a folder named drupal to hold your working copy of the repository, since the name of the repository is drupal.

The -r parameter stands for "revision." Typically, this will be a tag or a branch. I'll talk about what tags and branches are in a moment. In the preceding command, we're asking for the revision named DRUPAL-6-2, which is the tag corresponding to the Drupal 6.2 release. You can substitute the correct tag for whatever version of Drupal is current.

```
cvs -d:pserver:anonymous:anonymous@cvs.drupal.org:/cvs/drupal checkout -d
~/www/drupal6 -r DRUPAL-6-2 drupal
```

A list of all tags and branches for core is available at http://drupal.org/node/93997. And finally, drupal is the name of the repository to check out.

```
cvs -d:pserver:anonymous:anonymous@cvs.drupal.org:/cvs/drupal checkout -d
~/www/drupal6 -r DRUPAL-6-2 drupal
```

Branches and Tags

Tagging and branching are standard practices for many revision control systems. We will examine how these concepts are used within Drupal core and for contributed modules. Spend the time necessary to understand these concepts, as doing so will save you much time and grief.

Branches in Drupal Core

When a new version of Drupal is released, the maintainers create a *branch* within CVS, which is essentially a clone of the current HEAD codebase. This allows bleeding-edge development to continue on the original trunk of code while also allowing the community to stabilize a new release. This is how Drupal 6 was created, for example. The actual canonical branch names are DRUPAL-4-6-0, DRUPAL-4-7-0, DRUPAL-5, and DRUPAL-6 (notice that the naming convention changed in Drupal 5; the tertiary numbers have been removed).

Let's see how that works. In the following series of figures, note that time is on the vertical axis. As development of Drupal moves along, and bug fixes and new features are committed to the codebase, the leading edge (or cutting edge) of development is called HEAD, as shown in Figure 21-1.

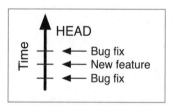

Figure 21-1. *Drupal development timeline*

When the code is complete enough to warrant a branch, the core committers create a stable branch on the tree for a given release. At this point, both copies are identical. Then new features and bug fixes continue to be added to the HEAD of the tree, and bug fixes are added to the stable branch, as shown in Figure 21-2. Stable branches, as a rule, receive only bug fixes; new features are reserved for HEAD. They are called "stable" branches, because they are guaranteed not to change suddenly.

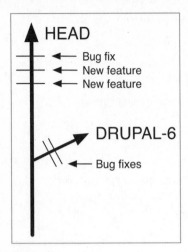

Figure 21-2. *A branch has been created.*

When enough bug fixes have been committed to the stable branch that the core committers decide there should be another official release of Drupal, a release is created. But the new release is created with tags, not branches, so let's take a look at tags.

Tags in Drupal Core

Tags are snapshots in time of a particular branch. In the Drupal world, tags are used to mark beta, bug-fix, and security releases. This is how we get minor versions such as Drupal 6.1 and 6.2. Canonical tag names are `DRUPAL-4-7-1`, `DRUPAL-4-7-2`, `DRUPAL-5-7`, `DRUPAL-6-0`, `DRUPAL-6-1`, and `DRUPAL-6-2` (again, notice that the naming convention changed in Drupal 5). For a complete list of tag names used by Drupal core, see `http://drupal.org/node/93997`.

When Drupal 6 was being developed, the core committers wanted to make a beta release so that people could test the code more easily. So they decided to create a tag called `DRUPAL-6-0-BETA-1`, shown in Figure 21-3.

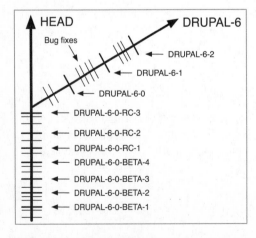

Figure 21-3. *A DRUPAL-6-0-BETA-1 tag has been created.*

The tag DRUPAL-6-0-BETA-1 refers to the code in a particular state; that is, a snapshot of exactly how the code was at one point in time. You could still download the beta 1 release of Drupal right now using CVS if you really wanted to.

As more bugs are fixed, one or more release candidates are tagged with tags like DRUPAL-6-0-RC-1 and DRUPAL-6-0-RC-2. A branch called DRUPAL-6 is created to split off development of Drupal 6 from development of the codebase that will become Drupal 7. Finally, the big day comes, and the DRUPAL-6-0 tag is created. Articles are written and the blogosphere goes into a frenzy. But back on the DRUPAL-6 branch, hordes of Drupal developers continue to fix bugs, which leads to the tags DRUPAL-6-1, DRUPAL-6-2, and so forth.

The -dev Suffix

Meanwhile, development has continued on HEAD. But rather than refer to it as HEAD, the Drupal community prefers to think of it as the next version of Drupal, because that's really what's being developed. As you can see in Figure 21-4, 7.x-dev is where development takes place for Drupal 7.

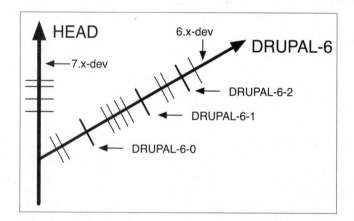

Figure 21-4. *-dev snapshots refer to the leading edge of development.*

When the time comes to push for a Drupal 7 release, the core committers will add a stable branch for Drupal 7 and that's where the tagging will happen. Note, therefore, that 7.x-dev is not a tag! That means it does *not* refer to code in a given state. Rather, it refers to continuing development along a branch. Every day, a packaging script on drupal.org takes a snapshot of the branch and makes it available as a "Development snapshot," shown in Figure 21-5. But this is done simply for convenience; it is not a feature of CVS.

Version	Date	Links	Status	
7.x-dev	2008-May-20	Download · Release notes	Development snapshot	✕
6.2	2008-Apr-09	Download · Release notes	Recommended for 6.x	✓
5.7	2008-Jan-29	Download · Release notes	Recommended for 5.x	✓

Figure 21-5. *Drupal makes the development snapshot of the next version available at http://drupal.org/download.*

Likewise, bug fixes continue on the stable branch. Look at the DRUPAL-6 branch in Figure 21-4. From the figure, you can see that a bug has been fixed after the DRUPAL-6-2 tag was created, but that no new tag has been created yet. A new tag is not created after every bug fix; a tag is created only when enough bug fixes have been released that the core committers determine a new release is warranted (the exception is security fixes, which usually result in an immediate release). When it's time, core committers create the new release by creating the DRUPAL-6-3 tag.

So, back to Figure 21-4, the code on the DRUPAL-6 branch that is past the DRUPAL-6-2 release but contains a postrelease bug fix is called 6.x-dev. That means it is the development version of Drupal 6.3; this code will become Drupal 6.3 when the core committers create the DRUPAL-6-3 tag. After that, the code at the end of the branch will be 6.x-dev, because that code will become Drupal 6.4.

Tip When developers refer to the code at the end of the branch, they don't always want to stop and check which actual version will be next (will it be 6.1? 6.2? 6.3?). In that case, they use an "x" in place of, for example, the "1" in "6.1" or the "2" in "6.2" and just call it 6.x-dev—that is, "x" refers to the code that will become the next version of Drupal 6, whatever version that may happen to be.

You should now understand the difference between a tag and a branch and how tags are related to releases for core. The information is summarized in Table 21-2.

Table 21-2. *The Relationship Among Tags, Branches, Releases, and Tarballs Available at* *http://drupal.org/download*

Tag	Appears on Branch	Release	Tarball
DRUPAL-5-7	DRUPAL-5	Drupal 5.7	drupal-5.7.tar.gz
DRUPAL-6-0	DRUPAL-6	Drupal 6.0	drupal-6.0.tar.gz
DRUPAL-6-1	DRUPAL-6	Drupal 6.1	drupal-6.1.tar.gz
DRUPAL-6-2	DRUPAL-6	Drupal 6.2	drupal-6.2.tar.gz
HEAD	None	7.x-dev	drupal-7.x-dev.tar.gz

Checking Out Drupal Using a Tag or Branch Name

I've already shown you how to get a version of code from a tag on the DRUPAL-6 branch in the "Checking Out Drupal from CVS" section. Here are some examples that use that code to retrieve various tags and branches and place them in a new folder named drupal in the current directory.

Check out a copy of the DRUPAL-6 branch exactly as it was during its first beta release:

```
cvs -d:pserver:anonymous:anonymous@cvs.drupal.org:/cvs/drupal checkout
   -r DRUPAL-6-0-BETA-1 drupal
```

Check out a copy of Drupal 6.2:

```
cvs -d:pserver:anonymous:anonymous@cvs.drupal.org:/cvs/drupal checkout
  -r DRUPAL-6-2 drupal
```

Check out a copy of 6.x-dev (that is, the latest code on the DRUPAL-6 branch including any bug fixes since the last release):

```
cvs -d:pserver:anonymous:anonymous@cvs.drupal.org:/cvs/drupal checkout
  -r DRUPAL-6 drupal
```

Check out a copy of the latest version of HEAD (that is, 7.x-dev). Note that no branch needs to be specified in this case:

```
cvs -d:pserver:anonymous:anonymous@cvs.drupal.org:/cvs/drupal checkout
  drupal
```

Updating Code with CVS

If you want to apply the latest Drupal code updates to your site or even upgrade to the next shiny new version, you can do it all with the cvs update command. To first test what changes a cvs update command would make, run the following command:

```
cvs -n update -dP
```

This shows you what will be changed without making the changes. To perform the actual update, use this command:

```
cvs update -dP
```

This brings your working copy of Drupal in sync with the latest changes of the branch you're following. CVS knows the branch you're following by looking at the CVS metadata stored within those CVS folders that was placed there when you did your initial checkout, so you don't have to specify it each time. The -d option creates any directories that exist in the repository if they're missing in your working copy. The -P option prunes empty directories as they aren't needed.

■**Note** Always back up your data before running any CVS command that will modify your files. Another best practice for moving these changes to production is to do a CVS update on the staging site and resolve any potential file conflicts before moving those changes into production.

Upgrading to a different version of Drupal is just a variation of the CVS update command. Let's assume you're at Drupal 5.7 and wish to upgrade to 6.2. Again, make sure that you are at the Drupal root directory before running the following commands.

Update to the last official release on the existing branch, which we will assume for the sake of this example is Drupal 5.7. You do not really need to specify DRUPAL-5-7 in the following command (since cvs will know your current branch), but it is helpful to be verbose to make sure you're making the changes you intended:

```
cvs update -dP -r DRUPAL-5-7
```

■**Caution** If you are upgrading to a new Drupal version, you should disable all noncore modules and themes before running the cvs update command, which updates core. See http://drupal.org/upgrade for detailed instructions.

Next, upgrade the core's code to Drupal 6. Let's assume that Drupal 6.2 is the latest version. Thus, the following command gets code from the DRUPAL-6 branch of the CVS tree that has been tagged DRUPAL-6-2:

```
cvs update -dP -r DRUPAL-6-2
```

Now you still need to go through the rest of the standard upgrade process such as updating contributed modules and themes and updating your database by visiting update.php, but now you don't have to download the new version of core and overwrite your core files.

Tracking Drupal Code Changes

Want to check if anyone on your development team has modified core files? Want to generate a report of any changes made to core code? The cvs diff command generates a human-readable, line-by-line output of code differences, that is, updates and modifications.

■**Note** On the Unix command line, the diff command (not the cvs diff command) compares two files and shows you the changes. You would use it by typing diff file1 file2. Instead of comparing two local files, the cvs diff command compares a local file with a file in a CVS repository.

Here's example output of cvs diff run using cvs diff -up:

```
Index: includes/mail.inc
===================================================================
RCS file: /cvs/drupal/drupal/includes/mail.inc,v
retrieving revision 1.8.2.2
diff -u -p -r1.8.2.2 mail.inc
--- includes/mail.inc 2 Apr 2008 08:41:30 -0000   1.8.2.2
+++ includes/mail.inc 15 May 2008 23:56:40 -0000
@@ -272,8 +272,8 @@ function drupal_html_to_text($string, $a
    $string = _filter_htmlcorrector(filter_xss($string, $allowed_tags));
```

```
      // Apply inline styles.
-     $string = preg_replace('!</?(em|i)>!i', '/', $string);
-     $string = preg_replace('!</?(strong|b)>!i', '*', $string);
+     $string = preg_replace('!</?(em|i)((?> +)[^>]*)?>!i', '/', $string);
+     $string = preg_replace('!</?(strong|b)((?> +)[^>]*)?>!i', '*', $string);

      // Replace inline <a> tags with the text of link and a footnote.
      // 'See <a href="http://drupal.org">the Drupal site</a>' becomes
```

The lines that begin with a single addition symbol (+) were added and the lines that begin with the single subtraction symbol (-) were removed. It looks like someone modified the regular expressions in the drupal_html_to_text() function.

Drupal uses *unified diffs*, indicated by the -u option. The -p option is also used; this prints the name of the function after the summary of changes. This is useful for quickly determining in which function the code appears when reading the output, as not all Drupal developers have memorized the line numbers in which functions appear. The following line, taken from the previous cvs diff output, reveals the function that was affected:

```
@@ -272,8 +272,8 @@ function drupal_html_to_text($string, $a
```

Resolving CVS Conflicts

If you've made changes to the Drupal core code, you risk creating conflicts when doing CVS updates. Files that have line conflicts will be marked with a "C" after running the cvs update command, and your site will no longer be operational as a result of these conflicts (the text inserted by CVS to mark the conflict is not valid PHP). CVS attempted to merge the new and old versions of the files but failed to do so, and now human intervention is needed to inspect the file by hand. Here's what you'll see somewhere in the file containing CVS conflicts:

```
<<<<<<< (filename)
your custom changes here
=======
the new changes from the repository
>>>>>>> (latest revision number in the repository)
```

You'll need to remove the lines you don't wish to keep and clean up the code by removing the conflict indication characters.

Cleanly Modifying Core Code

You should strive to never touch core code. But at some time, you may have to. If you need to hack, make sure you hack in a way that allows you to track your changes with precision. Let's take a simple example; we'll edit sites/default/default.settings.php. On line 143, you'll see the following code:

```
ini_set('session.cookie_lifetime', 2000000);
```

This value controls how long cookies last (in seconds). Let's assume that our sessions table in the database is filling up way too quickly, so we need to reduce the lifetime of these sessions. We could just go and change that value, but if that line changes on a subsequent CVS update, we'll get a conflict and need to manually resolve the problem.

A cleaner solution is to comment around the line of code we wish to change and duplicate the line a little further down in the file:

```
/* Original value - Changed to reduce cookie lifetime
ini_set('session.cookie_lifetime',  2000000);
*/
ini_set('session.cookie_lifetime',  1000000); // We added this.
```

The idea here is that CVS will not run into a conflict, because the original line of code has not changed.

Creating and Applying Patches

If you get the itch to fix a bug, test someone else's potential bug fix, or hack core code for one reason or another, you're going to run into the need to create or apply a patch. A *patch* is a human- and computer-readable text file that shows the line-by-line modifications made against the Drupal code repository. Patches are generated by the diff (or cvs diff) program, and you saw an example of one previously in the "Tracking Drupal Code Changes" section.

Creating a Patch

Here's an example of a patch that was made to clean up the documentation for the t() function in includes/common.inc:

```
Index: includes/common.inc
===================================================================
RCS file: /cvs/drupal/drupal/includes/common.inc,v
retrieving revision 1.591
diff -u -r1.591 common.inc
--- includes/common.inc      28 Mar 2007 07:03:33 -0000     1.591
+++ includes/common.inc      28 Mar 2007 18:43:18 -0000
@@ -639,7 +639,7 @@
  *
  * Special variables called "placeholders" are used to signal dynamic
  * information in a string, which should not be translated. Placeholders
- * can also be used for text that that may change from time to time
+ * can also be used for text that may change from time to time
  * (such as link paths) to be changed without requiring updates to translations.
  *
  * For example:
```

After making changes to the includes/common.inc file, the developer ran the following command from the Drupal root:

```
cvs diff -up > common.inc_50.patch
```

This command takes the output of cvs diff and puts it in a new file called common.inc_50.patch. Then the developer went to drupal.org and filed the bug here: http://drupal.org/node/100232.

Applying a Patch

Patches are the files created from output of the cvs diff or diff command. After you create or download a patch, navigate to your Drupal root and run the following command:

```
patch -p0 < path/to/patchfile/patchfile.patch
```

If the patch was created at the root of a Drupal installation, and you are applying it from the root of a Drupal installation, the paths will be the same so the -p0 (that's a zero) flag is used to tell the patch program to use the path found in the patch file (that is, to strip out zero segments from the path prefix).

If you run into problems when applying a patch, look for assistance at http://drupal.org/node/60116.

Sometimes, you may want to apply a patch to your production site for speed improvements or to add missing functionality. A best practice when doing this is to create a patches folder to store a copy of each patch after it is applied. If you haven't been doing this, you can always re-create the patch by running cvs diff -up on the file. You should also create a text file in that same folder to document the reasons each patch was applied. And you can use a naming convention to make it clear where a reference is for contextual information, for example:

```
modulename-description-of-problem-NODEID-COMMENTNUM.patch
```

Suppose you are using the workflow and token modules, but they are not playing well together. Someone has submitted a patch that fixes this, but the module maintainer has not yet incorporated the patch into a new release, yet you need it now because your site is going live tomorrow. You would name the patch:

```
workflow-conflict-with-token-api-12345-67.patch
```

That way, when it comes time to upgrade the site, whoever is responsible for upgrading can figure out the following:

- What parts of this installation are modified?

- Why were those modifications made?

- Has this patch already been applied upstream?

- If not, has someone come along and posted a better solution?

Maintaining a Module

In this section, we'll walk through an example of a developer creating and maintaining a module on drupal.org. We will cover the most common tasks.

Getting a Drupal CVS Account

Drupal has two CVS repositories: a Drupal core repository to which only a select few developers have commit access and a contributions repository that holds all the contributed modules, translations, and themes found on drupal.org, as well as some documentation and sandbox folders for developers to store code snippets. If you have a module, theme, or translation that you would like to contribute, you can apply for a CVS account to gain write access to the Drupal CVS contributions repository to share your code and contribute back to the community.

CVS accounts are not handed out like candy. You'll need to show that you really need one. You will be asked your specific motivation for getting an account. If you want to contribute a module, you will need to provide a copy of the module for review and demonstrate that it is substantially different than existing modules. (Spend some time using the search form on drupal.org to make sure your module truly is new and different. You can restrict searches to just contributions by checking the Project check box in the Advanced search form.) Also, make sure that you are OK with GNU General Public License (GPL) licensing, since all code in the contributions repository must be GPL licensed.

For details on how to apply, see http://drupal.org/node/59. Excellent documentation for committing and branching your own contributed modules can be found on the Drupal site at http://drupal.org/handbook/cvs/quickstart; plus we'll walk through some of the most common tasks next.

There are many other ways to contribute to Drupal as well, such as writing documentation and participating in the forums; see http://drupal.org/node/22286.

Checking Out the Contributions Repository

As I mentioned, drupal.org has two repositories, one for core code and one for contributed code including modules and themes. Only a handful of people have access to the former, but hordes of developers have access to the latter. You can check out the contributions repository as either an anonymous or a logged-in user. If you are checking out code from the contributions repository for a site (e.g., you're just using CVS to get a copy of a module so you can run it), check it out as an anonymous user. Otherwise, the next person to maintain that Drupal site you created will be frustrated when they want to update that module from CVS and are prompted to log in with your password!

You could check out the entire repository:

```
cvs -z6 -d:pserver:anonymous:anonymous@cvs.drupal.org:/cvs/drupal-contrib
  checkout contributions
```

However, this is discouraged because it puts a heavy load on the server infrastructure. A more targeted approach is better. Suppose you want to create a module and make it available to the Drupal community. That means you just need the modules subdirectory of the contributions repository. If you are going to be committing code to the repository, you'll need to log in (and you'll need your CVS account and password; see "Getting a Drupal CVS Account"). Here's how to log in, assuming that your CVS username is sproinx:

```
cvs -d:pserver:sproinx@cvs.drupal.org:/cvs/drupal-contrib login
```

You will be prompted for the password you provided when you applied for your CVS account. This password may not be the same as your `drupal.org` password.

■**Tip** You can change the password to your CVS account by logging into `drupal.org`, clicking "My account" ➤ Edit, and clicking the CVS tab.

Next, you check out the `modules` subdirectory of the contributions repository (the repository is named `drupal-contrib`). You could check out the `modules` subdirectory with all of the modules it contains, though this is rarely done unless you want a copy of all the thousands of modules available to peruse during a long plane flight:

```
cvs -z6 -d:pserver:sproinx@cvs.drupal.org:/cvs/drupal-contrib checkout
  contributions/modules
```

This will place a copy of the `modules` subdirectory on your local computer. It should look something like this:

```
contributions/
  CVS/
  modules/
    a_sync/
    aapi/
    about_this_node/
    abuse/
    ...
```

Or you could do what most developers do and just check out the `modules` subdirectory without any of the modules it contains:

```
cvs -d:pserver:sproinx@cvs.drupal.org:/cvs/drupal-contrib checkout
  -l contributions/modules
```

■**Note** At the time of this writing, the `modules` subdirectory contained about 300MB of data. That's a reason to use the `-z6` flag in the CVS command to check out the subdirectory (`-z6` compresses the data before sending it across the network) or just use the `-l` flag to omit checking out all those modules.

Notice that in the preceding CVS commands, the argument `-d:pserver:sproinx@cvs.drupal.org:/cvs/drupal-contrib` is repeated. Since typing this each time is not very handy, savvy developers put this into the `CVSROOT` environmental variable:

```
export CVSROOT=:pserver:sproinx@cvs.drupal.org:/cvs/drupal-contrib
```

From now on, the CVS commands will look a lot shorter. The preceding commands look like this after CVSROOT has been set:

```
cvs login
cvs -z6 checkout contributions/modules
cvs checkout -l contributions/modules
```

From now on, I'll assume that the CVSROOT environmental variable has been set.

Adding Your Module to the Repository

Now that you've got a copy of the modules subdirectory of the contributions repository, you might think that it's time to place your module among the thousands of others. But let's not be hasty! First, spend some time investigating the repository to see whether someone else has already written a module that solves your problem. Here are some resources to do that:

- http://drupal.org/project/Modules allows you to browse modules by category, name, or date and filter by major release compatibility (Drupal 6, Drupal 5, etc.).

- http://drupal.org/node/23789 outlines basic approaches for joining forces with others.

- http://drupalmodules.com offers easy searching of contributed modules as well as reviews and rankings.

If you are satisfied that your module is worth writing, it's time to develop it. Let's make a module.

Here's the .info file:

```
// $Id$
name = Foo
core = 6.x
```

And here's the module itself:

```
<?php
// $Id$

/**
 * @file
 * The greatest module ever made.
 */
```

So now the module's directory contains the preceding two files and looks like this:

```
foo/
  foo.info
  foo.module
```

Go ahead and copy the new module into your newly checked out contributions repository:

```
cp -R foo /path/to/local/copy/of/contributions/modules
```

Next, it's time to tell CVS about the new directory:

```
cd /path/to/local/copy/of/contributions
cvs add modules/foo
```

and the files within the directory

```
cvs add modules/foo/*
```

CVS will remind you that though the files have been scheduled for addition, you still have to commit them:

```
cvs add: use `cvs commit' to add these files permanently
```

If your module contains subdirectories, you will have to add those as well, because cvs add does not work recursively:

```
cvs add modules/foo/subdir1
cvs add modules/foo/subdir1/*
```

The Initial Commit

Now comes the big moment. It's time to commit your files to the repository! This is a time to get nervous. Check /path/to/local/copy/of/contributions/modules/foo to make sure that all of the files are there and that they actually contain the code you want to commit. Next, it's time to type the fateful command. Think up a succinct sentence that describes what your module does and then go ahead:

```
cvs commit -m "Initial commit of foo module. This module sends badgers to those
  who use it."
```

The -m flag means that what follows in quotes is a message to record along with the code commit. Provide useful information in your message. If you want to type several lines of text, it may be helpful to omit the -m flag if your installation of CVS automatically opens a text editor instead. On my OS X machine, this opens the vim editor, which gives me a screen like this:

```
CVS: -----------------------------------------------------------------
CVS: Enter Log.  Lines beginning with `CVS:' are removed automatically
CVS:
CVS: Committing in .
CVS:
CVS: Added Files:
CVS:    foo.info
CVS:    foo.module
CVS: -----------------------------------------------------------------
~
~
```

If you've never used vim before, this can be frightening. Use the down arrow key to navigate to the last line that begins with CVS: and press the "o" key (as in, "oh boy!"). Then type your longer commit message, and when you're done, press Esc and then type **:wq** to exit. You can substitute your favorite editor by setting the CVSEDITOR environment variable; for example, for emacs, set the variable like this:

```
export CVSEDITOR=emacs
```

or like this for Textmate:

```
export CVSEDITOR="mate -w"
```

Checking Out Your Module

Now that your module is in the repository like all the others, you can check it out from CVS and put it into your local development copy of Drupal (you may have to create the modules and contrib directories first).

```
cd /path/to/drupal
cd /sites/all/modules/contrib
cvs checkout -d foo contributions/modules/foo
```

If you receive an error like the following, you have not set your CVSROOT environment variable (see "Checking Out the Contributions Repository").

```
cvs checkout: No CVSROOT specified!  Please use the `-d' option
cvs [checkout aborted]: or set the CVSROOT environment variable.
```

Tip If you are maintaining a Drupal web site with modules that are checked out from CVS, investigate the CVS deploy module at http://drupal.org/project/cvs_deploy. It integrates the modules' CVS information with Drupal's built-in update status module, which reports when a module needs updating.

Creating a Project on drupal.org

Since you are sharing your module with the community, it makes sense to have a place where people can interact with you about your module in a structured way. That way, you won't be inundated with e-mail, and there will be a standard way of tracking requested features, bug fixes, and so on. After logging into drupal.org, go to http://drupal.org/node/add/project-project or use the site navigation menu to go to "Create content" ➤ Project, and fill in the form, paying particular attention to the "Full description" field where you describe your module (or theme). Once you have completed the form your project will be available at http://drupal.org/project/*yourprojectname*.

Caution Always create a project *before* you do any tagging or branching.

Committing a Bug Fix

If your checkout worked, you now have the following in `sites/all/modules/contrib`:

```
foo/
  CVS/
  foo.info
  foo.module
```

But oh, no! We've only just shared our code, and already someone has created an issue in our issue queue at `http://drupal.org/project/yourprojectname/issues`. User `flyingpizza` on `drupal.org` is pointing out in a post at `http://drupal.org/node/1234567` that we forgot to add a description line in our `.info` file! Let's add it now:

```
// $Id: foo.info,v 1.1 2008/05/22 14:15:21 jvandyk Exp $
name = Foo
description = Sends badgers to those who use it.
core = 6.x
```

Notice that the first line of the file has been changed by CVS from `// $Id$` to the actual identification information for the file. If you still see `// $Id$` there instead, you are not working with a version that has been checked out from CVS.

Before we commit this change, let's preview our changes by running the `cvs diff` command:

```
cvs diff -up
```

The output follows:

```
==================================================================
RCS file: /cvs/drupal-contrib/contributions/modules/foo/foo.info,v
retrieving revision 1.1
diff -u -u -p -r1.1 foo.info
--- foo.info  22 May 2008 14:15:21 -0000  1.1
+++ foo.info  22 May 2008 14:21:54 -0000
@@ -1,3 +1,4 @@
 // $Id: foo.info,v 1.1 2008/05/22 14:15:21 jvandyk Exp $
 name = Foo
+description = Sends badgers to those who use it.
 core = 6.x
```

Notice that the output shows the new line we added with a + character in front of it. Now let's go ahead and commit the change:

```
cvs commit -m "#1234567 by flyingpizza: Added missing description line."
```

The #1234567 in the commit message will be automatically changed to a hyperlink to `http://drupal.org/node/1234567` on commit logs viewable on `drupal.org` (e.g., at `http://drupal.org/cvs`).

■Tip Commit messages should be succinct but descriptive and should always give proper attribution to those who contributed. Include the node number of the issue and the name of the user who supplied a patch or was responsible for bringing this to your attention. That way, you can always cross-reference the discussion at node 1234567 on `drupal.org` from the CVS commit message. If you are in doubt about whether to include someone's username in the commit message, err on the side of generosity. It feels good to be given credit for the work you've done by pointing out or correcting a bug. Spread the love!

Excellent. Our development so far can be visualized in Figure 21-6.

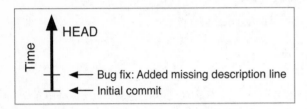

Figure 21-6. *Development of the foo module*

Viewing the History of a File

You can use the `cvs log` command to view the history of a file. Let's see the two commits that have happened to the `foo.info` file:

```
cvs log foo.info
```

```
----------------------------
revision 1.2
date: 2008-05-22 09:28:25 -0500;  author: jvandyk;  state: Exp;  lines: +2 -1;
  commitid: LYpsSr1ZkEut7Y3t;
"#1234567 by flyingpizza: Added missing description line.
----------------------------
revision 1.1
date: 2008-05-22 09:15:21 -0500;  author: jvandyk;  state: Exp;
  commitid: wcK48PdiMOyZ2Y3t;
Initial commit of foo.module. This module sends badgers to those who use it.
=============================================================================
```

Creating a Branch

Now we'll see how to create a branch for those poor sots who are still using Drupal 5.

■Caution Only create a branch for your module *after* you have created a project on `drupal.org` for your module.

First, you want to make sure you are using the latest version of HEAD:

```
cvs update -dP
```

Another way of checking is to issue the CVS status command. Let's check the status of our foo.info file:

```
cvs status foo.info
```

```
======================================================================
File: foo.info              Status: Up-to-date

   Working revision:    1.2    2008-05-22 09:28:25 -0500
   Repository revision:   1.2    / cvs/drupal-contrib/
contributions/modules/foo/foo.info,v
   Commit Identifier:     LYpsSr1ZkEut7Y3t
   Sticky Tag:         (none)
   Sticky Date:        (none)
   Sticky Options:     (none)
```

Notice that the status is listed as Up-to-date. That means that your local file is identical to the file in the repository. If you had changes in your local file that were not yet committed to the repository, or maybe some debugging code you forgot to remove, the status would read Locally Modified instead. Also, the value of the Sticky Tag field is (none), which confirms that you are using HEAD.

Creating a DRUPAL-5–Compatible Branch

Let's go ahead and create the branch:

```
cvs tag -b DRUPAL-5
```

Don't be confused by the use of the word tag. We're creating a branch, not a tag, as indicated by the -b option (for the purists out there: yes, a branch is a special kind of tag, but let's keep things simple here, OK?). After giving the command, the module development history with our brand new DRUPAL-5 branch looks like Figure 21-7.

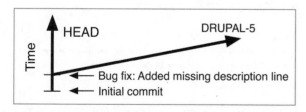

Figure 21-7. *Module development history after branching for Drupal 5*

Notice that the code is exactly the same in both branches at the moment, because we have not made any changes.

A creeping realization comes over you. Your module is dependent on the badger module being installed! Yet you haven't specified that in the `.info` file. Furthermore, Drupal 5 has a different syntax for describing dependencies than Drupal 6 and later. So let's add the Drupal 5 version to the DRUPAL-5 branch. But how do you determine what your local workspace contains? Are those files on your hard drive from the DRUPAL-5 branch or from HEAD? Let's specify that we want files from the DRUPAL-5 branch:

```
cvs update -dP -r DRUPAL-5
```

This says, "Give me the files from DRUPAL-5 branch, creating any new directories that are needed and pruning any empty directories that are no longer needed." Now let's change that `.info` file:

```
// $Id: foo.info,v 1.2 2008/05/22 14:28:25 jvandyk Exp $
name = Foo
description = Sends badgers to those who use it.
dependencies = badger
```

Let's view the changes:

```
cvs diff -up foo.info
```

```
===================================================================
RCS file: / cvs/drupal-contrib/contributions/modules/foo/foo.info,v
retrieving revision 1.2
diff -u -u -p -r1.2 foo.info
--- foo.info    22 May 2008 14:28:25 -0000   1.2
+++ foo.info    22 May 2008 16:40:53 -0000
@@ -1,4 +1,4 @@
 // $Id: foo.info,v 1.2 2008/05/22 14:28:25 jvandyk Exp $
 name = Foo
 description = Sends badgers to those who use it.
-core = 6.x
+dependencies = badger
```

Note that we removed the `core = 6.x` (since that's a Drupal 6 feature and we're putting this on the DRUPAL-5 branch), let's view the status:

```
cvs status foo.info
```

```
===================================================================
File: foo.info              Status: Locally Modified

   Working revision:    1.2    2008-05-22 09:28:25 -0500
   Repository revision:    1.2    / cvs/drupal-contrib/
contributions/modules/foo/foo.info,v
```

```
Commit Identifier:    LYpsSr1ZkEut7Y3t
Sticky Tag:    DRUPAL-5 (branch: 1.2.2)
Sticky Date:    (none)
Sticky Options:  (none)
```

Note the status is `Locally Modified` and the `Sticky Tag` field indicates that we are working with the `DRUPAL-5` branch.

Finally, let's commit the change:

```
cvs commit -m "Drupal-5-compatible dependency on badger module."
```

Figure 21-8 shows what our development history looks like now.

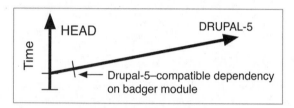

Figure 21-8. *Module development history after committing to the DRUPAL-5 branch*

Tagging and Creating a Release

Now the module is ready to go for Drupal 5. Let's go ahead and create a release. We'll do that by creating a tag.

■**Note** A tag is a label given to files that are in a specific state. When a user downloads the code that has been tagged, he or she will get the files in exactly the same state they were in when they were tagged. That is why tagging is useful to create a release.

Remember that a tag denotes a release. Since this is the first release of our code on the `DRUPAL-5` branch, we know that the tag needs to be `DRUPAL-5--1-0`. Figure 21-9 shows what that tag actually means.

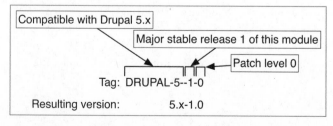

Figure 21-9. *Relationship between the tag name and resulting module version*

Before tagging, it's always wise to use `cvs status` to make sure that you're working with the set of files that you think you are. Then go ahead and create the tag:

```
cvs tag DRUPAL-5--1-0
```

Review the development history of your module, shown in Figure 21-10.

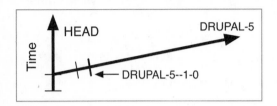

Figure 21-10. *Development history showing the tag on the DRUPAL-5 branch*

Creating a DRUPAL-6–Compatible Branch

You've created a branch for Drupal 5 and a tag on that branch. Now let's focus on Drupal 6 and add that dependency on the badger module. But first, there is a decision to be made. Should we branch immediately? Or should we simply use HEAD instead? We can create tags anywhere we like, so the question is, how useful is a DRUPAL-6 branch? Let's examine two different approaches.

Using HEAD for Releases

One approach for the new release is to edit the foo.info file on HEAD to add the dependency information. First, we need to get the files from HEAD into our local workspace, since we were working with files from the DRUPAL-5 branch. You would think that the following is what you need:

```
cvs update -dP -r HEAD
```

However, this will generate a sticky tag in your local workspace, and if you try to do a commit with the sticky tag set to HEAD, you will receive an error similar to this:

```
cvs commit: sticky tag `HEAD' for file `foo.info' is not a branch
cvs [commit aborted]: correct above errors first!
```

The solution is to use the following command, which resets sticky tags:

```
cvs update -A
```

Now, let's add the dependency information with the square bracket format that Drupal 6 uses:

```
// $Id: foo.info,v 1.2 2008/05/22 14:28:25 jvandyk Exp $
name = Foo
description = Sends badgers to those who use it.
dependencies[] = badger
core = 6.x
```

You can use `cvs diff` and `cvs status` to inspect the changes. Then commit the change:

```
cvs commit -m "Drupal-6-compatible dependency on badger module."
```

Figure 21-11 shows our latest change.

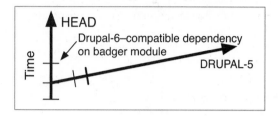

Figure 21-11. *Development history showing commit on HEAD*

As long as we are not doing any development for Drupal 7, we can keep things simple by just treating HEAD as the place where new development currently happens. That means one less branch to worry about. Fewer branches mean fewer places to commit bug fixes. Let's go ahead and make our first tag for Drupal 6. Since it's the first release that is compatible with the 6.x series of Drupal core, we call it DRUPAL-6--1-0:

```
cvs tag DRUPAL-6--1-0
```

This tag is created on HEAD, as shown in Figure 21-12.

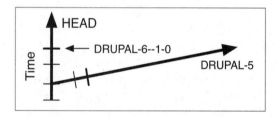

Figure 21-12. *A tag applied to the trunk of the CVS tree*

Suppose you continued updating the module and made several more commits and releases. Your development history would soon look like the one shown in Figure 21-13.

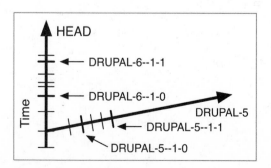

Figure 21-13. *Development using HEAD for Drupal 6 releases*

Creating a DRUPAL-6 Branch

When Drupal 7 comes out, you want to keep developing the module for Drupal 6. By now, your activity on the DRUPAL-5 branch has slowed to a crawl. But how are you going to develop for both Drupal 7 and Drupal 6 if all of your commits are happening on HEAD? It's time to create a branch for Drupal 6 and continue Drupal 6–specific development there. First, you want to make sure you are working with the latest version of HEAD. Then, create the branch for Drupal 6.

```
cvs update -A
cvs tag -b DRUPAL-6--1
```

Now your development history looks like Figure 21-14.

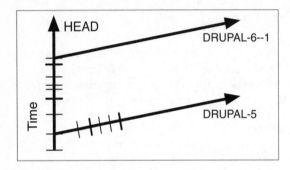

Figure 21-14. *Creating a branch for Drupal 6.*

Wait a minute! Why are we using DRUPAL-6--1 for the DRUPAL-6 branch instead of DRUPAL-6? The answer is simple: starting with Drupal 6, branch names are more specific about what they describe (see http://drupal.org/node/147493 for details). The tags that you will create along the DRUPAL-6 branch will be for the 6.x-1.x series of releases. That means releases that are compatible with any version of Drupal 6 and are in the first series of releases you do. Figure 21-15 shows tags that correspond to the 6.x-1.2 and 6.x-1.3 releases of your module; Figure 21-16 shows the releases that correspond with the tags.

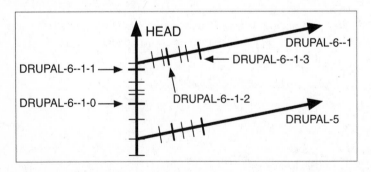

Figure 21-15. *The 6.x-1.x release series with tag names shown*

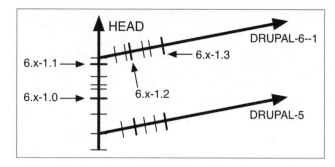

Figure 21-16. *The 6.x-1.x release series with release version numbers shown*

TAGS AND VERSION NUMBERS

There are two hyphens next to each other in branch names like DRUPAL-6--1 and tag names like DRUPAL-6--1-3. It is easy to think about this when you consider that the hyphen immediately after the 6 is a wildcard for a release of Drupal. That is, the DRUPAL-6--1-3 tag, which corresponds with the 6.x-1.3 release of your module, is compatible with any Drupal 6 release (Drupal 6.1, Drupal 6.2, Drupal 6.3, etc.). Think of the hyphen that follows the major version number in the tag name as translating to the x in the release number, as shown in the following illustration:

```
     Tag: DRUPAL - 6 - - 1 - 3
Module version:    6 . x - 1 . 3
```

Now that you have established a branch for Drupal 6, you can continue to use HEAD for Drupal 7 development—until Drupal 8 comes out, at which time, you'll create a branch for Drupal 7. Figure 21-17 shows how Drupal 7 development would look. Notice that this is exactly the same approach that we used previously when we started Drupal 6 development after creating the DRUPAL-5 branch.

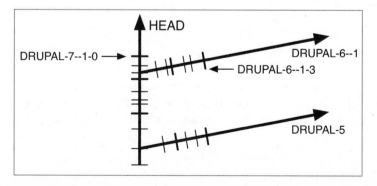

Figure 21-17. *Drupal 6 development on its own branch with Drupal 7 development on HEAD*

Advanced Branching

In the preceding examples, we have been assuming that only one major version of a module exists per major Drupal release, but that may not always be true. For example, suppose you've released version 6.x-1.3 of the foo module. Then inspiration strikes. You realize that a different approach will make the module faster with half as many lines of code. Yet, doing this will change the API so that modules that work with the foo module will all break. The solution is to release version 2.0 of your module with the new API. Since the module will still be compatible with Drupal 6, the tag you would use would be DRUPAL-6--2-0, and the corresponding release number would be 6.x-2.0.

You could just commit the code to the DRUPAL-6--1 branch and tell everyone that version 6.x-1.3 was the final release of the 1.x series of your module. But what happens if the security team finds a security hole in your module and you're forced to release a 6.x-1.4 version? No, using the DRUPAL-6--1 branch for the rewrite of your module is not a good idea.

The solution? Create a new branch on which you can release version 2.0 of your module. The branch will be called DRUPAL-6--2, and you can make it branch off of the existing DRUPAL-6--1 branch. First, make sure you have the latest versions of files from the DRUPAL-6--1 branch. Then make the new branch:

```
cvs update -dP -r DRUPAL-6--1
cvs tag -b DRUPAL-6--2
```

Your development history now looks like Figure 21-18.

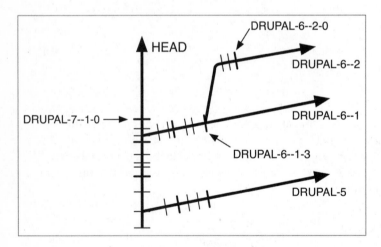

Figure 21-18. *Creating a branch off of an existing stable branch*

An alternative approach, if you are not yet doing any development for Drupal 7, would be to use HEAD for the development of your module's 2.0 release and eventually branch from HEAD (just like you did for the DRUPAL-6--1 branch) for your 2.0 series of releases. This approach is shown in Figure 21-19.

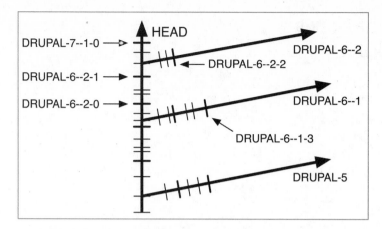

Figure 21-19. *Creating a branch off of HEAD for a second stable branch of a module supporting one major release of Drupal (Drupal 6)*

The approach you take is up to you. Generally, avoiding creating a new branch until you have to is most convenient. In Figure 21-19, the deciding factor as to when the DRUPAL-6--2 branch should be created is when development starts for Drupal 7. Without the DRUPAL-6--2 branch in place for development of the 2.0 series of the module to veer off onto, there would be no place on the CVS tree to do Drupal 7 development.

Creating a Release Node

In order for other people who are not as CVS savvy as you to download your module, you should create a release node on drupal.org. A release node provides information about a given release tag, and the packaging scripts on drupal.org will automatically build a tarball for you using the files indicated by that release tag. For example, you might create a release node for the DRUPAL-6--1-3 tag of your module. The packaging script would take the files from the DRUPAL-6--1 branch of your module exactly as they were when you created the DRUPAL-6--1-3 tag and create a tarball and a nice link so that visitors to drupal.org can download the tarball. The tarball would be called something like foo-6.x-1.3.tar.gz.

To create a release node, you go to the page of the project you created on http://drupal.org (see "Creating a Project on drupal.org") and click the "Add release" link. You then select the CVS tag that this release will represent and indicate whether the changes in this release are security updates, bug fixes, or new features.

In the body of the release node, the new capabilities of this particular release should be listed. Think of them as release notes. You should provide a list of issues addressed, preferably with links to the issues on drupal.org. Figure 21-20 shows a typical release node. A handy script at http://cvs.drupal.org/viewvc.py/drupal/contributions/tricks/cvs-release-notes can help you automatically generate the list of issues fixed.

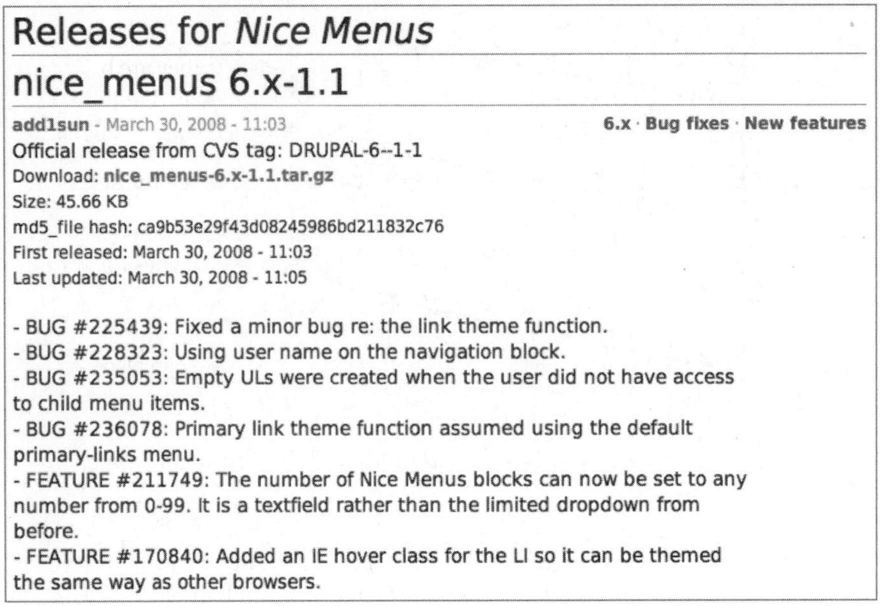

Releases for *Nice Menus*

nice_menus 6.x-1.1

add1sun - March 30, 2008 - 11:03   **6.x · Bug fixes · New features**
Official release from CVS tag: DRUPAL-6--1-1
Download: **nice_menus-6.x-1.1.tar.gz**
Size: 45.66 KB
md5_file hash: ca9b53e29f43d08245986bd211832c76
First released: March 30, 2008 - 11:03
Last updated: March 30, 2008 - 11:05

- BUG #225439: Fixed a minor bug re: the link theme function.
- BUG #228323: Using user name on the navigation block.
- BUG #235053: Empty ULs were created when the user did not have access
to child menu items.
- BUG #236078: Primary link theme function assumed using the default
primary-links menu.
- FEATURE #211749: The number of Nice Menus blocks can now be set to any
number from 0-99. It is a textfield rather than the limited dropdown from
before.
- FEATURE #170840: Added an IE hover class for the LI so it can be themed
the same way as other browsers.

Figure 21-20. *Release node for version 6.x-1.1 of the nice menus module*

Once a release node is created and the packaging script has run, the release node is added
to the project page, where anyone can download the tarball or read the release notes you have
entered, as shown in Figure 21-21.

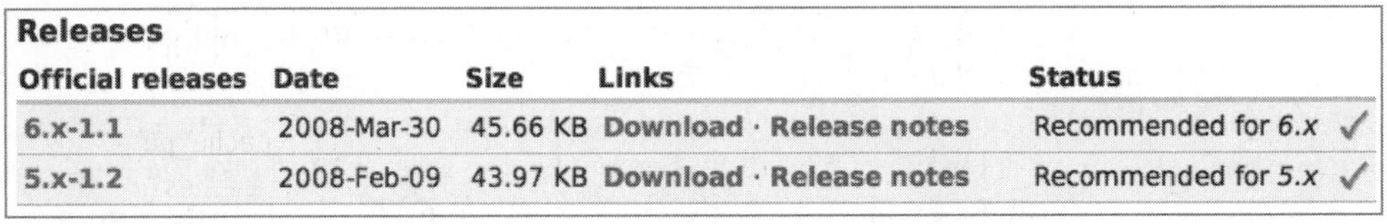

Releases

Official releases	Date	Size	Links		Status	
6.x-1.1	2008-Mar-30	45.66 KB	**Download · Release notes**		Recommended for *6.x*	✓
5.x-1.2	2008-Feb-09	43.97 KB	**Download · Release notes**		Recommended for *5.x*	✓

Figure 21-21. *Tarballs for releases are downloadable on the project page.*

Mixing SVN with CVS for Project Management

While the Drupal codebase is under CVS, the rest of your project may not be under any revision control at all or may be under a different revision control system.

A common practice is to use a second, nonconflicting revision control system such as
Subversion (SVN) and store the entire project (including Drupal and its CVS metadata!) in
its own repository. The idea is that you do a CVS update to Drupal (pulling changes from
cvs.drupal.org) and then turn around and do an SVN commit of those changes (which
pushes them into your SVN repository). You can use this SVN repository to store any custom modules, themes, images, or even the database schema for your project.

■**Note** More about Subversion can be found here: http://subversion.tigris.org.

Testing and Developing Code

Software tests are a way to isolate different parts of a program to determine if they are behaving as expected. Testing is a major goal for the next version of Drupal. In fact, testing is required for major changes in core as of Drupal 7. The benefits of testing include the following:

- Knowing instantly if code changes (e.g., through refactoring) have broken the software

- Automating the process of checking for errors in code. The automated test bed at `http://testing.drupal.org` is a project that aims to check incoming patches for core

- Ensuring that new code works as expected

For more information on testing, see `http://drupal.org/simpletest`. You can also become involved in the testing group at `http://groups.drupal.org/unit-testing`.

The devel Module

The devel module is a smorgasbord of developer utilities for debugging and inspecting bits and pieces of your code.

You can grab the module from `http://drupal.org/project/devel` (or do a CVS checkout and gain cool points). After it is installed, make sure the devel block is enabled. Here's a list of some of the more ambiguous links in the devel block and what each one does:

- *Empty cache*: This executes the `drupal_flush_all_caches()` function in `includes/common.inc`. This is the same thing that happens when you click the "Clear cached data" button at Administer ➤ Site configuration ➤ Performance. That is, CSS and JavaScript caches are flushed; the newly compressed CSS and JavaScript files are given new names to enforce download of the new files by clients; the theme registry is rebuilt; the menus are rebuilt; the `node_type` table is updated; and the database cache tables, which store page, menu, node, block, filter, and variable caches, are cleared. Specifically, the tables that are flushed are `cache`, `cache_block`, `cache_filter`, `cache_menu`, and `cache_page`. Any custom cache tables from modules that have implemented `hook_flush_caches()` (which returns an array of custom cache table names to clear) are flushed, too.

- *Enable Theme developer*: This link enables the theme developer module, which allows you to identify which template or theme function created a page element by pointing to it with your mouse (see Chapter 8).

- *Function reference*: This link supplies a list of user functions that have been defined during this request using PHP's `get_defined_functions()`. Click a function name to view its documentation.

- *Hook_elements()*: This link displays the results of calling `hook_elements()` in an easy-to-read format, which is useful when working with the form API.

- *Rebuild menus*: This one calls `menu_rebuild()`, which clears and then builds the `menu_router` table and updates the `menu_links` table (see Chapter 4).

- *Reinstall modules*: This link reinstalls a module by running hook_uninstall() and hook_install(). The schema version number will be set to the most recent update number. Make sure to first manually clear out any existing tables for modules that do not implement hook_uninstall().

- *Session viewer*: Use this link to display the contents of your $_SESSION variable.

- *Variable editor*: This link lists and allows you to edit the variables and their values currently stored in the variables table and the $conf array of your settings.php file. These variables are usually accessed with variable_get() and variable_set().

Displaying Queries

Head on over to http://example.com/?q=admin/settings/devel (or click "Devel settings" in the Development block if you have it enabled), and check the boxes next to "Collect query info" and "Display query log."

Once you save those settings, you'll see, at the bottom of each page, a list of all the queries that were used to generate the page you're on! What's more, the list tells you the function generating the query, the time it took to generate it, and how many times it was called.

You can use this information in many insightful ways. For example, if the same query is being called 40 times per page, you need to check for a bad control structure loop in your code. If that is fine, consider implementing a static variable to hold the database result for the duration of the request. Here's an example of what that design pattern might look like (taken from modules/taxonomy/taxonomy.module):

```
function taxonomy_get_term($tid) {
  // Define a static variable to hold data during this page request.
  static $terms = array();

  // Look in the static variable and only hit the database if the data
  // for this term ID has not already been retrieved.
  if (!isset($terms[$tid])) {
    $terms[$tid] = db_fetch_object(db_query('SELECT * FROM {term_data} WHERE tid =
      %d', $tid));
  }

  return $terms[$tid];
}
```

We create a static array to hold the result sets, so that if the query has already run, we've got the value and can return it rather than ask the database again.

Dealing with Time-Consuming Queries

Here's an example of how the devel module can help you speed up your site by identifying slow queries. Say you've written a custom node module called task, and you're making use of hook_load() to append extra information about task to the node object. The table schema follows:

```
CREATE TABLE task (
  nid int,
  vid int,
  percent_done int,
  PRIMARY KEY  (nid,vid),
  KEY nid (nid)
);
```

You notice that after running `devel.module` and looking at the query log that queries to the preceding table are bringing your site to a crawl! Note that queries that take more than 5 milliseconds are considered slow by default (you can change the value by going to Administer ➤ Site configuration ➤ Devel settings).

milliseconds	function	query
27.16	task_load	SELECT * FROM task WHERE vid = 3

So why is this query taking so long? If this were a more complex query with multiple table joins, we'd look into better ways of normalizing the data, but this is a very simple query. The first thing to do is use the `SQL EXPLAIN` syntax to see how the database is interpreting the query. When you precede a `SELECT` statement with the keyword `EXPLAIN`, the database will return information on the query execution plan:

```
EXPLAIN SELECT * FROM task WHERE vid = 3
```

MySQL gives the following report:

Id	select_type	table	type	possible_keys	key	key_len	ref	rows	Extra
1	SIMPLE	task	system	NULL	NULL	NULL	NULL	1	

The most important column in this case is the key column, which is NULL. This tells us that MySQL didn't use any primary keys, unique keys, or indexed keys to retrieve the result set; it had to look through every single row. So the best way to increase the speed of this query is to add a unique key to the `vid` column.

```
ALTER TABLE task ADD UNIQUE (vid);
```

You can find more information on MySQL's `EXPLAIN` reports here: http://dev.mysql.com/doc/refman/5.0/en/explain.html.

Other Uses for the devel Module

The devel module has other handy functions tucked away to increase your development acumen.

For example, you can switch the user that Drupal perceives is viewing the page in real time. This is useful for technical support and debugging other roles. To switch to another user, navigate to the URL http://example.com/?q=devel/switch/$uid, where $uid is the ID of the user you want to switch to. Alternatively, enable the "Switch user" block, which provides a set of links to do the same.

The devel module provides an additional block called Execute PHP that can be handy for entering and executing short snippets (and provides yet another reason for making sure the devel module is disabled on your production site!).

You can print out debug messages that are hidden from other users with the dpm(), dvm(), dpr(), and dvr() functions:

- dpm() prints a simple variable (e.g., a string or an integer) to the message area of the page. Think of it as meaning "debug print message."

- dvm() prints a var_dump() to the message area of the page. Use this for complex variables such as arrays or objects. Think of it as meaning "debug variable message."

- dpr() prints a complex variable (e.g., an array or object) at the top of a page using a special recursive function (dprint_r()) that gives nicely formatted output.

- dvr() prints a nicely formatted var_dump() to the top of the page.

The output of all of these functions is hidden from users who do not have "access devel information" permission, which comes in handy for real-time debugging.

An example usage follows:

```
dpr(node_load(5)); // Display the data structure of node 5.
dvr($user);        // Display the $user variable.
```

The Module Builder Module

There is a great module located at http://drupal.org/project/module_builder that makes it easy for you to build out the skeleton of your own modules. It asks you which hooks you want to create and creates them, along with example code. Then you can download the text and start building!

Application Profiling and Debugging

The following PHP debuggers and Integrated Development Environments (IDEs) offer some great tools for getting a sense of where Drupal's bottlenecks are; they also come in handy for discovering inefficient algorithms within your own modules:

- *Zend Studio IDE*: http://www.zend.com/

- *Komodo IDE*: http://www.activestate.com/Products/komodo_ide/

- *Eclipse IDE*: http://www.eclipse.org/

- *Xdebug PHP Extension*: http://www.xdebug.org/

In the following figures, we've used screenshots of Zend Studio (which arguably has the prettiest graphics), but the other IDEs can produce similar output. Figure 21-22 shows the graphical output from a Drupal request that was run through an application profiler. The results show the relative times spent in functions from each file. In this case, it looks like Drupal spent about half the time in includes/bootstrap.inc.

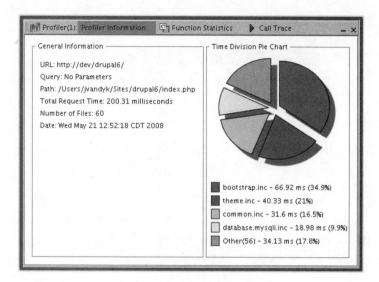

Figure 21-22. *Time division pie chart of a Drupal request in the Zend IDE*

In Figures 21-23 and 21-24, we drill down to see which functions consume the most relative processor time during a request. Such a feature is handy to determine where to focus your optimization efforts.

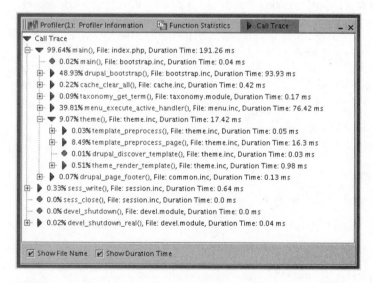

Figure 21-23. *Call trace of a Drupal request within the Zend IDE*

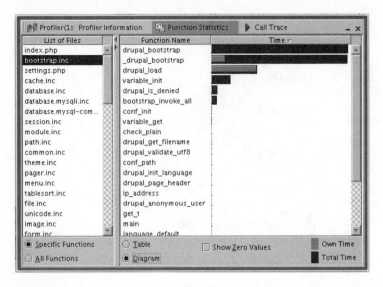

Figure 21-24. *Function statistics of a Drupal request within the Zend IDE*

Real-time debugging is a feature of PHP and not Drupal, but it's worth covering, since you can easily be identified as a Drupal ninja if a real-time debugger is running on your laptop.

Using a PHP debugger lets you pause the code execution of PHP in real time (i.e., set a breakpoint) and inspect what is happening step by step. Getting familiar with a PHP debugger is one of the best investments in your craft as a developer. Stepping through code execution frame by frame, like a movie in slow motion, is a great way to debug and become intimately familiar with a beast as complex as Drupal at the same time.

A rite of passage that budding Drupal developers go through is to grab a cup of tea, fire up the debugger, and spend a couple hours going through a standard Drupal request step by step, gaining invaluable first-hand knowledge of how Drupal works.

Summary

After reading this chapter, you should be able to

- Code according to Drupal coding conventions.

- Document your code so that your comments can be reused by the API module.

- Comfortably search through Drupal's codebase using egrep.

- Download Drupal and keep it updated using version control.

- Cleanly hack the Drupal core.

- Generate patches showing code changes using unified `diff` format.

- Apply patches that others have made.

- Maintain a contributed module using tagging and branching.

- Use `devel.module` to enhance your coding productivity.

- Identify Drupal coding ninjas by their best practices.

CHAPTER 22

■ ■ ■

Optimizing Drupal

Drupal's core architecture is lean and written for flexibility. However, the flexibility comes at a price. As the number of modules increases, the complexity of serving a request increases. That means the server has to work harder, and strategies must be implemented to keep Drupal's legendary snappiness while a site increases in popularity. Properly configured, Drupal can easily survive a Slashdotting. In this chapter, we'll talk about both performance and scalability. *Performance* is how quickly your site responds to a request. *Scalability* has to do with how many simultaneous requests your system can handle and is usually measured in requests per second.

Finding the Bottleneck

If your web site is not performing as well as expected, the first step is to analyze where the problem lies. Possibilities include the web server, the operating system, the database, and the network.

Initial Investigation

Knowing how to evaluate the performance and scalability of a system allows you to quickly isolate and respond to system bottlenecks with confidence, even amid a crisis. You can discover where bottlenecks lie with a few simple tools and by asking questions along the way. Here's one way to approach a badly performing server. We begin with the knowledge that performance is going to be bound by one of the following variables: CPU, RAM, I/O, or bandwidth. So begin by asking yourself the following questions:

Is the CPU maxed out? If examining CPU usage with top on Unix or the Task Manager on Windows shows CPU(s) at 100 percent, your mission is to find out what's causing all that processing. Looking at the process list will let you know whether it's the web server or the database eating up processor cycles. Both of these problems are solvable.

Has the server run out of RAM? This can be checked easily with top on Unix or the Task Manager on Windows. If the server has plenty of free memory, go on to the next question. If the server is out of RAM, you must figure out why.

Are the disks maxed out? If examining the disk subsystem with a tool like vmstat on Unix or the Performance Monitor on Windows shows that disk activity cannot keep up with the demands of the system while plenty of free RAM remains, you've got an I/O problem. Possibilities include excessively verbose logging, an improperly configured database that is creating many temporary tables on disk, background script execution, improper use of a RAID level for a write-heavy application, and so on.

Is the network link saturated? If the network pipe is filled up, there are only two solutions. One is to get a bigger pipe. The other is to send less information while making sure the information that is being sent is properly compressed.

■**Tip** Investigating your page serving performance from outside your server is also useful. A tool like YSlow (http://developer.yahoo.com/yslow/help/) can be helpful when pinpointing why your pages are not downloading as quickly as you'd like when you haven't yet hit a wall with CPU, RAM, or I/O. A helpful article on YSlow and Drupal can be found at http://wimleers.com/article/improving-drupals-page-loading-performance.

Web Server Running Out of CPU

If your CPU is maxed out and the process list shows that the resources are being consumed by the web server and not the database (which is covered later), you should look into reducing the web server overhead incurred to serve a request. Often the execution of PHP code is the culprit.

PHP Optimizations

Because PHP code execution is a big part of serving a request in Drupal, it's important to know what can be done to speed up this process. Significant performance gains can be made by caching PHP operation codes (opcodes) after compilation and by profiling the application layer to identify inefficient algorithms.

Operation Code Caching

There are two ways to reduce the CPU resources used to execute PHP code. Obviously, one is to reduce the amount of code by disabling unnecessary Drupal modules and writing efficient code. The other is to use an opcode cache. PHP parses and compiles all code into an intermediate form consisting of a sequence of opcodes on every request. Adding an opcode cache lets PHP reuse its previously compiled code, so the parsing and compilation are skipped. Common opcode caches are Alternative PHP Cache (http://pecl.php.net/package/APC), eAccelerator (http://eaccelerator.net), XCache (http://xcache.lighttpd.net/), and Zend Platform (http://zend.com). Zend is a commercial product while the others are freely available. The interface for APC is shown in Figure 22-1.

Because Drupal is a database-intensive program, an opcode cache should not be regarded as a single solution but as part of an integrated strategy. Still, it can give significant performance gains for minimal effort.

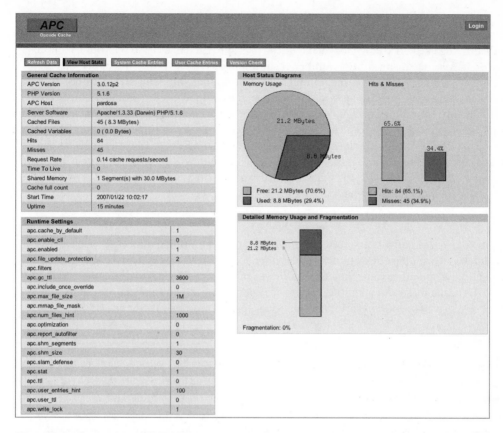

Figure 22-1. *Alternative PHP Cache (APC) comes with an interface that displays memory allocation and the files currently within the cache.*

Application Profiling

Often custom code and modules that have performed reasonably well for small-scale sites can become a bottleneck when moved into production. CPU-intensive code loops, memory-hungry algorithms, and large database retrievals can be identified by profiling your code to determine where PHP is spending most of its time and thus where you ought to spend most of your time debugging. See Chapter 21 for more information on PHP debuggers and profilers.

If, even after adding an opcode cache and optimizing your code, your web server cannot handle the load, it is time to get a beefier box with more or faster CPUs or to move to a different architecture with multiple web server frontends.

Web Server Running Out of RAM

The RAM footprint of the web server process serving the request includes all of the modules loaded by the web server (such as Apache's `mod_mime`, `mod_rewrite`, etc.) as well as the memory used by the PHP interpreter. The more web server and Drupal modules that are enabled, the more RAM used per request.

Because RAM is a finite resource, you should determine how much is being used on each request and how many requests your web server is configured to handle. To see how much real RAM is being used on average for each request, use a program like `top` to see your list of processes. In Apache, the maximum number of simultaneous requests that will be served is set using the `MaxClients` directive. A common mistake is thinking the solution to a saturated web server is to increase the value of `MaxClients`. This only complicates the problem, since you'll be hit by too many requests at once. That means RAM will be exhausted, and your server will start disk swapping and become unresponsive. Let's assume, for example, that your web server has 2GB of RAM and each Apache request is using roughly 20MB (you can check the actual value by using `top` on Unix or Task Manager on Windows). You can calculate a good value for `MaxClients` by using the following formula; keep in mind the fact that you will need to reserve memory for your operating system and other processes:

```
2GB RAM / 20MB per process = 100 MaxClients
```

If your server consistently runs out of RAM even after disabling unneeded web server modules and profiling any custom modules or code, your next step is to make sure the database and the operating system are not the causes of the bottleneck. If they are, then add more RAM. If the database and operating system are not causing the bottlenecks, you simply have more requests than you can serve; the solution is to add more web server boxes.

■**Tip** Since memory usage of Apache processes tends to increase to the level of the most memory-hungry page served by that child process, memory can be regained by setting the `MaxRequestsPerChild` value to a low number, such as 300 (the actual number will depend on your situation). Apache will work a little harder to generate new children, but the new children will use less RAM than the older ones they replace, so you can serve more requests in less RAM. The default setting for `MaxRequestsPerChild` is 0, meaning the processes will never expire.

Other Web Server Optimizations

There are a few other things that you can do to make your web server run more efficiently.

Apache Optimizations

Apache is the most common web server used with Drupal, and it can be tweaked to provide better performance. The following sections will suggest some approaches to try.

mod_expires

This Apache module will let Drupal send out `Expires` HTTP headers, caching all static files in the user's browser for two weeks or until a newer version of a file exists. This goes for all images, CSS and JavaScript files, and other static files. The end result is reduced bandwidth and less traffic for the web server to negotiate. Drupal is preconfigured to work with `mod_expires` and will use it if it is available. The settings for `mod_expires` are found in Drupal's `.htaccess` file.

```
# Requires mod_expires to be enabled.
<IfModule mod_expires.c>
  # Enable expirations.
  ExpiresActive On

  # Cache all files for 2 weeks after access (A).
  ExpiresDefault A1209600

  # Do not cache dynamically generated pages.
  ExpiresByType text/html A1
</IfModule>
```

We can't let mod_expires cache HTML content, because the HTML content Drupal produces is not always static. This is the reason Drupal has its own internal caching system for its HTML output (i.e., page caching).

Moving Directives from .htaccess to httpd.conf

Drupal ships with two .htaccess files: one is at the Drupal root, and the other is automatically generated after you create your directory to store uploaded files and visit Administer ➤ "File system" to tell Drupal where the directory is. Any .htaccess files are searched for, read, and parsed on every request. In contrast, httpd.conf is only read when Apache is started. Apache directives can live in either file. If you have control of your own server, you should move the contents of the .htaccess files to the main Apache configuration file (httpd.conf) and disable .htaccess lookups within your web server root by setting AllowOverride to None:

```
<Directory />
  AllowOverride None
  ...
</Directory>
```

This prevents Apache from traversing up the directory tree of every request looking for the .htaccess file to execute. Apache will then have to do less work for each request, giving it more time to serve more requests.

Other Web Servers

Another option is to use a web server other than Apache. Benchmarks have shown that, for example, the lighttpd web server generally serves more requests per second for Drupal. See http://buytaert.net/drupal-webserver-configurations-compared for more detailed comparisons.

Database Bottlenecks

Drupal does a lot of work in the database, especially for authenticated users and custom modules. It is common for the database to be the cause of the bottleneck. Here are some basic strategies for optimizing Drupal's use of the database.

Enabling MySQL's Query Cache

MySQL is the most common database used with Drupal. MySQL has the ability to cache frequent queries in RAM so that the next time a given query is issued, MySQL will return it instantly from the cache. However, in most MySQL installations, this feature is *disabled by default*. To enable it, add the following lines to your MySQL option file; the file is named my.cnf and specifies the variables and behavior for your MySQL server (see http://dev. mysql.com/doc/refman/5.1/en/option-files.html). In this case, we're setting the query cache to 64MB:

```
# The MySQL server
[mysqld]
query_cache_size=64M
```

The current query cache size can be viewed as output of MySQL's SHOW VARIABLES command:

```
mysql>SHOW VARIABLES LIKE 'query_cache%';
```

```
...
| query_cache_size              | 67108864
| query_cache_type              | ON
...
```

Experimenting with the size of the query cache is usually necessary. Too small a cache means cached queries will be invalidated too often. Too large a cache means a cache search may take a relatively long time; also, the RAM used for the cache may be better used for other things, like more web server processes, memcache, or the operating system's file cache.

■**Tip** In Drupal, visit Administer ➤ Reports ➤ "Status report," and click the MySQL version number to get a quick overview of the values of some of the more important MySQL variables. You can also check if the query cache is enabled from that page.

Identifying Expensive Queries

If you need to get a sense of what is happening when a given page is generated, devel.module is invaluable. It has an option to display all the queries that are required to generate the page along with the execution time of each query. See Chapter 21 for details on how to use devel. module to identify and optimize database queries using the EXPLAIN syntax.

Another way to find out which queries are taking too long is to enable slow query logging in MySQL. This is done in the MySQL option file (my.cnf) as follows:

```
# The MySQL server
[mysqld]
log-slow-queries
```

This will log all queries that take longer than 10 seconds to a log file at `example.com-slow.log` in MySQL's data directory. You can change the number of seconds and the log location as shown in this code, where we set the slow query threshold to 5 seconds and the filename to `example-slow.log`:

```
# The MySQL server
[mysqld]
long_query_time = 5
log-slow-queries = /var/log/mysql/example-slow.log
```

Identifying Expensive Pages

To find out which pages are the most resource intensive, enable the statistics module that is included with Drupal. Although the statistics module increases the load on your server (since it records access statistics for your site into your database), it can be useful to see which pages are the most frequently viewed and thus the most ripe for query optimization. It also tracks total page generation time over a period, which you can specify in Administer ➤ Reports ➤ "Access log settings." This is useful for identifying out-of-control web crawlers that are eating up system resources, which you can then ban on the spot by visiting Administer ➤ Reports ➤ "Top visitors" and clicking "ban." Be careful though—it's just as easy to ban a good crawler that drives traffic to your site as a bad one. Make sure you investigate the origin of the crawler before banning it.

Identifying Expensive Code

Consider the following resource-hogging code:

```
// Very expensive, silly way to get node titles. First we get the node IDs
// of all published nodes.
$sql = "SELECT n.nid FROM {node} n WHERE n.status = 1";

// We wrap our node query in db_rewrite_sql() so that node access is respected.
$result = db_rewrite_sql(db_query($sql));

// Now we do a node_load() on each individual node.
while ($data = db_fetch_object($result)) {
  $node = node_load($data->nid);
  // And save the titles.
  $titles[$node->nid] = check_plain($node->title);
}
```

Fully loading a node is an expensive operation: hooks run, modules perform database queries to add or modify the node, and memory is used to cache the node in `node_load()`'s internal cache. If you are not depending on modification to the node by a module, it's much faster to do your own query of the node table directly. Certainly this is a contrived example, but the same pattern can often be found, that is, often data is retrieved via multiple queries that could be combined into a single query, or needless node loading is performed.

■Tip Drupal has an internal caching mechanism (using a static variable) when a node is loaded more than once per request. For example, if node_load(1) was called, node number 1 is fully loaded and cached. When another call to node_load(1) is made during the same web request, Drupal will return the cached results for the previously loaded node having the same node ID.

Optimizing Tables

SQL slowness can result from poor implementation of SQL tables in contributed modules. For example, columns without indices may result in slow queries. A quick way to see how queries are executed by MySQL is to take one of the queries you've captured in your slow query log, prepend the word EXPLAIN to it, and issue the query to MySQL. The result will be a table showing which indices were used. Consult a good book on MySQL for details.

Caching Queries Manually

If you have very expensive queries that must be performed, perhaps the results can be manually cached by your module. See Chapter 15 for details on Drupal's cache API.

Changing the Table Type from MyISAM to InnoDB

Two common choices for MySQL storage engines, often called *table types*, are MyISAM and InnoDB. Drupal uses MyISAM by default.

MyISAM uses table-level locking, while InnoDB uses row-level locking. *Locking* is important to preserve database integrity; it prevents two database processes from trying to update the same data at the same time. In practice, the difference in locking strategies means that access to an entire table is blocked during writes for MyISAM. Therefore, on a busy Drupal site when many comments are being added, all comment reads are blocked while a new comment is inserted. On InnoDB, this is less of a problem, since only the row(s) being written get locked, allowing other server threads to continue to operate on the remaining rows. However, with MyISAM, table reads are faster, and data maintenance and recovery tools are more mature. See http://dev.mysql.com/tech-resources/articles/storage-engine/part_1.html or http://dev.mysql.com/doc/refman/5.1/en/storage-engines.html for more information on MySQL's table storage architectures.

To test whether table-locking issues are the cause of slow performance, you can analyze lock contention by checking the Table_locks_immediate and Table_locks_waited status variables within MySQL.

```
mysql> SHOW STATUS LIKE 'Table%';
```

```
+-----------------------+---------+
| Variable_name         | Value   |
+-----------------------+---------+
| Table_locks_immediate | 1151552 |
| Table_locks_waited    | 15324   |
+-----------------------+---------+
```

Table_locks_immediate is the number of times that a table lock was acquired immediately, and Table_locks_waited is the number of times a table lock could not be acquired immediately and a wait was needed. If the Table_locks_waited value is high, and you are having performance problems, you may want to split up large tables; for example, you might create a dedicated cache table for a custom module or consider ways to reduce the sizes or the frequency of the table lock commands. One way to reduce table sizes for some tables, such as the cache_*, watchdog, and accesslog tables, is by reducing the lifetime of the data. This can be done within the Drupal administrative interface. Also, making sure cron is being run as often as once an hour will keep these tables pruned.

Because Drupal can be used in many different ways, it is impossible to give an across-the-board recommendation as to which tables should use which engine. However, in general, good candidates for conversion to InnoDB are the cache, watchdog, sessions, and accesslog tables. Fortunately, the conversion to InnoDB is very simple:

```
ALTER TABLE accesslog TYPE='InnoDB';
```

Of course, this conversion should be done when the site is offline and your data has been backed up, and you should be informed about the different characteristics of InnoDB tables.

■**Note** Drupal 6 does not use the LOCK TABLES command in core code, though the database API offers the db_lock_table() and db_unlock_tables() functions for contributed modules that need them.

For MySQL performance tuning, check out the performance tuning script at http://www.day32.com/MySQL/, which provides suggestions for tuning MySQL server variables.

Memcached

Often the system takes a performance hit when data must be moved to or from a slower device such as a hard disk drive. What if you could bypass this operation entirely for data that you could afford to lose (like session data)? Enter memcached, a system that reads and writes to memory. Memcached is more complicated to set up than other solutions proposed in this chapter, but it is worth talking about when scalability enhancements are needed in your system.

Drupal has a built-in database cache to cache pages, menus, and other Drupal data, and the MySQL database is capable of caching common queries, but what if your database is straining under the load? You could buy another database server, or you could take the load off of the database altogether by storing some things directly in memory instead of in the database. The memcached library (see http://www.danga.com/memcached/) and the PECL Memcache PHP extension (see http://pecl.php.net/package/memcache) are just the tools to do this for you.

The memcached system saves arbitrary data in random access memory and serves the data as fast as possible. This type of delivery will perform better than anything that depends on hard disk access. Memcached stores objects and references them with a unique key for each object. It is up to the programmer to determine what objects to put into memcached.

Memcached knows nothing about the type or nature of what is put into it; to its eyes, it is all a pile of bits with keys for retrieval.

The simplicity of the system is its advantage. When writing code for Drupal to leverage memcached, developers can decide to cache whatever is seen as the biggest cause of bottlenecks. This might be the results of database queries that get run very often, such as path lookups, or even complex constructions such as fully built nodes and taxonomy vocabularies, both of which require many database queries and generous PHP processing to produce.

A memcache module for Drupal and a Drupal-specific API for working with the PECL Memcache interface can be found at `http://drupal.org/project/memcache`.

Drupal-Specific Optimizations

While most optimizations to Drupal are done within other layers of the software stack, there are a few buttons and levers within Drupal itself that yield significant performance gains.

Page Caching

Sometimes, it's the easy things that are overlooked, which is why they're worth mentioning again. Drupal has a built-in way to reduce the load on the database by storing and sending compressed cached pages requested by anonymous users. By enabling the cache, you are effectively reducing pages to a single database query rather than the many queries that might have been executed otherwise. Drupal caching is disabled by default and can be configured at Administer ➤ Site configuration ➤ Performance. For more information, see Chapter 15.

Bandwidth Optimization

There is another performance optimization on the Administer ➤ Site configuration ➤ Performance page to reduce the number of requests made to the server. By enabling the "Optimize CSS files" feature, Drupal takes the CSS files created by modules, compresses them, and rolls them into a single file inside a `css` directory in your "File system path." The "Optimize JavaScript files" feature concatenates multiple JavaScript files into one and places that file inside a `js` directory in your "File system path." This reduces the number of HTTP requests per page and the overall size of the downloaded page.

When storing a page in the page cache, Drupal will check if page compression is enabled. This feature is enabled by default and can be disabled at Administer ➤ Site configuration ➤ Performance. When enabled, Drupal checks for the presence of the `zlib` extension for PHP and uses `gzencode($data, 9, FORCE_GZIP)` to compress the page before storing it in the cache. When the page is retrieved from the cache, Drupal determines if the browser supports `gzip` encoding, and if it does, it simply hands over the cached, compressed page. Otherwise, the cached data is unzipped using `gzinflate()` before being sent. See `drupal_page_cache_header()` in `includes/bootstrap.inc` for details.

Pruning the Sessions Table

Drupal stores user sessions in its database rather than in files (see Chapter 16). This makes Drupal easier to set up across multiple machines, but it also adds overhead to the database for managing each user's session information. If a site is getting tens of thousands of visitors a day, it's easy to see how quickly this table can become very large.

PHP gives you control over how often it should prune old session entries. Drupal has exposed this configuration in its `settings.php` file.

```
ini_set('session.gc_maxlifetime',   200000); // 55 hours (in seconds)
```

The default setting for the garbage collection system to run is a little over two days. This means that if a user doesn't log in for two days, their session will be removed. If your `sessions` table is growing unwieldy, you'll want to increase the frequency of PHP's session garbage collection.

```
ini_set('session.gc_maxlifetime',   86400); // 24 hours (in seconds)
ini_set('session.cache_expire',     1440); // 24 hours (in minutes)
```

When adjusting `session.gc_maxlifetime`, it also makes sense to use the same value for `session.cache_expire`, which controls the time to live for cached session pages. Note that the `session.cache_expire` value is in minutes.

Managing the Traffic of Authenticated Users

Since Drupal can serve cached pages to anonymous users, and anonymous users don't normally require the interactive components of Drupal, you may want to reduce the length of time users stay logged in or, crazier yet, log them out after they close their browser windows. This is done by adjusting the cookie lifetime within the `settings.php` file. In the following line, we change the value to 24 hours:

```
ini_set('session.cookie_lifetime',   86400); // 24 hours (in seconds)
```

And here we log users out when they close the browser:

```
ini_set('session.cookie_lifetime',   0); // When they close the browser.
```

The default value in `settings.php` (2,000,000 seconds) allows a user to stay logged in for just over three weeks (provided session garbage collection hasn't removed their session row from the `sessions` database).

Pruning Error Reporting Logs

Drupal offers module developers the `watchdog()` function, which writes information to a log. Built-in support is available for logging to the database and to syslog.

Severity Levels

The severity levels to be used by PHP code that calls `watchdog()` are compliant with RFC 3164 and are shown in Table 22-1.

Table 22-1. *Constants and Severity Levels for Drupal's Watchdog System*

Drupal Constant	Integer	Severity Level
WATCHDOG_EMERG	0	Emergency: system is unusable
WATCHDOG_ALERT	1	Alert: action must be taken immediately
WATCHDOG_CRITICAL	2	Critical: critical conditions
WATCHDOG_ERROR	3	Error: error conditions
WATCHDOG_WARNING	4	Warning: warning conditions
WATCHDOG_NOTICE	5	Notice: normal but significant condition
WATCHDOG_INFO	6	Informational: informational messages
WATCHDOG_DEBUG	7	Debug: debug-level messages

Logging to the Database

Drupal ships with the Database logging module enabled by default. Entries can be viewed at Administer ➤ Reports ➤ Recent log entries. The watchdog table in the database, which contains the entries, can bloat fairly quickly if it isn't regularly pruned. If you find that the size of the watchdog table is slowing your site down, you can keep it lean and mean by adjusting the settings found at Administer ➤ Site configuration ➤ Logging and alerts ➤ Database logging. Note that changes to this setting will take effect when cron runs the next time. Not running cron regularly will allow the watchdog table to grow endlessly, causing significant overhead.

Logging to Syslog

The syslog module, which ships with Drupal core but is disabled by default, writes calls to watchdog() to the operating system log using PHP's syslog() function. This approach eliminates the database inserts required by the Database logging module.

Running cron

Even though it's step seven of Drupal's installation instructions, setting up cron is often overlooked, and this oversight can bring a site to its knees. By not running cron on a Drupal site, the database fills up with log messages, stale cache entries, and other statistical data that is otherwise regularly wiped from the system. It's a good practice to configure cron early on as part of the normal install process. See step seven of Drupal's INSTALL.txt file for more information on setting up cron.

■**Tip** If you are in a critical situation where cron has never been run on a high-traffic site or it simply hasn't been run often enough, you can perform some of what cron does manually. You can empty the cache tables (TRUNCATE TABLE 'cache', TRUNCATE TABLE 'cache_filter', and TRUNCATE TABLE 'cache_page') at any time, and they will be rebuilt automatically. Also, in a pinch, you can empty the watchdog and sessions tables to try to regain control of a runaway Drupal site. The implications of removing watchdog entries are that you'll lose any error messages that might indicate problems with the site. If you are concerned about holding on to this data, you can do a database dump of the watchdog table before truncating it. Truncating the sessions table will log out currently logged in users.

Automatic Throttling

Drupal includes a module called throttle.module as part of the core distribution. This module measures site load by sampling the number of current users and by turning off functionality if the sampling indicates that the threshold set by the administrator has been reached. It's a good idea to turn on this module when you configure a site, so you'll be ready when a page on the site makes the headlines and the masses pummel your server. The throttle module is not a panacea, however. It takes a good deal of overhead to actually perform the throttling. Other solutions, such as using memcached, should also be investigated.

Enabling the Throttle Module

When you enable the throttle module, you'll notice that an extra series of check boxes appears on the module administration page. That is, in addition to selecting whether a module is enabled, you can also select whether it will be throttled. *Being throttled* means that when module_list() returns a list of which modules are enabled and the throttle is on because of high traffic, that module will not be included; throttled modules are effectively disabled.

Obviously, you'll need to carefully choose which modules you wish to throttle. Good candidates are modules that do something nonessential but take up CPU time or perform many database queries. Core modules cannot be throttled (because they're necessary for Drupal to run correctly) but may understand throttling and offer their own options for reducing processing time when the site is being throttled. For example, the block module cannot be throttled, but individual blocks can be throttled, as shown in Figure 22-2.

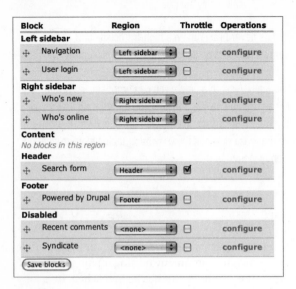

Figure 22-2. *When under a heavy load, this site will not display the search form in the header or the "Who's new" and "Who's online" blocks in the right sidebar, but it will always display the Navigation and "User login" blocks in the left sidebar and the "Powered by Drupal" block in the footer.*

Configuring the Throttle Module

In order for the throttle mechanism to kick in, you'll have to give it a threshold and a sampling frequency. When the throttle module is enabled, the thresholds can be set at Administer ➤ Site configuration ➤ Throttle.

Setting Thresholds

Two thresholds can be entered: the number of anonymous users at which throttling will begin and the number of authenticated users at which throttling will begin. Since anonymous users take fewer resources than authenticated users, the threshold for anonymous users should be higher. The actual values will depend on your individual site.

The number of users must be measured against a given time period. This time period is set in the "Who's online" block settings and stored as the Drupal variable `user_block_seconds_online`. If it has not been set, it defaults to 900 seconds (15 minutes), as shown in Figure 22-3.

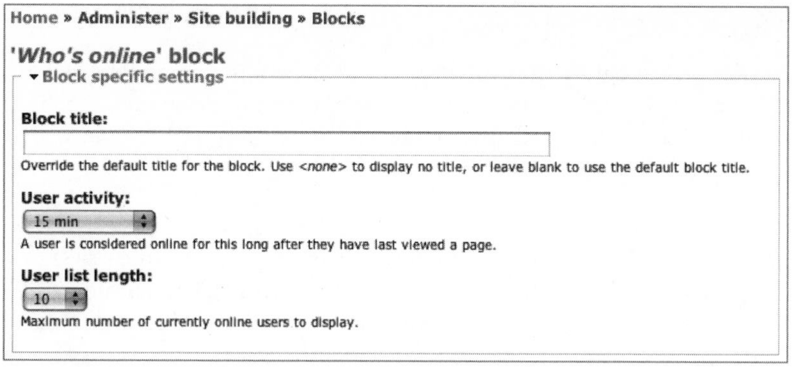

Home » Administer » Site building » Blocks

'*Who's online*' block
▾ Block specific settings

Block title:

Override the default title for the block. Use *<none>* to display no title, or leave blank to use the default block title.

User activity:
15 min ⬍
A user is considered online for this long after they have last viewed a page.

User list length:
10 ⬍
Maximum number of currently online users to display.

Figure 22-3. *The time period after a user's last visit during which a user is still considered "online" is determined by the User activity field in the "Who's online" block settings.*

Setting Sampling Frequency

To determine the load on the site to see if the throttle mechanism should be on or off, the throttle module must query the database. This puts additional load on the database server. The frequency of these checks (actually the probability that a check will occur on a given request) is set using the "Auto-throttle probability limiter" setting. For example, choosing the value 20 percent would sample on about 1 out of every 5 requests.

Making Modules and Themes Throttle-Aware

The throttle mechanism is either on or off. When writing your own modules and themes, you can respond to the throttle status, for example:

```
// Get throttle status.
// We use module_invoke() instead of calling throttle_status() directly
// so this will still work when throttle.module is disabled.
$throttle = module_invoke('throttle', 'status');

if (!$throttle) {
  // Throttle is off.
  // Do nonessential CPU-intensive task here.
}
```

■Tip If you have large media files that are nonessential but being served as part of your theme, you could use throttling to temporarily stop serving these files, decreasing the amount of bandwidth used when your web site is being hammered.

Architectures

The architectures available for Drupal are those of other LAMP-stack software, and the techniques used to scale are applicable to Drupal as well. Thus, we'll concentrate on the Drupal-specific tips and gotchas for different architectures.

Single Server

This is the simplest architecture. The web server and the database run on the same server. The server may be a shared host or a dedicated host. Although many small Drupal sites run happily on shared hosting, serious web hosting that expects to scale should take place on a dedicated host.

With single-server architecture, configuration is simple, as everything is still done on one server. Likewise, communication between the web server and the database is fast, because there is no latency incurred by moving data over a network. Clearly, it's advantageous to have a multicore processor, so the web server and database don't need to jockey as much for processor time.

Separate Database Server

If the database is your bottleneck, a separate and powerful database server may be what you need. Some performance will be lost because of the overhead of sending requests through a network, but scalability will improve.

■**Note** Any time you are working with multiple servers, you'll want to be sure that they are connected via a fast local network.

Separate Database Server and a Web Server Cluster

Multiple web servers provide failover and can handle more traffic. The minimum number of computers needed for a cluster is two web servers. Additionally, you need a way to switch traffic between the machines. Should one of the machines stop responding, the rest of the cluster should be able to handle the load.

Load Balancing

Load balancers distribute web traffic among web servers. There are other kinds of load balancers for distributing other resources such as a hard disks and databases, but here, I'm just talking about distributing HTTP requests. In the case of multiple web servers, load balancers allow web services to continue in the face of one web server's downtime or maintenance.

There are two broad categories of load balancers. Software load balancers are cheaper or even free but tend to have more ongoing maintenance and administrative costs than hardware load balancers. Linux Virtual Server (http://www.linuxvirtualserver.org/) is one of the most popular Linux load balancers. Hardware load balancers are expensive, since they contain more advanced server switching algorithms, and tend to be more reliable than software-based solutions.

In addition to load balancing, multiple web servers introduce several complications, primarily file uploading and keeping the codebase consistent across servers.

File Uploads and Synchronization

When Drupal is run on a single web server, uploaded files are typically stored in Drupal's files directory. The location is configurable at Administer ➤ Site configuration ➤ File system. With multiple web servers, the following scenario must be avoided:

1. A user uploads a file on web server A; the database is updated to reflect this.

2. A user views a page on web server B that references the new file. File not found!

Clearly, the answer is to make the file appear on web server B also. There are several approaches.

Using rsync

The rsync program is a utility that synchronizes two directories by copying only the files that have changed. For more information, see http://samba.anu.edu.au/rsync/. The disadvantage of this approach is the delay that synchronization incurs, as well as having duplicate copies (and thus storage costs) of all uploaded files.

■**Tip** If you have many files and are doing regularly scheduled rsync synchronizations, it might make sense to do a conditional synchronization by checking the file and upload tables and skipping the synchronization if they are unchanged.

Using a Shared, Mounted File System

Rather than synchronize multiple web servers, you can deploy a shared, mounted file system, which stores files in a single location on a file server. The web servers can then mount the file server using a protocol like Network File System (NFS). The advantages of this approach are that cheap additional web servers can be easily added, and resources can be concentrated in a heavy-duty file server with a redundant storage system like RAID 5. The main disadvantage to this system is that there is a single point of failure; if your server or file system mounts go down, the site is affected unless you also create a cluster of file servers.

If there are many large media files to be served, it may be best to serve these from a separate server using a lightweight web server such as lighttpd to avoid having a lot of long-running processes on your web servers contending with requests handled by Drupal. An easy way to do this is to use a rewrite rule on your web server to redirect all incoming requests for a certain file type to the static server. Here's an example rewrite rule for Apache that rewrites all requests for JPEG files:

```
RewriteCond %{REQUEST_URI} ^/(.*\.jpg)$ [NC]
RewriteRule .* http://static.example.com/%1 [R]
```

The disadvantage of this approach is that the web servers are still performing the extra work of redirecting traffic to the file server. An improved solution is to rewrite all file URLs within Drupal, so the web servers are no longer involved in static file requests. However, there is not a simple way to effect this change within Drupal core at this time.

Beyond a Single File System

If the amount of storage is going to exceed a single file system, chances are you'll be doing some custom coding to implement storage abstraction. One option would be to use an outsourced storage system like Amazon's S3 service.

Multiple Database Servers

Multiple database servers introduce additional complexity, because the data being inserted and updated must be replicated or partitioned across servers.

Database Replication

In MySQL database replication, a single master database receives all writes. These writes are then replicated to one or more slaves. Reads can be done on any master or slave. Slaves can also be masters in a multitier architecture.

The current difficulty with running Drupal in a replicated database environment is that Drupal does not distinguish between reads and writes. However, because all database queries go through the database abstraction layer, it is not hard to add this by scanning the query for the keywords ALTER, CREATE, DELETE, FLUSH, INSERT, LOCK, UPDATE, and so forth, and routing the query to the appropriate database. There are some examples of this approach that can be located by searching for "replication" on http://drupal.org, and an interesting blog post is at http://buytaert.net/database-replication-lag.

Database Partitioning

Since Drupal can handle multiple database connections, another strategy for scaling your database architecture is to put some tables in one database on one machine, and other tables in a different database on another machine. For example, moving all cache tables to a separate database on a separate machine and aliasing all queries on these tables using Drupal's table prefixing mechanism can help your site scale.

Summary

In this chapter, you learned the following:

- How to troubleshoot performance bottlenecks

- How to optimize a web server

- How to optimize a database

- Drupal-specific optimizations

- Possible multiserver architectures

CHAPTER 23

■ ■ ■

Installation Profiles

When you install Drupal, certain modules are enabled and certain settings are selected, but these defaults may not be what you need. Drupal's installer uses a default *installation profile* that determines all of these settings. By creating your own installation profile, you can customize the initial installation of Drupal to install your sites with all of the modules and settings you'd like. Maybe you work for a university and you'd like to create an installation profile that enables a custom module that ties in with your university's single sign-on infrastructure, creates a new role for the site administrator, and sends e-mail to you when installation is complete. Drupal's installer system allows you to customize what happens at installation by writing an installation profile. You'll learn how in this chapter.

Where Profiles Are Stored

Your Drupal site already contains an installation profile. It's the default installation profile that ships with Drupal, and you'll find it at `profiles/default/default.profile`. We want to create a new profile called `university`, so we'll create a new file at `profiles/university/university.profile`. For now, we'll just add a single function to the file:

```php
<?php
// $Id$

/**
 * Return a description of the profile for the initial installation screen.
 *
 * @return
 *   An array with keys 'name' and 'description' describing this profile,
 *   and optional 'language' to override the language selection for
 *   language-specific profiles, e.g., 'language' => 'fr'.
 */
function university_profile_details() {
  return array(
    'name' => 'Drupal (Customized for Iowa State University)',
    'description' => 'Select this profile to enable settings typical for a
      departmental website.',
  );
}
```

Note that we made the filename the same as the profile directory name plus a `.profile` suffix, and that all functions in the `university.profile` file will begin with the `university_` prefix.

Because the installation profile choice screen is presented before locale selection happens, there is not much point in translating the `name` and `description` strings. However, it should be noted that in the remainder of the installation profile, the `st()` function should be used where you'd normally use the `t()` function, because when the installer runs this code, Drupal has not yet completed a full bootstrap, so `t()` is not available. If someone wanted to make a French translation for our installation profile, the translation would go in `profiles/university/translations/fr.po` (see Chapter 18).

How Installation Profiles Work

When Drupal's installer begins, it scans the `profiles` directory for possible profiles. If it finds more than one, it will give the user the choice of which one to use. For example, after creating our `university.profile` file and adding the `university_profile_details()` function, going to `http://example.com/install.php` will result in a screen similar to the one shown in Figure 23-1. (Of course, the installation profile will not actually work yet—we've got more to do.)

Tip If Drupal finds only one profile, it will automatically choose that profile. Thus, if you want your own profile to run without presenting the screen in Figure 23-1, delete `profiles/default/default.profile`.

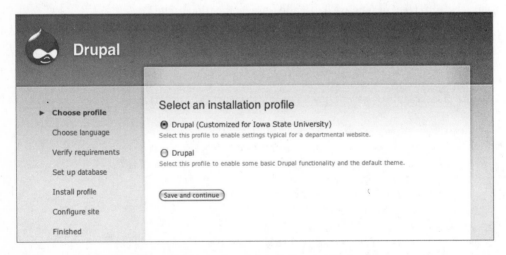

Figure 23-1. *Drupal presents a choice of which installation profile to use.*

Drupal's installer will come back to the installation profile later on, too. It will return once to find out any custom tasks the installation profile wants to perform (so it can add them to the list of steps on the left-hand side of the page). It will also ask which modules the profile wants enabled and will enable them automatically. Finally, at the end of the installation process, the installer will hand off execution to the installation profile to actually perform custom tasks. It is during this latter stage that further Drupal customization occurs. An overview of the process is shown in Figure 23-2.

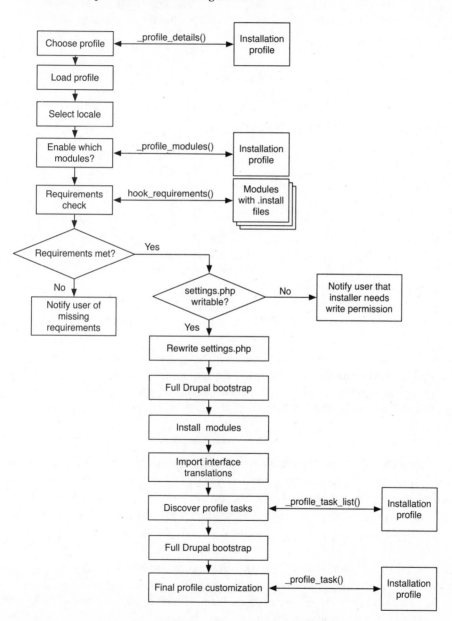

Figure 23-2. *How the installer interacts with the installation profile*

Indicating Which Modules to Enable

We'll tell Drupal which modules our installation profile wants enabled by adding the university_profile_modules() function (again, we know what the name of this function should be by concatenating the name of our profile with _profile_modules). The function should return an array of module names that the profile wants enabled. Take care to order the array so that modules with dependencies are listed after the modules on which they are dependent.

```
/**
 * Return an array of the modules to be enabled when this profile is installed.
 *
 * The following required core modules are always enabled:
 * 'block', 'filter', 'node', 'system', 'user'.
 *
 * @return
 *   An array of modules to be enabled.
 */
function university_profile_modules() {
  return array(
    // Enable optional core modules.
    'dblog', 'color', 'help', 'taxonomy', 'throttle', 'search', 'statistics',

    // Enable single signon by enabling a contributed module.
    'pubcookie',
  );
}
```

Before enabling the modules, the installer asks each module whether or not the system that Drupal is being installed on has all of the necessary requirements for the module. It does this by calling hook_requirements('install') for each module. If requirements are not met, the installer fails and reports on what's missing.

■**Note** The requirements hook is an optional hook that allows modules to test that the environment is okay before proceeding with installation. For example, a module may require that a minimum version of PHP be installed. The requirements hook must be placed in the module's .install file. For more on this hook, see http://api.drupal.org/api/function/hook_requirements/6.

The installer ensures that the modules are present before enabling them. It looks in several locations, which are shown in Table 23-1. Since we're enabling the pubcookie module (a module not included with Drupal core), we need to ensure that it's available in one of these locations before running our installation profile.

Table 23-1. *Directories Where Drupal Modules May Be Placed*

Directory	Modules Stored There
modules	Modules included with Drupal core
sites/all/modules	Third-party modules (for all sites)
profiles/*profilename*/modules	Modules included with the installation profile
sites/*/modules	Modules included within the same sites directory as your settings.php file

The installer also looks for modules stored wherever your site's settings.php file is located. If settings.php is found at sites/default, then Drupal looks for sites/default/modules. Similarly, if settings.php is located at sites/example.com, then Drupal looks for sites/example.com/modules.

Defining Additional Installation Tasks

Notice the list of tasks in the left sidebar of Figure 23-1 ("Choose profile," "Choose language," "Verify requirements," etc.). Let's add a few tasks to that list by defining them in our installation profile. We'll write a function that begins with the name of our profile and ends with _profile_task_list:

```
/**
 * Return a list of tasks that this profile supports.
 *
 * @return
 *   A keyed array of tasks the profile will perform during
 *   the final stage. The keys of the array will be used internally,
 *   while the values will be displayed to the user in the installer
 *   task list.
 */
function university_profile_task_list() {
  return array(
    'dept-info' => st('Departmental Info'),
    'support-message' => st('Support'),
  );
}
```

The tasks we define now show up when the profile is selected, as shown in Figure 23-3.

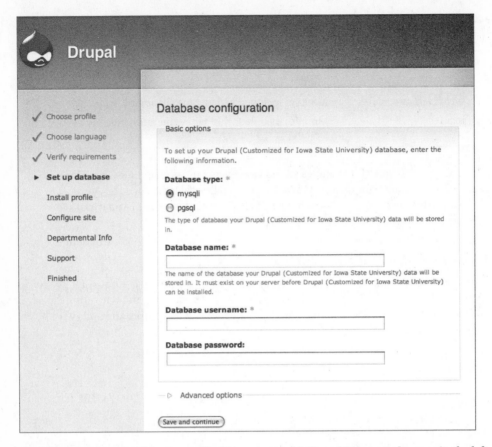

Figure 23-3. *Tasks defined by the profile (Departmental Info and Support) show up in the left sidebar.*

The installer runs through a series of tasks, including built-in tasks as well as tasks that your installation profile may define. The built-in tasks are listed in Table 23-2. Make sure that the keys you define for your array of tasks do not conflict with the task identifiers of the built-in tasks.

Table 23-2. *Names and Descriptions of Tasks Run by the Installer Listed in the Order in Which They Are Executed*

Task Identifier	Description
profile-select	Choose profile*
locale-select	Choose language
requirements	Verify requirements
database	Set up database
profile-install	Prepare batch of modules for installation and enabling
profile-install-batch	Install profile (modules are installed and enabled)
locale-initial-import	Prepare batch of interface translations for import

Task Identifier	Description
locale-initial-batch	Set up translations by importing .po files
configure	Configure site (user fills out form)
profile	Hand over control to installation profile's _profile_tasks() function
profile-finished	Prepare batch of remaining interface translations for import
locale-remaining-batch	Set up remaining translations
finished	Tell user that installation has completed
done	Rebuild menus, register actions, and display initial page

* If only the default profile is available, the "Choose profile" task is not shown in the user interface and the "Install profile" task is renamed "Install site."

The tasks you define indicate steps in the installation process; the purpose of defining the tasks here is so that Drupal can include them in the user interface. There is nothing to prevent you from having more tasks than are listed in university_profile_task_list() if you want to make your installation profile more modular but don't want to include names for the tasks in the user interface.

Running Additional Installation Tasks

The tasks you specify in university_profile_task_list() will be run during the profile phase of installation. During that phase, the installer will repeatedly call university_profile_tasks() and pass in a $task variable containing the task name and a URL for possible use in form functions. The first time the installer calls, $task will contain the string profile.

After each task, Drupal will ask the browser to do an HTTP redirect using install_goto() in includes/install.inc, then do a full bootstrap before going on to the next task. When all of your tasks have been completed, set $task to profile-finished, and the installer will stop calling university_profile_tasks() and move on.

Here is a skeleton of what university_profile_tasks() will look like:

```
function university_profile_tasks(&$task, $url) {
  if ($task == 'profile') {
    // The value of $task is 'profile' the first time we are called.
    // Set up all the things a default installation profile has.
    require_once 'profiles/default/default.profile';
    default_profile_tasks($task, $url);
    // Then do our custom setup here.

    // Set $task to the next task.
    $task = 'dept-info';
    // Display a form requesting some info.
    return drupal_get_form('university_department_info', $url);
  }
```

```
  if ($task == 'dept-info') {
    // Send email indicating that a site was set up.

    // Set $task to key of next task.
    $task = 'support-message';
    // Build some output.

    return $output;
  }

  if ($task == 'support-message') {
    // Return control to the installer.
    $task = 'profile-finished';
  }
}
```

Since we want almost the same kind of setup as a regular Drupal site, we load Drupal's default profile and just call `default_profile_tasks()`, rather than duplicating all of that code in our installation profile. Another approach would be to copy the code out of the default profile and paste it into the first task.

Tip A simple installation profile need not implement multiple tasks. It can just ignore the parameters that are passed to it and run code when it is called. When the installer sees that the `$task` variable has not changed, it will move on to the post-installation profile steps. Drupal's default installation profile is such a profile, which is why we can call `default_profile_tasks()` without worrying that it will change the value of `$task`.

Notice the structure of the preceding code. It consists of a series of `if` statements, one per task. At the end of each task, the `$task` variable, which was passed by reference, is changed, and any output is returned and will result in an additional screen for the user to interact with.

Since the database is up and running prior to custom installation tasks being run, the installer keeps track of the name of the current task in a persistent Drupal variable by calling `variable_set('install_task', $task)` at the end of each task. If you want to pass information from one of your tasks to another, you can use the same technique. Just remember to delete the variables you used by calling `variable_del()` at the end of your last task.

Let's examine a full-fledged version of the university installation profile's `university_profile_tasks()` function:

```
/**
 * Perform final installation tasks for this installation profile.
 */
function university_profile_tasks(&$task, $url) {
  if ($task == 'profile') {
    // $task is set to 'profile' the first time this function is called.
    // Set up all the things a default installation profile has.
    require_once 'profiles/default/default.profile';

    // Need constants defined by modules/comment/comment.module
    // to be in scope.
    require_once 'modules/comment/comment.module';

    default_profile_tasks($task, $url);
    // If the administrator enables the comment module, we want
    // to have comments disabled for pages.
    variable_set('comment_page', COMMENT_NODE_DISABLED);

    // Define a News Item node type.
    $node_type = array(
      'type' => 'news',
      'name' => st('News Item'),
      'module' => 'node',
      'description' => st('A news item for the front page.'),
      'custom' => TRUE,
      'modified' => TRUE,
      'locked' => FALSE,
      'has_title' => TRUE,
      'title_label' => st('Title'),
      'has_body' => TRUE,
      'orig_type' => 'news',
      'is_new' => TRUE,
    );
    node_type_save((object)$node_type);

    // News items should be published and promoted to front page by default.
    // News items should create new revisions by default.
    variable_set('node_options_news', array('status', 'revision', 'promote'));

    // If the administrator enables the comment module, we want
    // to have comments enabled for news items.
    variable_set('comment_news', COMMENT_NODE_READ_WRITE);
```

```php
  // Create a News Categories vocabulary so news can be classified.
  $vocabulary = array(
    'name' => st('News Categories'),
    'description' => st('Select the appropriate audience for your news item.'),
    'help' => st('You may select multiple audiences.'),
    'nodes' => array('news' => st('News Item')),
    'hierarchy' => 0,
    'relations' => 0,
    'tags' => 0,
    'multiple' => 1,
    'required' => 0,
  );
  taxonomy_save_vocabulary($vocabulary);

  // Define some terms to categorize news items.
  $terms = array(
    st('Departmental News'),
    st('Faculty News'),
    st('Staff News'),
    st('Student News'),
  );

  // Submit the "Add term" form programmatically for each term.
  $form_id = 'taxonomy_form_term';
  // The taxonomy_form_term form is not in taxonomy.module, so need
  // to bring it into scope by loading taxonomy.admin.inc.
  require_once 'modules/taxonomy/taxonomy.admin.inc';
  foreach ($terms as $name) {
    $form_state['values']['name'] = $name;
    $form_state['clicked_button']['#value'] = st('Save');
    drupal_execute($form_id, $form_state, (object)$vocabulary);
  }

  // Add a role.
  db_query("INSERT INTO {role} (name) VALUES ('%s')", 'site administrator');

  // Configure the pubcookie module.
  variable_set('pubcookie_login_dir', 'login');
  variable_set('pubcookie_id_is_email', 1);
  // ...other settings go here

  // Set $task to next task so the installer UI will be correct.
  $task = 'dept-info';
  drupal_set_title(st('Departmental Information'));
  return drupal_get_form('university_department_info', $url);
}
```

```
if ($task == 'dept-info') {
  // Report by email that a new Drupal site has been installed.
  $to = 'administrator@example.com';
  $from = ini_get('sendmail_from');
  $subject = st('New Drupal site created!');
  $body = st('A new Drupal site was created: @site', array(
    '@site' => base_path()));
  drupal_mail('university-profile', $to, $subject, $body, $from);

  // Set $task to next task so the installer UI will be correct.
  $task = 'support-message';
  drupal_set_title(st('Support'));
  $output = '<p>'. st('For support, please contact the Drupal Support Desk
    at 123-4567.') .'</p>';
  // Build a 'Continue' link that goes to the next task.
  $output .= '<p>'. l(st('Continue'), $url) .'</p>';
  return $output;
}

if ($task == 'support-message') {
  // Change to our custom theme.
  $themes = system_theme_data();
  $theme = 'university';
  if (isset($themes[$theme])) {
    system_initialize_theme_blocks($theme);
    db_query("UPDATE {system} SET status = 1 WHERE type = 'theme' AND
      name = '%s'", $theme);
    variable_set('theme_default', $theme);
    menu_rebuild();
    drupal_rebuild_theme_registry();
  }

  // Return control to the installer.
  $task = 'profile-finished';
}
}
```

Our first custom installation task displayed an interactive form to the user. Let's define that form now. We can use the standard form API, but we take care to set $form['#redirect'] to FALSE and set the form's action to the URL that is provided by the installer. The form is handled by a submit handler just like normal. Here is the form definition and the submit handler. The form is shown in Figure 23-4.

```
/**
 * Define form used by our dept-info installer task.
 *
 * @param $form_state
 *   Keyed array containing the state of the form.
 * @param $url
 *   URL of current installer page, provided by installer.
 */
function university_department_info($form_state, $url) {
  $form['#action'] = $url;
  $form['#redirect'] = FALSE;
  $form['department_code'] = array(
    '#type' => 'select',
    '#title' => st('Departmental code'),
    '#description' => st('Please select the correct code for your department.'),
    '#options' => array('BIOL', 'CHEM', 'COMP', 'DRUP', 'ENGL', 'HIST', 'MATH',
      'LANG', 'PHYS', 'PHIL'),
  );
  $form['submit'] = array(
    '#type' => 'submit',
    '#value' => st('Save and Continue'),
  );
  return $form;
}

/**
 * Handle form submission for university_department_info form.
 */
function university_department_info_submit($form, &$form_state) {
  // Set a persistent variable.
  variable_set('department_code', $form_state['values']['department_code']);
}
```

■**Note** We use `st()` instead of `t()` throughout the installation profile to allow the entire installation profile translation to be stored in an installation profile translation file. This is a `.po` file located in the optional `translations` directory of the installation profile. See Chapter 18 for more about `.po` files.

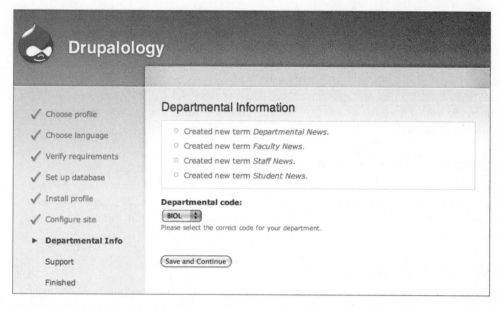

Figure 23-4. *The screen for our custom task*

Setting Drupal Variables

Drupal variables may be set by simply calling `variable_set()`:

```
variable_set('pubcookie_login_dir', 'login');
```

Creating Initial Node Types

If you need to create node types using Drupal's built-in content type support, a call to `node_type_save()` with a node type definition object is all it takes. In the previous example profile, we ended up with two node types: page for normal web pages (created by the default profile when we called `default_profile_tasks()`) and news for news items. We then used `variable_set()` to set node option defaults so that news items will appear on the front page when posted, whereas pages will not.

If you have enabled modules that provide node types, the node types will already be available to Drupal through the `node_info()` hook in those modules.

Saving Information to the Database

An installation profile may wish to tweak some database settings. Since the database connection is available, `db_query()` can be used to modify the database. In our example profile, we added a role to the Drupal site. In your profile, you may want to go beyond this by inserting permissions into the `permissions` table, for example.

An easy way to get the proper queries is to do a plain vanilla Drupal installation, then configure it exactly the way you want it to be when your installation profile finishes. This could even include a few nodes to act as placeholders, complete with URL aliases. The university department using this installation profile may want to have an About page, a Courses Taught page, and so forth. After this configuration has taken place, you can use your database tools to do an SQL dump of the site's database. You can then pick the insertion commands you wish to use from among the INSERT SQL commands in the dump and include them in your installation profile.

Submitting Forms Programmatically

Because Drupal supports programmatic form submission, you can use drupal_execute() to submit forms as if you were interacting with the web site. In the previous example, we used this approach to add taxonomy terms to the site. See Chapter 10 for more information about drupal_execute().

Setting a Theme During Installation

Drupal stores the value of the default theme in the persistent variable called theme_default. Thus, you can choose the initial theme for the site that will show up after installation by setting this variable. In the preceding example profile, we selected a custom theme named university.

```
// Change to our custom theme.
$themes = system_theme_data();
$theme = 'university';
if (isset($themes[$theme])) {
  system_initialize_theme_blocks($theme);
  db_query("UPDATE {system} SET status = 1 WHERE type = 'theme' AND
    name = '%s'", $theme);
  variable_set('theme_default', $theme);
  menu_rebuild();
  drupal_rebuild_theme_registry();
}
```

But there is some housekeeping that needs to be done. Calling system_theme_data() and checking whether $themes['university'] is defined ensures that Drupal has discovered our custom theme. Blocks in the new theme need to be set up, the theme itself needs to be enabled, and then the menu and theme registry need to be rebuilt.

The approach here is to find the function that takes care of the process you are interested in (in this case, enabling and setting a default theme), and then either calling the function or duplicating the functionality in your installation profile task. In the preceding example, the code was extracted from system_themes_form_submit() in modules/system/system.admin.inc.

Using the Batch API

Sometimes you need to run a series of tasks that may take a long time—long enough that PHP may time out. Fortunately, Drupal provides an API that makes this easy. You just specify what has to be done, then hand it off to the batch processor. This is usually done after a form submission, though that is not necessary. We will examine the use of the batch API in the installer and then see how it can be used from a form submission.

Using the Batch API to Enable Modules

The basic idea behind the batch API is that you define a set of operations and some information about which progress messages to display and how you'd like the operations to be run, then hand that to the batch engine. The engine will chug away through the operations, making HTTP refreshes and updating progress indicators as necessary. Then, when all operations are completed, it will call the final function that you indicated.

Here is a simplified version of how the installer uses the batch API to enable modules:

```
$operations = array();
foreach ($modules as $module) {
  $operations[] = array(
    '_install_module_batch', // Name of callback.
    array($module, $files[$module]->info['name']), // Array of parameters.
  );
}
$batch = array(
  'operations' => $operations,
  'finished' => '_install_profile_batch_finished', // Call this when done.
  'title' => st('Installing @drupal', array(
    '@drupal' => drupal_install_profile_name())
    ),
  'error_message' => st('The installation has encountered an error.'),
);
batch_set($batch);
batch_process($url, $url);
```

First, it creates an array of operations. Each operation consists of the name of a PHP function to be called and an array of parameters to pass along. The PHP function is referred to as a *callback* because it will be called back later, when processing happens.

Then, a *batch set* is defined. This includes the array of operations, the name of the callback to call when processing is finished, a title to use during processing, and an error message to use if things go horribly awry. The batch set is verified using batch_set(), and then processing begins by calling batch_process().

Tip In this case, all of the operations are calling the same function, just with different parameters. But the operations could be any function that you want to call.

Following is the code of the _install_module_batch() function from install.php that is run on each operation:

```
/**
 * Batch callback for batch installation of modules.
 */
function _install_module_batch($module, $module_name, &$context) {
  _drupal_install_module($module);
  // We enable the installed module right away, so that the module will be
  // loaded by drupal_bootstrap() in subsequent batch requests, and other
  // modules possibly depending on it can safely perform their installation
  // steps.
  module_enable(array($module));
  $context['results'][] = $module;
  $context['message'] = 'Installed '. $module_name .' module.';
}
```

Defining a Batch Set

As mentioned, a group of operations is called a batch set. The batch API can handle multiple batch sets without mixing them up. Batch sets are processed sequentially, with a new progress indicator for each batch set.

Let's dive into an example. Rather than make the example part of the installation profile, we will write it as a separate module. That way, you can test, debug, and play with it without having to wipe the database and reinstall Drupal every time. Keep in mind that you can use the same approach within your installation profile by kicking off batch processing in response to a form that you present to the user during one of your custom profile tasks.

For our scenario, let's take the common example of someone moving from a custom content management system to Drupal. There is an existing database table of users that would look like this if we were to dump out the SQL:

```
CREATE TABLE old_users (
  user_id int(32) NOT NULL,
  username varchar(32) NOT NULL,
  email varchar(32) NOT NULL,
  pass varchar(32) NOT NULL
);
INSERT INTO old_users VALUES (3, 'mary', 'mary@example.com', 'foo');
INSERT INTO old_users VALUES (4, 'joe', 'joe@example.com', 'bar');
INSERT INTO old_users VALUES (6, 'fred', 'fred@example.com', 'zou');
INSERT INTO old_users VALUES (7, 'betty', 'betty@example.com', 'baz');
INSERT INTO old_users VALUES (8, 'friedrich', 'freidrich@example.com', 'fre');
INSERT INTO old_users VALUES (9, 'martin', 'martin@example.com', 'aoi');
INSERT INTO old_users VALUES (10, 'fozzie', 'fozzie@example.com', 'lii');
INSERT INTO old_users VALUES (11, 'steve', 'steve@example.com', 'doi');
```

Let's set up a batch that will import these users as Drupal users when the administrator clicks a form like the one shown in Figure 23-5.

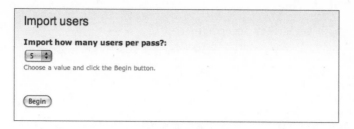

Figure 23-5. *Form for selection of how many users should be imported during one cycle*

Here is the .info file for our module, which you should put at sites/all/modules/custom/importusers/importusers.info:

```
; $Id$
name = Import Users
description = Imports users from a database using the batch API.
package = Pro Drupal Development
core = 6.x
```

We'll start out by implementing the menu hook, creating our form definition, and writing the handler for form submission. The initial code for sites/all/modules/custom/importusers/importusers.module follows:

```php
<?php
// $Id$

/**
 * @file
 * Example of using the batch API.
 */

/**
 * Implementation of hook_menu().
 */
function importusers_menu() {
  $items['importusers'] = array(
    'title' => 'Import users',
    'page callback' => 'drupal_get_form',
    'page arguments' => array('importusers_form'),
    'access arguments' => array('administer users'),
  );
  return $items;
}
```

```php
/**
 * Menu callback: define form to begin user importation.
 */
function importusers_form() {
  $form['size'] = array(
    '#type' => 'select',
    '#title' => t('Import how many users per pass?'),
    '#description' => t('Choose a value and click the Begin button.'),
    '#options' => drupal_map_assoc(array(1, 5, 10, 25, 50)),
  );
  $form['submit'] = array(
    '#type' => 'submit',
    '#value' => t('Begin'),
  );
  return $form;
}

/**
 * Handle form submission by beginning batch operation.
 */
function importusers_form_submit($form_id, &$form_state) {
  $size = $form_state['values']['size'];
  $batch = array(
    'operations' => array(
      array('importusers_import', array($size)),
      array('importusers_optimize', array()),
      ),
    'finished' => 'importusers_finished',
    'title' => t('Importing Users'),
    'init_message' => t('The user import process is beginning.'),
    'progress_message' => t('Imported @current of @total.'),
    'error_message' => t('The importation process encountered an error.'),
  );
  batch_set($batch);
  // batch_process() not needed here because this is a form submit handler;
  // the form API will detect the batch and call batch_process() automatically.
}
```

The menu hook and form definition functions should be old hat by now (if not, see Chapters 4 and 10, respectively). Where it gets interesting is in the importusers_form_submit() function, where we define our batch set. A batch set can have the following keys in its associative array. Only the operations key is required.

- `operations`: This is an array of arrays. Each array contains two members: the name of a callback function and an array of parameter values that will be passed to the callback when the operation is performed.

- `finished`: This is the name of a callback function that will be called when all operations are complete. This function will receive information about what happened during processing, so it can be analyzed, summarized via `drupal_set_message()`, or otherwise used.

- `title`: This is the title that should be shown on the page that displays progress information to the user. If no `title` is set, `t('Processing')` will be used.

- `init_message`: When the processing of the batch set is being initialized, this message is shown. If no `init_message` is set, `t('Initializing')` will be used.

- `progress_message`: This is displayed during the processing of the batch set. The following placeholders may be used in the progress message: `@current`, `@remaining`, `@total`, and `@percent`. These values are changed as the batch set is processed. If no `progress_message` is set, `t('Remaining @remaining of @total.')` will be used.

- `error_message`: This is displayed to the user if an error occurs during processing. If no error message is set, `t('An error has occurred.')` will be used.

- `file`: If the callback functions for `operations` and `finished` are not in scope during a normal Drupal request, the path of the file containing these functions must be given. The path is relative to the `base_path()` of the Drupal installation and can be conveniently built using `drupal_get_path()`. It is unnecessary to define `file` if the functions are already in scope.

The preceding batch set is quite simple and consists of only two operations. First, the batch engine will call `importusers_import($size)` repeatedly until that function indicates that all users are imported. Remember, the `$size` parameter is the number of users to import on each call. `$size` matters because it determines how much work is done within each request cycle, before the batch API has the client initiate another HTTP request. For example, if you had 100 users to import, setting `$size` to 1 would result in 100 HTTP requests, while setting it to 50 would result in 2 requests. How much work you try to do in each request will be determined by how powerful your server is, how busy the server will be, and how much work needs to be done.

A Batch Operation Callback

After users are imported, a call will be made to `importusers_optimize()`. Finally, when that operation is completed, the callback we specified in the finished key (`importusers_finished()`) will be called. Here is the `importusers_import()` function:

```
/**
 * Batch callback operation: Import users.
 *
 * @param $size
 *    Number of users to import in each operation.
 * @param $context
 *    Batch context containing state information.
 */
function importusers_import($size, &$context) {
  // Initialize sandbox the first time through.
  if (!isset($context['sandbox']['progress'])) {
    $context['sandbox']['progress'] = 0;
    $context['sandbox']['current_user_id'] = 0;
    $context['sandbox']['max'] = db_result(
      db_query('SELECT COUNT(DISTINCT user_id) FROM {old_users}'));
  }

  // Retrieve some users from the old_users table.
  $result = db_query_range("SELECT user_id, username AS name, email AS mail,
    pass FROM {old_users} WHERE user_id > %d ORDER BY user_id",
    $context['sandbox']['current_user_id'], 0, $size);

  // Transform them into Drupal users.
  while ($account = db_fetch_array($result)) {
    $new_user = user_save(array(), $account);

    // Update progress information.
    $context['sandbox']['progress']++;
    $context['sandbox']['current_user_id'] = $account['user_id'];
    $context['message'] = t('Importing user %username', array('%username' =>
      $new_user->name));

    // Store usernames in case the the 'finished' callback wants them.
    $context['results'][] = $new_user->name;
  }

  // Let the batch engine know how close we are to completion.
  if ($context['sandbox']['progress'] == $context['sandbox']['max']) {
    // Done!
    $context['finished'] = 1;
  }
  else {
    $context['finished'] = $context['sandbox']['progress'] /
      $context['sandbox']['max'];
  }
}
```

```
/**
 * Batch callback operation: Optimize users.
 * For now, this function does nothing.
 *
 * @param $context
 *   Batch context containing state information.
 */
function importusers_optimize(&$context) {
  // Code would go here.
  // Inform the batch engine that we are done.
  $context['finished'] = 1;
}
```

Notice that in addition to passing the parameter you indicated in the batch set operation array, importusers_import() is receiving another parameter called $context. This array, which is passed by reference, contains information from the batch engine on the state of the current batch set. The contents of $context are listed following:

- sandbox: This area is open to use by callback functions. You can store anything you need in here and it will persist. In our example, we store some information about the number of users to import, the user currently being imported, and so forth. Use this instead of $_SESSION for storing information during batch processing. If you use $_SESSION and the user opens a new browser window, bad things could happen.

- results: This is an array of results for use by the finished callback. For example, this might be used if the user wants to see a list of the usernames that were imported.

- message: This is a message to display on the progress page.

- finished: This is a floating point number between 0 and 1 indicating how much data has been processed. Set this to 1 when all the data has been processed to indicate to the batch processing engine that it may go on to the next operation.

Here is the callback that will be called when all of the batch operations have run:

```
/**
 * Called when all batch operations are complete.
 */
function importusers_finished($success, $results, $operations) {
  if ($success) {
    drupal_set_message(t('User importation complete.'));
  }
  else {
    // A fatal error occurred during batch processing.
    $error_operation = reset($operations);
    $operation = array_shift($error_operation);
    $arguments = array_shift($error_operation);
    $arguments_as_string = implode(', ', $arguments);
```

```
    watchdog('importusers', "Error when calling operation '%s'('%s')",
      array($operation, $arguments_as_string));
    drupal_set_message(t('An error occurred and has been recorded
      in the system log.'), 'error');
  }
}
```

Error Handling

Let's change the second operation, importusers_optimize(), to demonstrate what happens when things go bad.

```
/**
 * Batch callback operation. Demonstrate error handling.
 */
function importusers_optimize() {
  // Cause fatal error by calling nonexistent function.
  go_bananas();
}
```

The batch processing engine will actually catch the error and helpfully redirect the user to an error page. The error page is under the control of the finished callback shown in the preceding section.

Redirection

A final redirection will take place after batch processing is completed and the finished function has run. The destination of the redirection will be the $destination that was set when batch processing was begun. If that was not set, the value of $form_state['redirect'] from the form submit handler will be used. Failing that, $batch['redirect'] will be used, and finally, if all else fails, the redirect will be to the URL of the page the user was on when batch processing was initiated.

Progressive and Nonprogressive Batch Sets

A progressive batch set is a normal batch set that uses a progress indicator to provide feedback to the user. However, you wouldn't want that if you were submitting a form programmatically via drupal_execute(). So the form API recognizes programmatic execution and changes the batch set to nonprogressive in that case. A nonprogressive batch set executes all operations in a single request. The setup of progressive and nonprogressive batch sets is shown in Figure 23-6.

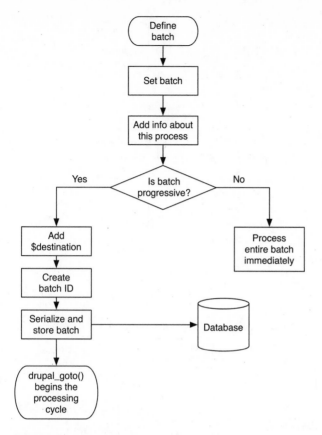

Figure 23-6. *Beginning the processing of progressive and nonprogressive batch sets*

The Batch Request Cycle

While operations are being performed, the batch engine takes care of refreshing the progress indicator page to avoid a PHP timeout. The cycle is shown graphically in Figure 23-7 and can be investigated by reading `includes/batch.inc`.

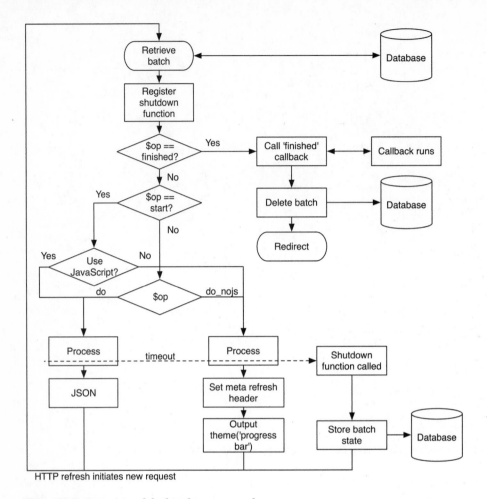

Figure 23-7. *Overview of the batch request cycle*

Resources

Writing installation profiles can be tricky. In our example, we needed to get the comment module into scope so that some of its constants could be used to set preferences, even though we did not include the comment module in university_profile_modules(). Likewise, we had to define a $form_state['clicked_button'] entry when programmatically submitting the form that enters taxonomy terms because the submit handler for that form expected it. Expect to spend some time working out details like that in your own installation profiles.

While such things may take extra time, you can gain it back by using an installation profile generator. See http://drupal.org/node/180078 for more information. If you are interested in advancing the current state of installation profiles (no pun intended), join the Distribution Profiles group at http://groups.drupal.org/distributions.

Summary

In this chapter, you learned the following:

- What an installation profile is

- Where installation profiles are stored

- How to set up a basic installation profile

- How to specify which modules should be installed

- How to specify profile tasks that should run during installation

- How to manipulate Drupal during the stage of installation when profile tasks run

- How the batch API is used in the installer

- How to create your own batch set

■■■

Database Table Reference

This appendix describes the database tables and fields that make up Drupal core. The descriptions are taken from the hook_schema() implementations in the core modules' .install files, with minor changes for clarity. The information is reproduced here for your convenience.

Primary keys are indicated by bold italic type; indices are indicated by bold type. Multi-column indices are not shown unless the index is the primary index for the table. You can find current table definitions in your Drupal installation within the schema hook of a module's .install file or using the contributed schema module, found at http://drupal.org/project/schema. Definitions for nonmodule core tables are in the modules/system/system.install file. If a table is used primarily by a specific module, that module is listed in parentheses after the table name. References to other tables show table names in curly brackets.

access (user module)

This table stores site access rules.

Name	Type	Null	Default	Description
aid	serial	No		Primary key: unique access ID
mask	varchar(255)	No	' '	Text mask used for filtering access
type	varchar(255)	No	' '	Type of access rule: name, mail, or host
status	int:tiny	No	0	Whether rule is to allow (1) or deny (0) access

accesslog (statistics module)

This table stores site access information for statistics.

Name	Type	Null	Default	Description
aid	serial	No		Primary key: unique accesslog ID
sid	varchar(64)	No	' '	Browser session ID of user who visited the page
title	varchar(255)	Yes		Title of the page visited

Continued

Name	Type	Null	Default	Description
path	varchar(255)	Yes		Internal path to the page visited (relative to Drupal root)
url	varchar(255)	Yes		Referrer URI
hostname	varchar(128)	Yes		Hostname of the user who visited the page
uid	int, unsigned	Yes	0	User {users}.uid who visited the page
timer	int, unsigned	No	0	Time in milliseconds that the page took to load
timestamp	int, unsigned	No	0	Timestamp of when the page was visited

actions (trigger module)

This table stores action information.

Name	Type	Null	Default	Description
aid	varchar(255)	No	'0'	Primary key: unique actions ID
type	varchar(32)	No	' '	The object that the action acts on (node, user, comment, system, or custom types)
callback	varchar(255)	No	' '	The callback function that executes when the action runs
parameters	text:big	No		Parameters to be passed to the callback function
description	varchar(255)	No	'0'	Description of the action

actions_aid (trigger module)

This table stores action IDs for nondefault actions and serves as a sequences table for configurable actions.

Name	Type	Null	Default	Description
aid	serial	No		Primary key: unique actions ID

aggregator_category (aggregator module)

This table stores categories for aggregator feeds and feed items.

Name	Type	Null	Default	Description
cid	serial	No		Primary key: unique aggregator category ID
title	varchar(255)	No	' '	Title of the category
description	text:big	No		Description of the category
block	int:tiny	No	0	The number of recent items to show within the category block

aggregator_category_feed (aggregator module)

This bridge table maps feeds to categories.

Name	Type	Null	Default	Description
fid	int	No	0	The feed's {aggregator_feed}.fid
cid	int	No	0	The {aggregator_category}.cid to which the feed is being assigned

aggregator_category_item (aggregator module)

This bridge table maps feed items to categories.

Name	Type	Null	Default	Description
iid	int	No	0	The feed item's {aggregator_item}.iid
cid	int	No	0	The {aggregator_category}.cid to which the feed item is being assigned

aggregator_feed (aggregator module)

This table stores feeds to be parsed by the aggregator.

Name	Type	Null	Default	Description
fid	serial	No		Primary key: unique feed ID
title	varchar(255)	No	' '	Title of the feed
url	varchar(255)	No	' '	URL to the feed
refresh	int	No	0	How often to check for new feed items, in seconds

Continued

Name	Type	Null	Default	Description
checked	int	No	0	Last time feed was checked for new items, as a Unix timestamp
link	varchar(255)	No	' '	The parent web site of the feed; comes from the <link> element in the feed
description	text:big	No		The parent web site's description; comes from the <description> element in the feed
image	text:big	No		An image representing the feed
etag	varchar(255)	No	' '	Entity tag HTTP response header; used for validating the cache
modified	int	No	0	When the feed was last modified, as a Unix timestamp
block	int:tiny	No	0	Number of items to display in the feed's block

aggregator_item (aggregator module)

This table stores the individual items imported from feeds.

Name	Type	Null	Default	Description
iid	serial	No		Primary key: unique ID for feed item
fid	int	No	0	The {aggregator_feed}.fid to which this item belongs
title	varchar(255)	No	' '	Title of the feed item
link	varchar(255)	No	' '	Link to the feed item
author	varchar(255)	No	' '	Author of the feed item
description	text:big	No		Body of the feed item
timestamp	int	Yes		Post date of the feed item, as a Unix timestamp
guid	varchar(255)	Yes		Unique identifier for the feed item

authmap (user module)

This table stores distributed authentication mapping.

Name	Type	Null	Default	Description
aid	serial	No		Primary key: unique authmap ID
uid	int	No	0	User's {users}.uid
authname	varchar(128)	No	' '	Unique authentication name
module	varchar(128)	No	' '	Module that is controlling the authentication

batch (batch.inc)

This table stores details about batches (processes that run in multiple HTTP requests).

Name	Type	Null	Default	Description
bid	serial	No		Primary key: unique batch ID.
token	varchar(64)	No		A string token generated against the current user's session ID and the batch ID; used to ensure that only the user who submitted the batch can effectively access it.
timestamp	int	No		A Unix timestamp indicating when this batch was submitted for processing. Stale batches are purged at cron time.
batch	text:big	Yes		A serialized array containing the processing data for the batch.

blocks (block module)

This table stores block settings, such as region and visibility settings.

Name	Type	Null	Default	Description
bid	serial	No		Primary key: unique block ID.
module	varchar(64)	No	' '	The module from which the block originates; for example, 'user' for the Who's Online block and 'block' for any custom blocks.
delta	varchar(32)	No	'0'	Unique ID for block within a module.
theme	varchar(64)	No	' '	The theme under which the block settings apply.
status	int:tiny	No	0	Block enabled status (1 means enabled and 0, disabled).
weight	int:tiny	No	0	Block weight within region.
region	varchar(64)	No	' '	Theme region within which the block is set.
custom	int:tiny	No	0	Flag to indicate how users may control visibility of the block (0 indicates that users cannot control it; 1 that the block is on by default but can be hidden; and 2 that the block is hidden by default but can be shown).
throttle	int:tiny	No	0	Flag to indicate whether or not to remove block when web site traffic is high (1 means throttle; 0 means do not throttle).
visibility	int:tiny	No	0	Flag to indicate how to show blocks on pages (0 means to show on all pages except listed pages, 1 to show only on listed pages, and 2 to use custom PHP code to determine visibility).

Continued

Name	Type	Null	Default	Description
pages	text	No		Contents of the "Pages" block; contains either a list of paths on which to include or exclude the block or PHP code, depending on the "visibility" setting.
title	varchar(64)	No	''	Custom title for the block (an empty string will use block default title; <none> will remove the title; text will cause block to use specified title).
cache	int:tiny	No	1	Binary flag to indicate block cache mode (-1 means do not cache; 1 means cache per role; 2, cache per user; 4, cache per page; 8, block cache is global). See Chapter 9 for an explanation of block cache modes.

blocks_roles (block module)

This table stores access permissions for blocks based on user roles.

Name	Type	Null	Default	Description
module	varchar(64)	No		The block's origin module, from {blocks}.module
delta	varchar(32)	No		The block's unique delta within module, from {blocks}.delta
rid	int, unsigned	No		The user's role ID from {users_roles}.rid

book (book module)

This table stores book outline information and connects each node in the outline to a unique link in the menu_links table.

Name	Type	Null	Default	Description
mlid	int, unsigned	No	0	The book page's {menu_links}.mlid.
nid	int, unsigned	No	0	The book page's {node}.nid.
bid	int, unsigned	No	0	The book ID is the {book}.nid of the top-level page.

boxes (block module)

This table stores the contents of custom-made blocks.

Name	Type	Null	Default	Description
bid	serial	No		The block's {blocks}.bid.
body	text:big	Yes		The block contents.
info	varchar(128)	No	''	The block description.
format	int:small	No	0	The block body's {filter_formats}.format; for example, 1 means Filtered HTML.

cache

The generic cache table is used to cache things not separated out into their own cache tables. Contributed modules may also use this to store cached items.

Name	Type	Null	Default	Description
cid	varchar(255)	No	''	Primary key: unique cache ID
data	blob:big	Yes		A collection of data to cache
expire	int	No	0	A Unix timestamp indicating when the cache entry should expire or 0 for never
created	int	No	0	A Unix timestamp indicating when the cache entry was created
headers	text	Yes		Any custom HTTP headers to be added to cached data
serialized	int:small	No	0	A flag to indicate whether content is serialized (1) or not (0)

cache_block (block module)

This is the cache table for the block module to store already built blocks, identified by module, delta, and various contexts that may change the block, such as the theme, locale, and caching mode defined for the block.

Name	Type	Null	Default	Description
cid	varchar(255)	No	''	Primary key: unique cache ID
data	blob:big	Yes		A collection of data to cache
expire	int	No	0	A Unix timestamp indicating when the cache entry should expire or 0 for never
created	int	No	0	A Unix timestamp indicating when the cache entry was created

Continued

Name	Type	Null	Default	Description
headers	text	Yes		Any custom HTTP headers to be added to cached data
serialized	int:small	No	0	A flag to indicate whether content is serialized (1) or not (0)

cache_filter (filter module)

The cache table for the filter module stores already filtered pieces of text, identified by input format and MD5 hash of the text.

Name	Type	Null	Default	Description
cid	varchar(255)	No	' '	Primary key: unique cache ID
data	blob:big	Yes		A collection of data to cache
expire	int	No	0	A Unix timestamp indicating when the cache entry should expire or 0 for never
created	int	No	0	A Unix timestamp indicating when the cache entry was created
headers	text	Yes		Any custom HTTP headers to be added to cached data
serialized	int:small	No	0	A flag to indicate whether content is serialized (1) or not (0)

cache_form

The cache table for the form system stores recently built forms and their storage data for use in subsequent page requests.

Name	Type	Null	Default	Description
cid	varchar(255)	No	' '	Primary key: unique cache ID
data	blob:big	Yes		A collection of data to cache
expire	int	No	0	A Unix timestamp indicating when the cache entry should expire or 0 for never
created	int	No	0	A Unix timestamp indicating when the cache entry was created
headers	text	Yes		Any custom HTTP headers to be added to cached data
serialized	int:small	No	0	A flag to indicate whether content is serialized (1) or not (0)

cache_menu

The cache table for the menu system stores router information as well as generated link trees for various menu/page/user combinations.

Name	Type	Null	Default	Description
cid	varchar(255)	No	' '	Primary key: unique cache ID
data	blob:big	Yes		A collection of data to cache
expire	int	No	0	A Unix timestamp indicating when the cache entry should expire or 0 for never
created	int	No	0	A Unix timestamp indicating when the cache entry was created
headers	text	Yes		Any custom HTTP headers to be added to cached data
serialized	int:small	No	0	A flag to indicate whether content is serialized (1) or not (0)

cache_page

This cache table is used to store compressed pages for anonymous users, if page caching is enabled.

Name	Type	Null	Default	Description
cid	varchar(255)	No	' '	Primary key: unique cache ID
data	blob:big	Yes		A collection of data to cache
expire	int	No	0	A Unix timestamp indicating when the cache entry should expire or 0 for never
created	int	No	0	A Unix timestamp indicating when the cache entry was created
headers	text	Yes		Any custom HTTP headers to be added to cached data
serialized	int:small	No	0	A flag to indicate whether content is serialized (1) or not (0)

cache_update

The cache table for the update module stores information, fetched from the central server, about available releases.

Name	Type	Null	Default	Description
cid	varchar(255)	No	' '	Primary key: unique cache ID
data	blob:big	Yes		A collection of data to cache
expire	int	No	0	A Unix timestamp indicating when the cache entry should expire or 0 for never
created	int	No	0	A Unix timestamp indicating when the cache entry was created
headers	text	Yes		Any custom HTTP headers to be added to cached data
serialized	int:small	No	0	A flag to indicate whether content is serialized (1) or not (0)

comments (comment module)

This table stores comments and associated data.

Name	Type	Null	Default	Description
cid	serial	No		Primary key: unique comment ID.
pid	int	No	0	The {comments}.cid to which this comment is a reply. If set to 0, this comment is not a reply to an existing comment.
nid	int	No	0	The {node}.nid to which this comment is a reply.
uid	int	No	0	The {users}.uid who authored the comment. If set to 0, this comment was created by an anonymous user.
subject	varchar(64)	No	' '	The comment title.
comment	text:big	No		The comment body.
hostname	varchar(128)	No	' '	The author's hostname.
timestamp	int	No	0	The time, as a Unix timestamp, that the comment was created or last edited by its author.
status	int:tiny, unsigned	No	0	The published status of a comment (0 mean published, and 1, not published).
format	int:small	No	0	The {filter_formats}.format of the comment body.
thread	varchar(255)	No		The vancode representation of the comment's place in a thread.

Continued

Name	Type	Null	Default	Description
name	varchar(60)	Yes		The comment author's name. Uses {users}.name if the user is logged in; otherwise, uses the value typed into the comment form.
mail	varchar(64)	Yes		The comment author's e-mail address from the comment form if user is anonymous and the "Anonymous users may/must leave their contact information" setting is turned on.
homepage	varchar(255)	Yes		The comment author's home page address from the comment form if user is anonymous and the "Anonymous users may/must leave their contact information" setting is turned on.

contact (contact module)

Contact form category settings are located in this table.

Name	Type	Null	Default	Description
cid	serial	No		Primary key: unique category ID
category	varchar(255)	No	' '	Category name
recipients	text:big	No		Comma-separated list of recipient e-mail addresses
reply	text:big	No		Text of the automatic reply message
weight	int:tiny	No	0	The category's weight
selected	int:tiny	No	0	Flag to indicate whether or not category is selected by default (1 for yes and 0 for no)

files (upload module)

This table stores information about uploaded files.

Name	Type	Null	Default	Description
fid	serial	No		Primary key: unique files ID
uid	int, unsigned	No	0	The {users}.uid of the user who is associated with the file
filename	varchar(255)	No	' '	Name of the file
filepath	varchar(255)	No	' '	Path of the file relative to Drupal root
filemime	varchar(255)	No	' '	The file MIME type
filesize	int, unsigned	No	0	The size of the file in bytes
status	int	No	0	A flag indicating whether file is temporary (1) or permanent (0)
timestamp	int, unsigned	No	0	Unix timestamp for when the file was added

filter_formats (filter module)

This table stores input formats, which are custom groupings of filters such as Filtered HTML.

Name	Type	Null	Default	Description
format	serial	No		Primary key: unique ID for format
name	varchar(255)	No	' '	Name of the input format (e.g., Filtered HTML)
roles	varchar(255)	No	' '	A comma-separated string of roles, references {role}.rid
cache	int:tiny	No	0	Flag to indicate whether format is cachable (1 for cachable and 0 for not cachable)

filters (filter module)

This table maps filters (e.g., HTML corrector) to input formats (e.g., Filtered HTML).

Name	Type	Null	Default	Description
fid	serial	No		Primary key: automatically incrementing filter ID
format	int	No	0	Foreign key: the {filter_formats}.format to which this filter is assigned
module	varchar(64)	No	' '	The origin module of the filter
delta	int:tiny	No	0	ID to identify which filter within the module is being referenced
weight	int:tiny	No	0	Weight of filter within format

flood (contact module)

This table controls the threshold of events, such as the number of contact attempts.

Name	Type	Null	Default	Description
fid	serial	No		Primary key: unique flood event ID
event	varchar(64)	No	' '	Name of event (e.g., contact)
hostname	varchar(128)	No	' '	Hostname of the visitor
timestamp	int	No	0	Timestamp of the event

forum (forum module)

This table stores the relationship of nodes to forum terms.

Name	Type	Null	Default	Description
nid	int, unsigned	No	0	The {node}.nid of the node
vid	int, unsigned	No	0	Primary key: the {node}.vid of the node
tid	int, unsigned	No	0	The {term_data}.tid of the forum term assigned to the node

history (node module)

This table stores a record of which users have read which nodes.

Name	Type	Null	Default	Description
uid	int	No	0	The {users}.uid that read the {node}.nid
nid	int	No	0	The {node}.nid that was read
timestamp	int	No	0	The Unix timestamp at which the read occurred

languages (locale module)

The languages table stores a list of all available languages in the system.

Name	Type	Null	Default	Description
language	varchar(12)	No	' '	Language code, for example, 'de' or 'en-US'
name	varchar(64)	No	' '	Language name in English
native	varchar(64)	No	' '	Native language name
direction	int	No	0	Direction of language (0 for left-to-right, 1 for right-to-left)
enabled	int	No	0	Enabled flag (1 for enabled, 0 for disabled)
plurals	int	No	0	Number of plural indexes in this language
formula	varchar(128)	No	' '	Plural formula in PHP code to evaluate to get plural indexes
domain	varchar(128)	No	' '	Domain to use for this language
prefix	varchar(128)	No	' '	Path prefix to use for this language
weight	int	No	0	Weight, used in lists of languages
javascript	varchar(32)	No	' '	Location of the JavaScript translation file

locales_source (locale module)

This table stores a list of the English source strings.

Name	Type	Null	Default	Description
lid	serial	No		Unique identifier of this string.
location	varchar(255)	No	''	Drupal path in case of online discovered translations or file path in case of imported strings.
textgroup	varchar(255)	No	'default'	A module-defined group of translations. See hook_locale().
source	text	No		The original string in English.
version	varchar(20)	No	'none'	Version of Drupal where the string was last used (for locales optimization).

locales_target (locale module)

This table stores translated versions of strings.

Name	Type	Null	Default	Description
lid	int	No	0	Source string ID, references {locales_source}.lid
translation	text	No		Translation string value in this language
language	varchar(12)	No	''	Language code, references {languages}.language
plid	int	No	0	Parent lid (lid of the previous string in the plural chain) in case of plural strings, references {locales_source}.lid
plural	int	No	0	Plural index number in case of plural strings

menu_custom (menu module)

This table holds definitions for top-level custom menus (for example, primary links).

Name	Type	Null	Default	Description
menu_name	varchar(32)	No	''	Primary key: unique key for menu. This is used as a block delta so the length is 32 to match {blocks}.delta.
title	varchar(255)	No	''	Menu title, displayed at top of block.
description	text	Yes		Menu description.

menu_links (menu module)

The menu_links table contains the individual links within a menu.

Name	Type	Null	Default	Description
menu_name	varchar(32)	No	''	The menu name. All links with the same menu name (such as 'navigation') are part of the same menu.
mlid	serial	No		The menu link ID is the integer primary key.
plid	int, unsigned	No	0	The parent link ID is the mlid of the link above in the hierarchy, or 0 if the link is at the top level in its menu.
link_path	varchar(255)	No	''	The Drupal path or external path this link points to.
router_path	varchar(255)	No	''	For links corresponding to a Drupal path (0 means external), this connects the link to a {menu_router}.path for joins.
link_title	varchar(255)	No	''	The text displayed for the link, which may be modified by a title callback stored in {menu_router}.
options	text	Yes		A serialized array of options to be passed to the url() or l() function, such as a query string or HTML attributes.
module	varchar(255)	No	'system'	The name of the module that generated this link.
hidden	int:small	No	0	A flag for whether the link should be rendered in menus (1 indicates a disabled menu item that may be shown on admin screens; -1, a menu callback; and 0, a normal, visible link).
external	int:small	No	0	A flag to indicate if the link points to a full URL starting with a protocol, like http:// (1 for external and 0 for internal).
has_children	int:small	No	0	Flag indicating whether any links have this link as a parent (1 means children exist; 0 means there are no children).
expanded	int:small	No	0	Flag for whether this link should be rendered as expanded in menus; expanded links have their child links displayed always, instead of only when the link is in the active trail (1 means expanded, and 0 means not expanded).
weight	int	No	0	Link weight among links in the same menu at the same depth.
depth	int:small	No	0	The depth relative to the top level. A link with plid == 0 will have depth == 1.
customized	int:small	No	0	A flag to indicate that the user has manually created or edited the link (1 means customized, and 0 means not customized).

Continued

Name	Type	Null	Default	Description
p1	int, unsigned	No	0	The first mlid in the materialized path. If N = depth, then pN must equal the mlid. If depth > 1, then p(N-1) must equal the plid. All pX where X > depth must equal 0. The columns p1 . . . p9 are also called the parents.
p2	int, unsigned	No	0	The second mlid in the materialized path. See p1.
p3	int, unsigned	No	0	The third mlid in the materialized path. See p1.
p4	int, unsigned	No	0	The fourth mlid in the materialized path. See p1.
p5	int, unsigned	No	0	The fifth mlid in the materialized path. See p1.
p6	int, unsigned	No	0	The sixth mlid in the materialized path. See p1.
p7	int, unsigned	No	0	The seventh mlid in the materialized path. See p1.
p8	int, unsigned	No	0	The eighth mlid in the materialized path. See p1.
p9	int, unsigned	No	0	The ninth mlid in the materialized path. See p1.
updated	int:small	No	0	Flag that indicates that this link was generated during the update from Drupal 5.

menu_router

This table maps paths to various callbacks (e.g., access, page, and title callbacks).

Name	Type	Null	Default	Description
path	varchar(255)	No	' '	Primary key: the Drupal path this entry describes.
load_functions	varchar(255)	No	' '	A serialized array of function names (like node_load) to be called to load an object corresponding to a part of the current path.
to_arg_functions	varchar(255)	No	' '	A serialized array of function names (like user_uid_optional_to_arg) to be called to replace a part of the router path with another string.
access_callback	varchar(255)	No	' '	The callback that determines the access to this router path; defaults to user_access.
access_arguments	text	Yes		A serialized array of arguments for the access callback.
page_callback	varchar(255)	No	' '	The name of the function that renders the page.
page_arguments	text	Yes		A serialized array of arguments for the page callback.
fit	int	No	0	A numeric representation of how specific the path is.
number_parts	int:small	No	0	Number of parts in this router path.

Name	Type	Null	Default	Description
tab_parent	varchar(255)	No	' '	Only for local tasks (tabs); the router path of the parent page (which may also be a local task).
tab_root	varchar(255)	No	' '	Router path of the closest nontab parent page. For pages that are not local tasks, this will be the same as the path.
title	varchar(255)	No	' '	The title for the current page or the title for the tab if this is a local task.
title_callback	varchar(255)	No	' '	A function that will alter the title; defaults to t().
title_arguments	varchar(255)	No	' '	A serialized array of arguments for the title callback. If empty, the title will be used as the sole argument for the title callback.
type	int	No	0	Numeric representation of the type of the menu item, like MENU_LOCAL_TASK.
block_callback	varchar(255)	No	' '	Name of a function used to render the block on the system administration page for this menu item.
description	text	No		A description of this menu item.
position	varchar(255)	No	' '	The position of the block (left or right) on the system administration page for this menu item.
weight	int	No	0	Weight of the element. Lighter weights are higher up; heavier weights move down.
file	text:medium	Yes		The file to include for this element, usually the page callback function lives in this file.

node (node module)

This is the base table for nodes.

Name	Type	Null	Default	Description
nid	serial	No		The primary identifier for a node
vid	int, unsigned	No	0	The current {node_revisions}.vid version identifier
type	varchar(32)	No	' '	The {node_type}.type of this node
language	varchar(12)	No	' '	The {languages}.language of this node
title	varchar(255)	No	' '	The title of this node, always treated as nonmarkup, plain text
uid	int	No	0	The {users}.uid that owns this node; initially, the user who created it

Continued

Name	Type	Null	Default	Description
status	int	No	1	Boolean value indicating whether the node is published (visible to nonadministrators)
created	int	No	0	The Unix timestamp when the node was created
changed	int	No	0	The Unix timestamp when the node was most recently saved
comment	int	No	0	Whether comments are allowed on this node: 0 means no; 1 means comments are read-only; and 2 means comments can be read or written
promote	int	No	0	Boolean value indicating whether the node should be displayed on the front page
moderate	int	No	0	Previously, a Boolean value indicating whether the node was "in moderation"; not currently used by core
sticky	int	No	0	Boolean value indicating whether the node should be displayed at the top of lists in which it appears
tnid	int, unsigned	No	0	The translation set ID for this node, which equals the node ID of the source post in each set
translate	int	No	0	A Boolean value indicating whether this translation page needs to be updated

node_access (node module)

This table identifies which realm/grant pairs a user must possess in order to view, update, or delete specific nodes.

Name	Type	Null	Default	Description
nid	int, unsigned	No	0	The {node}.nid this record affects.
gid	int, unsigned	No	0	The grant ID a user must possess in the specified realm to gain this row's privileges on the node.
realm	varchar(255)	No	' '	The realm in which the user must possess the grant ID. Each node-access node can define one or more realms.
grant_view	int:tiny, unsigned	No	0	Boolean value indicating whether a user with the realm/grant pair can view this node.
grant_update	int:tiny, unsigned	No	0	Boolean value indicating whether a user with the realm/grant pair can edit this node.
grant_delete	int:tiny, unsigned	No	0	Boolean value indicating whether a user with the realm/grant pair can delete this node.

node_comment_statistics (comment module)

This table maintains statistics of nodes and comments posts to show "new" and "updated" flags.

Name	Type	Null	Default	Description
nid	int, unsigned	No	0	The {node}.nid for which the statistics are compiled
last_comment_timestamp	int	No	0	The Unix timestamp of the last comment that was posted within this node, from {comments}.timestamp
last_comment_name	varchar(60)	Yes		The name of the latest author to post a comment on this node, from {comments}.name
last_comment_uid	int	No	0	The user ID of the latest author to post a comment on this node, from {comments}.uid
comment_count	int, unsigned	No	0	The total number of comments on this node

node_counter (statistics module)

This table stores access statistics for nodes.

Name	Type	Null	Default	Description
nid	int	No	0	The {node}.nid for these statistics
totalcount	int:big, unsigned	No	0	The total number of times the {node} has been viewed
daycount	int:medium, unsigned	No	0	The total number of times the {node} has been viewed today
timestamp	int, unsigned	No	0	The most recent time the {node} has been viewed

node_revisions (node module)

This table stores information about each saved version of a node.

Name	Type	Null	Default	Description
nid	int, unsigned	No	0	The {node} this version belongs to
vid	serial	No		The primary identifier for this version
uid	int	No	0	The {users}.uid that created this version
title	varchar(255)	No	' '	The title of this version

Continued

Name	Type	Null	Default	Description
body	text:big	No		The body of this version
teaser	text:big	No		The teaser of this version
log	text:big	No		The log entry explaining the changes in this version
timestamp	int	No	0	A Unix timestamp indicating when this version was created
format	int	No	0	The input format used by this version's body

node_type (node module)

This table stores information about all defined {node} types.

Name	Type	Null	Default	Description
type	varchar(32)	No		The machine-readable name of this type.
name	varchar(255)	No	' '	The human-readable name of this type.
module	varchar(255)	No		The module that implements this type.
description	text:medium	No		A brief description of this type.
help	text:medium	No		Help information shown to the user when creating a {node} of this type.
has_title	int:tiny, unsigned	No		Boolean value indicating whether this type uses the {node}.title field.
title_label	varchar(255)	No	' '	The label displayed for the title field on the edit form.
has_body	int:tiny, unsigned	No		Boolean value indicating whether this type uses the {node_revisions}.body field.
body_label	varchar(255)	No	' '	The label displayed for the body field on the edit form.
min_word_count	int:small, unsigned	No		The minimum number of words the body must contain.
custom	int:tiny	No	0	A Boolean value indicating whether this type is defined by a module (0) or by a user via a module like the Content Construction Kit (1).
modified	int:tiny	No	0	A Boolean value indicating whether this type has been modified by an administrator; currently not used in any way.

Name	Type	Null	Default	Description
locked	int:tiny	No	0	A Boolean value indicating whether the administrator can change the machine name of this type.
orig_type	varchar(255)	No	' '	The original machine-readable name of this node type. This may be different from the current type name if the locked field is 0.

openid_association (openid module)

This table stores temporary shared key association information for OpenID authentication.

Name	Type	Null	Default	Description
idp_endpoint_uri	varchar(255)	Yes		URI of the OpenID provider endpoint
assoc_handle	varchar(255)	No		Primary key: used to refer to this association in subsequent messages
assoc_type	varchar(32)	Yes		The signature algorithm used: HMAC-SHA1 or HMAC-SHA256
session_type	varchar(32)	Yes		Valid association session types: no-encryption, DH-SHA1, and DH-SHA256
mac_key	varchar(255)	Yes		The MAC key (shared secret) for this association
created	int	No	0	Unix timestamp for when the association was created
expires_in	int	No	0	The lifetime, in seconds, of this association

permission (user module)

This table stores permissions for users.

Name	Type	Null	Default	Description
pid	serial	No		Primary key: unique permission ID
rid	int, unsigned	No	0	The {role}.rid to which the permissions are assigned
perm	text:big	Yes		List of permissions being assigned
tid	int, unsigned	No	0	Originally intended for taxonomy-based permissions, but never used

poll (poll module)

This table stores poll-specific information for poll nodes.

Name	Type	Null	Default	Description
nid	int, unsigned	No	0	The poll's {node}.nid
runtime	int	No	0	The number of seconds past {node}.created during which the poll is open
active	int, unsigned	No	0	Boolean value indicating whether or not the poll is open

poll_choices (poll module)

This table stores information about all choices for all polls.

Name	Type	Null	Default	Description
chid	serial	No		Primary key: unique identifier for a poll choice
nid	int, unsigned	No	0	The {node}.nid this choice belongs to
chtext	varchar(128)	No	''	The text for this choice
chvotes	int	No	0	The total number of votes this choice has received by all users
chorder	int	No	0	The sort order of this choice among all choices for the same node

poll_votes (poll module)

This table stores per-user votes for each poll.

Name	Type	Null	Default	Description
nid	int, unsigned	No		The {poll} node this vote is for
uid	int, unsigned	No	0	The {users}.uid this vote is from, unless the voter was anonymous
chorder	int	No	-1	The {users}'s vote for this poll
hostname	varchar(128)	No	''	The IP address this vote is from, unless the voter was logged in

profile_fields (profile module)

This table stores profile field information.

Name	Type	Null	Default	Description
fid	serial	No		Primary key: unique profile field ID
title	varchar(255)	Yes		Title of the field shown to the end user
name	varchar(128)	No	' '	Internal name of the field used in the form HTML and URLs
explanation	text	Yes		Explanation of the field to end users
category	varchar(255)	Yes		Profile category that the field will be grouped under
page	varchar(255)	Yes		Title of page used for browsing by the field's value
type	varchar(128)	Yes		Type of form field
weight	int:tiny	No	0	Weight of field in relation to other profile fields
required	int:tiny	No	0	Whether the user is required to enter a value (0 for no and 1 for yes)
register	int:tiny	No	0	Whether the field is visible in the user registration form (1 for yes and 0 for no)
visibility	int:tiny	No	0	The level of visibility for the field (0 for hidden, 1 for private, 2 for public on profile pages but not on member list pages, and 3 for public on profile and list pages)
autocomplete	int:tiny	No	0	Whether form automatic completion is enabled (0 for disabled and 1 for enabled)
options	text	Yes		List of options to be used in a list selection field

profile_values (profile module)

This table stores values for profile fields.

Name	Type	Null	Default	Description
fid	int, unsigned	No	0	The {profile_fields}.fid of the field
uid	int, unsigned	No	0	The {users}.uid of the profile user
value	text	Yes		The value for the field

role (user module)

This table stores user roles.

Name	Type	Null	Default	Description
rid	serial	No		Primary key: unique role ID
name	varchar(64)	No	''	Unique role name

search_dataset (search module)

This table stores items that will be searched.

Name	Type	Null	Default	Description
sid	int, unsigned	No	0	Search item ID, for example, the node ID for nodes
type	varchar(16)	Yes		Type of item, for example, node
data	text:big	No		List of space-separated words from the item
reindex	int, unsigned	No	0	Set to force node reindexing

search_index (search module)

This table stores the search index and associates words, items, and scores.

Name	Type	Null	Default	Description
word	varchar(50)	No	''	The {search_total}.word that is associated with the search item
sid	int, unsigned	No	0	The {search_dataset}.sid of the searchable item to which the word belongs
type	varchar(16)	Yes		The {search_dataset}.type of the searchable item to which the word belongs
score	float	Yes		The numeric score of the word, higher being more important

search_node_links (search module)

This table stores items (like nodes) that link to other nodes; it is used to improve search scores for nodes that are frequently linked to.

Name	Type	Null	Default	Description
sid	int, unsigned	No	0	The {search_dataset}.sid of the searchable item containing the link to the node
type	varchar(16)	No	' '	The {search_dataset}.type of the searchable item containing the link to the node
nid	int, unsigned	No	0	The {node}.nid that this item links to
caption	text:big	Yes		The text used to link to the {node}.nid

search_total (search module)

This table stores search totals for words.

Name	Type	Null	Default	Description
word	varchar(50)	No	' '	Primary key: unique word in the search index
count	float	Yes		The count of the word in the index using Zipf's law to equalize the probability distribution

sessions

Drupal's session handlers read and write into the sessions table. Each record represents a user session, either anonymous or authenticated.

Name	Type	Null	Default	Description
uid	int, unsigned	No		The {users}.uid corresponding to a session or 0 for anonymous user.
sid	varchar(64)	No	' '	Primary key: a session ID. The value is generated by PHP's Session API.
hostname	varchar(128)	No	' '	The IP address that last used this session ID (sid).
timestamp	int	No	0	The Unix timestamp when this session last requested a page. Old records are purged by PHP automatically. See sess_gc().
cache	int	No	0	The time of this user's last post. This is used when the site has specified a minimum_cache_lifetime. See cache_get().
session	text:big	Yes		The serialized contents of $_SESSION, an array of name/value pairs that persists across page requests by this session ID. Drupal loads $_SESSION from here at the start of each request and saves it at the end.

system

The system table contains a list of all modules, themes, and theme engines that are or have been installed in Drupal's file system.

Name	Type	Null	Default	Description
filename	varchar(255)	No	' '	The path of the primary file for this item, relative to the Drupal root; e.g., modules/node/node.module.
name	varchar(255)	No	' '	The name of the item; for example, node.
type	varchar(255)	No	' '	The type of the item: module, theme, or theme_engine.
owner	varchar(255)	No	' '	A theme's "parent"; can be either a theme or an engine.
status	int	No	0	Boolean value indicating whether or not this item is enabled.
throttle	int:tiny	No	0	Boolean value indicating whether this item is disabled when the throttle.module disables items that can be throttled.
bootstrap	int	No	0	Boolean value indicating whether this module is loaded during Drupal's early bootstrapping phase (e.g., even before the page cache is consulted).
schema_version	int:small	No	-1	The module's database schema version number. -1 if the module is not installed (its tables do not exist). If the module is installed, 0 or the largest N of the module's hook_update_N() function that has either been run or existed when the module was first installed.
weight	int	No	0	The order in which this module's hooks should be invoked relative to other modules. Equally weighted modules are ordered by name.
info	text	Yes		A serialized array containing information from the module's .info file; keys can include name, description, package, version, core, dependencies, dependents, and php.

term_data (taxonomy module)

This table stores term information.

Name	Type	Null	Default	Description
tid	serial	No		Primary key: unique term ID
vid	int, unsigned	No	0	The {vocabulary}.vid of the vocabulary to which the term is assigned
name	varchar(255)	No	' '	The term name
description	text:big	Yes		A description of the term
weight	int:tiny	No	0	The weight of this term in relation to other terms

term_hierarchy (taxonomy module)

This table stores the hierarchical relationship between terms.

Name	Type	Null	Default	Description
tid	int, unsigned	No	0	Primary key: the {term_data}.tid of the term.
parent	int, unsigned	No	0	Primary key: the {term_data}.tid of the term's parent. 0 indicates no parent.

term_node (taxonomy module)

This table stores the relationship of terms to nodes.

Name	Type	Null	Default	Description
nid	int, unsigned	No	0	The {node}.nid of the node
vid	int, unsigned	No	0	Primary key: the {node}.vid of the node
tid	int, unsigned	No	0	Primary key: the {term_data}.tid of a term assigned to the node

term_relation (taxonomy module)

This table stores nonhierarchical relationships between terms.

Name	Type	Null	Default	Description
trid	serial	No		Primary key: unique term relation ID
tid1	int, unsigned	No	0	The {term_data}.tid of the first term in a relationship
tid2	int, unsigned	No	0	The {term_data}.tid of the second term in a relationship

term_synonym (taxonomy module)

This table stores term synonyms.

Name	Type	Null	Default	Description
tsid	serial	No		Primary key: unique term synonym ID
tid	int, unsigned	No	0	The {term_data}.tid of the term
name	varchar(255)	No	' '	The name of the synonym

trigger_assignments (trigger module)

This table maps triggers to hook and operation assignments from the trigger module.

Name	Type	Null	Default	Description
hook	varchar(32)	No	' '	Primary key: the name of the internal Drupal hook on which an action is firing; for example, nodeapi
op	varchar(32)	No	' '	Primary key: the specific operation of the hook on which an action is firing; for example, presave
aid	varchar(255)	No	' '	Primary key: the action's {actions}.aid
weight	int	No	0	The weight of the trigger assignment in relation to other triggers

upload (upload module)

This table stores uploaded file information and table associations.

Name	Type	Null	Default	Description
fid	int, unsigned	No	0	Primary key: the {files}.fid
nid	int, unsigned	No	0	The {node}.nid associated with the uploaded file
vid	int, unsigned	No	0	Primary key: the {node}.vid associated with the uploaded file
description	varchar(255)	No	' '	Description of the uploaded file
list	int:tiny, unsigned	No	0	Whether the file should be visibly listed on the node (1 for yes and 0 for no)
weight	int:tiny	No	0	Weight of this upload in relation to other uploads in this node

url_alias (path module)

This table contains a list of URL aliases for Drupal paths; a user may visit either the source or destination path.

Name	Type	Null	Default	Description
pid	serial	No		A unique path alias identifier.
src	varchar(128)	No	' '	The Drupal path this alias is for, for example, node/12.
dst	varchar(128)	No	' '	The alias for this path, for example, title-of-the-story.
language	varchar(12)	No	' '	The language this alias is for; if blank, the alias will be used for unknown languages. Each Drupal path can have an alias for each supported language.

users (user module)

This table stores user data.

Name	Type	Null	Default	Description
uid	serial	No		Primary key: unique user ID.
name	varchar(60)	No	' '	Unique username.
pass	varchar(32)	No	' '	User's password (MD5 hash).
mail	varchar(64)	Yes	' '	User's e-mail address.
mode	int:tiny	No	0	Per-user comment display mode (threaded vs. flat), used by the {comment} module.
sort	int:tiny	Yes	0	Per-user comment sort order (newest vs. oldest first), used by the {comment} module.
threshold	int:tiny	Yes	0	Previously used by the {comment} module for per-user preferences; no longer used.
theme	varchar(255)	No	' '	User's default theme.
signature	varchar(255)	No	' '	User's signature.
created	int	No	0	Timestamp for when user was created.
access	int	No	0	Timestamp for previous time user accessed the site.
login	int	No	0	Timestamp for user's last login.
status	int:tiny	No	0	Whether the user is active (1) or blocked (0).
timezone	varchar(8)	Yes		User's time zone.
language	varchar(12)	No	' '	User's default language.
picture	varchar(255)	No	' '	Path to the user's uploaded picture.

Continued

Name	Type	Null	Default	Description
init	varchar(64)	Yes	' '	E-mail address used for initial account creation.
data	text:big	Yes		A serialized array of name/value pairs that are related to the user. Any form values posted during user edit are stored and loaded into the $user object during user_load(). Use of this field is discouraged, and it will likely disappear in a future version of Drupal.

users_roles (users)

This table maps users to roles.

Name	Type	Null	Default	Description
uid	int, unsigned	No	0	Primary key: {users}.uid for user
rid	int, unsigned	No	0	Primary key: {role}.rid for role

variable

Named variable/value pairs created by Drupal core or any other module or theme are stored in this table. All variables are cached in memory at the start of every Drupal request, so developers should not be careless about what is stored here.

Name	Type	Null	Default	Description
name	varchar(128)	No	' '	Primary key: the name of the variable
value	text:big	No		The value of the variable

vocabulary (taxonomy module)

This table stores vocabulary information.

Name	Type	Null	Default	Description
vid	serial	No		Primary key: unique vocabulary ID
name	varchar(255)	No	' '	Name of the vocabulary
description	text:big	Yes		Description of the vocabulary
help	varchar(255)	No	' '	Help text to display for the vocabulary
relations	int:tiny, unsigned	No	0	Whether or not related terms are enabled within the vocabulary (0 for disabled and 1 for enabled)
hierarchy	int:tiny, unsigned	No	0	The type of hierarchy allowed within the vocabulary (0 for disabled, 1 for single, and 2 for multiple)
multiple	int:tiny, unsigned	No	0	Whether or not multiple terms from this vocabulary may be assigned to a node (0 for disabled and 1 for enabled)
required	int:tiny, unsigned	No	0	Whether or not terms are required for nodes using this vocabulary (0 for disabled and 1 for enabled)
tags	int:tiny, unsigned	No	0	Whether or not free tagging is enabled for the vocabulary (0 for disabled and 1 for enabled)
module	varchar(255)	No	' '	The module that created the vocabulary
weight	int:tiny	No	0	The weight of the vocabulary in relation to other vocabularies

vocabulary_node_types (taxonomy module)

This table stores which node types vocabularies may be used with.

Name	Type	Null	Default	Description
vid	int, unsigned	No	0	Primary key: the {vocabulary}.vid of the vocabulary
type	varchar(32)	No	' '	Primary key: the {node}.type of the node type for which the vocabulary may be used

watchdog (dblog module)

The watchdog table contains logs of all system events.

Name	Type	Null	Default	Description
wid	serial	No		Primary key: unique watchdog event ID
uid	int	No	0	The {users}.uid of the user who triggered the event
type	varchar(16)	No	' '	Type of log message, for example "user" or "page not found"
message	text:big	No		Text of log message to be passed into the t() function
variables	text:big	No		Serialized array of variables that match the message string and that is passed into the t() function
severity	int:tiny, unsigned	No	0	The severity level of the event; ranges from 0 (Emergency) to 7 (Debug)
link	varchar(255)	No	' '	Link to view the result of the event
location	text	No		URL of the origin of the event
referer	varchar(128)	No	' '	URL of referring page
hostname	varchar(128)	No	' '	Hostname of the user who triggered the event
timestamp	int	No	0	Unix timestamp of when event occurred

Resources

Many resources are available for the Drupal developer. The most useful of these are listed here.

Code

Some Drupal code resources follow.

Drupal CVS

`http://cvs.drupal.org`

Access to the CVS tree containing the Drupal core codebase and contributions repository has been covered in Chapter 21; however, a convenient web interface for browsing the repositories is available at the preceding URL. Especially nice is the ability to do color-coded diffs quickly.

Drupal API Reference

`http://api.drupal.org`

The comments from Drupal functions, as well as the documentation available in the `contributions/docs/developer` area of the Drupal contributions CVS repository, are available at `http://api.drupal.org`. Code is searchable, cross-referenced, and organized by major version. It's well worth your time to get familiar with this site. In fact, you can set up your own local version; instructions are at `http://drupal.org/node/26669`.

Security Advisories

`http://drupal.org/security`

Security advisories are available by e-mail or as an RSS feed from this page. You can subscribe to the advisories from this page when logged in to `http://drupal.org`.

Updating Modules

`http://drupal.org/update/modules`

When an API changes with a new release of Drupal, the technical implications of the change are documented here. This page is invaluable for keeping your modules in sync with changes to Drupal's codebase.

Updating Themes

`http://drupal.org/update/theme`

This page has the same kind of critical information as the "Updating Modules" page, but for themes. It's critical for updating themes from one version of Drupal to another.

Handbooks

The online handbooks at `http://drupal.org/handbooks` are constantly being updated and improved. Many HOWTO documents are posted here as well, providing step-by-step instructions.

Forums

The forums at `http://drupal.org/forum` are an excellent place to get help with Drupal. Usually someone else has experienced the problem you are having and has documented this on the forums. For problems that are clearly bugs with contributed modules, however, it is best to create an issue in the module's issue queue, since developers are more likely to see your bug report there than in the forums.

Tip Try using a search engine to constrain results to `http://drupal.org`. For example, the query `"installation profiles" site:drupal.org` on Google will search all of `http://drupal.org` for the string "installation profiles."

Mailing Lists

Many topic-specific mailing lists are available. Subscription management for these lists and archives is available at `http://lists.drupal.org/listinfo`.

development

This list is for Drupal developers and includes general discussion about Drupal's future direction, development-related questions, and merits of different approaches. If a major change is being made, it's usually discussed here. Hotly.

documentation

This list is for documentation writers. Documentation of Drupal's code and behavior is a never-ending task. Writing documentation is crucial to Drupal's success, and discussion of documentation improvements and changes happens here. New developers will benefit from some time spent on this list.

drupal-cvs

This list contains all CVS commit messages. It's useful for finding out what's happening in the CVS repositories. Alternatives include RSS feeds such as `http://drupal.org/cvs?rss=true&nid=3060` for Drupal's core repository and the list of recent commits at `http://drupal.org/cvs`.

infrastructure

This list is for those who volunteer their time maintaining the infrastructure on which the Drupal project runs, including the web server, the database server, the CVS repositories, mailing lists, and so on.

support

Although much support takes place in the `http://drupal.org` forums, there's also a mailing list where people can help one another get Drupal up and running.

themes

This list is for theme developers to discuss Drupal theming issues.

translations

This is a list for those translating Drupal's interface into other languages.

webmasters

This is a list for those who volunteer their time maintaining the web sites at `http://drupal.org`.

CVS-applications

CVS accounts for committing code to the contributions repository aren't available to just anyone. To receive an account, a new developer sends an application to this list justifying why an account is needed. The application is reviewed by seasoned developers and then approved or denied. See `http://drupal.org/cvs-account`.

consulting

This is for Drupal consultants and Drupal service and hosting providers to discuss topics related to for-pay Drupal services.

User Groups and Interest Groups

Local or regional user groups and those working on a particular aspect of Drupal can use the infrastructure at http://groups.drupal.org to organize and communicate. The site uses the organic groups module to provide functionality. Of particular interest to beginning developers is the Drupal Dojo group (http://groups.drupal.org/drupal-dojo). This group's goal is to teach Drupal skills to beginning developers and promises to "make you skilled like a ninja."

Internet Relay Chat

Internet Relay Chat (irc) is primarily used by Drupal developers as a real-time chat to help one another and to discuss issues related to Drupal. Not all developers are available on irc, and some believe that assistance given on irc is detrimental because answers to the questions asked aren't visible for others, as they would be had the question been asked on the forums at http://drupal.org or on a mailing list. Still, irc has its place when quick interaction on a topic is needed. It also serves to help developers get to know one another in an informal way. Several channels are related to Drupal. Occasionally, special channels are set up for code sprints (where a certain area of Drupal is worked on intensively) or bug squashing in preparation for a new release.

There is a particular culture on irc. In order to avoid making a faux pas, read the "How to Use IRC Effectively" page at http://drupal.org/node/108355.

All the channels in this section are available on the freenode network (http://freenode.net).

#drupal-support

This is a channel where volunteers answer questions about Drupal. The focus is on using Drupal through the web-based administrative screens or on figuring out which module does what. Coding questions are usually better asked in #drupal.

#drupal-themes

This is a discussion of Drupal theming, including creation, modification, and distribution of themes.

#drupal-ecommerce

This is a channel pertaining to using Drupal for e-commerce (see http://drupal.org/project/ecommerce).

#drupal

Chat about Drupal development on this channel. Many core developers hang out here. Coding questions are appropriate in #drupal. Noncoding support questions are not permitted in this channel; use #drupal-support or the http://drupal.org forums instead.

#drupal-dev

This channel is reserved for code discussions that need a quiet place. Developers often move here when #drupal is too noisy or when discussion of a specific module or feature is not of interest to the people on #drupal.

#drupal-consultants

Drupal consultants who provide paid support can be found in this channel (as well as on the paid Drupal services forum: http://drupal.org/forum/51). Any discussion of fees is done in private.

#drupal-dojo

Lessons for the Drupal Dojo group (see "User Groups and Interest Groups") are conducted here.

Videocasts

Sometimes, concepts are difficult to describe but easy to demonstrate. A growing collection of videocasts and screencasts are available at http://drupal.org/videocasts.

Weblogs

Weblogs are online journals. Many Drupal developers have weblogs in which they record their experiences with Drupal.

Planet Drupal

http://drupal.org/planet

Posts from weblogs related to Drupal are aggregated here. Reading this aggregator regularly is helpful for keeping your finger on the pulse of what's happening in the Drupal community.

Conferences

The Drupal community gathers at conferences that feature presentations, discussions, and lots of fun. Typically, a conference takes place in the spring in North America and in the fall in Europe. Conferences are a great way to learn about Drupal, make connections, and make new friends. If you have a chance to go, by all means take it. Details can be found at http://drupalcon.org. The #drupalcon irc channel is used before and during the conference to find and communicate with other attendees.

A code sprint is often scheduled before or after a Drupal conference.

Contribute

Contributors are Drupal's most valuable asset and are the reason why Drupal continues to move forward not only as a development platform but also as a community.

At `http://drupal.org/contribute`, you can contribute to Drupal not only through development but also through documentation, translations, usability, donations, marketing, and more. This page is the jumping-off point for contributing to the project at any level.

Index

You Need the Companion eBook

Your purchase of this book entitles you to buy the companion PDF-version eBook for only $10. Take the weightless companion with you anywhere.

We believe this Apress title will prove so indispensable that you'll want to carry it with you everywhere, which is why we are offering the companion eBook (in PDF format) for $10 to customers who purchase this book now. Convenient and fully searchable, the PDF version of any content-rich, page-heavy Apress book makes a valuable addition to your programming library. You can easily find and copy code—or perform examples by quickly toggling between instructions and the application. Even simultaneously tackling a donut, diet soda, and complex code becomes simplified with hands-free eBooks!

Once you purchase your book, getting the $10 companion eBook is simple:

❶ Visit **www.apress.com/promo/tendollars/**.

❷ Complete a basic registration form to receive a randomly generated question about this title.

❸ Answer the question correctly in 60 seconds, and you will receive a promotional code to redeem for the $10.00 eBook.

THE EXPERT'S VOICE™

2855 TELEGRAPH AVENUE | SUITE 600 | BERKELEY, CA 94705

Offer valid through 2/25/09.